PSYCHOLOGY—Part I

PSYCHOLOGY

PART I

HARDEEP KAUR SHERGILL
Consultant Counsellor and Psychotherapist

PHI Learning Private Limited
New Delhi-110001
2010

Rs. 350.00

PSYCHOLOGY, Part I
Hardeep Kaur Shergill

ISBN-978-81-203-3978-1

Published by Asoke K. Ghosh, PHI Learning Private Limited, M-97, Connaught Circus, New Delhi-110001 and Printed by Baba Barkha Nath Printers, Bahadurgarh, Haryana-124507.

To

My father

S. Balbir Singh Shergill

and

My daughter

Harnoor, with love

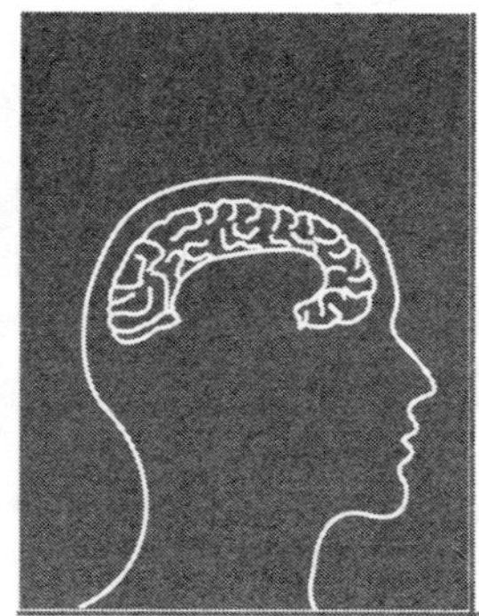

Contents

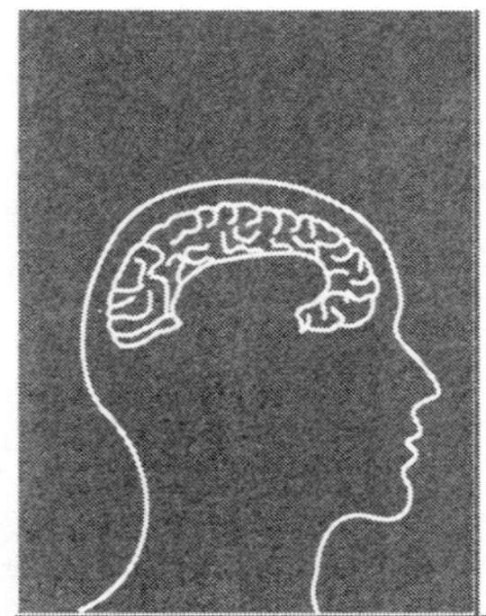

Preface

This book provides an introduction to Psychology to help create the most comprehensive text for the students. This book offers a full account of Psychology for all those with little or no previous knowledge of the subject. I hope this book will be of use to all students of Psychology. Though it is designed as per the syllabus of BA (Part I) of Guru Nanak Dev University, Amritsar, it will be equally useful to the undergraduate students of other universities.

I have worked to present the contents in a simple, clear, easy-to-understand, and illustrative manner. All topics covered in the text are informed and supplemented by the most recent information available. The goal of this book has been to produce the most accessible and complete study and teaching material. The book is divided into two parts, Part A and Part B to make study and teaching easy. The text is supplemented with interesting facts and health tips and studded with photographs of eminent psychologists. A number of sample questions taken from the question papers have been added at the end of each chapter according to the manner they are set in the question paper to help the students prepare in a better way for the examination. The questions having an asterisk are most important from the examination point of view and have beeen repeatedly asked in the examinations. Hindi words like *Chetna*, *Anna Brahman*, *Acharya*, *Siddhi*, etc. are written in MT bold script. In the book 'he' is referred to a genderless person. I wish the students are benefitted to the maximum by using the book.

All the best to the readers.

Hardeep Kaur Shergill

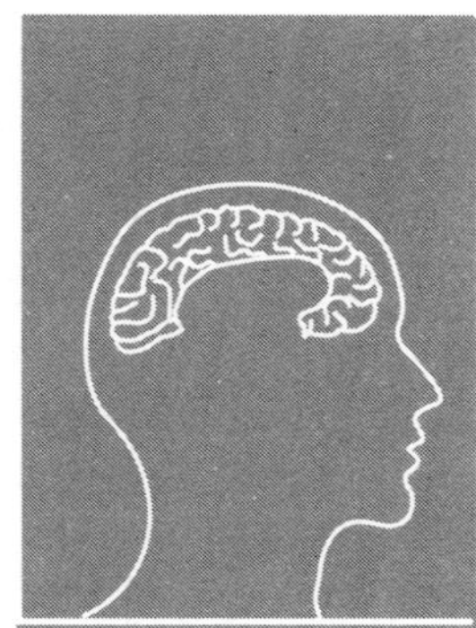

Acknowledgements

This book is very affectionately dedicated to my daughter Harnoor Shergill and my father S. Balbir Singh Shergill without whose inspiration, this work would not have been possible. I am greatly indebted to my near and dear ones for their enormous encouragement and support. I would like to acknowledge Mr. Sunny Arora for typing the manuscript. I would like to extend special thanks to **PHI Learning**, New Delhi for publishing this book.

Hardeep Kaur Shergill

PART A

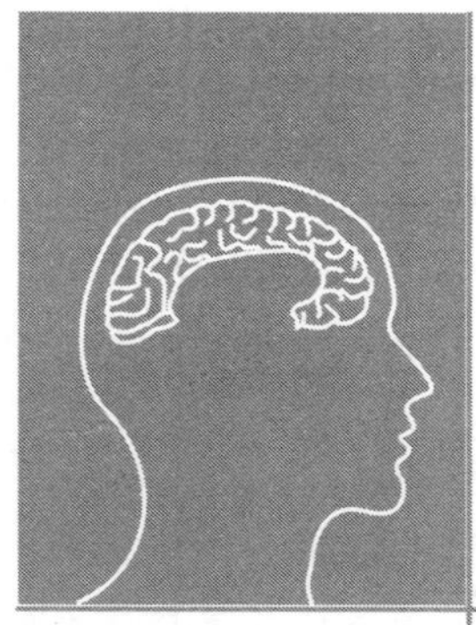

CHAPTER 1
Nature of Psychology

Psychology is concerned with the attempt to understand humans and other species. Psychology is all about human behaviour, different mental processes, and the context in which behaviour and mental processes occur.

The term "Psychology" is derived from two Greek words *psyche* and *logos*, which mean "soul" and "science" or "talk" or "study" or "discourse" respectively. Thus, the literal or etymological meaning of the word Psychology is the "science of soul".

Aristotle
(322–384 BC)

Plato
(347–429 BC)

Socrates
(399–469 BC)

Greek philosophers like, Aristotle, Plato and Socrates believed that soul, a spiritual entity, was responsible for the various mental activities such as learning, thinking, reasoning, and feeling etc. The Greek believed that the soul was controlling man's actions.

Aristotle (322–384 BC) was of the opinion that the heart is the seat of soul. Soul and body are indivisible. Soul is something mystical and speculative. It cannot be seen or touched.

David Hume (26 April, 1711–25 August 1776) regarded soul as something non-existent and Plato (347–429 BC) considered it as immaterial element. It does not exist in reality. Since, it is invisible; experiments cannot be conducted on this. Hence, this is beyond the reach of scientific investigation. Therefore, it was regarded as the talk about soul. Later on, it was observed that it was better to call Psychology the "science of soul" rather than "talk about soul", as science is a better term because of the following reasons:

David Hume
(1711–1776)

1. Science is more systematic and exhaustive than talk. Talk goes on carelessly and loosely. It is usually vague and indefinite.
2. Science implies well-established knowledge. It gives us some power of prediction.
3. Science gives us knowledge that is based on observation of facts. It gives us objective knowledge.
4. Science uses special terminology of its own or technical terminology.

Thus, literally Psychology means ***science of soul***. But it is not acceptable because of the following reasons:

1. Nature, origin, and place of soul are not known. It has no physical existence. It does not exist in reality. It cannot be seen or heard. It has no weight and volume. It is a metaphysical concept.
2. It makes Psychology more of religion than of science because it is a theological concept and implies certain theories of religion and relationship to God.
3. Soul makes our science a speculative science as it is not open to observation and experimentation and therefore not given to verification.

Therefore, this definition of Psychology as a science of soul is unscientific and hence this is discarded. Prof. Guilford says, "Psychology cannot be the science of soul because soul is not capable of scientific investigation."

René Descartes (31 March, 1596–11 February, 1650, French philosopher and mathematician, first modern philosopher) claimed that animals have no soul; therefore, they cannot feel anything. Human beings alone have both body and soul. Hence, we have feeling and emotions. We think, and therefore we know that we exist.

René Descartes
(1596–1650)

From the study of soul, Psychology changed into the study of Mind. The term Mind was considered better and it was substituted for soul.

(*a*) *A layman's view about Mind*: Mind is something in the body or in the heart, which thinks (cognitive activity), feels (affective activity), and acts (conative activity). If Mind means something mysterious inside us, it would be just the same as the soul. Hence, this definition would equally deserve to be rejected.

(*b*) *Psychologists' view about Mind:* Mind is the combination or sum total of mental processes and it stands for personal internal experiences of human beings, for example, pleasures and pains, hopes and wishes, dreams and desires.

Mind is a collection of mental functions and these are clearly based on the structure that is the brain.

In ancient times, Hindu philosophers thought of the Mind as the sixth organ along with the other five sense organs—eyes, ears, nose, tongue, and skin. According to them, Mind is the organ for thinking. We know the world through our five sense organs, and we can reflect on this knowledge through our Mind.

Later on, Psychology was considered as the science of consciousness (awareness). Since 1850 till 1878, Psychology was defined as the science of consciousness (awareness; ***chetana***). The first world-recognized Experimental laboratory was established in the year 1879 at Leipzig in Germany by Wilhelm Wundt, which gave Psychology the status of a science.

Sir Francis Galton
(1822–1911)

Later in 1882, Sir Francis Galton (1822–1911) formulated the first test laboratory in London. Consciousness is the unique characteristic of human thought. Consciousness means to be aware of the situation, to be fully alive to the situation or to be most wakeful to the situation. The Buddhists described this as mindfulness. Mindful, we must be of what we are doing at the moment. Consciousness stands for the inner experiences of man—his thoughts, feelings, and memories etc.

William James (1842–1910), an American scientist, considered the Father of American Psychology, wrote extensively about consciousness (our awareness of the environment and of ourselves). William James also developed a theory explaining that our emotional reactions arise from the way we perceive our physiological responses. William James wrote the following books—*Principles of Psychology* (1890), and *Psychology, Briefer Course* (1892).

According to Evans (1990), "The above-mentioned texts are probably the most significant psychological treatise ever written in America."

Edward Bradford Titchener (1867–1927), a structuralist, regarded Psychology as "The science of consciousness or the study of experience". Consciousness or experience can be broken or analyzed into three basic elements: physical sensations, feelings, and images—such as memories and dreams.

Sigmund Freud (1856–1939) compared the human mind to an iceberg. Only a small part of the iceberg rises above the surface of water. This portion is the conscious, which includes everything we are aware of at a particular moment. Consciousness is central to human functioning. "Consciousness" is often defined as an active awareness of all the many thoughts, images, perceptions, and emotions that occupies the mind at any given time (Natsoulas, 1983). Consciousness is what allows us to monitor our environments and ourselves as we make our way in the world. It is what enables us to exert some control over what we do and experience, to choose among alternative ways of thinking, feeling, and acting (Kihlstrom, 1984; Mandler, 1984). It is also, what gives us a sense of continuity, a way of linking experiences into a past, a present, and a future. Without Consciousness, in other words, we would have no sense of being, no sense of self (Rychlak, 1986).

Our "conscious experiences" refer to our sensory awareness of the environment and of ourselves. A conscious person actively processes a rich array of mental information.

Some additional material that is not in awareness at a particular time, can be retrieved or recalled or brought to consciousness/awareness with a little effort; this material is called *pre-conscious* or *sub-conscious*. An example of the pre-conscious would be the name of high school English teacher. The nature of material in the pre-conscious is not different from the material in the conscious, thoughts move easily from one state to the other (Cloninger, 1993).

Freud was especially interested in unconscious; this holds thoughts and desires that are far below the level of a person's awareness. Unconsciousness is the opposite of consciousness—being unaware, not attentive to events or ideas. Unattended objects or ideas soon fade away and are not remembered. Some memories are unconscious. They automatically show up without any effort. For example, memory of how to ride a bicycle comes back to us even after a lapse of few years during which we have not been on a bicycle.

Most of the iceberg lies below the surface of the water. Similarly, Freud argues that most psychic or mental processes are not conscious; they are hidden from the outside world. Your unconscious may hold particularly some traumatic or painful childhood memory. Although, a traumatic memory will not reach consciousness during normal daily activities, Freud proposed that it might influence your behaviour without your being aware of it. A mechanism called repression is supposed to be responsible for pushing unacceptable thoughts back into the unconscious rather than letting them emerge into awareness. Unconscious person is totally unresponsive to the outside world.

However, Psychology as a science of consciousness was discarded or rejected on the following grounds:

1. Consciousness forms a very negligible portion (that is, 1/10 portion) of our mind. The most important segments or portions that are pre-conscious or sub-conscious and unconscious exert a great influence on the development of personality.
2. We can be conscious of only of our own mental activities. We cannot know the consciousness of others. This method is very akin to introspection, which is the most subjective and least scientific or unscientific method. So, it cannot be accepted in the modern scientific age.
3. It cannot study conative or physical activities and these affect behaviour.

Early behaviourists (John Brodaeus Watson, B.F. Skinner, Edward Lee Thorndike, Karl S. Lashley, Edward C. Tolman, Clark C. Hull, and others) thought that if we cannot objectively see into consciousness to measure, to analyze its components, then, consciousness is not a proper subject for scientific study.

The current view of most (but not all) psychologists is that Psychology is the *science of human and animal behaviour*. However, psychologists are interested in the internal processes producing that behaviour. For example, psychologists studying aggression in adolescents do not only focus on their aggressive behaviour rather, they want to know why adolescents behave in anti-social manner or fashion.

Later on, Psychology was recognized as a *science of behaviour*. Behaviour, according to Drever is, "The total response of the organism to the situations of life." It includes physical as well as mental behaviour, human as well as animal behaviour, child as well as adult behaviour, normal as well as abnormal behaviour, etc. It includes all forms of processes, adjustments, activities, and experiences of the organism.

According to Robert Sessions Woodworth (17 October 1869–4 July, 1962), "Behaviour is the collective name for various types of activities: cognitive, affective, and conative corresponding to knowing, feeling, and doing. Behaviour includes cognitive activities like sensation, awareness, perception, thinking, learning, memory, imagination, problem solving, decision making, etc. "Cognitive activities" are the mental aspect of our experiences or behaviour. "Affective activities" include the effects or emotions involved in our experiences or behaviour like feelings, emotions, and sentiments. "Conative or psycho-motor activities" include the physical aspect involved in our experiences or behaviour like walking, jumping running, playing, swimming, dancing, digging, riding bicycle, etc. Thus, the word "Behaviour" covers not only our outer behaviour but also our inner experiences or mental processes. Behaviour expresses the entire life of an individual.

Behaviour is the expression of one's experience. Any manifestation of life is behaviour. Any activity on the part of an organism is her or his behaviour.

In a nutshell, "behaviour" refers to the entire life activities and experiences of all living organisms. "Behaviour" refers to all of a person's overt actions that others can directly observe, for example walking, speaking, and showing facial expressions.

1.1 PSYCHOLOGY AS SCIENCE OF BEHAVIOUR: DEFINITIONS

According to William Mc-Dougall (1908), "Psychology is a science which aims to give us better understanding and control of the behaviour of the organism as a whole."

According to Pillsbury (1911), "Psychology may be most satisfactorily defined as the science of human behaviour."

According to John Brodaeus Watson (1913), "Psychology is the positive science of behaviour. It deals with existing realities." A positive science studies facts as they are.

According to Norman L. Munn (1967), "Psychology today concerns itself with the scientific investigation of behaviour."

According to B.F. Skinner, "Psychology is a science of behaviour and experience."

According to Crow and Crow, "Psychology is the study of human behaviour and human relationships."

According to Garrison and others, "Psychology is concerned with observable human behaviour."

According to Bootzin and Bower (1991), "Psychology is the study of mental processes and behaviour."

According to Crooks and Stein (1991), "Psychology is the scientific study of the behaviour and mental processes of humans and other animals."

Wilhelm Wundt (1832–1920), a physiologist and a psychophysicist, is the founder of Modern Psychology and is regarded as the Father of Experimental Psychology. He published his first book on Psychology *Fundamentals of Physiological Psychology* in 1874 and established the first "University Institute of Experimental Psychology" (psychological laboratory) at Leipzig in Germany in the year 1879 and the first journal followed two years later. The birth date of Psychology is most often given as 1879.

Experimental Psychology aims at understanding the fundamental causes of behaviour. The experimental psychologists try to find out the variables or causes or factors which determine one's behaviour and experience, how behaviour is modified through learning and past experience, how memorization takes place, what are the causes of forgetting, what are the drives (desires, needs) which regulate or goad (motivate or direct) one's behaviour, how concepts are formed, etc. They also like to point out the manner in which the nervous system functions to produce behavioural results. The experimental psychologists are more interested in experimenting under controlled conditions.

One of the oldest methods that were widely used in Psychology was introspection. "Introspection" means "looking within." "Intro" means "within" and "spection" "means looking." Introspection was not very objective; however, one person's experience is not the same as another person". And hence, the use of this method led to many controversies.

- *Psychology can be defined as the scientific study of behaviour and mental processes.*

"Scientific study" means that psychologists use systematic, well-organized methods to learn about psychological processes. Psychologists do not gather or collect their data or information by casual speculation or observation. Instead, they use a variety of more careful methods that include experiments as well as objective observations.

"Behaviour" means physical action that can be seen or heard, such as touching or speaking aloud. The word "behaviour" in the definition of Psychology refers to anything a person or animal does that can be observed in some way. However, Psychology also includes mental processes, which cannot be seen or heard—for instance, perceiving, dreaming, remembering, and making decisions. "Mental processes" refer to the private thoughts, emotions, feelings, and motives that others cannot directly observe, for example, your private thoughts and feelings about your friend or your boss etc.

1.1.1 Psychology, An Interesting Subject

Psychology is an interesting subject because of the following reasons:

1. Most people are interested in understanding other people. They want to understand them better so that they can develop deeper, intimate, and more fulfilling relationships with them. They also want to understand themselves, in the hope that this will allow them to become happier and to cope and adjust better with the people and situations of their lives. Psychology is the only branch of knowledge which studies human and animal behaviour.
2. Psychology has numerous applications to our everyday life. Perhaps, the most important of such application is clinical psychology. Back in nineteenth century, Sigmund Freud argued that most people who were then regarded as "mad" or severely disturbed, were really suffering from one or other kind of mental disorder. He claimed that psychological forms of treatment such as psychoanalysis could allow such people to lead fuller and happier lives. Freud said that nobody is hundred percent normal. Clinical psychology has developed to a great extent since then and is of great value in treating various mental disorders.
3. Another application of Psychology is in the area of education. Educational psychologists make use of knowledge about human nature, and about the processes involved in learning to help children who are experiencing learning difficulties.
4. Fourth important application is that occupational psychologists are increasingly successful at devising programmes of stress management, which allow workers to function more effectively with less stress.
5. Psychology is also an interesting subject because psychologists are like detectives trying to make sense of various clues about human behaviour.

Robert Sessions Woodworth
(1869-1962)

Robert Sessions Woodworth (1869–1962), a devoted member of the behaviourist school of Psychology, took the initiation to develop a definition of Psychology in the line of John Brodaeus Watson, of course after rectifying his defects. Woodworth did not agree to limit the scope of Psychology either to outward behaviour (conative) or to consciousness (cognitive) as they were neither adequate nor comprehensive to explain Psychology. According to Watson, "Psychology is the positive science of behaviour it deals with existing realities." Behaviourism, a school started in the United States by John B. Watson (1913) argued that Psychology should just be the study of behaviour because behaviour is objective and observable.

While defining Psychology, one has to keep in mind the following points:

1. Psychology is a positive social science because it deals with existing realities. A positive science study facts as they are, and have little or no concern with what ought to be or should be. The "positive" is that which is given, that which is accepted as it is found.
2. It deals with cognitive activities like perception, imagination, learning, images, problem solving, decision making, and thinking etc. and affective activities which include various emotional experiences.

Thus, it was thought to be more appropriate to define Psychology as "The science of behaviour and experience in relation to the environment."

In Woodworth's opinion, therefore, in order to include various applications (aspects) of modern Psychology, one has to take into consideration organism as the intervening variable which in a major way, not only deals with cognitive and affective processes, but also understands, predicts, and controls human behaviour. So, Woodworth, by modifying the definition of Watson, defined Psychology as, "The scientific study of the activities of the organism in relation to the environment" or "Psychology is the science of the activities of the individual in relation to his or her environment."

In this definition, Woodworth attempted to include the interaction between the organism and the environment. However, he gave no greater weightage to either. He assumed that information from experiments with sub-human species could be generalized to the human organism.

Woodworth showed that S (stimulus)—O (organism)—R (response) concept clearly indicates how the interaction between stimulus and the organism determines responses or behaviour in a particular environmental set up.

$$R = f(s, o)$$

Response is a function of stimulus and organismic factors. The same stimulus may produce different response in different individuals and in the same individual under different environmental conditions. The uniqueness of Woodworth's definition is its dynamicity and recognition of the S—O—R organismic variables (variables inside an organism) which were ignored by predecessors (early behaviourists). Woodworth's definition is so clear and specific that it does not need further clarifications. Being the most accepted definition, it gives Psychology a scientific, objective, and unique status. Woodworth's definition is clear, specific, dynamic, recognizes S—O—R framework (behaviour), scientific, objective, unique, and comprehensive. That is why it is the most accepted one.

Let us understand the definition given by Woodworth by explaining different terms that are being used in it. "Psychology is science of the activities of the individual in relation to his or her environment." They are science, activities, individual (organism), environment, and interaction.

Study of Psychology as a Science

Wilhelm Wundt (a physiologist and a psychophysicist) gave Psychology a scientific status by opening the first laboratory at Leipzig in Germany in the year 1879. Science is a systematic body of knowledge gathered or collected by careful observation and measurement of events. A study cannot be called a science merely on the basis of its subject matter, what is more important is the scientific method. A science is not by what (subject matter) it studies but by how (method) its studies. Psychology may not seem as much of a science as biology or chemistry does. Psychologists, after all, often study things that cannot be put into test tubes or looked at under a microscope.

Science is defined not by what it studies but by how it studies. Psychologists, like other scientists, adopt a special approach to obtaining and organizing knowledge. They use systematic methods or scientific enquiry to gather data about the things that interest them. Once these data have been collected, they carefully analyze the data and interpret the meaning of their findings as objectively as they can. Along with conducting research, psychologists develop general laws and principles or theories about why things happen as they do. A "theory" is an attempt to fit all the known, relevant facts into a logical explanation. Once formulated, theory can serve as a framework for collecting more information.

Now, the essential elements of a science are as under:

1. **Explanation:** Explanation is the ultimate aim of science. Psychology deals with mental processes and activities of the organism in relation to his environment. It deals with experience and behaviour. The aims of Psychology precisely are to understand, describe, control, and predict human behaviour and

conditions and situations both in the world around him and within himself.

2. **Scientific procedure or experimental method:** It is mainly the scientific procedure adopted for the study of Psychology that gave it a scientific status. A subject in order to be considered a science at the outset requires a well-equipped laboratory, where experiments and investigations can be conducted under artificially controlled conditions, and through scientific procedures.

   Science uses methods like, objective observation, experiment, comparison and classification to investigate and collect data. Psychology uses both objective observation and experimentation, which are scientific procedures. Scientific procedure, according to Norman L. Munn (1950) involves, (a) "making systematic rather than aimless observations, (b) "being impersonal in one's search for truth, seeking information to test rather than to prove the ideas already held making it possible for others to repeat one's observations under essentially the same conditions and to confirm or modify them." Experiment is an observation of behaviour done under controlled conditions.

   The following are the steps of experimental method:

   1. Observation
   2. Recording observation
   3. Classification of facts
   4. Analyzing and generalizing
   5. Verification

   Science, in other words, uses experimental method for the purpose of investigation. Instead of mere observation, certain conditions or variables of the object of study are changed (independent or experimental variable) and the effect of these changes on the subject matter of study is noted. A science starts with some assumption or hypothesis and postulates about its subject matter (for example, personality, intellect, behaviour). The data obtained from the study verifies the hypothesis or assumption. If the data supports the assumption, the hypothesis is retained and if it does not, the hypothesis is rejected. In a scientific procedure like the experimental method, all the variables are controlled except the independent variable, that is whose effect we want to study. In addition to this, it must be systematic and the attitude should be for the search for truth. In scientific method, therefore, biases and prejudices are avoided.

3. **Science is systematic:** Psychology deals with systematic study of human behaviour under controlled conditions. It uses

experimental or scientific method for the purpose of investigation and inquiry, which deals with three essential characteristics of science, such as accuracy, certainty, and generality. Psychology, like any other science, tries to control all other conditions except one (independent variable) while conducting studies on human behaviour.

4. **Science must be quantitative:** Results obtained from a scientific study must be quantified or measured. Psychology uses statistical methods for the analysis of results. Fechner is associated with the development of various statistical techniques. Sir Francis Galton (1974) is associated with the development of various psychological tests. He established first laboratory of psychological tests in London in the year 1874. He measured individual differences by developing various intelligence and personality tests.
5. **Science can verify data:** In Psychology, verification of data is also done.

To sum up, Psychology is systematic study. It is impersonal in one's observations under essentially the same conditions. Psychology deals with the dynamic personality of the living organism. Since human personality is amenable to changes, the effect of a particular variable or factor cannot always be predictable as accurately as in other sciences. Different human beings may give different responses to same stimulus because of the differences in their personality, past experience, and learning. Due to these facts, in some cases, the predictions of the psychologists fail and their assumptions are not proved by their findings. But in a majority of cases, psychological predictions are supported by the data obtained from systematic investigations. Predictions, by and large, stand in most cases if not in all. Hypotheses are framed on the basis of previous findings. Many hypotheses are retained or accepted, while some are rejected.

Psychology qualifies as a science. Psychology can be called a science, as it uses many aspects of science. In view of these facts, Psychology has been rightly called a *positive social science*, which studies the activities of an individual in relation to his or her environment. Psychology is considered to be a science because psychologists attempt to understand people through careful, controlled observation. This reliance or dependence on rigorous scientific methods of observation is the basis of all sciences, including Psychology.

Activities

The second term used in Woodworth's definition of Psychology is the word "activities." Psychology studies the activities of the individual. The word "activities" according to him mean "any manifestation of life." The term activities include:

(i) Physical and motor activities (conative) like walking, running, jogging, playing, cycling, jumping, digging, etc.

(ii) Mental or intellectual activities (cognitive) like learning, perceiving, remembering, planning, thinking, problem-solving, decision making, etc.

(iii) Emotional activities (affective) like laughing, crying, etc.

Individual (Organism)

An individual is a psychophysical organism (having mind and body) or being. Psychology studies activities of all kinds of individuals—children, adolescents, adults, old people, normal and abnormal, intelligent and feeble-minded, humans and animals, males and females, alone or in group, etc.

Environment

The term "environment" stands for all those conditions or circumstances which influence the individual, since conception to death. Environment consists of physical, intellectual, social, moral, economic, political, and cultural forces. All these forces influence the activities, behaviour, and personality of the individual.

1. **Physical environment:** Food, temperature, climate, etc.
2. **Intellectual environment:** It consists of books around the student, libraries, laboratories, intellectual tastes and interest of the parents, teachers, recreation rooms, etc.
3. **Social environment:** It includes parents, other members of the family, teachers, friends, relatives, neighbours, and society at large.
4. **Emotional environment:** It consists of emotional nature of parents, members of family, friends, teachers, classmates, neighbours, etc.

Interaction

The individual has to depend on the environment for the development of his personality. The individual has to take active participation or participate actively in the environment. All his physical, mental, and emotional and other types of activities are influenced by the way he relates himself to the environment. A sort of interaction takes place between the individual and the environment. The individual influences the environment and the vice versa.

The best description of Psychology is to define it as the scientific study of the individual, which deals with behaviour and experience. Individual may be human being, animal, child, adolescent, adult, old, man, woman, normal, abnormal, gifted, mentally challenged, all alone or in group, whether his behaviour is good or bad, right or wrong, desirable or undesirable, moral or immoral, sociable or unsociable, it becomes the subject matter of Psychology. Psychology is the science of behaviour and mental processes that seek to describe and explain aspects of human thought, feelings, perceptions, and actions.

1.2 GOALS OR AIMS OF PSYCHOLOGY

Psychologists differ with respect to the goals, they emphasize. The following are the goals or aims of Psychology:

1. Describing (understanding) behaviour and mental processes based on careful, systematic observation. This goal of Psychology focuses on "What is..."
2. Explaining why these behaviours and mental processes occurred. This goal of Psychology focuses on "*How* and *Why* of behaviour."
3. Predicting future events on the basis of past events, and
4. Changing behaviours and mental processes so that they are more appropriate.

Offering explanations for behaviour or explaining how and why behaviours occur is just one of the goals of Psychology. Psychologists also seek to describe and predict people's behaviour. The following are detailed descriptions of the goals of modern Psychology:

1.2.1 Description/Understanding

Understanding human behaviour must begin with careful descriptions or understanding of how people think, feel, and act in specific situations. Psychologists collect descriptive data as objectively (systematic and organized) as they can. Ideally, they try to observe the behaviour of interest first hand, recording it precisely (carefully) in written notes or on tapes or video cassettes. Of course, in most incidents of sudden explosive violence, no curious psychologists are there to watch and record what happens. But researchers can carefully reconstruct such incidents through the testimonies or reports of participants and eyewitnesses. The information gathered through scientific research helps us describe psychological phenomena more accurately and completely. For example, information gathered in a survey on the frequency of sexual behaviour among college students without the protection of a condom would tell us whether they are at a high risk for the spread of sexually transmitted disease such as AIDS. We understand behaviour and mental processes when we can explain them. Because there is still much more to learn, our current explanations are always tentative. In other words, our explanations are theories, not truths. Theories are tentative explanations of facts and relationships in sciences. It is essential to understand this basic fact about science. The knowledge that is offered to us is always tentative. As the science of Psychology progresses through research, theories are always subject to revision.

1.2.2 Explanation

Describing human behaviour is not enough; however, psychologists also want to *Why* it happens, that is they want to explain it. Without insights (looking within) into why people think and act the way they do, psychologists would have purely descriptive information and no meaningful understanding of it. Theories, in themselves, are not enough either. Evidence is needed to support or to disconfirm those; otherwise, we would not be engaged in a science. Psychologists conduct studies and experiments for this purpose.

1.2.3 Prediction

A study designed to test a theory usually involves, making a prediction that people will behave in a certain set of circumstances. If the prediction is upheld, the theory is supported; if not, it is rejected or unsupported. Thus, the ability to make prediction—to say in advance how someone is likely to act—lies at the heart of doing certain kinds of psychological research.

When psychologists have a broad understanding of a particular behaviour, they can make many accurate predictions about it. For example, psychologists with a broad understanding of human violence should be able to predict with a fair degree of accuracy that is most likely to be involved in such behaviour that is violent behaviour (their age, gender, social class, personal histories, and so forth), what immediate circumstances tend to trigger it, and what if any factors can restrain it. Of course, no such predictions prove accurate all the time. Human behavior is highly complex and unanticipated factors can always influence it. But, if psychologists cannot predict a behaviour on some occasion, at least they are not very far along in understanding it.

In general, research psychologists focus on first three goals that is describing, explaining, and predicting human behaviour. In contrast, applied psychologists like clinical psychologists, educational psychologists, vocational psychologists, industrial and organizational psychologists, etc., have attained training in these three areas but they are more concerned with changing both actions and thoughts so that they are more appropriate.

The most important of applications of Psychology is Clinical Psychology. Clinical Psychology is the discipline, broadly concerned with the study, assessment, treatment, and prevention of abnormal behaviour. Clinical psychologists are trained to apply psychotherapeutic techniques and procedures to diagnose psychological disorders and to do research on the causes of these disorders. Psychology has been applied in numerous other areas also. Educational psychologists make use of knowledge about human nature, and about the processes involved in learning, to help children who are experiencing learning difficulties. Occupational psychologists focus on stress at work. Occupational psychologists are increasingly successful at devising programmes of stress management which allow workers or employees to function more effectively and with less stress. Now let us clarify these different goals with example of psychologists who study children's aggression. Some psychologists describe children's aggressive behaviour in classrooms. Others explain why children are more aggressive after watching violent movie. Still others might try to predict how aggressive each child will be in the first grade, based on her or his aggressiveness as a kindergartener. Finally, applied psychologist would attempt to change the children's behaviour reducing their level of aggression. In summary, a single Psychology topic can be explored or studied from a wide diversity or variety of perspectives or viewpoints.

1.2.4 Influence

Finally, psychologists hope to go beyond description, understanding, and prediction to influence behaviour in beneficial ways. What can we do to help a teenage boy or a girl climb out of a period of major stress? How can we help parents raise their rambunctious children better? What is the best way to help college students select a career? We can intentionally influence behaviour that Psychology completely fulfils its promise.

The goals of Psychology are to describe, understand, explain, predict, and influence or change or control behaviour and mental processes. Using the methods of science, we gather or collect information through systematic observation (planned, scientific, and controlled) that enables us to accurately describe psychological facts and relationships. When adequate descriptive information has been acquired, reasonably accurate predictions can be made and explanations proposed to help us understand these facts and relationships. Finally, when enough understanding and ability to predict has been acquired, we can sometimes intentionally influence people in ways that improve and enrich their lives.

Psychology is also a means of promoting human welfare, a body of information that can be applied to solve a variety of human problems. Probing the brain to discover which particular areas are involved in remembering information is an example of basic research. In contrast, researchers who use their knowledge of brain's mechanism of memory to help alleviate memory impairments are engaged in applied psychology or science.

Psychologists are involved in promoting human welfare in more direct ways too. They work as counsellors and clinicians in many settings—schools, hospitals, business, community health centres, and private practices. The main two professional organizations for American psychologists are American Psychological Association (APA) and the American Psychological Society (APS). The aims of both are to advance the basic science of Psychology and to promote the use of research findings to benefit society.

The application of knowledge to practical problems is an art. It is a skill or knack (the ability to do something skillfully) which is acquired by study, practice, and special experience. The psychotherapists talking to a worried client, the educational psychologist advising a school board on a new curriculum, the clinical psychologist supervising group therapy in a mental hospital and the social psychologist trying to lessen tensions between management and workers in a large industry are all practicing the art of Psychology. Just as a physician or an engineer develops skills in using scientific knowledge to solve practical problems, these psychologists have learned, through special training, the artistry, or knack, of applying Psychology. Of course, the ability to apply psychological principles and knowledge is a hard-won skill and special kinds of training and huge amounts of experience are needed for this purpose.

1.3 SCHOOLS OF PSYCHOLOGY

1.3.1 Structuralism

Wilhelm Wundt and his follower Edward Bradford Titchener helped the first systematic position, or school of thought, in Psychology—Structuralism, so called because it focuses on the structure of the mind. Wilhwelm Wundt was a powerful personality. He was the professor of biology in Germany. He is called the Founder of Modern Psychology and the first man who without reservation is properly called a psychologist (Edwin G. Boring, 1969). "When we call him the founder of Experimental Psychology, we mean both that he promoted the idea of Psychology as an independent science and that he is the senior among psychologists. In his first world recognized Experimental Laboratory at Leipzig (Germany) in 1879, he did experiments on sensations, emotions, reaction time, feelings, ideas, psychophysics, etc. His main contribution in P chology was

Wilhelm Wundt
(1832–1920)

Edward Bradford Titchener
(1867–1927)

recognition of Psychology as a science and he did work scientifically in his laboratory and studied several psychological problems experimentally. He did not conduct experiments on memory and learning. He wrote the first textbook, *Principles of Physiological Psychology* in 1874. He proposed that Psychology should focus on analyzing the contents of consciousness in order to determine its basic elements and the relationships between them—a view known as Structuralism. Structuralists argued that every experience could be broken down into its primitive components. Edward Bradford Titchener, a student of Wilhelm Wundt, who started a psychological laboratory at Cornell University, taught in the United States at Cornell University, regarded Psychology as the science of consciousness or the study of experience, believed that the job of psychologists was to analyze human consciousness in terms of its component parts, much as chemists analyze matter in terms of its component molecules and atoms. Consciousness or experience can be broken or analyzed into three basic elements: physical sensations, feelings, and images such as memories and dreams. Through his studies, Titchener concluded that the structure of the human mind was made up of more than 30,000 separate sensations, feelings, and images and nothing else. The principle components of consciousness, Titchener argued, were fundamental sensations and feelings, which ultimately combine to form the structure of the mind. He emphasized how mental structure is built up from parts. Complex experiences resulted from the joining together of a number of elementary or basic or primary sensations, images, and feelings. The task of Psychology or psychologists was to discover the basic elements of consciousness and to determine how they formed compounds. Psychology was often referred to as "mental chemistry." Like chemistry, Psychology consists of analysis—discovering the basic elements of conscious thought and synthesis—discovering connections between elements and the laws governing these connections. To qualify as an element, an experience has to be irreducibly simple. Titchener even dared to number the elements of consciousness and offered what one might view as a "periodic table" of the mind (Table 1.1).

Table 1.1 Titchener's (1910) periodic table of the mind

Elementary Sensations	*Number*
Colour	About 35,000
White to black range	600 to 700
Tones	About 11,000
Tastes	Just 4 (sweet, sour, bitter, and salty)
From the skin	Just 4 (pressure, pain, warmth, and cold)
From the internal organs	Just 4 (pressure, pain, warmth, and cold)
Smells	9 classes seem likely, but, there might be thousands of elements
Total elementary sensations	46,708 plus an indeterminate variety of smells

Elementary sensations had to be combined because as Wundt recognized, we experience conscious thought as a unity, not as a series of varied sensations of brightness, hue, shape, etc. Wundt's doctrine of apperception describes a process of "creative synthesis" by which elementary experiences are organized into a whole. And his law of psychic resultants posits that psychic compounds have new properties that are by no means the mere sum of the characteristics of the elements. Wundt put students through an arduous training in the method of introspection (looking inward or within) to single out those who could describe the elementary sensations of experience—colours, tones, tastes, and so on. But by the early twentieth century, introspection had been labelled "superstitious" by John Watson, the founder of behaviourism. In this way, Wilhelm Wundt and his followers like Titchener, known as Structuralists, tried to provide a systematic study of the mind through the study of its structure (identifying the basic units or elements of consciousness or experience along with the combinations in which they occur) by adopting introspection as the main technique. Wilhelm Wundt argued that this task (analyzing any experience into its various components) could be carried out by introspection—a method in which trained individuals report in detail on their conscious experiences in response to specific stimuli (for example, sounds, optical illusions, and other visual stimuli) that are presented to them under carefully controlled conditions. Neither the topics studied by Structuralists nor the methods they employed, have survived the test of time. However, the strict insistence by Wundt and his followers that Psychology adopts rigorous research methods, did survive and helped place Psychology on a firm scientific footing.

1.3.2 Functionalism

Structuralism's focus on identifying the elements (structure) of consciousness was soon challenged by William James (1842–1910) and other psychologists who felt that their view point should focus not on structure of consciousness, but on its functions. William James, an American scientist, was the pioneer of functional school of Psychology. A most important exponent of functionalism, and professor of biology at Harvard University William James argued that: "No one ever had a simple sensation by itself" (James, 1890). Instead, he proposed, the most important thing about consciousness is its continual flow, and coined the famous phrase "stream of consciousness", to emphasize this fact. From James' perspective, the function of consciousness is to guide behaviour that will help the organism adapt to the environment. He felt that consciousness must have some biological use or else it would not have survived. Not surprisingly, James saw Psychology as a biological science. Functionalism addressed the very practical question of what the mind, or mental processes, accomplish. The percept "thinking is for doing" is the hallmark of functionalism. Sensing and not sensations, thinking and not ideas, imaging and not images—these processes, it was asserted, should be the principal subject matter of the science of Psychology. William James considered the mind to be a recent development in the evolutionary process, the function of which was to aid man's adjustment to his environment.

William James
(1842–1910)

The consciousness or mental life, according to him, is a continuous and flowing unity, a stream that carries the organism in its adaptation to the environment. The notion of function is central to Charles Darwin's theory of evolution, as the physical characteristics of a species evolve to meet its requirements for survival. The idea that behaviour might also reflect adaptation to the environment soon followed. Functionalism was strongly influenced by Darwin's theory of natural selection. Proponents of functionalism argued that since consciousness is a uniquely human characteristic, it must serve important functions for us; otherwise it would have never been evolved. With this thought in mind, James and other functionalists focused on understanding the functions of consciousness—how it helps human beings cope with the challenging and changing world around them and began to focus on such topics as child development and the relative benefits of various educational practices. Functionalists opposed the exclusive emphasis on structure and who insisted with considerable vigor that the outstanding characteristics of the conscious mind are its active processes and not its passive contents.

After James, functionalism developed more formally as a school by John Dewey (1859–1952) and James Angell (1869–1949). Functionalism shifted attention away from the exclusive focus on private experience (consciousness) to include the study of objective, observable behaviour. Unlike structuralism, functionalism was not supplanted but provided a bridge for the emergence of the polar opposite of structuralism—a Psychology that focused on behaviour and eschewed study of the mind.

Functionalism argued that psychological processes are adaptive; they allow human beings to survive and adapt successfully to their surroundings and environment. James was admired for his textbooks, *Psychology, Briefer Course* (1892) and *Principles of Psychology* (1890), this textbook taught a whole generation of future psychologists (Hothersall, 1984). Taking twelve years to write and running to nearly 1400 pages, Principles of Psychology is filled with provocative insights about such topics as human habits, emotions, and consciousness. Professors referred to the longer version (*Principles of Psychology*, 1890) as "James" and they nick-named the shorter version (*Psychology, Briefer Course*, 1892) "Jimmy" (Hilgard, 1987). A century later, the two volume work has been called "Probably the most significant psychological treatise ever written in America" (Evans, 1990).

1.4 BEHAVIOURISM

The behaviourist perspective arose in the early twentieth century, led by the brilliant but brash young scholar John B. Watson (1878–1958). Watson argued personally for the view that Psychology should focus not on consciousness or experience but on behaviour—actions that can be observed and measured. Thus, if Psychology was to be a science, it must stop trying to study what goes in people's heads. Instead, it must be limited to the study of observable behaviour. Behaviorists, a large and vocal group asserted that mind is not amenable to investigation by the methods of science because it is too private and too subjective. They urged instead that Psychology be defined as the science of behaviour.

Ivan Petrovich Pavlov
(1849–1936)

John Brodaeus Watson
(1878–1958)

Watson and his associates were strongly influenced by the pioneering work of Great Russian Physiologist Ivan Petrovich Pavlov (1849–1936). Watson took the extreme position that all behaviours represent learned responses to particular stimuli. He rejected the notion of innate difference in ability or temperament. He believed that by controlling environmental stimuli, he could shape a person's character in any way he wished. "Give me a dozen healthy infants", Watson believed, "... and my own specified world to bring them up in, and I will guarantee to take any one at random and train him to become any type of specialist I might select—doctor, lawyer, artist, merchant-chief, and yes, even beggar-man and thief, regardless of his talents, tendencies, abilities, vocations, and race of his ancestors" (Watson, 1924).

The behaviourists' emphasis on observable behaviour led them to reject any kind of terms referring to mental events such as ideas, thoughts, mental images, soul, mind, mental life, etc. (covert or internal behaviour). In fact, early behaviourists classified thinking as simply a form of speech (implicit speech). They thought that they should be able to detect tiny movements of the tongue (an observable human behaviour) if they could develop the appropriate equipment. Behaviourists argued that vague, invisible constructs, such as thoughts were simply unnecessary.

Other American psychologists were also influential in developing the behaviourist thought or school. One was Edward Lee Thorndike (1874–1949), who conducted a series of studies with cats. This research emphasized the importance of rewards to learning. Thorndike argued that if an animal comes to associate a particular response with a reward that response would strengthen and increase in frequency (rate of occurrence). Conversely, if an animal comes to associate a particular response with punishment, that response will weaken and decrease in frequency.

Edward Lee Thorndike
(1874–1949)

B.F. Skinner
(1904–1990)

Behaviourist B.F. Skinner (1904–1990) like his predecessors Watson and Thorndike spent a good part of his carrier studying learning among animals. But Skinner went far beyond his predecessors (Watson and Thorndike) in arguing that behaviourism instead can and should be applied to human society as a whole. His widely-read novel *Walden Two*

Robert Sessions Woodworth
(1869–1962)

Albert Paul Weiss
(1878–1958)

Karl S. Lashley
(1890–1958)

Edwin Ray Guthrie
(1886–1959)

(1948) portrays a behaviourist Utopia—a small community, in which people are trained from birth to be productive and satisfied citizens. Utopia can be defined simply as a place where there is plenty of food. He or she tends to think that, if only guaranteed food for the rest of life, he or she tends to be defined happier in terms of eating. Skinner's brand of behaviourism is called "radical" because of his ideas about the role the mind plays in determining people's behaviour. To Skinner, the concept of

Clark H. Hull
(1884–1952)

Norman L. Munn
(1902–1993)

Joseph Wolpe
(1915–1997)

mind was totally unnecessary concept to explain why someone acts in a certain way. All that is needed is knowledge of the rewards and punishments that are affecting the person's behaviour. The critics charge that we cannot ignore people's thoughts and feelings, if we are to understand their activities.

1.4.1 The Psycho-Analytic or Psycho-Dynamic Perspective or Viewpoint or School

No discussion of modern Psychology would be complete without the mention of the psychoanalytic perspective developed by Sigmund Freud (1856–1939). Freud was born on May 6, 1856. He died on September 23, 1939 in London. The psychodynamic approach emphasizes the three central points:

1. Childhood experiences determine adult personality.
2. Unconscious mental processes influence everyday behaviour.
3. Conflicts underlies most of the human behaviour.

Freud was a physician (psychiatrist) in Vienna, Austria, who specialized in the disorders of the nervous system. He observed that some of his patients had nothing physically wrong with them, even though they had symptoms of physical illness like headache, exhaustion, insomnia (lack of sleep), etc. He suspected that mental conflicts or psychic conflicts lay behind these symptoms—conflicts that had been pushed out of normal awareness and into a part of the mind, Freud called unconscious. *Conflict* means being torn in two or more directions by opposing motives. Conflict is frustrating and stressful. Conflict may also be looked at as a type of frustration in which the barrier to achieving a goal is an opposing impulse or motive. Conflicts are discussed in detail in Chapter 10.

Sigmund Freud
(1856–1939)

Alfred Adler
(1870–1937)

Carl Gustav Jung
(1875–1961)

Freud was particularly exploring and was interested in the unconscious mind. Freud believed that if unconscious conflicts could be brought into awareness of the patient, they would lose their power to control that person's life. Freud suggested hypnosis to uncover unconscious conflicts but he became dissatisfied with it because often it did not reach deeply enough into a person's buried memories. Eventually, he developed a method called *free association*, in which the patients were asked to lie comfortably on a couch and say whatever came to their mind, no matter how irrelevant or foolish it sounded. The patient's apparently random talk, Freud believed, would eventually contain themes related to his unconscious conflicts. Freud also encouraged patients to talk about their dreams because he believed that dreams are full of symbolic hints as to what is bothering or troubling the dreamer. With these verbal cues, Freud helped his patients interpret and understand their symptoms. He called his approach to treatment, psychoanalysis. Freud said "Dreams are a royal road to unconscious."

Freud gradually developed an elaborate theory of personality based on his observations. According to Freud, human beings, like other animals, are driven by powerful biological urges, especially sexual ones. Freud used the term *sexual* in a broad sense to refer to almost anything pleasurable, from eating to painting. In humans, however, such urges often conflict with society's moral standards, so, people must learn to restrict and inhibit them. A major part of this learning, according to Freud, takes place during childhood, when the rules of society are first imposed. Thus, in Freud's view, psychological problems arise when early conflicts between society's demands and innate sexual urges are never satisfactorily resolved.

1.4.2 Humanistic Perspective or School

Behaviourism developed out of dissatisfaction with James' and Wundt's approaches, functionalism and structuralism respectively. Humanistic approach developed out of dissatisfaction with the two major theories that dominated the first half of the twentieth century, that is the psychoanalytic and the behaviourist approaches. The American psychologists such as, Carl Rogers and Abraham Maslow, argued that the

Carl Rogers
(1902–1987)

Abraham Maslow
(1908–1970)

psychoanalytic approach to personality and psychological disorders focused on the "sick" side of human beings. Furthermore, they pointed out that behaviourism only examined the simple behaviours. They preferred a theory that emphasized the more positive human qualities as well as more complex and noble human goals.

Psychologists who adopt a humanistic perspective reject the idea that people are not the masters of their own destinies. The humanists have sought to study the "whole" person in order to help her or him achieve a happier, more self-actualized, and creative existence. According to them, we are free to reach our fullest potential, to become whatever we are capable of being. The humanistic approach stresses that humans have enormous potential for personal growth. They have the ability to care deeply for other people and to establish meaningful, productive lives for themselves. The humanists, in fact, see a striving for self-actualization (for becoming all that we can be) as the pinnacle of human motivation.

Carl Rogers (1902–1987) believed that people could be helped to find self actualization when a therapist treats them with empathy and understanding, giving them emotional and psychological support regarding anything they want to be or do. Rogers stressed the positive side of human nature. He argued that when people are generally free, they are automatically constructive in their actions and seek to build caring and satisfying relationships with others. Roger's approach is called *client* or *person centred approach.*

Gordon Allport
(1897–1967)

Fritz Perls
(1893–1970)

Abraham Maslow (1908–1970) is probably best known for his theoretical exploration of self-actualization, the important tendency to realize our own potential. Maslow theorized that our human motives or needs are arranged in a hierarchy, with the most basic needs at the bottom and the more highly developed needs (esteem needs and self-actualization needs) at the top (Maslow, 1970). Maslow places physiological needs at the base of the hierarchy of needs. One step above is safety needs. Above the safety needs are the social needs (Bausmen, Ster Leary, 1995). Above the social needs in the hierarchy, Maslow proposes, are the esteem needs. Finally, at the top of the hierarchy are self-actualization needs.

1. *Physiological or biological needs:* Physiological or biological needs include need for food, water, sleep, air (oxygen), excretion of waste products from the body, bodily comforts, and sex etc.

   Biological needs or states of deprivation arising within our bodies create unpleasant states of arousal or drives—the subjective feelings associated with needs that we typically describe as hunger, thirst, fatigue, and so on. In order to eliminate such feelings and restore a balanced physiological state, known as *homeostasis*, we engage in certain activities. The term, *Homeostasis*, was coined by Walter Bradford Cannon (19 October, 1871–1 October 1945), a prominent Harvard University Physiologist. *Homeostasis* refers to the body's automatic efforts to maintain a constant, normal state of the blood stream. W.B. Cannon (1932) described this process for (i) the water content of the blood, (ii) salt content, (iii) sugar content, (iv) protein content, (v) fat content, (vi) calcium content, (vii) oxygen content, (viii) constant hydrogen-ion level (acid-base balance), and (ix) constant temperature of the blood. Obviously, this list could be extended to include other minerals, the hormones, vitamins, and so on. Homeostasis is a state of physiological balance within the body.

Rollo May
(1909–1994)

Victor Frankl
(1909–1994)

2. *Safety or security needs:* Safety or security needs include the need for security, protection, out of danger, physical security, avoidance of pain, stability, dependency, freedom from pain and fear, anxiety, and chaos, need for structure, order, law, and limits, strength in the protector, and so on.

   The peaceful, smoothly, running, stable, good society ordinarily makes its members feel safe enough from wild animals, extreme of temperature, criminal assaults, murder chaos, tyranny, and so on. The safety needs can become very urgent on the social scene whenever there are real threats to law, to order, to authority of society. The threat of chaos can be expected in most human beings to produce a regression from any higher needs to the more pre-potent safety needs.

3. *Belongingness and love needs:* Belongingness and love needs include needs for affiliation with others, affection, feeling loved, gaining the approval of others and achieving success. The love needs involve both giving and receiving affection. When they are unsatisfied, a person will feel keenly the absence of friends, mate, or children. Such a person will hunger for relations with people in general—for a place in the group or family and will strive with great intensity to achieve this goal. Now the pangs of loneliness, ostracism, rejection, friendlessness, and rootlessness are pre-eminent.

   In our society, the thwarting of these needs is the most commonly found cause in cases of maladjustment and more severe pathology. Practically, all theories of psychopathology have stressed thwarting of the love needs as basic in the picture of maladjustment.

4. *Esteem needs:* Esteem needs include need to respect ourselves and to win the esteem of others, to achieve, be competent, gain approval and recognition and be accepted.

   Maslow's initial conceptualization included only one growth need that is self-actualization. He later differentiated the growth need of self-actualization, specifically naming two lower-level growth needs prior to general level of self-actualization (Maslow and Lowery, 1998) and one beyond that level, that is self-transcendence (Maslow, 1971). They are:

5. *Cognitive needs:* Cognitive needs include need to know, to understand, and explore.
6. *Aesthetic needs:* Aesthetic needs include need for symmetry, order, and beauty.
7. *Self-actualization:* Self-actualization means attempting to reach her or his full potential or becoming all that one can be or realizing one's own potential.
8. *Self-transcendence:* Self-transcendence includes a spiritual sense of peace, belonging and oneness with the universe, to connect to something beyond the ego or to help others find self-fulfilment and realize their potential or how others could be edified.

Arthur W. Combs
(1912–1999)

Virginia Satir
(1916–1988)

According to Maslow, needs are of two kinds—deficiency needs and growth needs. *Deficiency needs* are the basic needs and must be satisfied before higher level of needs emerge. These include the four levels of hierarchy that is physiological or biological needs, safety or security needs, belonging and love needs, and esteem needs. The other category of human needs is the growth needs. *Growth needs* help in the growth of the human beings and help actualize their potentialities after deficiency needs are fulfilled and satisfied. Maslow's basic position is that as one becomes more self-actualized and self-transcendent, one becomes wiser (develops wisdom) and automatically knows what to do in a wide variety of situations. Daniels (2001) suggests that Maslow's ultimate conclusion that the highest levels of self-actualization are transcendent in their nature may be one of his most important contributions to the study of human behaviour and motivation.

Figure 1.1 shows Maslow's hierarchy of needs, in which each lower need must be satisfied before the next level of needs can be addressed.

The humanistic approach or the views of the humanistic psychologists have been criticized as vague and unscientific. This approach has been criticized for several other reasons also which are mentioned below:

(i) It relies upon the subjective experience. Some people have only limited ability to explain, so not real.

(ii) Studies are often inadequate. Only intelligent, verbally able and self-actualized people were studied.

(iii) It is too selfish. It emphasized self-liberation; no botheration about others.

(iv) It is too optimistic. Free man makes problem.

Despite these criticism and its weaknesses, humanistic psychology must be praised for its substantial strengths. An interesting phenomenon related to Maslow's work is that in spite of a lack of evidence to support his hierarchy, it enjoys wide acceptance. (Soper, Miford and Rosenthal, 1995; Wahba and Bridgewell, 1976).

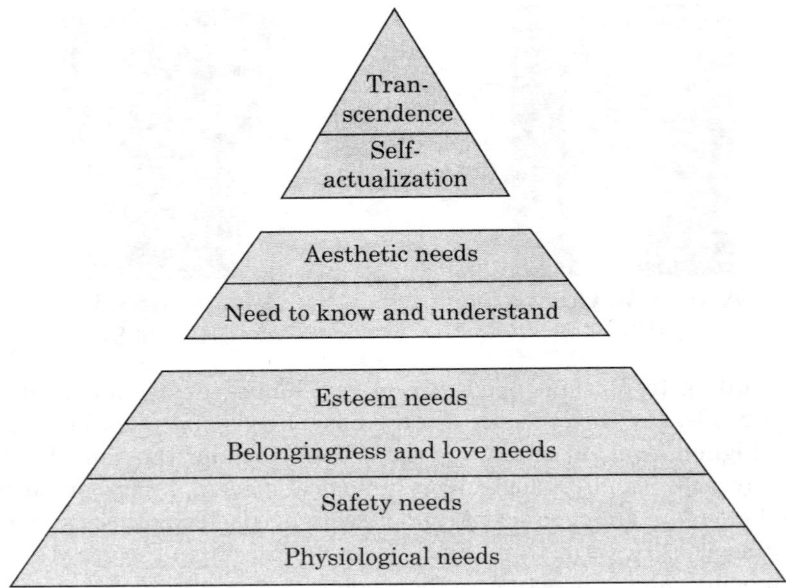

Figure 1.1 Maslow's hierarchy of needs.

Some Qualities or Characteristics of a Self-actualized Person or Self-actualizers

From his study and observations of self actualizers, Maslow also developed a profile of the self-actualizing personality. A summary of these characteristics is presented below:

Strengths

1. Maslow felt that self-actualizers had an acceptance of herself or himself, acceptance is applied to their attitudes towards themselves; were more likely to be satisfied with themselves.
2. An acceptance of other people, by which Maslow meant that these people would be more likely to take you as you are than try to change you into what they thought you should be.
3. Self-actualizing people have the ability to love others and to be loved by others. They have a capacity for deep interpersonal relationships. They enjoyed deeper personal relations with a few close friends and family members, rather than more shallow relationships with many people. Maslow found that self-actualizers have deeper and more profound interpersonal relations than any other people. Healthy people at least know how to love, can do so freely, easily, naturally and without getting wound up in conflicts or threats or inhibitions. Love is a complex psychological phenomenon. In philosophical language,

it is an aspect of being as well as of becoming and can be called B-love, that is, love for the Being of the others. Psychologists are often limited in their understanding of love.

Maslow (1971) describes love as primarily a "Feeling of tenderness and affection with great enjoyment, happiness, satisfaction, elation and even ecstasy in experiencing this feeling (if all is going well)." Within this definition, he also includes the desire for psychological and physical intimacy, the tendency to perceive one's mate as beautiful, the feeling of pleasure in her or his presence and depression in her or his absence, the desire to share pleasures, the need for privacy, feelings of generosity, the need to share secrets, the desire for fuller knowledge of one's partner, and the tendency to drop all defences and roles. This last characteristic was particularly important to Maslow because he felt that in true love relationships there wasn't the need to put one's "best foot" forward.

Theodore Reik
(1886–1969)

Theodore Reik (1957) has defined one characteristic of love as the absence of anxiety. Honesty in a relationship includes allowing one's faults, weaknesses, physical and psychological shortcomings to be freely seen by the partner. Other most important characteristics for love are good companionship, considerateness, affection, dependability, intelligence, kindness, being understanding, loyalty, and being interesting to talk to. Least valued characteristics for love are dominance, agnosticism (an agnostic is a person believing that nothing can be known about the existence of God), and being a night owl or being an early riser.

Maslow's writings make it evident that he understands the bonding between lovers, that he is able to objectively describe everyday love feelings, and that he appreciates the intensity of being sexual with someone you love. Maslow believed that sex and love are more perfectly fused with each other in healthy people. Furthermore, sexual pleasures are found in their most intense and ecstatic perfection in self-actualizing people. Whereas sex seemed to be wholeheartedly enjoyed far beyond the possibility of the average person. Maslow also found that it did not play any central role in the self-actualizer's philosophy of life.

4. They had a sense of humility and respect towards others—something Maslow also called democratic values—meaning that they were open to ethnic and individual variety, even treasuring it. They had a quality Maslow called *human kinship* or *Gemeinschaftsgefuhl*—social interest, compassion, humanity. And this was accompanied by strong ethics, which was spiritual but seldom conventionally religious in nature. They will not unnecessarily humiliate the other person, whether adult or child. Respect for another person acknowledges her or him as an independent entity and as a separate and autonomous individual.
5. Self-actualizing people will not casually use, control, or disregard the wishes of others.
6. Self-actualized person is involved in some cause outside of herself or himself.
7. A self-actualized person is self-aware, socially responsive, simple, spontaneous, creative, and autonomous, open to novelty and challenge. Maslow believed that self-actualizers were more spontaneous and natural in their behaviour than other people.
8. A self-actualized person has a good and unhostile sense of humour—preferring to joke at their own expense, or at the human condition, and never directing their humour at others. Maslow felt that self-actualizers had a more philosophical sense of humour.
9. A self-actualized person is focused on problems and solutions rather than her or him. Maslow discovered that self-actualizers focused most of their energies on problems and tasks outside of themselves.
10. The self-actualized persons are very spontaneous in both actions and emotions. They preferred being themselves rather than being pretentious or artificial.
11. A self-actualized person resists pressures to confirm. Maslow discovered that self-actualizers tended to have values that were often in opposition to the "mainstream" culture. Thus, they tended to resist "enculturation" or the transcendence of any particular culture. They resisted enculturation, that is, they were not susceptible to social pressure and cultural influences to be "well-adjusted" or "fit in"—they were in fact, non-conformists in the best sense.
12. A self-actualized person is creative, inventive, and original. Not surprisingly, every self-actualizer is deemed very creative.
13. The self-actualized persons have a concern about personal growth. They were strongly motivated to change negative qualities in themselves that could be changed.

14. These people had a certain freshness of appreciation, an ability to see things, even ordinary things, with wonder. According to Maslow (1970), "Self-actualizing people have the wonderful capacity to appreciate again and again, freshly and naively, the basic goods of life, with awe, pleasure, wonder, and even ecstasy, however stale these experiences may have become to others."
15. These people have the ability to have more peak experiences than the average person. Peak experiences are those profound and enlightening feelings that are so intense or illuminating that it is readily obvious that they are special events. A peak experience is one that takes you out of yourself, that makes you feel very tiny, or very large, to some extent one with life or nature or God. It gives you a feeling of being a part of the infinite and the eternal. It is also an active experience which is felt as self-validating, self-justifying, and inherently good. The emotional reaction has a special flavour of wonder, awe, reverence, humility, and surrender. Finally, the person at the peak feels god-like and loses all fear, anxiety, inhibition, defense, control, delay, and restraint. These experiences tend to leave their mark on a person, change them for the better, and many people actively seek them out. They are also called *mystical experiences*, and are an important part of many religious and philosophical traditions. Maslow discovered that self-actualizers have usually had feelings of being simultaneously more powerful and also more helpless than others; feelings of great ecstasy, wonder, and awe; feelings of being lost in time and space; and the feeling that something extremely important and valuable has happened to them, to such an extent that it has transformed and strengthened their everyday experiences.
16. A self-actualized person incorporates an outgoing freshness of appreciation of life. Maslow believed that self-actualizers have the wonderful capacity to appreciate the basic goods of life.
17. A self-actualized person has strongly developed a set of values.
18. The self-actualized persons have the need for privacy. Maslow found that self-actualizers preferred solitude and privacy much more than other people. The self-actualizers enjoyed solitude, and were comfortable being alone.
19. The self-actualizers enjoyed autonomy or independence of culture and environment, will, active agents; a relative independence from physical and social needs. Maslow believed that the self-actualizers depended solely on their resources for their development and continued growth.

20. The self-actualizers have more efficient perception of reality and more comfortable relations with it. Maslow felt that the self-actualizers were able to detect dishonesty in a better way and, in general, were better judges.
21. The self-actualizers can discriminate between means and ends, between good and evil. Maslow stressed that he could not characterize a single self-actualizer as someone who was chronically unsure about the difference between right and wrong.
22. The self-actualizers have a democratic character structure. Maslow discovered that self-actualizers are generally friendly with people regardless of class, education, political belief, race, or colour. As the matter of fact, Maslow often found that they acted as if they were unaware of these differences.

The self-actualizers have "genuine feelings for others" or *Gemeinschaftsgefuhl*. According to Maslow (1970), "This word, invented by Alfred Adler, is the only one available that describes well the flavour of the feelings for mankind expressed by self-actualizing subjects. They have for human beings in general a deep feeling of identification, sympathy, and affection in spite of... occasional anger, impatience, or disgust... Because of this they have a genuine desire to help the human race."

1.4.3 Gestalt Approach or School

Gestalt approach was prominent in Europe in the first decades of twentieth century (Hochberg, 1988). Gestalt school of Psychology was found in Germany in the 1910s. Some German psychologists tried to understand how, in spite of the limitations of the retinal image (retinal image is two-dimensional and very different in size and shape from the actual object), is our perception organized.

Max Wertheimer (1880–1943) **Kurt Koffka** (1886–1941) **Wolfgang Kohler** (1887–1967) **Kurt Lewin** (1890–1947)

Gestaltists protested that conscious experience could not be dissected without destroying the very essence of experience, namely, its quality of wholeness. Direct awareness, they said, consists of patterns or configurations and not of elements joined together. Gestaltists maintain that psychological phenomena could only be understood if they were viewed as organized, structured wholes (or Gestalten). They called themselves *Gestaltists*; this is based on the German word "Gestalt" meaning organized whole. According to the Gestalt approach, we perceive the object as a well-organized, whole structures instead of separate, isolated parts. A key assumption made by the Gestaltists is that "the whole is more than the sum of its parts." The Gestalt psychologists stressed that our ability to see object having shape and pattern is determined by interrelationships among the part (Greene, 1991). One area in which the Gestalt influence is still very prominent is in research on the figure-ground relationship (Figure 1.2), (Banks & Krajicek, 1991).

Figure 1.2 Reversible Figure-Ground.

"Figure and ground" refers to the most basic and elementary of all forms of perceptual structure. We perceive an object as a figure in a ground. We perceive a picture on a page. The picture is a figure and this page is ground. Edgar Rubin (6 September, 1886–3 May, 1951), a Gestalt and Danish psychologist and phenomenologist from Denmark, reached several conclusions (1915, 1958) about the figure-ground relationship. According to Edgar Rubin, "Figure and ground possess the following properties:

1. The figure seems closer to the viewer, with a clear location in space. In contrast, the ground seems farther away. It takes a clear location.
2. Figure has form, whereas ground is relatively formless. The figure has a definite, clear, distinct shape, whereas the ground seems vague, formless, and shapeless.

3. Figure has "thing like" qualities, whereas ground appears as more homogeneous and uniformed material.
4. Figure appears to be nearer to the observer than does the ground. The figure appears on the front, whereas the ground seems to continue behind the figure.
5. The figure is more easily identified or named than the ground.
6. The colour of the figure is more impressive.
7. The figure is more likely to be connected with meanings, feelings, and aesthetic values than is the ground.
8. The figure is bright, whereas the ground is dull".

In almost all cases, the figure-ground concept is clear art. We discriminate figure from ground, imposing one important kind of organization in our visual experiences. We also organize visual stimuli into patterns and groups. The Gestalt psychologists developed several laws of grouping that describe why certain objects seem to go together, instead of remaining isolated and independent.

Laws of organization or grouping or perception or principles of perceptual organization or Gestalt factors of perception

The Gestaltists argued that most perceptual organization depends on innate factors and brain processes or functions of the brain. The Gestaltists put forward several laws of perceptual organization. However, their most basic Law was the law of Pragnanz. This was expressed as follows by Koffka (1935): "Psychological organization will always be as 'good' as the prevailing conditions allow. In this definition the term 'good' is undefined." In fact, the Gestaltists regarded a "good" form as the simplest or most uniform of all the possible ways of organizing perceptual information.

1. *The law of proximity (or the law of nearness): Law of proximity* states that objects near each other tend to be perceived as a unit or the visual elements which are close to each other will tend to be grouped together (Figure 1.3). Law of proximity is also called *minimum-distance principle.*

Figure 1.3 Examples of the law of proximity.

In Figure 1.3 (a), a figure seen as three groups of two lines or (b), a figure seen as three groups of four dots.

2. *The law of similarity: Law of similarity* states that objects similar to each other tend to be seen as a unit or similar visual elements are grouped together (Figure 1.4).

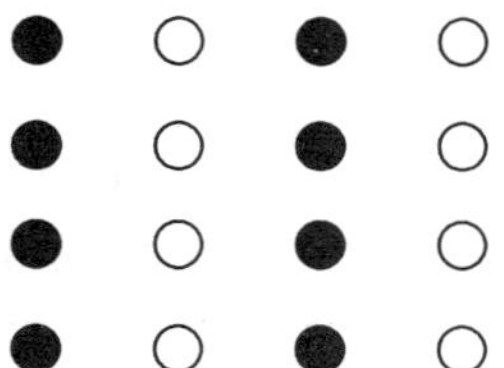

Figure 1.4 Example of law of the similarity.

Figure 1.4 is seen as two columns of one kind of dot and two columns of another; vertical columns rather than horizontal rows are seen.

3. *The law of good continuation: Law of good continuation* states that we tend to perceive smooth, continuous lines rather than discontinuous fragments or those visual elements producing the fewest interruptions to smoothly curving lines are grouped together (Figure 1.5(a) and (b).

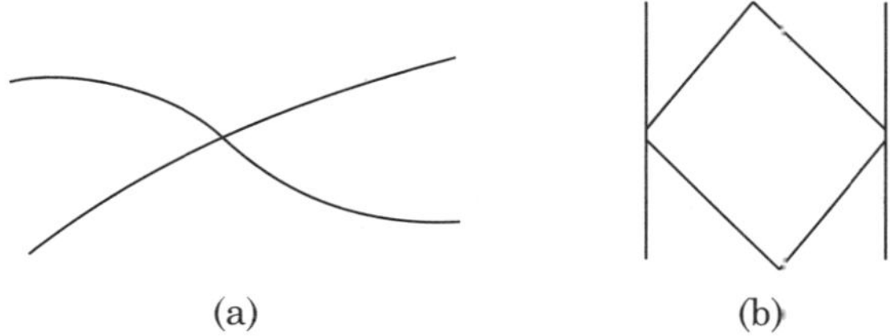

(a) (b)

Figure 1.5 Examples of the law of good continuation.

Figure 1.5 (a), we tend to see two crossing lines rather than V-shaped line and an inverted V-shaped line and Figure (b) is seen as a diamond between uprights and not as a W on top of an M.

4. *The law of closure: Law of closure* states that a figure with a gap will be perceived as a closed, intact figure or the missing parts of a figure are filled in to complete (Figure 1.6(a), (b) and (c).

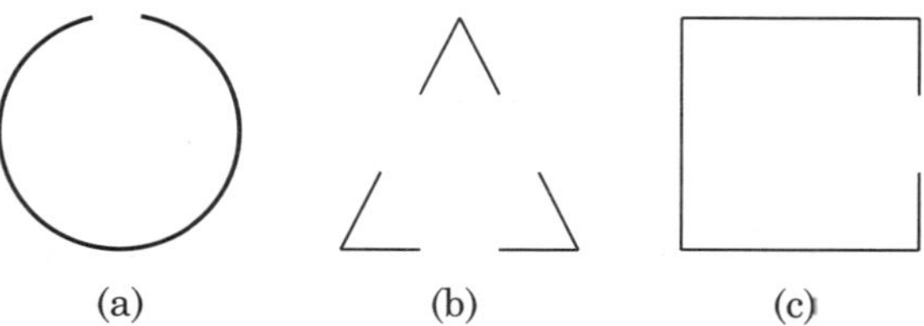

(a) (b) (c)

Figure 1.6 Examples of the law of closure.

Figure 1.6 shows a circle (a), triangle (b), and a square(c), although incomplete. It occurs because of our inclination or mindset to fill in the gaps or close the gaps and to perceive incomplete figures as complete. These non-existing lines, which are known as *subjective contours*, appear naturally as the result of the brain's automatic attempts to enhance and complete the details of an image (Kanisza, 1976).

5. *The law of symmetry: Law of symmetry* states that there is a tendency to organize things to make a balanced figure or symmetrical figure that includes all parts.
6. *The law of common fate: Law of common fate* states that those aspects of a perceptual field that function or move in similar manner tend to be perceived together.

The first four laws of organization of perceptual field discussed above are more specific statements and descriptions of the basic law of Pragnanz. The figure-ground relationship and these laws of grouping help organize our visual world and encourage pattern recognition.

Advantages of the Gestalt Approach

(i) The Gestaltists rightly recognized and emphasized the importance of perceptual organization.

(ii) The Gestaltists discovered figure-ground relationship and several laws of perception.

Disadvantages of the Gestalt Approach

(i) The laws of organization or grouping are only descriptive statements. They fail to explain why it is that similar visual elements or those close together are grouped.

(ii) It is difficult to apply the Gestalt laws of organization to certain complex visual stimuli (for example, stimuli in which similar elements are relatively far apart and dissimilar elements are close together).

(iii) The Gestaltists may have exaggerated the importance of innate factors.

(iv) The Gestaltists tried to identify some of the brain processes involved, but without any success.

EXERCISES

The below mentioned are some of the questions that have been asked in the examinations conducted by the Guru Nanak Dev University or can be asked. Knowledge of these answers can help the students to get success in the examinations.

Section A

Answer the following questions in **five** lines or 50 words.

1. Define Psychology.*
2. What is behaviour?*
3. Define Behaviourists.*
4. Write various goals of Psychology.*
5. What is Gestalt?
6. Who were Gestaltists?
7. What do you mean by Humanistic Psychology?
8. Explain the Law of Pragnanz.
9. Define Perception.
10. What do mean by peak experiences?
11. What is self actualization?*
12. What is Hierarchy of needs?
13. Write Woodworth's definition of Psychology.
14. Why definition of Psychology "as the study of soul' is not acceptable?
15. Write short note on the utility of Psychology.
16. What is cognitive behaviour?*
17. What is the contribution of Wilhelm Wundt in the history of Psychology?
18. Who, when, and where was the first experimental laboratory opened?
19. What is affective behaviour?
20. State—"Psychology is the science of ...."?
21. What is conative behaviour?
22. What is a science?*
23. What are the various kinds of behaviour?
24. Define 'activities' and write various kinds of activities.
25. Is Psychology a science?
26. Define structuralism.
27. Define functionalism.
28. What is 'Homeostasis'?
29. What are the goals of Psychology?*
30. What is organismic variable?

Section B

Answer the following questions up to **two** pages or 500 words.

1. Define Psychology.
2. Describe the nature of Psychology.
3. Define Psychology? Write its nature.
4. Why Psychology is called a 'science'.

   or

   Write in brief the nature of Psychology as a 'science'.

   or

   Is Psychology a science? Explain.
5. What is Psychology? Write briefly the various goals of Psychology.*
6. What is a science?
7. Write in detail Woodworth's definition of Psychology.*
8. Write a brief note on goals of Psychology.

   or

   Describe different goals of Psychology.
9. Discuss structuralism and functionalism in brief.
10. Describe structuralism.

    or

    Give a brief description of structuralism.
11. Give a brief description of Gestalt.

Section C

Answer the following questions up to **five** pages or 1000 words.

1. Write in detail the meaning and nature of Psychology.
2. Write in detail the nature and goals of Psychology.
3. Explain structuralism, functionalism, and Gestalt school of Psychology.
4. Discuss the various goals of Psychology.*
5. Write in detail the nature of Psychology as a science.*
6. What is 'Science'? Why Psychology is called a science?
7. Write about various schools of Psychology in short.*
8. Describe Psychoanalysis, Behaviourism, and Humanistic Psychology.
9. Give brief introduction to structuralism, psychoanalysis, Gestalt, and humanistic Psychology.

10. Describe the humanistic approach. What are its strengths? What are its weaknesses?
11. What are some of the strengths of Modern Psychology? What are some of its weaknesses?
12. Explain various schools of Psychology.

or

Write a detailed note on the schools of Psychology.

REFERENCES

Adler, A., *Practice and Theory of Individual Psychology*, New York: Harcourt Brace and World, 1927.

Adler, A., *Individual Psychology of Alfred Adler: A Systematic Presentation in Selections from his Writings*, New York: Harper Collins, 1989.

Allport, G., *Pattern and Growth in Personality,* New York: Holt, Rinehart and Winston, 1961.

American Psychological Association, *Ethical Principles of Psychologists and Code of Conduct,* American Psychologist, **47**, pp. 1597–1611, 1992.

Angell, J.R., *Psychology: An Introductory Study of the Structure and Function of Human Consciousness,* New York: Holt, 1904.

Bootzin, R., Bower, Crooker and Hall, *Psychology Today*, New York: McGraw-Hill, Inc, 1991.

Boring, E.G., *A History of Experimental Psychology* (2nd ed.), New York: Appleton-Century-Crofts, 1950.

Boring, E.G., Langfield, H.S., and Weld, H.P. (Eds.), *Foundations of Psychology*, New York: John Wiley & Sons, 1961.

Cannon, W.B., *Bodily changes in Pain, Hunger, Fear, and Rage* (2nd ed.), New York: Appleton-Century-Crofts, 1929.

Cannon, W.B., 'Hunger and Thirst,' in C. Murchinson (Ed.), *Handbook of General Experimental Psychology,* Worchester, MA: Clark University Press, 247–263, 1934.

Cannon, W.B., 'Reflections on the Man and His Contributions,' *International Journal of Stress Management*, Vol. **1** (2), 1994.

Crooks, R.L. and Stein, J., *Psychology, Science, Behaviour and Life,* London: Halt, Rinehart and Winston, Inc, 1991.

Crow, L.D. and Crow, A., *Educational Psychology* (3rd Indian reprint), New Delhi: Eurasia Publishing House, 1973.

Daniels, M., *Maslow's Concept of Self-actualization*, Retrieved February 2004, from http://www.mdani.demon.co.uk/archive/MD Maslowhtm, 2001.

Darwin, C., *The Origin of Species*, London: Murray, J. 1859.

Darwin, C., 'A Biographical Sketch of an Infant,' *Mind*, **2**, 285–294, 1877.

Dewey, J., 'The Reflex Arc Concept in Psychology,' *Psychological Review*, **3**, 357–370, 1896.

Drever, J., *Instincts in Man*, Cambridge: Cambridge University Press, 1917.

Frankl, V.E., *Man's Search for Meaning: An Introduction to Logotherapy,* New York: Washington Square Press, 1959, 1998.

Freud, S., *Introductory Lectures on Psychoanalysis*, Allen & Unwin, 1929.

Galton, F., 'Psychometric Experiments,' *Brain*, **2**, 149–162, 1879.

Galton, F., *Inquiries into Human Faculty and its Development*, London: Macmillan, 1883.

Greene, R.L., *The MMPI-2/MMPI: An Interpretative Manual,* Boston: Allyn Bacon, 1991.

Guilford, J.P., 'Creativity,' *American Psychologist*, **5**, 444–454. 1950.

Guilford, J.P., 'Factorial Angles to Psychology,' *Psychological Review*, **68**, 1–20. 1961.

Guilford, J.P., *Fields of Psychology*, New York: Van Nostrand, 1966.

Guthrie, E.R., 'Association and the Law of Effect,' *Psychological Review*, **47**, 127–148, 1940.

Guthrie, E.R., 'Association by Contiguity,' in S. Koch (Ed.), *Psychology: A study of a science* (Vol. 2), New York: McGraw-Hill, 1959.

Hilgard, E.R., *Theories of Learning* (4th ed.), New York: Appleton-Century-Crofts, 1976.

Hilgard, E.R., *Divided Consciousness: Multiple Controls in Human Thought and Action* (2nd ed.), New York: Wiley, 1986.

Hull, C.L., *Principles of Behaviour*, New York: Appleton-Century-Crofts, 1943.

James, W., *Principles of Psychology* (Vol. 2), New York: Henry Holt, 1890.

James, W., *Psychology: Briefer Course*, New York: Collier, 1892.

James, W., *Psychology: The Briefer Course*, New York: Henry Holt, 1892/1962.

James, W., *Psychology*, New York: Collier, 1962.

Jenkins, J.G., and Dallenbach, K.M., 'Obliviscence During Sleep and Waking,' *American Journal of Psychology*, **35**, 605–612, 1924.

Jung, C.G., *Conscious, Unconscious and Individuation,* in G. Adler, M. Fordham, and H. Read (Eds.), The Collected Works of C.G. Jung, London: Routledge, 1959.

Jung, C.G., *Psychological Types,* In Collected Works (Vol. 6). Princeton: Princeton University Press (First German edition, 1921), 1971.

Kihlstrom, J.F., 'The Psychological Unconscious,' in L.A. Pervin (Ed.), *Handbook of Personality Theory and Research* (pp. 445–464), New York: Guilford, 1990.

Koffka, W., *Principles of Gestalt Psychology*. New York: Harcourt Brace, 1935.

Kohler, W., *The Mentality of Apes*, New York: Harcourt Brace and World, 1925.

Kohler, W., *Gestalt Psychology*, New York: Leveright, 1929.

Kohler, W., *The Task of Gestalt Psychology*, Princeton, NJ: Princeton University Press, 1969.

Lashley, K.S., *Brain Mechanisms and Intelligence,* Chicago: University of Chicago Press, 1929.

Maslow, A.H., *Motivation and Personality* (2nd ed.), New York: Harper & Row, 1970.

Maslow, A.H., *The Farther Reaches of Human Nature*, New York: The Viking Press, 1971.

Maslow, A., and Lowery, R. (Ed.), *Toward a Psychology of being* (3rd ed.), New York: Wiley & Sons, 1998.

Mc Dougall, W., *Social Psychology*, London: Methuen, 1908.

Munn, N.L., *Handbook of Psychological Research on the Rat,* New York: Houghton Mifflin, 1950.

Munn, N.L., *Psychology: The Fundamentals of Human Adjustment* (5th ed.), Boston: Houghton Mifflin, 1966.

Munn, N.L., *An Introduction to Psychology* (2nd ed.), New Delhi: Oxford and IBH, 1967.

Pavlov, I.P., *Conditioned Reflexes*, London: Oxford University Press, 1927.

Pillsbury, W.B., *Essentials of Psychology*, New York: Macmillan, 1911.

Rogers, C.R., *A Way of Being*, Boston: Houghton Mifflin, 1980.

Rubin, E., *Synsoplevede Figurer*, 1915.

Skinner, B.F., *The Behaviour of Organism*, New York: Appleton-Century-Crofts, 1938.

Thorndike, E.L., *The Elements of Psychology*, New York: Seiler, 1905.

Tolman, E.L., *Purposive Behaviour in Animals and Men*, New York: Century, 1932.

Wahba, A., and Bridgewell, L., 'Maslow Reconsidered: A Review of Research on the Need Hierarchy Theory,' *Organizational Behaviour and Human Performance*, **15**, 212–240, 1976.

Watson, J.B., 'Psychology as a Behaviorist Views It,' *Psychological Review, Vol.* **20**, 1913.

Watson, J.B., *Behaviorism,* New York: Norton, 1925.

Weiss, A.P., 'Conscious and the Unconscious,' *Psychological Bulletin*, **16**, 9–12, 1919.

Wertheimer, M., 'Psychomotor Co-ordination of Auditory-Visual Space at Birth,' *Science*, **134**, 1692, 1962.

Wertheimer, M., *A Brief History of Psychology*, New York: Holt, Rinehart and Winston, 1970.

Woodworth, R.S., *Dynamic Psychology,* New York: Columbia University Press, 1918.

Woodworth, R.S., *Psychology.* New York: Holt, 1921, 1929, 1934, 1940.

Woodworth, R.S., *Dynamic Psychology*, in C. Murchison (Ed.), *Psychologies of 1930* (pp. 327–336), Worcester, UMA: Clark University Press, 1930a.

Woodworth, R.S., 'Robert S. Woodworth,' in C. Murchison (Ed.), *A History of Psychology in Autobiography*, (Vol. 2, pp. 359–380), Worcester, MA: Clark University Press, 1930b.

Woodworth, R.S., *Contemporary Schools of Psychology*, New York: Ronald Press, 1931, 1948.

Woodworth, R.S., *Experimental Psychology* (rev. ed.), New York: Holt, 1954.

Woodworth, R.S., *Dynamics of Behavior,* New York: Holt, Rinehart & Winston, 1958.

Woodworth, R.S., and Sheehan, M., *Contemporary Schools of Psychology* (3rd. ed.), New York: Ronald Press, 1964.

Wundt, W., *Fundamentals of Physiological Psychology*, 1874.

Wundt, W., *Grundzuge Der Physiologischen Psychologie* (Vol. 2), Leipzig: Englemann, 1874.

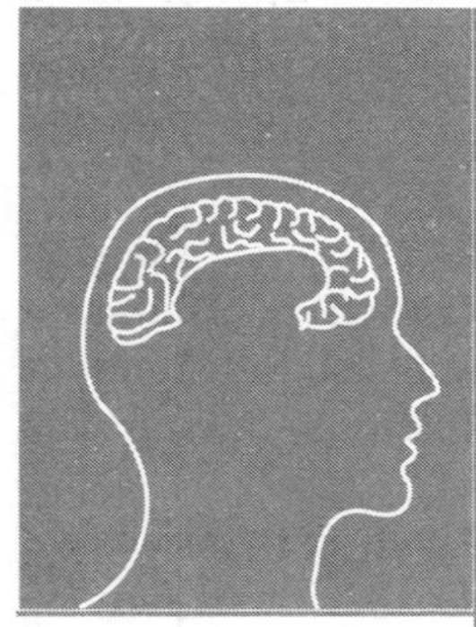

CHAPTER 2

Methods of Psychological Research

Psychological research is intended to accomplish one or more of three basic goals: to understand or to describe behaviour, to explain behaviour, and to predict the circumstances in which certain behaviours might occur again. Psychological research is based on the scientific method. The scientific method includes the following four basic steps:

1. Identify the research problem,
2. Design and conduct a study, gathering appropriate data,
3. Examine the data,
4. Communicate the results.

Psychologists use various methods to explore behaviour. Each method approaches the steps of the scientific method from a different perspective, and each method has strengths and weaknesses. By combining different approaches, researchers can achieve a much more complete picture of psychological processes. Various methods also differ in the amount of control the researchers can exercise when they conduct their studies. Different research methods, then, often complement one another, and together they enrich our understanding of human behaviour.

2.1 THE EXPERIMENT OR THE EXPERIMENTAL METHOD OR THE SCIENTIFIC METHOD

Experiment is an observation of behaviour done under controlled conditions. It is the most objective and scientific method. The word *experiment* is derived from the Latin word *experimentum*, which means a *trial* or *test*.

2.1.1 Definitions of an Experiment

According to Eysenck (1996) "An experiment is the planned manipulation of variables in which at least one of the variables that is the independent variable is altered under the predetermined conditions during the experiment."

According to Jahoda, "Experiment is a method of testing hypothesis."

According to Festinger and Katz, "The essence of experiment may be described as observing the effect of dependent variable after the manipulation of independent variable."

According to Bootzin (1991), "An experiment is a research method designed to control the factors that might affect a variable under study, thus allowing scientists to establish cause and effect."

The experimental method is the method of investigation most often used by psychologists. Experimental method allows us to study cause-and-effect relationship. An experiment is a controlled method of exploring the relationship between factors capable of change, called *variables*. A hypothesis tells what relationship a researcher expects to find between an independent variable and a dependent variable to study cause-and-effect relationship. The experiment is a research method designed to study or answer the questions about cause (independent variable) and effect (dependent variable), or to identify a cause-and-effect relationship. Its main advantage over other data gathering or collecting methods is that this method permits the researcher to control the conditions and so rules out—to as large an extent as possible—all influences on subject's behaviour except the factors or variables being examined.

In an experiment, researchers systematically manipulate a variable [Independent variable, (IV)] under controlled conditions and observe how the participants respond. For example, suppose some researchers want to study the effect of music on student's accuracy in solving mathematical problems. The researchers manipulate one variable (IV, for example, presence or absence of music) and they observe how the subjects or the participants respond (Dependent variable, DV, number of mathematical problems correctly solved). They try to hold constant the other variables that are not being tested but they can exert their influence on the variable being studied (IV). Variables which need to be controlled include light in the room, noise, fatigue, and type of math problems being solved etc. If the behaviour changes when only that manipulated variable is changed, then the researchers can conclude that they have discovered a cause-and-effect relationship, for example in this case between the presence of music and problem-solving.

In designing an experiment, the first step after framing of the problem is to state a hypothesis. "A hypothesis is a tentative set of beliefs about the nature of the world, a statement about what you expect to happen if certain conditions are true" (Halpern, 1989). A hypothesis is a presupposed answer to a problem. A hypothesis can be stated in an "If——— then ———" format. If certain conditions are true, then certain things will happen. For example, if music is present, then people solve a smaller number of math problems accurately.

Variable: A variable, as the name implies, is something which varies. The term *variable* means which can be changed or which can take up a number of values. *Variable* may be defined as those attributes, qualities, and characteristics of objects, events, things, and beings, which can be measured. In other words, variables are the characteristics or conditions that are manipulated, controlled or observed by the experimenter. Variable is any condition in a scientific investigation that may change in quantity and quality. Intelligence, anxiety, aptitude, income, education, authoritarianism, achievement, etc. are some examples of variables commonly employed or studied in Psychology, Sociology, and Education.

2.1.2 Definitions of Variable

According to Postman and Egan (1949), "A variable is a characteristic or attribute that can take a number of values."

According to D'Amato (2004), "Any measurable attribute of objects, things, or beings is called a variable." The measurability attribute need not be quantitative; it can be qualitative also such as race, sex, and religion."

Independent and dependent variable

Independent variable is the variable that the experimenter deliberately (wishfully) manipulates. Experimenter decides how much of that variable to present to the participant. The independent variable is described in the 'if' part of the "if ——— then ———" statement of the hypothesis. In the example discussed earlier, the independent variable is whether or not the music is presented to the participants or subjects of the study. The independent variable as the one which is selected, manipulated, and measured by the experimenter or researcher for the purpose of producing observable changes in the behavioural measure (DV). In other words, the independent variable is the variable on the basis of which the prediction about the dependent variable is made.

2.1.3 Definitions of Independent Variable

According to Kerlinger (1986), "An independent variable is the presumed cause of the dependant variable."

According to D'Amato (2004), Independent variable is "Any variable manipulated by experimenter either directly or through selection in order to determine its effect on a behavioural variable."

According to Townsend, "Independent variable is that variable which is manipulated by the experimenter in his attempt to ascertain its relationship to an observed phenomenon."

According to Ghorpade, "Independent variable is usually the cause whose effects are being studied. The experimenter changes or varies independent variable to find out what effects such change produced on dependent variable."

Underwood (1966) refers to the independent variable as the stimulus variable. Independent variable is indeed a stimulus to which a response from the participant or subject is sought. Independent variable is manipulated by the experimenter and its effect is observed or examined upon the dependent variable. Some experts, depending upon the method of manipulation used, have tried to divide the independent variable into Type-E independent variable and Type-S independent variable (D'Amats, 1970). Type-E independent variable is one which is directly or experimentally manipulated by the experimenter and Type-S independent variable is one which is not manipulated directly by the experimenter or researcher as these are difficult to be manipulated directly but manipulated through the process of selection only.

A research or investigation which involves the manipulation of the Type-E independent variable is called *experimentation*, no matter whether it is done in a laboratory or in a natural setting. Likewise, a research which involves the manipulation of the Type-S independent variable is called *correlation research*. A research in which there are no independent variables, is called *observation*.

The above classification of independent variables, according to Underwood was on the basis of method of manipulation. The independent variables or the stimulus can also be classified on the basis of nature of the variables. The following categories are there according to this classification:

1. **Task variables:** The *task variables* refer to those characteristics which are associated with a behavioural task presented to the subject or participant of the study. It includes the physical characteristics of the apparatus or instrument as well as many features of the task procedure or the method. The simplicity or the complexity of the apparatus or the instrument used in a research or study is likely to produce a change in behavioural measure or the behaviour of the subject or participant.

2. **Environmental variables:** The *environmental variables* refer to those characteristics or features of the environment, which are not physical parts of the task as such, but they tend to produce changes in the behavioural measure or the behaviour of the subject. Examples of such variables include noise, temperature, levels of illumination, and time of the day when experiment was conducted or done, etc.
3. **Subject variables:** The *subject variables* refer to those characteristics of the subjects (humans or animals) which are likely to produce changes in the behavioural measures. Examples of such variables include age, sex, height, weight, intelligence, anxiety of the subject, etc.

A dependent variable or behavioural measure concerns the responses that the participants make. It is the measure of their behaviour. Behaviour of the person or the subject or the participant is the dependant variable. Any measured behavioural variable of interest to the experimenter in a psychological investigation is the dependent variable. The dependent variable, which nearly always involves some form of behaviour, is what is expected to change when the independent variable is manipulated, provided the experimenter's hypothesis is right. Changes in the dependent variable depend on the changes in the independent variable.

2.1.4 Definitions of Dependent Variable

According to D'Amato, "Any measured behavioural variable of interest in the psychological investigation is dependent variable."

According to Townsend, "A dependent variable is that factor which appears, disappears, or varies as the experimenter introduces, or removes, or varies the independent variable."

According to Postman and Egan, "The 'phenomenon' with which we wish to explain and predict is dependent variable." Dependent variable is described in the "then" part of the "if ——— then ——— " statement or format of hypothesis. Underwood has referred to dependent variable as the response variable. In the example that we are discussing, the dependent variable is the problem-solving of the participants or the subjects, which we could measure in terms of the number of the problems correctly solved in a specified time. An "if ——— then ——— " statement stresses that a cause-and-effect relationship occurs in one direction only. Change in the independent variable causes change in the dependent variable but not vice versa. Because an experiment provides a means of establishing causality, it is the data gathering method of choice for many psychologists.

Experimental and controlled conditions or groups

In an experiment, the researcher must arrange to test at least two conditions that are specified by the independent variable. In the simple example of the music experiment, the researcher or the experimenter could test one group of subjects or participants of the study or research in a "no music condition" (controlled group) and the second group in a "music" condition (experimental group). An experimental group consists of those subjects who experience the experimental condition—"music". The independent variable that is music here is introduced in the experimental group. The experimental condition is changed in some way. Most experiments also use a control group to provide a source of comparison. Control subjects experience all the conditions that the experimental subjects do except the key factor the psychologist or researcher is evaluating, that is the independent variable (music). The control condition is left unchanged. A particular variable is present in the experimental condition that is absent in the control condition (music is either present or absent).

Control of variables

A good research design should control the effects of extraneous variables which are more or less similar to independent variable or variables that have the capacity to influence the dependent variable or variables. If left uncontrolled, such variables are called *independent extraneous variables* or simply *extraneous variables*.

There are various ways to control the effects of extraneous variables. Of these ways, randomization is considered by many as one of the best techniques of controlling the extraneous variables. Randomization is a very popular technique of controlling extraneous variables. "Randomization" refers to a technique in which each member of the population or universe at large has an equal and independent chance of being selected in the groups. There are three basic phases in randomization—random selection of subjects, random assignment of subjects into control and experimental groups, and random assignment of experimental treatments among different groups. Sometimes, it happens that for the researcher it is not possible to make random selection of subjects. In such situations, the researcher tries to randomly assign the selected subjects into different experimental groups. When this random assignment is not possible due to any reason, the researcher randomly assigns the different experimental treatments into experimental groups. Whatever the method may be, randomization has proved very useful in controlling the extraneous variables. A research design which fully controls the extraneous variable or variables is considered to be the best design for the research. This increases the internal validity of the research. Randomization helps in generalizing the findings.

Random assignment means that people are assigned to experimental group or groups using a system, such as slip system, coin tossing—which ensures that everyone has equal chance to be selected to any group or being assigned to any one group. Randomization is used where the experimenter or the researcher assumes that some extraneous variables operate, but she or he cannot specify them and, therefore, cannot apply the other techniques of controlling extraneous variables. The technique is also applied where the extraneous variables are known but their effects can't be controlled by known techniques.

The importance of randomization lies in the fact that this technique randomly distributes the extraneous effects over the experimental and control conditions. Such balancing occurs whether or not the experimenter has identified certain extraneous variables, because the effects of unknown or unspecified extraneous variables are said to be equally distributed across different conditions of the experiment when the experimenter randomly assigns subjects to the different groups or conditions.

If the number of participants or subjects in the study is sufficiently large, then random assignment usually guarantees that the various groups will be reasonably similar with respects to important characteristics like age, gender, intelligence, personality, aptitude, and other psychological traits. The participants used in an experiment consist of one or more samples drawn from some larger population. If we want the findings from a sample to be true of the population, then those included in the sample must be representative of the population. In more simple words, the sample must be true representative of the population. The best way to obtain a representative sample from that population would be to make use of random sampling. Another way of obtaining a representative sample is by using quota sampling, a sample that is chosen from a population so that the sample is similar to the population in certain ways, for example, proportion of females, proportion of graduates, etc. Random sampling and quota sampling are often expensive and time consuming. Accordingly, opportunity sampling can be used, which means participants are selected on the basis of their availability rather than by any other method. The extraneous variables can be controlled in several ways. Of these various ways, randomization, balancing, and counterbalancing are relatively more popular.

All experiments require some kind of comparison between conditions. If we have only one condition, we cannot draw conclusions about cause and effect. The music study could compare four conditions—no music (control condition) and three experimental conditions (low/soft, medium, and high/loud music).

Confounding variables

A *confounding variable* is any variable, other than the independent variable that is not equivalent in all conditions. These are variables that are mistakenly manipulated along with the independent variable. Confounding variables can lead researchers to draw incorrect conclusions. Researchers can guard against the confounding variables by the use of random assignment. Subjects are placed in either the experimental or the control group completely at random. According to the Dictionary of Psychology, “randomness” is a mathematical or statistical concept, and the term means simply that there is no detectable systematicity in the sequence of events observed. Strictly speaking, “random” refers not to a thing but to the lack of a thing, the lack of pattern or structure or regularity. The typical list of synonyms of the word random includes words or phrases like haphazard, by chance, occurring without voluntary control, aimless, purposeless, etc. This is a way of compensating for the fact that experimenters cannot possibly control for everything about their subjects. When a sample is sufficiently large, random assignment tends to produce a good shuffling, with regard to other factors that might otherwise bias experiment’s results. Consequently, any observed differences in the behaviour of the two groups are not likely to have been caused by inherent differences in the people who form these groups.

If researchers use precautions such as random assignment to reduce the effect of the confounding variables, then they have a systematic, planned, precised, well-organized, well-controlled, and a scientific study. With a well controlled study, researcher or the experimenter feels more confident and sure about drawing cause-and-effect relationship and conclusions in an experiment.

In experimental method, researchers manipulate a variable called *independent variable* and observe how the participants respond. If conditions in an experiment are carefully controlled and confounding variables are avoided, the researchers can conclude that a change in the independent variable actually caused or brought a change in the dependent variable.

2.1.5 Advantages of Experimental Method

(i) Experimental method is the only method that allows the experimenter to infer cause-and-effect relationship.

(ii) In experimental method, the experimenter can exercise control over other confounding variables.

(iii) It helps in conducting a systematic, objective, precised, planned, well-organized, and a well-controlled scientific study.

(iv) This method makes any subject a science because a subject is a science not by "what" it studies but by "how" it studies. This method makes Psychology a science.

2.1.6 Disadvantages of Experimental Method

(i) Its control is its weakness. It makes the set-up or the situation artificial. A situation in which all the variables are carefully controlled is not a normal, natural situation. As a result, the researcher or the experimenter may have difficulty generalizing the findings from observations in an experiment to the real world (Christensen, 1992). For example, researcher may not be able to generalize from a study conducted that examinee's memory for non-sense syllables presented on a computer screen in a psychological laboratory and draw conclusions about the student learning introductory Psychology in a college classroom. It is very difficult to know and control all the intervening variables.

(ii) All the psychological phenomena cannot be studied by this method.

(iii) The experimental method is a costly method, costly in terms of money and time. A well established laboratory and trained personnel are needed to conduct experiments.

2.2 OBSERVATION METHOD

"Observation can fairly be called a *method of scientific enquiry or investigation*. In the strict sense, observation implies the use of eyes rather than of the ear and voice." (C.A. Moser, 1958). In observation method, deliberate study is done. The observer is directly present and makes a full use of her or his eyes. Primary material for any study can be collected by this method. Observation method is an important method because by the help of which many psychological problems can be selected for the study. Careful observation of behaviour is a starting point of any scientific enquiry in any science, including Psychology.

2.2.1 Some Characteristics or Features or Qualities of Observation Method

All types of observation cannot be called scientific observation; only when the observation is based on *scientific manner*; it can be said *scientific observation*. It is necessary for the scientific observation to have the following characteristics:

1. Objectivity
2. Precision or accuracy
3. Specificity
4. Systematic
5. Qualitative
6. Verifiability
7. Reliability

2.2.2 Steps in Observation Method

1. *Adequate plan or aimful observation:* It is necessary for the study of observation method to construct appropriate planning for the behaviour and problem to be studied. Before making observations, the observer should first decide that what sort of behaviour is to be observed and which are the persons to be observed, she or he should plan beforehand all this. Prior planning makes the observation aimful and such planning helps in the attainment of relevant and correct data or information.
2. *Observation of behaviour:* After planning about the study, problem, tools, and apparatus, the observation is started by the help of pre-planned apparatus and eyes. An observer using this method of observation acts as a passive recorder of whatever happens. While observing the behaviour, those aspects are minutely observed which are related with the problem and are according to experimenter's plans. Along with the observations, the observer notes down the behaviour.
3. *Recording of behaviour or observation:* The observer notes down the behaviour along with her or his observations. To note the observation, she or he uses various apparatus and instruments like—by the help of movie camera, any sort of behaviour can be easily recorded. Similarly, the conversations related with behaviour can be recorded by the help of tape recorder. The observer notes down those points more carefully which are related specifically with the problem.
4. *Results or analysis of behaviour:* After noting her or his observations, the observer tries to convert her or his readings into numbers, makes tables and columns of them, and then analyzes the findings by using various statistical techniques and methods.
5. *Discussion, generalization, and interpretation:* After the analyses of the observed behaviour, it is discussed. If possible, the behaviour is discussed in the light of established laws and principles. The reasons of a particular behaviour are explained.

2.2.3 Types of Observation Method

1. *Simple or uncontrolled observation method:* When a phenomenon is observed in natural conditions and no control is put over natural conditions, such observation is known as *uncontrolled observation*. This kind of observation has no aim. As the event happens, the observer observes it. But uncontrolled observational method has its drawbacks, which are as follows:
   - (i) Mostly, this method lacks in providing accurate results because generally, we accept the results without observing the result minutely.
   - (ii) Because there is no control over the observer, the observations are biased. Bias results from observer's expectations.
   - (iii) It is seen that the same situation observed by different observers give different results.
   - (iv) Only external and observable behaviour can be observed. It is impossible to observe what is going on in the mind of the person being observed. Similarly, internal behaviour and contents of the unconscious mind are difficult to be observed.
   - (v) Not all natural situations can be observed as they cannot be repeated.
   - (vi) Attitude of the observer also affects the results. Interests, values, prejudices, liking, expectations, etc. of the observer may also distort the contents of the observation. An observer should have a scientific attitude or approach to observe behaviour. It means simply that orientation towards the study of phenomena that presumes that basic understanding is best achieved through the systematic application of the scientific method.
2. *Systematic or controlled or scientific or objective observation method:* When the observer and the phenomena both are kept under control and then observed, such method is called "controlled observation". This type of observation is done with some aim or goal in the mind of the observer or the experimenter. It is planned.
3. *Participant observation method:* In this method, the observer lives and adjusts with that group of people whose behaviour she or he wants to observe. The observer becomes a part of the situation. It is easy to do minute observation of small groups by this method. It becomes easier for the observer to observe the minute intricacies of the behaviour of people being observed. This type of observation is more pure and natural as the observer observes by being a participant.

4. *Non-participant observation method:* In this method, the observer keeps herself or himself away and unaffected from the group being observed and then observes. Large groups can be easily observed by this method. But because the observer remains aloof, detached, and unaffected from the group being observed, she or he is not able to observe minute and intricate details of their behaviour. The observer is also not able to exercise any kind of bias on the contents of the observation.

2.2.4 Importance or Advantages of Observation Method

(i) Observation method is basic to any scientific enquiry.

(ii) It is a simple method as compared to other methods.

(iii) It is natural, flexible, and economical method.

(iv) Observation method is used more at the time when the problems and hypotheses are to be framed or constructed.

(v) It is easy to study mutual relations (cause-and-effect) by this method.

(vi) The results obtained by this method are more reliable because the observer observes by using different apparatus, instruments, and by his own eyes. So, this kind of observation becomes objective and valid.

(vii) The results obtained through scientific and controlled observation method are objective. When this method is used scientifically and in a proper manner, the answer to such questions as how, what, and when can be obtained.

2.2.5 Limitations or Disadvantages of Observation Method

(i) The main defect of the observation method is that while observing, the observer maintains such pleasing relations with the subject that those relations affect observer's observations.

(ii) The observations of the observer are affected by her or his feelings and prejudices.

(iii) The results obtained by this method are not valid and reliable, and hence not scientific till the problem is studied by controlled observation and is preplanned. Otherwise, it will be an aimless observation.

(iv) Different observers reach at different results.

(v) The results obtained by this method are not verifiable specifically when the observations are done without prior planning.

2.3 INTERVIEW METHOD

Interview method is very often used in Psychology and is gaining popularity in the modern age, too. In this method, the interviewer (person who takes the interview) and interviewee (person who gives the interview) both sit face to face and the interviewer collects information regarding the problem from the interviewee. In this method, the interviewer sits in front of the interviewee and gathers information by the help of written or oral questions regarding the problem. This method is used independently and as a supporting or assisting tool. It is used in various types of studies or research. In Psychology, interviews are usually conducted either to collect or gather information or for therapeutic purposes like in clinical or counselling psychology.

2.3.1 Types of Interview Method

1. *Standardized or structured or active or preplanned interview:* In this method, the various questions regarding the problem are constructed before interview. The questions are asked in the predetermined order and series to the subjects. The series and order of the questions to be asked from the interviewee is not changed. Any interview with a preset organization in which the topics and questions and their order of use are all determined in advance, is called *structured interview*. The interview, however, must be preplanned if it is to be free from the interviewer's subjectivity and if it is to yield reliable and adequate data. A trained psychologist or an interviewer can accomplish this task. Structured interview method is more reliable as compared to unstructured because this is comparatively more accurate, and gives reliable results too and it also makes comparison easy.
2. *Unstructured or uncontrolled interview method: Unstructured interview* is an interview in which the topics to be covered are left unspecified at the outset and things are left to the unfolding interaction between the persons involved in the interview. In this method, neither the questions nor the number of questions are decided before. The experimenter or the interviewer is free to ask any question regarding the problem. It gives opportunity to understand the subject because of the freedom of questions and the way of putting them.

2.3.2 Importance or Advantages of Interview Method

The following are the advantages of the Interview method.

(i) This method has the advantage of first hand contact with the subject.

(ii) We can study those situations and problems which we are not able to see or which we cannot study by observation method.

(iii) The past events cannot be studied easily by this method.

(iv) If the interviewer is well-trained and collects the information with appropriate control, reliable results can be obtained.

(v) Because the interview is conducted in historical background, the information gathered by this method is not possible by any other method.

(vi) It is a useful method in the diagnosis of various psychological problems.

2.3.3 Limitations or Disadvantages of Interview Method

(i) This method has the disadvantage that only a segment of one's behaviour is examined.

(ii) It is difficult either to contact subjects for interview, they do not have time, or the time they have, does not suit the researcher.

(iii) When the problem is emotional in nature, the interviewees feel reluctant to say or share anything about their personal lives.

(iv) Many times, the information gathered or collected by using unstructured interview method is full of biases and prejudices. Interviewer bias is the contaminating effect of the interviewer's opinions, expectations or general lack of objectivity.

(v) Whatever information is collected about the problem being studied, it is difficult to test it. So, element of subjectivity is present.

(vi) Reliable information through this method can be collected only when the interviewer has a full knowledge of the technique.

(vii) If the time of the interview is short, full information cannot be gathered or collected.

2.4 QUESTIONNAIRE METHOD

According to W.J. Goode and P.K. Hatt (1952), "In general, the word "questionnaire" refers to a device for securing answers to questions by using a form which the respondent fills in himself." Questionnaire is a self-reporting technique. Questionnaire method has a preplanned list of aimful questions regarding the problem under study, by which answers are obtained from the study units and by the statistical analysis of the obtained answers, results are drawn. This method is used in the study of personality, interest, attitudes, etc. In a questionnaire, broadly, any set of questions dealing with any topic or group of related topics are designed and these have to be answered by the respondent. While constructing the questionnaire, following points should be kept in the mind:

1. The length and the number of questions should not be so long that the subject may feel exhausted by answering them. The questions should not be difficult and lengthy.
2. Questions should be clear.
3. Questions should be easy and attractive. The language of questionnaire should not be confusing or non-comprehensive, which makes it difficult to answer.
4. The difficulty level of the questions should rise gradually, which means that in the beginning of the questionnaire, simple and general questions should be asked and then the difficult and more specific questions can be put.

2.4.1 Types of Questionnaire

1. *Open questionnaire:* This questionnaire is such in which there is no restriction on the subject and she or he can answer freely.
2. *Closed questionnaire:* In this questionnaire, researcher lays restrictions on the subject. The subject has to answer out of selected answers only.
3. *Pictorial questionnaire:* In this, the questions are presented in the form of pictures.

2.4.2 Advantages of Questionnaire Method

(i) This method is economical in terms of time and money. This method makes possible the study of number of subjects in minimum of time and money because it can be administered on a number of subjects at a particular time.

(ii) We can obtain information many times from the same respondents and thus reliable data can be collected. Questionnaires are reliable and valid, that is these are standardized (objective, accurate, and precised measures).

2.4.3 Limitations or Disadvantages of Questionnaire Method

The main limitations of this method are as follows:

(i) The use of this method is restricted to literates only except in the case of a pictorial questionnaire.

(ii) Generally, the informant or the respondent leaves the questionnaire incomplete or in such a way that the written material or answers of the respondent is not readable, which makes it difficult for data collection.

(iii) Many informants either leave the questionnaire or information incomplete or fail to give in time or misplace the questionnaire schedule.

(iv) Respondents fill up the questionnaire according to their own will.

(v) If the questionnaire is not filled up in the presence of the experimenter, the information is not reliable.

(vi) The language of questionnaire should not be confusing or non-comprehensive which makes it difficult to answer.

2.5 CASE STUDY METHOD

According to Beisanz and Beisanz (1954), "......... The case study is a form of qualitative analyses involving the careful and complete observation of a person, a situation or an institution." This method emphasizes on the total process of the situation in which the behaviour took place.

Case study is a depth study method. It is also called *case history method*. It is the detailed account of a single individual. Case study is the intensive study of one or two individuals rather than the study of larger number of individuals or groups. It deeply studies the individual, family, institution, situation, group, and community. This method is most often used in psychotherapy, where a complete record of a single person as possible is compiled, including personal history, background, test results, ratings, interviews, etc. The life history of an individual is studied through her or his diaries, documents, autobiographies and the other things used in person's life so that important aspects of her or his behaviour can be collected. Parents, teachers, guardians, friends, etc. are interviewed to have information about the life of a person. The family background, the important events of her or his life, and the present or current situations, etc. are studied.

The following kind of data or information must be included in the case history:

1. Data about the family, neighbourhood, and community, and the sources from which such information is obtained.
2. Physical characteristics and selected items from the medical record of the individual.
3. Mental and physical development history of the individual.
4. The individual's school achievement (academic, behavioural, and co-curricular).
5. The individual's needs and the barriers which thwart them.
6. A record of the action taken as a result of the case study.
7. Follow-up reports at later periods.

2.5.1 Advantages of Case Study Method

The following are the advantages of the case study method.

(i) When the problem is studied by this method, the generalization is easier.

(ii) Deviant or abnormal persons can be discovered or found by this method.

(iii) Wider range of knowledge can be collected on the problem by this method.

2.5.2 Disadvantages of Case Study Method

This case study method has the following disadvantages

(i) The reliability of the collected data and results cannot be verified easily.

(ii) Lack of control makes this method more unscientific.

(iii) The information collected or gathered are unscientific and unverifiable.

(iv) More chances of biases are possible during data collection.

(v) Case studies usually do not allow researcher to draw conclusions or to make firm inferences about cause-and-effect.

(vi) Case study method is a subjective method.

(vii) Trained and competent investigators are needed to conduct case studies.

EXERCISES

The below mentioned are some of the questions that have been asked in the examinations conducted by the Guru Nanak Dev University or can be asked. Knowledge of these answers can help the students to get success in the examinations.

Section A

Answers the following questions in **five** lines or 50 words.

1. What is observation.
2. What do you mean by controlled observation?
3. What is unstructured interview?
4. What is case study method?
5. Explain debriefing *
6. Define voluntary informed consent.
7. Define an "experiment".*

   or

   What is an "experiment"?
8. What do you mean by introspection?
9. What are dependent and independent variables? *
10. What is questionnaire method?
11. What is independent variable?
12. What is scientific observation?
13. Define experimental method.
14. Distinguish between independent variable and dependent variable.*
15. What is a questionnaire?
16. What is a variable?
17. What is open-ended interview?
18. Define experimental control.*
19. What is natural observation?
20. What are the two important variables studied in an experiment?
21. Explain the demerits of interview.

Section B

Answer to the following questions up to **two** pages or 500 words.

1. What is case study method? Explain.
2. Describe interview as a method.

   or

   Explain interview method.

3. Discuss the advantages and disadvantages of experimental method.
4. Discuss observation as a method of Psychology stating its merits and demerits.
5. Write the various steps involved in an experiment.

   or

   Write the various steps of experimentation.
6. What is an experiment? Write its steps.*
7. Describe questionnaire and case study method.
8. Write briefly about the observation method.
9. What is an experiment?

   or

   Write a brief note on an experiment.
10. Write a note on observation method.
11. What is the importance of control in experimental method?*
12. Explain an experiment with the help of an example.
13. What is the basic nature of experimentation?
14. What is naturalistic observation?

Section C

Answers the following questions up to **five** pages or 1000 words:

1. What is the experimental method? Why has it been used so often in psychological research?
2. What are the main methods of investigation available to psychologist? What are the advantages of these methods? What are the disadvantages of these methods?
3. Explain experimental method.

   or

   Discuss experimental method in detail.

   or

   Write about experimental method.
4. Describe questionnaire and case study method.
5. What is the experimental method? Write its aims and essentials. State the steps involved in experimental method?
6. What is objective observation? Examine merits and limitations of observation method.
7. What are the various methods of Psychology?
8. Write experimental method in detail. Explain with the help of an example.*

9. What is the experimental method? Give its merits and demerits.

   or

   Explain the experimental method. Discuss its merits and limitations.
10. What are the different methods of investigation of behaviour in Psychology? Discuss any two methods in detail.
11. What are the various methods of Psychology? Which is the best method and why?
12. Explain the merits and demerits of any two of the following methods: observation, interview, questionnaire, experiment.

REFERENCES

Bootzin, R., Bower, Crooker and Hall, *Psychology Today*, New York: McGraw-Hill, INC, 1991.

Crow, L.D., and Crow, A., *Educational Psychology* (3rd Indian Reprint), New Delhi: Eurasia Publishing House, 1973.

D'Amato, M.R., *Experimental Psychology*, Delhi, Tata McGraw-Hill Publishing Company Limited, Delhi, 2004.

Eysenck, H.J., *The Biological Basis of Personality*, Springfield, IL: C.C. Thomas, 1967.

Eysenck, M.W., *Simply Psychology*, London: Psychology Press Publishers, 1996.

Ghorpade, M.B., *Essentials of Psychology*, Bombay: Himalaya Publishing House, 1999.

Goode, W.J., and Hatt, P.K., *Methods of Social Research*, New York: McGraw-Hill, 1952.

Hilgard, E.O., *Theories of Learning* (4th ed.), New York: Appleton-Century-Crofts, 1976.

Kerlinger, F.N., *Foundations of Behavioural Research* (3rd ed.), New York: Holt, Rinehart and Winston, 1986.

McDougall, W., *Social Psychology*, London: Methuen, 1908.

Munn, N.L., *An Introduction to Psychology* (2nd ed.), New Delhi: Oxford and IBH, 1967.

Pillsbury, W.B., *Essentials of Psychology*, New York: Macmillan, 1911.

Postman and Egan, J.P., *Experimental Psychology: An Introduction*, New York: Harper & Row, 1949.

Underwood, B.J., *Experimental Psychology*, New York: Appleton, 1966.

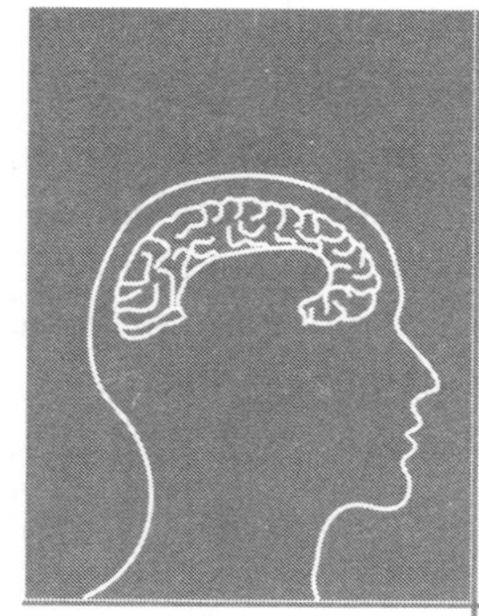

CHAPTER 3

Biological Bases of Behaviour

It was only after the publication of the book in 1859, *The Origin of Species* by Charles Darwin (1807–1882), a biologist, that the relevance of biology to psychology became accepted. Darwin's theory of evolution had at least four major effects on Psychology:

(i) Psychologists began to develop theories of human psychology from the biological perspective.

(ii) One of the lessons of the theory of evolution was that the study of animals could be of great value while studying the human behaviour. This led to the development of animal or comparative psychology.

Charles Darwin
(1807–1882)

(iii) Darwin argued that heredity is important in the development of a species, and that offsprings tend to be like their parents. These ideas led psychologists to explore the role of heredity in influencing human behaviour.

(iv) Darwin focused on variation among the members of species. According to his notion of survival of the fittest, evolution favours those members of a species who are best equipped to live in a given environment. These ideas led to an interest in individual differences, and to the study of intelligence and personality.

A number of books have been written on the biological bases of behaviour, however, in this book, a few selected topics related to biological bases of behaviour have been discussed. Glands are covered in this chapter and the nervous system, specially the brain, which is far more important than any other biological structure in influencing behaviour, is discussed in the fourth chapter.

3.1 GENES AND BEHAVIOUR

A child at birth, possesses a unique combination of genes from both parents. This inheritance provides a distinct biological blueprint and timetable for the development of an individual. The study of the inheritance of physical and psychological characteristics from ancestors is referred to as "Genetics".

Genes are the basic units of heredity. The child begins life as a single cell. This egg cell, produced in mother's reproductive organs, is a tiny round blob of material with a dark nucleus in its centre. The nucleus contains chromosomes. In humans, the genes are located on 23 pairs of chromosomes. Virtually, each cell in the body has 46 chromosomes carrying some genetic information that play a critical role in making one individual into oneself. One set of 23 chromosomes is contributed by the father; the other set comes from the mother. If you look through a microscope, each of these 46 chromosomes (23 pairs) looks like a long strand of coloured beads. These 46 chromosomes (23 pairs) are composed chiefly of a substance called DNA (deoxyribonucleic acid). By composition, DNA is an acid. It is nucleic acid because it is found chiefly in the nucleus of the cell. Our genes are composed chiefly of DNA molecules. DNA contains instructions for the production of proteins. These proteins regulate the body's physiological processes and the expression of phenotypic traits (body build, physical strength, intelligence, and other behavioural traits).

One of the 23 pairs of chromosomes determined whether one would be male or female, this pair is called the *sex chromosomes*. Females have a pair of sex chromosomes called X chromosome (symbolized XX). Males have one sex chromosomes called X and one called Y (symbolized XY). The Y chromosome is much smaller than the X chromosome. Ironically, then, a single chromosome pair determines a characteristic that most humans consider to be vitally important—whether one is male or female.

The 23rd chromosomes of the sperm cell can be either the larger X-type or the smaller Y-type. Whereas, the 23rd chromosome of the egg cell (of the female) is always a larger X-type. If the X-type sperm fertilizes the egg cell, the fertilized egg will have an XX 23rd chromosome pair and the infant will be a female. On the other hand, if a Y-type sperm fertilizes the egg, the 23rd chromosome pair will be XY and the infant will be a male. It proves that the sex of the child depends entirely on the chromosome of the sperm cell, that is, the father.

Every chromosome stores thousands of genetic commands; each engraved in a gene, the basic unit of hereditary transmission. The genes dictate much of the course of organism's development. An organism's full set of genes (genes inherited from both parents) is called its "genotype". The set of characteristics the organism actually develops by which individuals are recognized, its observable features like body build, eye colour, and other behavioural traits, etc. is called its "phenotype". The field of study that focuses on identifying the genetic bases of behavioural traits, such as intelligence, mental disorders, etc. is called "behaviour genetics".

It is observed that despite a similar heritage, children are different in their behaviour from their parents. There could be two reasons for the difference. First, children possess a unique combination of genes, unlike that of either parent. A mother and a father pass on to their child a part of what generations of their family lines have given them. Secondly, children grow up and live in different environment from those of their parents. Environment and genetic structure play equally important role in making us what we are today. This interaction between genes and environment or heredity and environment determines the uniqueness of the individual.

Our genetic heritage can also set a stage for important life experiences. For example, if you are born a female, you will be treated differently than a male and the behaviour pattern of the individual will also differ in accordance with the gender.

3.2 GLANDS AND HORMONES

The endocrine glands or ductless glands, muscles, and nervous system, play a crucial role in our behaviour and development. The glands are of two types: the endocrine or ductless glands and the exocrine or duct glands. The endocrine glands are called *ductless glands* because their products or secretions or chemicals are secreted directly into the circulatory system or bloodstream without intermediate passageways. Other type of glands—the exocrine glands or duct glands like salivary glands, tear glands, and sweat glands secrete their products through specific routes or ducts (tubes).

The endocrine system is a collection of glands (ductless) that release their chemicals directly into the bloodstream. The endocrine system is cleverly and economically designed to spread its messages through the bloodstream. The chemicals released by the endocrine system are called *hormones*. "Hormones" are chemical or bodily substances that originate in a gland or an organ, and are conveyed to other organic sites. Some behaviour is controlled through the action of hormones. The circulatory system is the passageway that carries hormones from the endocrine glands to the various organs and systems in the body.

Each hormone modulates or regulates the functioning of a target tissue or organ, located somewhere in the body. In the case of endocrine hormones, the influence may be specific to a localized region or area (as in Prolactin, the hormone that stimulates the production of milk in female mammary glands) or general to cells existing throughout the body (as in thyroxin, the hormone that regulates the metabolism rate for all bodily tissues). Some glands (such as the thyroid) secrete only one hormone (thyroxin), while others (the anterior pituitary) secrete many. Table 3.1 shows summary of some of important glands in the human body, their hormones, and general effects.

Table 3.1 Shows summary of some of important glands in the human body, their hormones, and general effects

Gland	*Hormone*	*General Effect*
1. Anterior pituitary	Growth hormone	Stimulation of growth
	Thyrotrophic	Stimulation of thyroid
	ACTH	Stimulation of adrenal cortex
	FSH	Development of germ cells
	LH	Stimulation of sex hormones
	Prolactin	Increases in milk production
2. Posterior pituitary	Vasopressin	Vasoconstriction, water control
	Oxytocin	Uterine contractions Increases in milk production
3. Thyroid	Thyroxin	Increases metabolism
4. Adrenal cortex	Corticoids	Control of body minerals Increases carbohydrate metabolism
5. Adrenal medulla	Norepinephrine	Increases sympathetic arousal
	Epinephrine	Stimulates ACTH release

The normal functioning of the glands and hormones is crucial to our behavioural well being. Over secretion of the hormones of a gland is called its "hyper-secretion" and under secretion of the hormones of a gland is called its "hypo-secretion". Without the delicately balanced secretion of hormones, the body would be unable to maintain the state of internal equilibrium that physiologists refer to as "homeostasis".

Hormonal influences upon behaviour do not exist independently of the central nervous system. The brain, specifically the hypothalamus, exerts or exercises enormous control over a host of endocrine glands in the secretion of important hormones. The central nervous system guides the patterns of endocrine hormone secretions via hypothalamic releasing hormones, while endocrine hormones themselves stimulate and maintain neural circuitry in the brain to guide gender-specific and perhaps other behaviours. Thus, the endocrine system and the central nervous system mutually interact. The nervous system is discussed in detail in Chapter 4.

Characteristics of hormones or the principles that govern the working of hormones:

1. Hormones do not initiate or stop the biological processes. Rather, hormones exert their influences on the body by regulating processes that are already ongoing.
2. There is variability in the secretion of hormones. Some hormones are secreted at a 24-hour period (as in the adrenal hormones), or a 28-day period (as in the female sex hormones), or a period measured in terms of years (as in growth hormone). Other hormonal secretions rise and fall according to internal situational demands (a rise in insulin after food intake) or to some environmental stimulation (a rise in corticoids or ATCH in times of danger).
3. Hormones have a catalytic quality. As catalysts, hormones influence biological or physiological processes without themselves being altered in any way. Hormones do not get "used up" as a result of their influence in a particular process.
4. The concentrations of hormones are far too small for any direct measurement. These infinitesimal qualities of hormones are measured through a technique called "Radio Immunological Assay" (RIA), developed in 1959.

3.3 THE PITUITARY GLAND

The most important gland in the endocrine system is the pituitary gland (Figure 3.1), a structure only about half an inch in diameter, which lies at the base of the brain just below a region called the *hypothalamus*. The anterior pituitary has historically been referred to as the "master gland" of the endocrine system because it directs the activities of most of the glands in our body. But now, it is evident that the anterior pituitary is itself controlled by the hypothalamus. It is, therefore, the hypothalamus that is ultimately the master gland. Despite its small size, the pituitary controls a wide range of body functions via its many hormones. The anterior pituitary and posterior pituitary secrete hormones and release

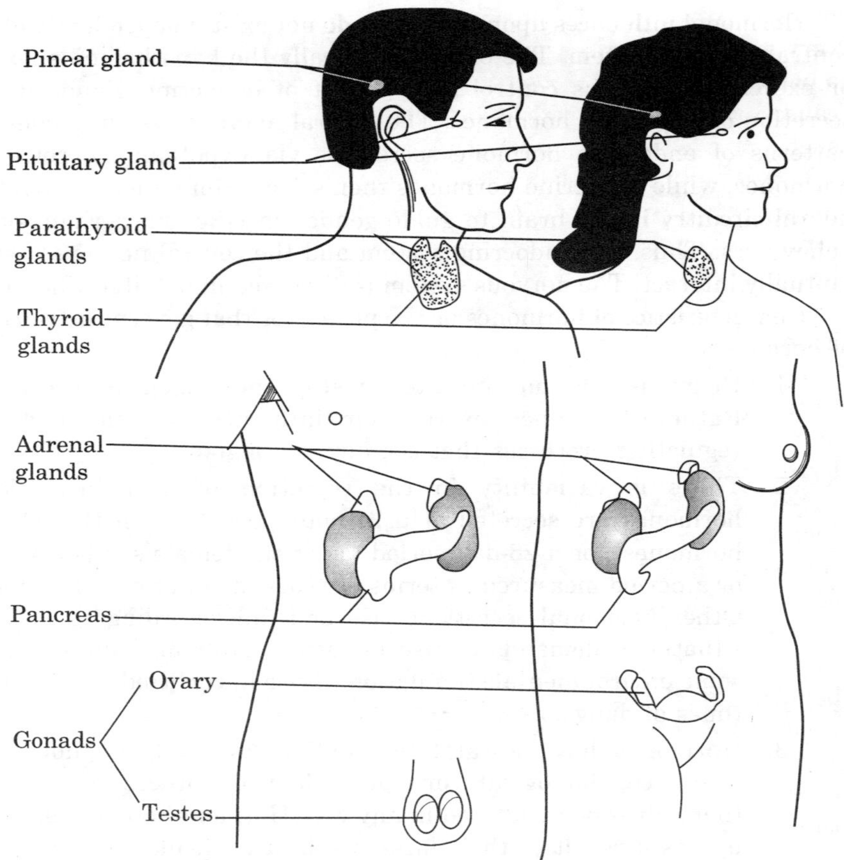

Figure 3.1 Location of important endocrine glands among major organs in the human body.

them at the appropriate time of life. Particularly important is growth hormone, (anterior pituitary hormone) which plays a key role in physical development. Primary function of growth hormone is to act directly upon the cells of the body, stimulating the growth process in these cells. The effects of growth hormone are seen dramatically in the formation of protein and the gradual enlargement of the large bones of the arm and leg. The functioning of growth hormone, however, goes beyond the process of growth itself. Evidence suggests that it influences the function of the thyroid, parathyroid, and sex glands at critical times in an individual's life. In addition, growth hormone plays a role in the metabolism of food.

Hypo-secretion of growth hormone early in life leads to a kind of miniaturization of the body. Dwarfism results from a severe deficit of growth hormone during childhood. Unlike the case of cretinism, however, the head-to-body ratio and all facial proportions are normal, and there is no evidence of mental retardation. Nevertheless, the overall body size is very small. If an excess of growth hormone is produced at an early age, a person will become a giant. Extreme hyper-secretion of growth hormone causes the body to grow to sizes well above normal. It is not unusual for such individuals to attain heights of 8 or 9 feet.

Prolactin (anterior pituitary hormone) prompts the production of milk in pregnant and nursing mothers. Gonadotrophic hormone (anterior pituitary hormone) controls the production of male and female sex hormones by prompting the testes in the males and ovaries in females. The principal tropic hormones (anterior pituitary hormones with indirect action; that is, they affect secretion of other endocrine glands) of the anterior pituitary are FSH (follicle-stimulating hormone) and LH (luteinizing hormone). Both of these hormones begin to be secreted only at the onset of the puberty and, like the other tropic hormones, are hypothalamic ally controlled by FSH–RH (FSH-releasing hormone) and LH–RH (LH–releasing hormone), respectively. As a result of FSH secretion, an ovum in the ovary begins to enlarge in size. At the same time, FSH induces the follicle cells to secrete estrogen into the blood. LH causes the follicle to rupture, releasing the ovum. If the ovum goes unfertilized or is fertilized too late or if implantation is prevented (for example, by an IUD) the walls of the uterus slough off and menstruation begins. LH is a hormone that, in the female, regulates progesterone production during the later stages of the menstrual cycle and, in the male, regulates the production of androgen. During the entire term of pregnancy (270 days on the average in the human), the levels of tropic hormones of the anterior pituitary, LH and FSH, are low.

The posterior pituitary, a gland lying immediately underneath the hypothalamus at the base of the brain, secretes two major hormones: the vasopressin and the oxytocin. Vasopressin is vital for bodily functions. Vasopressin is an important regulator of water balance in the body. When cells become dehydrated, vasopressin causes the kidney to reabsorb the water in the waste matter passing through it, so as to conserve the body's supply of fluid. Since this action is opposite to the passing off water in the urine, vasopressin is considered antidiuretic, and is often referred to as antidiuretic hormone (ADH). Inadequate vasopressin secretion results in a condition called *diabetes insipidus*, in which too much water passes through the urine without kidney reabsorption. The individual having this disorder develops an enormous thirst, since the body is not receiving sufficient fluids in order to function. A series of injections of posterior pituitary extract or of purified forms of vasopressin itself restores the functioning level of this hormone and effectively eliminates the symptoms.

At the onset of labour, oxytocin, secreted by the posterior pituitary, stimulates the uterus to contract and the birth canal to enlarge. When the child is delivered and, a few minutes later, the placenta expelled, the estrogen and progesterone levels fall to nearly zero. One effect of this sudden change is to cause the anterior pituitary to secrete Prolactin. As a result, the breasts are stimulated to begin producing milk. Oxytocin (posterior pituitary hormone) controls the release of milk during childbirth. The stimulation from the infant's sucking increases the secretion of oxytocin, causing the milk ducts to release milk through the nipples.

Estrogen and progesterone are related to female sexual development and reproduction. The function of the estrogens is to guide the sexual development of the female body, so that by the time of puberty (around the age of 10 to 14 years in humans), the individual not only possesses the secondary sex characteristics of a female (breast development, rounded body contours, a widened pelvis, etc.) but also possesses the primary sex characteristics related to reproduction itself. The onset of puberty is also often referred to as the age of menarche (first menstruation).

3.4 THE THYROID GLAND

The thyroid gland, located in the neck, lying on the sides of the throat at the level of the larynx (Figure 3.1), produces thyroxin that influences or regulates the body's metabolic rate. The steady secretion of thyroxin provides for the minimum rate at which body cells take in sources of energy, consume oxygen, and eliminate wastes. Thyroxin secretion is sensitive to external temperature changes. Exposure to cold environments increases thyroxin secretion rates, while exposure to hot environments decreases them. This hormone influences behaviour. Too much thyroid secretion or thyroxin or hyperthyroidism in a disorder called **Grave's disease** produces overexcitability, chronic insomnia, and a reduced capacity to focus upon a particular task. Patients with this problem show protruding or bulging eyes and often have a wild or staring appearance (Jensen, 1980). The corrective treatment of hyperthyroidism requires the surgical removal of a portion of the gland, so as to reduce the amount of thyroxin secretion. Too much thyroxin speeds up metabolism, causing individual to become highly active resulting in weight loss, an elevated body temperature, profuse sweating, intense thirst, accelerated heart rate, general excitability, and often difficulty in sleeping, and leads to a condition called *hyperthyroidism*.

The opposite disorder—too little thyroxin secretion or thyroxin or hypothyroidism in the early years of life can have devastating effects on an infant. Hypothyroidism results in a failure of the central nervous system, as well as other systems of the body, to develop normally. If untreated in newborns, it leads to a condition called *cretinism*, characterized by severely retarded mental and physical development. Due to inadequate skeletal and muscular development, the cretin body becomes dwarfed and grossly mishappens. The tongue protrudes from the mouth, the eyes are puffy, and the poor muscle tone causes the stomach and shoulders to sag. Mental retardation results from poor development of the nervous system. Prompt diagnosis of hypothyroidism and treatment through injections of extra thyroxin effectively restore the deficiency and renew the process of growth. If thyroid is removed in young animals, their growth is stunned and they fail to develop sexually. When occurring in adulthood, hypothyroidism shows symptoms that are less severe. The individual becomes sluggish or lazy in bodily movement, in the way the body maintains its internal temperature, and in general attitude. Therapy for this condition would be the same as that for childhood hypothyroidism, that is, injections of extra thyroxin. Too little thyroxin slows metabolism which leads to lethargy and weight gain and creates a range of related symptoms including obesity, a slowed heartbeat, lowered body temperature, reduced sweating, physical lethargy, and a lack of mental alertness.

An enlargement of the thyroid gland, along with a swelling in the neck, a condition called "goiter" can result from inadequate amounts of iodine in the diet. Iodine is an essential ingredient in the production of thyroxin. Goiter is a common occurrence in the areas of the world like high-altitude, mountainous regions, where crops grow in iodine-deficient soil. The addition of iodine to the diet through iodized salt or iodine-added salt prevents the development of goiter.

3.5 THE ADRENAL GLAND

Adrenals are a pair of glands that lie just above the kidney (Figure 3.1). Each adrenal actually consists of two glands, an inner region called the *medulla* and an outer region called the *cortex*.

The adrenal medulla produces epinephrine (adrenalin), nor-epinephrine (noradrenalin). In their roles, these hormones are also called *adrenalin* and *noradrenalin*. Both are involved in the body's reaction to stress. Through the two secretions of the adrenal medulla, circulated through the body via the bloodstream, the body undergoes the array of changes known as *sympathetic activation*: increased heart rate, constriction of blood vessels, increased muscle tone, and so forth. One of the functions of epinephrine and nor-epinephrine is to stimulate the anterior pituitary to secrete ACTH (adrenocorticotropic hormone) in the blood.

The other portion of the adrenal glands, the adrenal cortex, is probably the most diversified hormone factory in the body. It produces at least 50 hormonelike chemicals, and perhaps many others that scientists have not yet identified. Some of these help regulate the supply of sugar in the blood, others help regulate the relative concentrations of minerals and water in the body, still others act as sex hormones, chiefly male hormones, called *androgens*. Overproduction of adrenal androgens in women can promote the growth of facial and chest hair, deepening of the voice, and the development of muscular arms and legs.

The cortex region of the adrenal gland or adrenal cortex produces its own hormones called *corticoids* as a direct response to the level of ACTH in the blood. Two categories of corticoids dominate the output of the adrenal cortex: *mineralocorticoids* and *glucocorticoids*. Mineralocorticoids, as the name suggests, help regulate the level of minerals in the body, specifically sodium, potassium, and chloride. Since these minerals have a vital role in the way a neuron functions, disturbances in mineralocorticoids can have serious consequences in the nervous system. It is the glucocorticoids, however, that have been most intensively studied as hormones of stress. Their principal function is to promote the conversion of stored proteins and fats to glucose. These conversions are essential for the emergency requirements of increased energy and the repair of damaged tissue. One of the glucocorticoids in particular, 17-hydroxycorticoid (abbreviated 17-OHCS), has been extremely useful for psychologists to study as a physiological index of subjective feelings during stress. When measured either in blood or urine samples, 17-OHCS bears a close relationship to how stressed an individual feels at any particular time. Both ACTH and 17-OHCS remain at stable levels in the blood, when the individual is calm and unstressed. During times of stress, however, the picture is very different. Both ACTH and 17-OHCS, now rise together, as two components of the general stress reaction (Axelrod and Reisine, 1984)

A considerable number of physiological or bodily processes are controlled by the hormones secreted into the bloodstream by the endocrine glands. The organism's reaction to stressors, whether internal or environmental, is also controlled by the endocrine secretions or hormones. Hormones that play a key role in health are affected by emotions.

QUESTIONS

The below mentioned are some of the questions that have been asked in the examinations conducted by the Guru Nanak Dev University or can be asked. Knowledge of these answers can help the students to get success in the examinations.

Section A

Answer the following questions in **five** lines or 50 words.

1. Define endocrine system.
2. What are glands?
3. What are hormones?*

4. What is thyroid gland?*
5. What is adrenal gland?
6. Define genes.*
7. Name different hormones secreted by the pituitary gland.*
8. Explain adrenal gland's position and functions.
9. Name different hormones secreted by the thyroid gland.
10. Define thyroid or adrenal or pituitary gland.
11. What is "hypothyroidism"?

Section B

Answer the following questions up to **two** pages or 500 words.

1. Describe hormones and glands in relation to behaviour.
2. How pituitary glands affect human being?*
3. Write a short note on adrenal gland.
4. Give a brief description of endocrine glands.
5. Define the functions of any one of the following:
   Thyroid, Adrenal, Pituitary glands.

Section C

Answer the following questions up to **five** pages or 1000 words.

1. Describe biological mechanism of behaviour.
2. What is the endocrine system?
3. What are some of the parts of the endocrine system?*

REFERENCES

Axelrod, J., and Reisine, T.D., 'Stress Hormones: Their Interaction and Regulation,' *Science*, **124**, 452–459, 1984.

Darwin, C., *The Origin of Species*, London: Murray, J. 1859.

Darwin, C., 'A Biographical Sketch of an Infant,' *Mind*, **2**, 285–294, 1877.

Jensen, D., *The Principles of Physiology*, New York: Appleton-Century-Crofts, 1980a.

Jensen, D., *The Human Nervous System*, New York: Appleton-Century-Crofts, 1980b.

Rosenzweig, M. and Leiman, A., *Physiological Psychology* (2nd ed.), New York: Random House, 1992.

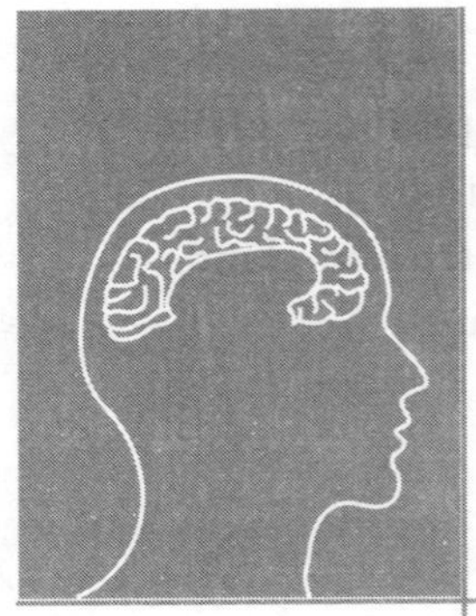

CHAPTER 4

Nervous System

Everything we think (cognitive activity), feel (affective activity) or do (conative activity) has a basis in biological processes and events and primarily in activities occurring in our brains and the other portions of our nervous system. Everything psychological is ultimately biological, in the sense that it is ultimately associated or linked with biological processes or events.

Psychologists realize that an understanding of these roots may often suggest effective treatments for behavioural problems. Science has made much progress in understanding the biological causes of mental disorders like depression, schizophrenia, and anxiety disorders, to name just a few, such knowledge, in turn, has led to the development of effective drugs for treating these disorders.

4.1 NEURONS

Neurons or nerve cells are specialized to conduct signals from one part of the body to another. They connect receptor cells (are embedded in the sense organs; are specialized) to receive various types of stimulation from the environment. During each waking second, receptor cells in our eyes, ears, skin, and other parts of body receive about 100 million signals, which are transmitted to the brain and then to the effector cells (are embedded in muscles and glands) and are specialized to contract the muscles and to stimulate the glands to secrete hormones. To perform even a relatively simple behaviour, for example, swinging a badminton racket, the brain must issue millions of commands via effector cells, directing and coordinating their activities. Neurons are the building blocks of the nervous system, and these building blocks, ultimately, compose our consciousness. Neurons are cells within our bodies that are specialized for the tasks of receiving, moving, and processing information. Even the smallest action, such as blinking the eyes, involves many thousands of neurons in the human body. In other words, the neuron is a specialized cell that processes, stores, and transmits information throughout the body. Scientists estimate that the human brain may contain more than 100 billion neurons, that is, 100,000,000,000 neurons (Hubel, 1979; Soper and Rosenthal, 1998; Thompson, 1985). The tissues we call nerves, which run throughout the body, are actually the long, fibrous parts of many neurons bundled together.

Neurons are tremendously varied in appearance, that is, neurons come in many sizes and shapes, depending on their functions in the nervouns system. Yet, most consist of three basic parts (Figure 4.1):

1. A cell body
2. The axon, and
3. The dendrites

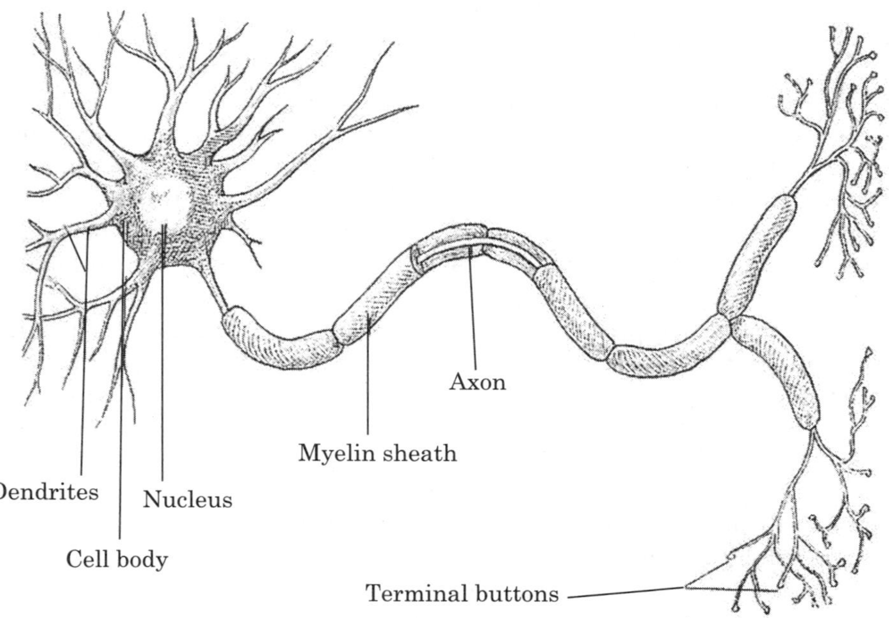

Figure 4.1 A schematic drawing of a neuron.

4.1.1 A Cell Body

The proponent central structure in the neuron is the cell body (Figure 4.1), the area of the neuron that contains the cell nucleus, as well as other structures that help the cell function properly. The cell body is the life-support centre of the cell or neuron and provides the energy for all the cell's or neuron's activities. The cell bodies found in mammals are usually less than 0.1 mm in diameter, barely visible to the human eye. (Kalat, 1992).

4.1.2 The Axon

The axon is a fibre that branch out from the cell body (Figure 4.1) and is involved in communications. The axon carries information away from the cell body, towards other neurons. Some axons are so short that they are not visible to the unaided eye; others are so long that they reach from the spinal cord to the toes. The relatively long axon can be thought of as the cell's "outgoing message line". It carries neural signals down its length to affect the muscle fibres, glandular cells, or other neurons with which its outer end connects.

4.1.3 The Dendrites

The dendrites of neurons are slender, branched fibres that carry impulses in the direction of the cell body in the neuron (Figure 4.1). The name "dendrite" comes from the Greek word for tree. The structure of the dendrites is like the branches of a tree. The greater the area of the dendrites, the more information they can receive from other neurons (Kalat, 1992). The dendrites are fibres that branch out from the cell body and are involved in communications. The numerous and relatively short dendrites can be thought of as the neuron's "antennae". They have specialized areas for receiving messages transmitted by other neurons.

The neural impulses (Figure 4.1) travel through the structures in the neuron in reverse alphabetical order: dendrite, cell body, axon (d, c, b, a). Dendrites carry information towards the cell body, whereas axons carry information away from it (cell body). Neurons are one-way channels of communication. Information usually moves from dendrites or all the cell body towards the axon and then outward along this structure.

In many neurons, the axon is covered by a sheath of fatty whitish substance known as the *myelin*. The myelin sheath (Figure 4.1) helps the action potential travel faster along the axon. It also helps insulate the axon from other nearby axons. Without the myelin sheath, the messages in neighbouring axons might become scrambled with each other. Obviously, a sophisticated message system must avoid scrambled communications. Multiple Sclerosis (MS) is a disease that destroys the myelin sheath causing numbness, weakness, visual disturbances, and motor problems. It also leads to jerky, uncoordinated movements in the affected person. The myelin sheath (fatty wrapping) is interrupted by small gaps (places where it is absent). Both the sheath and the gaps in it play an important role in the neuron's ability to transmit information. Damage to the myelin sheath surrounding axons can seriously affect synaptic transmission.

The myelin sheath is actually produced by another basic set of building blocks within the nervous system, glial cells. Glial cells are usually smaller than neurons and about ten times more numerous. Glia means "glue" and this word describes one of the functions that glial cells serve. They hold neurons in place. They serve several other functions in our nervous system. Glial cells carry nutrients to neurons, remove their waste products, and help repair damaged neurons in the peripheral nervous system, provide a barrier that protects neurons from certain harmful substances that can get into the blood, and play a role in the propagation of nerve impulses. They may even be involved in assembling and disassembling neural circuits (Hatton, 1985).

Glial cells, then are very important in enabling neurons to carry out their work, but neurons themselves play the major role in creating our perceptions, thoughts, feelings, and behaviours.

All the five qualities of the neuron would be wasted if there was no way for neurons to communicate with one another. Clearly, neurons must connect to other neurons. The location at which the axon of one neuron connects with the dendrite of a neighbouring neuron is called the "Synapse".

Neurons can be categorized according to the structures between which they conduct their signals. "Sensory neurons" carry information from the sense organs (eyes, ears, nose, tongue, skin) to the brain and spinal cord while "motor neurons" carry signals from the brain and spinal cord to the muscles and glands. "Interneurons" connect neurons to other neurons and integrate the activities of the sensory and motor neurons. It is the relationships among interneurons that somehow become translated into thoughts, feelings, perceptions, and memories. In humans, interneurons are much more in number than sensory and motor neurons. It has been estimated that for every motor neuron, there are more than 4,000 interneurons.

"Bipolar" neuron or cell is an electrode with two poles, one negative and one positive; such electrodes are commonly used in stimulating and recording from neural tissue. It is any neuron with two extensions or processes (axon and dendrite) running in opposite directions from the cell body. Almost always sensory in nature, they are found extensively in the retina where they form connections between the receptors and the ganglion cells.

"Uni-polar" neuron or cell is a neuron with a single stalk leading from the soma. This neural process branches with the dendrites at one end and the axonal terminals at the others. In unipolar neurons, unlike neurons with more than one pole, information is transmitted from dendrite to end button without passing through the somatic membrane.

The moving disturbance is called the *action potential*. It is the basic signal within our nervous system—the signal that is ultimately the basis of everything we sense, think, or do. Action potentials obey all-or-none law. Either it occurs at full strength or it does not occur at all; there is nothing in between. If the total input from all signals reaches the specified threshold, an action potential occurs, and the impulse is transmitted. If the total input falls short, no action potential occurs. In other words, nervous system does not allow any partial action potentials. Impressively, under ideal conditions, a neuron can produce as many as 1,000 action potentials per second.

4.2 THE NERVOUS SYSTEM

A part—a very important part—of the organism is the **nervous system**, which has as one of its characteristics a sensitivity to the organism's needs. If neurons are building blocks, the nervous system is the structure that they along with other types of cells, combine to erect. The nervous system is actually a complex network of neurons that regulates our bodily functions and permits us to react to the external world in countless ways. With its billions of interconnected cells that radiate throughout the body, the human nervous system is one of the most complex creations in the living world. You could never consciously control such a vast and intricate network with precise and ceaseless demands on the human nervous system, it is reassuring that it operates so automatically, without our conscious awareness, yet alone our conscious control. We can consciously use the brain, a central part of the nervous system, to explore this remarkable network and understand its complex workings.

The cells of the human nervous system are highly specialized. "Receptor cells", embedded in the sense organs, are specialized to receive various types of stimulation from the environment. During each waking second, receptor cells in the eyes, ears, skin, and other parts of the body receive about 100 millions signals, which are then transmitted to the brain. "Effector cells", in contrast, are embedded in muscles and glands, and are specialized to contract the muscles and to stimulate the glands to secrete hormones. To perform even a relatively simple behaviour, such as swinging a badminton racket, your brain must issue millions of commands via effector cells (Figure 4.2).

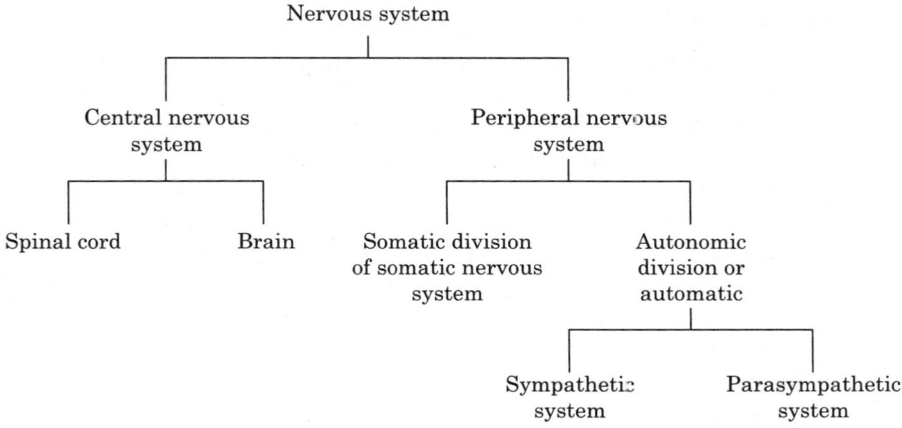

Figure 4.2 Major divisions of the nervous system.

Although the nervous system functions as an integrated whole, it is often viewed as having two major portions:

1. The central nervous system (CNS)
2. The peripheral nervous system (PNS)

These parts are further divided as illustrated in Figure 4.2.

4.2.1 The Central Nervous System (CNS)

The central nervous system (CNS) consists of the spinal cord and the brain, which lie within the bony casings of the spinal column and the skull, and is protected by bone and by fluid circulating it. It is so called (central) because it provides the ultimate control over all human behaviour. The nervous system contains all of the nerve cells in the body.

Spinal cord: The "spinal cord" is a column of neurons that runs from the base of the brain, through the middle of a bony column of hollow bones known as *vertebrae*, down the centre of the back. The spinal cord consists of a large collection of nerves running from the brain to the lower part of the neck. This collection of nerves is protected by the vertebrae of the backbone. A series of bones protects the spinal cord, just as the skull protects the brain. The spinal cord is the oldest part of the central nervous system, both in terms of evolution and in terms of developing embryo prior to birth (Bridgeman, 1988). Its basic organization is similar for all vertebrates. For humans, it performs more basic functions providing a gateway for signals to and from the peripheral nervous system. Damage to the spinal cord causes major disabilities.

The spinal cord has two major functions:

1. It carries sensory information via afferent (sensory) nerve fibres from receptors (sense organs) throughout the body to the brain and conducts information via efferent (motor) nerve fibres from the brain to muscles and glands. Receptor nerves transmit information to the brain via the spinal cord. Instructions from the brain are sent via the effector nerves. In other words, one function is to pass sensory information on from the peripheral nervous system to the brain, with receptor nerves being used to do this. The other main function is to transmit motor information from the brain to peripheral nerves, with effector nerves being used for this purpose. The spinal cord and the brain usually work in a coordinated fashion.
2. It plays a key role in various reflexes. Most of the movements we make are completely under our control but some of the reflex actions are not. A "reflex" is an automatic response to a stimulus. A reflex action is an action which takes place without any thought on our part. Look at the different dangers below and see how your reflexes work:

   For example,

   (i) Eyes blink if something comes too close or when a spec of grit gets into the eye.
   (ii) Hand pulls away quickly if it feels great heat.
   (iii) Foot quickly lifts up if it steps on something sharp.
   (iv) You cough if food goes down your throat the wrong way.
   (v) Your leg jerks forward when someone taps you on part of your knee.
   (vi) Your mouth waters when you think of certain foods.
   (vii) When we are tickled, we laugh and wriggle.
   (viii) Balancing ourselves when we walk.

Reflexes are automatic actions evoked rapidly by particular stimuli. With reflexes, information goes directly from receptor nerves to effector nerves without involving the brain. Withdrawing your hand from a hot object rapidly or blinking your eyes in response to a rapidly approaching object are common examples of reflex actions. If you were to touch something very hot, your hand would automatically be pulled away before you had realized that it was burning. This is because the nerves in your hand send a message to the brain, which immediately sends back the message which pulls the hand away—all in a split second. The knee-jerk reflex works very rapidly, and much faster than making a conscious decision to move your leg. Reflexes permit us to react to potential dangers much more rapidly than we could if the information first had to travel all the way to the brain. Reflexes have the advantage of speed, but they have the disadvantage of working in a rather rigid and inflexible way.

The Brain: The brain is the marvellous organ that is ultimately responsible for consciousness. Modern computers are impressive, but none can match the amazing abilities packed within three pounds of the human brain. And even if we could build a brilliant computer (as Deep Thought), it could not have the emotional experiences, imagery, insights, desires, motives, and creativity of the human brain. Our brain is a unique organ, indeed.

The impressive performance requires a complete organ and the brain certainly meets that description. The brain looks somewhat like a 3-pound lump of leftover lukewarm-oatmeal. Its texture is very soft and jellylike. In fact, it is so fragile that researchers have difficulty handling a fresh brain from a recently deceased human without damaging it (Carlson, 1998). The appearance of the brain is not particularly impressive (Figure 4.3).

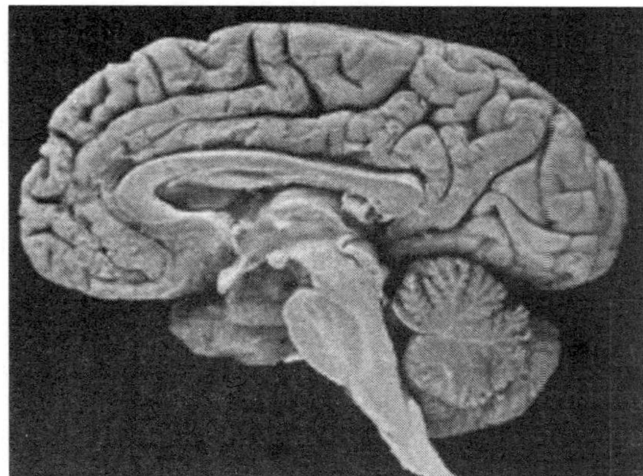

Figure 4.3 The human brain.

The first point that needs to be made about the brain is its complexity. Thousands of psychologists and other scientists have studied human brain, and yet there is still much about it that is unknown. However, the human brain is the most complicated object known (Cohen, 1985). The brain never rests, even when we are asleep. The various chemical and electrical systems in the brain keep on changing constantly. The brain is much more complex than the computers that have been developed so far, and computers cannot grow or change (Ornstein amd Thompson, 1984).

In order to understand the brain, we need to learn about its structure and about the functions of its different parts. It has proved rather easier to study structure than function. It is much harder to know what is going on inside the living brain. The study of brain physiology took on definite form from both the precise methodology and the coherent interpretation offered by Pierre Flourens (1794–1867). He assumed that six separate areas exist in the brain and, using his surgical skills, was able to identify the important functions of each area:

1. Cerebral Hemispheres: Willing, judging, memory, seeing, and hearing.
2. Cerebellum: Motor coordination.
3. Medulla Oblongata: Mediation of sensory and motor functions.
4. Corpora Quadrigemina (containing inferior and superior colliculi): Vision.
5. Spinal Cord: Conduction.
6. Nerves: Excitation.

Regions of the brain: At the most general level, the brain can be divided into three main regions: forebrain; midbrain; and hindbrain (Figure 4.4).

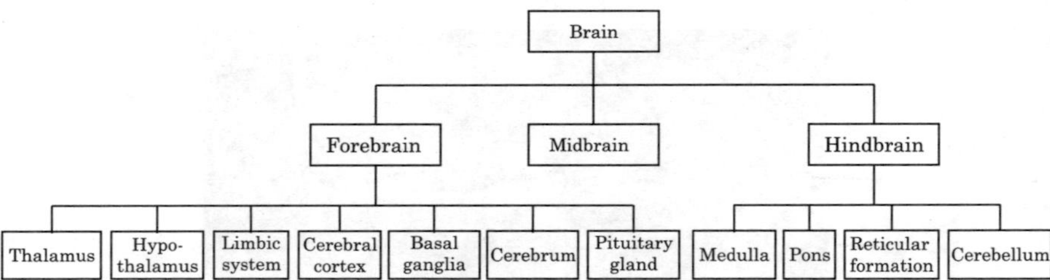

Figure 4.4 The major parts of the brain.

Because the forebrain is in many ways the most important part of the brain, we will start with it (Figure 4.5).

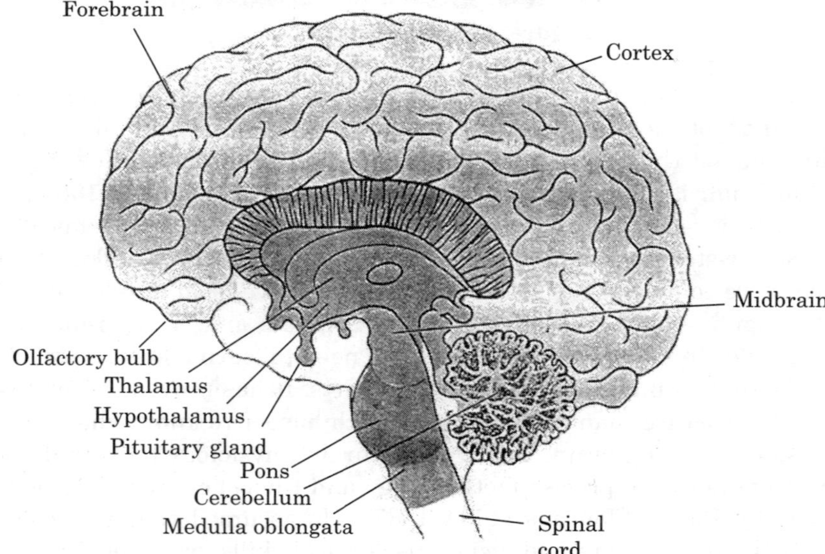

Figure 4.5 The human brain shows the forebrain, midbrain, and hindbrain.

(A) Forebrain: The forebrain is located towards the top and the front of the brain (Figure 4.5). In humans, the forebrain is the largest part of the brain. The forebrain is most important in perception, memory, thought, and social behaviour—those aspects of human life most relevant to Psychology. Important areas in the frontal part of the brain, or forebrain, are the thalamus, the hypothalamus, the limbic system, basal ganglia, the cerebral cortex, the cerebrum, and other structures, which are also critical in human behaviour.

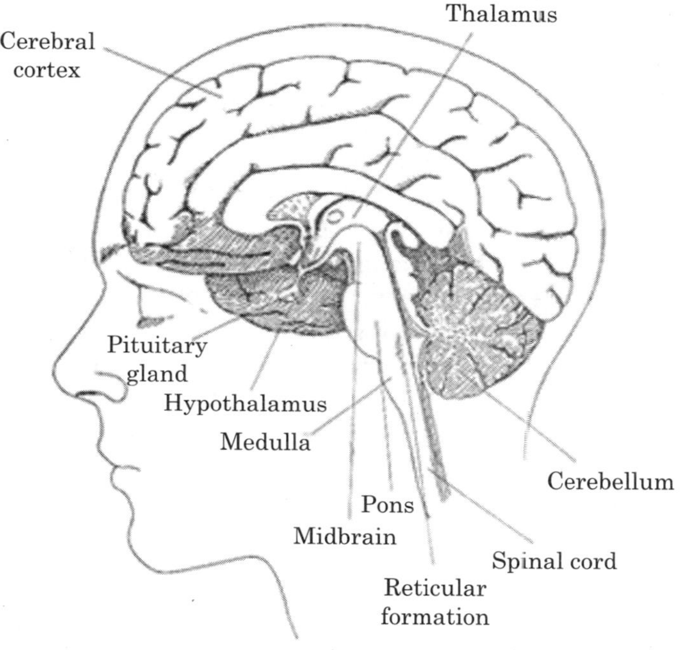

Figure 4.6 A schematic view of the human brain.

1. *The Thalamus:* The thalamus plays an important role in perception. The thalamus relays sensory information to the cortex, as from the eyes to the visual cortex (Figures 4.6, 4.8, and 4.9). Nearly all the information from the senses is processed by the thalamus on its route from the sensory receptors to the cerebral cortex (the one exception is smell, which travels a more direct route). The thalamus does not simply send messages along in a passive fashion. Instead, it organizes and transforms information. The thalamus is a major relay station for messages from all parts of the body. It passes information on to higher brain centres. The thalamus is also involved in wakefulness, sleep, and attention, in coordination with other structures, like

the Reticular Activating System (RAS). It is important in sensation of pain.

2. *The Hypothalamus:* The hypothalamus lies just below the thalamus (the prefix 'hypo' means 'under'). The hypothalamus is a tiny structure located between the thalamus and the pituitary gland (Figures 4.5, 4.6 and 4.8). Although the hypothalamus is less than one cubic centimeter in size, thin tiny structure exerts profound effects on our behaviour. The thalamus is vital in regulating body temperature, concentration of fluids, storage of nutrients, and motivation and emotion. Its functions include:
   (i) It controls and regulates the automatic or Autonomic Nervous System (ANS), which is responsible for glands, blood vessels, and internal organs, thus influencing reactions ranging from sweating and salivating to the shedding of tears, and changes in blood pressure, control of body temperature.
   (ii) It plays a key role in homeostasis—the maintenance of the body's internal environment at optimal level.
   (iii) By implanting electrodes in parts of the hypothalamus of animals and observing the effects when a current is switched on, researchers have found that the hypothalamus is involved in a range of motivational drives and behaviours, including hunger, thirst, sex, parenting behaviours, and aggression. The hypothalamus seems to play a role in the regulation of eating and drinking. The hypothalamus features several distinct clusters of neurons that regulate different kinds of motivated behaviour, such as eating, drinking, aggression, and activity level. It is also involved in the control of sexual behaviour and the endocrine (hormonal) system, and in reactions to stress.

   This structure is no longer than a kidney bean, and yet each of its regions is critically important to normal functioning.

3. *The Limbic System*: The hypothalamus along with parts of the thalamus and other structures, make up the limbic system. The limbic system consists of several related parts such as the hippocampus and the amygdala. The limbic system is classified as a system because the components are connected with one another and they work together in an integrated fashion. The limbic system plays a role in memory and in regulating the more basic drives involving hunger, thirst, and aggression. The limbic system helps regulate the emotions and it also plays a critical role in motivation, learning, and memory (Aggleton, 1992; Squire, 1991).

The largest of these structures, the hippocampus, plays a key role in the formation of memories (Eichenbaum and Bunsey, 1995; Gluck and Myers, 1995). It is of importance in learning also. The another main part, the amygdala, is involved in aspects of emotional control (anger and aggression) and in the limbic system—or in other parts of the brain that influence it—may play a role in human violence.

4. *The Cerebral Cortex:* The cerebral cortex is the outer layer or surface of the two cerebral hemispheres of the brain (Figures 4.5, 4.6, 4.8, and 4.9). It is only two millimeters deep, but has great importance for our ability to perceive, think, and use language. It processes all perceptions and complex thoughts. It is a thin layer of gray matter called the "cortex" (the term means "bark" or "outer covering"). The cortex is the most recent evolutionary development of the nervous system. It is only about a twelfth of an inch (2 millimeters) thick, but it has so many convolutions that it contains more than 9 billion neurons. If the human cortex were flattened out, its area would be about 2.5 square feet. It has wrinkled walnut like appearance (Figures 4.5, 4.6, 4.7, 4.8, and 4.9).

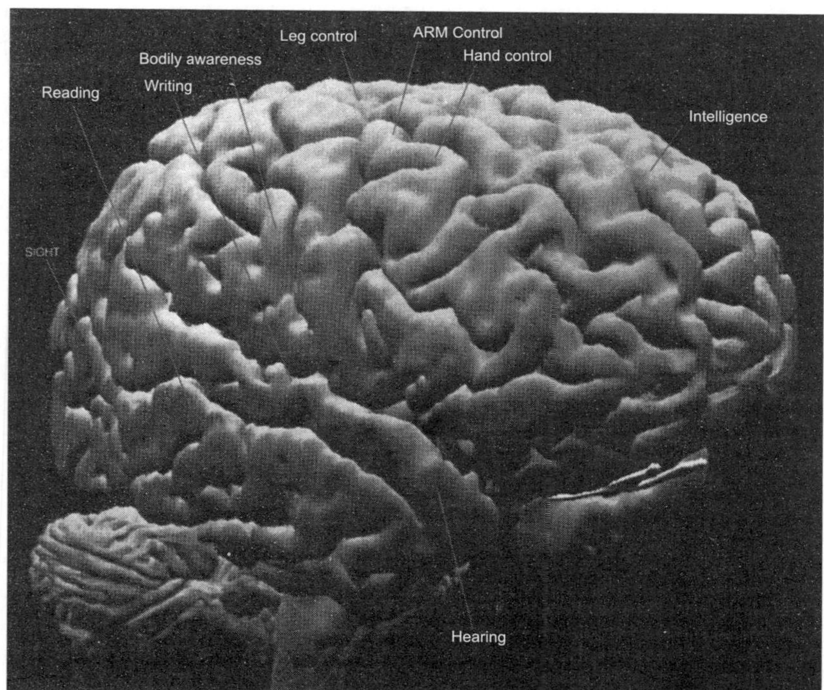

Figure 4.7 The Cerebral Cortex.

Parts of the cerebral cortex not involved in sensation of motor function are called "association areas". These areas make possible such higher functions as learning, thoughts, memory, and language. Figure 4.7 illustrates the areas of the cerebral cortex associated with different body functions.

The entire brain or the cortex is divided into two distinct hemispheres, discussed later in this chapter, and this has led psychologists to distinguish the left and right cerebral hemispheres.

5. *The Basal Ganglia:* The basal ganglia lie under the cortex in front of the thalamus (Figure 4.8) and help to regulate postural movements and coordination.
6. *The Cerebrum:* The cerebrum is your crowning glory. It is responsible for the shape of your delightfully rounded head. This contains 70% of all the neurons (nerve cells) in the central nervous system, and it plays a crucial role in thinking, use of language, and other cognitive skills. In particular, the development of the cerebrum and its outer layer, the cerebral cortex, distinguishes us from all other species.
7. *The Pituitary Gland:* Technically, the pituitary gland is not a part of the brain, but it is regulated by the nearby hypothalamus (Figures 4.5 and 4.6). The pituitary gland is discussed in detail in Chapter 3.

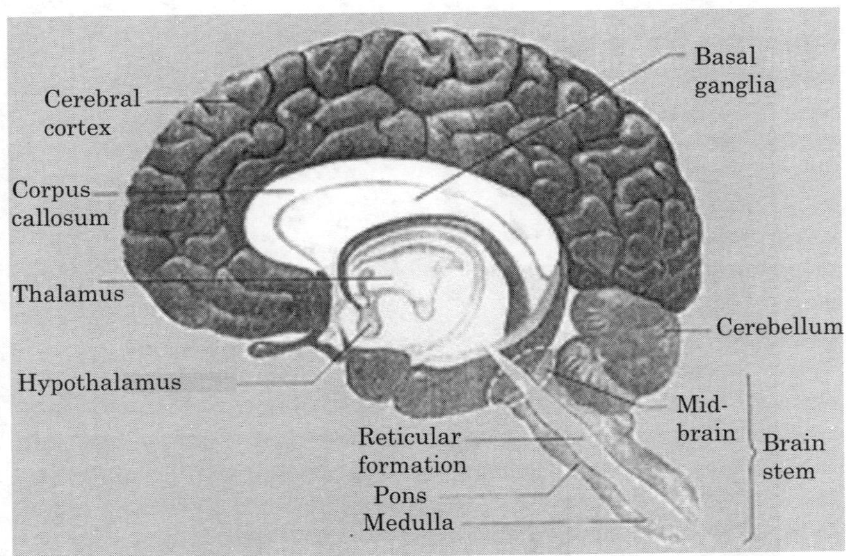

Figure 4.8 The right hemisphere of the brain as it would appear if the head were sliced exactly in half from front to back.

(B) Midbrain: Above the medulla and pons, near the end of the brain stem, is a structure called the "midbrain" (Figures 4.5, 4.6, and 4.8). All signals that pass between the spinal cord and the forebrain must pass through this structure. The midbrain plays a much less central role in human behaviour than the forebrain. It contains an extension of the reticular activating system as well as primitive centres concerned with vision and hearing: the superior colliculi (vision) and the inferior colliculi (hearing). The reticular activating system is an important structure in the control of consciousness. The midbrain also contains structures that play a role in such varied functions as the pain-relieving effect. Visual information passes through the midbrain in its route from the eyes to the forebrain. In the midbrain, visual information is also coordinated with motor movements and plays a role in sleep. One could not survive without one's midbrain or hindbrain.

(C) Hindbrain: In evolutionary terms, the hindbrain is a very old part of the brain. (Figures 4.5, 4.6, 4.8 and 4.9) Its brain structures are like those of reptiles, leading the hindbrain to be called the "reptile brain". The hindbrain or the lower part of the brain is located in the bottom portion of the brain and it includes several important structures:

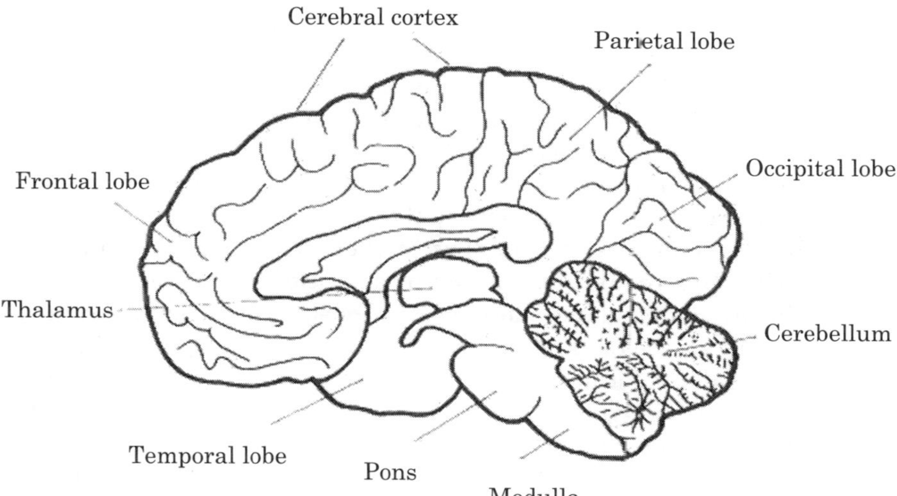

Figure 4.9 Cross-section of the human brain.

1. *The Medulla or The Medulla Oblongata:* The medulla can be found just above the spinal cord (Figures 4.5, 4.6, 4.8 and 4.9). It can be considered a broader, fancier extension of the spinal cord. Many nerves that link the spinal cord to higher brain levels pass through the medulla. This is a part of the reticular activating system. The medulla plays role in several important

and vital functions, such as controlling breathing or respiration, and heart rate, blood pressure, and also in sleep, sneezing, coughing, digestion, and swallowing. The medulla sounds rather dull, but one could not survive without it. The medulla contains several nuclei—collections of neuron cell bodies—that control vital other functions, as well, such as blood pressure, coughing, sneezing, etc. It is also the part of the hindbrain in which nerves from one side of the body cross to the other side of the brain.

2. *The Pons:* The pons is a bulging structure located above the medulla (Figures 4.5, 4.6, 4.8 and 4.9). The word 'pons' means 'bridge' and this structure serve the function of a bridge by connecting the lower brain regions with the higher brain regions. This is also part of the reticular activating system, being involved in the control of consciousness; it acts as a relay station passing messages between different parts of the brain; finally, cells associated with vision have been found in the pons, and it is very active during vivid dreams. The pons transmits information about body movement and is involved in functions related to attention, sleep, and respiration. The pons is important in muscle control, such as facial expression and the skillful use of our fingers (Glees, 1988).
3. *The Cerebellum:* Behind the medulla and pons is the cerebellum or "little brain" in Latin. Cerebellum looks like a miniature version of the entire brain, tacked on at the lower rear portion of the brain (Figures 4.5, 4.6, 4.8, 4.9, and 4.11). The cerebellum is one of the oldest structures in the evolution of mammals, nervous systems (Thompson, 1985). It is well developed in fish, birds, and lower animals. The cerebellum is primarily concerned with the regulation of motor activities. The cerebellum is involved in balance and motor (muscle) behaviour. Its main functions are the fine control of balance and bodily co-ordination generally; information about "over-learned" skills such as riding a bicycle or typing is stored in the cerebellum. Injury to the cerebellum may impair motor coordination and cause stumbling and loss of muscle tone. Damage to the cerebellum results in jerky, poor coordinated muscle functioning. If such damage is severe, it may be impossible for a person to stand, to walk, or run. It is important in maintaining posture and controlling motor movements. In addition, the cerebellum plays a role in certain cognitive processes such as learning (Daum et al., 1993).
4. *The Reticular Formation:* It turns up from the hindbrain, through to the midbrain (see Figures 4.6 and 4.8). Axons from the reticular formation even reach upward into the cerebral cortex at the top of the brain. The Reticular Activating System

(RAS) plays vital roles in attention, arousal, sleep, learning, and personality (introversion-extraversion). This structure is important in attention and in sleep, as well as in simple learning tasks (Mcginty and Szmusiak, 1988). RAS injury may leave an animal comatose. RAS stimulation triggers messages to the cortex that heighten alertness. Depressant drugs, such as alcohol, which dampen nervous system activity and lower RAS activity.

The brain is divided into four lobes or areas or regions (Figures 4.9 and 4.10), based on their structure and function. The lobes are anatomical regions named for the bones of the skull lying closest to them. The frontal lobe is at the front of the brain, and the occipital lobe is at the back of the brain. The two other lobes are in the middle of the brain, with the parietal lobe at the top of the brain and the temporal lobe below it. The four lobes of the cerebral cortex differ somewhat in terms of what they do. Robert Sternberg (1995) provided a good summary of their functions; "Higher thought processes, such as abstract reasoning and motor processing, occur in the frontal lobe, somatosensory processing (sensations in the skin and muscles of the body) in the parietal lobe, auditory processing in the temporal lobe, and visual processing in the occipital lobe."

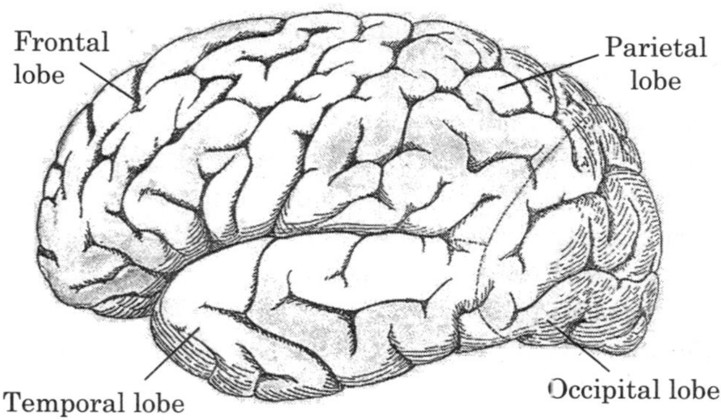

Figure 4.10 A schematic drawing of the cerebral cortex, as seen from the side.

(a) The Frontal Lobe: Important area here is the motor cortex. The cells in this region control voluntary movement for different parts of the body. Neurons in the motor area or motor cortex of the frontal lobe (Figures 4.9 and 4.10) are involved in controlling muscular responses, which enable us to move our limbs. This is involved in the planning and control of movements. Far more of the primary motor cortex is devoted to parts of the body that make very precise movements (for example, the fingers) than to those that do not (for example, the toes). In addition, the frontal lobe is also involved in learning, memory, speech, language, abstracting, thinking, and reasoning.

(b) The Parietal Lobe: The parietal lobe (Figures 4.9 and 4.10) is involved in determining our sense of body position. The parietal lobes contain the primary somatosensory cortex, the primary receiving area for the skin senses (touch, pressure, heat, pain) and for the sense of body position, body movement, and the location of body parts. This area receives information from various senses about temperature, pain, and pressure. The sensory area of the parietal lobe receives messages from skin senses all over the body. Those parts of the body most represented in the primary motor cortex also tend to be well represented in the primary somatosensory cortex.

(c) The Temporal Lobe: These are located on each side of the head. The auditory area of the cortex lies in the temporal lobe. The temporal lobes (Figures 4.9 and 4.10) contain the auditory cortex, which processes information about sound, speech, and music. The temporal lobe is involved in auditory processing. Sounds induce structures in the ear to vibrate, which relay messages to the auditory area. When activated, neurons in this area produce our experience of sound or hearing. The most important form of this processing is speech perception. Within the temporal lobe, some parts respond most to certain kinds of sounds (for example, those high or low in pitch). A person with a lesion in the left temporal lobe, may have difficulty understanding and producing language.

(d) The Occipital Lobe: It is located at the back of the head (Figures 4.9 and 4.10). An important part of this region of the brain is the visual cortex. The occipital lobe is primarily involved in vision. The occipital lobe is most concerned with visual processing. Information travels from the receptors in the eyes, through the thalamus, to the visual cortex. Nerve fibres from the right side of each eye go to the left occipital lobe, whereas those from the left side of each eye go to the right occipital lobe. When light stimulates the retinas of the eyes, neurons in the occipital lobe are activated creating the sense of sight. The occipital lobe plays a key role in vision, but the parietal and temporal lobes are also involved. Indeed, it has been estimated that as much as 50% of the entire cerebral cortex is devoted to visual processing.

It is important to note that none of the four lobes is devoted exclusively to the processes described so far. Large areas within each lobe are association areas, which link sensory and motor processing. Association areas integrate or organize different kinds of sensory information to produce appropriate behaviour. The frontal association area in the frontal lobes is of great importance. It is critically involved in complex planning and problem solving. Tulving (1985) found that the front part of the brain was most active when personal events were being thought about, whereas the back part of the brain was most active when he thought about his general knowledge of the world. This suggests that different parts of the brain are involved in thinking about different kinds of information in long-term memory. Table 4.1 shows brain structures and associated behaviours.

Volkow and Tancredi (1991) argued that brain functioning is based on three basic principles:

1. The first principle is that the brain is interconnected.
2. The second principle is that the organization of brain is hierarchical. Processing exists at a number of levels.
3. The third principle is that of functional differentiation, which means that any given brain area tends to be responsible for specific functions.

Table 4.1 Brain structures and associated behaviours

Brain Structures and Associated Behaviours	
Thalamus	Major relay station for messages from all parts of the body, important in sensations of pain
Hypothalamus	Regulation of metabolism, temperature, emotions
Limbic system	Attention, emotions, "fight or flight", memory
Medulla	Breathing, blood pressure, other vital functions
Cerebellum	Fine motor coordination, posture, and balance
Reticular formation	Arousal reactions, information screening
Frontal lobe	Learning, abstracting, reasoning, inhibiting
Parietal lobe	Soma esthetic and motor discriminations and functions
Temporal lobe	Discrimination of sounds, verbal and speech behaviour
Occipital lobe	Visual discrimination and some aspects of visual memory
Corpus collosum	Communication between the brain's right and left hemispheres
Sensory strip	Integration of sensory information from various parts of the body
Motor strip	Regulation of voluntary movement

4.2.2 The Peripheral Nervous System

The word "peripheral" refers to things that are not central. The peripheral nervous system consists of everything in the nervous system except the brain and the spinal cord. The peripheral nervous system transmits messages from the sensory receptors to the central nervous system (the spinal cord and the brain). It also transmits messages back out from the central nervous system to the muscles and glands. The peripheral nervous system is used to transmit information between the central nervous system and the receptors and effectors outside the central nervous system. The peripheral nervous system is linked up with receptors in external sensory organs such as the eyes and ears, and with receptors in internal structures such as the stomach. The peripheral nervous system is made up of nerves that receive and transmit sensory (messages from sense organs such as the eyes and ears) to the brain and spinal cord, and of nerves that transmit messages from the brain or the spinal cord to the muscles, causing them to contract, and to glands, causing them to secrete hormones. The communication between the two nervous systems typically takes place via nerves, which are bundles of axons from neurons in the peripheral nervous system.

The peripheral nervous system connects the brain to the outer world. Without the peripheral nervous system, people could not perceive the world or act on it. The peripheral nervous system is further divided into two parts:

1. The somatic division or the somatic nervous system.
2. The autonomic division or the autonomic nervous system.

The somatic division or the somatic nervous system

The somatic division consists of sensory neurons that transmit sensory information into the central nervous system, as well as motor neurons that carry motor commands out of the central nervous system to the muscles. The somatic nervous system transmits messages about sights, sounds, smells, temperature, body position, and so on, to the brain. Messages from the brain and spinal cord to the somatic nervous system regulate intentional body movements, like raising an arm, or walking, and subtle movements that maintain posture and balance. The somatic nervous system connects muscles to voluntary muscles throughout the body. The somatic nervous system controls the voluntary movements of our skeletal muscles. Nearly all of our movements, except those controlled by reflexes, involve the somatic nervous system. When you engage in almost any voluntary action, portion of somatic nervous system are involved, for example, scratching nose, chewing gum, or perform any other voluntary action.

The autonomic division or the autonomic nervous system

In contrast, Autonomic Nervous System (ANS) connects the central nervous system to internal organs and glands and to muscles over which we have little voluntary control. "Autonomic" means "automatic". Psychologists are particularly interested in the Autonomic Nervous

System because its activities are linked to emotional response. The Autonomic Nervous System regulates the glands and involuntary activities like heart rate, breathing, digestion, and dilation of the pupils of the eyes, even when we are sleeping. The autonomic division helps control the glands, blood vessels, the intestines, the heart, and other internal organs. The Autonomic Nervous System (ANS) usually works automatically for example, the muscles in the digestive system. The Autonomic Nervous System controls the movements of our non-skeletal muscles. The organs within the control of the Autonomic Nervous System include the heart, lungs, eyes, stomach, and the blood vessels of internal organs.

The autonomic division or the Autonomic Nervous System is further divided into two parts or branches: the Sympathetic Nervous System and the Parasympathetic Nervous System. These two systems provide neurons for each of the glands, blood vessels, and internal organs in the autonomic division. These branches have mostly opposing effects. Many organs and glands are served by both branches of the Autonomic Nervous System.

(i) The sympathetic system or the sympathetic nervous system: The Sympathetic Nervous System (SNS) is called into play in situations needing arousal and energy. It prepares the body for action. The sympathetic division is mostly involved in processes that draw body energy from stored reserves which helps prepare the person to fend off threats or dangers. It produces increased heart rate, reduced activity within the stomach, pupil dilation or expansion, and relaxation of the bronchi of the lungs. These changes make people ready for fight or flight. Its neurons' endings secrete epinephrine, which increases heart rate and dilates the pupils of the eye. It makes us sweat, blush. The sympathetic neurons also connect with hair follicles and with tiny arteries in the skin.

In general, this system prepares the body for using energy as in vigorous physical action. Thus, stimulation of this division increases heartbeat, raises blood pressure, releases sugar into the blood for energy, and increases the flow of blood to muscles used in physical activities.

(ii) The parasympathetic system or the parasympathetic nervous system: The Parasympathetic Nervous System (PNS) generally works in the opposite direction. The effects of activity in the Parasympathetic Nervous System are the opposite of those of activity in the Sympathetic Nervous System. The Parasympathetic Nervous System is involved when the body is trying to save energy. It tends to slow down your body functions and conserves energy. The parasympathetic division is most active during processes that replenish or refill energy reserves, like digestion. Activation of this system slows heartbeat, lowers blood pressure, constricts pupils, and diverts blood away from skeletal muscles (for example, muscles in the arms and legs) arms to the digestive system.

The Parasympathetic Nervous System produces increased activity within the stomach and constriction of the bronchi of the lungs. Its neurons secrete the neurotransmitter ach.

When we are afraid or anxious, the sympathetic branch of the Autonomic Nervous system accelerates the heart rate. When we relax, the parasympathetic branch decelerates the heart rate. The parasympathetic branch incites digestion, but the sympathetic branch constrains digestive activity. Because the sympathetic branch dominates when we are fearful or anxious, fear or anxiety can cause indigestion by interfering with digestion of consumed food.

The Sympathetic Nervous System and the Parasympathetic Nervous System are both important. Working together, these two systems ensure that your body maintains its balance. The Sympathetic system and the Parasympathetic System often work in an antagonistic (opposite) fashion, with one increasing and the other decreasing an organ's activity. This is true for the heart, the pupils, the intestines, and the lungs. The two systems work together to achieve homeostasis, or a constant, ideal internal environment.

While the Automatic Nervous System plays an important role in the regulation of bodily processes, it does so mainly by transmitting information to and from the Central Nervous System. Thus, it is the Central Nervous System, that is, the brain and the spinal cord that ultimately runs the show.

4.3 THE CEREBRAL HEMISPHERES

The brain has two cerebral hemispheres. The human activities of thought and language involve the two hemispheres of the cerebrum. Although, these two half-brains look nearly identical, they perform somewhat different functions. The cortex is divided into two distinct hemispheres (Figure 4.11).

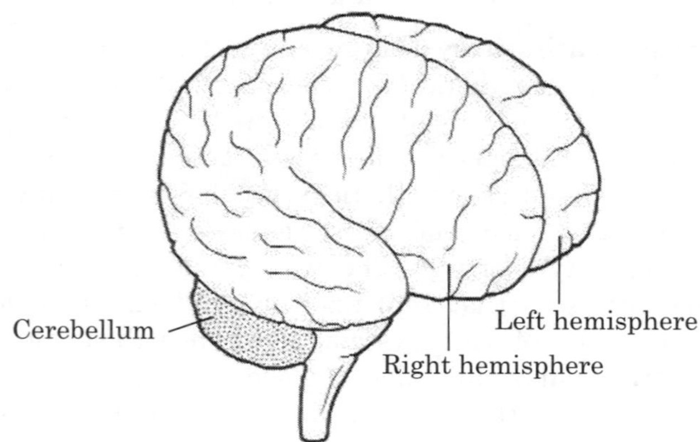

Figure 4.11 The hemispheres of the brain.

An important characteristic of the brain is that for the sensory and motor areas of the cortex, the right side of the cortex is more strongly connected with the left side of the body. Furthermore, the left side of the cortex is more strongly connected with the right side of the body. This crossover arrangement is called "contra-lateral arrangement." One who has had a stroke in the left cerebral cortex, his greatest difficulties involves the right side of the body. This person may have difficulty using the right hand due to left motor cortex damage and the right hand may also feel numb, due to left somatosensory cortex damage.

There is much "hemispheric specialization", meaning that the two hemispheres differ in their functions. This produces numerous situations in which there is "cerebral dominance", with one hemisphere being mainly responsible for processing information in that situation. Some of the earliest evidence about hemispheric specialization was obtained by Paul Broca in the 1860s. A few years later, Carl Wernicke conducted studies. The findings of Broca and Wernicke suggested that the left hemisphere is specialized for language. There is evidence that language is centered in the left hemisphere (Kandel, Schwartz, and Jessel, 1991; Kupferman, 1981; Levy et al., 1972; Roger Sperry, Michael Gazzaniga and their colleagues, 1982). There is more activity in the left hemisphere than in the right hemisphere when someone is carrying out a language-based task, but the opposite is the case during a spatial task (Kosslyn, 1994). According to Levy (1974), the right hemisphere usually processes information in a holistic fashion (as a whole), whereas the left hemisphere processes information in an analytic fashion (bit by bit). This characteristic of the brain is called "lateralization". "Lateralization" means that the two hemispheres have somewhat different functions. Table 4.2 shows some tasks on which one of the hemispheres shows superiority.

The hemispheres of the cerebral cortex are connected by the corpus callosum (Figure 4.8), a thick fibre bundle. The corpus callosum is the massive bundle of nerves that connects the two hemispheres (Bogen and Vogel, 1962). The normal brain features a bridge between the two hemispheres, called the corpus callosum, which is a thick bundle of about 800,000 axons (Trevarthen, 1987). The corpus callosum permits communication between the two hemispheres, so that a message received in one hemisphere can be quickly transmitted to the other hemisphere. For those having an intact corpus callosum, information is transferred from one hemisphere to the other in a few milliseconds. As a result, our two hemispheres normally function together in a co-operative fashion.

Table 4.2 Some tasks on which one of the hemispheres shows superiority

Tasks	*Left Hemisphere*	*Right Hemisphere*
Vision	Translation of letters into sounds	Recognition of faces
Hearing	Language sounds	Non-language sounds, music
Memory	Verbal memory	Visual memory
Language	Grammar, relations among words, concepts	Humour, emotional content, understanding beyond the level of the sentence
Mathematics	Arithmetic	Geometry
Problem-solving	Problems to be solved, analytically	Problems to be solved, holistically
Complex tasks	Tasks to be performed, one at a time	Tasks to be performed, all parts simultaneously

Patients with injuries to one hemisphere of the brain usually show sensory or motor deficits on the opposite side of the body because sensory and motor nerves cross in the brain and elsewhere. The left hemisphere controls functions on, and receives inputs from right side of the body. The right hemisphere controls functions on, and receives inputs from, the left side of the body.

In many ways, the hemispheres duplicate each other's functions but they are not fully equal. For most people, the left hemisphere contains language functions and is dominant (Rasmussen and Milner, 1977). We must conclude that both hemispheres can perform most tasks, but one hemisphere is usually faster and more accurate (Allen, 1983). As Levy (1985) concludes, "Normal people have not half a brain nor two brains but one gloriously differentiated brain, with each hemisphere contributing its specialized abilities."

4.4 A BRIEF INTRODUCTION TO MONITORING NEURAL ACTIVITY AND BIOFEED BACK OR WAYS OF STUDYING THE BRAIN OR NEUROPHYSIOLOGICAL SENSING TECHNIQUES

A few years ago, neurologists had only a few tools and techniques to use in the direct observation and exploration of the human brain. These included excising of tissue, electrical probes, EEG recordings, and postmortem examinations. Psychologists, on the other hand, invented a whole arsenal of techniques in which the mind revealed itself, such as the momentary presentation of stimuli and measuring of reaction time. Recently, however, new instruments have been invented that have profoundly accelerated our understanding of the brain and how it works. This progress is due to exciting technological advances. The new technology was originally developed for the diagnosis of brain disorders, but now it has become a valuable research tool.

Many recent models of the brain have been made possible because of technical developments in the field of neuroscience that have allowed a clearer view of the physical structures and internal workings of the human organism.

Before turning to recently developed methods, we will consider two methods invented several decades ago.

4.4.1 Electroencephalogram (EEG)

This is a technique for measuring the electrical activity of brain by electrodes placed at specific locations on the skull. The electroencephalogram (EEG) is based on electrical recordings taken from the scalp. It was first used by Hans Berger over 65 years ago. Very small changes in electrical activity within the brain are picked up by the electrodes placed on the scalp. These changes are shown on the screen of a cathode-ray tube by means of an instrument known as an *oscilloscope*. The pattern of changes is sometimes referred to as "brain waves".

Biofeedback is the information feedback about bodily function. Most information is mediated through normal sensory channels; for example, if you close your eyes and hold your arm out, kinaesthetic feedback informs you of its position and allows you to make adjustments to perform a task. Recent research has shown that biofeedback from an outside source can also be used to enable an organism to modify its functioning. For example, when EEG (Electroencephalogram) feedback is provided, people can maintain some degree of control over their alpha waves. Similar manipulations have been performed with heart rate, blood pressure, blood flow in the extremities, etc. Note that some of them have been taken to using the term as though it meant the direct control of internal, autonomic functions and activities. It should not be used in this fashion. It is merely a descriptive term for the process of providing an organism with information about its biological functions.

The EEG has proved useful in many ways. EEG research was of great importance in identifying the five stages of sleep. The EEG has also been of value in identifying the functions of the two hemispheres of the brain. In spite of these successes, the EEG is no longer used very much in research. The EEG is a rather blunt instrument in two ways. First, it measures electrical activity in several different areas of the brain at once, and so it is hard to work out which parts of the brain are more and less active. Second, it is an indirect measure of brain activity, because the recording electrodes are on the scalp rather than in the brain itself.

4.4.2 Evoked Potentials

Some years after the invention of the EEG, it was found that much could be learned about cognitive processes by using a related method known as "evoked potentials". Evoked potentials are based on averaging the EEG recordings from several presentations of the same stimulus. The method of evoked potentials has the great advantage that it provides a detailed moment-by-moment record of brain activity when a stimulus is being processed. However, there are two major limitations. First, it is not possible to identify with any precision that which parts of the brain are mainly responsible for the evoked potentials. Second, the method can only be used with simple stimuli. The evoked potential for complex stimuli would not show any clear pattern at all.

4.4.3 Brain Scanning

In recent years, various brain scanners have been developed. The scan produces a cross-sectional image of the brain. The impression is first enhanced by a computer, then colour added, and finally displayed on a video terminal. Photographs and/or hard copies of the display are often made. The important ones are discussed below:

1. **CAT or CT scans (Computerized Axial Tomography):** In order to take a scan, the individual lies on a table with her or his head in the middle of a doughnut-shaped ring that takes X-ray pictures. The more dense the material through which the X-ray pass, the less the radiation that is detected. The CAT scan rotates the X-ray beam 180 degrees, resulting in numerous pictures of the same organ. A CAT scan based on the X-ray produces a three-dimensional picture of a cross-section of the brain. This graphic cross section, called a "tomogram" has become critical in medical diagnosis. CAT scans have been used to detect tumours and other abnormalities of the brain. However, they do not show the actual functioning of the brain. Now, an ultra-fast CAT has been developed that speeds up processing so that previously blurred images are now clear. An even more sophisticated version of the CAT technique, the DSR (Dynamic Spatial Reconstructor), shows internal structures in three dimensions.
2. **MRI (Magnetic Resonance Imaging):** A method for studying the intact brain in which technicians obtain images by

exposing the brain to a strong magnetic field. MRI scans provide detailed information about brain structures. MRI scans are similar to CAT scans in some ways. However, they produce clearer and more detailed pictures. What happens in an MRI scan is that radio waves are used to excite atoms in the brain. This produces magnetic changes which are detected by an 11-ton magnet surrounding the individual or the patient. These changes are then interpreted by a computer and turned into a very precise three-dimensional picture. MRI scans can be used to detect very small brain tumours. They share the limitation of CAT scans of telling us about the structure of the brain rather than about the ways in which it functions.

Also, newer methods, called EPI (Echo-Planar MRI), are capable of high-resolution images of functional activity in the brain. It is likely that further developments will make EPI a practical tool for discrete visualization of brain structures and processes conducted in real time.

3. **PET or PETT scanning (Positron Emission Tomography or Positron Emission Transaxial Tomography):** Of all the new ways of studying the brain, the one that has attracted the most media interest is the positron-emission tomography (PET) scan. PET is an imaging technique that detects the activities of brain by measuring glucose utilization or blood flow. The technique is based on positrons, which are the atomic particles emitted by some radio-active substances. A radioactive form of glucose is injected into the body. When part of the brain becomes active, the radioactive glucose moves rapidly to that place. A scanning device then measures the positrons emitted from the radioactive glucose. A computer then translated this information into a motion picture of the activity levels of different parts of the brain. It may sound dangerous to inject a radioactive substance into someone, but only tiny amounts of radioactivity are involved.

   PET scans show us the brain in action, and this is an advance on CAT and MRI scans. PET scans differ from CAT scans in that they use detectors to measure radioactive particles in the bloodstream. However, PET scans are more limited than is sometimes realized. They tell us which areas of the brain are active, but they do not identify these areas with precision. Furthermore, PET scans indicate the activity levels in different areas of the brain over periods of time running into several seconds, but not on a moment-by-moment basis. PET or PETT scan is sometimes also called SPECT (Single-Photon Emission Computerized Tomography).

4. **CT or CTG scanning (Computerized Tomography):** A method scanning in which a series of X-ray images are synthesized and analyzed by the computer.
5. **SQUID (Super Conducting Quantum Interference Device):** An imaging technique that captures image of brain through its ability to detect changes in the magnetic fields in the brain.
6. **STA:** The device known as *Stereo Toxic Apparatus* enables psychologists to place tiny electrons within the brain of animals with a great precision.

Modern technology has provided impressive new tools for studying the living brain—for seeing where activity is centered as people solve problems, listen to music, reason, or memorize new information. (for example, Berson et al., 1998; Waltz et al., 1999). These tools have done for what microscope did for biology and medicine, and what the telescope did for astronomy. They have helped in understanding of how the brain works and the role it plays in complex behaviour, feelings, and experiences that make us human.

HEALTH TIPS

We spend lots of time in keeping ourselves healthy. The brain develops and gains strength during young age and later on it has to be maintained or allowed to degenerate. In diet, avoid fatty and fried foods that can cause blood arteries to block. Eat lots of fruits. Control negative emotions like fear, anger, jealousy, and emotional stress. Stay away from alcohol, tobacco, and other drugs. High risk life-styles include stress, smoking, pollution, alcohol, fast food, and processed food. Most of the negative changes to our bodies over time can be chalked up to disease-related aging (that is, changes accelerated by illness and conditions such as diabetes and heart disease). Reduce characteristics of Type-A behaviour pattern like excessive competitive drive, time urgency or impatience, hostility, inappropriate ambition, a reluctance to provide self-evaluation, a tendency to emphasize quantity of output over quality and a need for control. Type-A behaviour pattern is believed to be associated with increased incidence of coronary heart disease. World Health Organization estimated that by 2010, 60% of the cardiac patients in the world will be Indian. Meditation increases the thickness of the frontal lobe of the cerebral cortex, which is associated with cognitive activities like planning, decision-making, memory, etc. Reading is an excellent way to keep the working of the brain efficient. Puzzles, mental games, computer games, chess are good mental exercises. Physical exercises like walking, jogging, running improve the circulatory system and increase the supply of blood to the brain. Being physically active improves the quality of life as well. Physical exercises, meditation, aerobic activity, and yoga helps in keeping the body fit and also helps in relieving stress. Positive self-perceptions can prolong life expectancy. Optimists tend to look after their health better, be more focused, and know what they want, and are more likely to shun health-threatening behaviours. A healthy brain helps us to be mentally active, which is important in terms of longevity and a good life.

To conclude, it can be said that the science of staying healthy prescribes:

1. Proper nutrition
2. Regular exercise
3. Adequate rest
4. Positive attitude

QUESTIONS

The below mentioned are some of the questions that have been asked in the examinations conducted by the Guru Nanak Dev University or can be asked. Knowledge of these answers can help the students to get success in the examinations.

Section A

Answer the following questions in **five** lines or 50 words.

1. Define nervous system.*
2. What is central nervous system?
3. What is spinal cord?
4. Define peripheral nervous system.
5. Define sympathetic nervous system.
6. Defince Parasympathetic nervous system.
7. What is Cerebral cortex?*
8. What is forebrain?
9. What is midbrain?
10. What is hindbrain?
11. What is frontal lobe?
12. What is temporal lobe?
13. What is parietal lobe?
14. What is occipital lobe?
15. Explain reticular activating system.
16. What is CAT scan?
17. What is MRI scan?
18. What is PET scan?

19. What is Synapse?*

or

What do you understand by "Synapse"?
20. What is Cortex?
21. What is Neuron?*
22. Explain all or None Law.*

or

Define all or None principle.

or

What do you mean by all or none Law?
23. What is bio-feedback?*
24. What is neural activity?
25. Define effectors.*
26. What is bi-polar neuron?
27. What is unipolar neuron?
28. What do you understand by "axon"?
29. Write the functions of sympathetic nervous system.
30. What are receptors?*
31. What is multipolar neuron?
32. What is reflex action?
33. Write different functions of cerebrum.
34. What are the functions of receptors or effectors or conductors?
35. Define neuron.*
36. What is synapse?
37. What is thalamus?
38. What is hypothalamus?
39. What is neural activity?

Section B

Answer the following questions up to **two** pages or 500 words.

1. Describe the structure and functions of brain.
2. Give a brief description of peripheral nervous system.
3. Describe the structure and functions of a neuron.*
4. Describe the function of receptors.
5. Write about structure, functions, and types of neuron.
6. Describe the structure and types of neuron.*
7. Describe autonomic nervous system.

8. Define a neuron and describe its structure and functions.
9. Briefly discuss the functions of "receptors" in the body.
10. Describe the major parts of the brain with their functions.
11. Describe the structure and functions of spinal cord.
12. Explain 'all or none law'.
13. Define nervous system. Describe the functions of any one of the following:

    Receptors, Effectors, Conductors
14. What is the role of the cerebral cortex?
15. Give brief introduction to monitoring neural activity and bio-feedback.*

Section C

Answer the following questions up to **five** pages or 1000 words.

1. Describe the structure and functions of nervous system.*
2. What is the nervous system? What is it used for?
3. What are the main areas of the cerebral cortex? What is the function of each area?
4. What are the main functions of each hemisphere of the brain? What evidence is there for cerebral dominance and hemispheric specialization?
5. What methods have been developed for studying the brain? What are the advantages and disadvantages of these methods? *
6. Describe the functions of central nervous system.
7. Explain the peripheral nervous system.
8. Give a description of central nervous system.
9. What structures make up the central nervous system? What is the function of the spinal cord?
10. What two systems make up the peripheral nervous system? What are the roles of these two systems?
11. What are the functions of the sympathetic and parasympathetic nervous system?
12. What do you mean by neurons? What are their basic parts?
13. What are the functions of the hypothalamus and thalamus?
14. What methods are used by psychologists to study the brain and its role in behaviour?

REFERENCES

Broca, P., 'Perte de la parole, Ramollissement chrinique et destruction partielle du lobe anterieur gauche du cerveau,' *Bulletin de la Societe d' Anthropologie*, **2**, 135–237, 1861.

Broca, P., 'Sur le siega de la faculte du langage articule,' *Bulletin de la Societe d' Anthropologie*, **6,** 337–393, 1865.

Carlson, N.R., *Physiology of Behaviour* (3rd ed.), Longman Higher Education, 1977.

Carlson, N.R., *Physiology of Behaviour* (3rd ed.), Boston: Allyn & Bacon. 1986.

Carlson, N.R., *Physiology of Behaviour* (6th ed.), Needham Heights, MA: Allyn & Bacon, 1998.

Carlson, N.R., *Foundations of Physiological Psychology* (4th ed.), Boston: Allyn & Bacon, 1999.

Cohen, N.J., Eichenbaum, H., Deacedo, B.S., and Corkin, S.M., 'Different Memory Systems Underlying Acquisition of Procedural and Declarative Knowledge,' *Annals of the New York Academy of Sciences,* **444**, 54–71, 1985.

Daum, I., Ackerman, H., Schugens, M.M., Reimold, C., Dichgans, J., and Birbaumer, N., 'The Cerebellum and Cognitive Functions in Humans,' *Behavioural Neuroscience*, **104**, 411–419, 1993.

Eichenbaum, H. and Bunsey, M., 'On the Binding of Associations in Memory: Clues from Studies on the Role of the Hippocampal Region in Paired-associate Learning,' *Current Directions in Psychological Science*, **4**, 19–23, 1995.

Gazzaniga, M.S., 'Right Hemisphere Language: Remaining Problems,' *American Psychologist*, **39**, 1494–1495, 1984.

Gazzaniga, M.S., 'The Social Brain,' *Psychology Today*, pp. 29–38, 1985.

Gluck, M.A. and Myers, C.E., 'Representation and Association in Memory: A Neurocomputational View of Hippocampal Function,' *Current Directions in Psychological Science*, **4**, 23–29, 1995.

Hebb, D.O., 'Drives and the C.N.S. (Conceptual Nervous System),' *Psychological Review*, **62**, 243–254, 1955.

Hubel, D.H., 'Visual Cortex of the Brain.' *Scientific American*, **209**(5), 54–62, 1963.

Hubel, D.H. and Wiessel, T.N., 'Brain Mechanisms of Vision,' *Scientific American*, **241**, 150–162, 1979.

Kandel, E.R. and Schwartz, J.H., 'Molecular Biology of Learning: Modulation of Transmitter Release,' *Science*, **218**, 433–443, 1982.

Kosslyn, S., *Image and Brain,* Cambridge, MA: MIT Press, 1994.

Kosslyn, S.M., *Image and Brain: The Resolution of the Imagery Debate*, Cambridge, MA: MIT Press, 1994.

Levy, J., 'Cerebral Asymmetries as Manifested in Split-brain Man,' in M. Kinsbourne and W.L. Smith (Eds.). *Hemispheric Disconnection and Cerebral Function, Springfield,* IL: Charles C. Thomas, 1974.

Levy, J., Trevarthan, C., and Sperry, R.W., 'Perception of Bilateral Chimeric Figures Following Hemisphere Deconnection,' *Brain*, **95**, 61–78, 1972.

Ornstein, R., *Psychology of Consciousness* (2nd ed.), New York: Harcourt Brace Jovanovich, 1977.

Rosenzweig, M. and Leiman, A., *Physiological Psychology* (2nd ed.), New York: Random House, 1992.

Rasmussen, T. and Milner, B., 'The Role of Early Left Brain Injury in Determining Lateralization of Cerebral Speech Functions,' *Annuals of the New York Academy of Sciences,* **299**, 355–369, 1977.

Sperry, R.W., 'Hemispheric Deconnection and Unity of Conscious Experience,' *American Psychologist*, **29**, 723–733, 1968.

Sternberg, R.J., 'For Whom the Bell Curve Tolls: A Review of The Bell Curve,' *Psychological Science,* **6**, 257–261, 1995.

Squire, L.R., *Memory and Brain*, New York: Oxford University Press, 1987.

Squire, L.R., Closing remarks, in L.R. Squire and E. Lindenlaub (Eds.), *The Biology of Memory* (pp. 643–644), Stuttgart, Germany: F.K. Schattauer Verlag, 1991.

Squire, L.R., 'Biological Foundations of Accuracy and Inaccuracy of Memory,' in D.L. Schachter (Ed.), *Memory Distortions* (pp. 197–225), Cambridge, MA: Harvard University Press, 1995.

Thompson, R.F., *The Brain: An Introduction to Neuroscience*, San Francisco: Freeman, 1985.

Thompson, W. and Debold, R.C., *Psychology,* New York: McGraw-Hill Book Company, 1971.

Tulving, E., 'How Many Memory Systems are There?' *American Psychologist*, **40**, 385–398, 1985.

Tulving, E., 'Remembering and Knowing the Past,' *American Scientist,* **77**, 361–367, 1989.

Trevarthen, C., 'Analysis of Cerebral Activities that Generate and Regulate Consciousness in Commissuratomy Patients,' In S.J. Diamond and J.G. Beaumont (Eds.), *Hemispheric Function in the Human Brain*, New York: Halstead Press, pp. 235–263, 1974.

Weiss, A.P., 'Behaviour and the Central Nervous System,' *Psychological Review*, **29**, 329–344, 1922.

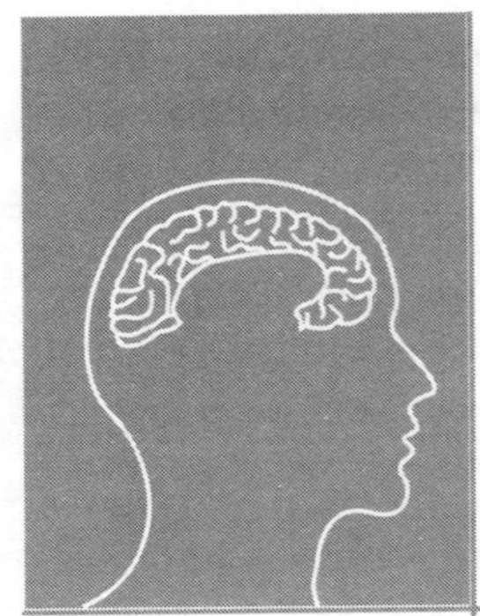

CHAPTER 5

Understanding Individual Differences

A psychological test is an objective, standardized measure of a sample of behaviour. Just as a laboratory technician makes observations on a sample of a person's blood, a psychologist collects a small sample of a person's behaviour (Anastasi, 1988). Psychological testing is challenging because we cannot simple peel back a person's scalp and watch all the existing psychological processes in action (Kail and Pallfgrino, 1985). Moreover, we cannot simply peep into people's head to assess their level of verbal ability or their extraversion. Instead, we must study mental processes by looking at a person's responses on standardized tests.

Psychological tests are tools. Traditionally, the function of psychological tests has been to measure the differences between individuals or between the reactions of the same individual under different circumstances. One of the earliest problems that stimulated the development of psychological tests was the identification of mentally retarded persons.

A psychological test is essentially an objective and standardized measure of a sample of behaviour. Whether or not the test adequately covers the behaviour under consideration obviously depends upon the number and the nature of the items in the sample.

The diagnostic or the predictive value of a psychological test depends upon the degree to which it serves as an indicator of a relatively broad and significant area of behaviour. The test items need not resemble closely the behaviour the test is to predict. It is necessary only that an empirical correspondence is demonstrated between the two. The degree of similarity between the sample and the predicted behaviour may vary widely. Prediction commonly connotes a temporal estimate, for example, individual's future performance on a job being forecast from their present test performance. The diagnosis of a present condition, such as mental retardation or emotional disorder, implies a prediction of what the individual will do in situations other than the present test. No psychological test can do more than measure behaviour, whether such behaviour can serve as an effective index of other behaviour, can be established only by empirical try out.

5.1 USES OF PSYCHOLOGICAL TESTS

The following are the purposes for which the psychological tests are put to use:

1. Psychological tests are used to measure differences between individuals or between the reactions of the same individual under different circumstances. Sir Francis Galton (1873) established the first test laboratory in England.
2. Psychological tests are used to identify and diagnose mentally retarded or intellectually deficient persons.
3. Psychological tests are used to diagnose persons with severe emotional disorders and other related behavioural problems.
4. Psychological tests are used in educational set up. At present, schools are among the largest test-users. The classification of children with reference to their ability to profit from different types of school instructions, the identification of outstandingly slow or fast learners, the educational and vocational counselling of high school and college students, and the selection of applicants for professional schools/colleges or cources are among the many educational uses of tests. Intelligence tests have been used to predict school or college performance. For example, an intelligence test will indicate that those with higher Intelligence Quotient (IQ) tend to have rather better academic performance than those with lower IQs. However, academic success also depends on motivation, personality characteristics, and parental encouragement.
5. The selection and classification of industrial personnel represent another major application of psychological testing. From the assembly—filling clerk to top management, there is scarcely a type of job for which some kind of psychological tests have not proved helpful in such matters as job assignment, transfer,

promotion or termination. Companies looking for additional staff often make use of a battery of tests, including tests of intelligence and personality. The effective employment of tests in many of these situations, especially in connection with high level jobs usually requires that the tests be used as an adjunct to skillful interviewing, so that scores may be properly interpreted in the light of other background information about the individual.

6. A closely related application of psychological testing is to be found in the selection and classification of military personnel. From simple beginnings in World War I, the scope and variety of psychological tests employed in military situations underwent a remarkable increase during World War II. Subsequently, research on test development has been continuing on a large scale on all branches of armed services.
7. Another use of psychological tests is in connection with career advice or vocational guidance. People who are successful in a given occupation, for example, teachers tend to possess certain characteristics. These characteristics include high IQ, more specific abilities, a certain type of personality, and interests.
8. The use of tests in individual counselling has gradually broadened from a narrow defined guidance regarding educational and vocational plans to an involvement with all aspects of the person's life. Emotional well being and effective interpersonal relations have become increasingly prominent objectives of counselling.
9. There is growing emphasis too, on the use of tests to enhance self-understanding and personal (personality) development. Test scores are part of the information given to the individual as aids to her or his decision-making process.
10. Psychological tests are currently being employed in the solution of a wide range of practical problems. Psychological tests are used on an applied basis in decisions about people's life chances and opportunities. These may be related to education, psychotherapeutic treatment or job selection.
11. Tests are also serving important functions in research.

Nearly all the problems in Psychology, for example studies on the nature and extent of individual differences, the organization of psychological traits, the measurement of group differences and the identification of biological and cultural factors associated with behavioural differences, etc. require testing procedures as a means of gathering data or data collection. Psychological tests provide standardized tools for investigating such varied problems as life span developmental changes within the individual, the relative effectiveness of different educational procedures, and the outcome of psychotherapy, the impact of community programmes, and the influence of environmental variables or factors on human performance.

5.2 FEATURES OR PROPERTIES OR CHARACTERISTICS OF GOOD PSYCHOLOGICAL TESTS

A proper psychological test has three important properties. A good test must be properly standardized and also both reliable and valid. All goals of Psychology that is understanding, explaining, predicting, and controlling human behaviour will not be fulfilled if the test is not an objective and a standardized tool and instrument. A psychological test should be reliable and also valid. Psychometric tests and other scales all need to be checked formally for their reliability and validity. They would also need to be standardized for general use.

5.2.1 Standardization

A psychological test is a standardized measure. A standardized test means that the test has been given to large, representative samples of the age groups covered by the test. As a result, the meaning of an individual's score on the test can be assessed by comparing it against the scores of those on whom the test was standardized. "Standardization" implies uniformity of procedure in administering and scoring the test. In the process of standardization, uniform procedures for giving and scoring a test are developed. Ideally, all people who take the test are subject to identical conditions, which mean the same instructions or directions, the same materials, the same time limits, and so forth. Without such standardized conditions, it would be impossible to say that different scores is not just a reflection of different testing situations.

Standardization also involves establishing norm or the standards of performance for the test. This is done by administering the test to a large group of people representative of those for whom the test is intended and then determining the distribution of their scores. These norms tell us if subsequent scores are high, low or in the middle range. It is essential that the group used to establish norms is representative of all those who will later be tested, otherwise subsequent scores may seem misleading high or low. To avoid the problem of unrepresentative norms, many tests are developed with norms for people of different ages, ethnic backgrounds, and social classes. Psychological tests have ethical importance as well, that is these tests must not discriminate, in a particular way, against some group of people. An extremely important consideration is that a test which is standardized on a particular population, can obviously not be used with confidence on a different population.

5.2.2 Reliability

A test is considered reliable if it consistently yields the same results. With an unreliable test, the same person may score very high on one occasion and very low on another, even though the two different occasions are close together in time. "Reliability" refers to the consistency of a person's scores. Reliability means that a test provides consistent findings. This consistency is established by re-examining the test takers with the same test on two occasions or by some other method for measuring the stability of the score (Anastasi, 1988).

Reliability is the accuracy of a test measure, in terms of producing the same results on different occasions. For example, if any scale or instrument does not give the same reading for the same material every time, the scale is not reliable, it is unreliable or the scale has poor reliability. We need to be confident that someone who obtains a given score on an intelligence test today will obtain a very similar score next week, next month, or next year. A psychological test or measure, such as personality or attitude questionnaire, is called reliable if it tends to produce or give the same scores from the same people at different times. If psychological research finding can be repeated, it is reliable. Repeating a research study in order to check on its reliability is called "replication". The effect found in an experiment can be said to be reliable if it occurs again in a replication of the original study.

The standards for Educational and Psychological Testing (hereafter referred to as the Standards: AERA/APA/NCME, 1985) describes "reliability" as an index that measures "the degree to which test scores are free from errors of measurement."

Unfortunately, few psychological tests are not ever hundred percent reliable because psychological characteristics are more difficult to measure than physical characteristics and people perform differently on different occasions for any number of reasons (for example, health). Still, reliability is one of the three qualities of a high quality psychological test.

Three major methods developed by researchers can be used to measure the reliability of a test:

(a) **Test-retest reliability:** "Test-retest" means that a group of people are tested once, then again some time later. The same people take the same test twice, and if their two scores are very similar, the test is considered reliable or the same test is administered on two occasions, usually one day to several weeks apart. The two sets of scores are correlated, to see whether people tend to get the same sort of scores on the second occasion. If the correlation is around 0.75–0.80, the test has high reliability.

People may not get similar or reliable scores on retesting on the same test because of (i) they may have forgotten their earlier answers (testing) and they answer differently on retesting (ii) people may wish to change the impression they made on first testing (iii) change in their attitude or perception.

(b) **Split-half reliability:** In split-half reliability, a psychological test which consists of several items or questions can be split so that items are randomly divided into two sets comprising half the complete test each. Every one takes just one test, but the items are split into two halves (often the even-numbered items versus the odd-numbered items). The person's scores on two halves are co-related. If the test is reliable, then subjects' scores on each half should be similar and the extent of similarity is assessed using correlation. If the test is reliable, the correlation co-efficient should be about +0.90, a very strong positive relationship or would be expected to exceed 0.90. This measure of reliability is sometimes called *internal consistency*. Internal consistency or reliability means "Is the test consistent within itself?" It is degree to which various parts of a test or other instrument measures the same variables, that is the degree to which a test can be said to be internally consistent. A test is internally consistent if a person responds much the same way to items that measure the same thing.

(c) **Alternate-form reliability:** Two alternate forms of tests are administered, usually one day to several weeks apart. The alternate forms reliability is high if each person's score is similar on the two tests. A good test is designed to make sure that nothing about the test itself—how it is given or how it is scored contributes to individuals' inconsistencies in performance.

5.2.3 Validity

"Validity" refers to a test's accuracy in measuring what it is supposed to measure, for example, if a test is a valid measure of intelligence, people's score on that test should be strongly correlated with their grades or achievement in college or school. Validity is that the test is really measuring what the researcher wants it to measure. Validity means that the test is measuring what it claims to be measuring. An experimental effect or any psychological test is valid if it demonstrates or measures what the researcher thinks or claims it does.

As the Standards (AERA/APA/NCME, 1985) point out, "test validation" is the process by which evidence is accumulated to support inferences that may be drawn from a test score. Various types of evidence may be produced, depending on the type of test and the purposes to which the test scores may be put.

Assessment of validity or kinds of validity

Validity can be assessed in many ways or there are many kinds of validity. Validity is more difficult to assess. However, in case of validity of intelligence tests, the fact that Intelligence Quotient (IQ) predicts academic success to some extent indicates that intelligence tests have reasonable validity. Validity of psychological tests can be assessed in the following ways:

(i) *Content validity:* "Content" is a test's ability to cover the complete range of material that it is supposed to cover. A test should not cover too much, and it also should not cover too little.

(ii) *Criterion-related validity:* Criterion validity is important for tests that are trying to identify people who have a specific trait or ability. The validity of a test of neuroticism might be established by first administering on group of people suffering from emotional problems and comparing the scores of these subjects with the scores of subjects or participants in the control group. Psychologists are referring to a test's ability to predict a person's performance on a second measure—that is, an independent criterion. The measure against which the test scores are compared is called the criterion, hence the term *criterion* validity.

(iii) *Concurrent validity:* If a test is validated by demonstrating correlation with a criterion immediately available, it is said to have a concurrent validity or if the new test is validated by comparison with a currently existing, it has concurrent validity.

(iv) *Predictive validity:* This is the type of validity a test has if results can be correlated with people's future performance. "Predictive validity" is the extent to which the scores on a test are predictive of actual performance. For example, a test designed to measure sales skills in people if it predicts who will and who will not be successful in the selling jobs.

5.3 TYPES OF PSYCHOLOGICAL TESTS—VERBAL AND NON-VERBAL TESTS

5.3.1 Verbal and Non-verbal Tests

Verbal tests

"Verbal tests" can be designated as reading or language test. It is, generally, any test that is ultimately linked in some way with language knowledge, verbal skills, etc. In verbal tests, reading and writing are required. The content of the test is verbal in nature like vocabulary, comprehension, etc. Unlike the non-verbal or non-reading or non-language tests, verbal test are unsuited for foreign language speaking or deaf testees. These tests can be administered to literates only.

Non-verbal tests

"Non-verbal tests" can be designated as non-reading or non-language tests. In non-verbal tests, neither reading nor writing is required. However, these tests make extensive use of oral instructions and communication on the part of the examiner. Such tests frequently measure verbal comprehension such as vocabulary and the understanding of sentences and short paragraph through the use of pictorial material supplemented with oral instructions to accompany each item. In non-verbal tests, figures, geometrical patterns, and designs are used. These tests can be administered to illiterate people and foreign language speaking or deaf testees. All non-verbal tests cannot be administered in group. According to Pillai (1972), "These cannot be used as group tests, chiefly because it is necessary to supervise the individual testee at work and give him necessary directions."

5.3.2 Individual Tests and Group Tests

Individual tests

"Individual test" is any test designed to be administered to one individual at a time. These are given to only one person at a time. For the administration of a test, it needs to be known whether the test can be administered to an individual or to a group. Individual tests enable the examiner to observe the subject's work methods, his social and emotional reactions. These tests also give the examiner a better opportunity to establish proper rapport, obtain co-operation, and maintain the interest of the subject in the test. "Rapport" means a comfortable, relaxed, unconstrained, mutually accepting interaction and relationship between a tester and a subject in psychological testing. Any special conditions, which may handicap the subject in his performance, can also be noted and removed (remedied). Individual tests generally require a highly-trained examiner. These are designed primarily as clinical instruments for the intensive study of individual cases.

Particularly, those non-verbal tests, which require the use of apparatus, become individual tests because it is not possible to conduct on 50–60 people using 50–60 equipments simultaneously. Since most of non-verbal tests need paper and pencil, they are usually administered in groups.

Group tests

"Group test" is any test that has been designed so that it can be administered to more than one person at a time. Group tests necessarily differ from individual tests in form and arrangement of items. Although, open ended questions calling for free response could be used-and were used in the early group tests—today the typical group test employs multiple-choice items. This is required for uniformity and objectivity of scoring. In group tests, items of similar content are arranged in increasing order in difficulty to try each type of items—such as vocabulary, arithmetic and spatial, and to complete the easier items of each type before trying the more difficult ones on which otherwise she or he may waste more time.

Most group tests are paper-and-pencil measures. There is no person-to-person interaction, as with individual tests. So the role of the test administrator is greatly simplified. The convenience and the economy of the group tests have led to their use in schools, employment offices, and many other mass-testing situations, one of the primary purposes of group tests is to classify a large number of people.

Advantages of group tests: Group tests are designed primarily as instruments for mass testing.

(i) Group tests can be administered simultaneously to as many persons as can be filled comfortably into the available space and reached through a microphone.

(ii) Group tests facilitated mass testing by greatly simplifying the examiner's role. Most group tests require only the ability to read simple instructions to the test takers and to keep accurate time. Some preliminary training sessions are desirable, of course. Scoring is typically more objective mostly in group testing. Most group tests can be scored by computers. So, group test are economical in terms of time and cost.

(iii) Group tests characteristically provide better established norms than do individual tests. According to Griffiths (1933), "The standard of measurement is the group performance."

(iv) Group tests are more objective as compared to the individual tests.

Disadvantages of group tests: Despite their economy in terms of time and administration, group tests have disadvantage also which are as follows:

(i) It is difficult to put the subjects at ease and to maintain their interest.

(ii) For group testing, the examiner has much less opportunity to establish rapport, to obtain their co-operation, which is essential.

(iii) In group testing, the examiner is also unlikely to detect illness, fatigue, worry, anxiety or other variable that may hinder test performance.

(iv) Group tests have been attacked or criticized because of the restrictions imposed on the examinee's responses. Criticisms have been directed particularly against multiple-choice items and against such standard item types as analogies, similarities and classification (Hoffman, 1991 and Lafave, 1966).

(v) Group tests lack flexibility, in sofar as every examinee is ordinarily tested in all items. Available testing time could be more effectively utilized if each examinee concentrated on items appropriate to her or his ability level.

3.5.3 Speed and Power Tests

Speed tests

"Speed test" is a general term for any test that measures ability by determining the number of problems that can be dealt with successfully within a fixed time period. A pure speed test is one in which individual differences depends entirely on speed of performance of the person. Such a test is constructed from items of uniformly low difficulty, all of which are well within the ability level of the person for whom the test is designed. The time limit is made so short that no one can finish all the items. Under these conditions, each person's score reflects only the speed with which she or he worked, for example clerical speed and accuracy test in Difference Aptitude Test Battery (DATB).

Power tests

"Power test" is a kind of test that measures ability by determining the degree of difficulty of material that can be mastered with no time pressures on the subject. A power test has a time limit long enough to permit everyone to attempt or complete all items. The difficulty of items is steeply or highly graded, and the test includes some items too difficult for anyone to solve, so that no one can get a perfect score.

Both speed and power tests are designed to prevent the achievement of perfect scores. The reason for such a precaution is that perfect scores are indeterminate; since it is impossible to know how much higher the individual's scores would have been if more items, or more difficult items, had been included. In actual practice, the distribution between speed and power test is one of degree, most items depending on both power and speed in varying proportions.

5.3.4 Paper and Pencil Tests and Performance Tests

Paper and pencil tests

A "paper and pencil" test is any test, whether achievement, aptitude, intelligence, etc. that uses only paper and pencil as testing instruments.

In the paper and pencil tests, the subject is provided with a test form or test booklet. The subject is required to fill in some empty spaces, to draw simple figures, and to point out similarities and dissimilarities.

Raven's Progressive Matrices test of Intelligence, verbal test of intelligence by Dr. S.S. Jalota, Chatterjee's Interest Preference Record, Differential Aptitude Test Battery (DATB) are some of the examples of paper-pencil tests.

Performance tests

"Performance test" is a test designed to rely on non-verbal performance. Performance tests require motor or manual response on the examinee's part generally but not always, involving manipulation of equipment or materials. Activities on the performance test include form boards, tracing a maze, block building, cube construction, to fit blocks in holes, picture completion, picture arrangement, puzzles, etc. They involve a minimal use of paper and pencil.

Performance tests are used in another sense, to denote tests, which are actually work samples. In this sense, they may include the use of paper and pencil. For example, in a performance in accounts or short hand, material other than paper and pencil may not be required but the test response will be called a *performance test*.

Alexander's battery of performance tests, Bhatia's battery of performance tests, the Pinter-Patterson scale, Arthur's point scale are all examples of performance tests.

Uses of performance tests: Performance tests are especially useful for:

1. Deaf testees as they are generally deficient in linguistic or language development.
2. Testees with speech defects who cannot give oral replies or are unable to take a paper-pencil test.
3. Illiterate testees, who cannot take the usual individual or group test that calls for a certain amount of reading and writing.
4. Foreign testees, who because of foreign language background may experience special difficulties in taking paper pencil tests.

Limitations of performance tests: Performance tests have some limitations.

(i) They have to be administered individually or in small groups. That way, they are time consuming.

(ii) No performance test can be totally culture-free or culture fair.

5.3.5 Essay and Objective Type Tests

Historically, the traditional school examinations consisted of a test of questions to be answered orally or in writing. In either case, the examinee composed and formulated the response. The term "Essay Question" came to be used broadly to cover all free-response questions, including not only those demanding a lengthy essay but also those requiring the examinee to produce a short answer or to work out the solution of a mathematical problem. By 1930, it was widely recognized that essay tests not only were more time consuming for examiners and examinees but also yielded less reliable results, thus "new type" of objective items.

"Objective questions" in contrast, were those that called for the choice of a correct answer out of the alternatives provided for each question. Although there are several kinds of items that require examinees to select a response, such as true-false and matching, the multiple choice questions test has been, by far the most widely used, the most thoroughly studied, and also the most frequently criticized type of test items.

Critics of multiple choice format argue that it promotes rote memorization and learning of isolated facts rather than the development of problem-solving skill and conceptual understanding.

5.4 ETHICAL ISSUES IN PSYCHOLOGICAL TESTING

In psychology, there are more major ethical issues associated with research than in any other subject. One reason for this is that all psychological experiments or research involve the study of organisms and living creatures (human beings and members of other species) and they have the right to be treated in a respectful, dignified, and caring manner.

Since 1970s there has been a heightened concern not only with ethical problems but also with broader questions of values in all fields of both theoretical and applied psychology (Bersoff, 1981; Diener and Crandall, 1978; Jacob and Hartshorne, 1991; Pope and Vasquez, 1991). The American Psychological Association (A.P.A) has issued several documents on the ethical standards for testing. Legislators have already enacted laws, and some corporations have voluntarily tightened their policies regarding employee-screening exam. Standards, a volume compiled by a joint committee on testing standards (AERA, APA, NCME, 1985), gives guidelines for a wide range of testing activities, from development tests to interpreting them (Jones and Applebaum, 1989).

Psychologists have become increasingly concerned about ethical issues in recent years. In the United Kingdom in 1990, the British Psychological Society issued its *Ethical Principles for Conducting Research with Human Participants.* These principles should be followed by everyone, including students who carry out experiments as part of their course. The key to conducting research in an ethical fashion is expressed in the following way in the principles: "The essential principle is that the investigation should be considered from the standpoint of all participants; foreseeable threats to their psychological well-being, health, values, and dignity should be eliminated." In other words, every effort should be made to make sure that participants do not experience pain, stress, or distress. Ethical treatment begins with the very first contact.

Some of the ethical concerns are as follows:

1. *Purpose of testing:* One concern is that people who choose tests choose, administer, and evaluate them properly (London and Bray 1980). Tests must be used only for appropriate purposes that are purposes for which the tests have been empirically demonstrated to be valid. Important decisions about a person should never be made on the basis of a test score alone. Information about the person should be supplemented by interview, objective observation, and other techniques.
2. *Obtaining voluntary informed consent:* Participants should be told precisely about what will happen in the experiment or research, before requesting that she or he gives voluntary informed consent, preferably written one, to take part. "Voluntary informed consent" is an ethical requirement involving making sure that the participants in a study agrees to take part knowing exactly what they will be asked to do. In the case of young subjects, necessary consent can be obtained from their parents or guardians.
3. *Avoiding potential harm:* Any experiment that is likely to cause permanent harm must be avoided. When researchers need to study physical pain in an experiment, they must participate in the experiment themselves before testing any participants. Reasearchers must avoid mental harm as physical harm. They must keep in mind the important principle of respecting the dignity of the other people (The Canadian Psychological Association, 1991).
4. *Avoiding unnecessary deception:* The relationship between the researchers and the participants must be based on openness and honesty. Whenever possible, the researcher must avoid deception. "Deception", generally means, action or speech designed to mislead another. In some studies, however, modest deception may be necessary. If the researchers describe precisely what will happen during the study or the experiment, the demand characteristics will distort the results and make them meaningless.
5. *Ensuring privacy:* "Privacy" means that people can decide for themselves whether they want to share their feeling, thoughts,

and personal information with others. Any personal information also must be kept confidential. Data must also be gathered anonymously, so that the researchers cannot identify which person supplied which data or information.

6. *Ensuring confidentiality:* Another important aspect of ethical research is confidentiality, which means that information about individual participants should not be revealed, not to give information about the names and performance of the individual participants. This ethical issue is regarding the disclosure of test results. Most ethics committees stress the test taker's right to confidentiality. They say that test scores should not be released to outside parties without subject's prior knowledge and often their expressed consent (London and Bray, 1980). The term "confidentiality" is most commonly used with respect to the legal and ethical issues which, in principle, protect this contract of trust, particularly as regards information passed during psychiatric or psychological therapy. The phrase "confidential communication" is the term used to cover such material.

   Participants have the right to withdraw from an experiment at any time without telling the reason. They can also insist that the data provided by them during the experiment or research should also be destroyed. But if the participants have decided to continue in the research, experimenter should provide what is known as *debriefing*.

7. *Debriefing:* An important part of any psychological research is debriefing. Proper debriefing requires telling the subject of an experiment what it was about. "Debriefing" means providing participants at the end of an experiment with information about it and reducing any distress. There are two aspects of debriefing: (i) provision of information about the experiment; and (ii) attempts to reduce any distress that may have been caused during the experiment. It also requires telling the participants afterwards about the purpose of the study, the nature of the anticipated results, and any deception used or when necessary, revealing any deception or withholding of information that may have been a necessary element in the study. This latter aspect is sometimes called *dehoaxing*. The purpose of debriefing is partially educational, if people donate their time to a project, they deserve to learn something from the experience. Milgram's (1974) research on obedience to authority is an example of good debriefing.

8. *Ensuring the ethical treatment of animals:* Research animals should be well treated, and all unnecessary pain must be avoided.

Most psychologists maintain that no animals should suffer needlessly, but that animal research is justified in producing results that may ultimately promote human welfare.

To summarize, ethical research requires the adequate purpose of testing, use of voluntary informed consent, avoiding potential harm, trying to avoid deception, providing the right to withdraw, adequate debriefing, and ensuring privacy and confidentiality in case of human being as participants, and proper treatment of animals, if they are used as subjects of any psychological research.

QUESTIONS

The below mentioned are some of the questions that have been asked in the examinations conducted by the Guru Nanak Dev University or can be asked. Knowledge of these answers can help the students get success in the examinations.

Section A

Answer the following questions in **five** lines or 50 words:

1. Define Cross-cultural differences.
2. What is deception?
3. What is informed consent?
4. What do you mean by standardization?*
5. Define the reliability of psychological tests.*
6. Define the validity of psychological tests.*
7. What is a standardized test?*
8. Explain performance tests.
9. Define verbal test.
10. Define non-verbal test.
11. What is speed test?
12. What is power test?
13. Define questionnaire.
14. Explain paper and pencil test.
15. Differentiate between verbal tests and non-verbal tests.
16. What is a psychological test?
17. State the characteristics of a good psychological test.*

Section B

Answer the following questions up to **two** pages or 500 words:

1. What ethical issues are raised by research with animals?
2. What are standardization, reliability, and validity?
3. What are a characteristics of good psychological tests?
4. What is the psychological test? Write various characteristics of a good psychological test.*
5. Write about various kinds of psychological tests.
6. What is a standardized test? What are the various ethical issues involved in psychological testing.*
7. What are the uses of psychological tests?*
8. Differentiate between speed and power test.*
9. Differentiate between verbal and non-verbal tests.
10. Write nature of psychological tests.
11. What is a psychological test? Discuss the different types of individual and group tests.

Section C

Answers to the following questions up to **five** pages or 1000 words:

1. What are the main features of ethical experimentation? Why is it important for experimenters to be ethical?
2. Describe different types of psychological tests.
3. Describe nature and uses of psychological tests.
4. What is the nature of a psychological test? Discuss in detail the various types of tests.
5. Describe the nature and characteristics of good psychological tests.*
6. What is a psychological test? Write its uses?
7. What is a psychological test? Write various types of tests.*

REFERENCES

Aiken, L.R., *Psychological Testing and Assessment*. New York: Allyn & Bacon.

American Psychological Association, 750 First Street, NE, Washington, DC 20002. (800) 374–2721. Web site: <http: //www.apa.org>, 2004.

Anastasi, A., *Psychological Testing* (6th ed.) , New York: Macmillan, 1988.

Bersoff, D.N., 'Testing and The Law,' *American Psychologist,* **36**, 1047–1056, 1981.

Bhatia, H.R., *Elements of Educational Psychology* (3rd ed.), Calcutta: Orient Longman, 968.

Bray, D.W., 'The Assessment Centre and the Study of Lives,' *American Psychologist*, **37**, 180–89, 1982.

British Psychological Society, 'Ethical Principles for Conducting Research with Human Participants,' *The Psychologist*, **3**, 270–72, 1990.

British Psychological Society, *Code of Conduct, Ethical Principles and Guidelines*. Leicester: British Psychological Society, 1998.

Diener, E. and Crandall, R., *Ethics in Social and Behavioural Research*, Chicago: University of Chicago Press, 1978.

Galton, F., *Inquiries into Human Faculty and its Development*, New York: AMS Press, 1863/1907/1973.

Galton, F., *Hereditary Genius: An Inquiry into its Laws and Consequences*, London: Macmillan, 1869/1892.

Griffiths, J.H., *The Psychology of Human Behaviour*, London: George Allen, 1933.

Griffiths, D., Dickinson, A., Clayton, N., *Episodic Memory: What can Animals Remember about their Past*? **3**, pp. 74–80, PMID 10234230, 1999.

Hoffman, L.W., 'The Influence of the Family Environment on Personality: Accounting for Sibling Differences,' *Psychological Bulletin,* **110**, 187–203, 1991.

Jacob, S. and Hartshorne, T.S., *Ethics and Law for School Psychologists,* Brandon, VT: Clinical Psychology Publishing Co., 1991.

Jones, L.V. and Applebaum, M.I., 'Psychometric Methods,' *Annual Review of Psychology*, **40**, 23–43, 1989.

Lafave, L., 'Essay vs. Multiple-choice, Which Test is Preferable?' *Psychology in the Schools,* **3**, 65–69, 1966.

Milgram, S., 'Nationality and Confirmity,' *Scientific American*, **205**, 45–51, 1961.

Milgram, S., 'Behavioral Study of Obedience,' *Journal of Abnormal and Social Psychology*, **67**, 371–378, 1963.

Milgram, S., *Obedience to Authority*, New York: Harper & Row, 1974.

Pope, K.S. and Vasquez, M.J.T., *Ethics in Psychotherapy and Counseling: A Practical Guide for Psychologists,* San Francisco: Jossey-Bass, 1991.

Raven, J.C., *Raven Progressive Matrices*, Los Angeles: Psychological Corp., 1977.

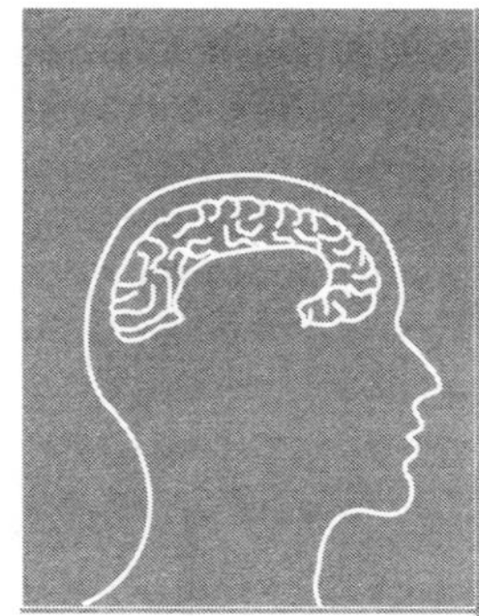

CHAPTER 6
Central Tendency

6.1 MEANING OF STATISTICS

The word Statistics seems to have been derived from the Latin word *Statista*, or the German word *Statistik*, or the French word *Statistique*, each of which means a "political state".

The word "Statistics" has been used to convey different meanings in singular and plural sense. When used as plural, statistics means numerical set of data and when used in singular sense, it means the science of statistical methods embodying the theory and techniques used for collecting, analyzing, and drawing inferences from the numerical data.

6.2 SOME DEFINITIONS OF STATISTICS

According to Webster's dictionary, "Statistics are the classified facts representing the confirmation of the people in a state...specially those facts which can be stated in number or in tables of numbers or in any tabular or classified arrangement."

According to A.L. Bowley, "Statistics may rightly be called the science of averages."

According to A.L. Bowley, "Statistics may be called the science of counting."

According to A.L. Bowley, "Statistics are numerical statements of facts in any department of enquiry placed in relation to each other."

According to Yule and Kendall, "By statistics, we mean quantitative data affected to a marked extent by multiplicity of causes."

According to Prof. Horace Secrist, "Statistics may be defined as the aggregate of facts affected to a marked extent of multiplicity of causes, numerically enumerated or estimated according to a reasonable standard of accuracy, collected in a systematic manner, for a predetermined purpose and placed in relation to each other."

From the definition of Prof. Horace Secrist, it can be concluded that:

"All statistics are numerical statements of facts but all numerical statements of facts are not statistics."

Statistics is the science which deals with the method of collecting, classifying, presenting, comparing, and interpreting numerical data collected to throw some light on any sphere of enquiry.

6.3 STATISTICS IN PSYCHOLOGY AND EDUCATION

Statistics has been used very widely in Psychology and education, too, for example, in the scaling of mental tests and other psychological data, for measuring the reliability and validity of test scores, for determining the Intelligence Quotient (IQ), in item analysis and factor analysis. The numerous applications of statistical data and statistical theories have given rise to a new field or discipline, called "Psychometry".

Statistics are a flexible tool and can be used for many different purposes. In Psychology, however, statistics are usually employed or used to accomplish one or more of the following objectives or tasks:

1. Summarizing or systematizing or describing large amounts of data.
2. Comparing individuals or groups of individuals in various ways.
3. Determining whether certain aspects of behaviour are related. (Whether they vary together in a systematic manner); and
4. Predicting future behaviour from current information.

6.4 MEASURES OF CENTRAL TENDENCY

The central tendency refers to the general trend of the group. This means that average or the central tendency represents the trend of the group. Measures of central tendency are those techniques of statistical analysis which help us to find one value from a series which represents the entire series. Measures of central tendency are those statistical methods with the help of which we get one value for a given series and this value represents the entire series. These measures are very useful in statistical analysis. Measures of central tendency help to reduce the complexity of data and make it comparable.

It is generally admitted that representative value lies in the centre of the distribution. That is why these techniques are called *measures of central tendency* or *measures of central value*. Some authors call these measures as *statistical averages*. Measures of a central tendency indicate the score that identifies the centre of the frequency distribution. Measure of a central tendency is a single representative measure used to characterize an entire distribution, commonly found near the middle of the score range.

6.5 SOME DEFINITIONS OF CENTRAL TENDENCY

According to Craxton and Cowden, "An average value is a single value within the range of the data that is used to represent all the values in the series. Since an average is somewhere within the range of the data, it is sometime called a *measure of central value.*"

According to L.L. Schkade, "Average is an attempt to find one single figure to whole of figure."

According to Simpson and Kaffca, "A measure of central tendency is a typical value around which other figures congregate."

6.6 CHARACTERISTICS OF A GOOD MEASURE OF CENTRAL TENDENCY OR AVERAGE OR AS MEASURES OF FIRST ORDER

Average is that value of a variable which represents the entire value of a variable or factor. Average must possess some qualities. Presence or absence of these qualities helps us to study whether any average is a good average or not. These characteristics or qualities or features are as follows:

1. *Familiarity:* Measure of central tendency should be familiar to layman or common people. Average or measure of central tendency should be such that common people are familiar with it. If it is not so, use of average will be limited.
2. *Simplicity:* Measure of central tendency should be simple and rapid to calculate and easy to understand. Only that measure or average becomes popular among the people which is simple to calculate and easy to understand. One of main objectives of average is to remove complexity. If average itself is complex, it will not serve the objective.
3. *True representative:* Measure of central tendency should be based on all the values of a variable or factor. Average can be true representative only if it is based on all the values of a variable or distribution or series. A single extreme score in the distribution can lead to a change in the average. If average ignores some of the given values it will not be a good representative of entire distribution.
4. *Rigid definition:* Measure of central tendency should be rigidly defined. Any average cannot be a good average if its definition is

not rigid. If definition is not rigid, many values of a variable may claim to be true representatives.

5. *Further algebraic or mathematical treatment:* Measure of central tendency should be capable of further algebraic treatment. Measures of central tendency are used in many other techniques of statistical analysis like measures of dispersion or variability, Correlation etc. The purpose can be solved only if a measure of central tendency or average is capable of further algebraic or mathematical treatment.
6. *Sampling stability:* Measure of central tendency should not be affected by fluctuations of sampling. It means that if different samples are taken from a population, the average of sample should be equal to the sample of the population. If the average of the sample is not equal to the average of the population, the sample is not true representative of the population. "Sample" means the participants actually used in a study, drawn from some larger sample. "Population" is a large collection of people from whom the sample used in a study is drawn. "Representative sample" is a sample that is chosen to be typical of the population from which it is drawn.
7. *Effect of extreme items/values/observations:* Measure of central tendency should not be unduly affected by presence of extreme values. For any average to be a good representative, this condition must be fulfilled. Extreme values or items or observations mean very small or very large scores in the distribution. If average is affected by the presence of any extreme score, it will not be representative of the population from which it is drawn and hence, not a good average.
8. *Open-end class intervals:* Measure of central tendency should be such that it can be calculated for open-end class intervals.
9. *Effect of skewness:* Measure of central tendency should not be affected by skewness. "Skewness" is the degree to which the curve of a frequency distribution departs from perfect symmetry.
10. *Qualitative problems:* A good measure of central tendency should be able to be found by both arithmetic as well as the graphic method.

Central tendency is the middle (centre) of the distribution of scores. Measures of central tendency are the tools by which the complexity of data is reduced and it is made more simple, comparable, and capable of further analysis or treatment. They give bird's eye view of the huge mass of statistical data. A measure of central tendency represents the whole series by one figure.

The three measures of central tendency, that is, Mean, Median, and Mode are the basic and most useful techniques of statistical analysis and are discussed below:

6.6.1 Mean or Average or Arithmetic Mean

Mean is an average, worked out by dividing the total of all participants' scores by the number of participants. Mean or average is a measure of central tendency derived by adding all the scores and dividing by the number of scores (N). Mean of a variable is defined as sum of the different values of a variable divided by number of these values. It is the sum of measurements divided by their number. Mean of a distribution of scores may be defined as the point on the scale of measurement obtained by dividing the sum of all the scores by the number of scores. Mean is generally referred to other averages as it is rigidly defind mathematically and is based upon all of the measures. The mean is the centre of gravity in the distribution, and each score contributes to its determination.

Calculation or computation of the mean when the data are ungrouped or for the individual series:

EXAMPLE 6.1: Suppose, a labourer earns Rs. 50, Rs. 60, Rs. 40, Rs. 90 on four consecutive days, his mean of daily wage is;

$$M = \frac{\Sigma X}{N}$$

where

M stands for mean

Σ is a Greek letter which stands for "sum of"

X stands for a score of other measures

N stands for number of measures in the series

$$M = \frac{X_1 + X_2 + X_3 + X_4 + \cdots + X_n}{N}$$

$$M = \frac{50 + 60 + 40 + 90}{4}$$

$$M = \frac{240}{4}$$

$$M = 60$$

In the above example, the mean or average daily wage of a labourer is Rs. 60.

EXAMPLE 6.2: Suppose, the time by your watch is 10.31 a.m. In checking with two friends, you find that their watches give the time as 10.25 a.m. and 10.34 a.m. Assuming that the three watches are equally good timepieces, what do you think is probably the "correct time"?

$$M = \frac{\Sigma X}{N}$$

$$X = 10.31, 10.25, 10.34$$

$$N = 3$$

$$M = \frac{10.31 + 10.25 + 10.34}{3}$$

$$M = \frac{30.90}{3}$$

$$M = 10.30$$

$$\text{Mean} = 10.30$$

In the above example, the mean or average "correct time" is 10.30 a.m.

Calculation or computation of the mean when the data are grouped or discrete series

(I) Long method of calculating mean:

$$M = \frac{\Sigma FX}{N} \quad \text{or} \quad M = \frac{\Sigma fx}{N}$$

where

M stands for mean
Σ is a Greek letter which stands for "sum of"
F or f stands for frequency of each class-interval
X or x stands for mid-point in each class-interval
N stands for total number of frequencies

EXAMPLE 6.3

Class-intervals	*Frequency*	*Mid-point*	*Frequency × Mid-point*
(CI)	*(F or f)*	*(X or x)*	*(FX or fx)*
90–94	2	92	184 (2 × 92)
85–89	2	87	174 (2 × 87)
80–84	4	82	328 (4 × 82)
75–79	8	77	616 (8 × 77)
70–74	8	72	576 (8 × 72)
65–69	12	67	804 (12 × 67)
60–64	9	62	558 (9 × 62)
55–59	7	57	399 (7 × 57)
50–54	5	52	260 (5 × 52)
45–49	1	47	047 (1 × 47)
40–44	2	42	084 (2 × 42)
$i = 5$	$N = 60$		ΣFX or $\Sigma fx = 4030$

Mid-point or mid-value of class-interval 90–94 $= \frac{90+94}{2}$

$= \frac{184}{2} = 92$

$$M = \frac{\Sigma FX}{N} \quad \text{or} \quad M = \frac{\Sigma fx}{N}$$

$$M = \frac{4030}{60}$$

$$M = 67.16$$

Mean = 67.16

EXAMPLE 6.4

Class intervals (*CI*)	*Frequency* (*F* or *f*)	*Mid-point* (*X* or *x*)	*Frequency × Mid-point* (*FX* or *fx*)
195–199	1	197	197 (1 × 197)
190–194	2	192	384 (2 × 192)
185–189	4	187	748 (4 × 187)
180–184	5	182	910 (5 × 182)
175–179	8	177	1416 (8 × 177)
170–174	10	172	1720 (10 × 172)
165–169	6	167	1002 (6 × 167)
160–164	4	162	648 (4 × 162)
155–159	4	157	628 (4 × 157)
150–154	2	152	304 (2 × 152)
145–149	3	147	441 (3 × 147)
140–144	1	142	142 (1 × 142)
$i = 5$	$N = 50$		ΣFX or $\Sigma fx = 8540$

Mid-point or mid-value of class-interval 195199 $= \frac{195+199}{2}$

$= \frac{394}{2} = 197$

$$M = \frac{\Sigma FX}{N} \quad \text{or} \quad M = \frac{\Sigma fx}{N}$$

$$M = \frac{8540}{50}$$

Mean = 170.80

EXAMPLE 6.5

Class-intervals	*Frequency*	*Mid-point*	*Frequency* × *Mid-point*
(CI)	(F or f)	(X or x)	(FX or fx)
100–109	5	104.5	522.5 (5 × 104. 5)
90–99	9	94.5	850.5 (9 × 94 .5)
80–89	14	84.5	1183.0 (14 × 84.5)
70–79	19	74.5	1415.5 (19 × 74.5)
60–69	21	64.5	1354.5 (21 × 64.5)
50–59	30	54.5	1635.0 (30 × 54.5)
40–49	25	44.5	1112.5 (25 × 44.5)
30–39	15	34.5	517.5 (15 × 34.5)
20–29	10	24.5	245.0 (10 × 24.5)
10–19	8	14.5	116.0 (8 × 14.5)
0–9	6	4.5	27.0 (6 × 4.5)
$i = 10$	$N = 162$		ΣFX or $\Sigma fx = 8979.5$

$$\text{Mid-point or mid-value of class-interval } 100 - 109 = \frac{100 + 109}{2}$$

$$= \frac{209}{2} = 104.5$$

$$M = \frac{\Sigma FX}{N} \quad \text{or} \quad M = \frac{\Sigma fx}{N}$$

$$= \frac{8979.5}{162}$$

$$\text{Mean} = 55.429$$

EXAMPLE 6.6

Class-intervals	*Frequency*	*Mid-point*	*Frequency* × *Mid-point*
(CI)	(F or f)	(X or x)	(FX or fx)
135.5–139.5	3	137.5	412.5 (3 × 137.5)
131.5–135.5	5	133.5	667.5 (5 × 133.5)
127.5–131.5	16	129.5	2072.0 (16 × 129.5)
123.5–127.5	23	125.5	2886.5 (23 × 125.5)
119.5–123.5	52	121.5	6318.0 (52 × 121.5)
115.5–119.5	49	117.5	5757.5 (49 × 117.5)
111.5–115.5	27	113.5	3064.5 (27 × 113.5)
107.5–111.5	18	109.5	1971.0 (18 × 109.5)
103.5–107.5	7	105.5	738.5 (7 × 105.5)
$i = 4$	$N = 200$		ΣFX or $\Sigma fx = 23888$

Mid-point or mid-value of class-interval 135.5 – 139.5 $= \frac{135.5 + 139.5}{2}$

$= \frac{275}{2} = 137.5$

$$M = \frac{\Sigma FX}{N} \quad \text{or} \quad M = \frac{\Sigma fx}{N}$$

$$= \frac{23888}{200}$$

$$\text{Mean} = 119.44$$

Calculation or computation of the mean for the grouped data or discrete series by the short method or the "assumed mean" method

The long method of finding the mean gives accurate results but often requires the handling of large numbers and entails monotonous calculation. Because of this, short method or the "Assumed mean" method can be used.

$$\text{Mean} = \text{AM} + ci$$

or

$$\text{Mean} = \text{AM} + \frac{\Sigma fx}{N} \times i$$

$$ci = \frac{\Sigma fx}{N} \times i$$

$$c = \frac{\Sigma fx}{N}$$

where

AM stands for the assumed mean or the guessed mean
c stands for correction in terms of class-interval
i stands for the length of class-interval

EXAMPLE 6.7

Class-intervals	*Mid-point*	*Frequency*	*Deviation*	*Frequency × Deviation*	
(CI)	(*X*)	(*f*)	(*x′*)	(*fx′*)	
90–94	92	2	+5	+ 8 (2 × 4)	+54
85–89	87	2	+4	+ 10 (2 × 5)	
80–84	82	4	+3	+ 12 (4 × 3)	
75–79	77	8	+2	+ 16 (8 × 2)	
70–74	72	8	+1	+ 8 (8 × 1)	
65–69	67 AM	12	0	0	
60–64	62	9	–1	–9 (9 × –1)	–52
55–59	57	7	–2	–14 (7 × –2)	
50–54	52	5	–3	–15 (5 × –3)	
45–49	47	1	–4	–4 (1 × –4)	
40–44	42	2	–5	–10 (2 × –5)	
i =5		N = 60		$\Sigma fx'$ = 2(54 – 52)	

$$N = 60$$

$$AM = 67$$

For assuming mean, the best plan is to take the mid-point of a class-interval somewhere near the centre of the distribution, and if possible the mid-point of that class-interval which contains the largest frequency. The mid-point having the highest frequency is assumed or guessed as the mean. The method gives constant results, no matter where the mean is tentatively placed or assumed.

$$\text{Mean} = \text{AM} + ci$$

or

$$\text{Mean} = \text{AM} + \frac{\Sigma fx'}{N} \times i$$

$$= 67 + \frac{2}{60} \times 5$$

$$= 67 + 0.16$$

$$= 67.16$$

$$\text{Mean} = 67.16$$

The process of calculating the mean by the short method may be summarized as follows:

Step 1: Tabulate the scores or measures into a frequency distribution.

Step 2: Find the mid-points or mid-value (X) of all class-intervals.

Step 3: Assume a mean as near the centre of the distribution as possible, and preferably on the class-interval containing the largest frequency. Mid-point of the class-interval having the highest frequency is assumed or guessed as the mean.

Step 4: Find the deviation (x') of the mid point of each class-interval from the AM (assumed mean) in units of interval.

Step 5: Multiply each deviation (x') by its appropriate f (the frequency opposite it).

Step 6: Find the algebraic (with signs) sum of the plus (+) and minus (–) fx' (frequency × deviation, and divide this sum by N, the number of cases. This gives c, the correction in units of class-interval.

Step 7: Multiply c by the interval length (i) to get ci, the score correction.

Step 8: Add *ci* algebraically to the AM (assumed mean) to get the actual mean. Sometimes, *ci* will be positive and sometimes negative depending upon where the mean has been assumed.

EXAMPLE 6.8

Class-interval	*Frequency*	*Mid-point*	*Deviation*	*Frequency* × *Mid-point*	
CI	f	X	x'	fx'	
0–10	6	5.0	–3	–18(6 × –3)	–36
11–20	5	15.5	–2	–10(5 × –2)	
21–30	8	25.5	–1	–8(8 × –1)	
31–40	15	35.5 (AM)	0	0	
41–50	7	45.5	1	7 (7 × 1)	28
51–60	6	55.5	2	12 (6 × 2)	
61–70	3	65.5	3	9 (3 × 3)	
$i = 10$	$N = 50$			$\Sigma fx' = -8(28 - 36)$	

$$\text{AM} = 35.5$$

$$N = 50$$

$$\Sigma fx' = -8$$

$$i = 10$$

$$\text{Mean} = \text{AM} + ci$$

or

$$\text{Mean} = \text{AM} + \frac{\Sigma fx'}{N} \times i$$

$$= 35.5 + \frac{-8}{50} \times 10$$

$$= 35.5 + \frac{-8}{5}$$

$$= 35.5 - \frac{-8}{5}$$

$$= 35.5 - 1.6$$

$$\text{Mean} = 33.9$$

EXAMPLE 6.9

Class-intervals	*Mid-point*	*Frequency*	*Deviation*	*Frequency × Deviation*	
(CI)	(X)	(f)	(x')	($f x'$)	
195–199	197	1	+5	+5(1 × 5)	43
190–194	192	2	+4	+8(2 × 4)	
185–189	187	4	+3	+12(4 × 3)	
180–184	182	5	+2	+10(5 × 2)	
175–179	177	8	+1	+8(8 × 1)	
170–174	172 AM	10	0	0	
165–170	167	6	–1	–6(6 × –1)	–55
160–164	162	4	–2	–8(4 × –2)	
155–159	157	4	–3	–12(4 × –3)	
150–154	152	2	–4	–8(2 × – 4)	
145–149	147	3	–5	–15(3 × – 5)	
140–144	142	1	–6	–6(1 × –6)	
$i = 5$		$N = 50$		$\Sigma fx' = -12$ (43 – 55)	

$$N = 50$$

$$\text{AM} = 172$$

$$c = \frac{\Sigma fx'}{N}$$

$$= \frac{-12}{50} = -0.240$$

$$i = 5$$

$$ci = -0.240 \times 5$$

$$= -1.20$$

$$\text{Mean} = \text{AM} + ci$$

or

$$\text{Mean} = \text{AM} + \frac{\Sigma fx}{N} \times i$$

$$= 172 + (-1.20)$$

$$\text{Mean} = 170.80$$

Use the mean

1. When the scores are distributed symmetrically around a central point, that is, when the distribution is not badly skewed. Skewness is the degree to which the curve of a frequency

distribution departs from perfect symmetry. A distribution is said to be "skewed" when the mean and the median fall at different points in the distribution, and the balance or centre of gravity if shifted to one side or the other—to right or left. Skewness is described as positive (or to the right) or negative (or to the left) depending upon whether the tail of the distribution extends towards those values relative to the mode. In positive skewness, the mean lies to the right of the median (Figure 6.1). In negative skewness, the mean lies to the left of the median (Figure 6.1).

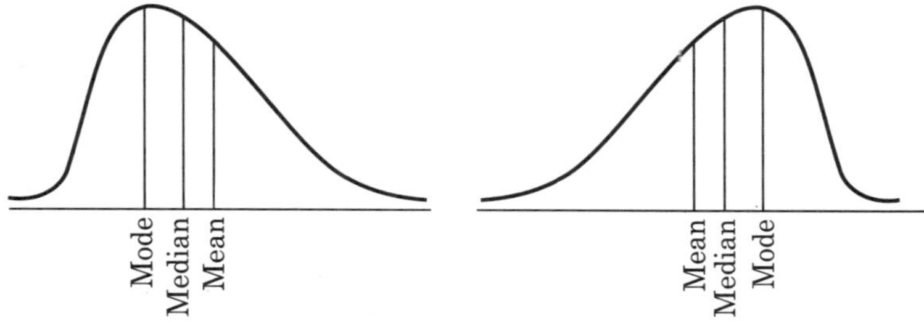

Figure 6.1 Locations of the Mean, Median, and Mode in positively and negatively skewed curves.

2. When the measure of central tendency or centre of gravity of a sample having the greatest stability is wanted.
3. When other statistics (for example, Standard Deviation—SD, Co-efficient of Correlation) are to be computed later. Many statistics are based upon the mean.
4. When group performances are to be compared with accuracy and precision.
5. When scores are to be properly interpreted or when standard scores are to be computed.
6. When there are no extreme cases to affect the measure of central tendency.
7. When there are no class-intervals of unspecified length.
8. When further algebraic treatment of the average is required.

Merits and demerits of mean

Merits of mean: The following are the merits of mean:

(i) Mean is the most familiar and popular measure.
(ii) It is simple to calculate and easy to understand.
(iii) It is rigidly defined.
(iv) It is definite.
(v) It is based on all the values or observations of a variable.

(vi) It is more accurate and reliable basis for comparison.
(vii) It is capable of further algebraic treatment.
(viii) It has maximum sampling stability.
(ix) It satisfies most of the conditions of a good or an ideal average.

Demerits of mean: The following are demerits of mean:

(i) Mean is highly affected by the presence of extreme scores or items or observations in the distribution. For example, mean of 4, 5, and 6 is 5. But if new value 85 is there, new mean of 4, 5, 6 and 85 will be 25.
(ii) It cannot be calculated in the case of open end class-intervals.
(iii) It sometimes gives us absurd values (for example, mean of family size or number of persons in a family or locality in fractions).
(iv) Its value sometimes does not exist in the series.
(v) It is highly affected by the presence of skewness in the distribution.
(vi) It cannot be determined graphically or by graphic method.
(vii) It cannot be used in the study of qualitative data which is incapable of numerical expression.

6.6.2 Median

Median is defined as that point on the scale of measurement above which is exactly one half of the cases and below which are the other half. When data have been arranged in rank order, this measure of central tendency may be found by locating a point that divides the whole distribution into two equal halves. Thus, median may be defined as "the point on the scale of measurement below and above which lie exactly 50 percent of cases." Median is defined as a point and not as a score or any particular measurement. In the Collins dictionary of statistics, median is defined as the middle value in a distribution, below and above which lie values with equal total frequencies or probabilities. According to Prof. L.R. Corner, "The median is that value of the variable which divides the group into two equal parts, one part comprising all values greater and the other all values less than median."

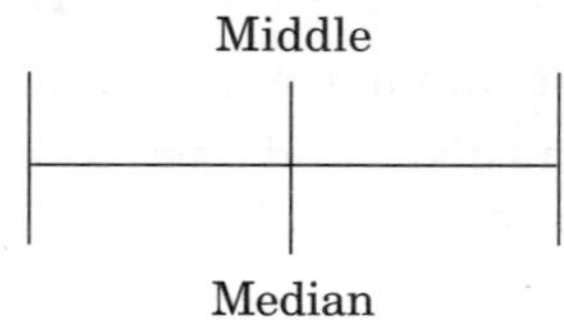

Calculation of the median when the data are ungrouped

(I) **When number of scores (N) is odd** (not divisible by 2):

EXAMPLE 6.10: For example, if there are seven scores as follows:

6, 10, 8, 11, 12, 7, 9

Arrange scores in ascending (small to large) or descending (large to small) order. On arranging them in ascending (or descending) order, we have the following arrangement of above-mentioned seven scores:

Ascending series → 6, 7, 8, ⑨, 10, 11, 12

Descending series → 12, 11, 10, ⑨, 8, 7, 6

9 is median because three scores, that is, 6, 7, 8 are on the left and three scores, that is, 10, 11, 12 are on the right of it or 12, 11, 10 are on the left and three scores, that is, 8, 7, 6 are on the right of it.

(II) When number of scores (N) is even (divisible by 2):

EXAMPLE 6.11: For example, if there are the following six scores:

6, 8, 9, 10, 11, 12

$$\text{Median} = \frac{N+1\text{th}}{2} \text{ term} \quad N = 6$$

$$= \frac{6+1}{2}$$

$$= \frac{7}{2}$$

$$= 3.5\text{th term}$$

Here, in order to find out 3.5th term, we have to find out the average of third score, that is, 9 and fourth score, that is, 10.

$$= \frac{\text{3rd + 4th score}}{2} \qquad \text{3rd score} \rightarrow 9$$

$$= \frac{9+10}{2} \qquad \text{4th score} \rightarrow 10$$

$$= \frac{19}{2}$$

$$= 9.5$$

9.5 is the median.

Median = 9.5

Calculation of median when data are grouped into a frequency distribution

The median in grouped scores or discrete series is said to be the point of distribution above which and below which lie 50% (half) of the scores.

$$\text{Median} = L + \frac{(N/2 - f_b)i}{f_p}$$

where

$L \rightarrow$ lower limit of class-interval in which the median lies

$\frac{N}{2} \rightarrow$ half of the total number of scores or cases

$f_b \rightarrow$ sum of scores below that interval in which the median lies

$f_p \rightarrow$ frequency which lies in the interval in which the median lies

$i \rightarrow$ length of the class-interval

EXAMPLE 6.12

Class-intervals	*Frequency*	*Cumulative frequency*
(CI)	(*F* or *f*)	(*cf*)
90–94	2	60
85–89	2	58
80–84	4	56
75–79	8	52
70–74	8	44
65–69	12(f_p)	36 → Median 30 lies here
60–64	9	24 (*fb*)
55–59	7	15
50–54	5	8
45–49	1	3
40–44	2	2
$i = 5$	$N = 60$	

$$\frac{N}{2} = \frac{60}{2} = 30$$

f_p = 12 (frequency which lies in the interval in which the median lies)

f_b = 24 (sum of scores below that interval in which the median lies)

$$\text{Median} = L + \frac{(60/2 - 24)5}{12}$$

$$= 64.5 + \frac{(30 - 24)5}{12}$$

$$= 64.5 + \frac{(6)5}{12}$$

$$= 64.5 + 2.5$$

$$\text{Median} = 67$$

Use the median

1. When the exact mid-point, the 50% point, of the distribution is wanted.
2. When there are extreme scores which would markedly affect the mean. Extreme scores do not affect the median. For example, in the series 4, 5, 6, 7, and 8, both mean and median are 6. But if 8 is replaced by 50, that is, 4, 5, 6, 7, and 50, the other scores remaining the same, the median is still 6, but the mean is 14.4.
3. When it is desired that certain scores should influence the central tendency, but all that is known about them is that they are above or below the median.

Merits and demerits of median

Merits of median: The following are the merits of median:

(i) Median is rigidly defined.
(ii) It is an ideal average.
(iii) It is not affected by the presence of extreme scores or items in the distribution.
(iv) It is generally used in the case of qualitative phenomena or problems where mean cannot be used.
(v) It can be used in the case of open-end class-intervals.
(vi) It can be determined graphically or by the graphic method.
(vii) It can be located easily in the ungrouped data.
(viii) It can be calculated in the case of open-end-class intervals.
(ix) It never gives absurd or fallacious results.

Demerits of median: The following are the demerits of median:

(i) Median is not familiar to common people or layman.
(ii) It is affected by the skewness in the distribution.
(iii) It is not based on all the scores or items or observations of the distribution; it may not be the true representative score.
(iv) It is not capable of further algebraic treatment.
(v) It cannot be used for computing other statistical measures, such as SD or Co-efficient of Correlation.
(vi) In comparison with mean, it is difficult to calculate.
(vii) In comparison with mean, it has less sampling stability.
(viii) The arrangement of scores in the ascending or descending order in sometimes very tedious and time consuming.

6.6.3 Mode

In statistics, mode is a measure of central tendency of a distribution of scores given by the score of the mid-point of the class-interval of scores with the highest frequency. Mode is the score in a given set of data that appears most frequently. In any series, mode is that value which has the maximum frequency. In any distribution, different frequencies show the popularity of different values in the distribution. That value is the most popular which has maximum frequency and that value is true representative of the distribution like in democracy, a popular leader is judged by voting, and is true representative of the population from which she or he is elected. Graphically, mode is the peak of a frequency distribution.

According to Kenny, "The value of the variable which occurs most frequently in a distribution is called the mode."

According to Croxton and Cowden, "The mode may be regarded as most typical of a series of a value."

Mode is generally represented by the symbol Z. In a simple ungrouped series of measures, the "crude" or "empirical" mode is that single score or measure which occurs most frequently. For example, in the series 10, 11, 11, 12, 12, 13, 13, 13, 14, 14, the most often recurring or frequently repeated score or measure, namely 13, is the crude or empirical mode.

When scores are grouped, mode is said to be the middle point of that class-interval which contains the maximum frequency. When data are grouped into frequency distribution, the crude mode is usually taken to be the mid-point of that interval which contains the largest frequency. While calculating the mode from a frequency distribution, we distinguish between "true mode" and the "crude mode". The true mode is the point (or "peak") of greatest concentration (because it has highest frequency) in the distribution, that is, the point at which more measures fall than at any other point. The crude mode is an unstable measure of central tendency. A crude mode is usually employed as a simple inspectional "average", to indicate in a rough way centre of concentration in the distribution.

Formula for calculating mode of the grouped data:

$$\text{Mode} = 3\ \text{Median} - 2\ \text{Mean} \qquad \text{Mean} = 67.16$$
$$= 3 \times 67 - 2 \times 67.16 \qquad \text{Median} = 67$$
$$= 201 - 134.32 \qquad \text{Mode} = 66.68$$
$$\text{Mode} = 66.68$$

Use the mode

1. When a quick and approximate measure of central tendency is all that is wanted.
2. When it is necessary to find out the point of maximum concentration.

3. When data is incomplete or the distribution is skewed, where most of the values are towards the extremes.
4. When the measure of central tendency should be the most typical value. When we describe the style of dress worn by the "average girl," for instance, the modal or most popular fashion is usually meant. In like manner, in speaking of the average wage in a certain firm, we often mean the modal wage under specified conditions.

Merits and demerits of mode

Merits of mode: The following are the merits of mode:

1. Mode is simple to locate.
2. It is based upon all the observations.
3. It gives the true representative value of the distribution as mode is the popular value.
4. It is not affected by the presence of extreme scores or items in the distribution.
5. It is not at all affected by skewness in the distribution.
6. It can be calculated in the case of open-end class-intervals.
7. It can be used in the case of qualitative phenomena or can be applied to qualitative problems.
8. It can be calculated graphically or by the graphic method.
9. It does have descriptive value, particularly when the distribution is bi-or multi-modal.
10. It, unlike the mean, it is a value which is found in the scores or series.
11. It helps in analyzing qualitative data.

Demerits of mode: The following are the demerits of mode:

1. Mode is the least important measure of central tendency.
2. It is not rigidly defined.
3. It is not familiar to common people.
4. It is not based upon all the scores or items of the distribution.
5. It is difficult to calculate.
6. It is not capable of further algebraic treatment.
7. It cannot be determined from unequal class-intervals.
8. It has very small sampling stability.

All the three measures of central tendency—the mean, the median, and the mode, discussed above, have their own merits and demerits. It is very difficult to say which of these measures is the best one and hence should be used in any statistical enquiry. The selection of an appropriate measure of central tendency or average for any problems or enquiry depends upon the nature of distribution available and purpose of the statistical enquiry. If simple and familiar measure is required, the mean is the best. Mean is also preferred to median and mode if further algebraic treatment is required. In the case of open-end class-intervals and in the case of extreme items, mean should be avoided. In these circumstances, median or mode should be used. Whenever skewness is present in the distribution, mode should be preferred to mean and median. In the case of qualitative phenomena, mean cannot be used; we should use either median or mode.

EXERCISES

The below mentioned are some of the questions that have been asked in the examinations conducted by the Guru Nanak Dev University or can be asked. Knowledge of these answers can help the students to get success in the examinations.

Section A

Answer the following questions in **five** lines or 50 words:

1. What do you mean by the term "statistics"?
2. What is mean?*
3. What is median?*
4. What is Mode?*
5. Define skewness.
6. What is the positive skewness?
7. What is the negative skewness?
8. Define central tendency.
9. How do we calculate mean and median for the ungrouped data?
10. What is the difference between grouped and ungrouped data?*
11. Write formulae for the various measures of central tendency.
12. Why statistics is used in psychology?*
13. What are the various measures of central tendency?
14. Define skewness and name two skewed curves.

Section B

Answer the following questions up to **two** pages or 500 words:

1. What are merits and demerits of measures of central tendency?*
2. Calculate mean of the following data:*

Class-interval (CI):	10–19	20–29	30–39	40–49	50–59	60–69
Frequency (*f*):	3	5	10	12	6	4

3. Calculate the median of the following data:

CI	*f*
77–82	2
71–76	5
65–70	6
59–64	8
53–58	4
47–52	2
41–46	0
35–40	1

4. Calculate the median of the following data:*

CI	*f*
45–49	2
40–44	3
35–39	5
30–34	6
25–29	3
20–24	3
15–19	2
10–14	1

5. What is statistics? Why is it used in Psychology?
6. Write about various measures of central tendency while discussing grouped and ungrouped data.
7. Calculate the mode of the following data:*

CI	*f*
50–54	1
45–49	2
40–44	4
35–39	6
30–34	8
25–29	3
20–24	2
15–19	1
10–14	1

8. Write the merits and demerits of mean, median, and mode.*
9. Write the formulae of calculating mean, median, and mode for grouped and ungrouped data separately. write the merits and demerits of all the measures of central tendency.

10. Calculate the median of the following data:

CI	f
70–71	2
68–69	2
66–67	3
64–65	4
62–63	6
60–61	7
58–59	5
56–57	4
54–55	2
52–53	3
50–51	1
	$N = 39$

11. What are various measures of central tendency? What are the characteristics of a good measure of central tendency?

Section C

Answer the following questions up to **five** pages or 1000 words:

1. What is statistics? Calculate mean for the following data by the short method:

CI	(f)
0–10	6
11–20	5
21–30	8
31–40	15
41–50	7
51–60	6
61–70	3
	$N = 50$

2. Calculate mean of the following data:

CI	f
77–82	2
71–76	5
65–70	6
59–64	8
53–58	4
47–52	2
41–46	0
35–40	1

3. Write down the essential characteristics of a good measure of central tendency.
4. Calculate the mode of the following data:

CI	f
150–154	1
145–149	2
140–144	4
135–139	6
130–134	8
125–129	3
120–124	2
115–119	1
110–114	1
	$N = 28$

5. Write the meaning and characteristics of a good measure of central tendency.*
6. What is statistics? What are the characteristics of a good measure of central tendency?
7. Find out Mode for the following data:

CI	f
0–5	4
5–10	8
10–15	12
15–20	19
20–25	11
25–30	10
30–35	5
35–40	3

8. Calculate the mean of the data given below by the short method:*

CI	f
40–44	1
35–39	0
30–34	3
25–29	5
20–24	3
15–19	10
10–14	1
5– 9	1
0– 4	4
	$N = 28$

9. What are the various measures of central tendency? Calculate median for the following data:

CI	f
155–159	1
150–154	3
145–149	4
140–144	5
135–139	8
130–134	10
125–129	6
120–124	4
115–119	5
110–114	4
105–109	3
100–104	2
	$N = 55$

10. Calculate median from the following data:

CI	f
41–45	1
36–40	3
31–35	5
26–30	6
21–25	8
16–20	4
11–15	3
6–10	0

11. Calculate mean from the following data by the assumed mean method:

Marks obtained: 80–84 75–79 70–74 65–69 60–64 55–59 50–54 45–49 40–44

No. of students: 2 3 3 7 9 8 6 4 2

12. Calculate mean from the following data by the long method:

CI	f
70–71	2
68–69	2
66–67	3
64–65	4
62–63	6
60–61	7
58–59	5
56–57	4
54–55	2
52–53	3
50–51	1
	$N = 39$

13. Calculate mean from the following data:

CI	f
90–94	2
85–89	2
80–84	4
75–79	8
70–74	6
65–69	11
60–64	9
55–59	7
50–54	5
45–49	0
40–44	2
	N = 56

14. Calculate median from the following data:

CI	f
120–122	2
117–119	2
114–116	2
111–113	4
108–110	5
105–107	9
102–104	6
99–101	3
96–98	4
93–95	2
90–92	1
	N = 40

15. Calculate mode of the following data:

Scores	f
15	1
14	2
13	3
12	6
11	12
10	15
9	22
8	31
7	18
6	6
5	2
4	2
	N = 120

16. Calculate the mean of the following data:

CI	f
120–139	50
100–119	150
80–99	500
60–79	250
40–59	50
	N = 1000

REFERENCES

Coolican, H., *Research Methods and Statistics in Psychology*, Sevenoaks, UK: Hodder and Stoughton, 1990.

Garrett, H.E., *Elementary Statistics*, New York: Longmans, Green and Co., 1956.

Garrett, H.E., *Statistics in Psychology and Education*, Vakils: Feffer and Simons, 1961.

Guilford, J.P., *Fundamental Statistics in Psychology and Education*, New York: McGraw-Hill Book Company, 1965.

Gupta, J.P., *Statistical Method*, New Delhi: Sultan Chand and Sons, 1991.

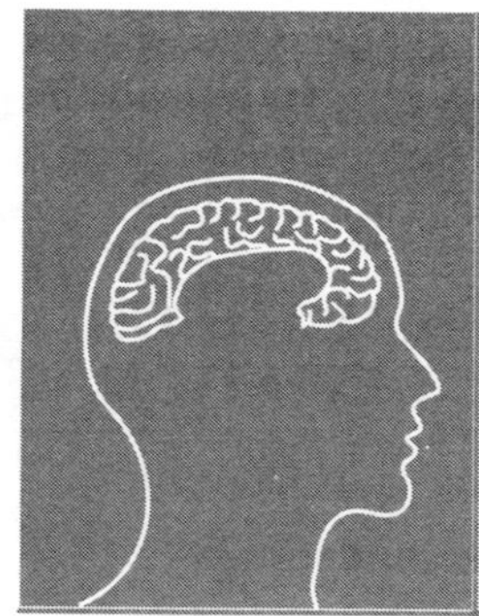

CHAPTER 7

Variability

Measures of variability or dispersion or deviation are those methods with the help of which variations in a given distribution are studied. Measures of variability are the measures of the "scatter" or "spread" of the separate scores around their central tendency. Measures of dispersion are called "averages of the second order" because the deviations of the size of items from a measure of central tendency are calculated (ignoring the signs) and then these deviations are averaged. The variability in the central value of a given series is termed dispersion. The property which denotes the extent to which the values are dispersed about the central value is also called *dispersion*. Dispersion is also known as scatter, spread, or variability.

7.1 DEFINITIONS OF DISPERSION

According to A.L. Bowley, "Dispersion is the measure of the variations of the item."

According to B.C. Brooks and W.F.L. Dicks, "Dispersion or spread is the degree of the scatter or variation of the variables about a central value."

According to L.R. Conner, "Dispersion is a measure of the extent to which the individual items vary."

According to M.R. Spieget, "The degree to which numerical data tend to spread about an average value is called *variation* or *dispersion* of the data."

According to Murray R. Spiegel, "The degree to which numerical data tend to spread about an average value is called the *variation* or *dispersion* of the data."

Dispersion, in general sense, also indicates the lack of uniformity in the size of items of a series.

7.2 CHARACTERISTICS OF A GOOD MEASURE OF VARIABILITY OR DISPERSION OR DEVIATION

A good measure of variability possesses the following characteristics:

1. It should be simple to calculate and easy to understand.
2. It should be rigidly defined.
3. It should be based on all the scores or items or observations of the series.
4. It should be capable of further algebraic treatment.
5. It should be familiar to common people.
6. It should not be affected by the presence of extreme scores in the distribution or by the fluctuations of sampling.
7. It should be such that it is possible to find variations even in the case of open-end class-intervals.
8. It should not be unduly affected by the presence of extreme items.

7.2.1 Importance of Measures of Variability

Measures of variability:

(i) help to ascertain the degree of variability or deviation or dispersion of the data.

(ii) supplement the information given by the measures of central tendency, which increases the accuracy of statistical analysis and interpretation, and helps to draw more dependable or reliable inferences or conclusions.

(iii) make possible comparison between different groups.

(iv) are very important in comparing and finding the remedies of many social problems and evils of different areas.

(v) serve as a useful check on drawing wrong conclusions from the comparison of averages or measures of central tendency.

(vi) are of great value in the statistical analysis of the data.

7.2.2 Functions or Objectives of Measures of Variability or Dispersion

The following are the functions or objectives of measures of variability or dispersion:

1. Dispersion determines variability in any distribution.
2. It compares the variability of two or more distributions.
3. It determines the reliability of statistical average.
4. It controls variability.
5. It helps in further statistical analysis.

For example, a test of verbal ability has been administered to a group of 50 girls and to a group of 50 boys and their scores is mentioned below:

Girls	*Boys*
$N = 50$	$N = 50$
Mean scores = 36.6	Mean scores = 36.5

So far as the mean goes, there is no difference in the performance of the two groups. If a group is homogeneous, that is, made up of individuals of nearly the same ability, most of its scores will fall around the same point on the scale, the range will be relatively short and the variability small. The less the range, the more the group will be homogeneous. If the variability is less, the dispersion is insignificant.

But, if the group contains individuals of widely differing capacities or abilities or potentialities, scores will be strung out from high to low, the range will be relatively wide and the variability large. The more the range, the less is the homogeneity of the group, and more the variability or dispersion or deviation. When the range is more, the group is more variable. For example, if the girls' scores are found to range from 15 to 51 and the boys' scores from 19 to 45. This difference in range shows that in a general sense, the girls "cover more territory or area or domain," are more variable than the boys; and thus great variability may be of more interest than the lack of a difference in the means.

Table 7.1 shows the frequencies of two groups of very different variability:

Table 7.1 Frequencies of two variable groups

Group A	*Group B*
Range from 20–80	Range from 40–60

Figure 7.1 shows two frequency distributions of the same N and the same mean, that is 50, but of very different of variability. Group A ranges from 20–80 and Group B ranges from 40–60. Group A is three times as variable as Group B—spreads over three times the distance on the scale of scores—though both distribution have the same central tendency.

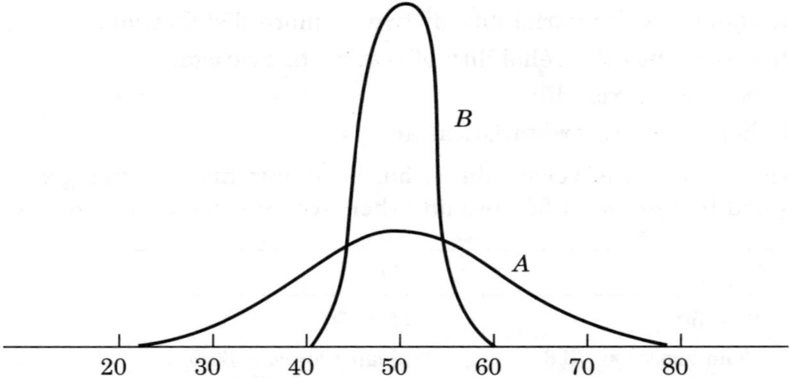

Figure 7.1 Two distributions of the same N and same mean (50) but of very different variability.

7.3 MEASURES OF VARIABILITY OR DISPERSION OR DEVIATION

Four measures have been devised to indicate the variability or dispersion or deviation within a set of measures:

1. The Range (R)
2. The Quartile Deviation (QD or Q)
3. The Average or Mean Deviation (AD or MD)
4. The Standard Deviation (SD)

7.3.1 The Range

The Range (R) is defined as the interval or "distance" between the lowest and the highest scores. The Range is defined as the difference between the maximum value of a variable and the minimum value. The Range is a measure or index of variability or dispersion or deviation or scatteredness of scores or observations. It is obtained by subtracting the lowest score from the highest score. According to the standard dictionary meaning, Range is the extent to which, or the limits between which, variation can occur. The Range is the most general measure of spread or scatter and is computed when we wish to make a rough comparison of two or more groups for variability. The Range takes account of the extremes of the series of scores and is unreliable when N is small or when there are large gaps, that is, zeros frequencies in the frequency distribution.

$$\text{Range} = \text{Maximum Value} - \text{Minimum Value}$$

or

$$\text{Range} = \text{Highest Score} - \text{Lowest Score}$$

Symbolically,

$$R = H_s - L_s$$

Calculation of range of the ungrouped data

EXAMPLE 7.1: The scores of ten girls on a test are:

48, 49, 51, 52, 55, 57, 50, 59, 61, and 62

In the above set of scores, the maximum value or the highest score is 62 and the minimum value or the lowest score is 48. So,

$$\text{Range} = 62 - 48$$

$$\text{Range} = 14$$

If the Range (14) of scores of ten girls is compared with the Range (60) of scores of ten boys in a test, the scores of girls do not vary much but the scores of boys are widely scattered. Thus, the variability of the scores of boys is much more than the variability of the scores of girls.

Calculation of range of the grouped data

EXAMPLE 7.2

Class-Interval	*Frequency*
70–79	3
60–69	6
50–59	12
40–49	11
30–39	8
20–29	5

In the above data, the upper limit of the highest class-interval 70–79 is 79.5 and the lower limit of the lowest class-interval 20–29 is 19.5. Therefore,

$$R = H_s - L_s$$

$$R = 79.5 - 19.5$$

$$R = 60$$

Use the range

1. When the data are too scant (spread over) or too scattered to justify the computation of a more precise measure of variability.
2. When knowledge of extreme scores or of total spread is all that is wanted.

Merits and demerits of the Range

Merits of range: The following are the merits of range:

1. Range is simple to calculate.
2. It is easy to understand.
3. It is a simplest measure of variability or dispersion or deviation.
4. It is the most familiar method.
5. It gives quick estimate of variability.
6. It is computed or calculated when we wish to make a rough comparison of two or more groups of variability.

Demerits of range: The following are the demerits of range.

1. Range is not based on all the scores, items, or observations of a series. It takes account of only the two extreme scores—the highest and the lowest.
2. It is not capable of further algebraic treatment.
3. It is highly or very greatly affected by the fluctuations of sampling.
4. It is a rough measurement.
5. It is highly affected by the presence of extreme scores or items.
6. It is of limited accuracy.
7. It is entirely unsuitable for precise and accurate studies.
8. It is unfit for the purposes of comparison, especially when the series are in two different units.
9. It cannot be used in the case of open end class-intervals.
10. It does not take into account the composition of the series.
11. It is quite unreliable when N is small or when there are large gaps in the frequency distribution.
12. It does not take into consideration the individual scores.

7.3.2 The Quartile Deviation

The Quartile Deviation (QD or Q) is a measure of variability or dispersion or deviation. The Quartile Deviation is based upon the interval containing the middle 50 percent of cases in a given distribution. It is also called *semi-interquartile range of a distribution*. The Quartile Deviation is one-half of the scale distance between the 75th (Q_3) and the 25th (Q_1) percentiles or centiles in a frequency distribution (Figure 7.2). The Quartile Deviation is defined as the difference between upper quartile (Q_3) and lower quartile (Q_1) divided by 2 (Figure 7.2).

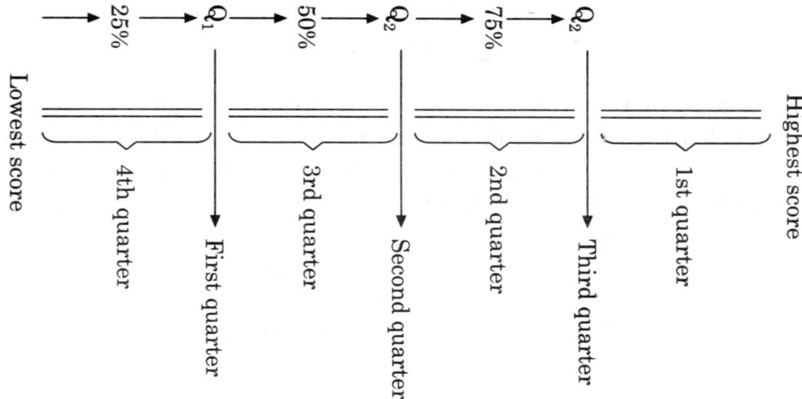

Figure 7.2 Showing quarters and quartiles.

The 75th percentile or Q_3 is the third quartile on the scores scale, the point below which lie 75% of the scores or cases.

Q_3 is the third or upper quartile; point below which lie 75% of the scores or cases

$$\frac{3N}{4}$$

The 25th percentile or Q_1 is the first quartile on the score scale, the point below which lie 25% of the scores or cases.

Q_1 is the first or lower quartile; point below which lie 25% of the scores or cases

$$\frac{N}{4}$$

Calculation or computation of quartile deviation of the ungrouped data

EXAMPLE 7.3 Find out the QD or Q of the following twenty scores: 21, 22, 23, 24, 25, 26, 27, 28, 29, 30, 31, 32, 33 34, 35, 36, 37, 38, 39, 40

$$N = 20$$

$$25\% \text{ of } N(20) = \frac{20}{4}$$

$$= 5$$

Q_1 is a point below which lie 25% of the cases. Here, Q_1 is a point below which 5 cases lie. From the ordered or arranged data given above, it is found that below 25.5, there are 5 cases. Thus, $Q_1 = 25.5$

$$75\% \text{ of } N\ (20) = \frac{3}{4} \times 20$$
$$= 15$$

Q_3 is a point below which lie 75% of the cases. Here, Q_3 is a point below which 15 cases lie. From the ordered or arranged data given above, it is found that below 35.5, there are 15 cases. Thus, $Q_3 = 35.5$

Formula for calculating QD or Q:

$$\text{QD or Q} = \frac{Q_3 - Q_1}{2}$$
$$= \frac{35.5 - 25.5}{2}$$
$$= \frac{10}{2}$$
$$\text{QD or Q} = 5$$

Calculation or computation of quartile deviation of the grouped data

EXAMPLE 7.4 Calculated the QD or Q for the data given below:

Class-intervals or intervals or scores	*f*	*Cum f*
195–199	1	50
190–194	2	49
185–189	4	47
180–184	5	43
175–179	8(f_q)	38(Q_3)
170–174	10(Q_3)	30 → cum f_1 (Q_3)
165–169	6	20
160–164	4(f_q)	14(Q_1)
155–159	4(Q_1)	10 → cum f_1 (Q_1)
150–154	2	6
145–149	3	4
140-144	1	1
	N= 50	

$$QD \text{ or } Q = \frac{Q_3 - Q_1}{2}$$

To find Q, it is clear that we must first compute the Q_3 (75th percentile) and Q_1 (25th percentile) quartile.

$$Q_3 = L + i\left(\frac{3N}{4} - \text{Cum } f_1\right)$$

$$Q_1 = L + i\left(\frac{N}{4} - \text{Cum } f_1\right)$$

where

L is the exact lower limit of the interval in which the quartile falls
i is the length of the interval
Cum f_1 is cumulative frequency upto the interval which contains the quartile
f_q is the frequency on the interval containing the quartile

Q_3 we count off 3/4 of N or $\frac{3 \times 50}{4}$ as N = 50 or 37.5 from the low-score end of the distribution

$$Q_3 = L + i\left(\frac{N}{4} - \text{Cum } f_1\right)$$

$$= 174.5 + \frac{5(37.5 - 30)}{4} \qquad L = 174.5$$

$$i = 5$$

$$= 174.5 + \frac{5(7.5)}{4} \qquad \frac{3N}{4} = 37.5$$

$$= 174.5 + 4.6$$

$$Q_3 = 179.19$$

$Q_1 \rightarrow$ we count off 1/4 of N or 50 as N = 50 or 12.5 from the low-score end of the distribution

$$Q_1 = L + i\left(\frac{N}{4} - \text{Cum } f_1\right)$$

$$= 159.5 + \frac{5(12.5 - 10)L}{4} \qquad L = 159.5$$

$$i = 5$$

$$= 159.5 + \frac{5(2.5)}{4} \qquad \frac{N}{4} = 12.5$$

$$= 159.5 + 3.12$$

$$Q_1 = 162.62$$

$$\text{QD or Q} = \frac{Q_3 - Q_1}{2}$$

$$= \frac{179.19 - 162.62}{2}$$

$$= \frac{16.57}{2}$$

$$\text{QD or Q} = 8.28$$

Use the Quartile Deviation (QD or Q)

1. When the median is the measure of central tendency.
2. When there are scattered or extreme scores which would influence the Standard Deviation (SD) disproportionately.
3. When the concentration around the median—the middle 50% of cases is of primary interest.
4. When the distribution is incomplete at either end.

Merits and demerits of Quartile Deviation

Merits of quartile deviation or QD or Q: The following are the merits of QD.

1. Quartile deviation is easy to calculate.
2. It is simple to understand.
3. It is rigidly defined.
4. It is a more representative and reliable measure of variability than the range.
5. It is the best measure in the case of open end class-intervals.
6. It is a good index of score density at the middle of the distribution.
7. It is used when extreme items are present.
8. As against range, which is based on two observations only, quartile deviation makes use of 50% of the data. Hence, it is better.
9. Quartiles are useful in indicating the skewness of the distribution.
10. Wherever median is preferred as the measure of central tendency, quartile deviation is preferred as a measure of variability or dispersion or deviation.

Demerits of quartile deviation or QD or Q: The following are the demerits of QD.

1. Quartile deviation is not capable of further algebraic treatment.
2. It is not based on all the observations of a series.
3. It has a very small sampling stability.
4. It gives a rough idea of dispersion.
5. It ignores the scores above the third quartile or Q_3 and the scores below the first quartile or Q_1. It simply speaks about the middle 50% of the distribution.
6. It only calculates the third and the first quartile. Hence, we cannot get a true picture about how the scores are dispersed from the central point or value.
7. It does not take into account the composition of the series.
8. It does not take into consideration the individual scores.

7.3.3 The Average Deviation or the Mean Deviation

The average deviation or AD (also written mean deviation or MD) is the mean deviations of all of the separate scores in a series taken from their mean (occasionally from the median or mode). In averaging deviations to find the AD, no account is taken of signs, and all deviations whether plus or minus are treated as positive. According to Garrett, "The Average Deviation (AD) or MD is the mean of the deviations of all the separate scores in a series taken from the mean." In averaging deviations to find the AD, no account is taken of signs, and all deviations whether plus or minus are treated as positive. AD or MD is defined as the arithmetic mean of the deviations of values of a variable from its average (mean, median, or mode) with signs ignored.

The average deviation or the mean deviation, as it is called sometimes, tends to remove a serious shortcoming of both methods (Range and quartile deviation). The average deviation is also called the *first moment of dispersion* and is based on all the items in a series. Average deviation is the arithmetic mean of the deviations of a series. Average deviation is the arithmetic mean of the deviations of a series computed from some measure of central tendency (mean, median or mode), all the deviations being considered positive. In other words, the average of the deviation or average deviation of all the values from the arithmetic mean is known as *mean deviation or average deviation*. Usually, the deviation is taken from the mean of the distribution.

AD or MD is always larger than the quartile deviation (QD or Q), which includes the middle 50% of the cases.

Calculation or Computation of the Average Deviation from Ungrouped Data

EXAMPLE 7.5: The mean of the five scores, that is, 6, 8, 10, 12, and 14 is 10

$$N = 5$$

$$\text{Mean} = \frac{\Sigma X}{N}$$

$$= \frac{6+8+10+12+14}{5}$$

$$= \frac{50}{5}$$

$$\text{Mean} = 10$$

And the deviations of the separate scores from their mean are:

$$\text{Deviation} = \text{Score} - \text{Mean}$$

or

$$x = X - M$$

$$-4 = 6 - 10$$

$$-2 = 8 - 10$$

$$0 = 10 - 10$$

$$2 = 12 - 10$$

$$4 = 14 - 10$$

The sum of these five deviations, disregarding signs, is 12.

$$\Sigma|x| = 4 + 2 + 0 + 2 + 4 = 12$$

Formula for calculating average deviation is:

$$\text{AD} = \frac{\Sigma|x|}{N}$$

in which || enclosing the x indicates that signs are disregarded in arriving at the sum. As always, x is a deviation of a score from the mean.

$$\text{AD} = \frac{12}{5}$$

AD = 2.4 is the mean of these five deviations from their mean.

Calculation or computation of the average deviation from grouped data or when data is grouped into frequency distribution

The average deviation or mean deviation is rarely used in modern statistics, but it is often found in the older experimental literature.

$$\text{AD or MD} = \frac{\Sigma|f_x|}{N}$$

EXAMPLE 7.6

Class-intervals or scores	*Mid–point*	*Frequency*	*frequency × mid-point*	*Deviation = mid-point – mean*	*frequency × deviation*
CI	X	f	f_x	X $(X - M)$	f_x
195–199	197	1	197(1 × 197)	26.20(197.00 – 170.80)	26.20(1 × 26.20)
190–194	192	2	384(2 × 192)	21.20(192.00 – 170.80)	42.40(2 × 21.20)
185–189	187	4	748(4 × 187)	16.20(187.00 – 170.80)	64.80(4 × 16.20)
180–184	182	5	910(5 × 182)	11.20(182.00 – 170.80)	56.00(5 × 11.20)
175–179	177	8	1416(8 × 177)	6.20(177.00 – 170.80)	49.60(8 × 6.20)
170–174	172	10	1720(10 × 172)	1.20(172.00 – 170.80)	12.00(10 × 1.20)
165–169	167	6	1002(6 × 167)	–3.80(167.00 – 170.80)	–22.80(6 × –3.80)
160–164	162	4	648(4 × 162)	–8.80(162.00 – 170.80)	–35.20(4 × –8.80)
155–159	157	4	628(4 × 157)	–13.80(157.00 – 170.80)	–55.20(4 × –13.80)
150–154	152	2	304(2 × 152)	–18.80(152.00 – 170.80)	–37.60(2 × –18.80)
145–149	147	3	441(3 × 147)	–23.80(147.00 – 170.80)	–71.40(3 × –23.80)
140–144	142	1	142(1 × 142)	–28.80(142.00 – 170.80)	–28.80(1 × –28.80)
$i = 5$		$N = 50$	$\Sigma fX = 8540$		$\Sigma f_x = 502$

$$\text{Mean} = \frac{\Sigma fx}{N}$$

$$= \frac{8540}{50}$$

$$\text{Mean} = 170.80$$

$$\text{AD or MD} = \frac{\Sigma |f_x|}{N}$$

$$= \frac{502}{50}$$

$$\text{AD or MD} = 10.04$$

AD or MD is always greater than QD or Q in this example, AD or MD is 10.04 and the QD or Q (calculated earlier) is 8.28.

Use the Average or Mean Deviation

1. When it is desired to measure all deviations from the mean according to their size.
2. When extreme deviations would influence standard deviation unduly or un-proportionately.
3. When it is required to know the extent to which the measures are spread out on either side of the mean.

Merits and Demerits of the Average or Mean Deviation

Merits of the average or mean deviation: The following are the merits of average or mean deviation.

1. Average or mean deviation is the simplest measure of dispersion.
2. It is rigidly defined.
3. It is easily comprehensible.
4. It is based on or takes into account all the values or observations in a given distribution or series.
5. It is not very much affected by the values of extreme items.
6. It is the average of the deviations of individual scores from the mean.
7. It tells the variability of the distribution around its central tendency in real sense.
8. In comparison with standard deviation, it is easy to calculate average or mean deviation.
9. In comparison with standard deviation, it is less affected by the presence of extreme items.
10. Average or mean deviation is preferred to standard deviation when extreme items are present.

Demerits of the average or mean deviation: The following are the demerits of average or mean deviation.

1. Average or mean deviation is rarely used in modern statistics; is not in common use.
2. It is not a very accurate measure of dispersion.
3. It is not capable of further algebraic treatment.
4. It cannot be calculated in the case of open end class-intervals.
5. It ignores the algebraic signs of the deviations which is seriously objectionable.

7.3.4 The Standard Deviation

The Standard Deviation (SD) or Root Mean Square Deviation is the most stable index and most frequently used measure of variability and is customarily employed in experimental work and in research studies. This measure of dispersion was given by Prof. Karl Pearson and is considered to be the best measure of dispersion. It is also called *root mean square deviation*. Standard deviation is defined as the square root of the mean of square of deviations from arithmetic mean. Standard deviation or SD is the square root of the mean of the squared deviations of the individual scores from the mean of the distribution. It is the only measure of variability or dispersion which is capable of further algebraic treatment. It is represented or denoted by the small Greek letter or by a conventional symbol σ (sigma).

In standard deviation, while calculating deviations of the items from the mean or average, instead of ignoring or neglecting algebraic signs, the deviations are squared, thereby making all of them positive.

Table 7.2 shows the differences between Standard Deviation and Average or Mean Deviation.

Table 7.2 Differences between Standard Deviation and Mean Deviation

SD	*AD* or *MD*
1. We avoid the difficulty of signs by squaring the separate deviations.	1. We disregard signs and treat all deviations as positive.
2. SD is capable of further algebraic treatment.	2. AD or MD is not capable of further algebraic treatment.
3. SD is most frequently and widely used measure of variability.	3. AD or MD is rarely used in modern statistics.
4. SD is affected least by sampling fluctuations.	4. AD or MD is used when extreme scores are present.

Calculation or computation of the standard deviation (SD) (σ) from ungrouped scores or when the data is ungrouped

EXAMPLE 7.7 There are five scores:

$$6, 8, 10, 12, 14 \qquad N = 5$$

$$\text{Mean} = \frac{\Sigma X}{N}$$

$$= \frac{6+8+10+12+14}{5}$$

$$= \frac{50}{5}$$

$$\text{Mean} = 10$$

Deviations of the separate scores from the mean are:

$$\text{Deviation} = \text{Score} - \text{Mean}$$

or

$$x = X - M$$

$$-4 = 6 - 10$$

$$-2 = 8 - 10$$

$$0 = 10 - 10$$

$$2 = 12 - 10$$

$$4 = 14 - 10$$

Deviations of the above-mentioned five scores from the mean are –4, –2, 0, 2, and 4. When each of these five deviations is squared, we get:

$$x^2 \text{ (square of deviations)} = (-4)^2, (-2)^2, (0)^2, (2)^2, (4)^2$$

$$x^2 = 16 + 4 + 0 + 4 + 16$$

$$x^2 = 40$$

$$\text{SD}(\sigma) = \frac{\sqrt{\Sigma x^2}}{N}$$

$$= \frac{\sqrt{40}}{5}$$

$$= \sqrt{8}$$

$$\text{SD}(\sigma) = 2.83$$

Calculation or computation of the standard deviation (SD or σ) from grouped data or when the scores are distributed into frequency distribution

$$\text{SD}(\sigma) = \frac{\sqrt{\Sigma fx^2}}{N}$$

(I) Calculation or computation of the Standard Deviation (SD or σ) by the long method

EXAMPLE 7.8

Class-intervals or scores	*Mid-point*	*Frequency*	*Frequency × mid-point*	*Deviation = mid-point – mean*	*Frequency × deviation*	$f_x \times x$
CI	*X*	*f*	f_x	*x*(*X* – *M*)	f_x	f_x^2
195–199	197	1	197(1 × 197)	26.20(197.00–170.80)	26.20(1 × 26.20)	686.44(26.20 × 26.20)
190–194	192	2	384(2 × 192)	21.20(192.00–170.80)	42.40(2 × 21.20)	898.88(42.40 × 21.20)
185–189	187	4	748(4 × 187)	16.20(187.00–170.80)	64.80(4 × 16.20)	1049.76(64.80 × 16.20)
180–184	182	5	910(5 × 182)	11.20(182.00–170.80)	56.00(5 × 11.20)	627.20(56.00 × 11.20)
175–179	177	8	1416(8 × 177)	6.20(177.00–170.80)	49.60(8 × 6.20)	307.52(49.60 × 6.20)
170–174	172	10	1720(10 × 172)	1.20(172.00–170.80)	12.00(10 × 1.20)	14.40(12.00 × 1.20)
165–169	167	6	1002(6 × 167)	–3.80(167.00–170.80)	–22.80(6 × –3.80)	86.64(–22.80 × –3.80)
160–164	162	4	648(4 × 162)	–8.80(162.00–170.80)	–35.20(4 × –8.80)	309.76(–35.20 × –8.80)
155–159	157	4	628(4 × 157)	–13.80(157.00–170.80)	–55.20(4 × –13.80)	76.76(–55.20 × –13.80)
150–154	152	2	304(2 × 152)	–18.80(152.00–170.80)	–37.60(2 × –18.80)	706.88(–37.60 × –18.80)
145–149	147	3	441(3 × 147)	–23.80(147.00–170.80)	–71.40(3 × –23.80)	1699.32(–71.40 × –23.80)
140–144	142	1	142(1 × 142)	–28.80(142.00–170.80)	–28.80(1 × –28.80)	829.44(–28.80 × –28.80)
i = 5		*N* = 50	Σf_x = 8540			Σf_x^2 = 7978

$$\text{Mean} = \frac{\Sigma fX}{N}$$

$$= \frac{8540}{50}$$

$$\text{Mean} = 170.80$$

$$\text{SD}(\sigma) = \frac{\sqrt{\Sigma fx^2}}{N}$$

$$= \frac{\sqrt{7978}}{50}$$

$$\text{SD}(\sigma) = 12.63$$

EXAMPLE 7.9

Class-interval	*Frequency*	*Mid-point*	*Frequency × mid-point*	*Deviation= (score – mean)*	*Frequency × deviation*	fx^2
CI	*f*	*X*	*fX*	*x (X – M)*	f_x	$f_x \times x$
41–45	1	43	43	16.83	16.83	283.25
36–40	3	38	114	11.83	35.49	1266.64
31–35	5	33	165	6.83	34.15	1166.22
26–30	6	28	168	1.83	10.98	120.56
21–25	8	23	184	–3.17	–25.36	643.13
16–20	4	18	72	–8.17	–32.68	1067.98
11–15	3	13	39	–13.17	–39.51	1561.04
6–10	0	8	0	–18.17	0	0
$i = 5$	$N = 30$		$\Sigma fX = 785$			$\Sigma f_x^2 = 6108.82$

$$\text{Mean} = \frac{\Sigma fX}{N}$$

$$= \frac{785}{30}$$

$$\text{Mean} = 26.17$$

$$\text{SD}(\sigma) = \frac{\sqrt{\Sigma x^2}}{N}$$

$$= \frac{\sqrt{6108.82}}{30}$$

$$= \sqrt{203.63}$$

$$\text{SD}(\sigma) = 14.27$$

EXAMPLE 7.10

Class-interval	*Frequency*	*Mid-point*	*Frequency × mid-point*	*Deviation= (score – mean)*	*Frequency × deviation*	fx^2
CI	f	X	fX	x $(X - M)$	f_x	$f_x \times x$
70–71	2	70.5	141.0	9.74	19.48	189.74
68–69	2	68.5	137.0	7.74	15.48	119.81
66–67	3	66.5	199.5	5.74	17.22	98.84
64–65	4	64.5	258.0	3.74	14.96	55.95
62–63	6	62.5	375.0	1.74	10.44	18.17
60–61	7	60.5	423.5	–0.26	–1.82	0.47
58–59	5	58.5	292.5	–2.26	–11.30	25.54
56–57	4	56.5	226.0	–4.26	–17.04	72.59
54–55	2	54.5	109.0	–6.26	–12.52	78.38
52–53	3	52.5	157.5	–8.26	–24.78	204.68
50–51	1	50.5	50.5	–10.26	–10.26	105.27
$i = 2$	$N = 39$		$\Sigma fX = 2369.5$			$\Sigma f_x^2 = 969.44$

$$\text{Mean} = \frac{\Sigma fX}{N}$$

$$= \frac{2369.5}{39}$$

$$\text{Mean} = 60.756 = 60.76$$

$$\text{SD}(\sigma) = \frac{\sqrt{\Sigma x^2}}{N}$$

$$= \frac{\sqrt{969.44}}{39}$$

$$= \sqrt{24.8574}$$

$$= \sqrt{24.86}$$

$$\text{SD}(\sigma) = 4.99$$

Calculation or computation of the Standard Deviation (SD or σ) by the short method or SD from a frequency distribution when deviations are taken from an assumed mean

$$\text{SD}(\sigma) = i\frac{\sqrt{\Sigma fx'^2}}{N} - c^2$$

where

i = length of class-interval

N = number of cases

c = correction in units of class-interval
ci = score correction or the correction in score units
$c \times i = c \times$ length of class-interval

EXAMPLE 7.11

Class-intervals or scores	*Mid-point*	*Frequency*	*Deviation*	*Frequency × deviation*	$f'_x \times x'$	
CI $f_x \times x$	X	F	x'	f'_x	f'^2_x	
195–199	197	1	+5	5(1 × 5)	25(5 × 5)	121
190–194	192	2	+4	8(2 × 4)	32(8 × 4)	
185–189	187	4	+3	12(4 × 3)	36(12 × 3)	
180–184	182	5	+2	10(5 × 2)	20(10 × 2)	
175–179	177	8	+1	8(8 × 1)	08(8 × 1)	
170–174	172(AM)	10	0	0(10 × 0)	0(0 × 0)	
165–169	167	6	–1	–6(6 × –1)	06(– 6 × –1)	–201
160–164	162	4	–2	–8(4 × –2)	16(– 8 × –2)	
155–159	157	4	–3	–12(4 × –3)	36 (–12 × –3)	
150–154	152	2	–4	–8(2 × –4)	32 (–8 × –4)	
145–149	147	3	–5	–15(3 × –5)	75 (–15 × –5)	
140–144	142	1	–6	–6(1 × –6)	36 (–6 × –6)	
$i = 5$		$N = 50$		$\Sigma f_x' = -55+43$ $\Sigma f_x' = -12$	$\Sigma f_x'^2 = 322$ (121 + 201)	

AM is assumed mean (mid-point of class-interval having the highest frequency is assumed as the mean)

Correction in units of class-interval:

$$c = \frac{\Sigma fx'}{N}$$

$$= \frac{-12}{50}$$

$$c = -\ 0.240$$

$$c^2 = c \times c$$

$$= -0.240 \times -0.240$$

$$c^2 = 0.0576$$

Correction in score units or score correction:

$$ci = c \times i$$

$$= -0.240 \times 5$$

$$ci = -1.20$$

$$SD(\sigma) = i\frac{\sqrt{\Sigma f_x'^2} - c^2}{N}$$

$$= i\frac{\sqrt{322} - 0.0576}{50}$$

$$SD(\sigma) = 12.63$$

Use the Standard Deviation (SD or σ)

1. When the statistics having the greatest stability is sought.
2. When the most accurate and reliable measure of variability is wanted.
3. When extreme deviations should exercise a proportionally greater effect upon the variability.
4. When co-efficient of correlation and other statistics are subsequently to be computed.
5. When other measures of reliability are to be computed.
6. When standard scores are to be computed.
7. When we want to test the significance of the difference between two means or statistics.
8. When co-efficient of variation, variance, etc. are to be calculated.
9. When scores are to be properly interpreted with reference to the normal curve.

Merits and demerits of the Standard Deviation (SD or σ)

Merits of standard deviation: The following are the merits of standard deviation:

1. Standard deviation is an important or master measure of variability or dispersion or deviation.
2. It is most frequently and widely used measure of variability.
3. It is the reliable measure of variability.
4. It is rigidly defined and its value is always definite.
5. It is based on all scores or values or observations of a series or distribution.
6. It is capable of further algebraic treatment.
7. It is used in further statistical analysis.
8. It provides accurate results.
9. It occupies a central position in statistics.
10. It is affected least by sampling fluctuations.
11. Signs are not ignored but made positive by taking square.

Demerits of standard deviation: The following are the demerits of standard deviation.

1. Standard deviation is difficult to calculate.
2. It is not easily understood.
3. It is not familiar to common people.
4. It is highly affected by the presences of extreme items.

EXERCISES

The below mentioned are some of the questions that have been asked in the examinations conducted by the Guru Nanak Dev University or can be asked. Knowledge of these answers can help the students to get success in the examinations.

Section A

Answer the following questions in **five** lines or 50 words:

1. Define variability.
2. Define deviation.*
3. Define quartiles and quartile deviation.
4. What is Range?*
5. What is mean deviation?*
6. What is quartile deviation?*
7. What is standard deviation?*
8. What are the various measures of variability?
9. Write formulae of all measures of variability.
10. Name all measures of variability.

Section B

Answer the following questions up to **two** pages or 500 words:

1. What is the difference between grouped and ungrouped data? What are different measures of variability?
2. What are the merits and demerits of variability?
3. Write briefly about different measures of variability while discussing grouped and ungrouped data?
4. Write formulae of different measures of variability?
5. What is variability? Mention its various measures?
6. What are various measures of variability? What are the characteristics of a good measure of variability?

7. Find out the standard deviation of the following data:

Class-interval (CI)	Frequency (f)
73–75	1
70–72	3
67–69	8
64–66	15
61–63	20
58–60	28
55–57	21
52–54	13
49–51	6
46–48	2
43–45	1

8. Calculate mean deviation of the following data:

CI	f
330–339	1
320–329	1
310–319	8
300–309	30
290–299	6
280–289	4
270–279	0
260–269	0
250–259	3
240–249	8
230–239	16
220–229	14
210–219	7
200–209	2
	N = 100

Section C

Answer the following questions up to **five** pages or 1000 words:

1. Define the terms "standard deviation" and "mean deviation". How is standard deviation a better measure of variability or dispersion than the mean deviation?
2. Calculate mean and mean deviation for the following frequency distribution:

Class-interval:	10–19	20–29	30–39	40–49	50–59	60–69
Frequency:	3	5	10	12	6	4

3. Find the mean deviation and standard deviation for the following frequency distribution:

X:	5	10	15	20	25	30
F:	2	7	10	15	11	5

9. What are the characteristics of a good measure of variability?*
10. What is statistics? Discuss about the various measures of variability giving formulae separately for the grouped and the ungrouped data?
11. What is variability? Find out the SD from the following data:*

CI	f
91–100	0
81–90	2
71–80	5
61–70	7
51–60	10
41–50	11
31–40	8
21–30	4
11–20	2
1–10	1
	N = 50

12. Calculate the Quartile Deviation from the following data:

CI	f
90–94	2
85–89	2
80–84	4
75–79	8
70–74	8
65–69	12
60–64	9
55–59	7
50–54	5
45–49	1
40–44	2
	N = 60

13. Calculate the Standard Deviation of the data given below:

Class-interval (CI)	Frequency (f)
195–199	1
190–194	2
185–189	4
180–184	5
175–179	8
170–174	10
165–169	6
160–164	4
155–159	4
150–154	2
145–149	3
140–144	1
	$N = 50$

14. Calculate the Standard Deviation:

CI	f
100–106	2
93–99	4
86–92	6
79–85	8
72–78	4
65–71	3
58–64	2

15. Calculate the Quartile Deviation of following data:

CI	f
45–49	2
40–44	3
35–39	5
30–34	6
25–29	3
20–24	3
15–19	2
10–14	1

16. Calculate the Standard Deviation (SD) for the following data by calculating mean by the long method:

CI	f
41–45	1
36–40	3
31–35	5
26–30	6
21–25	8
16–20	4
11–15	3
6–10	0
	N = 30

17. Calculate Mean Deviation from the following data:*

CI	f
70–71	2
68–69	2
66–67	3
64–65	4
62–63	6
60–61	7
58–59	5
56–57	4
54–55	2
52–53	3
50–51	1
	N = 39

18. Calculate the Quartile Deviation

CI	f
30–32	12
32–34	18
34–36	16
36–38	14
38–40	12
40–42	8
42–44	6
	N = 86

19. Find out Standard Deviation for the following data:

CI	f
150–200	25
200–250	160
250–300	50
300–350	30
350–400	20
400–450	10
450–500	5
	N = 300

20. Calculate Standard Deviation for the following data:

CI	f
95–99	1
90–94	3
85–89	4
80–84	5
75–79	8
70–74	10
65–69	6
60–64	4
55–59	5
50–54	4
45–49	3
40–44	2
	$N = 55$

21. Calculate the Quartile Deviation for the data:

CI	f
155–159	1
150–154	3
145–149	4
140–144	5
135–139	8
130–134	10
125–129	6
120–124	4
115–119	5
110–114	4
105–109	3
100–104	2
	$N = 55$

22. Calculate the Standard Deviation of the following data:

CI	f
50–54	1
45–49	2
40–44	4
35–39	6
30–34	8
25–29	3
20–24	2
15–19	1
10–14	1
	$N = 28$

REFERENCES

Coolican, H., *Research Methods and Statistics in Psychology*, Sevenoaks, UK: Hodder & Stoughton, 1990.

Garrett, H.E., *Elementary Statistics,* New York: Longmans, Green and Co., 1956.

Garrett, H.E., *Statistics in Psychology and Education*, Vakils: Feffer and Simons, 1961.

Guilford, J.P., *Fundamental Statistics in Psychology and Education*, New York: McGraw Hill Book Company, 1965.

Gupta, J.P., *Statistical Methods*, New Delhi: Sultan Chand and Sons, 1991.

PART B

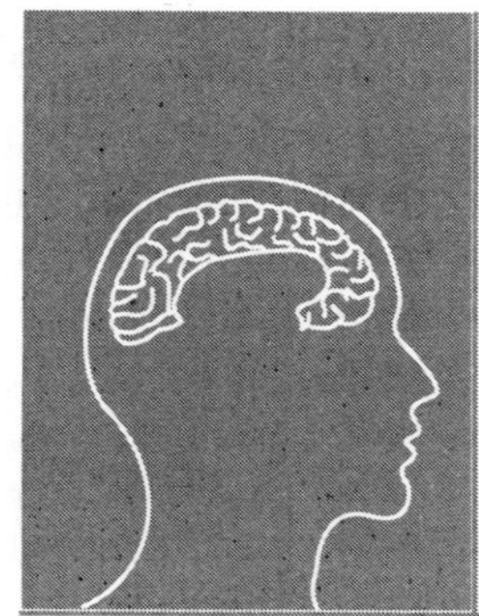

CHAPTER 8
Introduction to Learning

Any response that an organism is not born with is said to have been acquired or learned. From infancy, we are constantly learning new skills, gaining information, and developing beliefs and attitudes. All these are learned. Learning is very essential for the survival, development, and progress of human race. Learning goes on not only in a formal situation but throughout life. Learning, right or wrong, brings about relatively permanent and ephemeral changes in the behaviour of a person.

Learning is a key process in human behaviour. It refers to a spectrum of changes that takes place as a result of one's experience. Learning may be defined as "Any relatively permanent change in behaviour or behavioural potential produced by experience" (Gordon, 1989). Behavioural changes occurring due to the use of drugs or fatigue or emotions or alterations in motives, growth, or maturation are not considered learning. Systematic changes resulting due to practice and experience and relatively permanent are illustrative of learning.

8.1 DEFINITIONS OF LEARNING

According to Woodworth (1945), "Any activity can be called learning so far as it develops the individual (in any respect, good or bad) and makes him alter behaviour and experiences different from what they would otherwise have been."

According to Postman and Egan (1949), "Learning may be defined as the measurable changes in behaviour as a result of practice and condition that accompany practice."

According to Underwood (1966), "Learning is the acquisition of new responses or the enhanced execution of old ones."

According to Crow and Crow (1973), "Learning is the acquisition of habits, knowledge, and attitudes. It involves new ways of doing things, and it operates in an individual's attempts to overcome obstacles or to adjust to new situations. It represents progressive changes in behaviour. . . . It enables him to satisfy interests to attain goals."

According to Hilgard and Atkinson (1975), "Learning is a relatively permanent change in behaviour that occurs as the result of practice."

The phrase "relatively permanent" serves to exclude temporary or momentary behavioural change that may depend on such factors such as fatigue, satiation, and the effects of drugs or alteration in, motives. "Reinforced" is the crux of behaviourism. Without reinforcement, extinction will occur. "Practice" which means that for learning to emerge, sooner or later the behaviour must be emitted and repeated (reinforced) occurrences will improve learning. The notion of practice also allows for the exclusion of other behavioural changes of a relatively permanent kind that are generally not considered to be instances of learning, such as native tendencies of particular species (for example, imprinting) and maturational changes (for example, flying in birds).

According to Bandura (1977), "Learning is a change in acquired information (and hence in performance potential) that can occur just by virtue of being an observer in the world."

According to Morgan and King (1978), "Learning is defined as any relatively permanent change in behaviour which occurs as a result of practice and experience."

According to G.A. Kimble and Germazy (1984), "Learning is a relatively permanent change in a behavioural or response potentiality or tendency that occurs as a result of reinforced practice."

According to Bootzin (1991), "Learning is a long lasting change in an organism's disposition to behave in certain ways as a result of experience."

According to Crooks and Stein (1991), "Learning is a relatively enduring change in potential behaviour that results from experience."

According to Baron (1995), "Any relatively permanent change in behaviour potential resulting from experience is called *learning*."

According to Mangal (2002), "Learning stands for all those changes and modifications in the behaviour of the individual which he undergoes during his lifetime."

The term "learning" refers to the process by which experience or practice results in a relatively permanent change in behaviour. It is such a pervasive and continual process that we can easily overlook how much learning we actually do everyday.

8.2 CHARACTERISTICS OR FEATURES OF THE LEARNING PROCESS

The process of learning has certain distinctive characteristics which are mentioned below:

1. *Learning connotes change:* Learning is a change in behaviour, for better or worse. Throughout her or his life, an individual acquires new patterns of inner motivations or attitudes, and of overt (external) behaviour. These result from the changes taking place within her or him. At the same time, she or he may be strengthening attitudes and behaviour patterns that are in the process of formation, or weakening old patterns that already have been established.
2. *Learning is a complex process:* At one and same time, an individual is:
   (a) learning new skills or improving those that already are operating.
   (b) building a store of information or knowledge, and
   (c) developing interests, attitudes, and ways of thinking.
3. *Learning always involves some kind of experience:* One experiences an event occurring in a certain sequence on a number of occasions. If one event happens, then it may be followed by certain other events. For example, one learns that if the bell rings in the hostel after sunset, it means that dinner is ready to be served. They have learned that bell signalled the serving of the food. It is through repeated experience of satisfaction that leads to the formation of habit. Sometimes, one single experience can lead to learning, for example, child strikes a matchstick on the matchbox side and gets her or his fingers burnt. Such an experience makes the child learn to be careful in handling the matchbox in future.
4. *It is a change that takes place through practice or experience:* However, changes due to growth or maturation, drugs, fatigue, satiation, emotions, etc. are not learning.
5. *The behavioural changes that occur due to learning are relatively permanent:* Exactly, how long cannot be specified but it must last a fairly long time. Whatever is learnt is stored in memory and therefore becomes enduring, long lasting, and permanent.
6. *Learning is an inferred process and is different from performance:* Performance is an individual's observed behaviour or response of action. Let us understand the term "inference". For example, you are asked by your teacher to remember a multiplication table. You read that table a number of times. Then

you say that you have learnt the table. You are asked to recite that table and you are able to do it. The recitation of that table by you is your performance. On the basis of your performance, the teacher infers that you have learned that table. Learning that can be inferred from performance is called "potent learning". Learning becomes potent with practice and training. Whereas, learning that cannot be easily inferred from performance is called "latent learning". Learning has taken place but has not yet manifested itself in changes in performance. It occurs in the absence of changes in behaviour. This form of learning usually occurs when reward or positive reinforcement is not provided.

7. Learning is engaged in consciously or unconsciously; it may be "informal" in that it represents learning as an aspect of an individual's daily situational experiences, or "formal" to the extent that the learning situation is organized according to definite objective, planned procedures, and expected outcomes.
8. The direction of the learning can be vertical and or horizontal. "Vertical learning" applies to the addition of knowledge to that which already is possessed in a particular area of knowledge, the improvement of a skill in which some dexterity has been achieved, or the strengthening of development attitudes and modes of thinking. It is vertical if more facts are covered at higher levels so as to move towards perfection.

   "Horizontal learning" means that the learner is widening her or his learning horizons, competence in new forms of skills, gaining new interests, discovering new approaches to problem-solving, and developing different attitudes towards newly experienced situations and conditions. Learning is horizontal if more facts are covered at the same level. As learning proceeds both vertically and horizontally, that which is learned is integrated and organized as functioning units of expanding experiences.
9. Learning is cumulative, with no breaks, until a hundred percent mastery has been achieved.
10. Learning is an active process in which the learner, fully aware of the learning situation, is motivated to learn, has intention to learn, and participates in the learning process. A passive person cannot learn.
11. Learning is goal-directed. The nature of learning is purposeful. For meaningful and effective learning, the purpose of learning must be clear, vivid, and explicit.

12. Much of our learning consists of the formation of habit patterns as we are stimulated by conditions that surround us to imitate the behaviour of others or to try out various forms of response.
13. Enforced learning can have equally undesirable effects upon young people.

8.3 TYPES OF LEARNING

8.3.1 Trial and Error Learning

Trial and learning was put forward, initiated, and propagated by an American psychologist, Edward Lee Thorndike (1874–1949). E.L. Thorndike (1911) studied Animal Intelligence. Notable contributions of E.L. Thorndike include Instrumental Conditioning, the Law of Effect, and S–R analysis. McDougall, Lloyd, Morgan, Miller and Dollard also conducted experiments on trial and error learning. Thorndike (1898) conducted several experiment on cats, rats, chickens, fishes, dogs, monkeys, and human beings. According to Woodworth, "Trial and error learning consists in trying, failing, varying the procedure and gradually attaining success in a series of trials without the learner seeing clearly what the conditions of success are."

Edward Lee Thorndike
(1874–1949)

Thorndike first stated the elements of his theory of learning in 1913 saying that connections are formed in the nervous system between stimuli and responses. These connections formed are illustrated by the symbol S–R. Another word used to describe these connections is the word "bond" and hence, this theory is sometimes called a "Bond Theory of Learning". Thorndike has written, "Learning is connecting. The mind is man's connection system."

According to Thorndike, learning takes place by trial and error. Some people call it "Learning by selection of the successful variant." Accordingly, when no readymade solution of a problem is available to the learner, he adopts the method of Trial and Error. He first, tries one solution. If it does not help him, he rejects it. Then, he tries another, and so on. In this way, he eliminates errors or irrelevant responses which do not serve the purpose and finally, discovers the correct solution. Thus, in Trial and Error method, the learner makes random activities and finally reaches the goal accidentally. Here, one thing should be remembered that in Trial and Error also, there are often systematic and relevant responses. Activities are not wholly random. All these activities though apparently random, are suggested to him by the situation and the learner proceeds on accordingly. The stages through which the learner has to pass are goal, block, hindrances, random movements or multiple response, selection and fixation. When and how the connection is accomplished was stated in the laws of learning.

In one of his famous experiments, Edward Lee Thorndike put a hungry cat in a cage called “puzzle box”. The door of the puzzle box could be opened by correctly manipulating a latch and thus the cat could come out. The food for the animal that is some pieces of fish meat were kept outside the cage, which acted as a strong motive for the cat to come out of the puzzle box. Figure 8.1 illustrates Thorndike's cat trying to come out. When placed in the puzzle box, the cat becomes restless and moves randomly in the puzzle box. The situation is described by Thorndike as: “It tries to squeeze through every opening; it claws and bites at the bars or wires, it thrusts its paws through any opening and claws at everything it reaches.” The cat has a motive or purpose to come out of the puzzle box and eat the fish. In making random movements and attempts to open the door, in one of the random movements, the latch was manipulated accidentally, the door got opened, and the cat came out and ate the fish. Again the cat was put in the puzzle box. Again, the cat made random movements and attempts to open the door and eat the fish. But this time, incorrect responses such as biting, clawing, dashing, blind fumbling gradually decreased and the number of errors was less than the previous trial. Trial and Error learning states that when placed in a new situation,

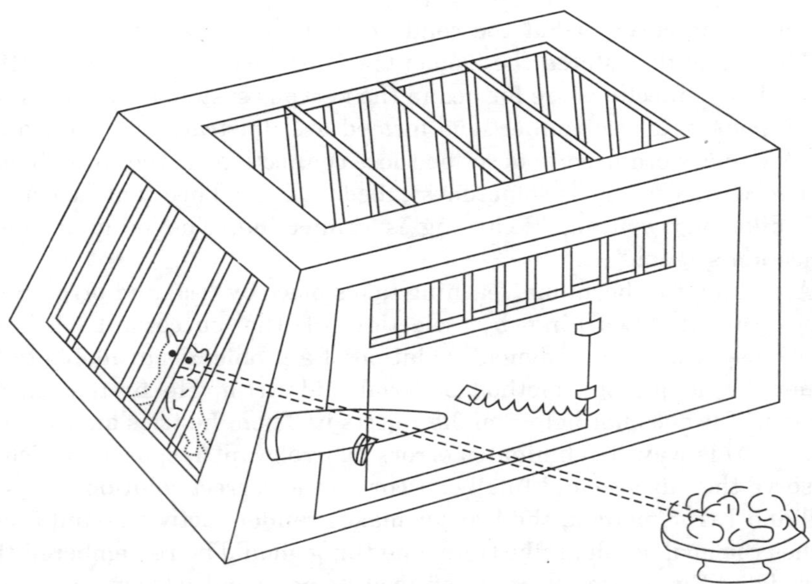

Figure 8.1 Thorndike's cat performing Trial and Error learning.

an individual makes random movements, those of which are unsuccessful are stamped out or eliminated and the successful movements are stamped in or fixed. The course of such learning is typified by the gradual elimination of ineffectual responses and the strengthening of those responses that are satisfactory. The trials continued till the errors reached zero. In this way, gradually, the cat learned to open the door and got its reward in form of fish.

According to Trial and Error learning, as the trial goes on increasing, the errors and time taken go on decreasing. Learning is incremental. The animal or the organism learns from mistakes and experiences. Thorndike interpreted learning in terms of connection or association between stimulus and response. According to Thorndike, learning is the result of the formation of a connection in the nervous system between the stimulus or stimuli and the response. Thorndike (1931) writes that learning is connecting. Thorndike argued that this process was central to the acquisition of complex acts, a position now totally abandoned. In the International Congress of Psychology in Newttaven in September 1929, Thorndike said, "I am wrong".

Steps or stages of Trial and Error learning

The following are the steps or stages of the Trial and Error learning:

1. Need or drive
2. Goal
3. Block or barrier
4. Random movements or responses or attempts
5. Chance success
6. Selection of proper and correct movements and elimination of wrong and incorrect responses
7. Repetition of successful movements or responses
8. Fixation or achievement of the goal

Laws of Trial and Error learning

Thorndike established and propounded the following laws of learning which explain the process, development, and causes of learning:

1. **Law of Readiness:** First primary law of learning, according to Thorndike is the "Law of Readiness" or the "Law of Action Tendency", which means that learning takes place when an action tendency is aroused through preparatory adjustment, set as attitude. "Law of Readiness" refers to the physical or psychological preparedness of a person to do a job or to attend to a stimulus. This law refers to the conditions that determine what will act as satisfiers and annoyers. According to Thorndike, "When any conduction unit is ready to conduct,

for it to do so is satisfying. When any conduction unit is not to in readiness to conduct, for it to conduct is annoying. When any conduction unit is in readiness to conduct, for it not do so is annoying."

"Readiness", according to Thorndike, is preparation for action and is essential for learning. Readiness means a preparation for action. Readiness is a position of preparedness in which an organism is set to act or to respond. Woodworth used the term "mental set" for readiness. Readiness for doing a work makes learning smooth, pleasant, and economical in terms of time and effort. If one is not prepared to learn, learning cannot be automatically instilled in her or him. For example, unless the typist in order to learn typing prepares himself to start, he would not make much progress in a lethargic and unprepared manner.

2. **Law of Exercise:** The second law of learning is the "Law of Exercise" which means that drill or practice helps in increasing efficiency and durability of learning and according to Thorndike's S–R Bond Theory, the connections are strengthened with trial or practice and the connections are weakened when trial or practice is discontinued. Practice makes one perfect. If an S–R (Stimulus-Response) connection is used repeatedly, the strength of that connection is increased and if an S–R connection in not used, the strength of that connection is weakened. Repetition, therefore, increases the strength of response and lack of repetition weakens it. Responses are connected to situations simply because they occur frequently in those situations (laws of use and disuse). The law of exercise, therefore, is also understood as the "Law of Use and Disuse" in which case connections or bonds made in the brain or cortex are weakened or loosened. Many examples of this are found in case of human learning. Learning to drive a car, typewriting, singing or memorizing a poem or a mathematical or multiplication table, and music etc. need exercise and repetition of various movements and actions many times. The law of exercise can be divided into two more laws:

(i) *Law of Use:* "Law of Use" refers to the strengthening of a connection with practice. Law of Use states that the strength of S–R connection is increased by exercise. It is a generalization that states that responses, functions, association, etc. which are practiced, exercised or rehearsed or used are strengthened relative to those which go unused. According to Thorndike, "When a modifiable connection is made between a situation and response that connection's strength is, other things being equal, increased."

(ii) *Law of Disuse:* "Law of Disuse" refers to the weakening of connection or forgetting when the practice is discontinued. Law of Disuse states that strength of S–R connection is decreased when it is not exercised. It is a generalization which states that a learned association will become weak by lack of use. According to Thorndike, "When a modifiable connection is not made between a situation and response, during a length of time, that connection's strength is decreased."

(iii) **Law of Effect or Law of Consequence of Result:** The third law is the "Law of Effect" according to which the trial or steps leading to satisfaction stamps in the bond or connection. Satisfying states lead to consolidation and strengthening of the connection, whereas dissatisfaction, annoyance and pain lead to the weakening or stamping out of the connections. "Law of Effect" refers to some kind of reward or reinforcement. It stresses the role of motivation in learning. According to Thorndike, "When a modifiable connection between stimulus and response is made and is accompanied or followed by a satisfying state of affairs, that connection's strength is increased. When made and accompanied or followed by an annoying state of affairs, its strength is decreased."

By "satisfying state of affairs", Thorndike means one which the animal does nothing to avoid, often doing things which maintain or renew it. It is something which the animal always tried to maintain. By "annoying state of affairs", Thorndike means one which the animal does nothing to preserve, often doing things which put an end to it. Responses are selected and connected to situations or are disconnected from situations depending upon the consequences they produce (satisfiers or annoyers).

"Law of Effect" refers to strengthening and weakening of connection, as a result of its consequences. When a modifiable connection is made and is followed by a satisfying state of affairs, the strength of the connection is increased. If a connection is made and is followed by an annoying state of affairs, the strength is decreased. The learning which gives satisfaction is repeated over and over again. Conversely, failure and dissatisfaction will create aversion for that learning. Strength of connection takes place in terms of result, that is, it depends upon the result. It can also be called the *law of consequence of result.* The satisfying consequences or results are retained and the dissatisfying ones are eliminated. In fact, the Law of Effect signifies that if the responses satisfy the subject, they are learnt and selected, while those which are not satisfying are eliminated. Teaching, therefore, must be pleasing. Greater the satisfaction, stronger will be the motive to learn. Thus, intensity is an important condition of the Law of Effect.

Three important views about the law of effect:

(i) "Law of effect is essential to learning." (Thorndike, Hull)

(ii) "Law of effect is incidental to learning." (Tolman, Gestaltists)

(iii) "Law of effect is of no importance." (Guthrie)

In addition to the above-mentioned laws or besides these three basic laws, Thorndike also gave or referred to the below discussed subsidiary laws (referring to the history of the learner) which further help to explain the learning process. These are:

1. *Law of Multiple Responses:* "Law of Multiple Responses" implies that there are a numbers of responses at the disposal of the O (organism). When one fails, the other is tried. The learner's behaviour is not random; she or he comes with a set of responses supplied by heredity or by past experience. According to it, the organism varies or changes its responses till an appropriate behaviour is hit upon. Without varying the responses, the correct response for the solution might never be elicited. If the individual wants to solve a puzzle, he is to try in different ways rather than mechanically persisting in the same way. Thorndike's cat in the puzzle box moved about and tried many ways to come out till finally it hit the latch with her paw which opened the door and it jumped out.
2. *The Law of Prepotency or Prepotency of Elements or Law of Piecemeal Activity*: According to this law, the learner reacts selectively to the important or essential elements in the situation and neglects the other elements which may be relevant part of the situation, makes analytical and insightful learning possible. The aspects of a situation that will be noticed depend upon the learner's species membership and past experience. In this law of prepotency of elements, Thorndike is really anticipating insight in learning which was more emphasized by the Gestaltists.
3. *Law of Associative Shifting*: According to this law, we may get any response of which a learner is capable, associated with any other situation to which she or he is sensitive. A transfer of responses to new stimuli takes place by their pairing with stimuli already connected to those responses. Thorndike illustrated this by the act of teaching a cat to stand up at a command. A fish was dangled before the cat while he said "stand up". After a number of trials by presenting the fish after uttering the command "stand up", he later ousted the fish and the overall command of "stand up" was found sufficient to evoke the response in the cat by standing up on her hind legs.
4. *Law of Attitude or Set:* Learning is guided by a total set or attitude of the organism, which determines not only what the person will do but what will satisfy or annoy him. For instance, unless the cricketer sets himself to make a century, he will not be able to score more runs. A student, similarly, unless she or he sets to get first position and has the attitude of being at the top, would while away the time and would not learn much. The

learner's behaviour is influenced by what she or he has been led to expect of a task and its outcome. This may come from instructions or from prior experience. Hence, learning is affected more in the individual if she or he is set to learn more or to excel.

5. *Law of Contiguity:* "Contiguity" means nearness of space and time. If two are experienced together, either due to the nearness of space or time, when one is experienced, the other immediately comes to our mind. For example, because of contiguity of space, chalk and blackboard; because of contiguity of time, thunder and lightening.
6. *Law of Frequency*: Law of Frequency and Law of Exercise are sometimes considered as having equal functions. It is the frequent occurrence that gives an advantage. When the nerve connections are frequently used, they leave a particular mark on our memory. This is suggested by Thorndike as a physiological change.
7. *Law of Recency:* Any act which has been performed recently has the advantage of being learnt and remembered more quickly than the older, far off, and distant experiences because:
   (i) neural pathways involved in recent experiences are the last to be activated and the impression in the nerves is fresh.
   (ii) they were the acts more nearer to the solution and satisfaction of the need.
8. *Law of Primacy:* First impressions last long. All first learnt things are better remembered. For example, first night of marriage, first day in a college, etc. The first things get enough time to be consolidated, and there is no proactive inhibition in this case while in the middle series, both proactive and retroactive inhibition operates.
9. *Law of Intensity:* If the experience is very intense and emotional, it is easily remembered and further learning may not be necessary to remember it. However, according to the theory of repression, if the experience is too shocking or unpleasant, it may be forgotten due to the operation of the mechanism of repression.
10. *Law of Belongingness:* It states that the effect is stronger, if it belongs to the stimulus-response connection. If there is S–R connection and the effect belongs to it, the influence is stronger. For example, when one is hungry, food belongs to the situation and so hunger-food connection makes learning more efficient. When one is hungry, water does not belong to it, only food belongs to it, only food can satisfy the need of hunger. The belongingness of reward and punishment depends upon the

appropriateness in satisfying an aroused motive or want in the learner and in its logical and informative relationship to the activities rewarded and punished. Thorndike says that effect is more efficacious when it is an effect with belongingness.

11. *Law of Response by Analogy:* According to this law, the individual makes use of old experiences or acquisitions while learning in a new situation. There is tendency to utilize common elements in the new situation as existed in a similar past situation. The learner's behaviour will depend in part on the similarity of the present situation to past situations (also called the *identical elements theory of transfer*). The learning of driving a car, for instance, is facilitated by the earlier acquired skill of driving a motor cycle or bike or even riding a bicycle, therefore the perspective of maintaining a balance and controlling the handle helps in steering a car.

Limitations of Trial and Error Learning

Trial and Error learning has some limitations which are mentioned below:

(i) It is random and mechanical.
(ii) It is slow.
(iii) It is temporary.
(iv) It is simple type of learning.
(v) It lays too much emphasis on motivation.
(vi) It depends upon practice.
(vii) It does not involve insight.
(viii) It does not explain all type of learning.

Thorndike's Trial and Error Theory is the oldest theory of learning. Despite its defects and limitations, it is still accepted in the field of learning and education. It explains the causes, process, and development of learning by emphasizing the role or importance of motivation. Thorndike's laws of learning have made a significant contribution to the field of educational psychology.

Wolfgang Kohler
(1887–1967)

8.3.2 Insight Learning

Wolfgang Kohler (21 Jan, 1887–1 June, 1967), a German psychologist, propounded a theory of learning called "Insightful Learning". According to this theory, the learner does not merely receive or make responses to the stimuli, but definitely processes, that is, he interacts with and does something about what he receives and his response is determined by that processing. An “insight” is a sudden recognition of relationship that leads to the solution of a problem or problems. Within Gestalt psychology, “insight” is the process by which problems are solved. In this sense, insight characterizes a sudden reorganization or restructuring of the pattern or significance of events allowing one to grasp relationships relevant to the solution. Here, insight represents a kind of learning. Insight is a higher and complex kind of learning involving cognitive processes.

According to Woodworth, “By insight meant a good observation, perception of the situation as a whole or perceiving those parts of the situation that provides route to the goal.”

According to Wertheimer, “Insightful learning involves exploratory procedure as examining parts of the whole, investigating the false leads and constant shifting of point of view.”

Types of Insight

1. *Foresight:* According to Kohler, insight involves foresight; foresight involves seeing the way to the goal before trying it.
2. *Hindsight:* According to Woodworth, hindsight is observing that a lead or a way is correct after trying it.

Kohler (1925) conducted experiments on chimpanzees and apes. Sultan was the most intelligent of Kohler’s chimpanzees. In one of his classic experiment (Figure 8.2), Kohler put the chimpanzee, Sultan, inside a cage. Sultan was kept hungry. A bundle of bananas was hung on the roof of the cage, beyond the reach of the chimpanzee. Some wooden boxes were kept inside the cage. The chimpanzee tried to reach the bananas by jumping but could not succeed. After some time, the solution flashed suddenly and the chimpanzee arrived at the solution. Kohler seemed to see insightful learning in terms of a sudden “Aha” or “a-ha” experience or a blot of lightening or a sudden flash. “A-ha” experience is a term used to describe the feeling that accompanies the moment of insight, that instance when the various disparate aspects of a problem-solving situation suddenly fit together to yield the solution. Insight depends upon intelligence, experience, maturity. Insight involves some trial and error behaviour. Sultan placed the boxes on the top of each other and used it as the platform by placing it just below the hanging bananas. So, by sudden solution of the problem and insight, chimpanzee, Sultan, solved his problem of reaching the bananas. In another experiment, Kohler made the problem more difficult requiring the specific arrangement of boxes by the chimpanzee.

Figure 8.2 Kohler's box problem.

In another more complicated experiment, Kohler put Sultan inside a cage. Two sticks were kept inside the cage. One stick was hollow at one end. Another stick could be thrust into it or attached to it to form a longer stick. A banana was kept at a distance outside the cage. It was not possible for the chimpanzee to pick the banana by any one of the sticks. The chimpanzee first tried to pull the banana towards him by using the sticks one by one but failed. Figure 8.3 illustrates how Kohler's chimpanzee, Sultan learns to assemble a long stick by joining two shorter ones. Suddenly, Sultan had an idea and joined the two ends of both sticks together and got a bigger one. Sultan then used that stick to reach the banana and pull the banana towards him. In this experiment, Sultan must have used his past experience or hindsight to solve the problem of reaching the banana.

Figure 8.3 Kohler's Chimpanzee Sultan learns to assemble a long stick by joining two shorter ones.

Stages of Insight

The following are the stages of an insight learning.

1. Need
2. Preparation
3. *Incubation:* In cognitive psychology, a period of time during which no conscious effort is made to solve a problem but which terminates with the solution. In insight learning, it is the stage or period of no progress, in which the organism silently thinks over the problem.
4. Inspiration
5. Verification

Insightful learning is purposeful and goal-directed. It requires the organization of the perceptual field and learning material. In insight learning, the learner has to be motivated by arousing her or his interest and curiosity for the learning situation and process. The learner has to understand the whole situation. Insight learning is relatively permanent because the solution to the problem is learnt by understanding the relationship between different parts of the situation.

8.4 CONDITIONING

Although the term "conditioning" is often used in a much wider context, it is more properly restricted to "simple" forms of learning, in particular to classical and instrumental conditioning, two very active areas of research interest. Psychologists often use the word "conditioning" as a synonym for learning in animals as well as in human beings. Generally, the term "conditioning" refers to acquiring a pattern of behaviour but psychologists have referred it as "Part of an expression that describes a specific process of learning" (C.G. Morris).

According to Srivastava, "Conditioning is a process by which a previously ineffective stimulus (or object or situation) becomes effective in eliciting a lateral response."

Drever defines conditioning as "A process by which a response comes to be elicited by a stimulus, object, or situation other than that to which it is the natural or normal response."

Underwood defines conditioning as a "Procedure for studying learning in which a discrete response is attached to more or less discrete stimulus."

In general, it can be said that when an individual learns to respond in natural manner to an unnatural stimulus, then it can be said that he has conditioned it. The form of learning in which the capacity to elicit a response is transferred from one stimulus to the other is called "conditioning". Conditioning can be both classical or Pavlovian or respondent conditioning as well as instrumental or operant conditioning.

Two models of learning demonstrated the research activities of learning psychologists during the early part of this century. One model was developed by Ivan Petrovich Pavlov (1849–1936) and is commonly called *classical conditioning*; the other model was suggested by Edward Lee Thorndike (1874–1949) and refined by B.F. Skinner (1904–1990) and is referred to as instrumental or operant conditioning. The initial experiments of both groups attempted to identify the conditions for learning, using non-human subjects. Pavlov used his famous salivating dogs, while Thorndike studied the effects of reward on the behaviour of cats. Skinner employed rats in his early experiments, then pigeons, and finally among other species, humans.

8.4.1 Classical Conditioning or Pavlovian or Simple or Respondent Conditioning

Classical conditioning was the first type of learning to be discovered and studied within the behaviourist tradition (hence the name classical). The term "classical" means "in the established manner" and "classical conditioning" refers to conditioning in the manner established by the Russian physiologist, Ivan Petrovich Pavlov (1849–1936), a Russian scientist trained in biology and medicine, the first investigator to study this process extensively in the laboratory. He was a major theorist in the development of classical conditioning. Notable contributions of Pavlov include discovery of Conditioned Reflexes; CS, US, CR, UR; Conditioned Inhibition; and Excitatory and Inhibitory Inhibition. The classical conditioning was first discovered by Pavlov (1895), while he was studying the digestive processes in animals. It is also known as *simple conditioning*; simple because the organism enters situation only in a high mechanical or automatic way.

Ivan Petrovich Pavlov
(1849–1936)

Association is an outstanding aspect of classical conditioning. Association is of central importance in classical conditioning. Here the organism learns to respond in a distinct manner even in the absence of the particular stimulus. It is crucial for an association to be formed between the unconditioned and the conditioned stimulus. For that to happen, it is important for the two stimuli to occur close together in time. Conditioning is usually greatest when the conditioned stimulus (tone) precedes the unconditioned stimulus (food) by a short interval of time (about half a second is ideal) and stays on while the unconditioned stimulus is presented. If the unconditioned stimulus (food) is presented shortly before the conditioned stimulus (tone), however, there is little or no conditioning. This situation is called *backward conditioning*. Conditioned stimulus (tone) allows the dog to predict that the unconditioned stimulus (food) is about to be presented. The tone provides a clear indication that food is about to arrive, and so it produces an effect or response, that is salivation.

Pavlov was not the first scientist to study learning in animals but he was the first to do so in an orderly and systematic way, using a standard series of techniques and a standard terminology to describe his experiments, and their results. In the course of his work on the digestive system of the dogs, Pavlov had found that salivary secretion was elicited not only by placing food in the dog's mouth but also by the sight and smell of food and even by the sight and sound of the technician who usually provided the food. He observed that dogs deprived of food began to salivate when one of his assistants walked into the room. He began to investigate this phenomenon and established the laws of classical conditioning. For Pavlov at first, these "psychic secretions" (because it is caused by psychological process, not by food actually being placed in the mouth) merely interfered with the planned study of digestive system. From about 1898 until 1930, Pavlov occupied himself with a study of this subject.

The best-known example of classical conditioning comes from the work of Ivan Pavlov. Pavlov used dogs as the experimental animals. Pavlov found he could train a dog to salivate to other stimuli, for example, a tone. He chose food as the stimulus and secretion of saliva as the response. Some neutral stimulus such as a bell (or tone or light) is presented just before some effective stimulus (food). Dogs (and other animals) salivate when food is put in their mouths. A response such as salivation, originally evoked or elicited only by the effective stimulus (food) eventually appears when initially neutral stimulus is presented. Pavlov's dogs began to salivate at the sound of the bell, which naturally does not make the dog salivate. The response is said to have become conditioned. But since they had learned that the bell signalled the appearance of food, their mouths watered on cue even in the absence of food. The dogs had been conditioned to the bell which normally wouldn't have caused salivation. Classical conditioning seems easiest to establish for involuntary reactions mediated by the autonomic nervous system.

Pavlov's experiments on conditioning employed a standard and simple procedure. A hungry dog was restrained on a stand and every two minutes was given some dry meat powder; an event signalled by an arbitrary stimulus, such as the ticking of a metronome. The food itself elicited plentiful (copious) salivation, but after a few trails, the ticking of metronome, which regularly preceded the delivery of food, also elicited salivation. He presented a tone (the training stimulus) just before food on a number of occasions, so that the tone signalled that food would be arriving soon. Finally, he presented the same tone (the test stimulus) on its own without any food following, and found that the dog salivated to the tone. In technical terms, the dog had learned a conditioned reflex, in which the conditioned stimulus (the tone) was associated with the unconditioned stimulus (food), and the conditioned response was salivation to the tone.

In Pavlov's terminology, the food is an unconditioned stimulus (US or UCS). Unconditioned or natural stimulus will naturally (without learning) elicit or bring about a reflexive or involuntary response. Classical conditioning starts with a reflex: an innate, involuntary behaviour, for example salivation, eye blinking, etc. It invariably (unconditionally) elicits salivation, which is termed as unconditioned response (UR or UCR). The ticking of a metronome or tone before conditioning is a neutral or orienting stimulus and during conditioning, it is repeatedly paired with the natural or the unconditioned stimulus. After conditioning, the ticking of a metronome or tone is a conditional stimulus (CS) because its ability to elicit salivation (now a conditional response, when it occurs in a reaction to the conditional stimulus alone on a particular set of experiences). The elicitation of the conditioned response (CR, salivation) by the conditioned stimulus (ticking of the metronome or tone) is termed conditioned reflex or response, the occurrence of which is reinforced by the presentation of the unconditioned stimulus (food). Now, the neutral or orienting stimulus (ticking of the metronome or tone) is transformed into a conditioned stimulus (CS), that is, when the CS is presented by itself, it elicits or evokes or produces or causes the CR (salivation, which is the same involuntary response as the UR; the name changes because it is elicited or evoked by a different stimulus).

The word "unconditioned" indicates that the connection between this particular stimulus (food) and response (salivation) does not have to be learned. The new or neutral stimulus, for example ticking of the metronome or tone that comes to elicit salivation (UR or UCR) is called *conditioned stimulus* (CS) and the animal's or dog's salivation in response to it is called *conditioned response* (CR). The word "conditioned" indicates that this new response (salivation to the ticking of the metronome or tone) is learned through an association of events (association between the tone and the arrival of food). Tone serves as the signal that the food is coming. Pavlov found that a large number of auditory or visual or tactile sensations, including the ticking of the metronome, the flash of a light, or a brush on the skin could serve as conditioned stimuli for salivation.

Paradigm of classical conditioning or specific model of classical conditioning or the three stages of classical conditioning:

US or UCS ⟶ Unconditioned stimulus
UR or UCR ⟶ Unconditioned response
CS ⟶ Conditioned stimulus
CR ⟶ Conditioned response

Stage 1 Before conditioning: In order to have classical or respondent conditioning, there must be present a stimulus that will automatically or reflexively elicit a specific response. This stimulus is called the *unconditioned stimulus* or US or UCS because there is no learning involved in connecting the stimulus and response. Here the US or UCS is food. There must also be a stimulus that will not elicit this specific response, but will elicit an orienting response (Figure 8.4). This stimulus is called a *neutral stimulus* or an *orienting stimulus*, for example sound of a bell or a tone.

Stage 1: Before conditioning

CS ⟶ No response or perk up ears (or orientation)
(sound of a bell or tone)

US or UCS ⟶ UR or UCR
(presentation of food) (salivation)

Stage 2: During conditioning: During conditioning, the neutral stimulus will first be presented, for example a bell or a tone, followed by the unconditioned stimulus, that is food (Figure 8.5). Over time, the

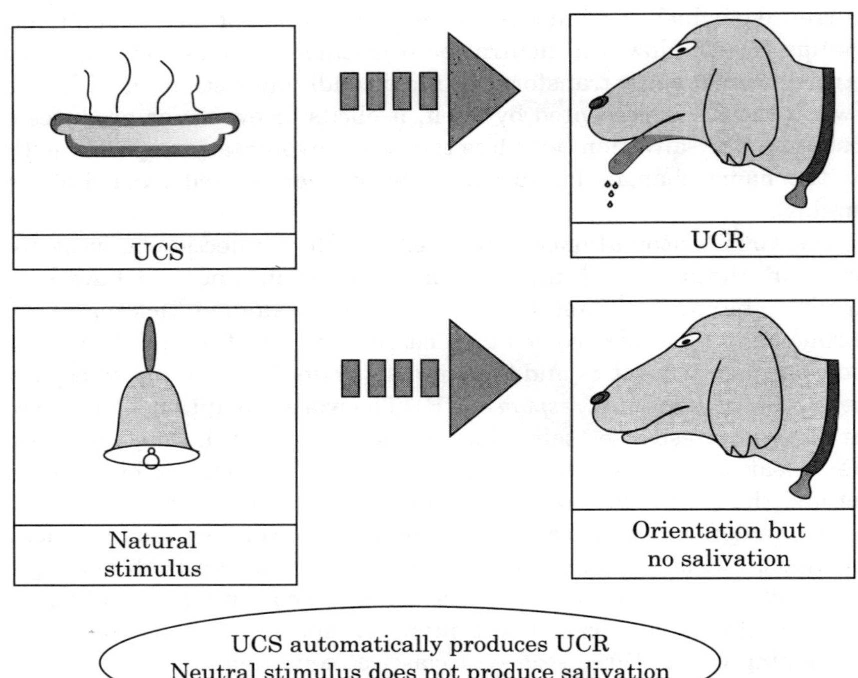

Figure 8.4 Classical conditioning: Before conditioning.

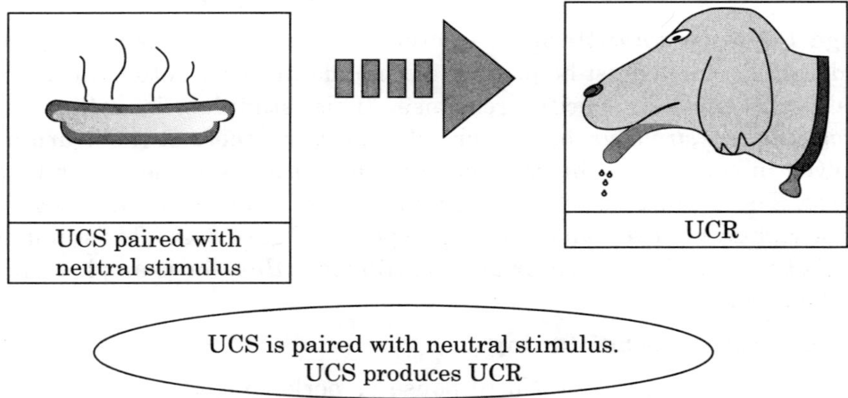

Figure 8.5 Classical conditioning: During conditioning.

learner will develop an association between these two stimuli, that is will learn to make a connection between the two stimuli, the bell and the food. An association is developed (through pairing) between the neutral stimulus, that is bell and the unconditional stimulus, that is food so that the animal or dog responds to both events and stimuli in the same way.

Stage 2: During Conditioning

CS + US or UCS ⟶ UR or UCR
(sound of a bell or tone) (food) (salivation)

Stage 3: After conditioning: After conditioning, the previously neutral or orienting stimulus, for example a bell or a tone will elicit the response previously only elicited by the unconditioned stimulus (food) that is salivation (Figure 8.6). The stimulus in now called a *conditioned stimulus* (CS) because it will now elicit a different response as a result of conditioning or learning. The response is now called a *conditioned response* (CR) because it is elicited by a stimulus as a result of learning. The two responses, unconditioned (salivation) and conditioned (salivation) look the same, but they are elicited or evoked or produced or caused by different stimuli and are therefore given different labels. After conditioning, both the US or UCS and the CS will elicit the same involuntary response. The animal or dog learns to respond reflexively to a new stimulus.

Stage 3: After conditioning

CS ⟶ CR
(sound of a bell or tone) (salivation)

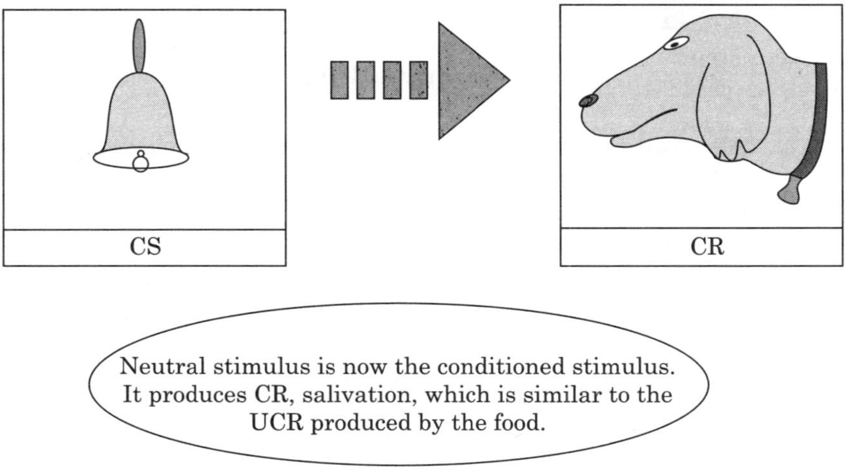

CS

CR

Neutral stimulus is now the conditioned stimulus. It produces CR, salivation, which is similar to the UCR produced by the food.

Figure 8.6 Classical conditioning: After conditioning.

Features of classical conditioning

1. **Generalization or stimulus generalization:** "Generalization" refers to the fact that the strength of the conditioned response, for example, salivation depends on the similarity between the test stimulus and the previous training stimulus. The conditioned response of salivation was greatest when the tone presented on its own was the same as the tone that had previously been presented just prior to food. However, a smaller amount of

salivation was obtained when a different tone was used. Stimulus generalization is performing a learned response in the presence of similar stimuli. For example, if the dog has been classically conditioned at the sound of a dinner bell, it will salivate to a ringing telephone or to high-pitched notes on a piano, etc.

John Brodaeus Watson
(1878–1958)

John Brodaeus Watson (1878–1958) and his student Rosalie Rayner showed how rapidly generalization occurs (Watson and Rayner, 1920). They classically conditioned an eleven month old boy named Albert to fear a harmless laboratory rat by repeatedly pairing presentation of the rat with the loud noise. Soon, little Albert began to show fear at the sight of the rat alone, without the noise following. Moreover, his fear appeared to generalize to other furry objects like a rabbit or a dog, a sealskin coat, even a bearded Santa Clause mask. More similar a subsequent stimulus is to the one that prevailed during learning; the more likely it is that generalization will occur.

2. **Discrimination or stimulus discrimination:** "Discrimination" is learning to make a particular response only to a particular stimulus. For example, experimenter trains the dog to salivate only when it hears a particular bell and to ignore all other bells.
3. **Experimental extinction:** The repeated presentation of the conditioned stimulus (tone) in the absence of the unconditioned stimulus (food) removes the conditioned response (salivation). When Pavlov presented the tone on its own several times without being followed by food, there was less and less salivation and will result in the gradual disappearance or extinction of the conditioned response. Extinction is an important process. It is the removal of reinforcement following the occurrence of some of the responses that have been reinforced in the past. Experimental extinction or disappearance of conditioned response or salivation occurs when the tone no longer predicts the arrival of the food.
4. **Spontaneous Recovery:** Extinction does not mean that the dog has totally lost the conditioned reflex or response. When dog is brought back to the experimental situation, it salivates to the conditioned stimulus that is tone. This is called *spontaneous recovery*.

8.4.2 Instrumental or Operant Conditioning

"A human fashions his consequences as surely as he fashions his goods or his dwelling. Nothing that he says or does is without consequences." (Norman Cousins). Learning to make or to withhold a particular response of its consequences has come to be called *operant conditioning*. An important difference between operant and classical conditioning usually involves reflexive or involuntary responses, whereas operant conditioning usually involves voluntary ones. It is the stimulus that follows a voluntary response that changes the probability of whether the response is likely or unlikely to occur again. There are two types of consequences: positive (sometimes called *pleasant*) and negative (sometimes called *aversive* or *unpleasant*). These can be added to or taken away from the environment in order to change the probability of a given response occurring again. Thorndike labelled this type of learning instrumental. Skinner renamed instrumental as operant because it is more descriptive (that is in this learning, one is "operant" on, and is influenced by the environment). "Operant conditioning", in other words, is learning to obtain reward or to avoid punishment. In classical conditioning, reward (food) is not response contingent. But in instrumental conditioning, the reward is response contingent. Laboratory experiments of such conditioning among small mammals or birds are common. Rats or pigeons may be taught to press levers for food; they also learn to avoid or terminate electric shock.

The major theorists for the development of operant or instrumental conditioning are Edward Lee Thorndike, John Brodaeus Watson, and B.F. Skinner. Among the American psychologists the credit must go to the E.L. Thorndike for initiating the study of instrumental conditioning. Thorndike began his studies as a young research student at about the times that Pavlov was starting his work on classical conditioning. Our environment, B.F. Skinner the leading behaviourist in modern Psychology argued, is filled with positive and negative consequences that mould or shape our behaviour as the piece of fish moulded the behaviour of Thorndike's cat. According to instrumental conditioning, consequences of any behaviour determine its probability of occurrence.

The best-known example of instrumental conditioning is provided by the work of B.F. Skinner (1904–1990). Notable contributions of B.F. Skinner include operant conditioning, operant chambers, schedules of reinforcement, and functional analysis. He placed a hungry rat in a small box (often called a Skinner box) containing a lever. When a rat pressed the lever, a food pellet appeared. The rat slowly learned that food could be obtained by pressing, and so it pressed the lever more and more often.

Our friends and families control us with their approval or disapproval. Our jobs control us by offering or withholding money. Our schools and colleges control us by passing or failing us thus affecting our offering access to jobs. To Skinner, infact, the distinctive patterns of behaviour that each person has, are merely the product of all the many consequences that person has experienced.

B.F. Skinner
(1904–1990)

Thorndike's typical experiment involved placing a cat inside a "puzzle box", an apparatus from which the animal could escape or get food only by pressing a panel, opening the door or pulling a loop of string. Thorndike measured the speed with which the cat gained its release from the box on successive trials. He observed that on early trials, the animal would behave aimlessly or even frantically, stumbling on the correct response purely by chance; with the repeated trials, however, the cat eventually would execute this response efficiently with a few seconds of being placed in the box.

One of the simplest ways of establishing that change in behaviour results from the temporal relationship (in relation to time) between the conditioned stimulus and the unconditioned stimulus in classical conditioning or between the response and the reinforcer in an instrumental conditioning case. A gap of even a few seconds between the rate of pressing the lever and the delivery of food will seriously interfere with the animal's ability to learn the connection.

However, though the operant behaviour is voluntary, they can still be influenced by external factors, in particular, by their own consequences. Consequences determine the fate of behaviour. In instrumental conditioning, the reward is response contingent. These consequences can either increase or decrease the frequency of operant response. A consequence that causes the behaviour to be repeated (to increase its frequency) is called *reinforcement* or *reward*. Much of instrumental conditioning is based on the law of reinforcement: the probability of a response occurring increases if that response is followed by a reward or positive reinforcer such as food or praise. The effect of a reward is greater if it follows shortly after the response has been produced than if it is delayed. A consequence that suppresses a behaviour (decreases its frequency) is called *punishment*. Punishment weakens behaviour by adding a negative stimulus. After a response, a negative or aversive stimulus is added which weakens the frequency or occurrence of the response. Of course, what is regarded as punishing, differs from person to person. It is much more objective to define reinforcement and punishment in terms of their effects on subsequent behaviour, that is whether they increase or decrease the frequency of the response.

Types of Reinforcement

Reinforcement is of two types which are mentioned below:

(a) **Positive Reinforcement:** In a positive reinforcement, when a hungry cat presses a lever and receives a pellet of food, lever pressing is being positive reinforcement and is likely to occur again. The frequency of a response increases because that response causes the arrival of a subjectively satisfying stimulus. The term "reinforcement" always indicates a process that strengthens behaviour; the word positive has two cues associated with it. First, a positive or pleasant stimulus is used in the process. Second, the reinforcer is added. In positive reinforcement, a positive reinforcer is added after a response and increases the frequency of the response or the rate of occurrence of the response or desired behaviour. There are two major types of positive reinforcers or rewards:

   (i) *Primary reinforcers:* "Primary reinforcers" are stimuli that are needed to live, for example foods, water, air, sleep, etc.

   (ii) *Secondary reinforcers:* "Secondary reinforcers" are rewarding because we have learned to associate them with primary reinforcers. Secondary reinforcers include money, praise, appreciation, and attention.

(b) **Negative Reinforcement:** In contrast, when behaviour is followed by the removal of an unpleasant stimulus, negative reinforcement occurs. The term "reinforcement" always indicates a process that strengthens behaviour; the word 'negative' has two cues associated with it. First, a negative or aversive stimulus is used in the process. Second, the reinforcer is subtracted. In negative reinforcement, after the response, the negative reinforcer is removed which increases the frequency of the response or the rate of occurrence of response or behaviour. Negative reinforcement tends to increase the frequency of the response that precedes it. There are two types of negative reinforcement: escape and avoidance. The organism tries to escape from or avoid the unpleasant stimulus by performing the behaviour that enabled it to do so before. In general, the learner must first learn to escape before she or he learns to avoid. A cause-and-effect relationship exists between a particular behaviour and the outcome that follows it. In a negative reinforcement, the frequency of the response increases because the response caused by the removal of some subjectively unpleasant stimulus. For example, when a rat presses a lever that turns off an electrical shock, lever pressing is negatively reinforced. Here the rat is engaging in escape learning, pressing the lever allows it to escape from the shock. Alternatively, pressing the lever might enable the rat to stop the shock from being turned on and so avoid it. This is called *avoidance learning*. Both escape and avoidance responses can be established through negative reinforcement.

Negative reinforcement and punishment both involve aversive stimuli, such as electric shock. Humans and other species learn to behave in ways that reduce their exposure to aversive stimuli just as they learn to increase their exposure to positive reinforcers or rewards. When behaviour is followed by the arrival of an unpleasant stimulus, punishment occurs. Punishment tends to decrease the frequency or occurrence of the response that precedes it. The organism tries to prevent the unpleasant stimulus from occurring another time by not performing the behaviour again. Instrumental conditioning in which a response is followed by an aversive or unpleasant stimulus is called *punishment training*. The aversive stimulus should occur shortly after the undesirable response otherwise the effects of the aversive stimulus are reduced.

Skinner claimed that punishment does not produce new learning, instead, suppresses certain behaviours temporarily. Estes (1974), through his research, suggested that effects of punishment are short-lived.

Schedules of reinforcement

"Schedule of reinforcement" is the way in which rewards are given for appropriate behaviour. A "continuous reinforcement schedule" is one in which the reinforcer or reward is given after every response. Continuous reinforcement is providing a reward each time the desired behaviour occurs. It works best for establishing a conditioned operant response. However, it is very rare in everyday life for our actions to be continuously reinforced. Continuous reinforcement leads to the lowest rate of responding. Once a response has been established, however, the best way to maintain is the partial reinforcement schedule. In partial reinforcement schedule, only some of the responses are rewarded. "Partial reinforcement schedule" is a pattern of reinforcement in which reinforcement occurs intermittently. There are four main schedules of partial reinforcement and are discussed below:

1. **Fixed Ratio Schedule:** The behaviour is rewarded after it occurs a specific number of times. Every nth, like every fifth or tenth response is rewarded. A reinforcer is given after a specified number of correct responses. This schedule is best for learning a new behaviour.
2. **Variable Ratio Schedule:** A reward might be given after ten responses, sometimes after seven, still other times fifteen or

twenty and so on. A reinforcer is given after a set number of correct responses. After reinforcement, the number of correct responses, necessary for reinforcement, changes. This schedule is best for maintaining behaviour.

3. **Fixed Interval Schedule:** A reward is delivered the first time the behaviour occurs after a certain interval of time has elapsed. The first correct response after a set amount of time (for example 60 seconds) has passed is reinforced, that is a consequence is delivered. The time period required is always the same.
4. **Variable Interval Schedule:** A reward may be given after a variable time interval has passed. The first correct response after a set amount of time (for example 60 seconds) has passed is rewarded or reinforced. After the reinforcement, a new time period (shorter or longer) is set with the average equalling a specific number over a sum total of trials. Table 8.1 demonstrates various schedules of reinforcement and their outcomes.

Table 8.1 Various Schedules of Reinforcement and their outcomes

Schedule	*Outcome*
Continuous	moderate rate of response; low response to extinction
Fixed-ratio	very high rate of response; low resistance to extinction
Variable-ratio	high rate of response; high resistance to extinction
Fixed-interval	slow rate of response; low resistance to extinction
Variable-interval	steady rate of response; high resistance to extinction

Variable schedules, especially variable ratio leads to very fast rates of responding. The probability of a response has been found to decrease if it is not followed by a positive reinforcer. This phenomenon is called *experimental extinction*. No longer reinforcing a previously reinforced response, using either positive or negative reinforcement, results in the weakening of the frequency of the response. Those schedules of reinforcement associated with the best conditioning also show the most resistance to extinction. It has been found that the rats who have been trained on the variable ratio schedule kept responding in extinction (in the absence of reward or reinforcer) longer than rats on any other schedule, whereas rats trained with continuous reinforcement stop responding the soonest.

8.4.3 Classical and Operant Conditioning: A Comparison

Two forms of conditioning—classical or Pavlovian or respondent and operant or instrumental have some similarities and differences.

Similarities

Some of the major similarities are as follows:

1. In classical conditioning, the organism learns that the conditioned stimulus (CS) is the signal or sign for the occurrence of unconditioned stimulus (US or UCS) because of their temporal and spatial contiguity. Likewise, in operant or instrumental conditioning, the subject (rat or pigeon) is placed in the Skinner box, which presents a new stimulus situation, and the organism learns to press the lever. The response may be considered as an action leading to food being dropped in the pellet. The stimulus in the box and the sight of the lever may be considered as conditioned stimulus (CS). Lever pressing is a conditioned response (CR) that is followed by food on the pellet. Thus, operant conditioning has some elements of classical conditioning. In both kinds of conditioning—classical and instrumental, food is used as the reward.
2. Both forms of conditioning are examples of simple learning. In both types of conditioning same kinds of processes such as extinction, generalization, discrimination, and spontaneous recovery are observed.

The major differences between classical and instrumental conditioning are given in Table 8.2.

Table 8.2 Differences between classical and instrumental conditioning

Classical Conditioning	*Instrumental Conditioning*
1. The responses are under the control of some stimulus because they are reflexes, automatically elicited by the appropriate stimulus. Such stimuli are selected as unconditioned stimuli and responses elicited by those are known as unconditioned responses. Thus, classical conditioning in which unconditional stimulus elicits response, is often called *response conditioning*. Involuntary responses are conditioned.	The responses are under the control of organism and are voluntary or operant responses. Voluntary responses are conditioned.
2. The unconditioned and conditioned stimuli are well defined.	The conditioned stimulus is not defined. Moreover, what is called reinforcer in the operant conditioning is called *unconditioned stimulus* in instrumental conditioning.

Table 8.2 Differences between classical and instrumental conditioning (*Contd.*)

Classical Conditioning	*Instrumental Conditioning*
3. The experimenter controls the occurrence of the unconditioned stimulus. Thus, for US or UCS in classical conditioning, the organism remains passive. A passive animal is presented with various conditions and unconditioned stimuli.	The occurrence of reinforcer is under the control of the organism. The subject has to be active in order to be reinforced. Learning involves the human or animal interacting actively with the environment.
4. In both forms of conditioning, the technical terms used to characterize the experimental proceedings are different. What is called reinforcer in instrumental or operant conditioning is called *unconditioned stimulus* in classical conditioning. A US or UCS has got two functions. In the beginning, it elicits the response and reinforces the response to be associated and elicited later on by the conditioned stimulus.	What is called unconditioned stimulus in classical conditioning is called *reinforcer* in instrumental conditioning.
5. The reward is not response contingent.	The reward is response contingent.

8.5 VERBAL LEARNING

Verbal learning is different from conditioning and is limited to human beings. Verbal learning is generally the study of learning using verbal stimulus materials and verbal responses. Verbal, here is a rather inclusive, covering printed and written as well as spoken material. Human beings acquire knowledge about objects, events, and their features largely in terms of words. Words become associated with one another. Psychologists have developed a number of methods to study this kind of learning in laboratory settings. Each method is used to investigate specific questions about learning of some kind of verbal material. Psychologists use a variety of materials to study verbal learning, that is familiar words like boat, head, etc., unfamiliar words like wrack, plump, etc., sentences, paragraph, and non-sense syllables like yol, kue, etc.

8.5.1 Methods Used in Studying Verbal Learning

Paired-Associate Learning: In this method, first a list of paired words are made. The first word of the pair will be the stimulus and the second word as response, for example ben-time, kug-lion, etc. The first word member of each pair may be from the same language or two different languages. This method is used in learning of some foreign language equivalent to mother tongue words. In the above list, the first member of the pairs (stimulus word) are non-sense syllables (a consonant-vowel-consonant combination, for example ben or kug) and the second words of the list are English nouns (response words), for example time and lion. The learner is first shown both the stimulus and response pairs together, and is instructed to remember and recall the response term after the presentation of each stimulus term. After that, the learning trial begins. One by one, the stimulus words are presented and the participant tries to give the correct response term. In case of failure, the learner is shown the response word. Trials continue until the participant or the learner gives all the response words without a single error.

Serial Learning: In this method, first, a list of verbal items like familiar words, unfamiliar words, non-sense syllables, etc. is prepared. The participant or the learner is presented the entire list and required to produce the items in the same serial order as in the list. In the first trial, the first item of the list is shown, and the participant has to produce the second. If the participant or the learner fails to do so in the prescribed time, the experimenter presents the second item. Now, the second item becomes the stimulus and the participant has to produce the third item that is the response word. This procedure is called *serial anticipation method*. Learning trials continue until the participant correctly anticipates all the items in the list.

Free Recall: In this method, the participants or the learners are presented a list of words, which they read and speak out. Each word is shown at fixed periods of exposure. Immediately after the presentation of the list, the participants or the learners are required to recall the words in any order they can. Studies indicate that the items placed in the beginning (primacy effect) or in the end (recency effect) of the lists are easier to be recalled than those placed in the middle which are more difficult to learn. In cognitive psychology, the common finding that in a free recall situation, the materials that are presented first in a series or items which are towards the beginning of the list (primary items) are better recalled than those that are presented in the middle of the list. This is also called the "law of primacy" or the "principle of primacy". Whereas, the common finding that in a free recall experiment, the items that are presented towards the end of a list, that is most recent in time at the point of recall are more likely to be correctly recalled than those in the middle of the list. This is also called "law or the principle of recency". The generalization that in a free recall experiment, the likelihood of an individual item from a list being recalled is a function of the location of that item in the serial presentation of the list during learning. This is called "*serial-position effect*".

8.5.2 Determinants or Factors of Verbal Learning

Verbal learning is influenced by a number of factors. The most important ones are the length of the list or material to be learned and meaningfulness of the material. Meaningfulness of material is measured in several ways. Thus, the number of associations elicited in a fixed time, familiarity of the material and the frequency, relation among the words in the list, and sequential dependence of each word of the list on the preceding words are used for this purpose. Non-sense syllables also can be used.

The longer the list or words with low association values in the list or lack of relations in the items on the list, the more time it takes to learn the list, and stronger will be learning. In this respect, psychologists have found that the total time principle operates. This principle states that a fixed amount of time is necessary to learn a fixed amount of material, regardless of the number of trials into which that time is divided. The more time it takes to learn, the stronger becomes the learning.

If participants are not restricted to the serial learning method and are allowed to give free recall, verbal learning becomes organizational. It implies that in free recall, participants recall the words not in their order of presentation, but in a new order or sequence. Bousfield demonstrated this experimentally. He made a list of sixty words that consisted of fifteen words drawn from each of four categories that is names, animals, professionals, and vegetables. These words were presented to participants one by one in random order. The participants were required to make free recall of the word. They recalled the words of each category together. He called it "category clustering". Though, the words were presented randomly, the participants organized them categorywise in recall. Free recall is organized subjectively. Subjectively organization shows that the participants organize words or items according to their personal ways and recall accordingly.

Verbal learning is used usually intentional but a person learns some features of the words unintentionally or incidentally. In this kind of learning, participants notice features, such as whether two or more words rhyme or start with identical letters or have some same vowels, etc. Thus, verbal learning is both intentional and incidental.

8.6 SOCIAL LEARNING OR OBSERVATIONAL LEARNING OR LEARNING BY IMITATION OR MODELLING

Much of human learning is based on imitation of the behaviour of others in social situations, and this type of learning was ignored by the behaviourists. It used to be thought that all learning occurred as the result of conditioning—classical or instrumental. The words "modelling, observational, and imitative" refer to a type of learning which results from observing other people's behaviour and its consequences for them. Earlier, social learning, which is based on observing the behaviour of others, was called by the name observational learning. Because animals or human beings acquire a great deal of knowledge largely through observation—looking, listening, touching, and so forth in the course of normal activities. This fashioning of our own behaviour by observing the behaviour of others is called "observational learning". In many situations, individuals do not know how to behave. They observe others and imitate their behaviour. That is why this form of learning is called "modelling".

According to social learning theory (also known as *social cognitive theory*), we acquire a wide variety of strategies or ways or methods, outlooks, and rules about behaviour that we imitate, avoid, or modify to our advantage. We need no particular reinforcement to accumulate this information. We do so naturally in the course of cognitively processing what those around us do. Examples of social or observational learning around in our social life include people imitating the models seen on television, fashion shows, and advertisements, magazines and newspapers, observing superiors and likeable persons and imitating their behaviour in a novel or new social situation is a common experience.

In order to understand the nature of social learning, we may refer to the studies of Albert Bandura (Born on 4 December, 1925). Albert Bandura's social learning theory is one of the most popular contemporary theories of behaviour. Bandura believes that most behaviour is learned through observation. Bandura's social learning theory assumes that people are neither driven by inner forces nor molded by environmental stimuli. Instead, they are a result of the reciprocal interaction of how they behave, in the past, and the environment they are in. This is the type of learning that Bandura (1977) believes accounts for our ability to acquire large integrated patterns of

Albert Bandura
(Born in 1925)

behaviour without having to go through the ritual of trial and error. In fact, Bandura believes that most behaviour is learned through observation not from actually performing the behaviour and then experiencing its consequences.

In one of his well-known experimental study, Bandura (1977), showed a film of five minutes duration to children. The film shows that in a large room, there were numerous toys including a large size doll. Now, a grown up boy enters the room and looks around. The boy starts showing aggressive behaviour towards the toys in general and the large size doll in particular. He hits the doll, throws the doll on the floor, and stamps it, sitting on it. After this, the film had three versions. The first version—a group of children saw a boy (model) being rewarded and praised for being aggressive to the doll by an adult. The second version—another group of children saw he was punished for aggressiveness. The third version—a group of children were not shown the boy being rewarded or punished.

After viewing a specific version of film, all the three groups of children were placed in an experimental room in which similar toys placed around, the children were allowed to play with toys. These groups were secretly observed and their behaviours were noted. It was found that those children having seen the aggressive behaviour being rewarded were most aggressive. Viewers who had seen the aggressive model being punished were least aggressive. So, consequences determine the fate of behaviour.

It may be noted that all the three groups had acquired the knowledge of aggressive behaviour and could produce the models of aggressive behaviour. Thus, in observational learning, observers acquire knowledge by observing model's behaviour, but performance is influenced by model's behaviour being rewarded or punished. Children observed adults' behaviour at home and during social ceremonies and functions. They exact adults in their games and play. Actually, they exact in their game what they observe in the society, in television, or by reading.

Children learn most of the social behaviour by observing and imitating others. Their ways to put on dress, hairstyle, and conduct oneself in society is learned through the observation of others. It has been shown that children learn and develop personality characteristics through observational learning like aggressiveness, politeness, etc. Obviously, we learn different things from different models. Moreover, some models are more effective in initiating observational learning than others.

According to Bandura (1977), the following steps are usually employed in social or observational learning:

1. Attending to and perceiving the behaviour of the model.
2. Remembering the behaviour.
3. Converting the memory into action.
4. Reinforcement of the imitated behaviour.

We are influenced, Bandura (1986) says, not only by the consequences of our behaviour but also by the consequences we see other people experiencing. Bandura called such "second hand" consequences acquired or learnt by vicarious reinforcement and punishment, and he points out that they have important effects on our behaviour. You are more likely to imitate a person or model that is being reinforced for her or his acts, than a model that is being punished. This type of learning is referred to as "vicarious". The "thinking" aspect of the person plays an important role in Bandura's social learning theory. Your perception is also influenced by your thinking. Thinking obviously influences behaviour.

In addition, Bandura stresses the importance of intrinsic reinforcement and punishment. By this, he means that our actions are regulated not just by the environmental consequences we observe but other creatures as well. People are motivated by internal factors such as curiosity or desire to feel competent. We measure our performance against our internalized standards of behaviour. If we exceed our own standards, we feel self-esteem, a powerful form of reinforcement. If we fall short, we feel self-reproach, a perfect form of punishment. But to Bandura, none of these various forms of reward and punishment is essential for learning to occur. For, learning is a change in acquired information and hence in performance potential that can be acquired just by virtue of being an observer in the world. Social learning was also studied by Rosekrans and Hartup (1967) showing the power of social learning.

8.7 CONCEPT LEARNING

A concept is a category that is used to refer to a number of objects and events. A concept is a name expressed in the words often, only in one word. Examples of concepts of categories are apple, cow, fan, etc. A concept may be used interchangeably with the word "category". A concept is defined as "A set of features or attributes or characteristics connected by some rule." Concepts are those objects, events, or behaviour, which have common feature or features. A "feature" is any characteristic or aspect of an object, event, or living organism that is observed in them and can be considered equivalent to some features observed or discriminated in other objects. Discrimination of features depends upon the degree of the observer's perceptual sensitivity. Properties as colour, size, number, shape, smoothness, texture, roughness, and softness are called *features*.

Rules that are used to connect the features to form a concept may be simple or complex. A rule is an instruction to do something. Psychologists have studied two types of concepts: natural and artificial concepts.

"Artificial concepts" are the concepts which are well defined and the rules connecting the features are rigid and precise. In a well-defined concept, the features that represent the concept are both singly necessary and jointly sufficient. Every object must have the entire features in order to become an instance of the concept. On the other hand, "natural concepts" or categories are usually ill-defined. Numerous features are found in the instances of the natural concepts or category. Such concepts include biological objects, real-world products, human artifacts such as tools, clothes, houses, etc.

The concept of a square is well-defind concept. It must have four attributes that is closed figure, four sides, and each side of equal length, and equal angle. Thus, square consists of these four features connected by rule. The features that are not included in the rule are considered irrelevant features.

8.8 FACTORS OF LEARNING OR VARIABLES INFLUENCING LEARNING

(I) Individual or organismic or physiological factors (factors associated with the learner)

Learning is self-initiated. Whatever change takes place within the supposed learner, however, depends upon what he does to bring about the change.

1. **Age:** Youth is the golden period for learning.
2. **Health:** The process of learning is greatly affected by the physical and mental health of the learner. Sickness of any kind can affect the rate of learning adversely. A tense, worried, emotionally excited, and mentally disturbed learner cannot show satisfactory progress and results in learning.

   Other physiological conditions such as hunger, thirst, etc. also affect learning adversely.
3. **Maturation:** Maturation is closely linked with the results and process of learning. According to Biggie and Hunt, "Maturation is a developmental process within which a person, from time to time, manifests different traits, the "blue-prints" of which have been carried in his cells from the time of his conception." For any kind of learning to take place, the learner has to be mature enough for that learning. For example, an infant of three months cannot learn or cannot be taught speech.
4. **Ability:** Learner's innate abilities, potentials, capabilities, and capacities for learning in terms of intelligence affect the rate and amount of learning.
5. **Motivation:** Motivation and adequate and reasonable level of aspiration plays an important role in learning. Learning is a modification of behaviour accompanying growth processes that

are brought about through adjustment to tensions initiated through sensory stimulation. All learning situations place the learner under stress that is the need for doing something about the situation or the necessity of resolving motivational conflicts. It further implies that the learner's habits of possibilities for action are inadequate to relieve these tensions except through adaptation or modification of behaviour.

6. **Interest:** Learner's interest is an important factor in learning. An individual puts in extra and special efforts in the tasks which she or he finds interesting even if the task is difficult.
7. **Goals:** Goals of one's life affect learning. Goals affect an individual's inclination and persistence in learning a task. Goals must match with the capacities, abilities, aptitudes, personality, etc. of the person. Repeated failures to reach the unachievable goals can result in lowered level of aspiration and also affect the physical as well as psychological well-being of the person, which further can play havoc with the personality of the person.
8. **Mental Set:** Mental set is an essential factor for learning. "Mental set" refers to the readiness to learn. Set arouses, sustains, and regulates the pattern of activity in an individual and leads to better attention, concentration, zeal, interest, attitude, motivation and hence better, effective, and productive learning. The attentive listener shuts out all distractions.
9. **Fatigue:** Fatigue affects the rate and amount of learning. "Fatigue" is an internal state or condition that results from extended effort and underlies the diminished capacity to perform. Fatigue causes a feeling of tiredness and weariness. Fatigue can be of different types. "Sensory fatigue" refers to the reduced responsiveness of a sense organ following prolonged exposure to stimulation. "Muscle fatigue" refers to the reduced capacity of muscle tissue to contract owing to a build-up of metabolic waste products such as lactic acid. Muscle and sensory fatigue are conveniently designated as bodily or physiological fatigue. "Neural or neuronal fatigue" is a heightened threshold of nerve fibres caused by previous neural activity. Neural or mental fatigue is generally referred to the central nervous system. "Mental fatigue" refers to a cognitive tired stemming from either extended mental concentration or boredom. "Emotional fatigue" is the general debilitated state resulting from excessive stress, conflicts, frustrations, anxieties, etc.
10. **Significance of the Task:** If the learner perceives the task to be learnt to be of significance, the learner feels enthusiastic to go ahead with the task.

11. **Drugs:** Excessive, improper, irresponsible, and self-damaging use of drugs results in severe physiological dysfunctions and affects all cognitive processes adversely, including learning.

(II) Task factors or variables (factors associated with the differences in tasks)

1. **Length of Material:** Length of the material or the task to be learnt determines the amount and rate of learning.
2. **Nature of Learning Material:** If the learning material is of easy nature, then it is learned quickly whereby difficult tasks take some time to be learned. Besides this, the serial position of material, shape, and meaningfulness also affect learning familiarity of the material influence learning.
3. **Difficulty Level:** Difficulty level of the material to be learnt also affects the learning. Krueger (1946) found that with easy material, learning is rapid at first and much slower in later trials. With difficult material, learning tends to be slower in the beginning and more rapid in later stages.
4. **Meaningfulness of the Material:** Learning of meaningful material is easy and economical in terms of trials needed to learn it. Learning for meaningless material or non-sense syllables is difficult. Guilford (1934) demonstrated this experimentally.
5. **Method or Methodology of Learning:** Learning depends upon the methods and techniques employed. Distributed practice yields greater learning and retention than massed practice. In "massed practice", the entire amount of time for learning involves one trial. When practice takes place over several time intervals, it is called "distributed practice".

With a reasonable length, whole method yields better results than the part method. When the material is too long or meaningless or nonverbal, the part method has proved most fruitful.

(III) Revision and practice

Revision and practice brings good results in terms of retention, reproduction, and utilization of the learnt material.

(IV) Knowledge of results

Knowledge of results facilitates learning. "Knowledge of results" refers to any feedback of information given to an individual about the correctness of her or his responses or in a learning situation about success or failure in mastering material. Knowledge of results acts as a powerful reinforcer.

(V) Learning situation

Socio-emotional climate like teacher-pupil relationship, pupil-pupil relationship, college-staff relationship, quality of the teacher, teaching skills, availability of appropriate learning material and facilities like books, audio-visual aids, etc. all affect the amount, rate, and quality of learning.

EXERCISES

The below mentioned are some of the questions that have been asked in the examinations conducted by the Guru Nanak Dev University or can be asked. Knowledge of these answers can help the students to get success in the examinations.

Section A

Answers the following questions in **five** lines or 50 words.

1. Explain learning.*
2. What is potent learning?
3. What is latent learning?
4. What is vertical learning?
5. What is horizontal learning?
6. What is conditioning?*
7. What is extinction?
8. Define spontaneous recovery.
9. What is generalization?
10. What are reinforcers?*
11. What is punishment?
12. What is law of exercise?*
13. Define trial and error learning.*
14. Define learning by insight.
15. What is verbal learning?
16. What is social learning?
17. What is concept learning?
18. What is stimulus generalization?*
19. Define the fixed-interval schedule.
20. What is variable-ratio schedule?*
21. Define concepts.*
22. What is conditioned response?
23. What is fixed interval schedule?
24. Explain spontaneous recovery.
25. Define primary reinforcers.

26. Explain negative reinforcement.
27. What is classical conditioning?
28. What is operant conditioning?
29. What is conditioned stimulus?
30. What is Artificial concepts?
31. Define learning. What are its characteristics?
32. What is aversive conditioning?
33. Define learning and age.
34. Define reinforcement.
35. Define serial learning.
36. Define maze learning.
37. What is the laws of learning?
38. Define Aha! Reaction or Experience.*
39. Distinguish between classical and instrumental conditioning.*

Section B

Answer the following questions up to **two** pages or 500 words.

1. What is learning?
2. What are schedules of reinforcement?
3. How does delay affect operant conditioning?
4. When is the use of continuous reinforcement desirable?
5. What is observational learning?
6. What is classical conditioning?
7. Upon what factors does acquisition of a classically conditioned response depend?
8. What is extinction?
9. What is the difference between stimulus generalization and stimulus discrimination?
10. What is operant conditioning?
11. How do negative reinforcement and punishment differ?

    or

    Differentiate between negative reinforcement and punishment?
12. What is conditioning? Explain with the help of an experiment.
13. What is the difference between "trial and error" and "insight"?
14. What are the differences between classical and instrumental conditioning?
15. Write about various schedules of reinforcement.*
16. Explain trial and error learning.

17. Write various laws of learning.
18. What is learning by insight? Explain with the help of an experiment.

    or

    Explain Insight Learning Theory.
19. Define conditioning. Differentiate between classical and instrumental conditioning?*
20. Describe the process of concept formation.
21. What is learning? Discuss the different laws of learning.
22. Describe trial and error learning.
23. With suitable experimental evidence, explain insight learning.
24. What is punishment and to what extent is it useful and effective?
25. Explain the process of concept learning.
26. Define learning? Give its characteristics.
27. Define concepts. Give their types.
28. Describe the laws of learning.*
29. Define learning. Explain one of the following methods of learning:

    Trial and Error, Insight, Conditioning.
30. Write a note on different types of concepts.
31. What is conditioning? What are the differences between classical and instrumental conditioning?
32. What is operant conditioning?
33. Write a note on social learning.*
34. Explain Insight Learning Theory.
35. Write brief note on concept learning.
36. Explain paradigm of classical conditioning with the help of an experiment.
37. Define verbal learning. Give its factors.*
38. Discuss the role of reinforcement in instrumental conditioning.

Section C

Answers the following questions up to **five** pages or 1000 words:

1. What is classical conditioning? What are some of the main phenomena of classical conditioning?*
2. What is instrumental learning? What are some of the ways in which it has been applied in the real world?
3. What is conditioning? Examine the contribution of Pavlov and Skinner to learning?

4. Define learning. Distinguish between learning by insight and trial and error learning.
5. Define learning operationally and describe the various processes of learning.
6. Explain the law of exercise and the law of effect in learning.
7. Discuss the role of reinforcement in instrumental conditioning.*
8. Discuss different types of schedules of reinforcement.
9. Define conditioning. Explain the main features of classical conditioning.
10. What are various types of learning? What are the merits and demerits of any one of the following methods:

    Trial and Error, Insight, Conditioning.
11. What is learning? Discuss verbal learning.
12. "Association is the key element in classical conditioning." Illustrate with the help of an experiment.*
13. What is the trial and error learning?
14. Explain Trial and Error Learning Theory with the help of experiment.*

REFERENCES

Bandura, A., 'Self-efficacy: Toward a Unifying Theory of Behavioural Change,' *Psychological Review,* **84** (2), 191–215. 1977a.

Bandura, A., *Social Learning Theory,* Englewood Cliffs, NJ: Prentice-Hall, 1977b.

Bandura, A., *Social Foundations of Thought and Action,* Englewood Cliffs, NJ: Prentice-Hall, 1986.

Baron, R.A., *Psychology*, New Delhi: Pearson Education, Asia (Singapore), 1995.

Biggie, M.L. and Hunt, M.P., *Psychological Foundations of Education,* New York: Harper and Row, 1968.

Bootzin, R., Bower, Crooker and Hall, *Psychology Today*, New York: McGraw-Hill, INC, 1991.

Bousfield, W.A., Whitmarsh, G.A., and Danick, J.J., 'Partial Response Identities in Verbal Generalization,' *Psychological Reports,* **4**, 703–713, 1958.

Crooks, R.L. and Stein, J., *Psychology, Science, Behaviour and Life*, London: Halt, Rinehart and Winston, INC., 1991.

Crow, L.D. and Crow, A., *Educational Psychology* (3rd Indian Reprint), New Delhi: Eurasia Publishing House, 1973.

Dollard, J., Doob, L., Miller, N., Mowrer, O.H., and Sears, R.R., *Frustration and Aggression,* New Haven, CT: Yale University Press, 1939.

Dollard, J. and Miller, N.E., *Personality and Psychotherapy: An Analysis in Terms of Learning, Thinking and Culture,* New York: McGraw-Hill, 1950.

Drever, J., *Instincts in Man,* Cambridge: Cambridge University Press, 1917.

Drever, J., *A Dictionary of Psychology*, Middlesex: Penguin Books, 1952.

Estes, W.K., 'Learning Theory and Intelligence,' *American Psychologist,* **29**, 740–749. 1974.

Gordon, W.C., *Learning and Memory,* Belmont, CA: Brooks/Cole Publishing Company, 1989.

Guilford, J.P., *Fields of Psychology*, New York: Van Nostrand, 1966.

Guthrie, E.R., 'Association and the Law of Effect,' *Psychological Review,* **47**, 127–148, 1940.

Hilgard, E.R., Atkinson, R.C. and Atkinson, R.L., *Introduction to Psychology*, New York: Hart Court Brace Jovanovich, INC, 1975.

Hull, C.L., *Principles of Behavior,* New York: Appleton-Century-Crofts, 1943.

Hull, C.L., *Essentials of Behavior*, New Haven: Yale University Press, 1951.

Hull, C.L., *A Behavior System,* New Haven: Yale University Press, 1952.

Kimble, G.A., *Hilgard and Marquis' Conditioning and Learning*, New York: Appleton-Century-Crofts, 1961.

Kimble, G.A., Germazy, N., and Zigler, E., *Principles of Psychology*, 6th ed., New York: Wiley, 1984.

Kohler, W., *The Mentality of Apes*, New York: Harcourt, 1925.

Mangal, S.K., *Advanced Educational Psychology*, 2nd ed., New Delhi: Prentice-Hall of India, 2002.

McDougall, W.G., *An Outline of Psychology*, 13th ed., London: Methuen, 1949.

Miller, G.A., 'The Magical Number Seven, Plus or Minus Two: Some Limits on our Capacity for Processing Information,' *Psychological Review,* **63**, 81–97, 1956.

Morgan, C.T. and King, R.A., *Introduction to Psychology*, New York: McGraw Hill Book Co., 1978.

Morris, C.G., *Psychology* (3rd ed.), Englewood Cliffs, New Jersey: Prentice Hall, 1979.

Pavlov, I.P., 'The Scientific Investigation of The Psychical Faculties or Processes in the Higher Animals,' *Science,* **24**, 613–619, 1906.

Pavlov, I.P., *Conditioned Reflexes*, London: Oxford University Press, 1927.

Postman and Egan, J.P., *Experimental Psychology: An Introduction*, New York: Harper & Row, 1949.

Rosekrans, M.A. and Hartup, W.W., 'Imitative Influences of Consistent and Inconsistent Response Consequences to a Model on Aggressive Behavior in Children,' *Journal of Personality and Social Psychology*, **7**, 429–434. 1967.

Skinner, B.F., *Walden Two*, New York: Macmillan, 1948.

Skinner, B.F., 'Are Theories of Learning Necessary?' *Psychological Review,* **57**, 193–216. 1950.

Skinner, B.F., *Science and Human Behaviour*, New York: Macmillan, 1953.

Skinner, B.F., *About Behaviorism*, New York: Knopf, 1974.

Skinner, B.F., 'Can Psychology be a Science of Mind?' *American Psychologist,* 1990.

Thorndike, E.L. 'Animal Intelligence: An Experimental Study of Associative Processes in Animals.' *The Psychological Review Monograph Supplements*, **2**, 4–160. 1898.

Thorndike, E.L., *Animal Intelligence: Experimental Studies,* New York: Macmillan, 1911.

Thorndike, E.L., *Educational Psychology* (Vol. II), *The Psychology of Learning*, New York: Teachers College, Columbia University, 1913.

Thorndike, E.L., *Educational Psychology (Briefer Course),* New York: Columbia University, 1914.

Thorndike, E.L., *Human Learning*, New York: Cornell University, 1931.

Thorndike, E.L., 'Reward and Punishment in Animal Learning,' *Comparative Psychology Monographs,* **8**, (4, Whole No. 39), 1932.

Thorndike, E.L., *Human Learning*, New York: Holt, 1965.

Tolman, E.C., *Purposive Behaviour in Animals and Men*, New York: Appleton-Century-Crofts, 1932.

Tolman, E.C., 'The Determiners of Behavior at a Choice Point,' *Psychological Review,* **45**, 1–41, 1938.

Underwood, B.J., *Experimental Psychology*, New York: Appleton, 1966.

Watson, J.B., *Psychology from the Stand-point of a Behaviourist*, Philadelphia: Lippincott, 1919.

Watson, J.B., *Behaviourism*, London: Kegan Paul, 1930.

Watson, J.B., *Behaviourism*, New York: Norton, 1970.

Watson, J.B., and Rayner, R., 'Conditioned Emotional Reactions,' *Journal of Experimental Psychology,* **3**, 1–14, 1920.

Wertheimer, M., 'Psychomotor Co-ordination of Auditory-visual Space at Birth,' *Science,* **134**, 1692, 1962.

Wertheimer, M., *A Brief History of Psychology*, New York: Holt, Rinehart and Winston, 1970.

Woodworth, R.S., *Psychology*, London: Methuen, 1945.

Woodworth, R.S., *Experimental Psychology*, New York: Holt, 1954.

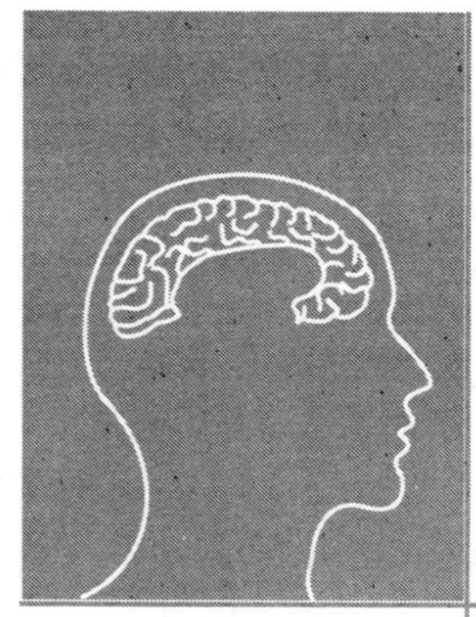

CHAPTER 9
Introduction to Memory

Memory is a subject that has been of interest for thousands of years. Memory is our cognitive storage system (or systems) in the brain or mind for storing and retrieving information. It is truly a crucial aspect of our cognition. If we did not possess memory, we would be unable to remember the past, retain new information, and solve problems or plan for future. We use memory for a large number of purposes. We are able to benefit from our learning and experience only because of our memory.

Memory involves storing information over time. Memory is very closely related to learning. Learning is very essential for the survival, development, and progress of human race. Whereas, learning is the process of acquiring new information or skills, memory is the retention of what you have learned as well as retrieval for future reference or use (Squire, 1995). Learning and memory, therefore, work together. You cannot really learn if you are unable to remember, and unless you acquire new data (that is, learn it); you have nothing for memory to store. "Memory" refers to the mental function of retaining information about stimuli, events, images, ideas, etc. after the original stimuli are no longer present. "Memory" may be defined as the retaining, recalling or reproduction of past events, impressions, and experiences without the presence of actual stimulus. The power that we have to "store" our experiences, and to bring them into the field of our consciousness sometime after the experiences have occurred, is termed "memory" (Ryburn, 1956).

9.1 SOME DEFINITIONS OF MEMORY

According to C.G. Morris, "Memory is a process by which learned material is retained."

According to Woodworth and Schlosberg, "Memory is the ability for doing it over again for what one has learnt to do."

According to Hilgard and Atkinson, "To remember means to show in present response some sign of earlier learned responses."

According to H.J. Eysenck, "Memory is the ability of an organism to store information, from earlier learned responses, experience, and retention and reproduce that information in answer to specific stimuli."

According to Lefton (1985), "Memory is the ability to recall or remember past events or previously learned information or skills."

According to Bootzin (1991), "Memory is the cognitive process of preserving current information for later use."

According to Crooks and Stein (1991), "The term memory has a dual meaning. It refers to the process or processes whereby we store and preserve newly acquired information for later recall." Here, the term memory describes either putting information into storage or pulling it back into conscious awareness.

According to Baron (1995), "Memory is the capacity to retain and later retrieve information."

The following are the general characteristics of human memory:

1. Human memory is active, rather than passive. Our memory does not record an event as accurately as a video recorder; instead, memory actively blends that event with other relevant information. For example, a memory of an event ten years old may be influenced by stories you have heard from other family members.
2. Human memory is a complex process involving factors like learning, retention, recall, and recognition.
3. Human memory is highly organized. The more organized the information or material in memory, the better we are able to remember it.
4. Memory accuracy depends upon how we encode material. For example, we will remember the definition for encoding if we think about its meaning; we will simply forget that definition if we simply glance at it.
5. Memory accuracy depends upon how we measure retrieval. It has been noticed that people's scores on multiple-choice test are higher than on a fill-in-the-blank test.

Recognizing the central role of memory, psychologists have studied it systematically for more than one hundred years. The ultimate goal of memory research is to produce theoretical accounts of memory which are of practical use. In fact, memory was the focus of some of the earliest research in Psychology—studies conducted by Hermann Ebbinghaus (24 January 1850–26 February 1909), a German psychologist, in the late nineteenth century. The credit for the first systematic experimental study of memory goes to Hermann Ebbinghaus (1885), who devised 23,000 nonsense syllables. In 1885, he published his first book on memory. Using himself as a subject, Ebbinghaus memorized and recalled hundreds of nonsense syllables—meaningless combination of letters, such teg or bom (consonant-vowel-consonant). Some of his findings about the nature of memory and forgetting have stood the test of time and are valid even today. He found that, at first we forget materials we have memorized quite rapidly but that later, forgetting proceeds more slowly. He was the first to plot a forgetting curve which shows the rate at which humans are able to retain lists of nonsense syllables after various intervals of time. And he found that distributed practice, in which we spread out our efforts to memorize materials over time, is often superior to massed practice, in which we attempt to do all our memorizing at once.

Hermann–Ebbinghaus
(1850–1909)

Criticism of Ebbinghaus' experiments:

(i) Ebbinghaus was both the subject and the experimenter of his experiments. His findings are said to be fallacious, unscientific, and biased.

(ii) Materials and methods used by Ebbinghaus could only be utilized by literate and educated persons and not by illiterates, animals, and children.

(iii) Recall method used by Ebbinghaus has least strength in measuring memory in comparison to other methods like recognition, relearning, and reconstruction. If one does not recall a material, it does not mean that she or he has forgotten it. It might have been repressed.

9.2 THE PROCESS OF MEMORIZING OR THE THREE STAGES OF MEMORY—ENCODING, STORAGE, AND RETRIEVAL

The information can be stored for less than a second or as long as your lifetime. For example, you use memory when you must store the beginning of a word (perhaps "mem"-) until you hear the end of the word (-ory). We also use memory when we recall the name of our favourite childhood teacher. Memory requires or involves three stages: Encoding, Storage, and Retrieval. Encoding, the first stage, includes the processes occurring at the time of learning. During *encoding*, we transfer sensory stimuli or the information coming to our senses into a form that can be placed in memory. During *storage*, the second stage, some of the information presented for learning is stored away in a long-term store, and we hold the information in memory for later use—perhaps less than a second, perhaps fifty years. During *retrieval*, the third stage, we successfully retrieve information or locate the item and use it. These three stages are closely linked together. To retrieve the information is necessary to store it previously.

Atkinson and Shiffrin (1968) proposed a highly influential model of memory, sometimes known as *Modal Model of Memory*. These researchers noted that human memory must accomplish three basic tasks:

9.2.1 Encoding

Encoding is converting information into a form that can be entered into memory. When you place information into memory, you often elaborate or transform it in some way. This elaboration process is part of what is called "encoding". "Encoding" is the act of converting sensory stimuli into a form that can be placed into memory, often using old information to analyze or manipulate the data. The methods we use to carry out this process such as naming objects or mentally picturing words or vivid imagery are called "encoding strategies".

Effortful encoding is an active process and involves willful or voluntary or deliberate attempt to put something into memory. We deliberately tried to encode the details of an event; we actively worked to place into short-term memory. A second kind of encoding, that is also very common, is automatic encoding; a kind of encoding that seems to happen with no deliberate effort. It is as if our memory just soaks up this kind of data with no conscious effort. Researchers have found that information about our location in mind and space and how often we experience different kinds of stimuli are among the things we typically encode automatically (Hasher and Zacks, 1984). Through practice, one can learn to encode other kinds of data automatically.

9.2.2 Storage

"Storage" means somehow retaining information over varying periods of time. Storage is a synonym of memory. Once information has been attended to and encoded, it must be kept active in short-term memory in order to be retained. Information entering short-term memory is lost rather quickly unless it is renewed through rehearsal.

Rehearsal usually involves some kind of speech either overt or covert as when you repeat a telephone number aloud or implicit, when you repeat a number mentally. Rehearsal, in other words, often maintains things phonetically: it is sounds of the words that are repeated and stored, (Baddeley, 1982).

Studies suggest that no more than half a minute new information stays in short-term memory (Brown, 1958; Peterson and Peterson, 1959). The exact duration depends on the amount of rehearsal they are able to squeeze in.

Other factors also affect the duration of short-term memory. Its duration depends on the degree to which new information or new material happens to be associated with the information held in long-term storage. On addition, the duration of short-term memory is affected by whether or not a person is motivated to remember.

In 1956, George Armitage Miller published a paper titled "*The magical number seven, plus or minus two*". In it, he summarized the results of many experiments, all of which indicated that a majority of people can hold only between 5 to 9 items in short-term memory at any one time. Most psychologists agree that the capacity of short-term memory is very near this range. We expand our limited capacity by chunking information. We see group of letters as word (small chunks), group of words as phrases (larger chunks), and series of phrases as sentences (even larger chunks). Short-term memory can hold about seven chunks, but each chunk may contain a great deal of information. Chunk is a familiar unit of information based on previous learning. "Chunking" is a term suggested by George A. Miller for the organization process whereby distinct "bits" of information are collected together perceptually and cognitively into larger, coordinated wholes, or "chunks". It means grouping pieces of data into units.

George Armitage Miller
(Born on 3 Feb., 1920)

Working memory is generally considered to have limited capacity. The earliest quantification of the capacity limit associated with short-term memory was the "magical number seven" introduced by Miller in 1956 (Hulme, Roodenrys, Brown, and Mercer, 1995). He noticed that the memory span of young adults was around seven elements, called *chunks*, regardless whether the elements were digits, letters, words, or other units.

Later research revealed that span does depend on the category of chunks used (for example, span is around seven for digits, around six for letters, and around 5 for words), and even on features of the *chunks* within a category. For instance, span is lower for long than for short words. In general, memory span for verbal contents (digits, letters, words, etc.) strongly depends on the time it takes to speak the contents aloud, and on the lexical status of the contents (that is whether the contents are words known to the person or not) (Cowan, 2001). Several other factors also affect a person's measured span, and therefore it is difficult to pin down the capacity of short-term or working memory to a number of chunks. Nonetheless, Cowan (2001) has proposed that working memory has a capacity of about four chunks in young adults (and less in children and old adults).

Long-term storage/storage in long-term memory

The way information enters the long-term memory is not completely understood. The process depends partly on the amount of time we rehearse things; the longer the rehearsal, the more likely is long-term storage. But even more important is the type of rehearsal. If we simply repeat something to ourselves without giving it thought (as when we rehearsal a telephone number), that information seldom becomes part of our long-term knowledge. In contrast, if we take a new piece of information and mentally do something with it, form an image of it, apply it to a problem, relate it to other things—it is more likely to be deposited in long-term storage. These different approaches can be described as shallow processing or mere maintenance rehearsal versus deep processing or elaborative rehearsal (Craik and Lockhart, 1972). "Maintenance rehearsal" involves a repetition of processes which have already been carried out (for example, simply repeating a word over and over again). On the other hand, "elaborative rehearsal" involves deeper processing of the stimulus material that is to be learned. The hypothalamus is a structure in the brain thought to be involved in the maintenance rehearsal or shallow processing of information. Emphasizing the meaning of a stimulus is especially conducive to deep processing.

9.2.3 Retrieval

"Retrieval" means locating and accessing information when it is needed at later times. It is the process or processes involved in remembering or gaining access to information stored in long-term memory. A good memory must reflect "an ideal revival" as Stout (1938) said "So far as ideal revival is merely reproduction.... . This productive aspect of ideal revival requires the object of past experiences to be re-instated as far possible in the order and manner of their original occurrence." Psychologists have studied two basic kinds of retrieval from long-term storage—recognition and recall (Brown, 1968).

"Recognition" involves deciding whether you have ever encountered a particular stimulus before or the awareness that an object or event is one that has been previously seen, experienced, or learned. Recognition is little more than a matching process. When asked if we recognize something, we consider its features and decide if they match those of a stimulus that is already stored in memory. In doing so, we tend to evaluate not the object as a whole, but rather its various parts (Adams, 1987). If all the parts match, the object is quickly recognized. If, however, some of the parts match while others do not, we are left with the feeling of only vague familiarity.

"Recall", in contrast, is the process of retrieving information from memory. It is an experimental procedure for investigating memorial processes whereby the subject must reproduce material previously learned. It entails retrieving specific pieces of information, usually guided by retrieval cues. Recall involves more mental operations than recognition does. When we try to recall something, we must first search through long-term memory to find the appropriate information. Then we must determine, as in recognition, whether the information we have come up with matches with the correct response. If we think it does, we give the answer, if we think it does not, we search again. Recall can be free recall or cued recall. In "free recall", you would be asked to say or recite or write down as many of the words of the list as you could remember in any order. In "cued recall", you might be given the first few letters of each word and asked to think of the appropriate list word (for example, mou... as a cue for the word mouth). Retrieval cues are especially important to the success of search components of recall.

9.3 TYPES OF MEMORY

The below discussed three types of memory—sensory memory, short-term memory, and long-term memory differ in terms of how long information or material is stored in them, in their storage capacity, and in terms of the way in which information is forgotten.

9.3.1 Sensory or Immediate Memory or Sensory Register or Sensory Stores

Sensory memory provides temporary storage of information brought to us by our senses. Information coming to our senses first enters the sensory memory, which is a storage system that records information from the senses with reasonable accuracy for a brief or small period of time. It can hold a large number of items, but each item fades away quickly—in less than two seconds.

Sensory memory or sensory register has two major purposes:

(i) We need to keep an accurate record of physical stimulus for a brief time while we select the most important stimuli for the further processing.
(ii) The stimuli that are bombarding your senses are constantly and rapidly changing.

Sensory memory is affiliated with the transduction of energy (change from one energy form to another). The environment makes available a variety of sources of information like light, sound, smell, heat, cold, etc., but the brain only understands electrical energy. The sense organs receive information from the senses and transform it to a form that can be received and understood by the brain. In the process of transduction, a memory is created. This memory is very short (less than half second for vision and about three seconds for hearing).

For the information to be transferred to the next level, that is short-term memory store, it is important that the information in the sensory memory store is attended to. Individuals are more likely to pay attention to a stimulus or information if it has an interesting feature. Second, individuals are more likely to pay attention if the stimulus activates a known pattern.

9.3.2 Short-Term and Long-Term Memory

William James (1842–1910), an American psychologist and philosopher at Harvard University, brother of the novelist Henry James, argued that we should distinguish two kinds of memory which he referred to as primary memory (is basically the psychological present, and consists of what is currently happening or what has just happened) and secondary memory (relates to the psychological past, recollection of events which may have happened days, weeks, or even years ago).

Richard C. Atkinson
(Born in 1929)

Richard M. Shiffrin

Richard C. Atkinson (Born in March, 1929) has had a long and distinguished career as an educator, administrator, and scientist. Richard C. Atkinson and Richard M. Shiffrin (an American psychologist) in 1968 distinguished between short-term (primary memory) and long-term (secondary memory) in their stage model of information processing or the multi-store model of memory or the stage theory or the multi-store approach. This model is widely accepted and the focus of this model is on how information is stored in memory.

Short-Term Memory (STM)

Short-term memory is also called "working memory" and relates to what we are thinking about at any given moment in time (Alan Baddeley and Graham Hitch, 1974). In Freudian terms, this is "conscious memory". Short-term memory may be thought of as a stage of conscious activity. STM contains only the small amount of material we are currently using. The name, working memory, for short-term memory is appropriate because it handles the material we are currently or presently working with, rather than the items that were unattended in sensory memory or the items stored away in the long-term memory (Baddeley 1986, 1990, 1992). The frontal lobes of the cerebral cortex are the structure associated with working memory. According to George Armitage Miller (1956), the capacity of short-term memory store is approximately seven items. According to him, an item is a chunk. Miller (1956) gave the number as 7 ± 2, but more recent research suggests the number may be more like 5 ± 2 for most things we are trying to remember. State-anxiety lowers the short-term memory ability.

Memories in short-term memory store are reasonably fragile (temporary) and they can be lost from within about thirty seconds unless they are somehow repeated or rehearsed. Organization and repetition play an important role in retaining information in short-term memory store. This is the memory system you use when you look up a telephone number and dial it. Short-term memory contains small amount of material for a brief period of time.

Atkinson and Shiffrin (1968) argued that information from the environment is initially received by sensory registers or modality-specific stores. Each of the senses can be regarded as a separate "modality". They suggested that we could have sensory memory or sensory register for all the senses—vision, hearing, smell, taste, and skin senses. However, researches have primarily concentrated on vision and hearing. Visual stimuli or information go to a special visual store (the iconic store), auditory stimuli or information go to a special auditory store (the echoic store), and so on for each of the senses. In short-term store, the information is selected and attended to and processed. The information that is not selected and attended to, simply fades away or decays rapidly.

Information from short-term memory or store goes to long-term memory or store through a process of rehearsal.

Long-Term Memory (LTM)

Long-term memory is also called "permanent memory". In Freudian terms, it is called *pre-conscious* and *unconscious memory*. "Pre-conscious" means that the information is relatively easily recalled with little effort. According to Atkinson and Shiffrin model, some information passes from short-term memory to long-term memory. Long-term memory has unlimited capacity. It allows us to retain vast or huge amounts of information for very long periods of time. It stores memories that are decades old, as well as memories that arrived a few minutes ago. Long-term memory contains a huge amount of very diverse information. These memories are also much more permanent than those that are in the sensory memory and short-term memory. And it is the long-term memory that allows us to remember factual information such as the capital of our country. Organization plays an important role in memory. Organization can make it easier to retrieve information (De Groot, 1966; Pearlstone, 1966). The effects of organization on memory occur because learners use their knowledge to make sense of the to-be-learned material. Material from the long-term memory is recalled category by category. The way in which presented information is structured and organized by the knowledge stored in long-term memory is called "categorical clustering".

According to Atkinson and Shiffrin (1968), the long-term memory storage of information usually depends on the amount of rehearsal; the greater the amount of rehearsal of to-be-learned material or information, the better that long-term memory becomes. Multi-store model of Atkinson and Shiffrin (1968) claims that all rehearsal leads to long-term memory; maintenance rehearsal usually leads to improved long-term memory. Whereas, Gus Craik and Robert Lockhart (1972), proponents of levels-of-processing theory, claims that elaborative rehearsal benefits or improves long-term memory, but maintenance rehearsal or rote rehearsal does not. The two processes most likely to move information into long-term memory are elaboration and distributed practice. Elaboration was important to memory. "Elaboration" refers to the amount of information that is processed at a particular level. Evidence for the importance of elaboration was reported by Craik and Tulving (1975). Imaging, method of loci, peg word method, rhyming, initial letter, etc. are several examples of elaboration that are commonly used in the teaching-learning process.

Atkinson and Shiffrin proposed that passing of information from one memory system to another involves the operation of active control processes that act as filters, determining which information will be retained. Information in sensory memory enters short-term memory when it becomes the focus of our attention, whereas sensory impressions which do not engage attention fade and quickly disappear. It is necessary to attend to material, information, or an event within the short-term store in order to remember it later (Moray, 1959). So, where memory is concerned, selective attention—our ability to pay attention to only some aspects of the world around us while largely ignoring others—often plays a crucial role (Johnston, MC Cann, and Remington, 1995; Posner and Peterson, 1990). In contrast, information in the short-term memory enters long-term memory storage through elaborative rehearsal (deep processing)—when we think about its meaning and relate it to other information already in long-term memory. Unless we engage in such cognitive effort, information or material in short-term memory, too, quickly fades away and is lost. In contrast, merely repeating information silently to ourselves (maintenance rehearsal) does not necessarily move information from short-term memory to long-term memory.

Recall is better if retrieval context is like the encoding context or situation (Begg and White, 1985; Eich, 1985; and Tulving, 1983). This is called "encoding specificity principle", a notion proposed by Endel Tulving, according to which remembering depends on the amount of overlap between the information contained in the memory trace and that available in the retrieval environment. The encoding specificity principle predicts that recall will be greatest when testing conditions match the learning conditions. In contrast, forgetting is more likely when the two contexts do not match.

It has been found that memory traces that are high in distinctiveness, that is unique in some way like a natural disaster are better remembered than those that are not distinct (Eysenck and Eysenck, 1983).

Some useful steps or tips to improve memory

- Really think about what you want to remember.
- Pay careful attention to what you have to remember.
- Minimize interference.
- Engage in distributed learning process.
- Use visual imagery and other mnemonic techniques.
- Give yourself extra retrieval cues.
- Develop your own shorthand codes.
- Meditate.

Types of Long-term Memory: Cohen and Squire argued that there are two long-term memory systems:

(i) *Declarative memory or knowledge:* "Declarative memory" is concerned with "knowing that". Our memory for this form of knowledge usually takes the form of conscious recollection. It generally refers to information we can talk about.

(ii) *Procedural memory or knowledge:* "Procedural memory" is concerned with "knowing how", learning and knowing of a variety of skills like driving a car, riding a bike, etc. Memory for procedural knowledge is demonstrated by skilled performance. During the course of skill acquisition, there is often an initial reliance on declarative learning followed by a switch to procedural learning.

Research demonstrates that patients with amnesic syndrome have very poor long-term memory for declarative knowledge. However, they show good long-term memory for procedural knowledge. In other words, these amnesic patients have a virtually intact ability to store procedural knowledge in long-term memory combined with a marked inability to store declarative knowledge.

Endel Tulving (Born on 26 May, 1927), a cognitive psychologist and a Canadian neuroscientist, in 1972 argued that a major distinction should be made between:

(i) *Episodic memory:* "Episodic memory" can best be thought of as memory for autobiographical or personal events that have happened to a person. Episodic memory is quite personal and connected with the episodes or events of one's life.

Endel Tulving
(Born on 26 May, 1927)

(ii) *Semantic memory:* "Semantic memory" consists of the organized knowledge that we possess about language and about the world. It includes facts and generalized information (concepts, principles, rules; problem-solving strategies; learning strategies). In general terms, semantic memories lack the specific information about time and place that typically characterizes episodic memories.

Most laboratory studies of human memory have investigated episodic rather than semantic memory (Parkin, 1982). Endel Tulving admits that the two memory systems are highly inter-dependent and inter-connected.

Graf and Schachter (1985) argued that there is an important distinction between:

(i) *Explicit memory:* "Explicit memory" is revealed when performance on a task requires conscious recollection of previous experiences. Traditional measures of long-term memory such as free recall, cued recall, and recognition are all measures of explicit memory.

(ii) *Implicit memory:* "Implicit memory" is revealed when performance on a task is facilitated in the absence of conscious recollection. Word completion, for example, is a test of implicit memory.

Studies of amnesic patients showed good implicit memory but poor explicit memory (Cohen, 1984; Graf, Squire and Mandler, 1984). The limitation of distinction between explicit and implicit memory is that the distinction is descriptive rather than explanatory.

9.4 FORGETTING

Forgetting is a very familiar and common phenomenon. Psychologists generally use the term "forgetting" to refer to apparent loss of information already encoded and stored in long-term memory. "Forgetting" (retention loss) refers to apparent loss of information already encoded and stored in an individual's long-term memory. Forgetting is the failure to recall what was once learnt, retained, and experienced.

Forgetting is a spontaneous or gradual process in which old memories are unable to be recalled from memory storage. It is subject to delicately balanced optimization which ensures that relevant memories are recalled. Forgetting can be reduced by repetition (or more elaborative cognitive processing information). Reviewing information in ways that involve active retrieval seems to slow the rate of forgetting.

9.4.1 Definitions of Forgetting

According to Aristotle, "Forgetting is fading of original experience with passage of time. It arises due to disuse."

According to Goddard, "Retention may be viewed in either positive or negative aspect and forgetting is negative aspect of retention."

According to Drever (1952), "Forgetting means failure at any time to recall an experience, when attempting to do so or to perform an action previously learned."

According to English and English (1958), "Forgetting: The loss or losing, temporary or permanent of something earlier learned, losing ability to recall, recognize or do something."

According to Munn (1967), "Forgetting is failing to retain or to be able to recall which has been acquired."

According to Stagner and Solley (1970), "Forgetting is the negative aspect of the memory. It is the failure to recall that which was once learned. How, to say that it is simply the failure to recall recognizes or retain... ."

9.4.2 Types of Forgetting

(i) *Natural or normal or passive and morbid or abnormal or active forgetting:* In "natural" or "normal" or "passive" forgetting, forgetting occurs in a normal way without making any effort or attempt with the passage or lapse of time or because of the disuse of the material learnt earlier. Whereas, in "morbid" or "abnormal" or "active" forgetting, a person deliberately forgets and consciously represses the unpleasant and painful material or information or experiences to be forgotten into the unconscious.

(ii) *General and specific forgetting:* In "general" forgetting, there is a total loss of previously learnt material. Whereas, in "specific" forgetting there is partial loss or loss of specific parts of previously learnt material.

(iii) *Physical or organic and psychological forgetting:* In "physical" or "organic" forgetting, certain physical illnesses, age, accidents, defects in the nervous system or brain can alter the functioning of the brain and nervous system and causes forgetting. Whereas in "psychological" forgetting, psychological factors like stress, anxiety, conflicts, emotional and psychological disorders cause forgetting.

Much of what we think we have forgotten does not really qualify "forgotten" because it was never encoded and stored in the first place. Memory has three major components; encoding, storage, and retrieval. Forgetting may occur due to failure at any of the stages. It may occur because of the failure of encoding, or storage, or retrieval.

9.4.3 Reasons for Forgetting

1. **Storage failure:** Forgetting from long-term memory takes place due to many factors. It may be due to decay of memory traces, because the stored material is not in use for a long period of time. Owing to disuse, the memory traces fade and ultimately become inaccessible. More often than not, memory trace is there in long-term memory, but interference in proper search for retrieval of information by situational factors leads us to think that the trace is lost forever. They appear to be lost, but memory traces, are never completely lost. Memory tracer deteriorates with time, if they are not in use. The course of forgetting is initially rapid, and then levels off with time (Wixted and Ebbensen, 1991).

2. **Retrieval Failure:** Forgetting is a process of fading of learned or memorized experiences with the passage of time. According to this view, forgetting is controlled by the time factor. Impressions fade away as the time passes. It is called the *theory of disuse* or *decay*. Psychologists believe

that learning results in neurological changes in the brain resulting in the formation of traces in the brain. These memory traces or impressions made on the brain get weaker and finally fade away or decay with the passage of time or by not using that information for a long period of time that is through disuse. There is progressive loss in retention with lapse of time. According to Albert Schweitzer (1875–1965), a physician, "Happiness is nothing more than health and a poor memory."

3. **Encoding Failure:** Age can affect encoding efficiency. The same brain areas jump into action when young adults are encoding new information, are less responsive among older adults. This slower encoding helps explain age-related memory decline (Grady and others, 1995).

4. **Interference:** Interference theory refers to the idea that forgetting occurs because the recall of certain items interferes with the recall of other items. Interference is an important cause of forgetting (Bushman and Bonacci, 2002). Interference is the negative inhibiting effect of one learning experience on another. It is the blurring of one memory by other memories that are similar to it and which compete with its recall and retrieval. In nature, the interfering items are said to originate from an over-stimulating environment. A vast amount of experimental evidence and everyday experience too indicates that learning new things interfere with our memory of what we learnt earlier and prior learning interferes with our memory of things learnt later. Interference theory exists in two branches, Retroactive and Proactive inhibition, each referring in contrast to the other. Memory interference resulting from activities that came after or subsequent to the events you are trying to remember is called *retroactive interference* or *inhibition*. "Retroactive inhibition" is when the later memory interferes with the past memory, causing it to change in a particular extent. It is called "retroactive" because the interference is with the memory of events that came before the interfering activity. Later learning disrupts memory for earlier learning. John Jenkins and Karl Dallenbach (1924) discovered the sleep benefits in a classic experiment. Jenkins and Dallenbach found that retention after sleep was far superior to retention after waking activities even when the time interval between learning and retention were identical. In the sleeping conditions, some activity is present as the subject does not always go to sleep immediately after the learning is complete. Even during sleep, many reactions like muscular movements, circulatory, digestive, and other bodily functions continue to occur. During sleep, though complete psychological vacuum may not be possible, almost all the activities of the "O" (organism) are at a minimum. Thus, fewer reactions occur which might interfere or inhibit with the recall of what was originally learned. So, forgetting is minimum during sleep.

Day after day, two people each learned some non-sense syllables, and then tried to recall them after up to eight hours of being awake or sleep at night. Forgetting occurred more rapidly after being awake and involved with other activities. The investigators surmised that forgetting is not so much a matter of the decay of old impressions and associations as it is a matter of interference, or obliteration of the old by the new. Later experiments have confirmed that the hour before a night's sleep (but not the minute before sleep) is a good time to commit information to memory (Fowler and others, 1973).

"Proactive interference" or inhibition, on the other hand, is due to events that come before the to-be-remembered information or material. Previous learning interferes with later learning and memory or retention. "Proactive interference" is when older memory interferes with the later memory, causing it to damage. The interference disrupts the various kinds of association between stimuli and responses formed during learning. Interference also somehow has its greatest effect on the memory of retrieval cues.

Both retroactive and proactive interference are greatest when two different responses have been associated with the same stimulus, intermediate when two similar stimuli are involved and least when two quite different stimuli are involved. In fact, probably only a small fraction of forgetting can be attributed to retroactive and proactive interference.

5. **Organic Cause:** Forgetting that occurs through physiological damage or dilapidation to the brain is referred to as "organic" causes of forgetting. Certain physical illnesses or diseases, age, accidents, etc. can cause some form of damage to brain tissues and can alter the functioning of the brain and nervous system which results in forgetting or amnesia. These theories encompass the loss of information already retained in LTM or the inability to encode new information (examples include Alzheimer's disease, Amnesia, Dementia), consolidation theory and the gradual slowing down of the central nervous system due to ageing.

6. **Confusion:** Atkinson and Shiffrin claimed that forgetting often occurs because of confusion among similar long-term memories. They argued that nearly all forgetting from long-term memory is due to an inability to find the appropriate memory trace rather than to the disappearance of the trace from the memory system.

7. **Trace-Dependent Forgetting and Cue-Dependent Forgetting:** According to Endel Tulving (1974), trace-dependent forgetting and cue-dependent forgetting are the only two major causes of forgetting. "Trace-dependent forgetting" occurs because the memory trace has deteriorated or decayed or required information or material has been lost from the memory system. Physiological traces in the brain are not available at the time of recall or retrieval.

"Cue-dependent forgetting" occurs when the memory trace still exists, but there is no suitable retrieval cue to trigger off the memory. The information is not accessible. It is a kind of forgetting in which the required information or material is in the long-term memory store, but cannot be retrieved without a suitable retrieval cue. The cues present at the time of learning are not present at the time of recall or interfering and competing cues are present and they block the memory. Cue-dependent or retrieval failure is the failure to recall a memory due to missing stimuli or cues that were present at the time the memory was encoded. It is one of the five cognitive psychology theories of forgetting. It states that memory is sometimes temporarily forgotten purely because it cannot be retrieved, but the proper cue can bring it to mind. The information still exists, but without these cues, retrieval is unlikely. Furthermore, a good retrieval cue must be consistent with the original encoding of the information. If the sound of the word is emphasized during the encoding process, the cue should also put emphasis on the phonetic quality of the word. Information is available, however, just not readily available without these cues.

8. **Trace Decay:** Trace decay focuses on the problem of availability caused when memories decay. Trace theory states that when something new is learned, a neuro-chemical, physical "memory trace" is formed in the brain, and over time, this trace tends to disintegrate, unless it is occasionally used. Hebb said that incoming information creates a pattern of neurons to create a neurological memory trace in the brain which would fade away with time. Repeated firing causes a structural change in the synapses. Rehearsal of repeated firing maintains the memory in STM until a structural change is made.

9. **Motivated Forgetting or Repression:** Theory on the relationship between motivation and forgetting or repressive (suppressive) forgetting states that unhappy memories are easily forgotten, that is forgetting is a motivated and intentional process. This theory was put forward by Sigmund Freud. According to him, forgetting is due to conscious repression or suppression by the person. "Repression" is a mental function which cushions the mind against the unpleasant effect of painful, traumatic, and unacceptable experiences, events, memories or conflicts. Freud claimed that repressed memories are traumatic and painful and are strongly associated with anxiety, guilt, or other negative emotions. The anxiety associated with memory is so great that the memory is kept out or pushed out of consciousness although it still exists in the unconscious mind.

Forgetting, like attention, is selective. Forgetting, in some sense, is good because if forgetting does not take place, our life will be burdened with useless and unpleasant information.

Memory researcher Daniel Schacter (1996) enumerates seven ways our memories fail us. He calls these seven sins of memory and are the following:

1. *Absent-mindedness:* Inattention to details produces encoding failure.
2. *Transience:* Transience includes storage decay over time. Information which is not used over time fades away.
3. *Blocking:* It includes inaccessibility of stored information or material.

   Three sins of distortion are as follows:
4. *Misattribution:* Misattribution includes confusing the source of information.
5. *Suggestibility:* Suggestibility is the lingering effect of misinformation.
6. *Bias:* Bias includes belief-coloured recollections.

   One sin of intrusion is as follows:
7. *Persistence:* Persistence includes unwanted memories.

9.4.4 Factors Affecting Forgetting

1. **Rate of original learning:** When an individual learns with speed, forgetting will be slow and when learning is slow, the individual tends to forget quickly.

2. **Over-learning:** Over-learning is the term used to describe the practice that continues after a perfect recall has been scored. Over-learning is essential for improving retention or retrieval. For example, nursery rhymes and multiplication tables.

3. **Periodic reviews:** Reviews, soon after the original learning, may prevent the very rapid forgetting that normally takes place immediately after practice.

4. **Meaningfulness:** The most effective method to improve retention is to make the subject matter meaningful. Meaningful material is forgotten less rapidly than the non-sense or meaningless material.

5. **Intention to learn:** Most people feel that we are more likely to remember something if we deliberately try to learn it. The learners' intention while learning affects both the retention of material and the rate of original learning. But Hyde and Jenkins (1973) reported that memory is determined by the nature of the processing that occurs at the time of learning rather than by the presence or absence of intention to learn the material.

6. **Spaced verses massed learning:** The spacing of repetition of practice period influences retention. One may learn the subject matter superficially for immediate use by cramming. But, for permanent retention, a time interval between repetitions is more effective.

9.4.5 The Curve of Forgetting

One of the first people to study the mechanisms of forgetting was a German psychologist Hermann Ebbinghaus (24 January 1850–26 February 1909). Ebbinghaus conducted his first set of memory experiments (1878–1879). He conducted second set of memory experiments (1883–1884). Ebbinghaus founded a psychology laboratory in Breslan in 1897. Notable contributions of Hermann Ebbinghaus include serial list learning, savings as a measure of memory, and nonsense syllables. Ebbinghaus developed the first scientific approach to the study of a higher psychological process called *memory*. He was the first person to use nonsense syllables in learning and memory research. He was the first to describe the "learning curve."

Hermann Ebbinghaus
(1850–1909)

Among the various experiments conducted by Hermann Ebbinghaus, in his pioneer works on memory (1885), the most often cited is his quantitative study of the loss of retention with the passage or lapse of time. His first significant study in this area was published in 1885, as *Uber das Gedachtnis* (later translated into English as Memory: A Contribution to Explain Psychology). He discovered the experimental nature of forgetting. The following formula can roughly describe the forgetting:

$$R = \frac{et}{s}$$

where

R is memory retention,
s is the relative strength of memory, and
t is time.

Ebbinghaus, a trace psychologist, believed that certain neural traces are formed due to learning. When these traces are later aroused, we remember the original materials and the failure of re-arousal of traces, is called *forgetting*. He himself worked as a subject for these studies. His procedure was to learn lists of non-sense syllables (two consonants and one vowel in the middle), lay them aside for a certain interval, relearn them and note the saving in time or number of readings, due to the partial retention of the effects of the first learning. In course of this investigation, he learned over 1200 lists each containing 13 non-sense syllables. A learning session lasted 18–20 minutes during which time he learned eight such lists. He took the first list and read it through and through at a steady rate of one syllable every 2/5 second till it could be recited twice without hesitation and with a consciousness of being correct. After a pause of fifteen seconds, another list was studied and so on till these eight lists had been learned. The total time to learn the eight lists was the original learning time for the unit of work. After a certain lapse of time, this same set of lists was relearned to the same criterion. After a lapse or gap of thirty one days, the relearning of a set of eight lists always showed some saving as compared with the original learning. If thousand and ten (1010) seconds were needed for the original learning of the eight lists and thirty one days later, eight hundred and three (803) seconds were needed to relearn them, the saving was 207 (1010 – 803 = 207) seconds was equal to 20.5% of the original time. Learning efficiency may differ at different hours of the day. Using himself as the sole subject in his experiments, he measured his own capacity to relearn a given list of words after a variety of given period.

The work of Ebbinghaus was very accurate and thorough in yielding the Ebbinghaus' curve. Its main characteristic is a rapid fall immediately after learning and a gradual flattening out as the interval is prolonged. He found that forgetting occurs in a systematic manner, beginning rapidly and than levelling off. The course of forgetting is initially rapid then levels off with time (Wixted and Ebbensen, 1991). Forgetting becomes more and more gradual as the time advances (Figures 9.1 and 9.2).

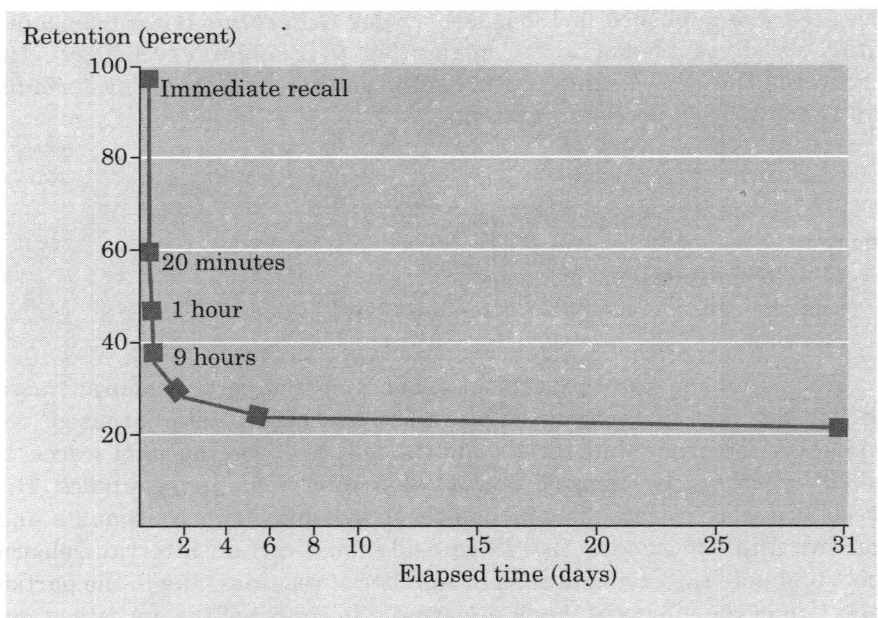

Figure 9.1 Curve of forgetting.

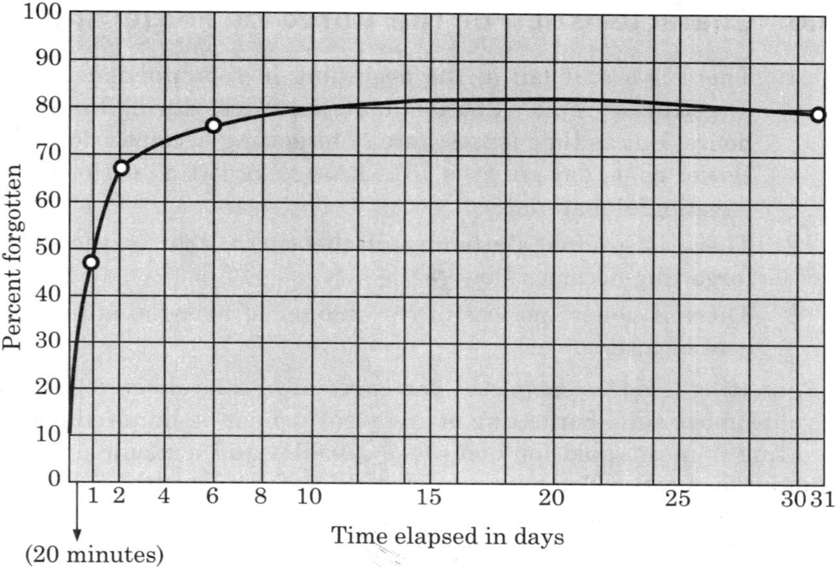

Figure 9.2 Ebbinghaus' curve of forgetting.

The speed of forgetting depends on a number of factors such as the difficulty of the learned material (for example, how meaningful it is), its representation, and physiological factors such as stress and sleep. The basal forgetting rate differs little between individuals.

Ebbinghaus memorized a list of non-sense syllables and then tested himself at intervals varying from 20 minutes to 31 days or a month to see how much of the list he remembered. Ebbinghaus described his results by plotting a curve of forgetting (Figures 9.1 and 9.2), which he obtained by plotting the amount forgotten as a function of time. He was the first to describe the shape of the forgetting curve. The forgetting curve illustrates the decline of memory retention in time. The related concept is the strength of memory that refers to the durability of the memory traces in the brain. The stronger the memory, the longer period of time a person is able to recall it. As shown in the curve, he found that he remembers less than 40% of the items after 9 hours, but that the rate of forgetting levelled off over time. The results in terms of the percentage of material forgotten with the lapse of time were as follows:

Time Elapsed	*Amount Forgotten*
20 minutes	47%
First 24 hours or one day	65%
Two days	72%
Six days	75%
Thirty-one days	79%

9.4.6 Characteristics of the Curve of Forgetting

1. There is a stiff fall in the beginning in reproduction. At first, forgetting is rapid as 65% of material is lost during the first 24 hours. But as time lapses, rate of forgetting becomes slower and slower as on day six, it is 75%. Rate of forgetting is slower with meaningful material.
2. There is gradual flattening of the curve, that is the rate of forgetting becomes slow.
3. There is almost no loss in the amount of material after a good deal of interval.

Forgetting is never complete. The curve always levels up off at some low value above zero. Forgetting of any thing cannot be hundred percent. Forgetting is most rapid for non-sense syllables and next for prose and minimum for poetry. The basic law that the rate of forgetting is rapid in the beginning, then slows down with the passage of time, holds good for all types of materials.

QUESTIONS

The below mentioned are some of the questions that have been asked in the examinations conducted by the Guru Nanak Dev University or can be asked. Knowledge of these answers can help the students to get success in the examinations.

Section A

Answers the following questions in **five** lines or 50 words.

1. Define memory.*
2. What is encoding?
3. What is storage?
4. What is retrieval?
5. What is multi-store model?
6. What is chunk?
7. What do you mean by confirmation bias?
8. Define elaboration.
9. What is the short-term memory?*
10. What is long-term memory?
11. Define proactive interference.*
12. Define retroactive interference.*

13. What is repression?*
14. What is recognition?
15. Define S.T.M.*
16. Define L.T.M.*
17. What is sensory memory?
18. What do you mean by motivated forgetting?
19. What is the strength of memory?
20. Define the maintenance rehersal.
21. Explain deep processing.

Section B

Answer the following questions up to **two** pages or 500 words:

1. What is sensory memory, short-term memory, and long-term memory?
2. What are episodic memory and semantic memory?
3. What is repression? What role does it play in memory?
4. Differentiate between short-term and long-term memory.*
5. What is forgetting? What are the causes of forgetting?*
6. Define memory. What are different types of memory?

Section C

Answer the following questions up to **five** pages or 1000 words:

1. Describe the short-term memory and long-term memory stores. What evidence supports that distinction?
2. Describe the interference theory of forgetting. What factors other than interference cause forgetting?
3. According to Atkinson and Shiffrin model, what basic tasks are carried out by memory?
4. What are retroactive interference and proactive interference? What role do they play in forgetting?
5. Define memory. What are different types of memory?*
6. Discuss the nature and types of memory.

REFERENCES

Adams, R.J., 'An Evaluation of Color Preference in Early Infancy,' *Infant Behavior and Development*, **10**, 143–150, 1987.

Atkinson, R., and Shiffrin, R., 'Human Memory: A Proposed System and its Control Processes,' in K. Spence and J. Spence (Eds.), *The Psychology of Learning and Motivation: Advances in Research and Theory*, Vol. 2, New York: Academic Press, 1968.

Baddeley, A.D., *The Psychology of Memory,* New York: Basic Books, 1976.

Baddeley, A.D., 'Working Memory,' *Science*, **255**, 556–559, 1992.

Baddeley, A.D., 'Exploring the Central Executive,' *Quarterly Journal of Experimental Psychology*, **49** A, 5–28, 1996.

Baddeley, A.D., *Essential of Human Memory*, Hove: Psychology, 1999.

Baddeley, A.D., and Hitch, G., 'Working Memory,' in G.H. Bower (Ed.). *The Psychology of Learning and Motivation,* Vol. 8, London: Academic Press, 1974.

Baron, R.A., *Psychology*, New Delhi: Prentice-Hall of India, 1995.

Bootzin, R., Bower, Crooker and Hall, *Psychology Today*, New York: McGraw-Hill, INC. 1991.

Brown, J., 'Reciprocal Facilitation and Impairment in Free Recall,' *Psychonomic Science*, **10**, 41–42, 1968.

Cohen, N.J., 'Preserved Learning Capacity in Amnesia: Evidence for Multiple Memory Systems,' in L.R., Squire and N. Butters, (Eds.), *Neuropsychology of Memory*, New York: Guilford Press, 1984.

Cowan, N., 'The Magical Number 4 in Short-term Memory: A Reconsideration of Mental Storage Capacity,' *Behavioral and Brain Sciences*, **24**, 87–185, 2001.

Craik, F.I.M. and Lockhart, R.S., 'Levels of Processing: A Framework for Memory Research,' *Journal of Verbal Thinking and Verbal Behavior*, Vol. **11**, 671–684, 1972.

Craik, F.I.M. and Tulving, E., 'Depth of Processing and the Retention of Words in Episodic Memory,' *Journal of Experimental Psychology: General*, **104**, 268–294, 1975.

Crooks, R.L. and Stein, J., *Psychology, Science, Behaviour and Life.* London: Halt, Rinehart and Winston, INC., 1991.

De Groot, A.D., 'Perception and Memory Versus Thought, in B. Kleinmuntz (Ed.), *Problem Solving*, New York: Wiley, 1966.

Drever, J., *Instincts in Man*, Cambridge: Cambridge University Press, 1917.

Ebbinghaus, H., *Grundzuge der Psychologie. 1. Band, 2. Their*, Leipzig: Veit & Co., 1902.

Ebbinghaus, H., *Memory,* (Trans. By H.A. Ruger and C.E. Bussenius), New York: Teachers College, Columbia University, 1913.

Ebbinghaus, H., *On Memory*, New York: Dover, 1964.

Ebbinghaus, H., *Memory: A Contribution to Experimental Psychology*, New York: Drever, 1885/1962.

Ebbinghaus, H., *Psychology: An Elementary Textbook*. New York: Alno Press, 1973/1908.

Eich, J.E., 'Levels of Processing, Encoding Specificity, Elaboration, and CHARM,' *Psychological Review*, **92**, 1–38, 1985.

Eysenck, H.J., *The Biological Basis of Personality*, Springfield, IL: C.C. Thomas, 1967.

Eysenck, H.J., and Eysenck, M.W., *Mindwatching: Why People Behave the Way They Do,* New York: Garden/Doubleday, 1983.

Eysenck, M.W., *Simply Psychology*, London: Psychology Press Publishers, 1996.

Eysenck, M.W., *Principles of Cognitive Psychology*, London: Psychology Press Ltd. Publishers, 1999.

Graf, P. and Schachter, D.L., 'Implicit and Explicit Memory for New Associations in Normal and Amnesic Subjects,' *Journal of Experimental Psychology: Learning, Memory, and Cognition*, **11**, 501–518, 1985.

Graf, P., Squire, L.R., and Mandler, G., 'The Information That Amnesic Patients Do Not Forget,' *Journal of Experimental Psychology: Learning, Memory, and Cognition*, **10**, 164–178. 1984.

Hebb, D.O., *The Organization of Behavior,* New York: Wiley, 1949.

Hilgard, E.R., Atkinson, R.C., Atkinson, R.L., *Introduction to Psychology*, New York: Hart Court Brace Jovanovich, INC., 1975.

Hulme, C., Roodenrys, S., Brown, G., and Mercer, R., 'The Role of Long-Term Memory Mechanisms In Memory Span,' *British Journal of Psychology*, **86**, 527–536, 1995.

Hyde, T.S., and Jenkins, J.J., 'Recall for Words as a Function of Semantic, Graphic, and Syntactic Orienting Tasks,' *Journal of Verbal Learning and Verbal Behaviour*, **12**, 471–480, 1973.

Jenkins, J.G. and Dallenbach, K.M., 'Obliviscence During Sleep and Waking,' *American Journal of Psychology*, **35**, 605–612, 1924.

Johnston, J.C., McCann, R.S., and Remington, R.W., 'Chronometric Evidence for Two Types of Attention,' *Psychological Science*, **6**, 365–369, 1995.

Miller, G.A., 'The Magical Number Seven, Plus or Minus Two: Some Limits on Our Capacity for Processing Information,' *Psychological Review*, **63**, 81–97, 1956.

Moray, N., 'Attention in Dichotic Listening: Affective Cues and the Influence of Instruction,' *Quarterly Journal of Experimental Psychology*, **11**, 59–60, 1959.

Morris, C.G., *Psychology*, 3rd ed., Englewood Cliffs, New Jersey: Prentice Hall, 1979.

Morris, P.E., 'Strategies for Learning and Recall,' in M.M. Gruneberg and P.E. Morris (Eds.), *Applied Problems in Memory*, London: Academic Press, 1979.

Munn, N.L., *Introduction to Psychology*, 2nd ed., Delhi: Oxford & IBH, 1967.

Munn, N.L., *Being and Becoming*, Adelaide, Australia: Adelaide University Union Press, 1980.

Parkin, A.J., 'Residual Learning in Organic Amnesia,' *Cortex,* **18**, 417–440, 1982.

Peterson, L.R. and Peterson, M.J., 'Short-term Retention of Individual Verbal Items,' *Journal of Experimental Psychology*, **58**, 193–198. 1959.

Posner, M.I. and Peterson, S.E., 'The Attention System of the Human Brain,' *Annual Review of Neuroscience*, **13**, 25–42, 1990.

Ryburn, W.M., *Introduction to Educational Psychology*, London: Oxford University Press, 1956.

Schachter, D.L., *Searching for Memory*, New York: Basic Books, 1996.

Schachter, D.L., *The Seven Sins of Memory: How the Mind Forgets and Remembers*, Boston: Houghton Mifflin. 2001.

Shiffrin, R.M., and Steyvers, M., 'A Model for Recognition Memory: REM: Retrieving Effectively from Memory,' *Psychonomic Bulletin and Review*, **4** (2), 145–166, 1997.

Squire, L.R., 'Biological Foundations of Accuracy and Inaccuracy of Memory,' in D.L. Schachter (Ed.), *Memory Distortions* (pp. 197–225), Cambridgem MA: Harvard University Press, 1995.

Tulving, E., 'Episodic and Semantic Memory,' in E. Tulving and W. Donaldson (Eds.), *Organization of Memory*, (pp. 381–403). New York: Academic Press, 1972.

Tulving, E., 'Cue-dependent Forgetting,' *American Scientist*, **62**, 74–82, 1974.

Tulving, E., *Elements of Episodic Memory*, Oxford: Oxford Clarendon Press/Oxford University Press. 1983.

Tulving, E., 'How Many Memory Systems are There?' *American Psychologist*, **40**, 385–398, 1985.

Tulving, E., 'Episodic Memory: From Mind to Brain', *Annual Review of Psychology*, **53**: 1–25. doi: 10. 1146/ annurev.psych 53, 100901.135114. PMID11752477, 2002.

Wixted, J., 'The Psychology and Neuroscience of Forgetting.' *Annual Review of Psychology*, **55**, 235–269, 2004.

Woodworth, R.S., *Dynamic Psychology,* New York: Columbia University Press, 1918.

Woodworth, R.S., and Schlosberg, H., *Experimental Psychology*, 2nd ed., New York: Holt, Rinehart and Winston, 1954.

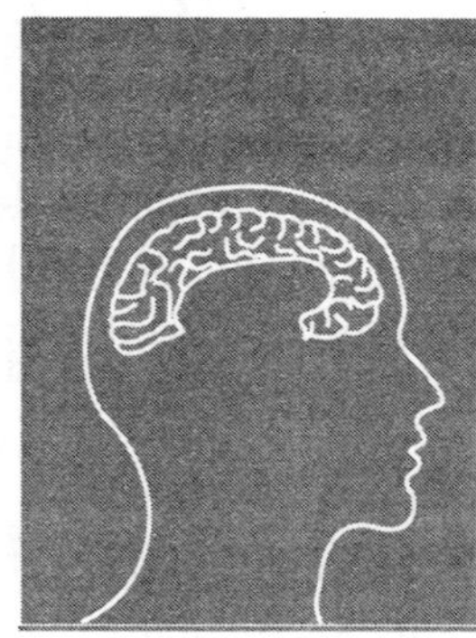

CHAPTER 10
Motivation

Motivation is the process of activating behaviour, directing it, and sustaining it towards a particular goal. Motivation is the process of activation and persistence of behaviour. Motivation may be regarded as something which prompts, compels, and energizes an individual to act or behave in a particular manner at a particular time for attaining some specific goal or purpose. Motivation focuses on why people behave in certain ways. By motivation, psychologists mean that which gives impetus to behaviour by arousing, sustaining, and directing it towards the attainment of goals (Madsen, 1959).

The concept of motivation is a central one in our attempt to understand the behaviour. The word "Motivation" comes from the Latin word "*movere*" meaning to "move". In the literal sense, it is a process which arouses the energy or drive in the individual to proceed in an activity. The activity aroused, fulfils the need, and reduces the drive or tension. Until it has not fulfilled the need, the drive is not reduced. The motivated behaviour is often of a vigorous or persistent nature and may persist over long period of time. Motivated people are responding to their own motivation—internal processes that cannot be directly observed, but which activate, guide, and maintain their overt behaviour. Therefore, "Motivation" is defined as an internal process that influences the direction, persistence, and vigour or energy, or enthusiasm of goal-directed behaviour.

Motivation helps us explain how internal factors seem to move animals and people toward certain goals. Whenever the causes of a specific form of behaviour cannot be readily observed in the immediate situation, many psychologists believe that it is reasonable to explain them in terms of various motives. "Motivation" refers to the processes that cannot be directly observed in the situation but which are real, nevertheless, and which serve to activate, guide and maintain people's actions. Motivation is the process of arousing action, sustaining activity in progress, regulating, and directing patterns of activity through energy transformations within the tissues of the organism (human or members of other species). Motivation is an internal process that activates, guides, and maintains behaviour.

The study of motivation lies at the heart of the psychologists' attempt to understand, explain, predict, and control behaviour (goals of Psychology). Human motivation is extremely complex, difficult to understand, interpret, predict, and control. It is neither practicable nor possible to bring human beings to the cage or laboratory for experimenting on their drives and motivational processes. So, most of the researches on motivation have been done on animal behaviour. Most of the inferences on human motivation have also been drawn from animal studies.

10.1 DEFINITIONS OF MOTIVATION

According to Atkinson (1958), "The term motivation refers to the arousal of a tendency to act, to produce one or more effects."

According to Guilford (1960), "Motivation is an internal factor or condition that tends to initiate and sustain activity."

According to Teitelbaum (1962), "Motivation is the urge to perform a particular act, to obtain a certain object, or to produce a desired outcome."

According to Brown (1965), "Motivation stands for non-directive energizing dimension of behaviour and for convenience one may refer to level of drive or arousal meaning points along the continuum from quiescence or inactivity to very high degree of activity."

According to P.T. Young (1973), "Motivation is the process of arousing an action, sustaining the activity in progress."

According to Bootzin (1991), "Motivation is a process that taken together energizes, maintains, and directs behaviour towards the goal."

According to Baron (1995), "Motivation refers to the internal process that can't be directly observed but that activates, guide, and maintain overt behaviour."

According to Morgan and King (2000), "Motivation refers to the driving and pulling forces which results in persistent behaviour directed towards a particular goal."

After gleaning the above definitions of motivation, a general consensus results, that motivation is an internal state or condition (sometimes described as a need, desire, or want) that serves to activate or energize behaviour and gives it direction (Kleinginna and Kleinginna, 1981). Motivation is

- an internal state or condition that activates behaviour and gives it direction;
- desire or want that activates behaviour and directs goal-oriented behaviour;
- influence of needs and desires on the intensity and direction of behaviour.
- Franken (1994) provides an additional component in his definition:
- the arousal, direction, and persistence of behaviour.

Most motivation theorists assume that motivation is involved in the performance of all learned response; that is, a learned behaviour will not occur unless it is energized. Like psychologists in other fields, those interested in motivation have developed a number of concepts that help guide their research.

10.1.1 Instinct

One of the earliest was the concept of instincts, innate motivations inherited through genes. Instinct—an instinct is an innate force, found in all members of a species, which directs behaviour in predictable ways when the right eliciting stimulus is present (Weiner, 1974, 1980). The word "instinct" has its root in the Latin, "instinctus" meaning "instigated" or "impelled", with the implication that such impulses are natural or innate. According to the dictionary of Psychology, there are four general, distinguishable meanings of the term:

(i) An unlearned response characteristic of the members of a given species.

(ii) A tendency or disposition to respond in a particular manner that is characteristic of a particular species. This disposition is the presumed underpinning of the observed behaviour.

(iii) A complex, coordinated set of acts found universally, or nearly so, within a given species that emerges under specific stimulus conditions and specific development conditions. This meaning is found primarily in ethology.

(iv) Any of a number of unlearned, inherited tendencies that are hypothesized to function as the motivational forces behind complex human behaviour. This sense, of course, is that expressed by classical psychoanalysis. The first school of

Psychology to make instinct a central concept was the Freudian. In his early writings, Freud outlined two classes of instincts: the life instinct (sexual)—Eros, and the death instinct (aggression)—Thanatos. Freud (1990) suggested that all action or behaviour is a result of internal, biological instincts that are classified into two categories.

Instincts are innate patterns of behaviour that are universal in a species, independent of experience, and elicited by specific stimuli or conditions. William James (1890), included, in his list of basic human instincts pugnacity or combativeness, acquisitiveness or greed, sympathy, and curiosity.

Ethnologists studying animal behaviour in its natural habitat have stressed the species-specific and biological aspects and have observed that bees communicate the location of food to other bees, birds build nests, and spiders spin webs. All this happens exactly the same way as their parents did. These are examples of instinctive behaviour that occurs in response to specific types of stimulations.

McDougall (1908) used the term "instinct" to denote an inherited disposition that has three components, that is, energizing, action, and goal direction. His list of human instincts included curiosity, gregariousness, self-abasement, fight, flight, repulsion, self-assertion, reproduction or sex or mating, acquisition, parental care, and pugnacity (a strong desire to fight or argue with other people), appeal, construction, submission, food-seeking, and laughter.

The idea of instinct as an explanation of human behaviour has been rejected. Today, most of the psychologists accept that human behaviour is the product of interaction of genetic and environmental factors.

10.1.2 Need and Drive

Psychologists now use the concept of need, wants, or desires to describe the motivational properties of behaviour. A need is a lack or deficit of some necessity within the individual. A "need" is a state of deprivation arising within our bodies. According to Boring, Lingfield, and Weld (1962), "Need is the necessity or deficiency of the body due to which tension or imbalance arise in the body." Needs are now viewed as dispositions toward action. They create a condition that is predisposed toward taking action or making a change and moving in a certain direction.

There is little agreement about the identification of basic human needs. Murray (1938, 1943) has given a list of 37 needs such as need for oxygen, food, water, rest, sleep, physical contact, love and affection, social approval, company, self-assertion, security, independence, etc. Ryan and

Deci (2000) suggest three needs—the need for autonomy, the need for competence, and the need for relatedness. Grace and Cohen (2001) state that the most important needs for children are connection, recognition, and power. Nohria, Lawrence, and Wilson (2001) provide evidence from a sociobiology theory of motivation that humans have four basic needs: (i) acquire objects and experiences; (ii) bond with others in long-term relationships of mutual care and commitment; (iii) learn and make sense of the world and of ourselves; and (iv) to defend ourselves, our loved ones, beliefs, and resources from harm. The Institute for Management Excellence (2001) suggests that there are nine basic human needs: (i) security, (ii) adventure, (iii) freedom, (iv) exchange, (v) power, (vi) expansion, (vii) acceptance, (viii) community, and (ix) expression.

Human needs can be broadly classified into biological needs and socio-psychological needs. Biological needs include need for food, water, oxygen, rest when tired, action when rested, regular elimination of waste products from the body, having an even internal body temperature, sleep after periods of wakefulness, protection from threats of the physical environment like haphazards of the weather, natural calamities, wild animals, satisfaction of the sex urge or desire to seek sex experiences, needs associated with the demands of our senses, need for physical contact, sensory stimulation, etc. In addition to biological needs, human beings have psychological and social needs. We are motivated to have power, freedom or gaining independence, need to achieve, security, prestige, love, and affection. We try to seek affiliation, company, self-assertion, self-expression or self-actualization, recognition, and approval from others or social approval, and self-transcendence. In fact, these psychological needs make human beings different from animals. The continuous struggle in our life to accomplish various goals draws our attention to the centrality of needs in regulating and organizing human behaviour.

The condition of need leads to drive. For any drive to occur, need is essential. A "drive" is an internal state of tension or arousal or energy produced by a need. A drive is an unpleasant state of arousal within our bodies. The term "drive" was first introduced to Psychology by Woodworth in 1918. Hull (1952) viewed drive as "Hypothetical resultant of tissue needs and wants. One frequent effect of drive arousal is an increase in the activity of an organism." Hull distinguished between primary or biological drives and secondary or learned drives. Drive energizes random activity. When one random activity leads to a goal that reduces the drive then the organism stops being active. The organism returns to a balanced state. Thus, the sequence of motivational events is as follows (Figure 10.1):

Need → Drive → Goal directed behaviour → Goal achievement → Drive reduction

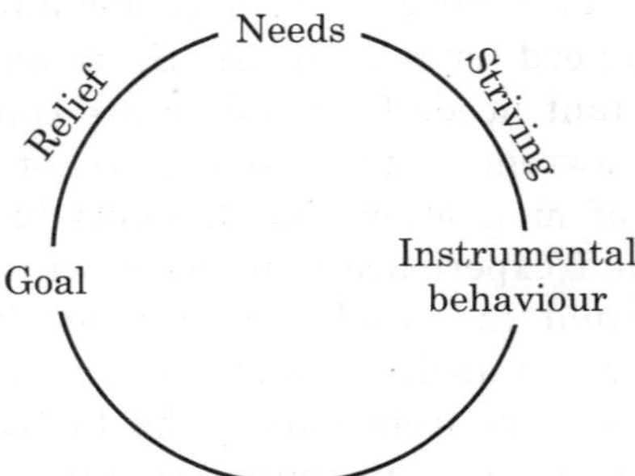

Figure 10.1 Motivational cycle.

Drive is stimulated by biological factors, but behaviours that reduce a drive may be learned. In this kind of reasoning, maintaining a normal state of balance or homeostasis is the main concern. Drives may also be induced by intense, internal or external stimuli in addition to the primary drives, which do not depend upon learning, there are secondary drives. Neutral stimuli paired with strong drives can acquire motivating properties. Drives learned through conditioning are called "acquired drives". Fear is a good example of acquired drive. Organism can be energized by the external stimuli. These stimuli may attract or repel us. Much of our behaviour is directed towards seeking pleasurable consequences and avoiding unpleasant ones. Eating food when hungry and drinking water when thirsty provide satisfaction.

10.1.3 Motive

"Motive" is a state of arousal that impels an organism to action. Motive may be considered as an energy or force or tendency (learned or innate) within the individual to compel, persuade, or inspire her or him to act either for the satisfaction of basic needs or for the attainment of some goal or purpose. McDougall said "All motives are purposeful and directed towards a goal."

According to Fisher, "A motive is an inclination or impulsion to action plus some degree of orientation or direction."

According to Carroll (1966), "A need gives rise to one or more motives. A motive is a rather specific process which has been learned. It is directed towards a goal."

According to Rosen, Fox, and Gregory (1972), "A motive may be defined as a readiness or disposition to respond in some ways and not others to a variety of situations."

A motive becomes the reason for certain course of action whether conscious or unconscious. The motive is a concept, it is not an object. It may be also stated as the source of energy used to produce motion or behaviour in an organism. Motive, generally, is the cause of behaviour. Motivated behaviour is based upon our needs and it is directed for achieving a goal. Generally, motives are expressed in three forms. The clearest expression of any motive is complete fulfilment. The behaviour is directed for the fulfilment of the immediate need of the organism, for example, eating, drinking, etc. The second expression is instrumental which involves action upon the environment. The act which should secure what will satisfy the motive. The stronger motive makes the organism to act vigorously to have it satisfied. The third expression of the motive is not going to be fulfilled immediately, for example in the case of people who were deprived of good food for a long time; they express their motive for food in some other forms. The organism is directed towards the goal and the strong desire provides more energy for the behaviour.

Types of motives

Human behaviour is activated by a variety of motives and is discussed below:

(A) Biogenic or Biological Motives: Some motives are largely biological, emphasizing bodily needs such as hunger, thirst, fatigue, need for sleep, sex, pain, maternal behaviour, and excretion. These are rooted primarily in body tissue needs. These motives propel or move us to satisfy physiological needs. These are biological or primary needs, as they are concerned with the survival and sustenance of the individual. Some of the biological motives are discussed below:

1. *Hunger:* Hunger occupies the most prominent position among all biological drives and obviously most of the studies have been done on hunger drive. In addition, food has been considered as God (*Anna Brahman*) and for hungry person, the overriding concern is to get food and satisfy hunger in any way. This shows the value attached to food, hunger, and feeding. The survival of the organism depends upon the satisfaction of the hunger need. Though, hunger is usually produced by food deprivation, stimulus conditions (presence of food, taste, appearance, and aroma or smell) also contribute to its arousal. A growling stomach or hunger pangs caused by the contractions of the stomach are taken as hunger signals. The common belief that deprivation of food substances in the stomach leads to stomach contractions and lowered level of food sugar has been refuted by certain recent evidences. According to the findings of Keys, Brozek, Henschel, Micelson, and Taylor (1950), "Although awareness of hunger under such conditions may have been associated with strong stomach contractions, it is obvious that it was not caused by emptiness of stomach." Tsang (1938) indicates that hunger exists in the absence of stomach contractions.

The study conducted by Ehrlich (1964) suggests that the most significant physiological factor in regulating hunger is the hypothalamus, which regulates the amount of food taken into the stomach. On the basis of laboratory findings, it has been now agreed that the physiological key to hunger lies in the chemical composition of the blood and a structure in the brain called the *hypothalamus*. The sugar, glucose which is present in our blood helps to provide energy to the body. It can be stored in the liver only in small quantities and for a short time. When the amount of glucose in the blood, the blood-sugar level drops, below a certain point, a message is sent to the hypothalamus which in turn alerts the body to its need for food. After eating, when the blood-sugar level rises the hypothalamus works for inhibition of the hunger messages. Two areas of the hypothalamus that are involved in the hunger mechanism have been identified. The lateral hypothalamus controls the "on" switch and thus sends out hunger signals, while the ventromedial hypothalamus performs the task of inhibition by controlling the "off" switch. Recent researches have suggested that number of other parts of the brain such as limbic system and the temporal lobe may also play a major role in the human hunger drive.

It has also now been experimentally proved that besides the chemical composition and brain mechanism, certain other personal, social, cultural, and psychological factors like choice or preference for a specific food, one's biological predisposition, boredom, loneliness, nervousness, insecurity, anxiety, depression, socio-cultural demands, acquired food habits and similar other factors also govern the eating behaviour of human beings.

Walter Bradford Cannon
(1871–1945)

All in combination, act with external factors to help you to understand that you are hungry. Here it is pertinent or important to mention that deprivation of a specific food substance leads to an increased preference for that substance. For example, when the blood sugar level drops, the hypothalamus structure in the brain, glands, stomach organs, and other body parts sends out signals which activate a hunger drive and make one feel hungry. After food has been consumed by the individual's body, it returns to a state of balance. This maintenance of overall physiological balance is called "Homeostasis".

The term or concept "Homeostasis," was coined or formulated by Walter Bradford Cannon (19 October, 1871–1 October 1945), a prominent Harvard University Physiologist, in the years 1929–1932. W.B. Cannon (1932) suggested that our body system constantly works towards an optimum level of functioning, maintaining a normal state of balance between input and output. According to Weiner (1980), "Homeostasis is the tendency towards the maintenance of a relatively stable internal environment." Homeostasis refers to the body's automatic efforts to maintain a constant, normal state of the bloodstream.

Thus, it can be said that our food intake is regulated by a complex feeding—satiety system located in the hypothalamus, liver and other parts of the body. They are equipped with special detectors that respond to variations in the concentration of various nutrients in the blood. It has been suggested that our bodies work to maintain a critical level of body fat called the set point. Your personal set point is the weight you maintain when you are making no effort to gain or loose weight. When your body weight goes below this level, you feel hungry. The set point is determined partly by one's genetic make-up and partly by the early feeding practices. Cultural considerations often determine what, when, and how much to eat, and food intake also is determined by social values and moral training. The idea of same food may induce hunger pangs in some and the feeling of nausea in others. It shows that while hunger is of biological origin, it is uniquely shaped by culture, personal experiences, moral training, and cognitive factors also.

2. *Thirst:* Like hunger, thirst is a periodic drive. People may survive without food for several weeks but without water may die in a few hours. Thirst is often felt sooner than hunger. Strength of thirst is also more than the hunger drive. Water loss occurs through evaporation, breathing, perspiration, and urination. Without sufficient water, our bodies become hostile environments to the individual cells within our bodies. According to Cannon's theory, dryness of the mucus lining of the mouth and throat elicit thirst drive. This is because of deprivation of water for several hours. This dryness is a sign of dehydration of the tissues. Thus, thirst drive is aroused by dehydration of the body tissues, particularly tissues of the oral cavity due to want or need of water. Lowering the amount of water in blood reduces the saliva secreted into the mouth and the throat. By taking water, these dried tissues of the oral cavity become wet and the thirst sensation or drive subsides or is satisfied. But if instead of putting water inside the throat directly, the water is sent to the stomach by the help of a tube, relatively greater time will be required for the cessation or the satisfaction of the thirst drive. On the other hand, a few drops of water put inside the mouth to wet tissues of the mouth, would be able to subside the thirst experience temporarily.

The physiological key to the thirst motive lies in the imbalance of fluid in the body tissues and the hypothalamus. Imbalance of fluid in the body has been linked to the level of salt (sodium chloride) in the blood stream as salt caused dehydration. A high level of salt in the blood upsets the fluid balance in the tissues which in turn calls for the supply of fluids to them. This message is conveyed to the lateral hypothalamus and the thirst drive is activated. After getting the supply of fluid in the form of a drink, the body's chemical balance is restored. This activates the thirst satiety centre situated in the hypothalamus which in turn switches off the thirst drive.

Human behaviour depends not only on one's biological predispositions and chemical imbalance of the body tissues and is, to a large extent, a function of social learning. Why we drink, what we drink, when we drink, and how we drink somehow or the other, depends upon personal, social, and cultural factors and environmental learning.

3. *Sleep:* Sleep, like food and water, is a basic necessity of life. Sleep is one of our important bodily or physiological functions, so much so that *Ayurveda* has included sleep in three support pillars of life, the other two being food and the sexual discipline. Acharya Charka has defined it as a stage when physical and mental exertion lowers the activity of the mind, resulting in its dissociation with the sense objects. Need for sleep arises, particularly, when the individual or the organism is tired. Sleep acts as a type of rest by providing the cell bodies to recover the energy used in activity. Sleep is considered the most effective way to give absolute rest to the body and the mind. Adequate rest is a vital need for the body and the mind. Hence, sleep is essential for health. Studies show that not getting enough sleep or getting poor quality of it on a regular basis can play havoc with our health. Sound sleep makes the person fresh and fit, as it reduces the effect of fatigue and tiredness by providing rest to cell bodies. Due to continuous physical work, the muscles accumulate lactic acid. Most probably, this stimulates certain receptors and the person wants to take rest by the way of sleep.

Though not enough studies have been done on sleep as a biological drive, certain investigations do indicate that certain parts of the brain; specially the reticular formation of the lower brain controls and regulates the drive for sleep and rest. Insomnia seems to be caused by excessive metabolic activity in the brain's frontal cortex. Cooling the brain reduces metabolic activity. For deep, refreshing sleep to occur, the frontal cortex has to rest, said Dr. Eric Nofzinger, a professor of psychiatry at the University of Pittsburgh. Although sleep is necessary to reduce fatigue and tiredness, it has been observed that a person can remain awake continuously for more than hundred hours. But, one will definitely experience feeling of drowsiness, headache, nausea (vomiting tendency), and lack of appetite, etc. following the days of sleepless nights than when a person had a comfortable sleep at night. Research shows that sleep deprivation mainly affects attention (Adler, Tina, 1993). There are related psychological problems, however, including impaired memory formation, which in part may reflect lessened motivation to focus on details. Affecting our overall performance, poor quality sleep can lead to low immunity, poor digestion, constipation, hypertension, anxiety, and depression. Insufficient sleep is also responsible for mood swings, irritability, and other behavioural disorders resulting in reduced productivity and troubled relationships. Sleep affects health, relationships, and decision making. If parents want their children to thrive academically, "Getting them to sleep on time is important as getting them to school on time", said psychologist Gahan Fallone, who conducted the research at Brown Medical School.

Sleep researcher Wilse Webb (1993) notes that when we are sleep-deprived for several nights, aspects of psychological functioning such as attention, learning, and memory deteriorate notably. Webb (1993) also notes that many people sleep late or nap on their days off. Perhaps, they suffer from mild sleep deprivation during the week and catch up on the week end. The amount of sleep we need seems to be in part genetically determined, like our heights (Webb, 1993). People also tend to need more sleep during periods of change and stress such as a change of job, an increase in workload, or an episode of depression. Perhaps, sleep helps us recover from the stresses of life.

The need for sleep not only varies from person to person, it also keeps changing throughout the life cycle. Most adults need six to eight hours of sleep daily per night, whereas a newly born infant sleeps between sixteen and eighteen hours. School-going children need at least seven or eight hours of sleep daily. It is believed that all of us spend one-third of our life in sleep or deep slumber. As the old age approaches, people often get less sleep. Old people are more often seen wanting for it. Michael Gardner found perhaps most surprising, the worst sleep seems to occur in men and women ages 18 to 24. "The story with age is fascinating," Gardner said. "Usually, the common knowledge is that as you get older you have more sleep problems, We found pretty much the opposite."

A good sleep has a wide range of positive effects on our body and mind. Sleep is relaxing and freshening for the body and the mind. Good sleep enjoyed at proper time and for an adequate time period tends to improve all biological or physiological functions. "Sleep is related to everything", said Michael Gardner a fellow at the Centre for Sleep and Respiratory Neurobiology at the University of Pennysylvania. It is said that happiness and misery of a person can be judged from that person's sleep pattern. According to the Upanishads, "A man with a hundred desires sleeps uneasy."

Because of complex lives, full of stresses, long working hours, deadline or target pressure, and coping with increasing competitiveness, sound sleep is becoming a remote possibility. Difficulty in sleeping is not unusual when under stress, fears, aggravation, or other negative emotions that lead to higher body activity. Income, employment status, relationship satisfaction, and hobbies all affect sleep, according to research. Surveys report that sixty percent of the adult urban population in our country either sleeps during wrong hours like late in the night till late in the morning or suffers from poor quality of rest inviting many health problems especially psychosomatic disorders. Sleep is something that the body generates and depends on many factors. Not getting enough sleep is linked to many problems, from car-crash to crippled memory and inhibited creativity. Narcolepsy is a very common sleep disorder characterized by recurrent, uncontrollable, brief episodes of sleep.

Sleep specialist Cornelius Kellner said "It's normal to be awake at night occasionally." People suffering from sleeplessness can help themselves by modifying their daily routine. Follow a regular relaxing bedtime routine. Arrange your schedule so you go to sleep at the same time each night. Make it a point to get up at the same time each day. Avoid exposure to bright light before bedtime. They can include adequate physical exercise like a walk in the early morning or evening, and adopting relaxation techniques like meditation, yoga, and deep breathing. Exercise everyday, but not just before going to sleep. Exercise regularly. At least three hours before bedtime. Food is best avoided two to three hours before going to bed. Avoid drinking too much towards the end of the evening. One should exclude foods containing caffeine like tea, coffee, chocolates, cola, etc. Coffee, nicotine, and alcohol also impede falling asleep and, therefore, should not be consumed before going to bed. While initially both caffeine and alcohol might not affect your sleep, in due course it does. One should reduce the intake of fried foods, television viewing till late at night, stimulating music, or using computers before going to bed. Read something pleasant or relaxing just before going to sleep. If you can not sleep, get up. Read or watch television until you feel tired. That way you will not feel frustrated by your inability to sleep. Take a warm bath or have a massage before retiring to bed or going to sleep. Setting a regular sleep schedule and sticking to it, even on weekdays helps. Do not nap during the day. All this helps in managing sleep disorders. Having a good sleep is the practice of a disciplined life style. Early to bed and early to rise holds the key to good health. So, better sleep, better health.

Figure 10.2 Maternal affection.

4. *Maternal behaviour:* The love, affection, care, devotion, sympathy, concern, worries, and anxiety of the mother for the welfare of her child is almost universally observed (Figure 10.2). Hormones play an important role in activating the maternal drive. The presence of the hormone named "Prolactin" secreted by the pituitary gland seems to have effect upon the brain of the mother. This brings

profound changes in the mother's behaviour. Such behaviour is characterized by a strong desire to remain in close proximity with the child, particularly, when the child is separated from the mother, to take care of the child, to protect the child at the cost of her own life, to be elated at child's success, and unhappy over child's failure, to show anxiety and concern for her child's welfare and so on.

The maternal drive is stimulated both by biological, as well as psychological factors interrelated with learning. A hormone Progesterone has been found to be important in maintaining pregnancy. Another hormone, Prolactin, produced by the pituitary gland, directs the mammary glands to secrete milk for the newborn. The stimuli responsible for activating maternal drive and behaviour spring from a variety of sources: from one's physical environment, or socio-cultural background, from one's mother and grandmother, from observing the behaviour of friends and neighbours, from books, movies, and television, etc. However, much depends upon the impact of social learning and earlier experiences which leave an indelible impression on the mind of the mother justifying the finding that being a good and loving mother, depends considerably on one's having had a good and loving mother for oneself.

5. *Pain:* Pain is said to be an aversive motive. It refers to avoidance drive. Any stimulus that is painful to the organism, invites avoidance or aversion tendency for it. Loud voices, electric shocks, pricking of pin, etc. give pain to the individual. So, they are usually avoided. When pain is prolonged and continuous, and can be escaped by developing appropriate action, it proves to be most effective and useful. Many bad habits are unlearned and good habits are learned by useful application of a painful stimulus. Chronic pain can also impair the immune system (Page et al., 1993).

Pain is unpleasant and we all want to avoid it. Pain alerts us to problems occurring somewhere within our bodies. Our feelings of pain are private sensations—they are difficult to share or describe to others (Verillo, 1975). Many stimuli can cause pain. Very intense stimulation of virtually any sense receptor can produce pain. Too much light, very strong pressure on the skin, excessive temperatures, very loud sounds, and even too many "hot" spices can all result in our experiencing pain. The stimulus for pain need not be intense. Under the right circumstances, even a light pin prick can be very painful.

Our skin seems to have many receptors for pain, but pain receptors can also be found deep inside our bodies—consider stomach aches, lower back pain, headaches. Pain is experienced in our brains; pain is the only "sense" for which we can find no one specific centre in the cerebral cortex.

A theory of pain that still attracts attention from researchers is Melzack & Wall's Gate-Control Theory (Melzack, 1973). Melzack believes that pain signals are allowed in or blocked from the brain by neural "gates" in the spinal cord and brain stem. It suggests that our experience of pain happens not so much at the level of the receptor (say, in the skin), but within the central nervous system. The theory proposes that a gate-like structure in the spinal cord responds to stimulation from a particular type of nerve—one that "opens the gate" and allows for the sensation of pain by letting impulses on up to the brain. Other nerve fibres can offset the activity of the pain-carrying fibres and "close the gate" so that pain messages are cut off and never make it to the brain.

The sensation of pain is transmitted along two different nerve pathways in the spinal cord—rapid and slow neural pathways. This is why we often experience "first and second pain" (Melzack and Wall, 1965; Sternbach, 1978). The "first pain" is clear, localized feeling that does not "hurt" much, but it tells us that which part of the body has been hurt and what kind of injury has occurred. The "second pain" is more diffuse, a long-lasting pain that hurts in the emotional sense.

There are several situations in which this theory of opening and closing a gate to pain seems reasonable. One of the things that happen when we are exposed to persistent pain is that certain neurotransmitters—endorphins—are released in the brain (Hughes et al., 1975; Terenius, 1973). Endorphins (plural because there may be a number of them) naturally reduce our sense of pain and generally make us feel good. When their effects are blocked, pain seems usually severe. Endorphins stimulate nerve fibres that go to the spinal cord and effectively close the gate that monitors the passage of impulses from pain receptors.

One situation that seems to fit the gate-control theory is abnormally persistent pain. Some patients who have received a trauma to some part of their body, for example through accident or surgery continue to experience pain even after the initial wound is completely healed. Abnormal pain is also found in the so-called "phantom limb" pain experienced by some (about 10 percent) of amputees. These patients continue to feel pain in an arm or leg, even after that limb is no longer there. Recent thinking is that severe trauma of amputation overloads and destroys the function of important cells in the spinal cord that normally act to close the gate for pain messages, leaving the pain circuits uninhibited (Gracely, Lynch, and Bennett, 1991; Laird and Bennett, 1991)

Think of some of the other mechanisms that are useful in moderating the experience of pain. Hypnosis and cognitive self-control (just trying very hard to convince yourself that the pain you are experiencing is not that bad and will go away) are effective (Litt, 1988; Melzack, 1973). That pain can be controlled to some extent by cognitive training, is clear from the success of many classes aimed at reducing the pain of childbirth. The theory is that psychological processes influence the gate-control centre in the spinal cord. We also have ample evidence that placebos (an inactive substance that works because a person has to come to believe that it will be effective) can be effective in treating pain. A "placebo" is a substance (perhaps in pill or tablet form) that a person believes will be effective in treating some symptom, when, in fact there is no active pain-relieving ingredient in the substance (placebo). When subjects are given a placebo that they genuinely believe will alleviate pain, endorphins are released in the brain which, again, help to close the gate to pain-carrying impulses (Levine et al., 1979).

Another process that works to ease the feeling or experience of pain, particularly pain from or near the surface of the skin, is called "counterritation". The idea here is to stimulate forcefully (not painfully, of course) an area of the body near the location of the pain. Dentists have discovered that rubbing the gum near where a novocaine needle is to be inserted significantly reduces the patient's experience of the pain of the needle. Again, as you might have guessed, the logic is that all the stimulation from the nearby rubbing action serves to close the pain gate so that needle has little effect. And speaking of needles, the ancient oriental practice of acupuncture can also be tied to the Gate-Control Theory of pain. There also is evidence that acupuncture releases endorphins in the brain. Perhaps, each or all of these functions serve the major purpose of controlling pain by closing off impulses to the brain. New research shows that men and women with so-called dispositional optimism—defined as having positive expectations for the future—were less sensitive to pain.

6. *Pleasure*: Although pleasure (Figure 10.3) is an important drive or motive, it has received relatively less attention for systematic physiological study. Some studies by Delged, Roberts, and Olds have located a pleasure centre in the septal area of the brain.

Figure 10.3 Pleasure.

7. *Sex or Sex Motive:* Sex is a psycho-physical motive. Sex is said to be a powerful biological drive, though it is not necessary for survival like food, water, oxygen, etc. Satisfaction of the sex urge or desire to seek sex-experiences is although not essential for the survival of an individual. It is the strongest human urge in the satisfaction to which lies the proper growth and development, and well-being of an individual. Its satisfaction results in feeling of immense happiness and well-being in an individual. Moreover, it is essential for the continuation and survival of the human species. Sex drive in the civilized and urban societies is particularly suppressed by the social traditions and cultural restrictions. But suppression of sexual drive is dangerous for good health and normal personality development.

The studies indicate that the strength of the sexual drive depends upon the chemical substances present in the blood. Investigations also show that secretion from the sex gland produces strong sex drive. Hormones from the endocrine glands produce change in sex drive. Hormone called *Testosterone* secreted in the testes of the males and *Estrogens* secreted in the ovaries of the females are considered responsible for the sexual drive and sexual behaviour. Lindgren and Petsinoich observed that the human sex drive seems to be stimulated by three classes of events: (i) the presence of sex hormones, (ii) external stimulation, (iii) cerebral activity. Human sex motive is termed as a complex blend of innate as well as acquired tendencies.

Much of motivation in the form of sexual arousal and behaviour is rooted in earlier experiences and social learning and controlled by lesions in the hypothalamus, the sub-cortical structure in the brain. In practice, the sex game is more psychological than biological or organic. The other variables or factors related to one's socio-cultural environment, sexual experiences, and learning also play a significant role in guiding and deciding the mode or method and nature of the sex drive and behaviour in human beings independently of their fertility period and secretion of hormones. Cognitive factors such as our thoughts, feelings, fantasies, perceptions, attitudes, and memories, etc. play a powerful role in sexual motivation.

8. *Fear and Anger:* Fear and anger are considered as two motivational behaviours. The drives for fear and anger are expressed through bodily and behavioural changes. Fear is an important drive because it can be learned easily. It is said to be a drive because it motivates the learning and performance of new responses like hunger, thirst, and other drives. It is assumed that, possibly, fear may be related to pain avoidance, another basic and primitive drive. The fear or general excitement found for loud noise is innate and universally found. Fear and anger are discussed in Chapter 11.

9. *Aggression:* Aggressiveness is said to be an aversive motive. It is related to the need to defend the organism from attack. It may be relatively more complex drive than pain avoidance. Ulrich (1967) has shown that painful stimulations lead to aggressive behaviour. It is also a common experience in our everyday life. It has been found that when animals are put together in an enclosure and are subjected to electric shock, they start fighting with each other. Feshbach and Delgardo have made certain studies in this area of human motivation.

(B) Sociogenic or Psycho-Social Motives: These are also called *secondary motives*. These motives are learnt or acquired. At birth and soon after, almost all drives and needs of the body are generally physiological in nature, aimed with the purpose to fulfil the basic needs to survive. His entire behaviour is guided and regulated by these physiological needs such as need for food, water, air, bathing, sleep, excretion of waste products from the body, etc.

The social motives are learned from others. The infant or the baby learns from others when and how these physiological needs are to be fulfilled and when and where to ask for food and where not to. He, therefore, slowly but steadily learns to fulfil his needs and motives in a socialized manner, according to his family customs, group norms, and according to the values of the society, etc.

The social motives are called "secondary motives" because they involve interaction with others and are learned due to social conditioning, in social context. There are a large number of social motives, which are purely acquired and developed due to habit and conditioning. Morgan and King state that social motives are general, persisting characteristics of a person and since they are learned motives; their strength differs greatly from one individual to another.

1. *Gregariousness:* "Gregariousness" refers to the motive to keep contact with other people. It is the human tendency to belong to a certain group or to derive satisfaction from group activity or group work. This desire to be attached to some persons, groups, or associations is so very commonly found in every human, that it has been thought by many as an inborn or universal motive.

But gregariousness is due to social conditioning or learning. Right from the moment of birth, the human baby due to her or his helpless condition depends upon others for the satisfaction of her or his needs. And because of this dependence, she or he comes in contact with other people and interacts with them. Gregariousness develops out of this habit to remain with others and interact with them from the beginning of life. It is universally found because all go through a period of helplessness and dependence upon others and learn it through the process of growth. In addition to this motive, there are two other motives, which have their roots in the helplessness of the human baby: (i) imitativeness, (ii) the tendency to appeal to powers superior to oneself.

2. *Self-Assertiveness:* The self-assertiveness is also called *mastery motive*. The strong desire to master oneself, to get recognition in the society, to show dominance over others varies from society to society. This motive is expressed in a wide variety of behaviours like the motive for leadership, power, self-display, to compete with others, etc. In societies, the child is taught and encouraged from the early childhood to develop these motives. There are other social motives like co-operation, competition, self-esteem, etc. Murray (1938) on the basis of his findings has referred several social motives like abasement, affiliation, achievement, aggression counteraction, exhibition, etc.

3. *Need for Achievement:* Need for achievement was one of the first social motives to be studied in detail (McClelland et al., 1953), and research into

this motive continues even today (Spence, 1989). As characterized by D.C. McClelland and J.W. Atkinson, "The need for achievement (n-ach) is the desire to compete with a standard of excellence."

According to Atkinson and Feather (1966), "The achievement motives is conceived as a latest disposition which is manifested in overt striving only when the individual perceives performance as instrumental to a sense of personal accomplishment."

According to Irving Sarnoff, "Achievement motive is defined in terms of the way an individual orients himself towards objects or conditions that he does not possess. If he values those objects and conditions, and he feels that he ought to possess them, he may be regarded as having an achievement motive."

People in whom need for achievement is strong, seek to become accomplished, and to improve their task performance. They are task-oriented and prefer to work on tasks that are challenging, and on which their performance can be evaluated in some way, either by comparing it with other people's performance or in terms of some other standards. "Achievement is task-oriented behaviour that allows the individual's performance to be evaluated according to some internally or externally imposed criterion, that involves the individual in competing with others, or that otherwise involves some standards of excellence" (Smith, 1979; Spence and Helmreich, 1983). Achievement motivation can be seen in many areas of human behaviour, on the job, in homemaking, or athletic competition. Individual high in achievement motivation tend to get higher grades in school, earn more rapid promotions, and attain greater success in running their own businesses than persons low in such motivation (Andrews, 1967; Raynor, 1970). Social motives like need for achievement are learned motives. Difference in early life experiences lead to variation in the amount of achievement motivation (and other social motives, as well). Children learn by imitating or copying the behaviour of their parents, teachers, elder siblings, friends, and other important people who serve as models.

The expectations that the parents have for their children are said to be important in the development of achievement motivation (Eccles, 1977). Parents who expect their children to work hard and to strive for success encourage them to do so and will praise them for achievement. Studies have shown that the children whose independent training starts at an early age and who get more autonomy within a cooperative, encouraging, and less authoritarian family environment, usually develop an achievement-oriented attitude. Later on, the experiences and learning based on the circumstances and situations in her or his life may lead an individual to provide a level for the intensity of her or his achievement motive to struggle for attaining the standards of excellence desired by her or him.

It has been suggested that need for achievement is related to the society's economic and business growth (McClelland et al. 1961, 1971).

Regarding the gender differences in achievement motivation, Horner (1970, 1972) suggested that many women actually fear success: they realize that striving for achievement can reduce their femininity in the eyes of others. Fortunately, these results have not been replicated in subsequent investigations (Cherry and Deaux, 1975).

The degree, to which people with strong underlying achievement motivations show achievement-oriented behaviour, depends upon fear of failure also. Fear of failure inhibits the expression of achievement behaviour (Atkinson, 1958; Atkinson and Birch, 1978).

Achievement motivation is negatively related to leaders' effectiveness because persons high in such motivation frequently want to take total charge and run the show in all respects. Need for achievement is generally measured with a projective test, using, specially, several pictures similar to those from Murray's Thematic Apperception Test (TAT).

Some characteristics of people having high n-ach:

1. People having high need for achievement prefer to work on moderately challenging tasks or jobs, which promise success. Persons high in achievement motivation tend to prefer situations involving moderate levels of risk or difficulty to ones that are either very low or very high in risk or difficulty (Atkinson and Litwin, 1960). They do not like to work on easy tasks, where there is no challenge, nor do they like very difficult task, where the likelihood of their success is very low. They are very realistic on work.
2. People having high need for achievement like tasks in which their performance can be compared with other people.
3. People having high need for achievement tend to be persistent on working jobs they perceive as career related.
4. When high needs for achievement people are successful, this tends to raise their level of aspiration in a realistic way so that they will move on to slightly challenging and difficult tasks.
5. People having High needs for achievement like to work in situations in which they have some control on the outcome.
6. People having high need for achievement strongly dislikes failures. Atkinson and Atkinson found that person with high need for achievement have two active tendencies: (i) tendency to achieve success, and (ii) tendency to avoid failure.

The work on goal theory of achievement motivation has differentiated three separate types of goals: mastery goals (also called *learning goals*), which focus on gaining competence or mastering a new set of knowledge or skills; performance goals (also called *ego-involvement goals*), which focus on achieving normative-based standards, doing better than others, or doing well without a lot of effort; and social goals, which focus on relationships among people (Ames, 1992; Dweck, 1980; Urban and Maehr, 1995). In the context of school learning, which involves operating in a relatively structured environment; students with mastery goals outperform students with either performance or social. However, in life success, it seems critical that individuals have all three types of goals in order to be very successful.

One aspect of this theory is that individuals are motivated to either avoid failure (more often associated with performance goals) or achieve success (more often associated with mastery goals). In the former situation, the individual is more likely to select easy or difficult tasks, thereby either achieving success or having a good excuse for why failure occurred. In the latter situation, the individual is more likely to select moderately difficult tasks which will provide an interesting challenge, but still keep the high expectations for success.

4. *Power motivation:* Winter (1973) has defined social power as "The ability or capacity of a person to produce (consciously or unconsciously) intended effects on the behaviour or emotions of another person." Motivation to be in-charge, have high status, and exercise or exert influence over others is called "power motivation". The goals of power motivation are to influence, control, persuade, lead, and charm others, and to enhance one's own reputation in the eyes of other people. People with strong motivation derive satisfaction from achieving these goals.

Power motivation or the need for power (n-power) varies in strength from person to person. Power motivation can be expressed in many ways; the manner or way of expression depends greatly on the person's socio-economic status (Hoyenga & Hoyenga, 1984), sex (Hoyenga & Hoyenga, 1979), level of maturity (McClelland, 1975), and the degree to which the individual fears her or his own power. People with high power motivation express themselves (Hoyenga, 1984):

(i) By impulsive and aggressive action, especially by men in lower social economic level. Physical violence between spouses occurs in almost one-third of all marriages (Russel, 1988).
(ii) By participation in competitive sports such as hockey, football, etc. especially by men in lower social economic background, and by college men.
(iii) By joining organizations and holding office in these organizations.
(iv) Among men, by drinking and sexually dominating women.
(v) By obtaining and collecting possessions such as fancy cars, gems, elaborate stereo sets, etc.

(vi) By associating with people who are not particulary popular with others and who perhaps, are more easily controlled by high n-power persons because they depend on her or him for friendship.

(vii) By choosing occupations such as teaching, diplomacy, business, etc.—occupations in which high n-power people believe they have a chance to have an impact on other beings.

(viii) By building and disciplining their bodies. This seems especially a characteristic of women with high power needs.

5. *Human Aggression:* "Aggressive motivation" is the desire to inflict harm on others and often results in behaviour directed towards the goal of injuring another living being who is motivated to avoid such treatment (Baron and Richardson, 1994).

Direct provocation from others is an important cause of aggression. It is based on the principle of reciprocity, meaning that we tend to treat others in the manner they have treated us. Perhaps, the most common everyday source of aggression is a verbal insult or negative evaluation from another person (Buss, 1961). If insult is perceived as intended, and if harmful intent is attributed to the insulter, the insult is interpreted as an aggressive act. This aggressive act arouses aggression in the person being insulted, and this person responds with counteraggression, especially in public situations. Social learning theory stresses the role of imitation of others' behaviour as a cause of aggression (Bandura, 1873, 1877, 1883). Exposure to aggressive models, for example by watching television, elicits aggressive behaviour.

Another important cause of aggressive motivation is frustration. "Frustration" is the thwarting or blocking of goal-directed behaviour. People behave aggressively when others prevent them from achieving their goals or what they want. "Frustration-aggression hypothesis" states that aggression always stems from frustration and that frustration always produces aggression (whether overt or covert). Aggressive behaviour is always an indication of frustration.

Aggressive behaviour can also stem from negative affect—unpleasant feelings produced by a wide range of social or environmental conditions (Berkowitz, 1993). High temperature (Baron, 1997), intensive or loud noise (Donner Stein and Wilson, 1976), crowding (Freedman, 1986; Schopler and Stock Dale, 1977), intake of alcohol, and Type A behaviour pattern increase aggression, particularly, in people who have already been angered in some way.

10.2 INTRINSIC AND EXTRINSIC FRAMEWORK

Explanation regarding the source or sources of motivation can be categorized as intrinsic—internal to the person or extrinsic—out side the person (Figure 10.4).

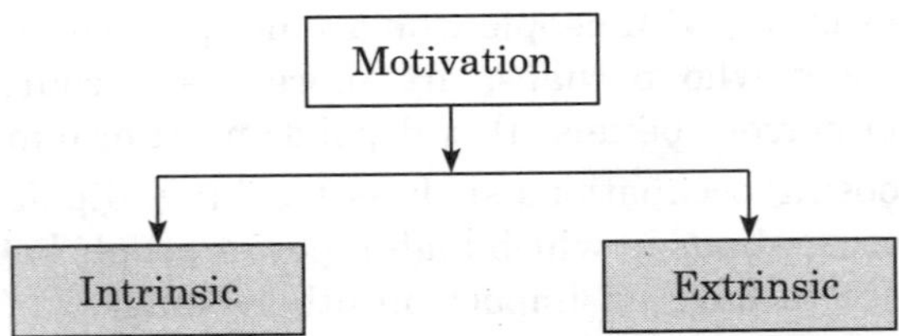

Figure 10.4 Intrinsic-Extrinsic Motivation.

10.2.1 Intrinsic Motivation

The concept of "intrinsic motivation" was originally proposed by Robert White (1959), who argued that many behaviours such as play, fun, and exploration do not need to be reinforced in order to be performed. White also argued that people, even young children, have an internal force that encourages them to be competent and effective. For instance, a child at age one, playing with an old stool that she has turned upside down. She would climb in and beam with pride at her accomplishment. Then she would climb out grinning once again about her sense of mastery. She did not look to her parents for approval. Competent interaction with her environment was its own reward (Deci and Ryan, 1985).

"Intrinsic motivation" is the term used to refer to the motivation for any behaviour that is dependent on factors that are internal in nature. Intrinsic motivation usually derives from feelings of satisfaction and fulfilment, not from external rewards. A person or an animal is motivated to act because of a driving tension, an emotional state triggering an opposite emotional state, or some internal force that encourages competence and inquiry. Researchers have discovered that enjoyment in life is correlated with experiencing activities as intrinsically motivating. In one study, 107 working men and women rated the extent to which their work was intrinsically motivating, as well as their sense of well-being (Graef et al., 1983). The correlation between intrinsic motivation and happiness was + 0.28, which was statistically significant.

10.2.2 Extrinsic Motivation

In contrast, motivation that originates on factors outside the individual is called "extrinsic motivation". It includes behaviour that is motivated by rewards and/or a punishment administered by outside forces is extrinsically determined, for example students striving hard in school for the extrinsic reward of good grades. Incentive theory emphasizes how external goals motivate us to respond and to act. An incentive occurs before we actually do something, and it energizes us to do something—if the incentive is attractive, or not to do something—if the incentive is unattractive (Reeve, 1992). Incentive theory is consistent with the principles of operant or instrumental conditioning. Incentive theory, agues, that the probability of engaging in a particular activity depends both on the expectation of obtaining a particular goal, and the value of that goal.

The below mentioned is a technique of motivation by Locke and Latham (1990):

1. Set specific goals
2. Set difficult goals
3. Set attainable goals
4. Reward yourself for reaching each goal
5. Become committed to your goals

10.3 THE NEED HIERARCHY MODEL (Hierarchy of Needs: A Theory of Human Motivation)

Abraham Maslow (1908–1970), was born on April 1, 1908 in Brooklyn, New York. He received his BA in 1930, his MA in 1931, and his Ph.D from the University of Wisconsin in 1934, all in Psychology. Maslow served as the chair of the Psychology department at Brandeis from 1951 to 1969. He spent his final years in semi-retirement in California, until, on June 8, 1970, he died of a heart attack after years of ill health.

Abraham Maslow
(1908–1970)

Abraham Maslow, a humanistic psychologist, believed that "Human life will never be understood unless its highest aspirations are taken into account." To Maslow, this meant intensive study of growth, self-actualization, the striving toward health, the quest for identity and autonomy, and the yearning for excellence. Although Maslow also believed that there are regressive, fearful, and self-diminishing tendencies, he sought to describe a system of values that was intrinsically good and desirable. Maslow (1970) proposed that human motives are arranged in a hierarchy. According to him, human motives or needs may exist in a hierarchy, so that we must satisfy those that are more basic before moving on to ones that are less linked to biological needs. Maslow's theory of motivation consists of needs, with each need being prepotent to the need above it. For instance, the lowest needs are physiological, such as hunger and thirst, and must be satisfied in order for the next higher need of safety (avoidance of pain, desire for security) to be considered.

Abraham Maslow (1970) is probably best known for his theoretical exploration of self-actualization, the important tendency to realize our own potential. Maslow theorized that our human motives or needs are arranged in a hierarchy, with the most basic needs at the bottom and the more highly developed needs (esteem needs and self-actualization needs) at the top (Maslow, 1970). Maslow places physiological needs at the base of the hierarchy of needs. One step above is safety needs. Above the safety needs are the social needs (Bausmen, Ster Leary, 1995). Above the social needs in the hierarchy, Maslow proposes, are the esteem needs. Finally, at the top of the hierarchy are self-actualization needs (Figure 10.5).

1. *Physiological or biological needs:* Physiological needs or biological needs include the need for food, water, sleep, air (oxygen), protein, salt, sugar, calcium, and other minerals and vitamins, excretion or elimination of waste products from the body, or to get rid of wastes (carbon dioxide, sweat, urine, and faeces), bodily comforts like warmth, pain avoidance, and to have sex or sexual release, etc. They also include the need to maintain a pH balance (getting too acidic or base will kill you) and temperature (98.6 or near to it). Also, there are the needs to be active, to rest, and to sleep.

Biological needs or states of deprivation arising within our bodies create unpleasant states of arousal or drives—the subjective feelings associated with needs that we typically describe as hunger, thirst, fatigue, and so on. In order to eliminate such feelings and restore a balanced physiological state, known as homeostasis, we engage in certain activities. The term, "Homeostasis," was coined by W.B. Cannon, a prominent Harvard University physiologist. "Homeostasis" refers to the body's automatic efforts to maintain a constant, normal state of the bloodstream. Cannon (1932) described this process for (i) the water content of the blood, (ii) salt content, (iii) sugar content, (iv) protein content, (v) fat content, (vi) calcium content, (vii) oxygen content, (viii) constant hydrogen-ion level (acid-base balance), and (ix) constant temperature of the blood. Obviously, this list could be extended to include other minerals, the hormones, vitamins, and so on. Homeostasis is a state of physiological balance within the body. Homeostasis is the principle by which your furnace thermostat operates: when it gets too cold, it switches the heat on; when it gets too hot, it switches the heat off. In the same way, your body, when it lacks a certain substance, develops a hunger for it; when it gets enough of it, then the hunger stops. Maslow simply extends the homeostatic principle to needs, such as safety, belonging, and esteem that we do not ordinarily think of in these terms.

2. *Safety or security needs:* Safety or security needs include the needs for feeling safe and secure in one's life. The list of safety or security needs include the need for security, protection from environment, housing, clothing, out of danger, desire for security, stability, protection, physical

security, crime security, avoidance of pain, dependency, freedom from pain and fear, anxiety, and chaos, need for structure, order, law, and limits, strength in the protector, and so on.

When the physiological needs are largely taken care of, this second layer of needs come into play. You will become increasingly interested in finding safe circumstances, stability, and protection. You might develop a need for structure, for order, some limits. The peaceful, smoothly, running, stable, good society ordinarily makes its members feel safe enough from wild animals, extremes of temperature, criminal assaults, murder, chaos, tyranny, and so on. In the ordinary adult, this set of needs manifest themselves in the form of our urges to have a home in a safe neighbourhood, a little job security, and a good retirement plan and a bit of insurance and so on. The safety needs can become very urgent on the social scene whenever there are real threats to law and order and authority of society. The threat of chaos can be expected in most human beings to produce a regression from any higher needs to the more prepotent safety needs. Utopia can be defined simply as a place where there is plenty of food. She or he tends to think that if only guaranteed food for the rest of life, she or he tends to be defined happier in terms of eating.

3. *Social needs or the belongingness and love needs:* The belongingness and love needs include needs to have friends, a sweetheart, children, to be loved and appreciated, affectionate relationships in general, communion with neighbourhood and friends, etc., and to belong to and fit into a network of social relationships or a sense of community. The list of social needs or the belongingness and love needs include the need for intimate relationships, social groups, friends, affiliation with others, affection, feeling loved, gaining the approval of others and achieving success. The love needs involve both giving and receiving affection. In our day-to-day life, we exhibit these needs in our desires to marry, have a family, be a part of community, a member of a religious institution, a brother in the fraternity, a part of a gang or a bowling club, etc. When they are unsatisfied, a person will feel keenly the absence of friends, mate, or children. Such a person will hunger for relations with people in general—for a place in the group or family and will strive with great intensity to achieve this goal. Now the pangs of loneliness, ostracism, rejection, friendlessness, and rootlessness are pre-eminent.

In our society, the thwarting of these needs is the most commonly found cause in cases of maladjustment and more severe pathology. Practically, all theories of psychopathology have stressed thwarting of the love needs as basic in the picture of maladjustment.

4. *Esteem needs:* Esteem needs include the need to respect ourselves or develop self-respect, the desire for high evaluation, self-respect, gain the approval of others, to win the esteem of others, be competent, to achieve

success, recognition, prestige, status, and be accepted. Ambition and the need for the achievement are closely linked to esteem needs.

Next, we begin to look for a little self-esteem. Maslow noted two versions of esteem needs, a lower one and a higher one. The lower one is the need for the respect of others, the need for status, fame, glory, recognition, attention, reputation, appreciation, dignity, even dominance. The higher form involves the need for self-respect, including such feelings as confidence, competence, achievement, mastery, independence, and freedom. This is the "higher" form because, unlike the respect of others, once you have self-respect, it is a lot harder to lose! The negative version of these needs is low self-esteem and inferiority complexes.

Maslow felt that Alfred Adler (1870–1937) was really onto something when he proposed that these were at the roots of many, if not most, of our psychological problems. In modern society, most of us have what we need in regard to our physiological and safety needs, we, more often than not, have quite a bit of love and belonging, too. It is a little respect that often seems so very hard to get!

Alfred Adler
(1870–1937)

Maslow's initial conceptualization included only one growth need that is self-actualization. He later differentiated the growth need of self-actualization, specifically naming two lower-level growth needs prior to general level of self-actualization (Maslow and Lowery, 1998) and one beyond that level, that is self-transcendence (Maslow, 1971). They are:

5. *Cognitive needs:* Cognitive needs include the needs to know, to understand and to explore. It also includes novelty and curiosity.

6. *Aesthetic needs:* Aesthetic needs include the need for symmetry, order, beauty, structure, art.

7. *Self-actualization:* Self-actualization means attempting to reach one's full unique potential (self-fulfilment), the desire to become all that one can be or is capable of becoming, realizing one's own potential, and discernment.

Perhaps the best known of Maslow's rights or tenets is the term 'self-actualization." Although very rarely achieved, it is described as the full use and exploitation of talents, capacities, and personality. That is, self-actualizers are people who fulfil themselves and are doing the best that they are capable of doing (Maslow, 1970). Maslow reports that his interest in self-actualizing people was initially a consequence of his admiration for two of his teachers: Max Wertheimer, the founder of Gestalt psychology, and Ruth Benedict, a prominent cultural anthropologist (Maslow, 1971).

Maslow (1962) studied self-actualization by focusing on peak experiences. Maslow assumed that self-actualized individuals would report more peak experiences than other people. Self-actualization was described in the following way by Maslow (1954): "A musician must make music, an artist must paint, a poet must write, if he is to be ultimately at peace with himself. What a man can be, he must be. This need we may call self-actualization."

According to Carl Ransom Rogers (1902–1987), the path to self-actualization requires getting in touch with our genuine feelings, accepting them as ours, and acting upon them. We are happiest when our goals seem attainable, almost within our grasp, and we are striving with confidence to achieve them. Self-actualization can be measured by the questionnaires such as the index of self-actualization.

Carl Ransom Rogers
(1902–1987)

When looking for self-actualizers or people who were using their potential to its fullest, Maslow avoided the tendency to look for "perfect" people—that is, people without mistakes. Abraham Lincoln and Albert Einstein were identified as famous examples of people who were self-actualized. Maslow's list of self-actualizers include Aldous Huxley, Eleanor Roosevelt, Jane Addams, Schweitzer, Spinoza, and William James.

8. *Self-transcendence:* The need of self-transcendence includes a spiritual sense of peace, belonging and oneness with the universe, to connect to something beyond the ego or to help others find self-fulfilment and realize their potential or how others could be edified. It involves higher states of consciousness such as comic vision, experiencing oneself as a part of the universe. Most clearly defined by Victor Frankl, it is an outgrowth of our natural tendencies to care about our children, our families, friends, and lovers, and our innate capacity for empathy. It includes altruism, love, compassion, and Adler's social concern. Perhaps, it also includes other experiences that take us out of ourselves, such as music, art, literature, dance, and the beauty of nature.

According to Maslow, needs are of two kinds—deficiency needs and growth needs. Deficiency needs or D-needs are the basic needs and must be satisfied before higher level of needs emerge. All the needs towards the bottom of the hierarchy were regarded as deficiency motivation needs. This is because they are designed to reduce inadequacies or deficiencies. These include the four levels of hierarchy, that is physiological or biological needs, safety or security needs, social needs or belongingness and love needs, and esteem needs. They are the basics and must be satisfied before higher level of motivation, or growth needs can emerge.

The other category of human needs is the growth needs or growth motivation or being needs (B-needs). Growth needs help in the growth of the human beings and help actualize their potentialities after deficiency needs are fulfilled and satisfied. Growth needs are towards the top of the hierarchy and represent growth motivation, and are designed to produce personal growth. Growth motivated people welcome uncertainty, increased tension, pain, and are revolutionary (likes change), etc. According to Maslow (1968), "Satisfying deficiencies avoids illness, growth satisfactions produce positive health." Maslow's basic position is that as one becomes more self-actualized and self-transcendent, one become wiser (develops wisdom) and automatically knows what to do in a wide variety of situations.

Daniels (2001) suggests that Maslow's ultimate conclusion that the highest levels of self-actualization are transcendent in their nature, may be one of his most important contributions to the study of human behaviour and motivation. Maslow's initial conceptualization included only one growth need that is self-actualization. He later differentiated the growth need of self-actualization, specifically naming two lower-level growth needs prior to general level of self-actualization that is the cognitive and aesthetic needs (Maslow and Lowery, 1998) and one beyond that level that is self-transcendence (Maslow, 1971).

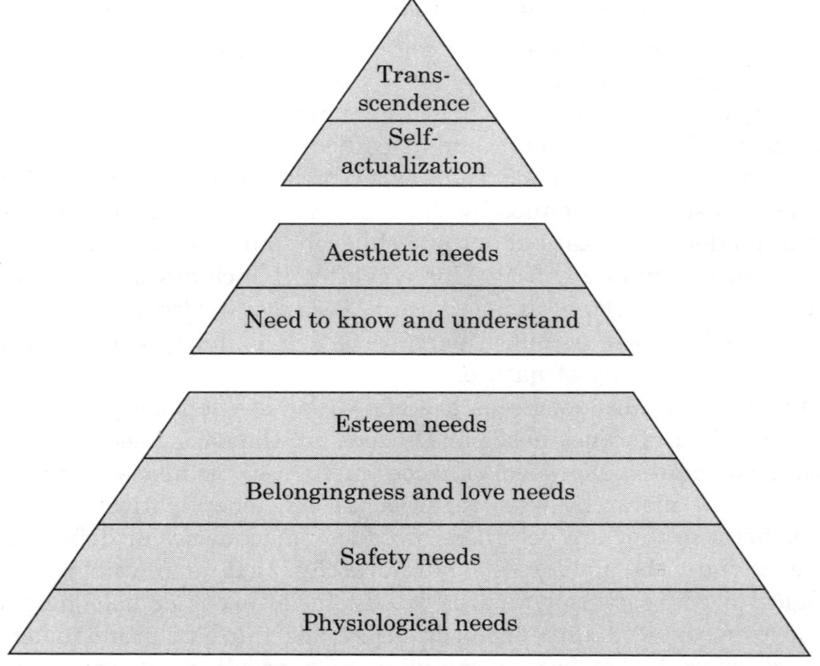

Figure 10.5 Maslow's hierarchy of needs.

Figure 10.5 shows Maslow's hierarchy of needs, in which each lower need must be satisfied before the next level of needs can be addressed. Norwood (1999) proposes that Maslow's hierarchy can be used to describe the kinds of information that individuals seek at different levels. For example, individuals at the lowest level that is physiological needs seek coping information in order to meet their basic needs. Information that is not directly connected to helping a person meets her or his needs in a very short time span, is simply left unattended. Individuals at the safety level, need helping information. They seek to be assisted in seeing how they can be safe and secure. Enlightening information is sought by individuals seeking to meet their belongingness needs. Quite often, this can be found in books or other material on relationship development. Empowering information is sought by people at the esteem level. They are looking for information on how their ego can be developed. Finally, people in the growth levels of cognitive, aesthetic, and self-actualization seek edifying information. While Norwood does not specifically address the level of transcendence, W. Huitt (2001) believes it safe to say that individual at this stage would seek information on how to connect to something beyond themselves or to how others could be edified.

There is little agreement about the identification of basic human needs. Murray (1938, 1943) has given a list of 37 needs such as need for oxygen, food, water, rest, sleep, physical contact, love and affection, social approval, company, self-assertion, security, independence, etc. The few major studies that have been completed on the hierarchy seem to support the proposals of William James (1892/1962), and Mathes (1981) that there are three levels of human needs James (1892/1962) hypothesized the levels of material (physiological, safety), social (belongingness, esteem), and spiritual. Mathes (1981) proposed the three levels were physiological, belongingness, and self-actualization; he considered security and self-esteem as unwarranted. Alderfer (1972) developed a comparable hierarchy with his ERG (existence, relatedness, and growth).

Ryan and Deci (2000) suggest three needs—the need for autonomy, the need for competence, and the need for relatedness. Grace and Cohen (2001) states that the most important needs for children are connection, recognition, and power. Nohria, Lawrence, and Wilson (2001) provide evidence from a sociobiological theory of motivation that humans have four basic needs: (i) acquire objects and experiences; (ii) bond with others in long-term relationships of mutual care and commitment; (iii) learn and make sense of the world and of ourselves; and (iv) to defend ourselves, our loved ones, beliefs, and resources from harm. The Institute for Management Excellence (2001) suggests there are nine basic human needs: (i) security, (ii) adventure, (iii) freedom, (iv) exchange, (v) power, (vi) expansion, (vii) acceptance, (viii) community, and (ix) expression.

Maslow's work lead to an additional attempt to develop a grand theory of motivation—a theory that would put all of the factors influencing motivation into one model. Leonard, Beauvais, and Scholl (1995) proposed five factors as the sources of motivation: (i) instrumental motivation (rewards and punishers) (ii) intrinsic process motivation (enjoyment, fun), (iii) goal internalization (self-determined values and goals), (iv) internal self-concept based motivation (matching behaviour with internally developed ideal self), (v) external self-concept based motivation (matching behaviour with externally developed ideal self). Individuals are influenced by all five factors, though in varying degrees that can change in specific situation.

Factors one and five mentioned above are both externally-oriented. The main difference is that individuals who are instrumentally motivated are influenced more by immediate actions in the environment (for example, operant or instrumental conditioning), whereas individuals who are self-concept motivated are influenced more by their constructions of external demands and ideals (for example, social cognition). Factors two, three, and four are more internally-oriented. In the case of intrinsic process, the specific task is interesting and provides immediate internal reinforcement (for example, cognitive or humanistic theory). The individual with a goal-internalization orientation is more task-oriented (for example, humanistic or social cognition theory), whereas the person with an internal self-concept orientation is more influenced by individual constructions of the ideal self (humanistic or psychoanalytic theory).

The Maslow's theory or the humanistic approach has been criticized as vague and unscientific. This approach has been criticized for several other reasons also which are mentioned herein below:

(i) It relies upon the subjective experience. Some people have only limited ability to explain, so not real. Humanistic psychologists tend to be anti-scientific in their approach, relying on phenomenology or subjective experiences.

(ii) The most common criticism concerns his methodology: picking a small number of people that he himself declared self-actualizing, then reading about them or talking with them, and coming to conclusions about what self-actualization is in the first place does not sound like good science to many people.

(iii) Another criticism, a little harder to respond to, is that Maslow placed such constraints on self-actualization. Maslow limits it to something only two percent of the human species. Maslow saw it as something achieved only rarely by the young, whereas Carl Rogers felt that babies were the best examples of human self-actualization.

(iv) Studies are often inadequate. Only intelligent, verbally able and self-actualized people were studied.

(v) It is too selfish. It emphasized self-liberation; no botheration about others.

(vi) It is too optimistic. Free man makes problem.

(vii) The important processes going on below the level of conscious awareness are ignored.

(viii) It may not be true that everyone has the potential to become a self-actualizer; people who are intelligent, well-educated, and talented are much more likely than others to become self-actualizers.

(ix) It is in some ways anti-scientific or unscientific, in that humanistic psychologists deny the value of carefully observing the behaviour under laboratory conditions. As a result, it has not been possible to test Maslow's theory by means of experimental studies.

(x) Humanistic psychologists do not believe that physiological and biological factors or processes are of any significance in human behaviour. Humanistic psychologists deny the importance of physiology and biology.

So, the idea that needs arise and are satisfied in a particular order has not been confirmed. For this reason, Maslow's theory should be viewed mainly as an interesting but unverified framework for understanding motives.

Despite these criticism and its weaknesses, Maslow's need hierarchy model is one of the most popular and often cited theories of human motivation and must be praised for its substantial strengths. Maslow focused on issues of great importance to human beings, such as their self-concept and their major motivating forces. Millions of people feel depressed and unfulfilled in spite of having all their basic physiological needs satisfied, indicating the importance of growth motivation. Humanistic approach is very cognitive. In the words of Cartwright (1979), humanistic psychology "is concerned with topics that are meaningful to human beings, focusing especially upon subjective experiences and the unique, unpredictable events in individual human lives." An interesting phenomenon related to Maslow's work is that inspite of a lack of evidence to support his hierarchy, it enjoys a wide acceptance (Soper, Miford, and Rosenthal, 1995; Wahba and Bridgewell, 1976). Maslow's theory is intuitively appealing, but research designed to test it has yielded mixed results. Some results suggest that growth needs come into play only after people have satisfied lower-level needs (Betz, 1982). But other findings indicate that people sometimes seek to satisfy higher-order need's even when ones lower-needs in the hierarchy have not been met (Williams and Page, 1989).

10.3.1 Some Qualities or Characteristics of a Self-actualized Person or Self-actualizers

From his study and observation of self-actualizers, Maslow also developed a profile of the self-actualizing personality. A summary of these characteristics is presented below:

Strengths of Self-Actualizers

1. Maslow felt that self-actualizers had an acceptance of herself or himself, acceptance is applied to their attitudes towards themselves; were more likely to be satisfied with themselves.
2. An acceptance of other people, by which Maslow meant that these people would be more likely to take you as you are than try to change you into what they thought you should be.
3. Self-actualizing people have the ability to love others and to be loved by others. They have a capacity for deep inter-personal relationships. They enjoyed deeper personal relations with a few close friends and family members, rather than more shallow relationships with many people. Maslow found that self-actualizers have deeper and more profound inter-personal relations than any other people. Healthy people at least know how to love, can do so freely, easily, naturally and without getting wound up in conflicts or threats or inhibitions. Love is a complex psychological phenomenon. In philosophical language, it is an aspect of being as well as of becoming and can be called B-love, that is, love for the Being of the others. Psychologists are often limited in their understanding of love.

   Maslow (1971) describes love as primarily a "Feeling of tenderness and affection with great enjoyment, happiness, satisfaction, elation and even ecstasy in experiencing this feeling (if all is going well)." Within this definition, he also includes the desire for psychological and physical intimacy, the tendency to perceive one's mate as beautiful, the feeling of pleasure in her or his presence and depression in her or his absence, the desire to share pleasures, the need for privacy, feelings of generosity, the need to share secrets, the desire for fuller knowledge of one's partner, and the tendency to drop all defences and roles. This last characteristic was particularly important to Maslow because he felt that in true love relationships, there wasn't the need to put one's "best foot" forward.

   Theodore Reik (1957) has defined one characteristic of love as the absence of anxiety. Honesty in a relationship includes allowing one's faults, weaknesses, physical and psychological shortcomings to be freely seen by the partner. Other most important characteristics for love are good companionship, considerateness, affection, dependability, intelligence, kindness, being understanding, loyalty, and being interesting to talk to. Least valued characteristics for love are dominance, agnosticism (an agnostic is a person believing that nothing can be known about the existence of God), and being a night owl or being an early riser.

Theodore Reik
(1886–1969)

Maslow's writings make it evident that he understands the bonding between lovers, that he is able to objectively describe everyday love feelings, and that he appreciates the intensity of being sexual with someone you love. Maslow believed that sex and love are more perfectly fused with each other in healthy people. Furthermore, sexual pleasures are found in their most intense and ecstatic perfection in self-actualizing people. Whereas sex seemed to be wholeheartedly enjoyed far beyond the possibility of the average person, Maslow also found that it did not play any central role in the self-actualizer's philosophy of life.

4. They had a sense of humility and respect towards others—something Maslow also called *democratic values*—meaning that they were open to ethnic and individual variety, even treasuring it. They had a quality Maslow called "human kinship" or *Gemeinschaftsgefuhl*—social interest, compassion, humanity. And this was accompanied by strong ethics, which was spiritual but seldom conventionally religious in nature. They will not unnecessarily humiliate the other person, whether adult or child. Respect for another person acknowledges her or him as an independent entity and as a separate and autonomous individual.
5. Self-actualizing people will not casually use, control, or disregard the wishes of others.
6. Self-actualized person is involved in some cause outside of herself or himself.
7. A self-actualized person is self-aware, socially responsive, simple, spontaneous, creative, and autonomous, open to novelty and challenge. Maslow believed that self-actualizers were more spontaneous and natural in their behaviour than other people.
8. A self-actualized person has a good and unhostile sense of humour—preferring to joke at their own expense, or at the human condition, and never directing their humour at others. Maslow felt that self-actualizers had a more philosophical sense of humour.

9. A self-actualized person is focused on problems and solutions rather than her or him. Maslow discovered that self-actualizers focused most of their energies on problems and tasks outside of themselves.
10. Self-actualized persons are very spontaneous in both actions and emotions. They preferred being themselves rather than being pretentious or artificial.
11. A self-actualized person resists pressures to confirm. Maslow discovered that self-actualizers tended to have values that were often in opposition to the "mainstream" culture. Thus, they tended to resist "enculturation" or the transcendence of any particular culture. They resisted enculturation, that is, they were not susceptible to social pressures and cultural influences to be "well-adjusted" or "fit in"—they were in fact, non conformists in the best sense.
12. A self-actualized person is creative, inventive, and original. Not surprisingly, every self-actualizer was deemed very creative.
13. Self-actualized persons have a concern about personal growth. They were strongly motivated to change negative qualities in themselves that could be changed.
14. These people had a certain freshness of appreciation, an ability to see things, even ordinary things, with wonder. According to Maslow (1970), "Self-actualizing people have the wonderful capacity to appreciate again and again, freshly and naively, the basic goods of life, with awe, pleasure, wonder, and even ecstasy, however stale these experiences may have become to others."
15. Self-actualized people have the ability to have more peak experiences than the average person. Peak experiences are those profound and enlightening feelings that are so intense or illuminating that it is readily obvious that they are special events. A peak experience is one that takes you out of yourself, that makes you feel very tiny, or very large, to some extent one with life or nature or God. It gives you a feeling of being a part of the infinite and the eternal. It is also an active experience which is felt as self-validating, self-justifying, and inherently good. The emotional reaction has a special flavour of wonder, awe, reverence, humility, and surrender. Finally, the person at the peak feels godlike and loses all fear, anxiety, inhibition, defence, control, delay, and restraint. These experiences tend to leave their mark on a person, change them for the better, and many people actively seek them out. They are also called *mystical experiences,* and are an important part of many religious and philosophical traditions. Maslow discovered that self-actualizers have usually had feelings of being simultaneously more powerful

and also more helpless than others; feelings of great ecstasy, wonder, and awe; feelings of being lost in time and space; and the feeling that something extremely important and valuable has happened to them, to such an extent that it has transformed and strengthened their everyday experiences.

16. A self-actualized person incorporates an outgoing freshness of appreciation of life. Maslow believed that self-actualizers have the wonderful capacity to appreciate the basic goods of life.
17. A self-actualized person has strongly developed set of values.
18. Self-actualized persons have the need for privacy. Maslow found that self-actualizers preferred solitude and privacy much more than other people. Self-actualizers enjoyed solitude, and were comfortable being alone.
19. Self-actualizers enjoyed autonomy or independence of culture and environment, will, active agents; a relative independence from physical and social needs. Maslow believed that self-actualizers depended solely on their resources for their development and continued growth.
20. Self-actualizers have more efficient perception of reality and more comfortable relations with it. Maslow felt that self-actualizers were better able to detect dishonesty and, in general were better judges.
21. Self-actualizers can discriminate between means and ends, between good and evil. Maslow stressed that he could not characterize a single self-actualizer as someone who was chronically unsure about the difference between right and wrong.
22. Self-actualizers have a democratic character structure. Maslow discovered that self-actualizers are generally friendly with people regardless of class, education, political belief, race, or colour. As the matter of fact, Maslow often found that they acted as if they were unaware of these differences.
23. Self-actualizers have "genuine feelings for others" or *Gemeinschaftsgefuhl.* According to Maslow (1970), "This word, invented by Alfred Adler, is the only one available that describes well the flavour of the feelings for mankind expressed by self-actualizing subjects. They have for human beings in general a deep feeling of identification, sympathy, and affection in spite of....occasional anger, impatience, or disgust.... Because of this they have a genuine desire to help the human race."

10.4 CONFLICTS (CONFLICT OF MOTIVES)

"Conflict" means being torn in two or more directions by opposing motives. When the organism has to choose between two equally attractive goals, he faces the problem of conflict. He is in conflict as he is unable to decide which goal to pursue for both have equal attraction and strength in fulfilling his motive. Goal can be attractive or desirable and unattractive or undesirable. Attraction value of a goal is called its "valence". People approach or sought or are attracted towards goals with positive valence. People avoid, fear, or run away from goals with negative valence. When two forces become equally strong like the desire in an adolescent to smoke a cigarette and the fear of being severely scolded by parents, there is conflict of these two motives.

"Conflict" refers to any situation in which there are mutually antagonistic or opposite motives, impulses, needs, desires, events, purposes, behaviours, etc. Conflict, though frustrating and stressful, is a common occurrence in our lives. Conflict may also be looked at as a type of frustration in which the barrier to achieving a goal is an opposing impulse or motive. Frustration that often causes the most persistent and deep-seated frustration in many individuals is motivational conflict. It is a situation that arises when two or more motives drive behaviour towards incompatible goals.

However, when one force becomes weak, the other proceeds on and is accepted as a goal. Those motives, which are not very strong, usually do not reappear. But in other cases, where the motive was equally strong, the motive may reappear again when occasion demands. In any case, if a final decision is not taken, the person loaded with tension and anxiety may show neurotic symptoms. This psychological state, where the organism is unable to decide whether to respond to stimulus X or to stimulus Y, is called a *state of nervous breakdown*. In our day-to-day life, we face such conflict of motives, needs, desires, urges, demands, and wishes daily.

This kind of frustration can be the most important in determining a person's anxieties or "hang-ups". On analysis, it seems that this kind of frustration can arise from four major kinds of conflict, which have been called, approach-approach conflict, avoidance-avoidance conflicts, approach-avoidance conflict, and double or multiapproach-avoidance conflict.

10.4.1 Approach-Approach Conflict

Approach-approach conflict results from being drawn towards *two* equally desirable but mutually incompatible goals (Figure 10.6). An approach-approach conflict is a conflict between two positive goals—goals that are equally attractive at the same time. In this type of conflict, two almost equally and equidistant positive or desirable valences or alternatives give birth to this type of conflict. This type of conflict is simple conflict and is easiest to resolve. This conflict is generally resolved when one get closer to or approaches one of the two goals having positive valence, since

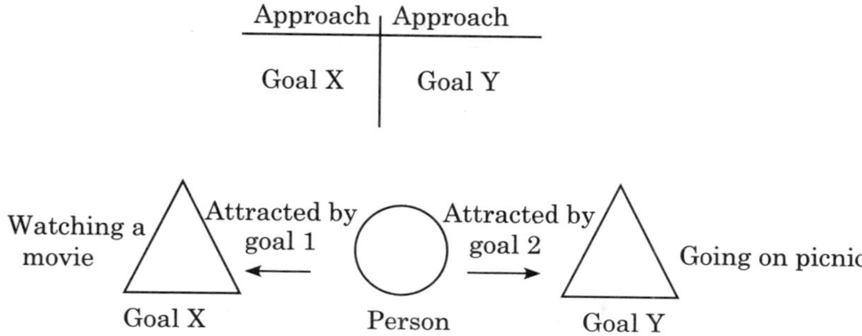

Figure 10.6 Approach-approach conflict.

desirability typically increases with proximity. For example, a psychological conflict arises when a person is hungry and sleepy at the same time. In the social context, a conflict may arise when a person wants both to watch a movie and go on a picnic, and to go to both a political rally and a party scheduled for the same night. Such conflicts are usually resolved either by satisfying first one goal and then the other for example, eating and then going to bed, if a person is both hungry and sleepy, or by choosing one of the goals and giving up the other. Compared with other conflict situations, approach-approach conflicts are usually easy to resolve and generate little emotional behaviour. This type of conflict is least stressful form of conflict.

10.4.2 Avoidance-Avoidance Conflict

Avoidance-avoidance conflict results from being repelled by *two* undesirable goals when there are strong pressures to choose one or the other. The individual in this kind of conflict, avoidance-avoidance, involves two negative goals, and is fairly a common experience. Two almost equally strong and equidistant negative or undesirable valences or alternatives work to force the individual to leave the field or escape from the situation. This conflict results in longer hesitation and indecision. The individual is caught between two repelling threats, fears, or situations. In addition to the negative goals, there are usually barriers in the periphery of the situation that prevents the person from "leaving the field" in order to escape from the conflict. This type of conflict is more stressful because the individual is motivated to avoid each of two negative goals (Figure 10.7).

For example, a boy must do his homework or get a spanking. Which one to avoid? The student must spend the next two days studying for an examination or face the possibility of failure.

Such conflicts are capsuled in the saying, "Caught between the devil and the deep blue sea". We can all think of things we do not want to, but

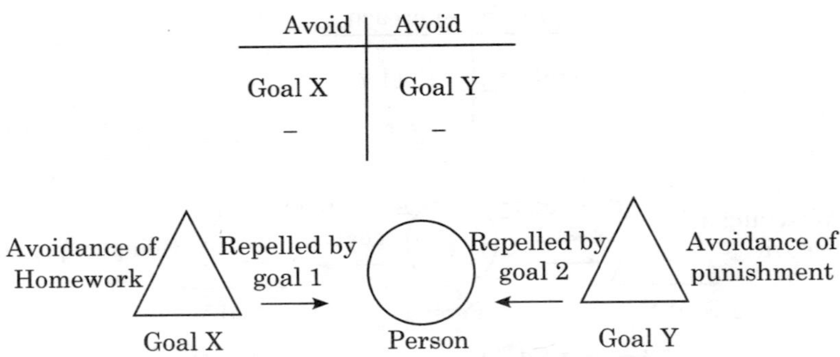

Figure 10.7 Avoidance-avoidance conflict.

must do or face even less desirable outcomes. This conflict means caught up in an unpleasant situation which prompts the individual or the person to select the "lesser of two evils".

Two kinds of behaviour are likely to be conspicuous or noticeable in this conflict. One is vacillation of behaviour and thought, meaning that people are inconsistent in what they think and do: they do first one thing and then another. Vacillation occurs because the strength of a goal increases as a person nears it. As one of the negative goals is approached, a person finds it increasingly repellent and consequently retreats or withdraws from it. But when this is done, the person comes close to other negative goal and finds it, in turn, unbearably obnoxious or unpleasant.

A second important feature of this kind of conflict is an attempt to leave the conflict situation. When the conflict is intense, a person may simply "leave the field" and refuse to choose between the alternatives. Theoretically, a person can escape from an avoidance-avoidance conflict by running away—and people do, indeed, try this. In practice, however there are often additional negative forces in the periphery of the situation ("the field") that prevent them from leaving. For example, a boy who does not want to either do his homework or get a spanking might think of running away from home. But the consequences of running away are even worse than his other alternatives, and so he does not do it (run away).

People in avoidance-avoidance conflicts may try a different means of running away. They may rely on their imaginations to free them from the fear and anxiety generated by the conflict. They may spend much of their time day-dreaming—conjuring up an imaginary world, where there are no conflicts. This way of leaving the conflict is called *regression*.

Many intense emotions are generated by avoidance-avoidance conflicts. If the two negative goals are fear-producing and threatening, a person caught between them will experience fear, or the individual may be angry and resentful at being trapped in a situation where the goals are negative.

10.4.3 Approach-Avoidance Conflict

Approach-avoidance conflict results from being both drawn and repelled by the same *one* goal. The person is equally attracted and repelled by the same goal for the desire to attain some object. Which one to choose or avoid? Approach-avoidance conflict is often the most difficult to resolve because in this type of conflict, a person is both attracted and repelled by the same goal object. Because of the positive valence or quality of the goal, the person approaches it, but as it is approached, the negative valence become stronger. If, at some point during the approach to the goal, its repellant aspects become stronger than its positive aspects, the person will stop before reaching the goal. Because the goal is not reached, the individual is frustrated. For example, a woman in a situation in which she is being offered a job with attractive salary but a substantial increase in workload. Another example is where a student wants to run a race for announced prize and at the same time not wanting to participate for fear of spoiling new dress.

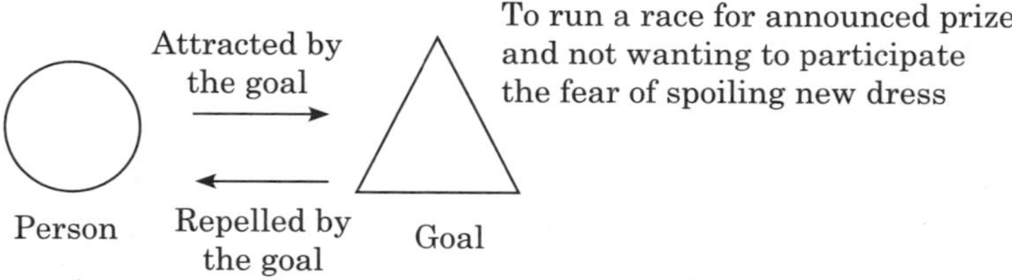

Figure 10.8 Approach-avoidance conflict.

People in these conflicts approach the goal until the negative valence becomes too strong, and then back away from it. Often, however, the negative valence is not repellant enough to stop the approach behaviour, whether a person is frustrated by reaching a goal slowly or by not reaching it at all, emotional reactions such as fear, anger, and resentment commonly accompany approach-avoidance conflicts.

10.4.4 Double Approach-Avoidance Conflict

In double approach-avoidance conflict situation, the individual is faced with a choice between *two* goals each of which has both a negative and a positive valence. This conflicts results from the situation in which each of the two exclusive goals are present with both positive and negative aspects. This conflict is a variation on the simple approach-avoidance conflict (Figure 10.9).

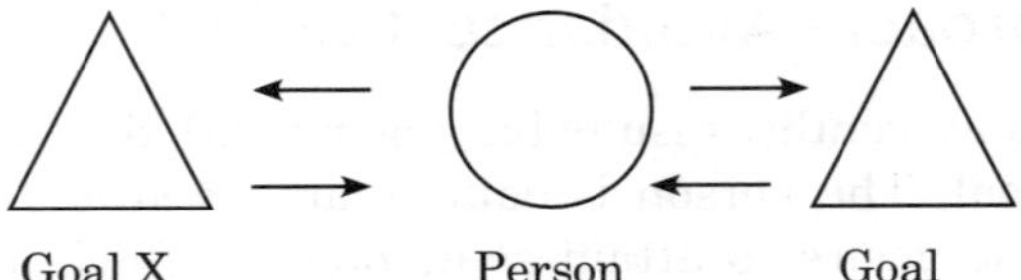

Figure 10.9 Double approach-avoidance conflict.

10.4.5 Multiple Approach-Avoidance Conflict

Multiple approach-avoidance conflict is a common, annoying, and stressful experience. This conflict result from the situation in which there are more than two or several goals or alternatives, each having positive and negative valence. The most complex form of conflict is the multiple approach-avoidance conflict, in which each of several alternative courses of action has its promising and distressing aspect.

10.5 FRUSTRATION

The term "frustration" refers to the blocking of behaviour directed towards a goal. Frustration is the thwarting or blocking of a motive to attain a goal. It is the act of blocking, interfering with or disrupting behaviour that is directed to some goal. The behaviour may be almost anything from overt, physical movement to covert, cognitive process. Frustration is usually increased as the importance or strength or urgency of the blocked motive or goal increases. An individual becomes more frustrated when obstacle or barrier comes on his way when he is about to reach the goal or is very near the goal (Figure 10.10).

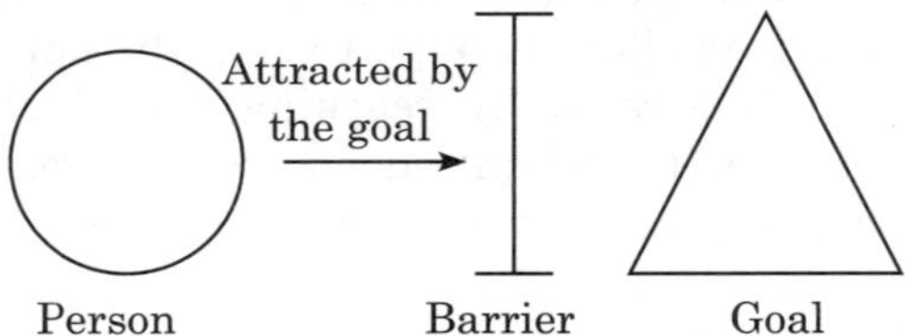

Figure 10.10 Frustration.

Frustration is the source of stress. "Frustration" also refers to the emotional state resulting from the frustrating act and has motivational properties that produce behaviour designed to bypass or surmount the block. Conflicts among simultaneously aroused motives are perhaps the most important reason why goals are not reached. If motives are frustrated, or blocked, emotional feelings and behaviour often result into depression. People who cannot achieve their important goals feel depressed, fearful, anxious, guilty, or angry. Often they are simply unable to derive ordinary pleasure from living.

10.5.1 Definitions of Frustration

According to Coleman, "Frustration is the result of the block of motive either by some obstacles that impedes progress towards a desired goal or by the absence of appropriate goal object."

According to Gilmer, "Frustration is the state of an organism resulting when the satisfaction of a motivated behaviour is made difficult or impossible, when the way to goal is blocked."

According to Kalesnik, "Frustration is the feeling of being blocked in satisfying a need or attaining a goal that the individual perceives as significant."

According to Kisker, "Frustration is a psychological state resulting from the blocking of goal directed activity."

10.5.2 Sources of Frustration

The causes of frustration are to be found in:

1. Environmental forces that block motive fulfilment (external frustration),
2. Personal inadequacies and characteristics that make it impossible to reach goals, and
3. Conflicts between and among motives.

1. **Environmental or external frustration:** By making it difficult or impossible for a person to attain a goal, environmental obstacles can frustrate the satisfaction of motives. An obstacle may be something physical, such as a locked door of one's house on a rainy day when a person returns from work or traffic jams or lack of money or it may be people—parents, teachers, relatives, friends, colleagues, superiors, etc. who prevent us from achieving our goals. External frustration results from failure, loss, delay, rejection of motives.

2. **Personal frustration:** Unattainable goals can be important source of original frustration. These are largely learned goals that cannot be achieved because they are beyond a person's abilities. Thus, people are often frustrated because they aspire to goals and have a level of aspiration beyond their capacity to perform. Repeated failures, apart from being frustrating and stressful, lowers a person's level of aspiration and feelings of self-worth or self-esteem.

3. **Conflict-produced frustration:** A major cause of frustration or stress is found in motivational conflict, in which the expression of one motive interferes with expression of other motives. In expressing aggression, for example, people are often caught in such a conflict. On the one hand, they would like vent or express their rage or anger, on the

other, they fear the social disapproval, which will result if they do. Aggression is thus in conflict with need for social approval.

According to Coleman (1969), the following are the reactions to frustration:

1. Fight—attack and aggression
2. Flight—escape and withdrawal
3. Compromise and substitution
4. Use of defence-mechanisms

QUESTIONS

The below mentioned are some of the questions that have been asked in the examinations conducted by the Guru Nanak Dev University or can be asked. Knowledge of these answers can help the students to get success in the examinations.

Section A

Answer the following questions in **five** lines or 50 words.

1. Explain the hierarchy of needs.*
2. Define motivation.*
3. Define instinct.*
4. What is motivational cycle?
5. Write different types of motives.
6. What is need?
7. What do you mean by intrinsic motivation?*
8. What do you mean by extrinsic motivation?
9. Define frustration.*
10. Define conflict.
11. Define drive.
12. What are primary needs?
13. What do you mean by self-actualization?*
14. What do you mean by conflict of motives?
15. What are acquired motives?

Section B

Answer the following questions up to **two** pages or 500 words.

1. Explain the meaning and nature of motivation.
2. What is motivation? Explain the various biological motives?
3. What is motivation? Explain various social motives?

4. Define motivation? Explain its nature.*
5. What is a motive? Explain the importance of biological motives in human life.
6. What are the basic ideas behind Maslow's needs hierarchy theory?*
7. What factors play a role in the regulation of eating?
8. What role do hormones play in human sexual motivation?
9. What social factors facilitate aggression?
10. What environmental factors contribute to aggression?
11. What is achievement motivation?
12. What is intrinsic motivation?
13. In Maslow's theory, what is self actualization?
14. Explain need-hierarchy theory of motivation.
15. Define motivation. What are its types?
16. What is frustration?*
17. What is conflict? How can it be avoided?

Section C

Answer the following questions up to **five** pages or 1000 words.

1. Describe the humanistic approach. What are its strengths? What are its weaknesses?
2. What is motivation? Discuss briefly the different types of motives?*
3. What is motivation? Explain sociogenic motives.
4. What is motivation? What is the need-hierarchy theory of motivation?*

REFERENCES

Alderfer, C., *Existence, Relatedness, and growth*, New York: Free Press, 1972.

Ames, C., 'Classroom Goals, Structures, and Student Motivation,' *Journal of Educational Psychology*, **84**(3), 261–271, 1992.

Andrews, J.D.W., 'The Achievement Motive and Achievement in Two Types of Organization,' *Journal of Personality and Social Psychology*, **6**, 163–168, 1967.

Atkinson, J.W., (Ed.). *Motives in Fantasy, Action, and Society,* Princeton: Van Nostrand, 1958.

Atkinson, J.W., and Birch, G., *An Introduction to Motivation* (2nd ed.), New York: Van Nostrand. 1978.

Atkinson, J.W. and Feather, N.T., (Ed.), *A Theory of Achievement Motivation*, New York: Wiley, 1966.

Bandura, A., *Principles of Behaviour Modification*, New York: Holt, Rinehart and Winston, 1969.

Bandura, A., *Self-efficacy: The Exercise of Control*, New York; W.H. Freeman, 1970.

Bandura, A., *Aggression: A Social Learning Analysis*, Englewood Cliffs, New Jersey: Prentice-Hall, 1973.

Bandura, A., 'Behaviour Theory and the Models of Man,' *American Psychologist*, **29** (12), 859–869, 1974.

Bandura, A., *Social Learning Theory*, Englewood Cliffs, N.J.: Prentice Hall,1977.

Bandura, A., *Self-efficacy: The Exercise of Control,* New York: W.H., Freeman, 1997.

Baron, R.A., *Psychology* (15th ed.), Delhi: Pearson Education Asia Pvt Ltd., 1995.

Baron, R.A., 'The Sweet Smell of...Helping, Effects of Pleasant Ambient Odors on Helping in Shopping Malls,' *Personality and Social Psychology Bulletin*, **2**, 498–503, 1997.

Baron, R.A., and Richardson, D., *Human Aggression* (2nd ed.), New York: Plenum, 1994.

Berkowitz, L., *Aggression: Its Causes, Consequences, and Control*, New York: McGraw-Hill, 1993.

Betz, E.L., 'Need Fulfillment in The Career Development of Women,' *Journal of Vocational Behaviour*, **20**, 53–66, 1982.

Bootzin, R., Bower, Crooker and Hall, *Psychology Today*, New York: McGraw-Hill, Inc, 1991.

Brown, R., *Social Psychology*, New York: The Free Press, 1965.

Coleman, J.C., *Psychology and Effective Behaviour,* Bombay: D.B., Tara Porevala Sons and Co. Pvt. Ltd., 1969.

Cannon, W.B., *Bodily Changes in Pain, Hunger, Fear, and Rage* (2nd ed.), New York: Appleton-Century-Crofts, 1929.

Cannon, W.B., *Hunger and Thirst,* In C., Murchinson (Ed.), Handbook of General Experimental Psychology, Worchester, MA: Clark University Press, 247–263, 1934.

Cannon, W.B., 'Reflections on the Man and His Contributions,' *International Journal of Stress Management*, Vol., **1** (2), 1994.

Carroll, J.B., 'Factors of Verbal Achievement,' in A. Anastasi (Ed.), *Testing Problems in Perspective* (pp. 406–413). Washington, DC: American Council on Education, 1966.

Carroll, J.B., 'Factor Analytic Investigations of Cognitive Abilities,' in S.E. Newstead, S.H. Irvine, and P.L. Dann (Eds.), *Human Assessment: Cognition and Motivation*, Nyhoff: Dordrecht, 1986.

Carroll, J.B., *Human Cognitive Abilities: A Survey of Factor-analytic Studies,* New York: Cambridge University Press, 1993.

Daniels, M., *Maslow's Concept of Self-actualization*, Retrieved February 2004, from http://www.mdani.demon.co.uk/archive/MD Maslowhtm., 2001.

Dweck, C.S., and Licht, B.G., 'Learned Helplessness and Intellectual Achievement,' in M.E.P. Seligman and J. Garber (Eds.), *Human Helplessness: Theory and Application*, New York: Academic Press, 1980.

Eccles, J.C., *The Understanding of the Brain* (2nd ed.), New York: McGraw-Hill, 1977.

Fisher, S., and Greenberg, R.P., *The Scientific Credibility of Freud's Theories and Therapy,* New York: Basic Books, 1977.

Franken, R., *Human Motivation* (5th ed.), Pacific Grove, CA; Brooks/ Cole, 2001.

Freedman, J.L., *'Television Violence and Aggression: A Rejoinder,' Psychological Bulletin*, **100**, 372–378, 1986.

Freud, S., *An Outline of Psychoanalysis*, London: Hogarth Press, 1953.

Freud, S., *Beyond the Pleasure Principle*. New York: W.W. Norton and Company, 1990.

Hughes, J.R., Smith, T.W., Kosterlitz, H.W., Fothergill, L.A., Morgan, B.A., and Morris, H.R., 'Identification of Two Related Pentapeptides from the Brain with Potent Opiate Agonist activity,' *Nature*, **258**, 577–581, 1975.

Huitt, W., *Motivation to Learn: An Overview*, Educational Psychology Interactive, Valdosta, GA: Valdosta State University. Retrieved from http ://chiron.valdosta.edu/whuitt col motivation/motivate.html., 2001.

Hull, C.L., *Principles of Behaviour*, New York: Appleton-Century-Crofts, 1943.

Hull, C.L., *A Behaviour System,* New Haven: Yale University Press, 1952.

Institute for Management Excellence, 'The Nine Basic Human Needs,' *Online Newsletter*, Retrieved February, 2004 from http://www. itstime.com/print./jun 97p.htm, 2001.

James, W., *Psychology: Brief Course*, London: Collier Macmillan Ltd., 1890.

James, W., *Psychology: The Briefer Course*. New York: Henry Holt, 1892/1962.

Kleinginna, P., Jr., and Kleinginna, A., 'A Categorized List of Motivation Definitions, with Suggestions for a Consensual Definition,' *Motivation and Emotion*, **5**, 263-291, 1981.

Leonard, N., Beauvair, L., and Scholl, R.A., *Self-concept Based Model on Work Motivation*, Paper presented at the Annual Meeting of the Academy of Management, August, Retrieved: December 1999, from http://www.cba.uri.edu/scholl/papers/self-concept motivation.htm, 1995.

Levine, J.D., Gordon, N.C., and Fields, H.L., 'The Role of Endorphins in Placebo Analgesia,' in J.J. Bonica, J.C. Liebeskind, and D. Albe-Fessard (Eds.), *Advances in Pain Research and Therapy,* Vol. 3, New York: Raven Press, 547–557, 1979.

Litt, M.D., 'Self-efficacy and Perceived Control: Cognitive Mediators of Pain Tolerance, '*Journal of Personality and Social Psychology*,' **54**, 149–160, 1988.

Maslow, A.H., 'A Theory of Human Motivation,' *Psychological Review,* **50**, 370–396. Retrieved June 2001, from http://psychclassics.yorku.ca/Maslow/Motivation.htm. 1943.

Maslow, A.H., *Motivation and Personality*, New York: Harper & Row, 1954.

Maslow, A.H., *Toward a Psychology of Being*, New York: Van Nostrand, 1962.

Maslow, A.H., 'Toward a Humanistic Biology,' *American Psychologist,* **24**(8), 734–735, 1969.

Maslow, A.H., *Motivation and Personality* (2nd ed.), New York: Harper & Row, 1970.

Maslow, A.H., *The Farther Reaches of Human Nature*, New York: The Viking Press, 1971.

Maslow, A., and Lowery, R. (Ed.), *Toward a Psychology of Being* (3rd ed.), New York: Wiley & Sons. 1998.

Mathes, E., 'Maslow's Hierarchy of Needs as a Guide for Living,' *Journal of Humanistic Psychology,* **21**, 69–72, 1981.

McClelland, D.C., *The Achieving Society*, New York: Van Nostrand, 1961.

McClelland, D.C., *Human Motivation,* New York: Scott, Foresman, 1985.

McClelland, D.C., Atkinson, J.W., Clark, R.A., and Lowell, E.L., *The Achievement Motive,* New York: Appleton-Century-Crofts, 1953.

McDougall, W., *Social Psychology*, London: Methuen, 1908.

McDougall, W., *Social Psychology*, Boston: John Luce, 1921.

McDougall, W.G., *Psychology—The Study of Behaviour*, New York: Henry Holt, 1908.

Melzack, R., 'Pain: Past, Present, and Future,' in M. Weisenberg and B. Tursky (Eds.), *Pain: New Perspectives in Therapy and Research,* New York: Plenum, 1976.

Melzack, R., 'Pain: Past, Present, and Future,' *Canadian Journal of Experimental Psychology,* **47,** 615–629, 1993.

Melzack, R., 'Folk Medicine and the Sensory Modulation of Pain,' in P.D. Wall and R. Melzack (Eds.), *Textbook of Pain* (pp. 1209–1217). Edinburgh: Churchill Livingstone, 1994.

Melzack, R. and Wall, P.D., 'Pain Mechanisms: A New Theory,' *Science,* **150**, 971–979, 1965.

Morgan, C.T. and King, R.A., *Introduction to Psychology*, New York: McGraw-Hill Book Co., 2000.

Murray, H., *Explorations in Personality*, New York: Oxford University Press, 1938, 1943.

Murray, H.A., *The Thematic Apperception Test*, Cambridge: Harvard University Press, 1943.

Nohria, N., Lawrence, P., and Wilson, E., *Driven: How Human Nature Shapes Our Choices,* San Francisco; Jossey-Bass, 2001.

Norwood, G., *Maslow's Hierarchy of Needs*, The Truth Vectors (Part I). Retrieved May 2002, from http://www.deepermind.com/20maslow. htm., 1999.

Raynor, J.O., 'Relationships Between Achievement-related Motives, Future Orientation, and Academic Performance,' *Journal of Personality and Social Psychology,* **15**, 28–33, 1970.

Rosen, E., Fox, Ronald, and Gregory, E., *Abnormal Psychology* (3rd ed.), Philadelphia: Saunders, 1972.

Ryan, R. and Deci., 'Self-determination Theory and the Facilitation of Intrinsic Motivation, Social Development, and Well-being,' *American Psychologist,* **55**(1), 68–78. Retrieved February 2004, from http:// www.psych.rochester.edu/ SDT/publications/documents/2000RyanDeci SDT.pdf. 2000.

Smith, S.M., 'Remembering In and Out of Context,' *Journal of Experimental Psychology: Human Learning and Memory,* **5**, 460–471, 1979.

Spence, A.P., *Biology of Human Ageing,* Englewood Cliffs, NJ: Prentice-Hall, 1989.

Stipek, D., *Motivation to Learn: From Theory to Practice,* Englewood Cliffs, NJ: Prentice Hall, 1988.

Teitelbaum, P., 'The Use of Operant methods in the Assessment and Control of Motivational States,' in W.K. Honig (Ed.), *Operant Behaviour: Areas of Research and Application,* New York: Appleton-Century-Crofts, pp. 565–608, 1966.

Teitelbaum, P. and Epstein, A.N., 'The Lateral Hypothalamic Syndrome: Recovery of Feeding and Drinking after Lateral Hypothalamic Lesions,' *Psychological Review,* **69**, 74–90, 1962.

Terenius, L., 'Characteristics of the "Receptor" for Narcotic Analgesics in Synaptic Plasma Membrane Fraction from Rat Brain,' *Acta Pharmacologia Toxicologia,* **32**, 377–384, 1973.

Wahba, S., and Bridgewell, L., 'Maslow Reconsidered: A Review of Research on the Need Hierarchy Theory,' *Organizational Behaviour and Human Performance,* **15**, 616–612, 1976.

Wall, P.D., 'Neurophysiological Mechanism of Pain,' In G. Adelman (Ed.), *Encyclopedia of Neuroscience,* Boston: Birkhauser, 904–906, 1987.

Weiner, B., *Achievement Motivation and Attribution Theory*, Morristown, NJ: General Learning Press, 1974.

Weiner, B., *Human Motivation*, New York: Holt, Rinehart Winston, 1980.

Weiner, B., *Human Motivation*, Hillsdale, NJ: Erlbaum, 1989.

Webb, W.B., (Ed.)., *Sleep: An Active Process,* Glenview, IL: Scott, Foresman, 1973.

Webb, W.B., *Sleep: The Gentle Tyrant*, Englewood Cliffs, NJ: Prentice-Hall, 1975.

White, R.W., 'Motivation Reconsidered: The Concept of Competence,' *Psychological Review,* **66**, 297–333, 1959.

Williams, D.E. and Page, M.M., 'A Multi-dimensional Measure of Maslow's Hierarchy of Needs,' *Journal of Research in Personality,* **23**, 192–213, 1989.

Winter, D.G., *The Power Motive,* New York: The Free Press, 1973.

Woodworth, R.S., *Dynamic Psychology,* New York: Columbia University Press, 1918.

CHAPTER 11

Emotion

Emotions are so much a part of daily existence that it is difficult to imagine a life without them. Emotions set the tone of our experiences and give life vitality and variety. Emotions make life interesting as well as distressing, pleasant as well as unpleasant, happy as well as unhappy. Without the ability to feel joy, anger, grief, and love, we would hardly recognize ourselves as humans. But sometimes emotions bring distress and disaster in human life and disorganize, and disturb the entire life pattern. At other times, it rebuilds functions and organizes activity. Emotions are important part of human personality and play a significant role in understanding human beings and their actions. Emotions not only describe and illuminate causes or reasons of human behaviour or actions but also motivate human beings to act in the manner they do.

Emotion is important in personal and social life (Izard, Kagan, and Zajonc, 1989), is very complex (Young, 1996), and has been an important topic of study throughout most of the history of Psychology (Lazarus, 1993). The emotions in our daily lives are rich, varied, complex, and complicated experiences. Without emotions, life would have been dull and colourless, devoid of charm. Emotions make life pleasurable as well as miserable. Emotion has got both integrating and disintegrating roles in life. These complicated experiences include cognitive, physiological, and behavioural reactions. Reiman and his associates (1997) have recently demonstrated that particular parts of the brain are associated with different aspects of emotion. The term "emotional intelligence" has been coined to describe attributes and skills related to this concept" (Koonce, 1996).

The English word "emotion" is derived from the French word *e' mouvoir.* This is based on the Latin word *emovere or E-Movere* where e- (variant of ex-) means "out" and "movere", which means "to move", "to excite", "to stir up", or "to agitate". Literally, emotion refers to movement. This arousal of self creates an urge towards action. The moving experience involves both physiological reactions as well as stirred up feelings. So, literally, emotion can be referred to as an agitated or disturbed or stirred up state of mind and body of an organism which moves, initiates, and directs behaviour. Emotion is a very complex, disturbed state of the organism and intricate psychological process. Entire organism is disturbed both physiologically and psychologically, activated and excited.

11.1 DEFINITIONS OF EMOTION

According to McDougall (1908), "Emotion is an affective experience that one undergoes during an instinctive excitement". For example, when a child perceives a bull coming towards him (cognition), he experiences an affective experience in the form of the arousal of accompanied emotion of fear and consequently tries to run away (conative aspect of one's behaviour)."

According to Drever (1917), "Emotion involves bodily changes of a widespread character—in breathing, pulse, gland secretion, etc. and, on the mental side, a state of excitement or perturbation, marked by a strong feeling, and usually an impulse towards a definite form of behaviour."

According to Carr (1949), "Emotion is a form of energy mobilization."

According to Woodworth (1954), "Emotion is a "moved" or "stirred up" state of an organism. It is a stirred up state of feeling that is the way it appears to the individual himself. It is a disturbed muscular and glandular activity that is the way it appears to an external observer."

According to Titchener, "Emotion is an affected state of the organism." By "affective state", he means to say joy, sorrow, love, hatred, etc.

According to Crow and Crow (1973), "Emotion is an affective experience that accompanies generalized linear adjustment and mental and physiological stirred up states in the individual and that shows itself in his overt behaviour."

According to Charles G. Morris (1979), "Emotion is an affective experience that involves diffuse physiological changes and can be expressed overtly in characteristic behaviour patterns."

According to P.T. Young, "Emotion is an acute disturbance of the organism, as a whole psychological in origin involving behaviour, conscious experience, and visceral functioning."

According to Kleinginna and Kleinginna (1981), "Emotion is an indefinite subjective sensation experienced as a state of arousal. Emotion occurs as a result of an interaction between perception of environmental stimuli, neural/hormonal responses to these perception (often labelled feelings), and subjective cognitive labelling of these feelings."

According to Izard (1990), "Emotions are complex reactions involving: (i) physiological changes within our bodies—shifts in heart rate, blood pressure, and so on; (ii) subjective cognitive states—the personal experiences we label as emotions; and (iii) expressive behaviours—outward signs of these internal feelings."

An "emotion" is a term for mental and physiological state associated with a wide variety of feelings, thoughts, and behaviour. Emotion is any number of extremely complex phenomena that are a synthesis of subjective experience, expressive behaviour, and neuro-chemical activity. Emotions are subjective experiences, or experienced from an individual's point of view. Emotion is often associated with mild temperament, personality, and disposition. Though psychologists have not found a simple yet comprehensive definition of emotion, they have generally agreed that emotions entail to varying degrees, awareness of one's environment or situation, bodily reaction, and approach or withdrawal of behaviour. Psychologists define emotion as a state of complex pattern of changes consisting of physiological arousal, cognitive processes, behavioural reactions, facial expressions, gestures, and subjective feelings in response to a situation perceived as personally significant in some way.

Reviewing the literature on emotions, Paul and Anne Kleinginna (1981) found many different definitions, but general consensus is on three points:

1. Emotions involve physiological changes.
2. Emotions often, but not always, lead to expressive goal directed behaviour, and
3. Perhaps more obviously, emotions are subjective experiences or internal states, often brought on by external circumstances.

Although everyone experiences emotions, scientists do not all agree on what emotions are or how they should be measured or studied. Emotions are complex and have both physical and mental components. Generally researchers agree that emotions have the following parts: subjective feelings, physiological (bodily) responses, and expressive behaviour.

The component of emotions that scientists call "subjective feelings" refer to the way each individual or person experiences feelings, and this component is the most difficult to describe or measure. Subjective feelings cannot be observed; instead, the person experiencing the emotion must describe it to others, and each person's description and interpretation of a feeling may be slightly different. For example, two people falling in love will not experience or describe their feelings in exactly the same ways.

"Physiological responses" are the easiest part of emotion to measure because scientists have developed special tools to measure them. A pounding heart, sweating, blood rushing to the face, or the release of adrenaline in response to a situation that creates intense emotion, can all be measured with scientific accuracy. People have very similar internal responses to the same emotion. For example, regardless of age, race, or gender, when people are under stress, their bodies release adrenaline; this hormone helps prepare the body to either run away or fight, which is called the "fight or flight" reaction. Although the psychological part of emotions may be different for each feeling, several different emotions can produce the same physical reaction.

"Expressive behaviour" is the outward signs that an emotion is being experienced. Outward signs of emotions can include fainting, a flushed face, muscle tensing, facial expressions, tone of voice, rapid breathing, restlessness, or other body language. The outward expressions of an emotion gives other people clues to what someone is experiencing and helps to regulate social interactions.

Michael W. Eysenck (1994) identified the following components of emotion:

1. **Cognitive or thinking:** Emotions are usually directed towards people or objects or situations. For example, in the emotion of fear, the cognitive or subjective component is "I feel afraid".

2. **Physiological:** There are generally a number of bodily changes involved in emotion; many of them such as increased heart-rate, increased blood-pressure, increased respiration-rate, sweating, etc. occur because of arousal in the sympathetic division of the autonomic nervous system. For example, in the emotion of fear, there is increased heart-rate and heavy breathing, heart pounds, sweaty palms, tremors.

3. **Experiential:** The feeling that is experienced or the conscious experience of emotion, which can only be assessed in the human beings by means of self-report measures.

4. **Expressive:** The non-verbal aspect of emotion, facial expressions and other aspects of non-verbal behaviour such as gestures, bodily posture. A facial expression results from one or more motions or positions of the muscles of the face. These movements convey the emotional state of the individual to observers. Facial expressions are a form of nonverbal communication. They are primary means of conveying social information among humans, but also occur in most other mammals and some other animal species. Evidence suggests there is a small core of emotions (perhaps 6 or 8) that are uniquely associated with a specific facial expression (Izard, 1990). This implies that there are a small number of unique biological responses that are genetically hard-wired to specific facial expressions.

5. **Behavioral:** The behavioral pattern associated with each emotional state; the pattern of behaviour such as fight or flight produced by an emotional state. For example, in the emotion of fear, a strong urge to escape.

According to Lang (1985), "These components are only loosely coupled."

Human emotions run the gamete from sorrow and despair, through envy and hate, to joy and intense delight (ecstasy). Thus, emotions may be defined as patterns of reactions that include physiological and bodily changes, expressive behaviour, and or goal-oriented behaviour and subjective experience.

11.2 CHARACTERISTICS OF EMOTION

1. Emotion is a complex affective experience.
2. Emotion is a "moved" or "stirred up" state of an organism. It involves diffused physiological changes. Emotion is an acute or strong disturbance of the body.
3. The core or important aspect of an emotion is feeling. When feelings become intense or strong, they develop into emotions.
4. Emotion is very brief. It starts very abruptly and ends soon after the incident is over. Since emotion involves physiological changes, it disappears after the emotional outburst is over.
5. The disturbed state produced by an emotional experience creates bodily changes within the organism which are physiological in nature, which takes place in the entire body system.
6. Each emotion has a different physiological pattern.
7. The disturbance due to emotion has a psychological origin, that is, a stimulus either external or internal, always produces the emotional reaction.
8. Emotions are the product of perception.
9. Emotion is a conscious experience—thoughts and perceptions of which a person is aware. The person facing the emotion-provoking situation must perceive it as significant. Then only the emotion can be produced.
10. Emotions are different from bodily appetites, such as hunger, thirst, etc. Emotional experiences are associated with some instincts or biological drives or forces within an organism.
11. Emotions are distinct or different from mood.
12. Emotions have cognitive and conative aspects. For example, if a person perceives a bear coming towards him (cognition), he

experiences or undergoes an affective experience in the form of the arousal of the accompanied emotion of fear and consequently tries to run away (flight, conative aspect of one's behaviour).

13. Emotions are expressed overtly or externally in characteristic behaviour patterns.
14. Emotions bring changes in the chemical composition of our blood like, (i) increase in the amount of adrenaline, (ii) increase in the amount of sugar level, (iii) changes in the number and proportion of red corpuscles or red blood cells.
15. During emotions, there are significant changes in the secretion of duct or exocrine and ductless or endocrine glands. The flow of these secretions in the form of tears, sweat or perspiration, saliva, etc. can be externally observed.
16. The muscles of our body hardened and get tense during an emotional current or influence. It may bring destabilization and inequilibrium to our body functioning. The twisting and hardening of the muscles may be easily detected from external observation.
17. Differences in heredity and environment cause different emotional behaviour.

Paul Ekman (1973) found that people in many different countries all have very similar facial expressions for six basic emotions: happiness; anger; disgust; sadness; fear; and surprise. This was true even in tribes that had little contact with the West or with mass media. The main exception is that there are some cultures, especially in the Far East, in which people are taught not to display certain emotions. Chalesworth and Kreutzer (1973) found that even individuals blind from birth showed the normal facial expressions when experiencing different emotions.

Paul Ekman
(Born in 1934)

11.2.1 What Happens During the Moment We Experience an Emotion

Emotion can occur very quickly. It can begin in a fraction of a second (even though in some people it often takes much longer). A second distinguishing aspect (distinguishing emotion from other mental phenomena) is automatic appraising. The evaluation that turns on an emotion, happens so quickly that we are not aware that it is occurring.

We are not a witness to the process of evaluation that generates the emotion. We typically become aware that we are afraid, or angry, or sad, after the emotion begins, not before. "The moment we become aware, is a half-second or a quarter second after the emotion begins, not before." That's what is meant by automatic appraising. In other words, we can be in the grip of an emotion before we have noticed it starting.

Emotions are public, not private. This means that the expression signals to others, in the voice, face, and in the posture, what emotion we feel. Our thoughts are private; our emotions are not. Others know how we feel—and that is very important for how people get along with each other.

When an emotion begins, it generates changes. It generates changes in our expression, our face, our voice, changes in the way we think, impulses to action. These occur involuntarily, and if we do not go along with them, we experience it as struggle. We struggle to control, to not show, or to not speak, or to not act. A defining aspect of emotion is the fact that it takes us over for a moment, or some time many moments. According to Paul Ekman, "Emotion can be very brief. It is possible for an emotion to last no more than a second or two. I can be happy one moment and angry the next, and sad right after that. Or an emotion can continue over some length or time."

11.2.2 Emotion and Feeling

"Feeling", most generally, is experiencing, sensing, or having a conscious process. It is a sensory impression, a sensation. It is an affective state as in the case of a sense of well-being. Feeling is an internal experience, not felt by any particular part. It is in other words, not localized in any part of the body. Feeling involves the entire body. Wundt suggested, "The state of a person's feeling at any moment may be described by telling how pleasant or unpleasant it is, how excited, and how tense or expectant." Feeling is a mild state of the organism. It is always used for various kinds of experiences such as feeling of pleasure, familiarity, excitement, happiness, worry, tension, depression, etc. Feeling is a dimension of an emotion. When our feelings become intense, they become emotions. Emotions, often called feelings, include experiences such as love, hate, anger, trust, joy, panic, fear, and grief.

Wundt's Tridimensional theory of feeling: Wundt has classified feeling into different conditions:

1. Excited versus depressed
2. Tensed versus relaxed
3. Pleasant versus unpleasant

Characteristics of feelings according to Wundt are as follows:

1. Each feeling whether pleasure, depression, excitement, moroseness or moodiness can be said to have a certain pleasant or unpleasant tone.
2. All feelings have a tone of excitement or numbness (pleasant-excitement; sadness-numbness).
3. Feeling can either be of tenseness or relaxation (expectancy-tenseness; no more expectancy-relief).

Table 11.1 shows the difference between feeling and emotion.

Table 11.1 Differences between feeling and emotion

Feeling	*Emotion*
1. Mild and dull	1. Acute and strong
2. Organism is not stirred physiologically or psychologically. It is only a mild disturbance. There are no bodily changes and overt expressions.	2. The entire organism is completely stirred, disturbed, and in main cases disorganized with typical physiological changes and bodily reactions.
3. Feeling has a longer continuation.	3. Very brief and continues for a short duration.
	4. Are more disturbing than feeling.

11.2.3 Emotion and Mood

"Mood" refers to a relatively pervasive and sustained emotional state. A mood is a heightened tendency to feel a particular emotion. Mood persists for a longer time. Emotions are related to, but different from, mood. Emotions are specific reactions to a particular event that are usually of fairly short duration. Mood is a more general feeling such as happiness, sadness, frustration, contentment, or anxiety that lasts for a longer time.

Moods are related to but different from emotions. The most obvious way they differ is in their duration. Emotions could come and go in a matter of seconds or minutes, but a mood can last a whole day. The first distinction between emotions and moods is that while emotions last for a short time may be a few seconds or even less, moods and their cognates last for a longer duration.

The second and more important distinction is that unlike moods, emotions have objects, for example, one is pleased or angry with something or someone. Mood is an impact left over from an emotional occurrence. Usually, when we have an emotion, we can say what produced it. We can specify the event that triggered it, that brought our emotion forth. Often with a mood, we can not. Moods are produced by internal changes that do not relate to what is happening to us on the outside. For example, when we wake up in a very positive mood or in an irritable mood; we wake up very happy or apprehensive or sad, for no reason that we know. There certainly are conditions that create moods. They are usually opaque to us—they are out of our awareness and so we don't know why we feel the way we do.

Another way how a mood occurs is that if we have a very dense emotional experience. If we experience amusement again and again in a short period of time, the consequence will be a very euphoric mood. If we are furious again and again, we will then have a long period in which we are irritable. So, these are the two different routes to a mood.

According to Paul Ekman, professor of Psychology, and the director of the Human Interaction Laboratory at the University of California Medical School in San Francisco and also a master of the face and of reading emotions, "When we are in a mood, it biases and restricts how we think. It makes us vulnerable in ways that we are normally not. So, the negative mood creates a lot of problems for us, because they change how we think. If I wake up in an irritable mood, I'm looking for a chance to be angry. Things that ordinarily would not frustrate me, do. The danger of a mood is only that it biases thinking but that it increases emotions. When I'm in an irritable mood, my anger comes stronger and faster, lasts longer, and is harder to control than usual. It's terrible state... one I would be glad never to have."

11.3 THE SOURCES OF EMOTION

Scientists have developed several theories about how emotions are generated based on subjective feelings, physiological responses, and expressive behaviour (Figure 11.1).

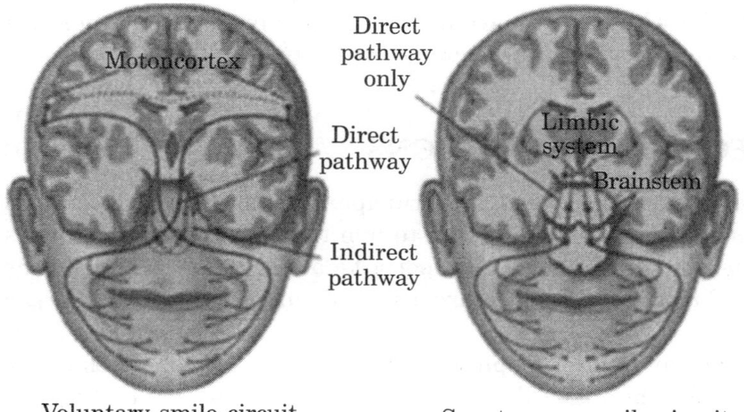

Figure 11.1 The sources of emotion.

The facial muscles involved in emotional expression are governed by nerves following a complex system of direct and indirect pathways to and from the motor cortex (voluntary smile circuit under conscious control) and the limbic system and brainstem (spontaneous smile circuit not under conscious control). This may explain why people's faces can express emotions like happiness, fear, and disgust without their being aware of it.

11.3.1 Why Do We Have Emotions?

Emotions appear to serve several physical and psychological purposes. Some scientists believe that emotions are one of the fundamental traits associated with being human. Emotions colour people's lives and give them depth and differentiation. For many people, strong emotions are linked to creativity and expression. Great art, music, and literature, on a fundamental level, deal with arousing emotions and creating an emotional connection between the artist and the public. Some scientists also believe that emotions serve as motivation to behave in specific ways.

Physiologically, emotions aid in survival. For example, sudden fear often causes a person to freeze like a deer caught by a car's headlights. Because animals usually attack in response to motion, at its simplest level, fear reduces the chances of attack. When someone froze in response to a car racing by her or him, this was an example of a physical response to an emotion that improved her or his chances of survival.

Emotions also help people monitor their social behaviour and regulate their interactions with others. Every person unconsciously learns to "read" the outward expressions of other people and apply past experiences to determine what these outward signs indicate about what the other person is feeling. If a person sees a man approaching who is walking very aggressively, holding his body stiffly and frowning, the person might correctly assume that the man is angry. Using this information, the person can decide whether to leave or to stay or what tone of voice and body language to use when approaching the man.

11.4 THEORIES OF EMOTIONS

A "theory" is a systematic general principle or set of principles that explain how separate facts are related to one theory. A theory organizes facts, must predict new facts, and permits a degree of control over phenomenon. Theories enable researchers to fit many facts into a larger framework.

All most modern theories emphasise the functional aspect of behaviour (Smith, 1989; Smith and Ellsworth, 1985; Tomkins, 1981) that is, emotions can also be adaptive. Earlier theorists believed that emotions might be disruptive (earlier theorists like Angler, 1927). According to this view, people become emotional when they are unable to cope up with the situations and their emotions make them even more confused further undermining their ability to cope.

The common sense holds that emotions cause physiological arousal and behaviour (Figure 11.2). When we see a mysterious figure in the passage, we feel frightened and this emotion (fear) causes heart to pound, and we run. In other words, events in the environment trigger a psychological state in an emotion, which in turn gives rise to physiological responses.

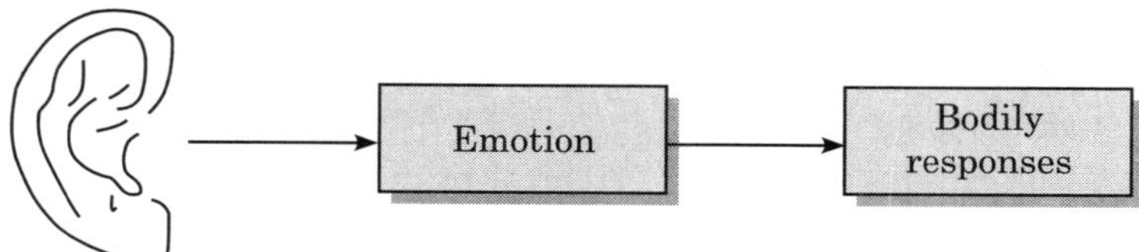

Figure 11.2 Commonsense view about emotion.

11.4.1 The James-Lange Theory

A particularly influential early theory of emotion was proposed independently by the American scientist and psychologist, also considered father of American Psychology, William James (1842–1910) and the Danish physician, scientist, and psychologist Carl George Lange (1834–1900). William James and Carl George Lange proposed one of the earliest theories on how our emotions worked. Both studied the relationship between emotion and physical changes in the body. In about 1885, they independently proposed that feeling an emotion is dependent on two factors: the physical changes that occur in the body and the person's understanding of the body's changes after the emotional event. James and Lange believed that physical changes occur first, and then interpretation of those physical changes occurs. Together, they create the emotion.

This has been called the James–Lange theory. James turned the above-mentioned commonsense notion upside down, the James–Lange assumption formally lingers the mental state to physiological processes. It holds that an emotion is a perception of phenomena within the body. According to James (1890), "I see a bear, I run away, I feel afraid." "We do not weep because we feel sorrow: we feel sorrow because we weep" (James, 1890). James himself put it, "We feel sorry because we cry, angry because we strike, and afraid because we tremble." When a person sees frightening sight, for example, the body immediately responds in certain way (for example, the heartbeat rate increases, sweaty palms, tremors) the perception of bodily response to the original stimulus constitutes the emotion of fear according to the James–Lange view. The James-Lange

Theory (1929) states that a stimulus immediately affects the autonomic nervous system and then the message is sent to the brain (Figure 11.3). Thus, people are happy because they smile, sad because they cry, and afraid because they flee. Smiling increases happiness, and frowning increases anger. Smiling is associated with happiness, crying with misery, and running away with fear.

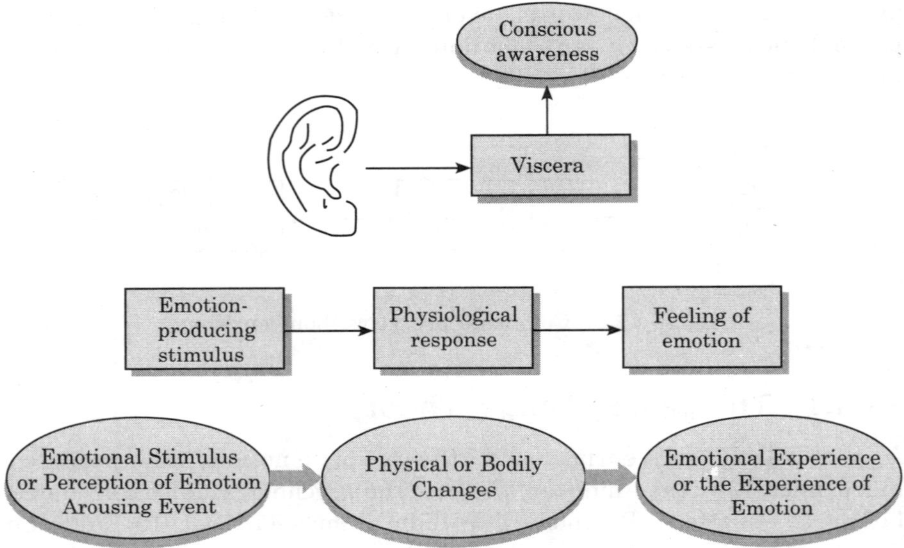

Figure 11.3 James–Lange view about emotion.

According to James, then, we do not act because we feel rather we feel because we act. Our perception of certain stimuli (what James called "existing facts") triggers changes in the body. These changes cause sensory messages to be sent to the brain and produce the actual experience of emotion. If you want to change your feelings (that is, your physiological functioning) you can do so by changing your facial expressions. That is, if you are motivated to change how you feel and your feeling is associated with a specific facial expression, you can change that feeling by purposively changing your facial expression. Since most of us would rather feel happy than otherwise, the most appropriate facial expression would be a smile.

James held that each emotional state is signalled by a unique physiological pattern. In his original work, James proposed that feelings might arise from changes in the viscera (vital internal organs), perspiration, circulation of blood, the skin temperature, the muscles, and even some of the postures. Where James depicted emotion as a whole body experience, Lange located emotions in the autonomic nervous system and the viscera. The ideas that emotions arise from perception of bodily changes become known as James–Lange Theory. (Lange and James, 1922) According to this theory, when a person experiences a threatening situation (almost being hit by a car), one's body first sent out chemical messengers, like adrenaline, that caused physical changes such as increased breathing and a faster heartrate. That person's brain then sensed these physical changes and interpreted them as the emotion–fear. Adrenaline (a-DREN-a-lin), also called epinephrine, (ep-e-NEF-rin), is a hormone, or chemical messenger, that is released. In response to fear, anger, panic, and other emotions, it readies the body to respond to threat by increasing heart rate, breathing rate, and blood flow to the arms and legs. These and other effects prepare the body to run away (flight) or fight.

Emotions are accompanied by physiological changes manifested by excitation of the sympathetic nervous system, especially these changes can be deducted in the Galvanic Skin Response (GSR), in which the electrical conductivity of the skin varies and also in the heart rate, blood pressure, blood circulation and others. But according to this view, these physiological changes would themselves be simulated by a perception. It is argued that, by the time a signal from the senses reaches the appropriate centre in the brain, physiological changes have already been taken place to cause the signal, which then produces the feeling of emotion.

More evidence providing some support for the James–Lange Theory was reported by Hohmann (1966) and Laird (1984). The findings of these studies suggest that bodily changes can affect emotional experience as predicted by James–Lange Theory. Some early evidence against the James–Lange Theory was reported by Sherrington (1906).

Advantages of the James-Lange Theory

(i) An emotional situation and bodily changes are both usually associated with emotional experience.

(ii) Physiological changes do sometimes occur before we experience emotion, as is predicted by the theory.

Disadvantages of the James-Lange Theory

(i) One of the problems with the James–Lange theory is that emotions seem to happen too quickly to be accounted for by the release of chemical messengers and the changes they cause.

(ii) Another problem is that different emotions (for example, fear and anger) have been shown to cause the same physical responses.

(iii) This theory is mainly criticized because there is very little difference between the physiological patterns of arousal in a number of emotions such as anger, fear, and sadness, yet our facial expression, body reaction, and the way we rate the experience differ a lot.

(iv) We often experience emotion before the bodily changes have occurred, which simply should not happen according to the theory. Visceral changes take place slowly.

(v) The assumption that there is a distinctive pattern of bodily changes for each emotional state is too simple; many different emotions are associated with a broadly similar state of arousal of the autonomic nervous system.

(vi) Visceral changes, by themselves, may not be sufficient to produce emotion. For example, a person who is doing any physical exercise like walking, jogging, running, cycling, etc. has an increased heart and respiration rate but may not experience the emotion of fear or anger, either.

11.4.2 The Cannon-Bard Theory

In 1927, about 40 years after the James–Lange Theory was developed, Harvard physiologist Walter Bradford Cannon (19 October 1871–1 October, 1945) and his colleague Philip Bard (1898–1977) developed a new theory that related the workings of the nervous system to the expression

Walter Bradford Cannon
(1871–1945)

Philip Bard
(1898–1977)

of emotions. An American psychologist Walter B. Cannon and later an American physiologist Philip Bard (25 October 1898–5 April, 1977) proposed a theory that became one of the chief arguments and an alternative against James–Lange view. Walter Cannon, the physiologist who first discovered the "fight or flight" syndrome saw the experience of emotion as entirely separate from its physiological correlates. In 1929, Cannon argued that the arousal response was general, not specific to different emotions. According to Cannon's model, an emotion producing stimulus produces a generalized fight or flight response.

Cannon and Bard found that people could experience emotion without getting physical feedback from chemical messengers. They proposed that upon experiencing a stimulating event, information about the event is collected by the body's senses and is sent through the nervous system to the brain. In the brain, the message is sent to two places at the same time. The message is sent to the cortex, which creates emotions (Figure 11.4); for example, almost being hit by car situation, it created fear. At the same time, the message also goes to the hypothalamus (hy-po-THAL-ah-mus). The hypothalamus is the part of the brain that controls automatic body responses. It tells the body to send out chemical messengers that cause the body to respond. Some of these responses are experienced as behaviours such as shaking, rapid breathing, and crying.

Cannon (1929) showed that subjects reacted emotionally even when nerves connecting the central nervous system to various organs were severed or cut off suggesting that physiological changes were not necessarily the primary cause of emotion. This theory rejects the view that physiological arousal alone leads to the perception of an emotion. Cannon proposed that signals from the senses might be received by the thalamus, which performs the dual function of providing the emotional content to the appropriate centre and transmitting the stimulus to other parts of the body.

Further research has called into question Cannon's view of the pre-eminence of the thalamus for the emotion. But the basic insight of this theory continues to be upheld, with more sophisticated support. Cannon's successors examined the structure of the reticular formation in the centre of the brainstem. Electrical activity throughout the brain was accompanied by electrical activity in reticular formation. Emotion is the result of certain level of reticular formation activation, a level less than that necessary to sustain such great functions as perception and behaviour. Because the reticular formation serves to integrate virtually all brain activity, any perception or action is necessarily infused with emotional content.

Thus, according to Cannon–Bard theory, an important mediator in emotional experience is the thalamus, a part of brain that receives messages from the sensory receptors. When a person is in an emotional situation, a part of brain known as *thalamus* is activated. The thalamus, in turn, sends separate messages to the autonomic nervous system and to the cortex. For example, you do not have to wait for your stomach to churn before your cortex knows that you are terrified. Instead, both events occur at the same time. For several decades, the Cannon–Bard Theory was more popular than the James-Lange approach. However, Cannon–Bard Theory is very limited, it tells us nothing about how the cognitive system decides whether a given situation is emotional.

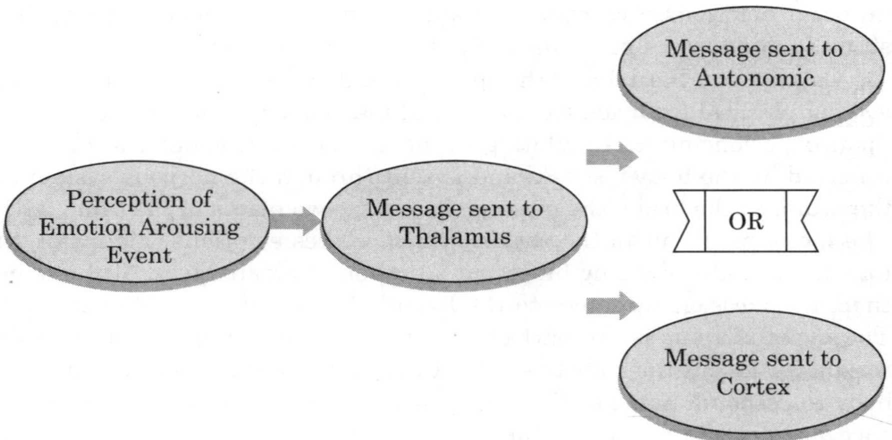

Figure 11.4 Cannon's theory of emotion.

Lie detector test: A lie detector test or more properly a polygraph examination, simultaneously measures several autonomic changes such as blood pressure, pulse rate, breathing patterns, and skin conductance. These measures are taken by a person on a structured series of questions. The examiner notes the pattern of arousal and decides on the basis of these that whether the person being tested is innocent or guilty (Saxe et al., 1985). Note that the polygraph does not really detect lies rather emotional arousal. An innocent person should show minimum arousal of the autonomic nervous system and an official who examines the polygraph should conclude that she or he is indeed "innocent". A guilty person should show strong arousal and an examination of polygraph should lead to the conclusion "guilty". Unfortunately, the research on the polygraph shows that the results do not correspond perfectly with reality. People who can control their physiological reactions can successfully lie and beat the test. On the other hand, other people with overly reactive autonomic nervous system may be telling the truth, yet the examiner would conclude "guilty". The problem is that these polygraph tests are simply too unreliable to be trusted.

11.5 BIOLOGICAL BASIS OF EMOTIONS

Emotions are complex reactions, involving not only the intense subjective feelings (joy, sorrow etc.) but also, outward emotional expressions and the ability or abilities to understand emotional information, (for example, to "read" the emotional reaction of others). Research on the biological and neural basis of emotion indicates that portions of the brain play a significant role in each of these components.

According to Harrington (1995), the right cerebral hemisphere plays an important role in emotional functions. The right hemisphere seems to be specialized for processing emotional information. Individuals with damage to the right hemisphere have deficiency in understanding the emotional tone of another person's voice or in currently describing emotional scenes (Heller, 1997; Nitscheke and Miller, 1998). Similarly, among healthy persons with no damage to their brains, individuals do better at identifying others' emotions, when such information is presented to their right hemisphere rather than to their left hemisphere (Ladavas, Umitta, Ricci-Bitti, 1980). The right hemisphere also seems to be specialized for the expression of the emotion. Patients with damage to the right hemisphere are less successful at expressing emotions through the tone of their voice than persons without such damage express (Borod, 1993).

There appear to be important differences between the left and right hemisphere of the brain with respect to two key aspects of emotions (i) *valence:* the extent to which an emotion is pleasant or unpleasant and; (ii) *arousal:* the intensity of emotion. Activation of left hemisphere is associated with approach, response to reward and positive affect (that is "positive" or positive feeling), whereas activation of the right hemisphere is associated with avoidance, withdrawal from aversive stimuli and negative affect. Further, anterior regions of the hemispheres (right and left) are associated primarily with valence (pleasant, unpleasant) dimensions while posterior regions are associated primarily with arousal (intensity). For example, depression and anxiety—both disorders involve negative feelings or emotions but depression is usually associated with low arousal (depression people lack energy), while anxiety is associated with high arousal (if you have ever experienced anxiety from right before an examination or an interview for a job, you know this well). Persons suffering from depression should show reduced activity in the right posterior region while persons suffering from anxiety should show increased activity in that brain region. These results have been conformed in several studies (Heller, Etienne, and Miller, 1995). Our growing knowledge of the neural basis of emotion has important practical as well as scientific implications.

Additional research indicates that structures deep within the brain too, play an important role in emotions. In particular, amygdala seems to be involved in our ability to judge the intensity although not the valence of other's emotion (Adolphs).

11.6 CONCEPT OF DEVELOPMENT OF EMOTIONS OR EMOTIONAL DEVELOPMENT

Bridges (1932) and others tried to study the development of emotions systematically (Figure 11.5). Analysis of this figure indicates that with the progress in age, emotional responses become more specific, differentiated, less diffused, and less random. Different emotions become more specialized and directed emotions and a mature level of emotional behaviour towards specific situations. As the child becomes older and older, linguistic responses increase and motor responses decrease especially in fear and anger provoking situations. According to Bridges (1932), emotional development has got a genetic sequence. With the undifferentiated general excitement due to intense stimulation present at birth, all emotional responses are derived as result of maturation and learning. Experimental studies indicate that maturation of the frontal lobe is responsible for matured emotional behaviours. Certain endocrine glands, like adrenal glands, which are comparatively inactive at birth, become more active at later stages, which lead to the development of emotions.

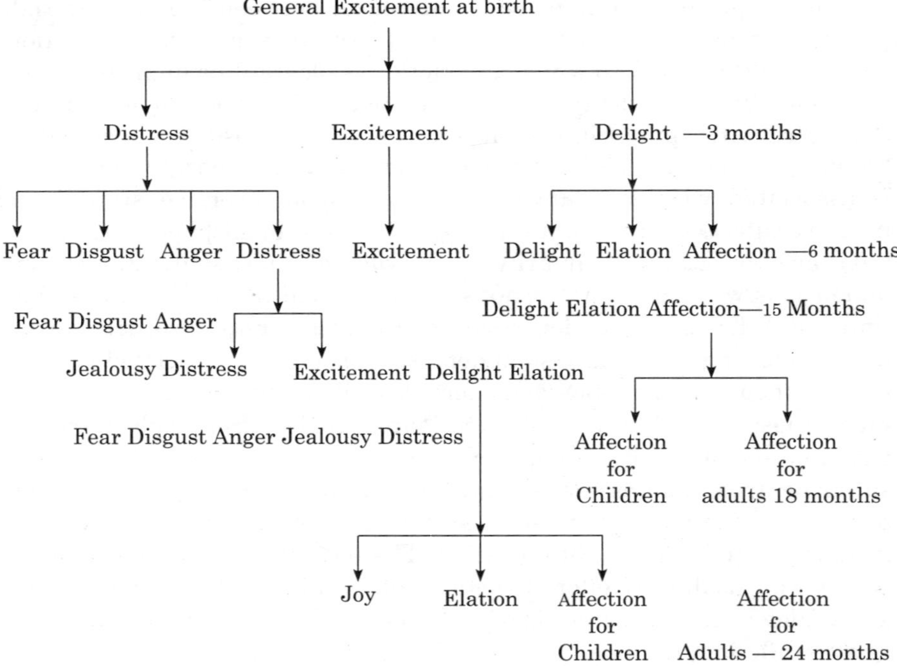

Figure 11.5 Development of emotions.

The process of maturation and learning play an effective role in the development of emotions in the human beings. As a child grows, she or he may acquire various positive and negative emotions through her or his environmental experiences and training. With age, there is an increase in intellectual development which enables the child to perceive meaning and become responsive to various stimuli. Emotions or emotional behaviour are in all sense, the learned and acquired patterns of our behaviour.

Therefore, at the time of birth, a child does not show the presence of any specific emotions except a sort of general excitement in the form of crying or smiling. This state of general excitement showing pleasure or displeasure to the concerned stimuli remains with the infant up to six months. Therefore, it can be safely said that a child begins her or his journey towards the development of her or his emotional behaviour with the help of two distinct emotions that is emotion of distress (displeasure) and emotion of delight (pleasure). "Distress" means suffering or unhappiness. "Delight" means a great pleasure or pleases greatly. When an infant completes his six months, distress further becomes more specific into negative emotions. Negative emotions like fear, disgust, anger etc. take the lead. Fear is an unpleasant sensation caused by nearness of danger or pain. And delight give rise to positive emotions. Positive emotions like elation, affection or love, sympathy, enjoyment, etc. creep in. Jealousy is seen around fifteen months. The emotions of joy and affection appear around eighteen months. Affection becomes further differentiated to children and adults from the age of eighteen months. Generally, up to two years, almost all emotions, positive and negative, take their shape and become quite distinct in children. However, the age at which differentiation of the various emotions take place varies somewhat from child to child. Differences in health and environment produce individual variations in the frequency, intensity, and duration of emotions.

Emotional development, after the stage of infancy, is thus totally concerned with the development of the ways and manners of expressing various positive and negative emotions. These ways and means of emotional expressions are learned through environmental experiences, formal as well as informal education, and specialized training given to an individual right from her or his childhood. Conditioning and imitation influence the development of emotional patterns in childhood. Conditioning of many irrational fears occurs easily and quickly during the early years of life because the young child lacks reasoning ability and experience.

Whatever, experience, education, or training a person may get for the expression of his emotional behaviour during expression of his emotional behaviour during his childhood and adolescence, and we expect from him a quite mature behaviour in terms of his emotional expression during his adulthood. Besides, attaining maturity in terms of his physical and mental development, and adult should also demonstrate adequate maturity in terms of his emotional development. In other words, he must be emotionally mature and exhibit it in his behaviour.

"Emotional maturity" means the state in which one's emotional reactivity is considered appropriate and normal for an adult in a given society. It is the power of self-control and the ability to suppress extreme emotional reactions. In its broadest sense, emotional maturity means the degree to which the person has realized his potential for richness of living and has developed his capacity to enjoy things, to relate himself to others, to love and to laugh; his capacity for whole-hearted sorrow when an occasion for grief arises....and his capacity to show fear when there is occasion to be frightened, without feeling a need to use a false mask of courage.

The following are some of the characteristics of an emotionally matured person:

1. An emotionally matured person can express her or his emotions in an appropriate and socially desirable manner.
2. An emotionally matured person has self-control over sudden outburst of her or his emotions.
3. An emotionally matured person faces the reality and accompanying emotions courageously.
4. An emotionally matured person takes decisions of her or his life logically.
5. An emotionally matured person respects other people and has self-respect and self-esteem.
6. An emotionally matured person is stable and honest in her or his behaviours.

11.7 PHYSIOLOGICAL CORRELATES OF EMOTIONS OR BODILY CHANGES IN EMOTION

Bodily changes mean physiological changes. Because of the excessive activation of different organs during emotional stages, physiological changes occur. However, each emotion has a typical behavioural pattern. It also varies from culture and from individual to individual. In spite of these variations, there are some common bodily changes, which can be divided into overt and covert or external and internal bodily changes.

11.7.1 External or Overt or Observable Bodily Changes

Facial Expressions

Face is the most expressive organ of the human body. Face, to some extent, is said to be the index of human beings and so of emotions. It is thus said to be the barometer of emotions. The muscles in the forehead, around the eyes, nose, and mouth are used differently with each emotion. Facial expressions vary from emotion to emotion, even for a particular emotion it varies from person to person.

Facial expressions of infants of some basic emotions recognized by Carroll Izard (1977):

1. Joy: mouth forms a smile, cheeks are lifted, twinkle in the eyes.
2. Anger: eyebrows drawn together and downward, eyes fixed, mouth squarish.
3. Interest: eyebrows raised or knitted, mouth softly rounded, lips may be pursed.
4. Disgust: nose wrinkled, upper lip raised, tongue pushed outward.
5. Surprise: eyebrows raised, eyes widened, mouth rounded in oval shape.
6. Sadness: eyebrows' inner corners raised, mouth corners drawn down.
7. Fear: eyebrows level, drawn in an up, eye-lids lifted, mouth corners retracted.

Facial expressions and non-verbal communication, however, cannot be understood as sufficiently, objectively, reliably, and valid instrument for the identification and measurement of one's emotions. The basis for the correlations of facial expressions and emotions may be discovered both in one's innate dispositions and socio-cultural environment.

However, it is not always easy to judge accurately one's emotion from his facial expressions, particularly of adults. Besides, some do not show any definite pattern of facial expressions for a particular emotion. Munn states that it is much easier to differentiate facial expression of pleasant emotions to unpleasant ones than it is to differentiate expressions of specific emotions. In joy, the eyes may shine, in grief they get dimmed. In anger, the face becomes red; the nostrils may expand or contract. In happiness, the lips may smile. The cheeks may be red in anger or when one blushes in shyness. In fear, the mouth gets dry, the face is full of sweat and the body shakes.

Postural changes

Different emotions arouse different postures. In emotion of love, there is movement towards or in the direction of the lover or the beloved. Fear involves flight. Violent anger involves not flight but fight or aggressive movements, which may either be abusive or involve actual attack. In anger, the body stiffens. In grief, we bow. We lean forward when we are anxious and expect something. In sorrow, there is a general slumping posture; while in joy the opposite is involved, that is the head is held high and chest out. There is movement of hands. The importance of postural reactions in emotional experiences is emphasized by James–Lange theory of emotion.

Vocal expressions or changes in voice

Voice is a powerful indicator of different kinds of emotional experiences. Change in loudness, pitch etc. may represent different kinds of emotions.

Laughing, weeping, speaking in a loud voice with an unusual high pitch, crying, talking slowly with some hesitation, feeling difficulty in speaking, uttering abusive language, speaking in a very sweet and affectionate manner, whistling, murmuring, etc. are some of the examples and ways through which we demonstrate different emotions. Loud laughter indicates joy and happiness, a slow and monotonous voice expresses defeat and dejection, and a high pitch voice indicates anger. In anger, the increase of body tension leads to more tension in the vocal cords. In fear, there is suffering. Therefore, from the verbal expressions of a person, his emotional state can easily be detected in addition to his facial expression, postural, and other expressions.

However, it is also not a reliable method for the identification of one's emotional experience simply on the ground that many of the emotional experiences may demonstrate similarities in terms of voice or vocal expressions.

11.7.2 Physiological or Covert or Internal Bodily Changes

In our day to day experience of emotion, we find the body undergoing various physiological changes like heart rate, breathing, pulse, skin conductance, muscular tension, sinking feeling in the stomach, general feeling of weakness, sweating, blood pressure, perspiration, and other physiological changes.

Glandular responses

Glands play an important role during different emotional states. In anger, the adrenal gland secretes excessive amount of adrenaline and it is responsible for many characteristics of strong emotional experiences. The level of sugar rises in the blood because of excessive secretion of this hormone. This increases heartbeat. Blood pressure increases due to the release of glycogen from liver. Many research studies have shown that adrenaline produces emotional responses in the organism.

Changes in the heart beat

It is a well-known fact that heartbeat increases during the emotional states. It has been studied experimentally with the help of instruments like Electro Cardiographer that there is always an increase in heartbeat when we are in anger, excitement, or in a fearful situation.

In general, heart rate is most accurate in discriminating among emotions (Z.A. Jonick and McIntosh, 1992). Anger is the only emotion associated with accelerated heart rate and low skin temperature. Fear is also associated with accelerated heart beat and low skin temperature (Levenson, 1992; McIntosh, 1992). The very different emotions—happiness, disgust, and surprise are all associated with low heart rate.

Changes in the Blood Pressure

Whenever we are excited or emotional, there is a change in the blood pressure and this disturbance is due to the disturbance in the circulation of blood. Side by side, there are changes in the pulse rate also. Generally, it increases but in some cases as of fear, anxiety, and shock, it may also reduce considerably. Instrument called *Sphygmomanometer* is used to measure blood pressure. Diastolic blood pressure is the pressure at a moment when the heart relaxes to permit the inflow of blood. Blood pressure is different for different age groups. For children, the normal is 50–80 (diastolic-systolic); for adults 70–120; for old people 90–140. Systolic blood pressure is the pressure at a moment when the heart relaxes in the process of pumping out blood and is obtained by adding 90 to the age of the person. For example, if the age of the person is 30 years, his normal systolic blood pressure is 120 (30 + 90). Table 11.2 shows the normal systolic and diastolic blood pressure for different age groups:

Table 11.2 Normal systolic and diastolic blood pressure for different age groups

Age	*Diastolic*	*Systolic*
20	78	118
25	80	120
30	82	122
35	48	124
40	86	127
45	88	130

Changes in the respiration process

During the emotional states, the intake of oxygen is also affected. Breathing process is disturbed and there is a change in the total respiratory function. Generally, it increases but in cases like excessive fear, happiness, shocks, and excitements, it may go down to the extent of becoming nil.

Changes in the response of pupil

Many psychologists believe that the problem of eye-blinking is related closely to emotional states. There are some instruments which can measure the movements of the pupil of the patients suffering from emotional problems.

Pupillometrics is a novel or new technique of measuring physiological changes during emotional stages. The pupil of the eye, during emotional state, dilates in response to stimuli, which arouse a favorable reaction and contrasts in response to an unpleasant and disliked stimuli.

Changes in the gastro-intestinal responses or digestive system

There are also changes in gastro-intestinal functions during emotional behaviour. Gastro-intestinal functions are usually measured by the help of balloons inserted into the stomach or intestines. By observing the stomach directly, gastro-intestinal functions can be measured. Digestive system is adversely affected by emotions. Experimental studies have concluded that under the current of emotions, our stomach and intestines work quite slowly and sometimes become inactive. The secretion of the digestive glands, including saliva, decreases considerably resulting in malfunctioning and inactivity on the part of the digestive system. That is why, most of the emotionally charged individuals are found to suffer from digestive problems.

Changes in the galvanic skin responses

The galvanic skin responses are measured by an apparatus or instrument called *psycho-galvanometre* or galvanic skin reflex instrument. It measures the electrical resistance in the skin, technically called *electrodermal* changes. These changes result from the activity of the sweat glands. Normal body temperature fluctuates. At the time of intense excitement, it generally goes down. There is a decrease in the case of emotions like distress, disgust, anger which results into sweating or perspiration. On the other hand, there is increase in the case of emotions like fear, love, wonder, etc. which results into the erection of the body hairs. These differences in skin temperature are almost universal.

Changes in the nervous system

Our nervous system plays an important role during emotions or emotional states. The autonomic nervous system is intimately associated with emotional behaviour. The autonomic nervous system sends fibres to visceral organs of the chest, abdomen, pelvis, and other structures containing smooth muscles or glandular tissues.

The autonomic nervous system has two parts: (a) Sympathetic and (b) Para-sympathetic divisions. Most of the vital functions of the body are controlled by the para-sympathetic division. The sympathetic division has a very minor role, while the para-sympathetic division carries everyday vital functions of life. The sympathetic division acts only during emergency. The two systems work in opposition or antagonistic manner. While one accelerates one particular function, the other retards it.

According to Ruch, "The sympathetic division takes over under three states—during cold, so extreme as to threaten life, during any violent effort or exercise, during fear and violent anger."

During fear and anger, the sympathetic system is full of activity. It speeds up the heartbeat, raises blood pressure, and dilates the pupils of the eyes. It distributes blood to the exterior muscles. The blood supply is contracted to other parts of the body and is diverted to the muscles.

11.7.3 The Role of Hypothalamus in Emotion

Hypothalamus plays a significant role in emotional behaviour. This is substantiated by various experimental studies on animals. Observations show that when the hypothalamus is seriously impaired by an accident or any other reason, apathy occurs, that is there is no emotional reaction. Lashley remarked that although it is clear that the hypothalamus plays a role in the motor expressions of emotion, its role in relation to feeling aspects is widely disputed (Figure 11.6).

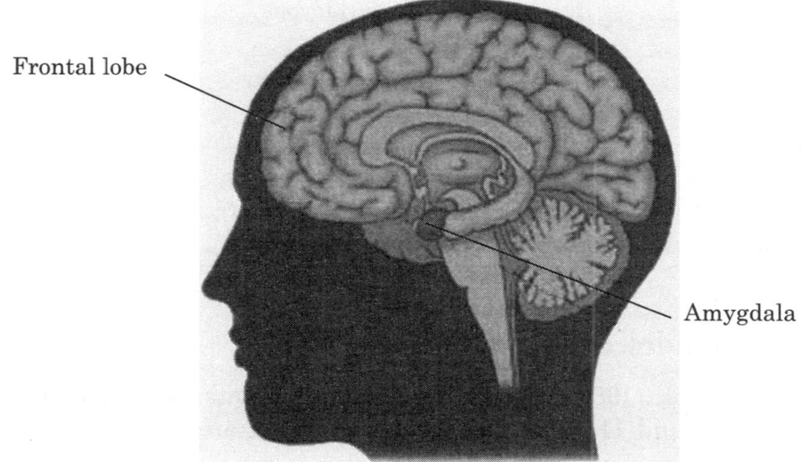

Figure 11.6 Structures affecting emotions.

Changes in the pattern of the brain potentials during emotion indicate the important involvement of cerebral cortex in emotional behaviour. The cognitive factors depend upon the cortical functioning.

11.8 TYPES OF EMOTIONS

Paul Ekman had done more than thirty years of world-class research and has a very unique personal mastery—almost a *siddhi* (extraordinary human capacity). According to him, there are up to ten emotions: 1. Anger, 2. Fear, 3. Sadness, 4. Disgust, 5. Contempt, 6. Surprise, 7. Enjoyment, 8. Embarrassment, 9. Guilt, 10. Shame. Carroll Izard (1977) isolated ten such basic emotions: 1. Joy, 2. Interest-excitement, 3. Surprise, 4. Sadness, 5. Anger, 6. Disgust, 7. Contempt, 8. Fear, 9. Shame, 10. Guilt, most of which are present in infancy. Izard reported that other emotions are combinations of these ten (Table 11.3 and Figure 11.7). Phillip Shaver and his colleagues (1994) believe that love, too, may be a basic emotion, Izard viewed it as a mixture of joy and interest-excitement.

Table 11.3 The basic human emotions

Carroll Izard (10)	*Paul Ekman and Wallace Frisen* (7)	*Robert Plutchik* (8)	*Silvan Tomkins* (9)
Fear	Fear	Fear	Fear
Anger	Anger	Anger	Anger
Disgust	Disgust	Disgust	Disgust
Surprise	Surprise	Surprise	Surprise
Joy	Happiness	Joyous	Enjoyment
Shame	–	–	Shame
Contempt	Contempt	–	Contempt
Sadness	Sadness	Sadness	–
Interest	–	Anticipation	Interest
Guilt	–	–	–
–	–	Acceptance	–
–	–	–	Distress

11.8.1 Wheel of Emotions

Robert Plutchik (1980) identified eight basic emotions. Basic emotions (Figures 11.7 and 11.8) and their basic opposites are mentioned below:

Basic emotion	*Basic opposite*
Joy	Sadness
Acceptance	Disgust
Fear	Anger
Surprise	Anticipation
Sadness	Joy
Disgust	Acceptance
Anger	Fear
Anticipation	Surprise

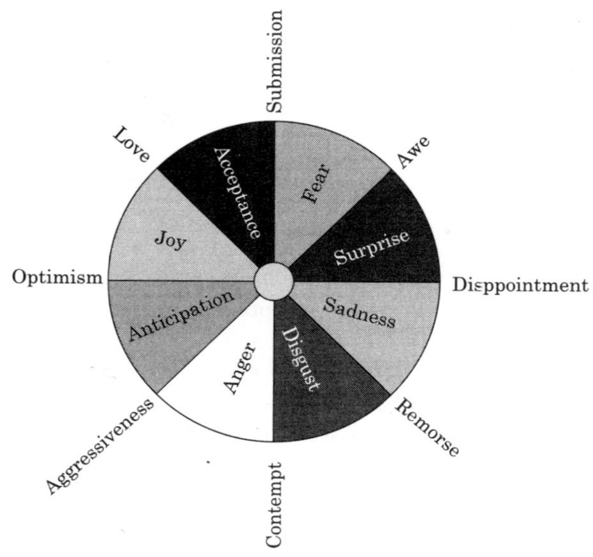

Figure 11.7 A Model of the emotions.

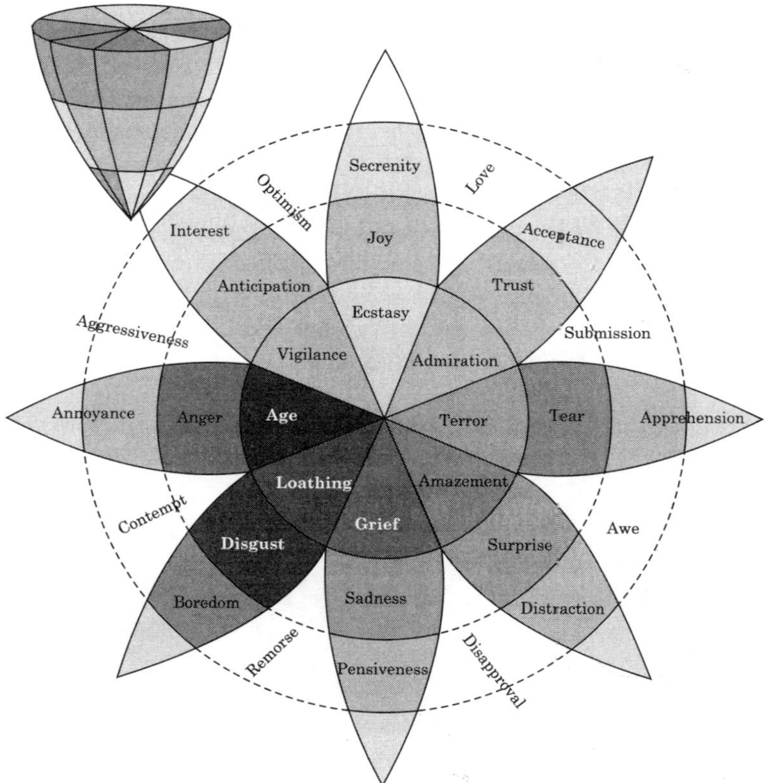

Figure 11.8 Wheel of emotions.

Psychologists recognize five basic emotions

1. Fear, 2. Anger, 3. Disgust, 4. Surprise, 5. Joy. There are twelve possible emotions in existence. Table 11.4 shows eight advanced emotions, each composed of two basic emotions:

Table 11.4 Shows eight advanced emotions, each composed of two basic emotions

Advanced Emotions	*Composed of*	*Advanced Opposite*
Optimism	Anticipation + Joy	Disappointment
Love	Joy + Acceptance	Remorse
Submission	Acceptance + Fear	Contempt
Awe	Fear + Surprise	Aggressiveness
Disappointment	Surprise + Sadness	Optimism
Remorse	Sadness + Disgust	Love
Contempt	Disgust + Anger	Submission
Aggressiveness	Anger + Anticipation	Awe

There are mainly two types of emotions in regard to the valence of emotion that is the pleasantness or unpleasantness of the emotion. They are positive emotions or negative emotions.

Positive emotions

Positive emotions fuel upward spirals.

1. **Joy, Pleasure, and Delight:** All these are positive emotions and they generally belong to joy. Such emotions always give pleasure to the individual (Figure 11.9). Joy depends upon good health and general bodily conditions.

Figure 11.9 Jumping for joy.

According to Carroll Izard (1977), facial expressions of infants in joy include mouth forming a smile, cheeks lifted, twinkle in the eyes (Figure 11.10). Joy is generalized and undifferentiated rather than specific.

Figure 11.10 A great smile.

Leuba found that laughter, smiling, etc. appear between six to seven months of age. Watson studied five situations causing laughter in children of six months to three years of age. These children were observed constantly from waking to sleeping time. He found that certain situations like being played with, running, chasing, playing with other children, teasing other children, watching other children play, cause laughter in children (Figure 11.11).

Figure 11.11 Sunny delight.

In order to release the strain of pent-up emotions, such as the negative emotions like anger and fear, the pleasant emotions like joy, pleasure, and delight etc. are required to be expressed.

2. **Affection:** Affection is positive and pleasant emotion directed towards a person or a thing. One who gives joy and satisfaction usually receives this emotional response. Young children express their affection to both objects and persons. Simpson, in a study of parent preferences, found that children as they grow older show more affection towards the mother than the father, perhaps because the mother is a constant companion of the child and fulfills all her or his needs.

3. **Happiness:** Happiness is a positive emotion. Happiness is an emotion associated with feelings ranging from contentment and satisfaction to bliss and intense joy. In everyday life, we use the word "happiness" in at least two rather different ways. One way refers to brief feeling of joy ("I was so happy at the party last night"), and the other way is the sense of long-lasting satisfaction or contentment ("last year was a happy year for me"). Happiness is considered mostly in the sense of long-term contentment.

One's state of happiness or unhappiness colours everything. People who are happy perceive the world as safer, make decisions more easily, rate job applicants more favorably, are more cooperative, and live healthier and more energized and satisfied lives (Lyukomirsky & others, 2002; Myers, 1995), let your mood brighten and your thinking broadens and becomes more playful and creative (Frederiksen, 1994). Happier people live longer, get fewer infections, and feel less pain.

Individual differences occur in degree of happiness. Some people are much happier than others. So, many factors play a role in enjoying a happy life, like deeper relationship with other people, more friends, more interesting and secure jobs, good health, positive attitudes, empathy, genuineness, forgiveness, self-esteem, success, and so on. People with lots of money are somewhat happier than those with just enough to afford life's necessities (Di Tella and others, 2001). People in rich countries are also somewhat happier than those in poor countries (Steel and Ones, 2002). Yet, in the long run, increased affluence hardly affects happiness. Wealth is like health: its utter absence can breed misery, yet having it is no guarantee of happiness. Another study found that very happy university students are not distinguished by their money but by their "rich and satisfying close relationship" (Diener and Seligman, 2002). The need to belong runs deeper, it seems, than any need to be rich.

Happiness may be related to the functioning of the body in key processes, such as those of the cardiovascular system and controlling hormone levels, a new study reveals. Happier individual showed lower levels of cortical, a stress hormone related to conditions (such as diabetes and hypertension). Happier individuals also had lower heart rate over the day and evening, which suggests good cardiovascular health. So, positive well-being is directly related to the biological processes relevant to health. Studies of pairs of twins carried out by psychologist David Lykken (1992) suggest that people even inherit a tendency toward a certain level of happiness. Despite the ups and downs of experience, people tend to drift back to their usual level of cheerfulness or grumpiness. Factors such as availability of money, level of education, and marital status may be less influential when it comes to human happiness.

Paul Ekman recognizes the following seven types of happiness:

(i) Amusement
(ii) Fiero (the delight of meeting a challenge)
(iii) Relief
(iv) Excitement, novelty
(v) Awe, wonder
(vi) Sensory pleasures (in each of the senses)
(vii) Calm peacefulness

Happiness is expressed through laughter (Figure 11.12). Laughter often termed an "internal message" is not merely a smile that has burst, it is much more. Laughter reveals one's sense of humour, smoothens human relationships, facilitates interaction during work, prolongs life, and above all, acts as a free medicine.

Figure 11.12 A smiley face is a well-known symbol of happiness.

Down the ages, ancient wisdom has slotted laughter as a prescription for good health. The smiley face is a well known symbol of happiness as shown in Figure 11.12. Physical as well as psychological research support the idea that laughter is much more than medicine. Dr. Thomas Houston who believes laughter is a strong positive emotion says, "Laughter stimulates the heartrate and circulation, exercises the lungs, and relaxes the muscles. Laughing even increases the endorphin level—those natural opiates that produce euphoria and well-being."

The humourist Robert McNabb believes a good joke often helps combat aggression. He sees laughter as a valuable tool in the workplace. He says, "People are drawn to people who laugh easily. Good-tempered people are like well-tempered steel." Conversely, a lack of sense of humour blocks communication. He says, "When people are making important decisions, a laugh is a break. After laughing, you can begin a new thought process. The mind moves in a new, perhaps better direction. One's perspective is changed." So, hearty guffaw contributes to longevity and he who laughs, lasts.

Apart from the fact, that happiness lies in biological function, personality plays an important role in one's happiness. Happy people tend to have a certain types of personality. Happy people experience many pleasant emotions, but very few unpleasant ones. Research supports the view that those who are high on Extraversion (E), a personality dimension of Eysenck's personality theory, measured by the test, Eysenck's Personality Questionnaire–R (EPQ–R) experience much more pleasant emotions than those who are low on extraversion. The following are some of the characteristics of extraverts:

- Outgoing
- Lively experience
- Quite social, sociable
- Take interest in other people
- Optimistic
- Jolly people
- Practical kind of people
- Helpful
- Very talkative
- Have many friends
- Adventurous
- Take interest in outward activities
- Not easily offended or embarrassed
- Sportive
- Magnify their success and ignore their failures
- Show much long to the external world, physical and social objects
- It is easier to make friendship with such people because they do not set up defensive attitude
- Men of action

Researchers have found that happy people tend to:

- Have high self-esteem
- Be optimistic, outgoing, and agreeable
- Have close friendships or satisfying relationships
- Have work and leisure that engages their skills
- Have a meaningful religious faith
- Sleep well and exercise

Psychologists also found that another dimension of our personality, which is also measured by the test (EPQ–R), is also related with one's happiness and that is Neuroticism (N). Neuroticism is a personality dimension involving being anxious and depressed. It refers to a person's general moodiness, stability versus instability. Those individuals high on extraversion (E) and low on neuroticism (N) were happy with their lives, whereas those who were low on extraversion and high on neuroticism were unhappy (Costa and McCrae, 1980). They found that those who are high on extraversion experience much more pleasant emotions than those who are low on extraversion. They also found that those who are high on neuroticism experience more negative emotions than those who are low on neuroticism. The following are the some of the characteristics of neurotics:

- Anxious
- Worrying individual
- Moody and frequently worried
- Likely to sleep badly and to suffer from various psychosomatic disorders
- Overly emotional, reacting too strongly to all sorts of stimuli and find it difficult to get back on an even keel after each emotionally arousing experience.
- React in irrational, sometimes rigid ways
- Main characteristic is a constant preoccupation with things that might go wrong, and a strong emotional reaction of anxiety to these thoughts.

If the high N individual (neurotic) has to be described in one word, one might say that she or he is a "worrier".

The experiences that we have obviously influence our level of happiness, and this is most true of our close relationships. Winning a fortune produces increase in happiness and disease (like paralysis, AIDS, cancer, etc.) reduces happiness considerably. Age, gender, education levels, parenthood, physical attractiveness seem not much related to happiness. Research has identified a number of correlates associated with happiness. These include religious involvement, parenthood, marital status, age, and income.

Carl Rogers, a humanist, considered self-concept to play an important role in happiness. "Self-concept" consists of our thoughts and feelings about ourselves, both as individuals and in relation to others. Happy people have a much smaller gap between the self-concept and the ideal-self than unhappy people. "Ideal-self" is the self-concept that an individual would most like to have. "The summit of happiness is reached when a person is ready to be what she or he is" or "It is the first point of happiness that a man is willing to be what she or he is."

Values also play an important role in happiness. Values should be defined to discover happiness. Values are motivating factors in human behaviour. Values provide a basis for judgment, discrimination, and analysis and it is these qualities that make intelligent choices possible between alternative courses of action. A person who holds a particular set of values can easily weigh different options in the light of these values and derive satisfaction. Various motivating values of human behaviour can be health, love, ambition, comfort, desire for knowledge, play, act, etc. Values like hygiene, manners, self-reliance, helpfulness, safety, co-operation, caring, sportsmanship, truth, responsibility, love, forgiveness, and patriotism to name just a few, definitely results into personality development. All school teachers, principals, teaching fraternity, parents, elders, are requested to instill these values in impressionable minds of their students. Happiness can be built only on virtue and its foundation should be laid on truth. Values give meaning to life as one discovers a great moral strength when she or he finds good values associated with her or his personality, which usually provides an able direction in one's life. Instead of aping the West, we need to inculcate traditional values in our children.

The happiest people are those who freely, generously, and willingly give off themselves in order to make others happy. When we feel happy, we are more willing to help others. Psychologists call it the "feel-good, do-good phenomena" (Salovey, 1992). Happiness does not just feel good; it does "good." But, one cannot give to others what one does not have!

So, happiness grows at our own fire-sides and is not to be picked from stranger's garden. A man as a physical being is always turned towards the outside, thinking that her or his happiness lies outside her or him. However, she or he finally turns inward and discovers that the source is within her or him. Accept life unconditionally. Most people ask for happiness on condition. Happiness can only be felt, if you do not set any condition. Like other things in life, happiness also does not come to the lazy. We have to strive for it diligently. That action is best which procures the greatest happiness for the greatest numbers.

Some important conditions contributing to happiness in childhood include: (i) Good health, (ii) An environment in which children have opportunities to use and develop their abilities and capabilities to the maximum, (iii) A disciplinary policy, (iv) A regular schedule, (v) Encouragement of creativity in play, (vi) Avoidance of criticism and ridicule specially in front of others, (vii) Parents being good role models, (viii) An atmosphere of cheerfulness, (ix) Having no unrealistic demands and expectations.

We all want to be happy in our life but it is said, "It is simple to be happy, but difficult to be simple." Happiness is not far to seek. Our happiness, to some extent, is under our direct personal control. Here are some research-based suggestions for being happier and increasing your satisfaction with life:

1. Act happy.
2. Give priority to your close relationships.
3. Do good to other people, those in need.
4. Develop values.
5. Make best use of your time.
6. Realize that happiness does not come from materialism.
7. Relax
8. Develop faith, hope, and purpose in life.
9. Nurture your spiritual self. Meditate.

Negative emotions

Negative emotions make our lives miserable and drive us to seek help.

1. **Anger:** Anger is said to be negative and unpleasant emotion. Anger is a common emotion experienced by all of us. In the beginning, generalized, undifferentiated, and mass anger responses are found, but gradually, it is distinguished and differentiated. According to Anna Wierzbicka (1988), anger is an emotion, "subjectively experienced as an arousal state of antagonism toward someone or something perceived to be the source of an aversive event."

Anger, the sages said, is "a short madness" (Horace, 8–65 BC) that "carries the mind away" (Virgil, 19–70 BC) and that can be "many times more hurtful than the injury that caused it" (Thomas Fuller, 1654–1734). A common metaphor for the physiological aspect of anger is that of a hot fluid in a container. Anger is troublesome when it leads to excessive arousal or self-defeating aggression. Prolonged arousal is stressful, maladaptive, and may lead to diseases of adaptation such as high blood pressure, coronary heart disease. But sages have also said, "noble anger" (William Shakespeare, 1564-1616), "makes any coward brave" (Cato, 149–234 BC), and "brings back.... strength" (Virgil, 19–70 BC). Anger and aggression are not necessarily bad; it is our anger at social injustices, for example, and aggressive action to correct them, that makes for positive social changes. Anger does communicate strength and competence

(Tiedens, 2001). Anger is viewed as "A natural and healthy response that has evolved to enable us to deal with threats."

Anger is more frequent emotional response in children than fear, as the anger-provoking stimuli are more than fear-provoking stimuli in child's environment. When the natural desires and motives are not freely fulfilled, but obstructed, anger is shown. Anger is the best way to fulfil her or his desires and get the attention of others. Anger is a fairly strong emotional reaction which accompanies a variety of situations, such as being physically restrained, being interfered with, having one's possessions removed, being attacked or threatened, blocking of activities in progress, denial of wishes, plans, and purposes. In many species, including humans, anger produces overt or implicit attack.

Anger is similar to sadness. The world is not as it should be. When we act on our anger, it becomes aggression. While anger is an emotion, aggression is the behavioural aspect of anger. Aggression can be learnt by observing and imitation. Parents, teachers, and other elders who give harsh treatment and punishment are effective aggressive models for the young minds. Violent visuals on television and movies have a negative impact on children. Unrealistic anger, the kind we hang on to despite the suffering it causes us and the people around us, could be labelled "hostility". Hostility differs from anger in that it is an enduring trait.

Types of anger: One type of anger is connected to the impulse for self-preservation, occurring when the person or animal is tormented or trapped. Second type of anger is a reaction to perceived deliberate harm-doing or unfair treatment by others. Irritability, sullenness, and churlishness are examples of the third type of anger, which is related more to character traits than to instincts or cognitions.

Causes of anger: The causes of anger are the interference and restriction at any time or due to frustrations. This frustration may be due to personal, physical, or social causes. A child reacts with anger if her or his favourite toy is snatched away. Rickettes has pointed out certain other causes of anger like, conflict over playthings, interruption of interesting activities like pressurizing the child to leave play or stop watching television and study etc., conflict over toilet and dressing. Tohes has found that in three to five year old children, anger is created over their daily toilet habits, dressing, going to school, etc. But by and large, the main cause of anger both in children and adults is the interference in the fulfilment of wishes and desires. Rapid social changes, break-up of the joint family system, complexity of life can be attributed as the causes of increasing aggression.

Anger usually occurs in response to stressors such as social provocation. The angry person usually finds the cause of her or his anger in an intentional, personal, and controllable aspect of another person's behaviour. Provocations occur immediately before the anger experience. Anger usually involves cognitions to the effect that world has no right to be the way it is (in the case of frustration) or that another person has no right to treat us in a certain way (in the case of social provocation). Anger is a common emotional response to negative feelings such as frustration (Berkowitz, 1989), and to social provocation such as insults or threats. The anger was often a response to friends' or loved ones' perceived misdeeds and was especially common when another person's act seemed wilful, unjustified, and avoidable. But blameless annoyances—foul odours, high temperatures, traffic jam, aches and pains—also have the power to make us angry (Berkowitz, 1993). Biologically, anger can cause both sympathetic and para-sympathetic arousal.

The external expressions can be found in facial expressions such as eyebrows drawn together and downward, eyes fixed, mouth squarish, redness of the face, body language (such as stiffened body), physiological responses (such as increase in heartrate preparing the person to move, increase of the blood flow to the hands preparing them to strike or attack, perspiration increases, hands get hot, jaws tend towards clenching), and at times in public acts of aggression while most of those who experience and explain its arousal as a result of "what happened to them." Psychologists point out that an angry person can be very well mistaken: anger causes a loss in self-monitoring capacity and objective observability. (Novaco, 2000).

Coping with anger or the treatment of anger: Checking or repression of anger is undesirable. Anger should be channelled in socially acceptable ways and manners rather than being suppressed, repressed or restricted. Impulses connected with aggression have to be channellized and regulated into socially accepted ways such as debates, games, sports etc. In general, obtaining a clear picture of all factors by removing the irritating factors and redirecting child's motives can treat anger. Anger can be reduced by using the following techniques and suggestions:

1. *Relaxation:* Allow the bodily sensations of relaxation to "flow in" and replace feelings of anger. Think about some pleasant activities or events. Calm yourself by exercising, meditation, yoga, playing an instrument, or confiding your feelings to a friend. To control anger, the body needs a chance to use up the adrenaline through exercise, relaxation techniques, or the well-known admonition to count to ten.
2. *Self-reward:* When you have coped with frustrations or social provocations or other stressors without becoming enraged or furious and aggressive, pat yourself on the back. Tell yourself "You did a fine job". Novaco (1977) suggests some additional self-rewarding thoughts:

"I handled that one pretty well. That's doing a good job."
"I could have gotten more upset than it was worth."
"My pride can get me into trouble, but I'm doing better at this all the time."
"I actually got through that without getting angry."

When we commit ourselves to monitoring and working on our negative feelings, we take direct charge of our emotional lives rather than condemning ourselves to passively riding out the winds of whatever emotion is driving us from moment to moment.

3. *Assertive behaviour:* "Assertive behaviour" entails expressing genuine feelings and sticking up for one's rights. Assertive behaviour does not include insulting, threatening, or attacking. However, it is assertive (not aggressive) to express strong disapproval of another person's behaviour and to ask that person to change her or his behaviour. Assertiveness training involves a variety of techniques commonly used in the treatment of a lack of assertiveness. Civility means not only keeping silent about trivial irritations but also communicating important ones clearly and assertively.
4. *Removing rewards:* Aggressive behaviour can be extinguished by discontinuing reinforcement. People behave aggressively because their aggressive behaviour is reinforced or rewarded. One way in which this can be done is by the use of time-out technique. Children who behave aggressively are prevented from continuing with such behaviours, for example by sending them to their rooms.

   Another way of removing rewards is the incompatible-response technique. In this technique, children's aggressive behaviour is ignored to remove attentional reward. For example, when a child shows temper tantrums to get the attention of others. Here attending the child's aggressive behaviour is being reinforced. If parents or other people who are observing the child's aggressive behaviour ignore the behaviour when it appears, there will be no reinforcement of aggressive behaviour and its frequency of occurrence will decrease in future.
5. *Positive reinforcement:* Positive reinforcement like praise and approval can do wonders when an aggressive child is able to control herself or himself. Psychologists suggest extinction or removal of any stimulus that can be the precursor to aggressive behaviour. Some suggest the removal of the aggressive child to a quieter place till the child cools down.
6. *Modelling:* Albert Bandura, a social learning theorist, claimed that most behaviour, including anger, is learned. Children

imitate the behaviour of other people. The implication of this theory is that if children imitate or copy or model the behaviour or actions of other people, then exposure to non-aggressive models should reduce anger and aggressive behaviour. This was found to be true experimentally by Baron (1970) and Baron and Kepner (1970).

7. *Fostering empathy:* Empathy is a cognitive awareness and understanding of the emotions and feelings of another person. It is the ability to read emotions in someone else. The term "empathy" is used to refer to the ability to understand the feelings of others or "putting oneself into other person's shoes." Empathy can be learned. Aggressive children tend to focus on the wrongs (real or imagined) that another person has done to them. Zahavi and Asher (1978) tried to use increased empathy as a way of controlling the aggressive behaviour of boys. The boys were told that aggression often hurts other people, that it causes resentment, and that it makes other people unhappy. This training produced a substantial reduction in aggressive behaviour and a large increase in desirable behaviour.

   Anything that makes clear the plight of the victim can increase empathy and reduce aggression. Baron (1977) also found supporting results.

8. *Forgiveness:* Research suggests that age-old response of forgiveness may be helpful in reducing anger. Without letting the offender off the hook or inviting further harm, forgiveness releases anger and can calm the body. Charlotte Witvliet and her co-researchers (2001) found that as the students mentally rehearsed forgiveness, their negative feelings—and their perspiration, blood pressure, heartrate, and facial tension—were all lower than when they rehearsed their grudges.

9. *Catharsis:* The word "catharsis" is derived from the Greek, meaning purification, purging. In Freud's psychoanalytic theory, it refers to the release of tension and anxiety resulting from the process of bringing repressed ideas, feelings, wishes, desires, and memories of the past into consciousness. In order to reduce anger, an individual, can "vent anger" or "letting off steam".

   The catharsis hypothesis maintains that we reduce anger by releasing it through aggressive action or fantasy. Experimenters report that this sometimes occurs. When people retaliate against someone who has provoked them, they may indeed calm down—if their counterattack is directed against the provoker, if their retaliation seems justifiable, and if their target is not intimidating (Geen and Quanty, 1977; Hokanson .nd Edelman, 1966). In short, expressing anger can be temporarily calming if it does not leave us feeling guilty or anxious. It follows from this theory that it is better for people to find relatively harmless ways of acting aggressively, for example playing sport, rather than allow their aggressive energy to increase to the level at which they become violent. It means rechannelizing a person's responses to constructive responses.

Most of the evidence fails to support the catharsis hypothesis (Mallick and McCandless, 1966; Walters and Brown, 1963). More often, expressing anger breeds more anger. When provoked, people hit a punching bag believing it will be cathartic, the effect is the opposite—misleading them to exhibit more cruelty (Bushman and others, 1999). "Venting to reduce anger is like using gasoline to put out a fire", concluded the researcher, Brad Bushman (2002). It may also arouse retaliation, which may transform a minor conflict into a major dispute or confrontation. Expressing anger can also magnify anger. Violent gestures increase anger. Thus, although "blowing off steam" may temporarily calm us, it may also amplify the underlying hostility.

10. *Wait:* Experts suggest that an individual can bring down the level of physiological arousal by waiting. "It is true of the body as of arrows", noted Carol Tavris (1982), "What goes up must come down. Any emotional arousal will simmer down if you just wait long enough."
11. Stop the anger process early.
12. Try a cooling-off period.
13. Do something to get you off the anger track.
14. Seek positive explanations for the things others say or do that make you angry.

2. **Jealousy:** Jealousy is a negative outgrowth of anger (Figure 11.13). It is an attitude of resentment directed to other people only, while anger can be directed towards other people, self, and other things.

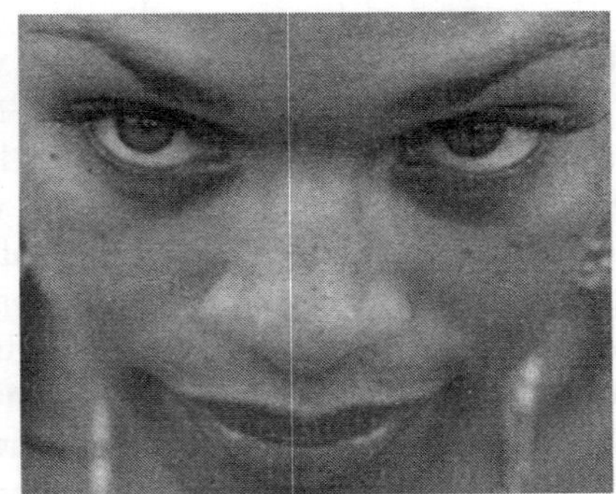

Figure 11.13 Facial expressions of jealousy.

Arousal of jealousy depends upon the training and the treatment that one gets from others. It involves people especially for whom the child has some liking or affection. Child rearing practices have got a lot to do with the development of jealousy. Jealousy is a common emotional experience in young children, originating with the birth of younger siblings. The older child thinks that she or he no longer gets the affection and attention from mother and other family members as all seem to attend more to the newly born. Hence, she or he feels neglected and becomes resentful towards newly born baby, mother, and others. Similarly, the young child is jealous of the older one because of the importance and privileges given to the older one. Children also show jealousy towards parents, especially towards the father when they see him showing affection towards their mother.

Characteristic expression of jealousy includes hurting others, reverting to infantile behaviour like bed-wetting, thumb-sucking, attention catching or attention-seeking. In older people, jealousy is expressed in verbal quarrel, gossiping, nickname calling, and taunting jokes. Jealousy is indirectly expressed in day dreams. According to Foster, girls are found more jealous than boys are. More jealousy is found in children of higher intellectual level.

Jealousy is often a product of home situation and particularly it grows because of the attitudes of parents and the discipline they use. Over protecting and greater attention lead to more jealousy. Overprotective attitude has a negative impact on the growth of personality. Jealousy is produced by unfavourable comparisons by the parents of their children. Levy says, "Jealousy of the child is a direct product of excessive attachment of the mother." Parental favouritism for attractive, affectionate, lucky, or the gifted child creates jealousy in children. According to Jersild, "Competitive attitude of parents, that is comparing one child's performance with another, is responsible for developing jealousy in children." The child is also jealous of other children if they have more possessions, like having more toys, more clothes, or more stationary, etc.

3. **Fear:** Fear is an emotional response to threats and dangers. "Fear" is an emotional state in the presence or anticipation of a dangerous or noxious stimulus. Fear is usually characterized by an internal, subjective experience of extreme agitation, and a desire to flee or attack. Fear is the most damnable, damaging thing to human personality. Fear can be poisonous and contagious. As Bridges (1932) says, at first fear is generated more like a state of panic, excitement than of any specific form. Gradually, with the development of language, fear increases and is expressed in many other linguistic expressions than by crying alone. Facial expressions of fear include—eye brows level, drawn in an up, eye-lids lifted, mouth corners retracted. Fear appears clearly at the age of six

months. It is supposed to be a very early emotion and in most cases, very dangerous for the normal personality development.

Fear is adaptive. It is an alarm system that prepares our body to flee away from danger. It protects us from any potential harm. Fear binds people together.

People can be afraid of almost anything—"afraid of truth, afraid of fortune, afraid of death, and afraid of each other", observed Ralph Waldo Emerson. Psychologists note that we can actually learn to fear almost anything.

The arousal of fear depends upon different situations, loss of support, sudden approach of anything, and loud noise leads to inherent fear. A five-year-old child has fear of darkness, dogs, doctor, skeletons, machines, death, fainting persons, dead bodies, being left alone, deep-water, etc. All these are not natural but acquired fears. Fear for animals, fire, etc. occurs because of conditioning and habit. Our fears may reflect not only our own past traumas but also the fears we learn from our parents and friends. We humans quickly learn to fear snakes, spiders, and cliffs—fears that probably helped our ancestors survive. We are less predisposed to fear cars, electricity, bombs, and global warming, all of which are now far more dangerous (Lumsden and Wilson, 1983; McNally, 1987).

Fear for animals is more found in childhood but for non-animals (for example, diseases), it increases with age. The stimulus itself does not create fear; the way it is presented creates a fear response. Phobia is an irrational fear and when it develops to great extent, it becomes abnormality. The sex of the child, age, social status, and intellectual development all affect the development or occurrence of fears.

A key to fear learning lies in the amygdala, that limbic system neural centre deep in the brain. The amygdala plays a key role in associating various emotions, including fear, with certain situations (Barinaga, 1992). Genes influence our emotional reactivity. Even among identical twins reared separately, one twin's level of fearfulness is similar to the other's (Lykken, 1982). Scientists recently isolated a gene that influences the amygdala's response to frightening situations (Hariri and others, 2002). People with a short version of this gene have less of a protein that speeds the reuptake of the neurotransmitter serotonin. With more serotonin available to activate their amygdala neurons, people with this short gene exhibit a revved-up amygdala response to frightening pictures.

Fear is often differentiated from anxiety on one (or both) of two grounds: (i) fear is treated as involving specific objects or events, while anxiety is regarded as a more general emotional state; (ii) fear is considered a reaction to a present danger, anxiety to an anticipated or imagined one.

Causes of fear: The following are some of the causes which are responsible for causing fear.

1. *Suggestions and imitation:* Dreadful stories narrated by parents or grandparents particularly at night cause greater fear in children. Whenever the mother sees a rat or cockroach, she screams in fear as if she sees a lion and the child imitates that fear. Most of our childhood fears are particularly due to imitation and observing others.
2. *For getting attention:* One shows fear for getting attention also.
3. *Overtraining:* Overprotected and sheltered homelife presents emotional immaturity. When the mother or other family member make it a point to accompany the child whenever she or he goes and wherever she or he goes to protect, in future she or he cannot go anywhere alone.
4. *Symbolic and imaginary fears:* To repress fear for one thing, they show fear for other thing. Fear for spider, bunch of hair, small rats, are mostly symbolic fears. Since these are harmless stimuli one should not show fear to these stimuli.
5. *Negative expectations:* Fear occurs when we have negative expectations.

The following are the physiological changes that accompany fear:

1. *The vascular changes:* The blood vessels leading to the stomach and intestines would constrict and digestion would virtually stop. At the same time, the vessels leading to the larger skeletal muscles would expand diverting the oxygen and nutrients carried in the blood to where they might be needed for flight or fight.
2. *Hormonal changes:* Whenever we are under fear, pancreas would secrete the hormone glycogen, which would stimulate the liver to release stored sugar into the bloodstream. The sugar would supply the extra energy to the skeletal muscles.
3. *Respiratory changes:* Breathing becomes deeper and more rapid and bronchioles (the small air passages leading to the lungs) would expand. These changes would increase the supply of oxygen to the blood—oxygen is needed to burn the sugar being sent to the skeletal muscles.
4. *Circulatory changes:* Heart rate would increase, perhaps more than doubling. Thus, spreading the circulatation of blood and the passing of oxygen and nutrients and delivering into skeletal muscles.
5. *Visual changes:* The pupils of the eyes would dilate thereby taking in more light.

6. *Sweat gland changes:* The activity of the sweat gland would increase. Sweating occurs. The sweat gland on the palms of the hands, in particular, would secrete moisture. In fear, hands get cold.
7. *Muscular changes:* The tiny muscles just beneath the surface of the skin at the roots of the hair would contract causing the hairs to stand on end and produce the effect we call "goose-pimples" or goose-flesh because fear causes the skin to look like that of a plucked goose. The muscles of the neck and shoulders would quickly tense, orienting our eyes and face towards the source of threat, and the muscles over the eyebrows would contract, pulling together and pushing them out, partially covering our eyes.

Prevention and elimination of fear: Joes found two broad categories of preventing fear: social imitation and direct conditioning.

1. *Social imitation:* Just as fear develops by social imitation, it can also be eliminated by imitation. Similarly, fear for different domestic animals, dark places, high places, rivers, water, and crowded places can be eliminated by imitation. Thus, fear can be removed by allowing child to observe others.
2. *Direct conditioning:* Conditioning can eliminate fears. Associating the feared object with a stimulus that the child wants or desires to get, fear can be eliminated. Presentation of fear by conditioning can be done in a time of one or two days. It is a gradual and a slow process, which requires patience, time, and understanding of the child's current desires and needs.
3. *Flooding:* In this method, a person is exposed to a fear evoking but harmless stimulus until fear is extinguished. Flooding is effective but unpleasant.
4. *Systematic desensitization:* In this method, people are gradually or slowly exposed to fear-evoking stimuli under circumstances in which they remain relaxed. This technique is highly effective. It takes longer to work but is less unpleasant.
5. *Counterconditioning:* In counterconditioning, one pairs a pleasant stimulus with the fear-evoking object in order to counteract the fear response by remaining relaxed in the presence of fear-evoking stimuli. We associate or condition feelings of relaxation to these stimuli. Feelings of relaxation then counteract our fear responses—hence the term counterconditioning.
6. *Optimism:* An effective way to shun fear is to substitute the negative thoughts with the positive ones. Research shows that ninety-five percent of the people think in negative ways. An optimist sees opportunity in each eventuality.

Fear can be removed by other techniques also like:

7. The child must not be allowed or told or read or heard horrible and dreadful stories as they imagine these stories in reality and develop tremendous fear.
8. Curiosity and heroism should be developed in the child to avoid fear.
9. Verbal appeal and reassurance combined with practical demonstrations reduce fear by developing good health.
10. Diverting the attention of the child from something she or he might fear.
11. Helping the child or creating an opportunity for the child to be acquainted with un-familiar objects. The acquaintance must be gradual and free from coercion or compulsion.
12. Explaining and assuring the child about the harmlessness of the objects or the individual.
13. Teaching some reactions to actual fearful situations.
14. Relaxation techniques can work wonders. Deep breathing is life-enhancing.

QUESTIONS

The below mentioned are some of the questions that have been asked in the examinations conducted by the Guru Nanak Dev University or can be asked. Knowledge of these answers can help the students to get success in the examinations.

Section A

Answer the following questions in **five** lines or 50 words.

1. Define emotion.*
2. What to you mean by behavioural component of emotion?
3. What is experiential component?
4. What is cognitive appraisal?
5. Define cognitive component of emotion.
6. Explain expressive component of emotion?*
7. What is happiness?*
8. What do you mean by physiological component of emotion?*
9. What is fear?
10. What is anger?*
11. Define facial expressions.

12. What is joy?
13. What do you mean by catharsis?*
14. Explain the Aha! reaction or Experience.*
15. Define emotions and heart.

Section B

Answers the following questions up to **two** pages or 500 words.

1. Explain external physiological co-relates of emotions.*
2. Write a note on development of emotions.
3. Explain different types of emotions.
4. What is emotion? Discuss in brief different types of emotions.
5. What is emotion? Write its nature.
6. What are different physiological correlates of emotions?*

Section C

Answers the following questions up to **five** pages or 1000 words.

1. What is emotion? How it can be measured?
2. Describe briefly two major theories of emotion. What are the strengths of these theories? What are the weaknesses of these theories?
3. How do the Cannon–Bard and James–Lange theories of emotion differ?
4. Compare James–Lange and Cannon-Bard theory of emotions.*
5. What is emotion? Discuss the various physiological changes for different types of emotions.*
6. Describe James–Lange theory of emotion.

REFERENCES

Adolphs, *The Human Amygdala and Emotion,* The Neuroscientist (in Press).

Adolphs, R., Russell, J.A., and Tranel, D., 'A Role for the Human Amygdala in Recognizing Emotional Arousal from Unpleasant Stimuli,' *Psychological Science,* **10**, 167–171, 1999.

Bandura, A., 'Self-efficacy: Toward a Unifying Theory of Behavioral Change,' *Psychological Review,* **84**, 191–215, 1977.

Bandura, A., *Social Learning Theory,* Englewood Cliffs, NJ: Prentice-Hall, 1977.

Bandura, A., *Self-efficacy: The Exercise of Control,* New York: Freeman, 1997.

Bard, P., 'On Emotional Expression After Decortication with Some Remarks on Certain Theoretical Views, Part 1 and II,' *Psychological Review,* **41**, 309–329, 424–449, 1934.

Baron, R.A., 'Attraction Toward the Model and Model's Competence as Determinants of Adult Imitative Behavior,' *Journal of Personality and Social Psychology,* **14**, 335–344. 1970.

Baron, R.A., *Human Aggression,* New York: Plenum, 1977.

Berkowitz, L., 'Frustration-aggression Hypothesis: Examination and Reformulation,' *Psychological Bulletin,* **106**, 59–73, 1989.

Berkowitz, L., *Aggression: Its Causes, Consequences, and Control,* New York: McGraw-Hill, 1993.

Borod, 'J.C., Cerebral Mechanisms Underlying Facial, Prosodic, and Lexical Emotional Expressions. A Review of Neuropsychological Studies and Methodological Issues,' *Neuropsychology,* **7**, 445–463, 1993.

Bushman, B.J., Baumeister, R.F., and Stack, A.D., 'Catharsis, Aggression, and Persuasive Influence: Self-fulfilling or Self-defeating Prophecies?' *Journal of Personality and Social Psychology,* **76**, 367–376, 1999.

Canon, W.B., 'The James–Lange Theory of Emotions: A Critical Examination and an Alternative Theory,' *American Journal of Psychology,* **39**, 106–124, 1927.

Cannon, W.B., *Bodily Changes in Pain, Hunger, Fear, and Rage* (2nd ed.), New York: Appleton-Century-Crofts, 1929.

Cannon, W.B., 'Hunger and Thirst,' in C. Murchinson (Ed.), *Hanbook of General Experimental Psychology,* Worchester, MA: Clark University Press, pp. 247–263, 1934.

Cannon, W.B., "Voodoo" death, *Psychosomatic Medicine,* **19**, 182–190, 1957.

Carr, A.C., 'An Evaluation of Nine Nondirective Psychotherapy Cases by Means of the Rorschach,' *Journal of Consulting Psychology,* **13**, 196–205, 1949.

Costa, P.T., Jr., and McCrae, R.R., 'Still Stable after all these Years: Personality as a Key to Some Issues in Adulthood and Old Age,' in P.B. Baltes and O.G. Brim, Jr. (Eds.), *Life-Span Development and Behavior* (Vol. 3), New York: Academic Press, 1980.

Crow, L.D. and Crow, A., *Educational Psychology* (3rd Indian Reprint), New Delhi: Eurasia Publishing House, 1973.

Drever, J., *Instincts in Man*, Cambridge: Cambridge University Press, 1917.

Ekman, P., *Darwin and Facial Expression: A Century of Research in Review*, New York: Academic Press, 1973.

Ekman, P., 'Facial Expressions of Emotion: New Findings, New Questions,' *Psychological Science,* **3**, 34–38, 1992.

Ekman, P., and Friesen, M.V., 'The Repertoire of Nonverbal Behaviour, Categories, Origins, Usage, and Coding,' *Semiotica,* **1**, 49–98, 1969.

Eysenck, M.W. *Individual Differences: Normal and Abnormal,* Hove, UK: Lawrence Erlbaum Associates Ltd., 1994.

Frederiksen, N., 'The Integration of Testing with Teaching: Applications of Cognitive Psychology in Instruction,' *American Journal of Education,* **102**, 527–564, 1994.

Harrington, A., 'Unfinished Business: Models of Laterality in the Nineteenth Century,' in R.J. Davidson and K. Hugdahl (Eds.), *Brain Asymmetry* (pp. 24–37). Cambridge, MA: MIT Press, 1995.

Heller, W., *Emotion,* In M.T. Banich (Ed.), *Neuropsychology: The Neural Bases of Mental Function* (pp. 398–429), Boston: Houghton Mifflin, 1997.

Heller, W., Etienne, M.A., and Miller, G.A., 'Patterns of Perceptual Asymmetry in Depression and Anxiety: Implications for Neuropsychological Models of Emotion and Psychopathology,' *Journal of Abnormal Psychology,* **104**, 327–333, 1995.

Hohmann, G., 'Some Effects of Spinal Cord Lesions on Experienced Emotional Feelings,' *Psychophysiology,* **3**, 143–156, 1966.

Hokanson, J.E., *The Physiological Basis of Motivation,* New York: Wiley, 1969.

Izard, C.E., *The Face of Emotion,* New York: Appleton-Century-Crofts, 1971.

Izard, C., *Human Emotions*, New York: Plenum, 1977.

Izard, C., 'Facial Expressions and the Regulation of Emotions,' *Journal of Personality and Social Psychology*, **58**, 487–498, 1990.

Izard, C.E., *The Psychology of Emotions,* New York: Plenum, 1991.

Izard, C., Kagan, J., and Zajonc, R., *Emotions, Cognition, and Behaviour,* New York: Cambridge University Press, 1989.

James, W., *Psychology: Brief Course,* London: Collier Macmillan Ltd., 1890.

Kleinginna, P., Jr., and Kleinginna, A., 'A Categorized List of Emotion Definitions, with Suggestions for a Consensual Definition,' *Motivation and Emotion,* **5**, 345–379. 1981.

Ladavas, E., Umilta, C., and Ricci-Bitti, P.E., 'Evidence for Sex Differences in Right-Hemisphere Dominance for Emotions,' *Neuropsychologia,* **18**, 361–366, 1980.

Laird, J.D., 'The Real Role of Facial Responses in the Experience of Emotion: A reply to Tourangeua and Ellsworth, and Others,' *Journal of Personality and Social Psychology*, **47**, 909–917, 1984.

Lazarus, R.S., *Psychological Stress and the Coping Process*, New York: McGraw-Hill, 1966.

Lazarus, R.S., 'From Psychological Stress to the Emotions: A History of Changing Outlooks,' *Annual Review of Psychology,* **44**, 1–21, 1993.

Levenson, R.W., 'Autonomic Nervous System Differences Among Emotions,' *Psychological Science,* **3**, 23–27, 1992.

Levy, L., *Psychological Interpretation,* New York: Holt, Rinehart & Winston, 1963.

Lykken, D.T., 'Controversy: The Fight-or-Flight Response in Homo Scientificus,' in P. Suedfeld and P.E. Tetlock (Eds.), *Psychology and Social Policy* (pp. 309–325), New York: Hemisphere, 1992.

Lykken, D. and Tellegen, A., 'Happiness is a Stochastic Phenomenon,' *Psychological Science*, **7**, 186–189, 1996.

McDougall, W., *Social Psychology*, London: Methuen, 1908.

Morris, C.G., *Psychology* (3rd ed.), Englewood Cliffs, New Jersey: Prentice-Hall, 1979.

Munn, N.L., *An Introduction to Psychology* (2nd ed.), New Delhi: Oxford and IBH, 1967.

Myers, D.G. and Diener, E., 'Who is Happy?' *Psychological Science,* **6**, 10–19, 1995.

Plutchik, R., 'Emotions, Evolution, and Adaptive Processes,' in M.B. Arnold (Ed.), *Feelings and Emotions: The Loyola Symposium*, New York: Academic Press, 1970.

Plutchik, R., *Emotion: A Psychoevolutionary Synthesis*. New York: Harper & Row, 1980.

Plutchik, R., "*The Nature of Emotions*", Retrieved on 2008-05-08.

Reber, A.S, and Reber, E., *The Penguin Dictionary of Psychology*, London: Penguin Books, 2001.

Rogers, C.R., *A Way of Being,* Boston: Houghton Mifflin, 1980.

Salovey, P., 'Mood-induced Self-focused Attention,' *Journal of Personality and Social Psychology,* **62**, 699–707, 1992.

Saxe, L., Dougherty, D., and Cross, T., 'The Validity of Polygraph Testing: Scientific Analysis and Public Controversy,' *American Psychologist,* **40**, 355–366, 1985.

Schachter, S., and Singer, J.E., 'Cognitive, Social, and Physiological Determinants of an Emotional State,' *Psychological Review,* **69**, 379–399, 1962.

Seligman, M.E.P., *Helplessness: On Depression, Development and Death,* Dan Francisco: W.H. Freeman, 1975.

Shaver, P.R., and Hazan, C., *Attachment,* in A.L. Weber and J.H. Harvey (Eds.), *Perspectives on Close Relationships* (pp. 110–130), Boston: Allyn and Bacon, 1994.

Simpson, E., 'Moral Development Research: A Case Study of Scientific Cultural Bias,' *Human Development,* **17**, 81–105, 1974.

Smith, C.R., *Review of the Classroom Environment Scale* (2nd ed.), Tenth Mental Measurements Yearbook, 174–177, 1989.

Smith, M.B. and Anderson, J.W., Henry A. Murray *(1893–1988), American Psychologist,* **44**, 1153–1154, 1989.

Tavris, C., *The Mismeasure of Woman, Feminism and Psychology,* **3**(2), 149–168, 1993.

Tomkins, S.S., 'The Quest for Primary Motives: Biography and Autobiography of an Idea,' *Journal of Personality and Social Psychology,* **41**, 306–329, 1980.

Watson, J.B., *Behaviorism,* New York: Norton, 1924.

Woodworth, R.S., *Experimental Psychology* (rev. ed.), New York: Holt, 1954.

Wundt, W., *Fundamentals of Physiological Psychology*, 1874.

Wundt, W., *Grundzuge der Physiologischen Psychologie* (Vol. 2), Leipzig: Englemann, 1874.

Young, C., *Emotions and Emotional Intelligence*, Cornell University. Retrieved April 1999, from http: // trochim.human.cornell.edu/ gallery/ young/ emotion, HTM, 1996.

Young, P.T., *Emotion in Men and Animal* (2nd ed.), Huntington, New York: Krieger, 1973.

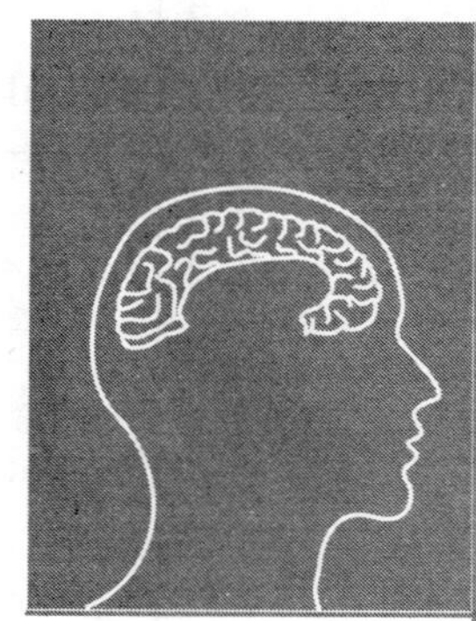

CHAPTER 12
Intelligence

Intelligence is an important human characteristic. Intelligence is one of those concepts that are easier to recognize than to define. We often refer to others' intelligence, describing people as bright, sharp or quick, on one hand, or as slow, dull, and even stupid or idiot on the other hand. The term "Intelligence" refers to individual's abilities to understand complex ideas, to adapt effectively to the environment, to learn from experience, to engage in various forms of reasoning, to overcome obstacles by careful thought (Neisser et al., 1996).

12.1 DEFINITIONS OF INTELLIGENCE

One of the first definitions of intelligence was developed by the French psychologist responsible for the development of the first intelligence test, Alfred Binet (11 July, 1857–18 October, 1911) and an American psychologist Herbert Alexander Simon (15 June, 1916–9 February, 2001).

Binet, the inventor of the individual intelligence test, felt that intelligent behaviour would be manifested in such abilities as reasoning, imagination, insight, judgment, and adaptability, so he designed his tests to evaluate just these functions. Binet and Simon (1905) argued that the essence of intelligence is: "To judge well, to comprehend well, to reason well."

According to Stern (1914), "Intelligence is a general capacity of an individual consciously to adjust his thinking to new requirements. It is the general mental adaptability to new problems and conditions of life."

Alfred Binet Herbert
(1857–1911)

Alexander Simon
(1916–2001)

According to Thorndike (1914), "Intelligence may be defined as the power of good responses from the point of view of truth or fact." Intelligence is of three kinds—social intelligence, concrete intelligence, and abstract intelligence. "Social intelligence" is the ability to understand and deal with other people, such as sensitivity to social cues, interest of one's surroundings, and a concern for important norms.

Lewis Madison Terman (1916), described intelligence as "The ability to carry on abstract thinking."

According to Terman A. Merril (1921), "An individual is intelligent in the proportion that he is able to carry on abstract thinking."

According to Thurstone (1924–1973), "Intelligence, considered as a mental trait, is the capacity to make impulses focal at their early, unfinished stage of formation. Intelligence is therefore the capacity for abstraction, which is an inhibitory process."

According to Wagnon (1937), "Intelligence is the capacity to learn and adjust to relatively new and changing conditions."

According to Burt (1941), "Intelligence is a fixed, inherited cognitive ability."

According to Stoddard (1943), "Intelligence is the ability to undertake activities that are difficult, complex and abstract and which are adaptive to a goal, and are done quickly and which have social value and which lead to the creation of something new and different."

According to David Wechsler (1944), "Intelligence is the aggregate or global capacity of an individual to act purposefully, to think rationally, and to deal effectively with his environment." Wechsler also provided a criterion for defining intelligent behaviour in terms of four characteristics, that is it involves awareness, is goal-directed, rational, and has value.

According to Woodworth and Marquis (1948), "Intelligence means intellect put to use. It is the use of intellectual abilities for handling a situation or accomplishing any task."

According to Jean Piaget (1952), "Intelligence is the ability to adapt to one's surroundings."

Heim, in 1970, argued that "Intelligent activity consists in grasping the essentials in a situation and responding appropriately to them."

According to Sandra Scarr (1981), "Intelligence includes a wide range of cognitive skills, including perception, learning, memory, problem-solving, and reasoning."

According to Estes (1982), "Intelligence is a property of behaviour, jointly determined by cognitive functioning and motives. We perform an intelligent act, or ask an intelligent question."

According to Howard Gardner (1983, 2003), "Intelligence is the ability to solve problems, or to create products, that are valued within one or more cultural settings."

According to Sternberg (1985), "Intelligence is a mental activity directed towards purposive adaptation to, and selection and shaping of, real-world environments relevant to one's life."

According to Flynn (1987), "Intelligence is the ability to think abstractly and to learn readily from experience."

According to Locurto (1991), "Intelligence is the ability to master information and skills needed to succeed within a particular culture."

According to Wortman and Loftus (1992), "Intelligence is the capacity to acquire and retain knowledge and to understand concepts and relationships, capacities that an intelligent person uses effectively when solving problems and communicating."

According to Goleman (1998), "Intelligence is related to important outcomes—how quickly individuals can master new tasks and adapt to new situation, how successful they will be in school and in various kinds of jobs, and even how well they can get along with others." We need intelligence in everyday life.

According to Sternberg and Kaufman (1998), "Intelligence is a socially constructed concept. Cultures deem "intelligent" whatever attributes enable success in those cultures."

According to Mangal (2002), "Intelligence is a sort of mental energy, in the form of mental or cognitive abilities, available with an individual which enables him to handle his environment in terms of adaptation to face novel situations as effectively as possible."

According to Myers (2004), "Intelligence is the ability to learn from experience, solve problems, and use knowledge to adapt to new situation."

According to Dr. C. George Boeree of Shippensburg University, intelligence is a person's capacity to (i) acquire knowledge (that is, learn and understand), (ii) apply knowledge (solve problems), and (iii) engage in abstract reasoning. It is the power of one's intellect, and as such is clearly a very important aspect of one's overall well-being. Psychologists have attempted to measure it for well over a century.

Psychologists used to define "intelligence" narrowly as thinking, reasoning, and problem-solving ability. Perhaps, the single characteristic that has received the most attention is the ability to think abstractly. It was generally agreed that those who were good at abstract reasoning, problem-solving and decision-making are more intelligent than those who were poor at these mental activities. However, psychologists now accept that the notion of intelligence is broader than that, and should include skills like street-wisdom, social intelligence, and emotional intelligence that are valued by the society or culture in which one lives. To improve our understanding of intelligence, many psychologists agree that we must consider the broader social contexts in which intelligent behaviour occurs.

To conclude, it can be said that intelligence is an ability (or set of abilities) or capacity or characteristic. Intelligence is the ability to:

- learn quickly,
- master information and skills,
- solve difficult problems,
- perform tasks accurately and quickly,
- take decisions,
- engage in various forms of reasoning,
- understand complex ideas,
- profit from experience,
- overcome obstacles by careful thought,
- adapt or adjust effectively to the environment.

Representative characteristics of an ideally intelligent person, as judged by experts in the field of intelligence (Sternberg et al., 1981) are:

(I) *Verbal intelligence:*
  1. Displays good vocabulary.
  2. Reads with high comprehension.
  3. Displays curiosity.

(II) *Problem-solving ability:*
  1. Enables us able to apply knowledge to problems at hand.
  2. Makes good decisions.
  3. Poses problems in an optimal or best possible way.

(III) *Practical intelligence:*
  1. Sizes up the situations well.
  2. Determines how to achieve goals.
  3. Displays awareness of the world around her or him.

Some of these characteristics focus on verbal intelligence, whereas others stress problem-solving ability. Interestingly, however, the experts also judge some less academic, more practical considerations to be more important (Sternberg et al., 1981).

Lewis Madison David
(1877–1956)

Terman Wechsler
(1896–1981)

12.2 INTELLIGENCE: UNITARY OR MULTI-FACETED

Is intelligence a single characteristic or does it involve several different components? Some scientists or psychologists viewed intelligence as a single characteristic or dimension along which people vary. One early supporter of this view was Charles Edward Spearman (10 September 1863–17 September, 1945), a British psychometrician, who believed that performance on any cognitive task depended on a primary general factor (which he termed "g") and one or more specific factors related to a particular task. Spearman identified it on the basis of the various components of an intelligence test. Spearman (1927) found that although tests of intelligence often contain different aspects of intelligence, scores on these items often correlate highly to each other. No matter how intelligence was measured, it was related to a single, primary factor. Spearman's view of intelligence resulted from his observation that people who scored high or low on one kind of test tended to score at a similar level on other tests. He argued that all abilities are only manifestations of a single underlying factor (the so-called General Factor) which is presumed to be at the root of all intellectual functioning.

In contrast, other researchers believed that intelligence is composed of many separate abilities that operate more or less independently. According to this multi-factor view, a given person can be high on some components of intelligence but low on others and vice versa. One early supporter of this position was Louis Leon Thurstone (1887–1955). Thurstone (1938) suggested that intelligence is composed of seven distinct primary mental abilities. Included in his list were: Verbal meaning—understanding of ideas and word meanings; Number—speed and accuracy in dealing with numbers; and Space—the ability to visualize objects in three dimensions. Alfred Binet (11 July, 1857–18 October, 1911), a French psychologist and the inventor of the individual intelligence test, felt that intelligent behaviour would be manifested in such abilities as reasoning, imagination, insight, judgment, and adaptability, so he designed his tests to evaluate just these functions. Other theoreticians have argued that only three fundamental cognitive processes are identifiable—abstraction, learning, and dealing with novelty.

Most modern theories of intelligence adopt a position or viewpoint somewhat in-between these extremes (Spearman's and Thurstone's view points). They recognize that intelligence may involve a general ability to handle a wide range of cognitive tasks and problems, as Spearman suggested, but also that intelligence is expressed in many different ways and that persons can be high on some aspects of intelligence but low on others.

12.3 THEORIES OF INTELLIGENCE

12.3.1 Psychometric Theories

Psychometric theorizing was the primary approach to the study of intelligence from about 1900 to 1950. Many of those working within this approach based their measures on the theory of Charles Edward Spearman (1927), who conceived of intelligence as a single, general ability. Thurstone (1938) distinguished among primary mental abilities such as verbal comprehension, number ability, and reasoning.

Psychometric tests sometimes confuse different mental abilities that they purport to measure. Verbal analogies, for example, often used to assess verbal reasoning. But if a student does not know the meaning of a word used in an analogy item, the student's failure on the item will be due to a lack of word knowledge rather than to a verbal reasoning error. It appears necessary to separate the measurement of different kinds of process (verbal versus spatial) and also to separate the measurement of mental processes from the measurement of knowledge. The two main psychometric theories are discussed below:

Spearman's Theory of Intelligence

Different researchers have drawn different conclusions about the particular factors that are involved in intelligence. Some believe that a general intelligence factor exists, one that is measured by every item on an intelligence test. A leading proponent of this viewpoint was the British educational psychologist and the great psychometrician Charles Edward Spearman (10 September 1863–17 September 1945).

Spearman (1927) made use of a statistical technique known as *factor analysis*. "Factor analysis" is a statistical procedure to locate a smaller number of dimensions, clusters, or factors in a larger set of independent variables or items. The first step in factor-analysis is to give a series of tests to a large number of individuals, and to obtain scores for each individual on each test. The inter-correlations between the tests are then calculated. If two tests correlate highly with each other, this means that those who perform well on one test tend to perform well on the other test. The key assumption is that when two tests correlate highly with each other, they are measuring the same aspect of intelligence. In contrast, if two tests do not correlate, then it is assumed that they measure different aspects of intelligence. The pattern of inter-correlations is used to identify the main aspects of intelligence (or factors as they are generally known). The psychologists who try to identify the factors involved in intelligence are known as *factor theorists*.

Charles Edward Spearman
(1863–1945)

His factor-analysis suggested that scores on a wide variety of mental tests are, to some extent related. That is, many people who scored high on tests of verbal ability also do fairly well on tests of mathematical reasoning, spatial-perceptual skills, and so forth. Spearman (1927) concluded that a general intelligence factor, which he called "g" factor, accounts for these positive correlations. Spearman's influence can be seen in contemporary IQ tests, for example, Culture Fair: Test of "g", scale 3, form A and B by R.B. Cattell and A.K.S. Cattell, that yield a single score indicating general intelligence.

Spearman's views, which have come to be called "g" factor theory, are reflected in intelligence tests that yield a single score, such as an Intelligence Quotient (abbreviated as IQ). Intelligence Quotient is a measure of intelligence level. The notion that intelligence can be largely summed up with one score is closely related to Spearman's idea that intelligence consists of one general ability or factor.

The MA/CA ratio yield the Intelligence Quotient (IQ), a concept proposed by German psychologist William Stern (29 April, 1871–27 March, 1938) in 1912. Stern coined the abbreviation "IQ", a translation of the German *Intelligenz-Quotient* ("Intelligence Quotient"), proposing that an individual's intelligence level can be measured as a quotient of their estimated mental age and their chronological age. An Intelligence Quotient or IQ is a score derived from one of several different standardized tests attempting to measure intelligence. MA is mental age, determined by a standardized test, and CA is chronological age. CA (chronological age) is the actual age of a person in years or months. It is simply age that is time since birth. For children up to three or four years old, CA is generally given strictly in months; from here until adolescence, the figure is usually presented in years and months, denoted, for example as 10–6, standing for ten years and six months; after adolescence, the months are generally considered negligible.

William Stern
(1871–1938)

Intelligence Quotient is a number obtained by dividing CA into MA and multiplying by 100. MA (mental age) is a type of score expressing mental development in terms of the age level at which a child is performing. MA is the level of intellectual development as measured by an intelligence test. For example, if a five year old boy does as well on an intelligence test of an average child of seven years, his MA (mental age) is 7.

For example, if two children both obtain an MA (mental age—an individual's performance on the test can be expressed as MA score) of five years, but one child is four years old and the other is six years old, obviously the younger child is developing intellectually at a much faster rate. To express this fact in the form of IQ's, we take the ratio of MA to CA and multiply with 100 to eliminate the problem of decimal.

$$IQ = \frac{MA}{CA} \times 100$$

$$\text{Child one, younger child (Bright child)} = \frac{5}{4} \times 100$$

$$= 125$$

$$IQ = 125$$

$$\text{Child two, elder child (Slow child)} = \frac{5}{6} \times 100$$

$$= 83$$

$$IQ = 83$$

Intelligence adds to our longevity. Smarter children may enjoy longer lives, the results of a new study (2005) by the experts from the Harvard School of Public Health suggest. The study, which followed elderly adults deemed, gifted by childhood IQ tests, found that higher their IQs were, the longer they lived—up to a point, at least. Though the reasons for the link between IQ and longevity are not clear, it does not appear to be merely a reflection of income and social position. For one, these children may be more likely to take up healthy habits like regular exercise, while shunning health risks like smoking, alcohol etc. They are also more likely to get high-paying jobs as adults, with all the advantages that confer.

IQs of 163 or higher is not seen often. It is an intelligence level few people reach. Marilyn Vos Savant, who appeared in the Guinness Book of World Records, obtained a ratio IQ of 228. IQ scores have been shown to be associated with such factors as morbidity and mortality, parental social status, and to a substantial degree, parental IQ. While its inheritance has been investigated for nearly a century, controversy remains as to how much is inheritable, and the mechanisms of inheritance are still a matter of some debate. The average IQ is 100, and children who score above 130 are considered "gifted". Causes of lower IQ associated with poverty and prolonged malnutrition are poor physical health, low birth weight, premature birth, higher risk of prenatal exposure to drugs, higher risk of lead poisoning, and less environmental stimulation in the home environment.

In a new, long-term study (2008), researchers at Harvard School of Public Health (HSPH) found that children with lower IQs showed an increased risk of developing psychiatric disorders as adults, including schizophrenia, depression, and generalized anxiety disorder. Lower IQ was also linked to psychiatric disorders that were more persistent and an increased risk of having two or more diagnoses at the age of 32. The study participants were members of the Dunedin Multidisciplinary Health and Development Study, a cohort or group of children born in 1972–1973 in Dunedin, New Zealand. At the initial assessment at age 3, the study had 1,037 children. The participants were also interviewed and tested on their overall health and behaviour at ages 5, 7, 9, 11, 13, 15, 18, 21, 26 and at age 32, when 96 per cent of the original cohort participated. IQs were assessed at ages 7, 9, and 11.

Research shows that general intelligence plays an important role in many valued life outcomes. The American Psychological Association's report *Intelligence: Knowns and Unknowns* (Neisser et al., 1995) states that wherever it has been studied, children with high scores on tests of intelligence tend to learn more of what is taught in school than their lower-scoring peers. The correlation between IQ scores and grades is about .50. However, this means that they explain only 25% of the variance. Successful school learning depends on many personal characteristics other than intelligence, such as persistence, interest in school, and willingness to study.

Correlations between IQ scores and total years of education are about .55, implying that differences in psychometric intelligence account for about 30% of the outcome variance. Many occupations can only be entered through professional schools which base their admissions at least partly on test scores: the MCAT, the GMAT, the GRE, the DAT, the LSAT, etc. Individual scores on admission-related tests such as these are certainly correlated with scores on tests of intelligence. It is partly because intelligence test scores predict years of education that they also predict occupational status, and income.

In addition to academic success, IQ correlates to some degree with job performance, socioeconomic advancement (for example, level of education, occupation, and income), and "social pathology" (for example, adult criminality, poverty, unemployment, dependence on welfare, children outside of marriage). Recent work has demonstrated links between general intelligence and health, longevity, and functional literacy. Correlations between "g" and life outcomes are pervasive, though IQ does not correlate with subjective self-reports of happiness. IQ and "g" correlate highly with school performance and job performance, less so with occupational prestige, moderately with income, and to a small degree with law-abiding behaviour. IQ does not explain the inheritance of economic status and wealth. According to Schmidt and Hunter, "For hiring employees without previous experience in the job, the most valid predictor of future performance is general mental ability" (Schmidt and Hunter, 1998). The validity depends on the type of job and varies across different studies, ranging from 0.2 to 0.6 (Hunter and Hunter, 1984). However, IQ mostly correlates with cognitive ability only if IQ scores are below average and this rule has many (about 30%) exceptions for people with average and higher IQ scores (Diaz-Asper, Schretlen, Pearlson, 2004). Also, IQ is related to the "academic tasks" (auditory and linguistic measures, memory tasks, academic achievement levels) and much less related to tasks where even precise hand work ("motor functions") are required (Warner, Ernst, Townes, Peel, and Preston, 1987). The American Psychological Association's report *Intelligence: Knowns and Unknowns* (Neisser et al., 1995) states that other individual characteristics such as interpersonal skills, aspects of personality, etc. are probably of equal or greater importance, but at this point, we do not have equally reliable instruments to measure them.

Sex and Intelligence: Some studies found that men outperform women on average by 3–4 IQ points (Stumpf and Jackson, 1994). Studies illustrate consistently greater variance in the performance of men compared to that of women, that is men are more represented at the extremes of performance (Deary, Irwing, Der, and Bates, 2007), and that men and women have statistically significant differences in average scores on tests of particular abilities, which even out when the overall IQ scores are weighted (Douglas, Jackson and Rushton, 2006; Lynn and Irwing, 2004). General classification of people according to their IQ is as shown in Table 12.1.

Table 12.1 General classification of people according to their IQ

IQ	*Category*
above 140	Very superior
120–140	Superior
110–120	High average
90–110	Normal or average
80–90	Low normal
70–80	Borderline defective
50–70	Moron
25–50	Imbecile

L.L. Thurstone's Theory of Intelligence

Not all researchers who have conducted factor-analysis have agreed with the concept of a "g" factor. One who took a different view was an American psychologist, Louis Leon Thurstone (1887–1955).

Thurstone's (1938) factor-analysis of scores from 56 different cognitive tests suggested that there are seven major intelligence factors, each relatively independent of the others. Table 12.2 shows the seven factors of Intelligence and the kinds of tests used to measure seven factors. The seven factors are discussed below:

1. **Numerical Ability:** The ability to calculate is usually known as the mathematical ability.

2. **Verbal Fluency:** This is the ability to deal with relationships expressed in words. It also includes the ability in the use of words.

3. **Verbal Comprehension:** This refers to one's vocabulary or the knowledge of words and their meanings.

4. **Rote Memory:** This is the ability to memorize verbal materials as measured by the usual methods of recall and recognition.

5. **Perceptual Speed:** By this is meant the ability to find out quickly similarities and differences in groups of designs.

6. **Spatial Relations:** This deals with one's ability to find out relationships among objects in space by quickly visualizing the three-dimensional factor or space.

7. **Reasoning:** "Inductive reasoning" is the ability which is usually dealt with in logic while examining a series of facts of data to find out a general principle running through them.

"Deductive reasoning" is an ability which is commonly dealt with in logic. This deals with one's ability to apply a given general principle to a particular situation. The form of reasoning is called "syllogism".

Table 12.2 Seven factors of intelligence and the kinds of tests used to measure seven factors

Ability or factor	*Measure or test*
Verbal comprehension	Test of vocabulary.
Verbal fluency	Test that requires listing in a limited time as many words as possible that start with a given letter.
Inductive reasoning	Test of analogies and number series.
Spatial visualization/relations	Tests requiring mental rotation of pictures of objects.
Number or numerical ability	Tests of computation and simple mathematical problem solving.
Memory	Tests of pictures and word recall.
Perceptual speed	Tests that require finding small differences in pictures.

Thurstone's influences can be seen in modern IQ tests that produce not one, but several scores, each for a different mental ability.

12.3.2 Cognitive Theories

These theories of intelligence tried to analyze and describe intelligence in terms of certain fundamental cognitive processes. Cognitive components approach deals with a level of complexity that is at least equal to the dimensions being measured on a test. One can investigate the speed and accuracy, with which each component of information processing is performed, and assess how adequately the process is carried out. The cognitive-component approach offers a new means of examining information processing but does not fundamentally challenge or alter the content of conventional intelligence tests. They believe that intelligence is much more integrated and complicated than psychometric and information processing theories suggest. Rather than search for static or even dynamic processes that produce relatively stable assessment of individual abilities, they attempt to understand an integrated whole consisting of various parts. Two good examples of systems theorizing and the important theories falling in this category are:

Gardner's Theory of Multiple Intelligences

Howard Gardner (Born on 11 July, 1943), an American psychologist, argues that the traditional IQ tests assess only the standard academic kinds of intelligence. Gardner (1983, 1988) suggested that not only people in the middle of intelligence dimension should be studied but also ones at the extremes—acclaimed geniuses and those who might be described as possessing special mental "gifts", for example, athletes or dancers.

Howard Gardner
(Born on 11 July, 1943)

Howard Gardner's Theory of Multiple Intelligences (1983) proposes that intelligent behaviour does not arise from a single unitary quality of the mind, as the "g"-based theories, but rather that different kinds of intelligence are generated from separate metaphorical pools of mental energy. Each of these pools enables the individual "To solve problems or to create products that are valued within one or more cultural settings" (Gardner 1983, 2003). Gardner derived this conceptualization of intelligence in part from his experiences working with members of extreme populations, in which certain cognitive abilities are preserved (often to a remarkable degree) even in the absence of other, very basic abilities. For example, some autistic savants display extraordinary musical or mathematical abilities despite severely impaired language development and social awareness. Likewise, individuals with localized brain damage often demonstrate severe deficits that are circumscribed to a single cognitive domain (Gardner 1983, 2003).

The seven intelligences proposed by Gardner are linguistic, logical-mathematical, spatial, bodily-kinesthetic, musical, interpersonal, and intrapersonal. "Linguistic intelligence" enables individuals to read, write and speak well. "Logical-mathematical intelligence" encompasses logical thinking (as might be used in chess or deductive reasoning, for example) as well as mathematical and scientific problem-solving. "Spatial intelligence" makes its appearance when an individual navigates an unfamiliar set of streets, or when an architect visualizes her or his plans for a building. "Musical intelligence" generates the set of skills that allow musicians to play a tune by ear, or to execute a phrase with sensitivity and grace. "Bodily-kinesthetic intelligence" is necessary for problem-solving that requires the individual to use her or his physical body, as would be necessary for performing a complex surgical procedure, executing a series of dance steps or catching a fly ball. "Interpersonal intelligence" drives social skills and things like empathy and intuition about what motivates other people—a type of understanding that is necessary for salespersons, teachers, and clergy, for example. "Intrapersonal intelligence" involves a similar set of abilities, but these are turned towards the self; individuals who have high intrapersonal intelligence have an accurate self-understanding, and can use this to their advantage in problem-solving. Gardner asserts that logical-mathematical and linguistic intelligences are overemphasized in traditional models of human intelligence, but that this is a cultural artifact; in different life circumstances, different intelligences would gain higher priority (Gardner, 1993)

Howard Gardner (1985) argued that there are several independent intelligences. Gardner proposed that we actually have different intelligences. This theory is based on the idea that the mind is not a holistic entity, but instead consists of distinct independent modules, having its own distinct by logical source in the brain. Gardner's theory of multiple intelligences proposes seven different components or parts of intelligence. In total, he identified seven intelligences:

1. **Language Ability or Linguistic Intelligence:** This is used in reading, writing, and speaking or comprehending speech. This type of human intelligence is responsible for all kinds of linguistic competence—abilities, talents, and skills, available in human beings. This type of intelligence is most often seen in lecturers, teachers, lawyers, writers, lyricists, and a number of other professionals exhibiting linguistic intelligence.

2. **Logical-Mathematical Thinking or Intelligence:** This is of special value in handling abstract problems of a logical or mathematical nature, carrying out calculations, and logical reasoning. It can be broken down into components like inductive reasoning, deductive reasoning, solving of logical puzzles. Professional like mathematicians, philosophers, physicists, etc. are found to exhibit this type of intelligence in abundance.

3. **Spatial Thinking or Intelligence:** This is used when deciding how to go from one place to another, in arranging objects spatially, as well as in visual art, and finding one's way around. Painters may be seen to demonstrate this type of intelligence. This is also true of professionals like land surveyors, architects, engineers, mechanics, sculptures, and chess players, who are found to rely upon the spatial intelligence in their own way.

4. **Musical Thinking or Intelligence:** It is the ability to perceive and create rhythmic patterns. This is used for playing an instrument, singing, and appreciating and composing music. Musical intelligence is the kind of intelligence shown by individuals who, without any formal training, can play any tune on the piano. This ability is seen in a quite large proportion in professionals like musicians and composers.

5. **Bodily-Kinesthetic Thinking or Intelligence:** It is the ability possessed by an expert person. This is used in the fine control of bodily movements or simply everyday movement and dexterity. It is a sort of intelligence shown by the dancers, actors, Olympic athletes, gymnasts, surgeons.

6. **Inter-Personal Thinking or Intelligence:** It is the ability to understand others and the ability to get along well with others. This includes communication with, and understanding of others' needed for social interactions. This is used in relating to others, interpreting social signals, and predicting social outcomes. In practical life, this type of intelligence is exhibited by teachers, psychotherapists, religious leaders, politicians, and sales people.

7. **Intra-Personal Thinking or Intelligence:** It is the ability to understand oneself or insight into oneself, understanding of one's own cognitive strengths, styles, and mental functioning. This form of intelligence is concerned with sensitivity to one's own abilities and emotional states. This type of intelligence is said to be personal or private kind of intelligence. This is used in understanding and predicting one's own behaviour, and in identifying aspects of the self and one's own personality. This type of intelligence is demonstrated by *yogis* and saints.

We are accustomed to individual differences in the first three areas. However, think of people who shine on other four skills, perhaps some one who can play the piano very well or a person who excels in sports. Someone skilled in intra-personal thinking has a highly accurate understanding of her or him.

Gardner's ideas about multiple intelligences have aroused considerable interest, and they have encouraged expanding our ideas about the constituents of intelligence (Kautrowitz, 1993). However, critics wonder if the last four skills really should be classified as components of intelligence. Also, the various abilities may not be as independent as Gardner suggested. For instance, logical-mathematical thinking and spatial thinking tend to be highly correlated (Sternberg, 1985).

Advantages of Gardner's Theory of Multiple Intelligences:

(i) There is reasonable evidence for the seven intelligences proposed by Gardner.

(ii) Gardner is right to argue that intelligence tests fail to consider all aspects of intelligence.

(iii) It seems better able to encompass some of the oddities about human intelligence than other theories, such as the existence of musical genius.

Disadvantages of Gardner's Theory of Multiple Intelligences:

(i) Gardner's approach tends to fall back on anecdotes as part of his evidence.

(ii) Musical and bodily-kinaesthetic intelligences are less important in everyday life than are the other intelligences: you can be tone-deaf and poorly coordinated and still lead a very successful life.

(iii) Those who score highly on some intelligence tend to score highly on the other intelligences as well; this suggests that the seven intelligences are not really independent of each other as Gardner argued.

(iv) Social factors are generally ignored in Gardner's theory, except for inter-personal intelligence itself.

Sternberg's Triarchic Theory of Intelligence (1985, 1988)

Robert J. Sternberg and Richard Wagner (1993) also argued that the traditional intelligence tests are too narrow in their emphasis on academic intelligence, rather than more practical, real-world kinds of intelligence. He noticed an interesting fact: some people who are good at critical thinking are not very creative—they rarely have good, original ideas of their own. He then come to the realization that some people who are not high on either of these dimensions seem to be "street smart"—they are able to adapt to changing situations in ways that enhance their intellectual strengths and compensate for their weaknesses.

As a cognitive psychologist, Robert J. Sternberg (Born on 8 December, 1949), an American psychologist and psychometrician, began with a view of intelligence emphasizing the ability to think critically (Trotter, 1986). He concentrated on what happens inside people's heads when they reason and process information effectively This theory proposes that there are three distinct aspects to human intelligence, working together to produce what we consider to be intelligent behaviour or intelligent action on the part of a given individual. According to this theory, known as the "Triarchic" theory of intelligence, there are actually three basic types of human intelligence. Triarchic is a theory suggesting that there are three basic forms of intelligence. Sternberg's (1985) triarchic theory of intelligence specifies three important factors of intelligence: (i) Componential (analytical) intelligence involves the abilities to think critically and analytically,

Robert J. Sternberg
(Born on 8 December, 1949)

(ii) Experiential (creative) intelligence emphasizes insights and the ability to formulate new ideas, (iii) Contextual (practical) intelligence. People can excel in one, two, or all three kinds of intelligence. Brief explanations of the various factors of intelligence given by Sternberg (1985) are as follows:

1. **Componential (Analytical) Intelligence:** It corresponds most closely with traditional notions of intelligence. This includes the cognitive skills that help you plan and devise strategies. Componential intelligence is all about the cognitive mechanisms which underlie intelligent functioning. This kind of intelligence also includes the kinds of skills used in solving an intellectual problem and getting the work done. For example, doing a research for a term paper and actually writing the paper. Persons high on this dimension usually excel on standard tests of academic potential and make excellent students. Componential intelligence emphasizes effectiveness in information processing. Persons high on this dimension are able to think critically and analytically.

2. **Experiential (Creative) Intelligence:** It is focused on how people perform on tasks with which they have either no previous experience or great experience. Creativity involves creating something novel (new) and useful. For example, you may have a friend with average grades, who was able to figure out what to do when he lost his ticket; he seems to thrive in new, unfamiliar settings. She or he quickly learns to drive, having extra cognitive ability for other more interesting activities, such as listening to music or talking. A person who is high in experiential intelligence also figures out how to perform familiar tasks more automatically. Experiential intelligence is all about how someone's own past experience influences how they go about a given task or situation. It addresses the way that we accumulate skills and knowledge as a result of our personal life-experiences. Different types of life-situations make different demands on us, and the experience we have had, will affect our ability to handle them. In short, experiential intelligence focuses on both our familiar and unfamiliar tasks. This is the kind of intelligence shown by many scientific geniuses and inventors such as Newton, Alexander Fleming (who discovered penicillin), and Edison. Experiential intelligence emphasizes insight and the ability to formulate new ideas.

3. **Contextual (Practical) Intelligence:** In Sternberg's triarchic theory, the third major kind of intelligence is contextual or practical intelligence in everyday life—that is street smarts. This aspect makes the triarchic theory distinctive among theories of intelligence. More formally, contextual intelligence requires adapting to, selecting, and sharing one's real-world context or environment. Part of contextual intelligence is called *practical intelligence* or knowing the pathway to success in your culture or occupation. Practical intelligence can be valuable in many contexts.

Persons high on this dimension are intelligent in practical sense. They quickly recognize what factors influence success on various tasks and are adept at both adapting to and shaping their environment. The other part of contextual intelligence is social intelligence, or the ability to understand others and interact successfully with them. You certainly know people who are high in other kinds of intelligence, yet, they are socially inept or inexpert. Contextual intelligence is concerned with intelligence within its socio-cultural setting. It proposes that intelligent acts take place within a context, and we do them for a reason. For example, such people who ask too many questions in the class, appearing to be completely unaware that neither the professor or teacher nor other students are charmed. Persons high on contextual intelligence are intelligent in a practical, adaptive sense. They are what many would term "street smarts" and are adept or skillful at solving problems of everyday life. According to Sternberg, "Solving practical problems require different intelligence from that required for success in school or other intellectual pursuits."

Conclusion: Whose factor analysis provides the most accurate picture of human intelligence? Unfortunately, even after years of study, psychologists still cannot come to a consensus. The reason is that different mathematical techniques, equally valid, can produce different results and lead to different conclusions (Gardner, 1983). Consequently, it is hard to decide whose idea about the factors underlining intelligence is the best. All theories explain the nature of intelligence in their own way.

12.4 EMOTIONAL INTELLIGENCE

Howard Gardner (1983), in his theory of multiple intelligences, suggest that there are seven "intelligences", or domains of talent: linguistic, logical-mathematical, spatial, musical, bodily-kinesthetic, intra-personal, and inter-personal. These talents are relatively independent, and each one may even have its own neural structures. People with brain damage often lose one of the seven without losing their competence in the others.

Among the most influential theorists of intelligence to point out the distinction between intellectual and emotional capacity was Howard Gardner, Harvard psychologist who in 1983 proposed a widely regarded model of "multiple intelligences". His list of seven kinds of intelligence included not just the familiar verbal and mathematical abilities but also two personal varieties: knowing one's inner world (understanding ourselves—intra personal intelligence) and social adeptness (understanding other people—inter personal intelligence).

Gardner's last two "intelligences" correspond to what some psychologists call emotional intelligence: the ability to identify your own and other people's emotions accurately, express your emotions clearly, and regulate emotions in yourself and others (Goleman, 1995; Mayer and Salovey, 1997). There is another kind of intelligence quite different from that measured by IQ tests.

Daniel Goleman (1995, 1998) has argued strongly that this kind of intelligence is more important for a happy, productive life than IQ. Daniel Goleman (Born on 7 March, 1946), an author, psychologist, and science journalist, terms this kind of intelligence as emotional intelligence (Emotional Quotient or EQ) and defines it as a cluster of traits or abilities relating to the emotional side of life. "Emotional Intelligence" refers to the capacity for recognizing our own feelings and those of others, for motivating ourselves, and for managing emotions well in us and in our relationships. Emotional Intelligence is the ability to perceive, express, understand, and regulate emotions (Peter Salovey and John Mayer, 1994; Salovey and others, 2002). Peter Salovey and John Mayer defined Emotional Intelligence in term of being able to monitor and regulate one's own and others' feelings, and to use feelings to guide thought and action. Emotional Intelligence refers to people's ability to monitor their own and other people's emotional states and to use this information to act wisely in relationships.

Daniel Goleman
(Born on 7 March, 1946)

Emotional intelligence describes abilities distinct from, but complimentary to, academic intelligence, the purely cognitive capacities measured by IQ tests. Many people who are book smart but lack emotional intelligence end up working for people who have lower IQs than they have but who excel in emotional intelligence skills. The term "emotional intelligence" describes such qualities as the abilities to motivate one, to persist in the face of frustrations, to control impulses, to delay gratification, to regulate one's mood, and to keep distress from swamping the ability to think, empathized, and hope (Goleman, 1995). This concept recognizes the fact that brain power as measured by tests of intelligence and standardized achievement tests is not necessarily as important for success as the qualities just outlined, which have gone unrecognized.

Many people do not even recognize which emotion they are experiencing. For example, they may not realize that they are actually angry at a person for dying or consider a parent who yells at a child who has just run into the street. Recognizing which emotions we are feeling is a key element of emotional intelligence because it helps individuals understand how their thinking can be affected by the emotions they are experiencing.

Some impulses appear easier to control than others; anger is one of the hardest to control, perhaps because of its evolutionary value in priming people to action. Dwelling on anger actually increases its power. To control anger, the body needs a chance to use up the adrenaline through exercise, relaxation techniques, or the well-known admonition to count to ten. Understanding how anger can affect our behaviour is an excellent example of emotional intelligence in action (Goleman, 1995). In fact, education may someday include training in self-awareness, self-control, and empathy, and the acts of listening, resolving conflicts, and co-operation (Sleek, 1997). To those who argue that schools or educational institutions have too much to teach to students already without adding instruction in emotional intelligence, proponents of such instruction suggest that it would be easier to teach students who can maintain their emotional equilibrium in the face of a wide variety of stressors at home and in the community (Sleek, 1997). The concept of emotional intelligence includes such abilities as motivating oneself, persisting in the face of frustration, and controlling impulses, as well as being aware of the emotions one is experiencing.

Emotional intelligence is a critical part of social intelligence and is not necessarily related to academic aptitude. Emotionally intelligent people are self-aware. They manage their emotions without being hijacked by overwhelming anger, anxiety, or depression. They can delay gratification in pursuit of long-range rewards, rather than being over taken by immediate impulses. Their empathy enables them to read others' emotions. They handle others' emotions skillfully, knowing what to say to a grieving friend, how to encourage colleagues, and how to manage conflicts well. Simply said, they are emotionally smart, and thus they often succeed in careers, parenting where other academically smarter (but emotionally less intelligent) people fail.

People with high emotional intelligence use their emotions in beneficial ways, to motivate themselves and others, spur creative thinking, and to deal empathically with others. People who are low in emotional intelligence are often unable to identify their own emotions; they may insist that they are not depressed when an intimate relationship ends, for example, but meanwhile they start drinking too much, become extremely irritable, and stop going out with friends. They express emotions inappropriately, such as by acting violently or impulsively when they are angry or worried. And they misread non-verbal signals from others, for example, they will give a long-winded account of all their problems even when the listener is obviously bored.

Emotional intelligence contributes to school achievement. Children who have difficulty in interpreting non-verbal emotional signals from others are less likely to do well academically and this is especially true of boys (Nowicki and Duke, 1983). Perhaps, children who can not read emotional cues from their teachers and classmates, or who can not regulate their own emotions, have trouble learning because they feel anxious, confused, or angry (Goleman, 1995).

These two different kinds of intelligence: intellectual and emotional intelligence—express the activity of the different parts of the brain. The intellect is based solely on the working of the neo-cortex, the more recently evolved layers at the top of the brain. The emotional centers are lower in the brain in the more ancient sub-cortex; emotional intelligence involves these emotional centres at work, in concert (combination) with the intellectual centers. In extreme cases, brain damage may diminish emotional intelligence while leaving academic intelligence intact.

Cognitive research on "intelligence" is starting to have practical benefits. Robert Sternberg and Howard Gardner have worked together with others to develop a practical intelligence curriculum being used in hundreds of classrooms (Sternberg, Okagaki, and Jackson, 1990; Williams et al., 1996). Children are taught three kinds of tacit knowledge necessary for success in school: how to manage themselves (for example, by avoiding procrastination); how to manage tasks (for example, by using different strategies when studying for multiple-choice and essay exams); and how to get along with others (for example, by convincing a teacher that an idea is worthwhile). Children receiving the curriculum have shown greater improvement in reading, writing, homework, performance, and test-taking ability than those not receiving it (Sternberg et al., 1995).

Emotional intelligence is the ability to perceive, express, understand, and regulate emotions (Peter Salovey and John Mayer, 1994; Salovey and others, 2002). Emotional intelligence refers to a set of skills that we use to deal with emotion-relevant information. Salovey, Hsee and Mayer (1993) suggest that it is concerned with:

(i) the appraisal and expression of emotion;
(ii) the use of information based on emotion; and
(iii) of particular importance how we learn to regulate our own emotions.

Salovey and colleagues argue that emotional self-regulation depends on two factors. The first is how disposed we are to regulate our own emotions. This in turn depends on emotional awareness and our thoughts about our own moods. Secondly, it depends on strategies that can be used to affect our own feelings. For example, we might manipulate what we feel by spending a day helping other people, or perhaps by completing the less pleasant tasks of the day early on, saving the more pleasant things for later. Thomson (1990, 1991) links changes in emotional self-regulation to the development of cognitive skills, allowing emotion to be seen as analyzable and capable of change. No doubt, such capacities themselves depend on a mixture of genetic influences and the development of language and social behaviour.

As emotional intelligence and the ability to self-regulate develop, so does a child's on way of thinking about emotions. This, in turn, will be influenced by socialization. So, emotional intelligence and self-regulation may to some extent depend on the attachment style and child experiences and how well socialized she or he becomes. Emotional intelligence is, of course, also concerned with accurately interpreting and dealing with others' emotions.

A comprehensive theory of emotional intelligence was proposed in 1994 by two psychologists: Peter Salovey and John Mayer. Another pioneering model of emotional intelligence in 1980's by Reuven Bar-on, an Israeli psychologist. And in recent years several other theorists have proposed variation on the same idea.

Researchers are beginning to develop tests that can measure emotional intelligence. Scientists who study emotions generally believe that people with high emotional intelligence usually work well in cooperative situations and are good at motivating and managing others. People with low emotional intelligence often misinterpret emotional signals and have difficulty with relationships. Although emotional intelligence probably has an inherited component, many psychologists believe that people can be guided into making better use of the emotional intelligence that they possess.

Emotional intelligence has five parts:

1. *Self-awareness:* recognizing internal feelings.
2. *Managing emotions:* finding ways to handle emotions that are appropriate to the situation.
3. *Motivation:* using self-control to channel emotions toward a goal.
4. *Empathy:* understanding the emotional perspective of other people.
5. *Handling relationships:* using personal information and information about others to handle social relationships and to develop interpersonal skills.

12.4.1 Major Components or Parts or Constituents or Elements of Emotional Intelligence

Daniel Goleman (1995) suggests that emotional intelligence consists of five major parts:

1. Knowing our own emotion,
2. Managing one's emotions,

3. Motivating our emotions,
4. Recognizing the emotions of others, and
5. Handing relationships.

Each of these elements, Daniel Goleman contends, plays an important role in shaping the outcomes we experience in life.

1. **Knowing our own Emotions:** Emotions are often powerful reactions, so it would seem at first glance that everyone ought to be able to recognize their own feelings. In fact, however, this is not always the case. Some persons are highly aware of their own emotions and their thoughts about them, but others seem to be almost totally unaware to these. Such differences exist because, (i) to the extent individuals are not aware of their own feelings, they cannot make intelligent choices ((ii) because, such persons are not aware of their own emotions, they are often low in expressiveness—they do not show their feelings clearly through facial expressions, body language, or other cues most of which are used to recognize others' feelings (Malandro, Barker and Barker, 1994). This can have adverse effects on their inter-personal relationships, because other people find it hard to know how they are feeling or reacting. For these reasons, this first component of emotion seems to be quite important.

This component includes perceiving emotions by recognizing emotions conveyed by various faces, musical excerpts, graphic designs, and stories; and understanding emotions by recognizing how emotions change overtime, predicting differing emotions (for example, the emotions of a person whose car hit a scooter and the emotions of the scooter's owner), and apprehending how emotions blend.

2. **Managing or Handling or Controlling or Regulating our own Emotions:** We regulate emotions by rating alternative strategies that we could use when facing various real-life situations demands. We often try to manage our emotions—to regulate their nature, intensity, and expression (Zillmann, 1996). Doing so is very important for our own mental health and from the point of view of interacting effectively with others.

3. **Motivating Ourselves:** Hard work and aspects of emotional intelligence, such as being able to motivate oneself to work along and hard on a task, remaining enthusiastic and optimistic about the final outcome, and being able to delay gratification—to put off receiving small rewards now in order to get larger ones later on (Shoda, Mischel, Peake, 1990). Being high in such skills can indeed contribute to success in many different contexts or situations.

4. **Recognizing and Influencing others' Emotions:** Another aspect of emotional intelligence, as described by Goleman, is the ability to "read" others accurately—to recognize the mood they are in, and what emotion

they are experiencing. This skill is valuable in many practical settings. For example, if you can accurately know or gauge another person's current mood, you can tell whether it is the right time to ask her or him for a favour. Similarly, persons who are skilled at generating strong emotions in others are often highly successful in such field as sales and politics. They can get other people to feel what they want them to feel.

5. **Handling Relationships:** Some people seem to have a knack or skill for getting along with others. Most people who meet these people like them, and as a result, they have many friends and often enjoy high levels of success in their careers. In contrast, others seem to make a mess of virtually all their personal relationships. According to Goleman (1995), "Such differences are another reflection of differences in emotional intelligence or as some researchers would phrase it, difference in inter-personal intelligence" (Hatch, 1990).

Inter-personal intelligence involve such skills as being able to coordinate the efforts of several people and to negotiate solutions to complex interpersonal problems, being good at giving others feedback that does not make them angry or resentful (Baron, 1993) and being a team player. Again, these skills are clearly distinct from the ones needed for getting good grades or scoring high on tests of intelligence, but they often play a key role in important life outcomes.

12.4.2 Evidence on the Existence of Emotional Intelligence and Effects

Most of the evidences Goleman offer concerning the existence and impact of emotional intelligence that is anecdotal or indirect in nature. Psychologists, of course, strongly prefer more concrete kinds of evidence. Accordingly, researchers have put the concept of emotional intelligence to the test, trying to determine whether the distinct skills described by Goleman cluster together as the single (if multi-facet) factor and whether this factor influences the important life outcomes.

With respect to the first of these issues, evidence is mixed. Some researchers have reported findings consistent with Goleman's suggestions, and with their own, similar definitions of emotional intelligence, others have obtained less encouraging results. In a recent and carefully conducted study, Davies, Stankou, and Roberts (1998) indicated that only one of the components emphasized by Goleman and other advocates of emotional intelligence emerged as clear and independent; emotion perception—the ability to accurately read others' emotions.

Another interpretation of existing evidence concerning emotional intelligence is that at present, there are no adequate methods for measuring all aspects of emotional intelligence. These components may, in fact, be somewhat independent of each other. Thus, it may not be possible to assign individuals to single overall Emotional Quotient (EQ) score comparable to the single IQ score yielded by many intelligence tests.

Other research offers support for the view that some of the components included in emotional intelligence—especially emotion perception—can indeed have measurable effects. Gideon Markman and Baron (2003) found that persons who are adept or skillful at "reading" others accurately and who adapt easily to new social situations or who are high on social adaptability are significantly more successful, financially, than people who score lower on these skills. To the extent that these two traits are related to emotional intelligence, this finding can be viewed as offering indirect support for the view that EQ influences the outcomes people experience in practical contexts. But the idea of emotional intelligence is an appealing one with important implications.

12.5 NATURE OR NURTURE ISSUE IN INTELLIGENCE OR THE ROLE OF HEREDITY AND ENVIRONMENT IN HUMAN INTELLIGENCE

That people differ in intelligence is obvious. Are they largely a matter of heredity—differences in the genetic materials and codes one inherit from one's parents? Or are they primarily the result of environmental factors—conditions (favourable or unfavourable) in the world around us that affect our intellectual development? Both types of factors (hereditary and environmental) are involved. Human differences in intelligence may depend on heredity, or on environment, or on a mixture of heredity and environment. The issue of the roles played by heredity and environment in determining intelligence has been looked at by many psychologists, and is sometimes known as the *nature-nurture issue*. Human intelligence is clearly the result of the complex interplay between genetic factors and a wide range of environmental conditions (Plomin, 1997). It is now quite widely accepted that genes and environment share a role in explaining individual variability in individual IQ (Snyderman and Rothman, 1987). Human intelligence appears to be the product of an extremely complex interplay between genetic factors and environmental conditions (Plomin, 1989; Weinberg, 1989).

Much of the researches on the nature-nurture question have been conducted on twins (Bouchard et al., 1990). The role of genes and environment (nature and nurture) in determining IQ is reviewed in Plomin et al. (2001, 2003). Robert Plomin (Born in 1948), an American psychologist is best known for his work in twin studies and behaviour genetics. Until recently heritability was mostly studied in children.

Robert Plomin
(Born in 1948)

Various studies find the heritability of IQ between 0.4 and 0.8 in the United States (Lichtenstein, McClearn, Pedersen, Plomin, 1994) that is, depending on the study, a little less than half to substantially more than half of the variation in IQ among the children studied was due to variation in their genes. The remainder was thus due to environmental variation and measurement error. Heritability in the range of 0.4 to 0.8 implies that IQ is "substantially" heritable. Identical twins or monozygotic twins have the same heredity, inheriting the same genes. Identical twins not only look the same, but they also share exactly the same genetic make up. If heredity is an important determinant of intelligence, then we would expect to discover that identical twins are more likely than fraternal twins in intelligence. The degree of similarity in intelligence shown by pairs of twins is usually reported in the form of correlations. A correlation of + 1.00 (perfect correlation) would mean that both twins in a pair obtain exactly the same IQ, whereas a correlation of 0.00 (no correlation or zero correlation) would mean that there was no relationship at all between the IQs of twins. Studies by Bouchard and McGue (1981) have demonstrated that correlations between the IQ scores for identical twins average + 0.86 when they are reared in the same household; that correlation is remarkably high. Higher correlations indicate closer relationships between variables. When identical twins are reared in separate households for example, because they were adopted by different couples and different families, the correlation averaged + 0.72. This data tells us two things: (i) nature is important, because the correlation remains very high, even when the twins have different nurturing experiences, (ii) nurture is important because the correlation is higher when twins are raised in the same environment than when raised in different environments.

This difference might be due to the greater genetic similarity of identical twins or the greater environmental similarity for identical twins than for fraternal twins. Loehlin and Nichols (1976) found that the parents of identical twins were much more likely than those of fraternal twins to have tried to treat them exactly the same.

In addition, consider fraternal twins or dizygotic twins (twins who came from two separate eggs and are thus no more genetically similar in their heredity than two siblings or ordinary brothers and sisters), whose genetic overlap is fifty percent—the same as for any two siblings. When fraternal twins are reared together, the correlations between their IQ scores averaged +0.60. This correlation is substantially lower than the +0.86 correlation for identical twins (people whose genetic overlap is 100%). These data, then, provide additional evidence that nature is important.

A study of French children adopted between the ages of 4 and 6 shows a possible continuing interplay of nature and nurture. The children came from poor backgrounds with IQs that initially averaged 77, putting them near retardation. Nine years later after adoption, they retook the IQ tests, and all of them did better. The amount they improved was directly related to the adopting family's status. "Children adopted by farmers and labourers had average IQ scores of 85.5; those placed with middle-class families had average scores of 92. The average IQ scores of youngsters placed in well-to-do homes climbed more than 20 points, to 98" (Kirp, 2006). On the other hand, the degree to which these increases persisted into adulthood is not clear from the study.

There are a number of points to consider when interpreting heritability:

- A high heritability does not mean that the environment has no effect on the development of a trait, or that learning is not involved. Vocabulary size, for example, is very substantially heritable (and highly correlated with general intelligence) although every word in an individual's vocabulary is learned. In a society in which plenty of words are available in everyone's environment, especially for individuals who are motivated to seek them out, the number of words that individuals actually learn depends to a considerable extent on their genetic predispositions (Neisser et al., 1995).
- A common error is to assume that because something is heritable, it is necessarily unchangeable. This is wrong. Heritability does not imply immutability. As previously noted, heritable traits can depend on learning, and they may be subject to other environmental effects as well. The value of heritability can change if the distribution of environments (or genes) in the population is substantially altered. For example, an impoverished or suppressive environment could fail to support the development of a trait, and hence restrict individual variation. Differences in variation of heritability are found between developed and developing nations. This could affect estimates of heritability (Neisser et al., 1995). Another example is Phenylketonuria (PKU: a genetic disorder of amino-acid metabolism in which the enzyme phenylalanine hydroxylase, necessary for the oxidizing of phenylalanine, is missing) which previously caused mental retardation for everyone who had this genetic disorder. Today, this can be prevented by following a modified diet (Neisser et al., 1995).

- On the other hand, there can be effective environmental changes that do not change heritability at all. If the environment relevant to a given trait improves in a way that affects all members of the population equally, the mean value of the trait will rise without any change in its heritability (because the differences among individuals in the population will stay the same). This has evidently happened for height: the heritability of stature is high, but average heights continue to increase.
- Even in developed nations, high heritability of a trait within a given group has no necessary implications for the source of a difference between groups (Neisser et al., 1995; Turkheimer, Haley, Waldron, Onofrio, Gottesman II, 2003).

12.5.1 Evidence for the Influence of Heredity

Several lines of research offer support for the view that heredity plays an important role in human intelligence. First, consider findings with respect to family relationship and measured IQ. If intelligence were indeed determined by heredity, we would expect that that the more closely the two persons are related, the more similar their IQ's will be. This prediction has generally been confirmed (Bouchard and McGue, 1981; Erlenmeyer-Kimling and Jarvik, 1963; McGue 1993; Neisser, 1996). The IQ of identical twins raised together co-relate almost +0.90, those of brothers and sisters about +0.50, and those of cousins about +0.15. Higher correlations indicate closer relationships between variables.

Relationship Sources	Co-relation between IQ Scores
Identical twins, reared together	0.88
Identical twins, reared apart	0.72
Brothers and sisters, reared together	0.43
Brothers and sisters, reared apart	0.22
Parent and child, living together	0.42
Foster parents and child	0.22
Unrelated persons, reared together	0.20
Unrelated persons, reared apart	0.00

Additional support for the impact of heredity on intelligence is provided by studies involving adopted children who are brought up by foster parents. Such twins are very important, because they would appear to have very similar heredity but dissimilar environment. If intelligence is strongly affected by genetic factors and if heredity is of major importance, the IQ of adopted children should resemble those of their biological parents more closely than those of their adoptive parents. If environment is of primary importance, there should be little or no similarity in intelligence. Those who believe in the importance of heredity would expect there to be a closer link with the biological parents than with the foster parents. This prediction too, has been confirmed (Bouchard, 1984, 1987; Bouchard et al., 1990; Gross, 1992; Jencks, 1972; Munsinge, 1978; Plomin et al., 1997).

Plomin et al. (1997) in a long term study found that the co-relations between the intelligence of adopted children and that of their biological parents, and between the intelligence of children living at home and that of their biological parents, increased over time. In contrast, the co-relations between the intelligence of adopted children and that of their adopted parents decreased over time. The adopted children came to resemble their biological parents, but not their adoptive parents more closely in intelligence over time. These findings suggest that genetic factors play an important role in intelligence.

On average, the IQ's of adopted children correlate about +0.5 with those of their biological mothers, compared with only +0.2 with those of their foster mothers. This evidence is consistent with the finding that from twin studies in suggesting some involvement of heredity in the determination of intelligence. While the IQs of adopted children correlate about +0.40 to +0.50 with those of their biological parents, they correlate only about +0.10 to +0.20 with those of their adoptive parents (Jencks, 1972; Munsinger, 1978; Plomin et al., 1977).

Growing evidence from the burgeoning or budding field of behavioural genetics does seem to point to the possibility that genetic factors may be more important in some respects than environmental ones (Plomin, 1989). Indeed, a growing body of evidence obtained primarily through large-scale studies of twins raised apart suggests that genetics play a crucial role in a variety of intellectual factors, including IQ, cognitive abilities, and academic achievement. Actually, increasing evidence suggests that genes do not fix behaviour but rather establish a range of possible responses to a given environment—a range referred to as malleability (Weinberg, 1989).

12.5.2 IQ and the Brain

Intelligence is linked in general to the thickness of the "gray matter"—the cerebral cortex of the brain, which plays a key role in memory, thought, language, and consciousness.

In 2004, Richard Haier, professor of Psychology in the Department of Pediatrics and his colleagues at University of California, Irvine and the University of New Mexico used MRI to obtain structural images of the brain in 47 normal adults who also took standard IQ tests. The study demonstrated that general human intelligence appears to be based on the volume and location of *gray matter* tissue in the brain. Regional distribution of gray matter in humans is highly heritable. The study also demonstrated that, of the brain's gray matter, only about 6 percent appeared to be related to IQ (Haier, 2004).

Many different sources of information have converged on the view that the frontal lobes are critical for *fluid intelligence*. Patients with damage to the frontal lobe are impaired on fluid intelligence tests (Duncan et al., 1995). The volume of frontal gray (Thompson et al., 2001) and white matter (Schoenemann et al., 2005) have also been associated with general intelligence. In addition, recent neuroimaging studies have limited this association to the lateral prefrontal cortex. Duncan and colleagues (2000) showed using Positron Emission Tomography that problem-solving tasks that correlated more highly with IQ also activate the lateral prefrontal cortex. More recently, Gray and colleagues (2003) used Functional Magnetic Resonance Imaging (FMRI) to show that those individuals that were more adept at resisting distraction on a demanding working memory task had both a higher IQ and increased prefrontal activity (Gray and Thompson, 2006).

A study involving 307 children (age between six to nineteen) measuring the size of brain structures using magnetic resonance imaging (MRI) and measuring verbal and non-verbal abilities has been conducted (Shaw et al., 2006). The study has indicated that there is a relationship between IQ and the structure of the cortex—the characteristic change being the group with the superior IQ scores starts with thinner cortex in the early age then becomes thicker than average by the late teens (Wade, 2006).

There is "a highly significant association" between the CHRM2 gene and intelligence according to a 2006 Dutch family study. The study concluded that there was an association between the CHRM2 gene on chromosome 7 and Performance IQ, as measured by the Wechsler Adult Intelligence Scale-Revised. The Dutch family study used a sample of 667 individuals from 304 families (Gosso, Van Belzen, De Geus et al., 2006). A similar association was found independently in the Minnesota Twin and Family Study (Comings et al., 2003) and by the Department of Psychiatry at the Washington University (Dick, Aliev, Kramer et al., 2007).

Significant injuries isolated to one side of the brain, especially those occurring at a young age, may not significantly affect IQ (Bava, Ballantyne, Tranner, 2005).

Studies reach conflicting conclusions regarding the controversial idea that brain size correlates positively with IQ. Jensen and Reed claim no direct correlation exists in non-pathological subjects (Reed and Jensen, 1993). A more recent meta-analysis suggests otherwise (McDaniels, 2005).

An alternative approach has sought to link differences in neural plasticity with intelligence (Garlick, 2002) and this view has recently received some empirical support (Shaw, Greenstein, Lerch et al., 2006).

Once thought immutable, recent research suggests that certain mental activities can change the brain's raw ability to process information, leading to the conclusion that intelligence can be altered or changed over time. Studies into the neuroscience of animals indicate that challenging activities can produce changes in gene expression patterns of the brain. *Training Degus to Use Rakes* (Okanoya, Tokimoto, Kumazawa, Hihara, Iriki, 2008) and Iriki's earlier research with macaque monkeys indicating brain changes—a study published in April 2008 by a team from the Universities of Michigan and Bern demonstrated the transfer of fluid intelligence from specifically designed working memory training (Jaeggi, Buschkuehl, Jonides, Perrig, 2008).

Further research will be needed to determine the extent and duration of the transfer.

12.5.3 Evidence for the Influence of Environmental Factors

In human intelligence, environmental factors, too, are important. In some investigation involving adopted children, the IQ's of adopted children have been observed to become increasingly similar to those of their adoptive or foster parents over time (Scarr and Weinberg, 1976). These findings indicate that environmental factors, too, play an important role. Evidence of the powerful effects that environment can have on intelligence was provided by Gordon, 1923; Schiff et al., 1978; Wheeler, 1940.

The effect of environment on intelligence often begins before birth. Performance on IQ tests has increased substantially around the world at all age levels in recent decades. This phenomenon is known as *Flynn Effect* (Flynn, 1987, 1996). The average IQ scores for many populations have been rising at an average rate of three points per decade since the early 20th century with most of the increase in the lower half of the IQ range: a phenomenon called the *Flynn effect*. Since the twentieth century IQ scores have increased at an average rate of around three IQ points per decade in most parts of the world (Flynn 1999). This phenomenon (the "Lynn–Flynn effect") has been named after *Richard Lynn* and *James R. Flynn*. Attempted explanations have included improved nutrition, a trend towards smaller families, better education, greater environmental complexity, and heterosis (also called hybrid vigour; increased strength, size, vigour, and growth rate resulting from cross-breeding of genetically dissimilar members of the same species) (Mingroni, 2007). Tests are, therefore, renormalized occasionally to obtain mean scores of 100, for example WISC–R (1974), WISC–III (1991) and WISC IV (2003). This adjustment specifically addresses the variation over time, allowing us to compare scores from different times. Some researchers argue that the Flynn Effect may have ended in some developed nations starting in the mid 1990s, namely in Denmark (Teasdale, Thomas, Owen, 2005) and in Norway (Teasdale, Thomas, Owen, 2006).

It is disputed whether these changes in scores reflect real changes in intellectual abilities, or merely methodological problems with past or present testing. Such increases have averaged about 3 IQ points per decade world wide; but in some countries, they have been even larger. These gains can be interpreted, only as stemming from environmental factors—changes in living standards and educational opportunities for millions of human beings. As a result of these gains in performance, it has been necessary to re-standardize widely used tests so that they continue to yield an average IQ of 100. What is termed "average" today is actually a higher level of performance that was true in the past as exhibited in the following data.

	1952	1962	1972
Britain	87	93	95
Netherlands	79	85	92
Norway	77	83	88

The following variables or factors have been suggested as possible contributors to the continuing rising IQ (Flynn, 1999; Williams, 1998):

1. Better nutrition
2. Increased urbanization
3. The advent of television
4. More and better education
5. More cognitively demanding jobs
6. Exposure to computer games

Environmental factors play a role in determining IQ. Proper childhood nutrition appears critical for cognitive development; malnutrition can lower IQ.

A recent study found that the FADS2 gene, along with *breastfeeding*, adds about 7 IQ points to those with the "C" version of the gene. Those with the "G" version of the FADS2 gene see no advantage (Capsi, Williams, Kim-Cohen et al., 2007; Turkheimer, Haley, Waldron, Onofrio, Gottesman II, 2003).

Musical training in childhood also increases IQ (Schellenberg, 2004). Recent studies have shown that training in using one's working memory may increase IQ (Jaeggi, Buschkuehl, Jonides, Perrig, 2008; Klingberg et al., 2002).

In sum, many forms of evidence support the view that intelligence is determined at least in part by environmental factors. Especially, when these are extremes, they may slow or accelerate children's intellectual growth, and this effect, in turn, can have important implications for the societies in which those children will become adults.

Additional evidence for the role of environmental factors in intelligence is provided by the findings of the studies on environmental enrichment and environmental deprivation. With regard to enrichment, removing children from sterile, restricted environments and placing them in more favourable settings seems to enhance their intellectual growth (Skeels, 1938, 1966). In terms of deprivation, some findings suggested that intelligence could be reduced by the absence of key forms of environmental stimulation early in life (Gottfried, 1984). It has been found that intelligence can be reduced by high levels of chaos and noise in the home (Wachs and Gruen, 1982).

Several studies report that firstborns tend to have higher IQ's than second-borns, who tend to have higher IQ's than third-borns, and so on (Zajonc and Markus, 1975). One possibility is suggested by Confluence theory (Zajonc, 1976, 1986). According to this theory, each individual's intellectual growth depends to an important degree on the intellectual environment in which she or he develops. A firstborn child benefits from the fact that for some period of time, until the birth of another child, she or he lives with a parent or parents who provide a relatively advantaged intellectual environment. Secondborn children, in contrast, live with adults who divide their attention between first and secondborn; thus the average level of the child's intellectual environment is somewhat diluted. Such effects become even stronger for thirdborns and continue to grow as the number of children in a family rises. Zajonc's interpretation of the correlation between birth order and intelligence, however, has not met with universal acceptance and in fact has been the source of heated debate (Blake, 1989; Galbraith, 1982; Rodgers, 1988).

Striking evidence that environmental factors like discrimination prevent American blacks from realizing their intellectual potential was obtained by Scarr and Weinberg (1976).

While most recent and carefully controlled efforts to increase intelligence through environmental interventions have produced beneficial results (Bryant and Maxwell, 1997; Collins, 1983; Guralnick, 1997). Ramey and Ramey (1998) noted recently such changes are most likely to occur when the following conditions are met:

1. The interventions begin early and continue for a long time.
2. The programs are intense, involving home visits several times per week.
3. The children receive new learning experience delivered directly to them by experts rather than indirectly through their parents.
4. The interventions are broad in scope, using many different procedures to enhance children's development.
5. Environmental supports for example an excellent school is put in place to support and maintain the positive attitudes towards learning the children gain.

Research on the role of the environment in children's intellectual development has demonstrated that a stimulating environment can dramatically increase IQ, whereas a deprived environment can lead to a decrease in IQ. A few such research studies are listed below. They confirm that IQ is all but a fixed quantity.

A particularly interesting project on early intellectual stimulation involved twenty-five children in an orphanage. These children were seriously environmentally deprived because the orphanage was crowded and understaffed. Thirteen babies with an average age of nineteen months were transferred to the Glenwood State School for retarded adult women and each baby was put in the personal care of a woman. Skeels, who conducted the experiment, deliberately chose the most deficient of the orphans to be placed in the Glenwood School. Their average IQ was 64, while the average IQ of the twelve who stayed behind in the orphanage was 87.

In the Glenwood State School, the children were placed in open, active wards with the older and relatively bright women. Their substitute mothers overwhelmed them with love and cuddling. Toys were available, they were taken on outings and they were talked to a lot. The women were taught how to stimulate the babies intellectually and how to elicit language from them.

After eighteen months, the dramatic findings were that the children who had been placed with substitute mothers, and had therefore received additional stimulation, on average showed an increase of 29 IQ points. A follow-up study was conducted two and a half years later. Eleven of the thirteen children originally transferred to the Glenwood home had been adopted and their average IQ was now 101. The two children who had not been adopted were re-institutionalized and lost their initial gain. The control group, the twelve children who had not been transferred to Glenwood, had remained in institution wards and now had an average IQ of 66 (an average decrease of 21 points). Although the value of IQ tests is grossly exaggerated today, this astounding difference between these two groups is hard to ignore.

More telling than the increase or decrease in IQ, however, is the difference in the quality of life these two groups enjoyed. When these children reached young adulthood, another follow-up study brought the following to light: "The experimental group had become productive, functioning adults, while the control group, for the most part, had been institutionalized as mentally retarded."

In the late 1960s, under the supervision of Rick Heber of the University of Wisconsin, a project was begun to study the effects of intellectual stimulation on children from deprived environments. In order to find a "deprived environment" from which to draw appropriate subjects for the study, Heber and his colleagues examined the statistics of different districts within the city of Milwaukee. One district in particular stood out. The residents of this district had the lowest median income and lowest level of education to be found in the city. This district also had the highest population density and rate of unemployment of any area of Milwaukee. There was one more statistic that really attracted Heber's attention: Although this district contained only 3 percent of the city's population, it accounted for 33 percent of the children in Milwaukee who had been labelled "mentally retarded".

At the beginning of the project, Heber selected forty newborns from the depressed area of Milwaukee he had chosen. The mothers of the infants selected, all had IQs below 80. As it turned out, all of the children in the study were black, and in many cases the fathers were absent. The forty newborns were randomly assigned, 20 to an experimental group and 20 to a control group.

Both the experimental group and the control group were tested an equal number of times throughout the project. An independent testing service was used in order to eliminate possible biases on the part of the project members. In terms of physical or medical variables, there were no observable differences between the two groups.

The experimental group entered a special program. Mothers of the experimental group children received education, vocational rehabilitation, and training in homemaking and childcare. The children themselves received personalized enrichment in their home environments for the first three months of their lives, and then their training continued at a special centre, five days a week, seven hours a day, until they were ready to begin first grade. The program at the centre focused upon developing the language and cognitive skills of the experimental group children. The control group did not receive special education or home-based intervention and enrichment.

By the age of six all the children in the experimental group were dramatically superior to the children in the control group, in terms of IQ. This was true on all test measures, especially those dealing with language skills or problem solving. The experimental group had an IQ average of 120.7 as compared with the control group's 87.2.

At the age of six the children left the centre to attend the local school. By the time both groups were ten years old and in fifth grade, the IQ scores of the children in the experimental group had decreased to an average of 105 while the control group's average score held steady at about 85. One possible reason for the decline is that schooling was geared for the slower students. The brighter children were not given materials suitable for their abilities and they began to fall back. Also, while the experimental children were in the special project centre for the first six years they ate well, receiving three hot, balanced meals a day. Once they left the centre and began to attend the local school, many reported going to classes hungry, without breakfast or a hot lunch.

Additional support for the role of environmental factors in intelligence is provided by the finding that many biological factors that children encounter while growing up can affect their intellect. Prolonged malnutrition can adversely affect IQ (Sigman, 1995), as can exposure to lead, either in the air or lead-based paint which young children often eat because it tastes sweet (Baghurst et al., 1992).

Finally, a wide range of other environmental factors have also been found to be related to IQ scores. To mention just a few, these include nutrition, family background such as parents' education and income; and quality of education (Bouchard and Segal, 1985), type of job, and socio-economic status. Chipeur et al. and Loehlin conclude that the postnatal rather than the prenatal environment is most important. Persons with a higher IQ have generally lower adult *morbidity* and *mortality*. Post-Traumatic Stress Disorder, (Breslan, Lucia, Alvarado, 2006) severe *depression*, (Mandelli, Serreti, Colombo et al., 2006; Sackeim, Freeman, McElhiney, Coleman, Prudic, Devanand, 1992) and schizophrenia (Woodberry, Ginliano, Seidman, 2008; Zinkstok, De Wilde, Van Amelsvoort, Tanck, Baas, Linszen, 2007) are less prevalent in higher IQ bands.

In terms of the effect of one's intelligence on health, high childhood IQ correlates with one's chance of becoming a vegetarian in adulthood (Gale, 1970) and inversely correlates with the chances of smoking (Taylor, 1932).

EXERCISES

The below mentioned are some of the questions that have been asked in the examinations conducted by the Guru Nanak Dev University or can be asked. Knowledge of these answers can help the students to get success in the examinations.

Section A

Answer the following questions in **five** lines or 50 words.

1. Define "Intelligence".*
2. What is Intelligence Quotient (IQ)?*
3. Define factor-analysis.
4. What is the nature/nurture issue?
5. Explain the triarchic theory.
6. What do you mean by componential intelligence?
7. What is experiential intelligence?
8. What is contextual intelligence?
9. What is emotional intelligence?*

10. What is "G" factor?*
11. What is "S" factor.
12. What do you mean by the psychometric theories?
13. Define the cognitive theories.
14. Distinguish between "Intra-personal" intelligence and "Inter-personal" intelligence.
15. What are the factors of Gardner's theory of intelligence?
16. Explain Thurstone's seven factors of intelligence?
17. What do you mean by the mental age?
18. What do you mean by the chronological age?
19. Define heredity.
20. Explain constancy of IQ.

Section B

Answers the following questions up to **two** pages or 500 words.

1. What is intelligence?*
2. Describe Spearman's theory of intelligence?
3. What is Gardner's theory of multiple intelligences?
4. What is Sternberg's triarchic theory of intelligence?
5. What evidence suggests that intelligence is influenced by genetic factors?
6. What evidence suggests that intelligence is influenced by environmental factors?
7. What is "emotional intelligence"?*
8. What evidence suggests the existence of emotional intelligence?
9. What is intelligence? Discuss Spearman and Thurstone's theories.
10. Define intelligence. Write Gardner and Sternberg's theories of intelligence.
11. Discuss nature and nurture issue in intelligence.*
12. Discuss the concept of "emotional intelligence".
13. What is emotional intelligence? Give its characteristics.
14. What is emotional intelligence? Give its main elements.
15. Write note on emotional intelligence.
16. Explain Thurstone's theory of intelligence.*
17. Describe Spearman's theory of intelligence.*
18. Do Spearman and Thurstone's theories of intelligence differ from each other? How?

19. Define intelligence. Discuss Spearman's two factor theory of intelligence.
20. Write a note on primary mental abilities?
21. Define intelligence and explain Thurstone's primary mental abilities.

Section C

Answers the following questions up to **five** pages or 1000 words.

1. What is IQ? How can it be measured?*
2. What is the nature/nurture issue in intelligence? What evidence supports the importance of nature? What evidence supports the importance of nurture?
3. What is intelligence? Discuss in detail the various theories of intelligence.*
4. Define intelligence. Discuss the concept of emotional intelligence.
5. What is emotional intelligence? Discuss nature and nurture issue in intelligence.
6. What is heredity? What is the role of heredity in the development of intelligence?
7. What is intelligence? Discuss various theories of intelligence.
8. What is the role of heredity and environment in the development of intelligence?*
9. Compare Spearman and Thurstone's theories of intelligence.*
10. Write psychometric theories of intelligence.
11. Write Gardner and Sternberg's theories of intelligence. Discuss nature and nurture issue in intelligence.
12. What is "emotional intelligence"? Write various components of "emotional intelligence".*
13. Write Spearman and Thurstone's theories of Intelligence. Discuss nature and nurture issue in the Intelligence.
14. What is "emotional intelligence"? Write various components of "emotional intelligence".

REFERENCES

Baghurst, P.A., McMichael, A.J., Wigg, N.R., Vimpahni, G.V., Robertson, E.F., Roberts, R.J., and Tongs, S.L., 'Environmental Exposure to Lead and Children's Intelligence at the Age of Seven Years: The Port Pirie Cohort Study,' *New England Journal of Medicine,* **327**, 1279–1284, 1992.

Baron, R.A., 'Criticism (Informal Negative Feedback) as a Source of Perceived Unfairness in Organizations: Effects, Mechanisms, and Countermeasures,' in R. Cropanzano (Ed.), *Justice in the workplace: Approaching Fairness in Human Resource Management* (pp. 155–170). Hillsdale, NJ: Erlbaum,1993a.

Baron Reuven, *The Emotional Quotient Inventory (EQ-i), A Test of Emotional Intelligence*, Toronto: Multiple-Health Systems, 1996.

Bava, S., Ballantyne, A.O., Trauner, D.A., 'Disparity of Verbal and Performance IQ Following Early Bilateral Brain Damage,' *Cogn Behav. Neurol* **18**(3): 163–70. PMID 16175020, http://meta.wkhealth.com/pt/pt-core/template-journal/lwwgateway/media/landingpage.htm?issn=15433633&volume=18&issue=3&spage=163, September 2005.

Binet, A., and Simon, T., 'Methodes Nouvelles Pour Le Diagnostic Du Niveau Intellectuel Des Anormaux,' *Annee Psychologique,* **11**, 191–244, 1905.

Binet, A., and Simon, T., *The Development of Intelligence in Children*, Baltimore: Williams and Wilkins, 1916.

Bouchard, T.J., 'Twins Reared Together and Apart: What They Tell us about Human Diversity,' in S.W. Fox (Ed.), *Individuality and Its Determinism*, New York: Plenum Press, 1984.

Bouchard, T.J., 'Genetic and Environmental Influences on Adult Intelligence and Special Mental Abilities,' *Hum. Biol,* **70** (2): 257–79. PMID 9549239, April 1998.

Bouchard, T.J., Lykken, D.T., McGue, M., Segal, N.L. and Tellegen, A., 'Sources of Human Psychological Differences: The Minnesota Study of Twins Reared Apart,' *Science,* **250**, 223–228, 1990.

Bouchard, T.J., and McGue, M., 'Familial Studies of Intelligence: A Review,' *Science,* **212**, 1055–1059, 1981.

Breslan, N., Lucia, V.C., Alvarado, G.F., 'Intelligence and other Predisposing Factors in Exposure to Trauma and Posttraumatic Stress Disorder: A Follow-up Study at Age 17 Years,' *Arch. Gen. Psychiatry* **63** (11): 1238–45, doi:10.1001/archpsyc.63.11.1238. PMID 17088504, November 2006.

Bryant, D., and Maxwell, K., 'The Effectiveness of Early Intervention for Disadvantaged Children,' in M., Guralnick (Ed.), *The Effectiveness of Early Intervention* (pp. 23–46). Baltimore: Brookes, 1997.

Burt, C.L., *The factors of the Mind,* New York: Macmillan, 1941.

Carroll, J.B., 'Factor Analytic Investigations of Cognitive Abilities,' in S.E. Newstead, S.H. Irvine, and P.L. Dann (Eds.), Human Assessment: *Cognition and Motivation,* Nyhoff: Dordrecht, 1986.

Carroll, J.B., *Human Cognitive Abilities: A Survey of Factor-Analytical Studies*, New York: Cambridge University Press, 1993.

Caspi, A., Williams, B., Kim-Cohen, J., et al., 'Moderation of Breastfeeding Effects on the IQ by Genetic Variation in Fatty Acid Metabolism,' *Proceedings of the National Academy of Sciences,* **104**: 18860, doi:10.1073/pnas.0704292104, PMID 17984066, 2007.

Cattell, R.B., *The Cattell Intelligence Test Scales 1, 2, and 3,* London: Harrap, 1933.

Cattell, R.B., *Intelligence: Its Structure, Growth, and Action*, New York: Elsevier, 1987.

Cattell, R.B., 'Some Theoretical Issues in Adult Intelligence Testing,' *Psychological Bulletin*, 38, 592, 1941.

Cattell, R.B., *Abilities: Their Structure, Growth and Action*, Boston: Houghton-Mifflin, 1971.

Cattell, R.B., *An Open Letter to the American Psychological Association*, 1997.

Davies, M., Stankov, L., and Roberts, R.D., 'Emotional Intelligence: In Search of an Elusive Construct,' *Journal of Personality and Social Psychology,* **75**, 989–1015, 1998.

Dick, D.M., Aliev, F., Kramer, J., et al., "*Association of CHRM2 with IQ: Converging Evidence for a Gene Influencing Intelligence*". *Behav. Genet,* **37**(2): 265–72. doi:10.1007/s10519-006-9131-2, PMID17160701, March 2007.

Deary, I.J., Irwing, P., Der, G., and Bates, T.C., 'Brother–Sister Differences in the g Factor in Intelligence: Analysis of Full, Opposite-Sex Siblings from the NLSY1979,' *Intelligence,* **35**(5): 451–456, 2007.

Devlin, B., Daniels, M. and Roeder, K., "*The Heritability of IQ*", Nature **388**(6641): 468–71. doi:10.1038/41319, PMID9242404, July 1997.

Diaz-Asper, C.M., Schretlen, D.J. and Pearlson, G.D., 'How Well Does IQ Predict Neuropsychological Test Performance in Normal Adults?' J Int Nehttp://en.wikipedia.org/w/index.php?title=Intelligence_quotient&action=edituropsychol Soc **10** (1): 82–90. doi:10.1017/S1355617704101100. PMID14751010. January 2004.

Douglas, N., Jackson and Rushton, J.P., 'Males Have Greater g: Sex Differences in General Mental Ability from 100,000 17 to 18 year-olds on the Scholastic Assessment Test,' *Intelligence*, Volume **34**, Issue 5, pages 479–486, September–October 2006.

Duncan, J., Burgess, P. and Emslie, H., 'Fluid Intelligence After Frontal Lobe Lesions,' *Neuropsychologia* **33**(3): 261–8, doi:10.1016/0028-3932(94)00124-8, PMID 7791994, 1995.

Duncan, J., Seitz, R.J., Kolodny, J., et al., 'A Neural Basis for General Intelligence,' *Science* **289**(5478): 457–60. doi:10.1126/science.289.5478.457, PMID 10903207, 2000.

Eysenck, M.W., *Individual Differences: Normal and Abnormal*, Hove, U.K: Lawrence Erlbaum Associate Ltd., 1994.

Flynn, J.R., 'The Mean IQ of Americans: Massive Gains 1932 to 1978,' *Psychological Bulletin*, **95**, 29–51, 1984.

Flynn, J.R., 'Massive IQ Gains in 14 Nations: What IQ Tests Really Measure,' *Psychological Bulletin*, **101**, 171–191, 1987.

Flynn, J.R., 'Skodak and Skeels: The Inflated Mother-child IQ Gap,' *Intelligence*, **17**, 557–661, 1993.

Flynn, J.R., 'Group Differences: Is The Good Society Impossible?,' *Journal of Biosocial Science*, **28**, 573–585, 1996.

Flynn, J.R., 'Searching for Justice: The Discovery of IQ Gains Over Time,' *American Psychologist*, Vol. **54**, pp. 5–20, 1999.

Gale, C.R., 'IQ in Childhood and Vegetarianism in Adulthood: 1970 British Cohort Study,' *British Journal of Medicine*, **334** (7587): 245, 1970.

Gardner, H., *Frames of Mind: The Theory of Multiple Intelligences*, New York: Basic Books, 1983/2003.

Gardner, H., *The Unschooled Mind: How Children Think and How Schools Should Teach*, New York: Basic Books, 1991.

Gardner, H., *Multiple Intelligences: The Theory in Practice*, New York: Basic Books, 1993.

Gardner, H., *Intelligence Reframed*, New York: Basic Books, 1999.

Gardner, H., *The Disciplined Mind: Beyond Facts and Standardized Tests, The K–12 Education That Every Child Deserves*, New York: Penguin Putnam, 2000.

Gardner, H., *The Disciplined Mind: Beyond Facts and Standardized Tests, The K–12 Education That Every Child Deserves*, New York: Penguin Putnam, 2000.

Garlick, D., 'Understanding the Nature of the General Factor of Intelligence: The Role of Individual Differences in Neural Plasticity as an Explanatory Mechanism,' *Psychol. Rev.*, **109** (1): 116–36, PMID 11863034, http://content.apa.org/journals/rev/109/1/116. January 2002.

Golemen, D., *Emotional Intelligence*, New York: Bantam Books, 1995.

Golemen, D., *Emotional Intelligence: Why It Can Matter More Than IQ*. Bantam Books, 1996.

Golemen, D., *Working with Emotional Intelligence,* New York: Bantam Books, 1998.

Goleman, D., *Social Intelligence: The New Science of Social Relationships,* Bantam Books, 2006.

Goleman, D., *How to Help: When can Empathy Move us to Action?* Greater Good, Science Center, 2008.

Gottfredson, L.S., *"Why g Matters: The Complexity of Everyday Life."* Intelligence, **24**(1), 79–132, PDF, 1997.

Gottfredson, L.S., 'The General Intelligence Factor,' Scientific American Presents, **9**(4):24–29, PDF, 1998.

Gottfried, A.W., *Home Environment and Early Cognitive Development,* San Francisco: Academic, 1984.

Goleman, D., *Emotional Intelligence: Why It Can Matter More Than IQ,* New York: Bantam Books, 1995.

Goleman, D., *Working with Emotional Intelligence*, New York: Bantam Books, 1998.

Gosso, M.F., Van Belzen, M, De Geus, E.J., et al., 'Association Between the CHRM2 Gene and Intelligence in a Sample of 304 Dutch Families,' *Genes Brain Behav*, **5**(8): 577–84, doi:10.1111/j.1601-183X.2006.00211.x, PMID 17081262, November 2006.

Gray, J.R., Psychology Department, Yale University, and Thompson, P.M., Laboratory of Nero Imaging, Department of Neurology, University of California, Los Angeles School of Medicine, *"Neurobiology of Intelligence: Science and Ethics"* (PDF), Nature Publishing Group, Volume **5**, Retrieved on August 6, 2006, June 2004.

Griffith, J.H., *The Psychology of Human Behaviour*, London: George Allen, 1933.

Gross, R.D., *Psychology: The Science of Mind and Behavior* (2nd ed.), London: Hodder and Stoughton Educational, 1992.

Guilford, J.P., *The Nature of Human Intelligence*, New York: McGraw-Hill, 1967.

Guilford, J.P., *Intelligence has Three Facets,* Science, **160**, 615–620, 1968.

Guilford, J.P., 'Cognitive Psychology's Ambiguities: Some Suggested Remedies,' *Psychological Review*, **89**, 48–59, 1982.

Guilford, J.P., and Hoepfner, R., *The Analysis of Intelligence,* 1971.

Guralnick, M.J. (Eds.), *The Effectiveness of Early Intervention*, Baltimore: Brookes, 1997.

Haier, R., 'Human Intelligence Determined by Volume and Location of Gray Matter Tissue in Brain,' Brain Research Institute, UC Irvine College of Medicine, Retrieved on August 6, 2006, July 19, 2004.

Hatch, T., *Social Intelligence in Young Children.* Paper presented at the meeting of the American Psychological Association, 1990.

Hohmann, G., 'Some Effects of Spinal Cord Lesions on Experienced Emotional Feelings,' *Psychophysiology*, **3**, 143–156, 1966.

Hunter, J.E., and Hunter, R.F., 'Validity and Utility of Alternative Predictors of Job Performance,' *Psychological Bulletin*, **96**, 72–98, 1984.

Jaeggi, S.M., Buschkuehl, M., Jonides, J., and Perrig, W.J., 'Improving Fluid Intelligence with Training on Working Memory,' *Proc. Natl. Acad. Sci.* U.S.A. **105** (19): 6829–33, doi:10.1073/pnas.0801268105, PMID 18443283, May 2008.

Jencks, D., *Inequality: A Reassessment of the Effect of Family and Schooling in America*, New York: Basic Books, 1972.

Klingberg, T., Forssberg, H., Westerberg, H., 'Training of Working Memory in Children with ADHD,' *J. Clin. Exp Neuropsychol.* **24** (6): 781–91, PMID 12424652, 2002.

Kirp, D.L., 'After the Bell Curve,' *New York Times Magazine*, Retrieved on August 6, 2006, July 23, 2006.

Koonce, R., 'Emotional IQ, A New Secret of Success?,' *Training and Development,* **50** (2), 19, 1996.

Loehlin, J.C., Lindzey, G. and Spuhler, J.N., *Race Difference in Intelligence*, San Francisco: W.H. Freeman, 1969.

Loehlin, J.C., and Nichols, R.C., *Heredity, Environment, and Personality: A Study of 850 Sets of Twins,* Austin; University of Texas Press, 1976.

Lynn, R., 'Race Differences in Intelligence: A Global Perspective,' *Mankind Quarterly,* **31**, 254–296, 1991a.

Lynn, R., 'The Evolution of Racial Differences in Intelligence,' *Mankind Quarterly*, **32**, 99–121, 1991b.

Lynn, R., 'Sex Differences in Intelligence and Brain Size: A Paradox Resolved,' *Personality and Individual Differences*, **17**, 257–271, 1994.

Lynn, R., 'Racial and Ethnic Differences in Intelligence in the United States on the Difference Ability Scale,' *Personality and Individual Differences*, **17**, 271–273, 1994.

Lynn, R., and Irwing, P., 'Sex Differences on the Progressive Matrices: A Meta-Analysis,' *Intelligence*, **32**, 481–498, 2004.

Malandro, L.A., Barker, L., and Barker, D.A., *Nonverbal Communication* (3rd ed.), New York: Random House, 1994.

Mandelli L., Serretti A., Colombo C., et al., 'Improvement of Cognitive Functioning in Mood Disorder Patients with Depressive Symptomatic Recovery During Treatment: An Exploratory Analysis,' *Psychiatry Clin. Neurosci.*, **60**(5): 598–604. doi:10.1111/j.1440–1819.2006.01564.x. PMID 16958944, http://www.blackwell-synergy.com/doi/abs/10.1111/j.1440-1819.2006.01564.x., October 2006.

Mayer, J.D. and Salovey, P., 'What is Emotional Intelligence?,' in P. Salovey and D. Suter (Eds.), *Emotional Development, Emotional Literacy, and Emotional Intelligence*, New York: Basic Books, 1997.

Mc Crae, R.R. and Costa, P.T., 'Updating Norman's "Adequate Taxonomy": Intelligence and Personality Dimensions in Natural Language and in Questionnaires,' *Journal of Personality and Social Psychology*, **49**, 710–721, 1985.

McDaniel, M.A., 'Big-brained People are Smarter: A Meta-analysis of the Relationship Between in Vivo Brain Volume and Intelligence,' *Intelligence*, **33**, 337–346, PDF, 2005.

McGue, M., Bouchard, T.J., Jr., Jaconon, W.G., and Lykken, D.T., 'Behavioral Genetics of Cognitive Ability: A Life-span Perspective,' in R. Plomin and G.E. McClearn (Eds.), *Nature, Nurture, and Psychology* (pp. 59–76), Washington, DC: American Psychological Association, 1993.

Mingroni, M.A., *Resolving the IQ Paradox: Heterosis as a Cause of the Flynn Effect and Other Trends*, pp. 806–829, 2007.

Munsinger, H.A., 'The Adopted Child's IQ: A Crucial Review,' *Psychological Bulletin*, Vol. **82**, 623–659, 1978.

Neisser, U., 'Never a Dull Moment,' *American Psychologist,* **52**, 79–81, 1997.

Neisser et al., 'Intelligence: Knowns and Unknowns,' *Board of Scientific Affairs of the American Psychological Association*, Retrieved on August 6, 2006, August 7, 1995.

Neisser, U., Boodoo, G., Bouchard, T.J., Jr., Bykin, A.W., Brody, N., Ceci, S.J., Halpern, D.F., and Urbina, S., 'Intelligence: Knowns and Unknowns,' *American Psychologist*, **51**, 77–101, 1996.

Nowicki, S. Jr., and Duke, M.P., *The Nowicki-Strickland Life-span Locus of Control Scales: Construct Validation,* in H.M. Lefcourt (Ed.), Research with the Locus of Control Construct (Vol. 2, pp 13–51), Orlando, FL: Academic Press. 1983.

Okanoya, K., Tokimoto, N., Kumazawa, N., Hihara, S., and Iriki, A., 'Tool-use Training in a Species of Rodent: The Emergence of an Optimal Motor Strategy and Functional Understanding,' PLoS ONE 3 (3): e1860, doi:10.1371/journal.pone.0001860. PMID 18365015, 2008.

Piaget, J., *The Origins of Intelligence in Children*, New York: W.W. Norton & Company, Inc., 1936, 1963.

Piaget, J., *The Origins of Intelligence in Children*, New York: International Universities Press, 1952.

Piaget, J., *The Psychology of Intelligence*, New York: Routledge, 1963, 2001.

Plomin, R., 'Genetics and Intelligence: What's New?,' *Intelligence,* **24**, 45–65, 1997.

Plomin, R., DeFries, J.C., McClearn, G.E., and McGuffin, P., *Behavioral Genetics* (4th Ed.)., New York: Worth Publishers.ttp://www.springerlink.com/content/t0844nw244473143/, Retrieved on 6 August 2006, 2001.

Plomin, R., Fulker, D.W., Corley, R., and DeFries, J.C., 'Nature, Nurture, and Cognitive Development from 1 to 16 years: A Parent-offspring Adoption Study,' *Psychological Science,* **8**, 442–447, 1997.

Plomin, R., Pedersen, N.L., Lichtenstein, P., and McClearn, G.E., 'Variability and Stability in Cognitive Abilities are Largely Genetic Later in Life,' *Behavior Genetics,* **24**(3): 207, doi:10.1007/BF01067188, h Plomin, R., DeFries, J. C., Craig, I. W., and McGuffin, P. (2003), Behavioral Genetics in the Postgenomic Era, Washington, DC: American Psychological Association, 05 1994.

Ramey, C.T., and Ramey, S.L., 'Early Intervention and Early Experience,' *American Psychologist*, **53**, 109–120, 1998.

Reed, T.E. and Jensen, A.R., 'Cranial Capacity: New Caucasian Data and Comments on Rushton's Claimed Mongoloid-Caucasoid Brain-size Differences,' *Intelligence*, **17**, 423–431. 1993.

Sackeim, H.A., Freeman, J., McElhiney, M., Coleman, E., Prudic, J., and Devanand, D.P., 'Effects of Major Depression on Estimates of Intelligence,' *J., Clin Exp. Neuropsychol.,* **14** (2): 268–88, PMID 1572949, March 1992.

Salovey, P., and Mayer, J.D., 'Emotional Intelligence,' *Imagination, Cognition, and Personality*, **9**, 185–211, 1990.

Salovey, P., and Mayer, J.D., 'Some Final Thoughts about Personality and Intelligence,' in R.J. Sternberg (Ed.), *Personality and Intelligence* (pp. 303–318), New York: Cambridge University Press, 1994.

Scarr, S., *Race, Social; Class, and Individual Differences in IQ: New Studies of Old Issues,* Hillsdale, NJ: Erlbaum, 1981.

Scarr, S. and Weinberg, R.A., 'IQ Test Performance of Black Children Adopted by White Families,' *American Psychologist*, **31**, 726–739, 1976.

Schellenberg, E.G., 'Music Lessons Enhance IQ,' *Psychol Sci.* **15**(8): 511–4, 2004.

Schmidt, F.L. and Hunter, J.E., 'The Validity and Utility of Selection Methods in Psychology: Practical and Theoretical Implications of 85 years of Research Findings,' *Psychological Bulletin*, **124**, 262–274, 1998.

Schoenemann, P.T., Sheehan, M.J. and Glotzer, L.D., 'Prefrontal White Matter Volume is Disproportionately Larger in Humans than in other Primates,' *Nat. Neurosci.*, **8**(2): 242–52, doi:10.1038/nn1394, PMID 15665874, 2005.

Shaw, P., Greenstein, D., Lerch, J., et al., 'Intellectual Ability and Cortical Development in Children and Adolescents,' *Nature*, **440** (7084): 676–9. doi:10.1038/nature04513, PMID 16572172, March 2006.

Shoda, Y., Mischel, W., and Peake, P.K., 'Predicting Adolescent Cognitive and Self-Regulatory Competencies from Preschool Delay of Gratification,' *Developmental Psychology*, **26**, 978–986, 1990.

Sigman, M., 'Nutrition and Child Development: More Food for Thought,' *Current Directions in Psychological Science*, **4**, 52–55, 1995.

Skeels, H.M., 'Mental Development of Children in Foster Homes,' *Journal of Consulting Psychology*, **2**, 33–43, 1938.

Skeels, H.M., *Ability Status of Children with Contrasting Early Life Experience,* Society for Research in Child Development Monographs, **31**(3), 1–5, 1966.

Spearman, C., 'General Intelligence,' Objectively Determined and Measured, *American Journal of Psychology*, **15**, 201–293, 1904.

Spearman, C., *The Nature of Intelligence and the Principles of Cognition*, London: Macmillan, 1923.

Spearman, C., *The Abilities of Man*, London: Macmillan, 1927.

Stern, W., *The Psychological Methods of Intelligence Testing* (G. Whipple, Trans.), Baltimore: Warwick and York, 1914.

Sternberg, R.J., *Intelligence, Information Processing, and Analogical Reasoning,* 1977.

Sternberg, R.J., *Beyond I.Q.: A Triarchic Theory of Human Intelligence*, London: Cambridge University Press, 1985a.

Sternberg, R.J., *Human Abilities: An Information-processing Approach,* New York: Freeman, 1985b.

Sternberg, R.J., *The Triarchic Mind: A New Theory of Human Intelligence,* New York: Penguin, 1989.

Sternberg, R.J., *Metaphors of Mind: Conceptions of the Nature of Intelligence*, 1990.

Sternberg, R.J. and Wagner, R.K., *Practical Intelligence: Origins of Competence in the Everyday World,* New York: Cambridge University Press, 1986.

Sternberg, R.J., Wagner, R.K., Williams, W.M., and Horvath, J.A., 'Testing Common Sense,' *American Psychologist*, **50**, 912–927, 1995.

Stoddard, G.D., *The Meaning of Intelligence*, New York: Macmillan, 1943.

Stumpf, H. and Jackson, D.N., 'Gender-related Differences in Cognitive Abilities: Evidence From a Medical School Admissions Program,' *Personality and Individual Differences*, **17**: 335–344, doi:10.1016/0191-8869(94)90281-X, 1994.

Taylor, M.D., 'Childhood IQ and Social Factors on Smoking Behaviour, Lung Function and Smoking-related Outcomes in Adulthood: Linking the Scottish Mental Survey 1932 and the Midspan Studies,' 1932.

Teasdale, Thomas, W., and David, R., Owen., 'A Long-term Rise and Recent Decline in Intelligence Test Performance: The Flynn Effect in Reverse,' *Personality and Individual Differences*, **39** (4):837–843, 2005.

Teasdale, Thomas, W., and David R. Owen, 'The End of the Flynn Effect, A Study of Secular Trends in Mean Intelligence Scores of Norwegian Conscripts During Half a Century,' Retrieved on August 6, 2006.

Terman, L.M., 'The Discovery and Encouragement of Exceptional Talent,' *American Psychologist*, **9**, 221–230, 1954.

Terman, L.M., and Merrill, M.A., *Measuring Intelligence*, Boston: Houghton Mifflin, 1937.

Thompson, G.H., *The Factorial Analysis of Human Ability*, London: London University Press, 1939.

Thompson, P.M., Cannon, T.D., Narr, K.L., et al., 'Genetic Influences on Brain Structure,' *Nat. Neurosci*, **4**(12): 1253–8, doi:10.1038/nn758, PMID 11694885, 2001.

Thomson, G.H., *The Factor Analysis of Human Ability,* (3rd ed.), Boston: Houghton Mifflin, 1948.

Thorndike, E.L., *Animal Intelligence*, New York: Macmillan, 1911.

Thurstone, L.L., *The Nature of Intelligence*, London: Routledge, 1924/1973.

Thurstone, L.L., 'The Vectors of the mind, Address of the President Before the American Psychological Association,' Chicago Meeting, September, 1933, First Published in *Psychological Review*, **41**, 1–32, 1934.

Thurstone, L.L., *Primary Mental Abilities*, Chicago: University of Chicago Press, 1938.

Thurstone, L.L., *Multiple-Factor Analysis*, Chicago: University of Chicago Press, 1947.

Thurstone, L.L. and Thurstone, T.G., *Factorial Studies of Intelligence*, Chicago: University of Chicago Press, 1941.

Turkheimer, E., Haley, A., Waldron, M., D'Onofrio, B. and Gottesman II, 'Socioeconomic Status Modifies Heritability of IQ in Young Children,' *Psychol Sci.,* **14** (6):6238, PMID14629696,http://www.blackwellsynergy.com/openurl?genre=article&sid=nlm:pubmed&issn=0956-7976&date=2003&volume=14&issue=6&spage=623, November 2003.

Wade, N., 'Scans Show Different Growth for Intelligent Brains,' *Brain Research Institute*, UCLA. Retrieved on August 6, 2006, March 30, 2006.

Warner, M.H., Ernst, J., Townes, B.D., Peel, J. and Preston, M., 'Relationships between IQ and Neuropsychological Measures in Neuropsychiatric Populations: Within-Laboratory and Cross-Cultural Replications Using WAIS and WAIS-R,' *J. Clin. Exp. Neuropsychol*, **9** (5): 545–62. PMID 3667899, October 1987.

Wechsler, D., *The Measurement of Adult Intelligence* (3rd ed.), New York: Williams and Wilkins, 1944.

Wechsler, D., *Manual for the Wechsler Adult intelligence Scale*, New York: Psychological Corporation, 1981.

Wechsler, D., *Wechsler Adult Intelligence Scale-Third Edition*, San Antonio, TX: The Psychological Corporation, 1997.

Wechsler, D., *Wechsler Intelligence Scale for Children-Fourth Edition*, San Antonio, TX: The Psychological Corporation, 2003.

Whalley, L.J., Starr, JIM., Athawes, R, Hunter, D., Pattie, A. and Deary, I.J., 'Childhood Mental Ability and Dementia,' *Neurology,* **55**(10): 1455–9, PMID 11094097, http://www.neurology.org/cgi/pmidlookup?view=long&pmid=11094097, November 2000.

Wheeler, R.H., *The Science of Psychology* (2nd ed.), New York: Crowel, 1940.

Williams, G.C., Grow, V.M., Freedman, Z.R., Ryan, R.M., and Deci, E.I., 'Motivational Predictors of Weight Loss and Weight-Loss Maintenance,' *Journal of Personality and Social Psychology*, **790**, 115–126, 1996.

Woodberry, K.A., Giuliano, A.J., and Seidman, L.J., 'Premorbid IQ in Schizophrenia: A Meta-Analytic Review,' *Am. J. Psychiatry.,* **165(**5): 579–87, doi:10.1176/appi.ajp.2008.07081242, PMID 18413704, May 2008.

Woodworth, R.S., *Racial Differences in Mental Traits, Science,* 31 (788), 171–186, 1910.

Wortman, C.B., Loftus, E.F., Marshall, M.E., *Psychology* (4th Ed.), New York: McGraw-Hill, Inc., 1992.

Zajonc, R.B., *Family Configuration and Intelligence*, Science, Vol. 192, 226–236, 1976.

Zajonc, R.B., *Mining New Gold from Old Research*, Psychology Today, 1986.

Zillman, D., *Anger,* In Encyclopedia of Mental Health. New York: Harcourt Brace, 1996.

Zinkstok, J.R., de Wilde, O., van Amelsvoort, T.A., Tanck, M.W., Baas, F. and Linszen, D.H., *"Association Between the DTNBP1 Gene and Intelligence: A Case-Control Study in Young Patients with Schizophrenia and Related Disorders and Unaffected Siblings",* Behav Brain Funct **3**:19, doi:10.1186/1744-9081-3-19, PMID 17445278, PMC: 1864987, http://www.behavioralandbrainfunctions.com/content/3/1/19, 2007.

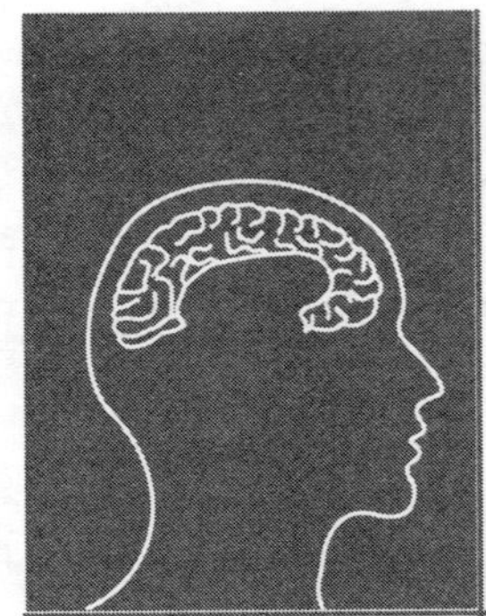

CHAPTER 13
Personality

Interest in personality is as old as civilization. Ancient philosophers and poets often speculated about why individuals were unique and why they differed from each other in so many ways. Personality usually refers to that which is unique about individuals—the characteristics that distinguish one person from its group. Personality implies predictability about how a person will act or react under different circumstances.

13.1 LITERAL MEANING OF THE TERM "PERSONALITY"

The term "Personality" is derived from the Latin word "*Persona*", which means a theatrical mask used by actors or worn by actors in those days to indicate their role in theatrical play.

People ordinarily think that personality means reputation or physical attractiveness, overall charm of a person. They think that Personality is a thing or quality possessed by all of us on the basis of the physical make-up. Personality does not simply mean the outward appearance of a person. In addition to the outer self, it also refers to her or his inner self. So, personality is the totality of a man, both his inner and outer qualities interacting with each other.

Personality is a pattern of characteristic feelings, thoughts, and behaviours that persists across time and situations. Personality is "The underlying causes within the person of individual behaviour and experience" (Cloninger, 1993 and Phares, 1979).

Personality is an individual's unique and relatively stable patterns of behaviour, thoughts, and emotions (Nelson and Miller, 1995; Zuckerman, 1995). Personality is the psychological forces that make people uniquely themselves (Friedman and Schustack, 1999).

Warren states that "Personality is the entire mental organization of a human being at any stage of development." This refers to the organization of personal traits. Every human being and personality is a completely integrated functioning unit or a complete whole.

When psychologists define personality, they tend to refer to qualities within a person, characteristics of a person's behaviour or both.

13.2 DEFINITIONS OF PERSONALITY

Morton Prince (1929) tried to give personality a broader base by accepting the role of both environmental and hereditary factors in constituting what is termed "personality". In his words, "Personality is the sum total of all the biological innate dispositions, impulses, tendencies, appetites, and instincts of the individual and the dispositions and tendencies acquired by experience."

Personality cannot be described through merely summing up the various elements involved in it. This definition was criticized on the ground that it does not present an integrated and organized view of personality. It would be like describing a house as a collection of bricks.

John Broadus Watson (1930), the founder of behaviourism, on the basis of behavioural studies, concluded—Personality is the sum of activities that can be discovered by actual observations over a long enough period of time to give reliable information. He tried to make "personality" synonymous with the consistent behaviour patterns of an individual. This, however, reflected a very narrow meaning of the term "personality".

According to Dashiell (1949), an individual's personality is the "Total picture of his organized behaviour, especially as it can be characterized by his fellow men in a consistent way."

Woodworth (1958) defined Personality as the "quality of the individual's total behaviour."

Munn (1967) gave a more comprehensive analysis pointing out that personality is the "Most characteristic integration of an individual's structure and activities." It is characteristic in a dual sense because (i) it is unique, thus differentiating the individual from all others, and (ii) it is fairly consistent, representing the customary integration of a particular individual's structures and activities.

According to Cattell (1975), "Personality is that which permits a prediction of what a person will do in a given situation."

According to Child (1975), personality consists of "More or less stable, internal factors that make one person's behaviour consistent from one time to another and different from the behaviour other people would manifest in comparable situations." There are four key terms used in this definition: Stable—Personality remains relatively constant or unchanging over time; Internal—Personality lies within us, but the ways in which we behave are determined in part by our personality; Consistent—if personality remains constant over time, and if personality determines behaviour, then we would expect that people would behave in fairly consistent ways; Different—when we talk of personality, we assume that there are considerable individual differences, which lead different people to behave differently in similar situations.

According to Eysenck (1971), "Personality is the more or less stable and enduring organization of a person's character, temperament, intellect, and physique, which determine his unique adjustment to the environment."

S.R. Maddi (1976), an American psychologist in his work, "*Personality Theories—A Comparative Analysis*", views personality as an organized and integrated whole of definite characteristics and tendencies within the individual which makes him. According to Maddi, "Personality is the stable set of characteristics and tendencies that determine commonalities and differences in the psychological behaviour (thoughts, feelings, and action) of people that have continuity in time and that may not be easily understood in terms of the social and biological pressures of the immediate situation alone."

After evaluating 49 different definitions from the literature, Gordon W. Allport (1937, 1948, and 1961) concluded "Personality is the **dynamic organization** within the individual of those **psycho-physical systems** that **determine** his characteristic behaviour and thought (or **unique adjustment to the environment**)." A brief explanation of the key terms used in Allport's definition is given below:

(i) *Dynamic:* "Dynamic" refers to the constantly evolving or changing nature of personality. The changes are not radical nor are they necessarily permanent.

(ii) *Organization:* "Organization" emphasizes the patterning of the independent parts of the personality structure, each of which has a special relation to the whole. A normal healthy personality is a highly correlated structured person. The abnormal personality shows disorganization.

(iii) *Psycho-physical systems:* A "psycho-physical system" is composed of habits, attitudes, emotional states, sentiments, motives, and beliefs, all of which are psychological but have a physical basis in the individual's neural, glandular, or general bodily states. As Allport (1961) said, "This term reminds us that personality is neither exclusively mental nor exclusively neural (physical). Its organization entails the functioning of both "mind" and "body" in some inextricable unity."

(iv) *Determine:* The word "determine" emphasizes the motivational role of the psycho-physical systems. Allport, "All the systems that comprise personality are to be regarded as determining tendencies. They exert a directive influence upon all the adjustive and expressive acts by which the personality comes to be known."

(v) *Unique:* Strictly speaking, every adjustment of every person is unique in time, place, and quality. In this sense, the activities as well as the potentialities of two seemingly alike persons are actually very different in quality, though the difference is generally with certain area or field.

(vi) *Adjustment to the environment:* This aspect is related to the functional and evolutionary significance of personality which depicts dealing with the environment. How does a person adjust to physical, geographical, social, and environmental surroundings express his personality. It is only a reactive adjustment, which is made on animal level. It is spontaneous and creative behaviour, sometime passively surrendering to, sometimes actually mastering the situation.

Although, Allport tried to give a comprehensive definition of the term "personality" by recognizing its dynamic nature and organizational aspects and by emphasizing the role it can play in an individual's adjustment to his environment. Allport's definition suffered from serious defects. In emphasizing the dynamic organization within the individual, he seems to view personality as somewhat different from the individual, within him, rather than as an integrated unity of mind and body. Personality, to him, is something put into the individual like water is put into a jug and it takes the shape of the jug.

Psychologist Walter Mischel (1977) mentioned both these processes and behaviour but emphasized behaviour. Personality, he wrote, consists of "The distinctive patterns of behaviour (including thoughts and emotions) that characterize each individual's adaptation to the situations of his or her life."

According to Burger (1990), Byrne and Shulte (1990), "Personality is generally defined as individual's unique and relatively stable patterns of behaviour, thoughts, and emotions."

Psychologists who investigate personality tend to define it as the reasonable stable patterns of emotions, motives, and behaviour that distinguish people from one another (Prigatano, 1992).

According to Bootzin (1997), "Personality is an individual's characteristic and distinctive patterns of thinking, feeling, and behaving."

Personality is usually defined as an individual's distinctive and relatively stable patterns of behaviour, motives, thoughts, and traits, characteristics that describe a person across situations (Wade and Tavris, 1998).

No single definition of personality is acceptable to all psychologists. However, most agree that personality includes the behaviour patterns a person shows across situations or the psychological characteristics of the person that lead to those behaviour patterns. Personality, deeply ingrained, is relatively enduring patterns of thought, feeling, and behaviour.

Characteristics of Personality

Personality has so many characteristics. Some of these characteristics are mentioned below:

1. It is stable.
2. It is dynamic.
3. It is unique and specific.
4. It is consistent.
5. It is persistent.
6. It is integrated.
7. It is all pervasive.
8. It is the product of heredity and environment.
9. It is assessable and measurable.
10. It is goal-directed.
11. It is a collection of many traits and attributes.
12. It is an organization of some psycho-physical systems or behavioural characteristics.
13. It is capable of change and modification.
14. It is different from character and temperament.
15. It exhibits self-consciousness.
16. It includes all behaviour patterns—cognitive, affective, and conative.

Character

Allport showed that traditionally the word "character" has implied some code of behaviour in terms of which individuals or their acts are appraised. Thus, in describing an individual's character, the word "good" or "bad" is often employed. Allport (1961) suggested that character is an ethical concept and stated that "We prefer to define character as personality evaluated, and personality as character devaluated." Character is shaped more by congenial environment.

Temperament

"Temperament" ordinarily refers to those dispositions that are closely linked to biological or physiological determinants and that consequently show relatively little modification with development. The role of heredity is naturally somewhat greater here than in the case of some other aspects of personality. Temperament is believed to be determined mainly by heredity. According to H.J. Eysenck, "Temperament refers to an individual's typical moods and activity level, and it is usually assumed that temperament is determined mainly by heredity." Temperament is the raw material along with intelligence and physique out of which Personality is fashioned or shaped. Eysenck's theory of Personality can be regarded as a theory of temperament as well as of personality.

13.3 DETERMINANTS OF PERSONALITY (BIOLOGICAL AND SOCIOCULTURAL DETERMINANTS) OR FACTORS AFFECTING PERSONALITY

13.3.1 The Concept of Personality Determinants

"Personality determinants" are the forces which modify and channel the expression of our basic needs and which, in fact, predetermine certain needs and motives. These are the forces and conditions that make each of us resemble all other persons, some other persons, and no other persons. The patterns we can discover in our inheritance and in those events and forces in our life that have affected us may be called the *determinants of personality*. Psychologists, sociologists, anthropologists use several systems for classifying these determinants.

An individual is the by-product of heredity and environment. An individual is the by-product of constant interaction of hereditary and environmental factors. These two factors contribute to the development of an individual. The way an individual is like or different from other individuals in her or his performance and personality is due to these factors. The factors affecting personality can be divided into two classes—biological and social. A few specifically important forces that determine the structuring, developing, shaping, and organizing of personality are being discussed here below:

Biological Determinants or Genetic Determinants or Biological-Constitutional Determinants (forces and tendencies that are physiological in nature)

Biological-constitutional determinants are those that are inherited like traits, tendencies, and limitations, as well as those that have to do with a bodily defect, such as an amputation or a sight or hearing loss resulting from disease or illness. Biological-constitutional determinants have to do with the physiological characteristics that affect our lives.

The organism is born with certain biological inheritance. Genetic factors are basic that determine the personality development of an individual. Physiological determinants such as ductless glands, nervous system, emotions, and motivation all play an important role in the development of an individual's personality.

1. **Glandular Development and Activity of Ductless Glands or Endocrine Glands:** Glandular development and activity affect personality in a number of ways. Ductless or endocrine glands, so called because they discharge their secretions or hormones directly into the bloodstream or send their secretions directly to the blood without ducts (tubes), influence the behaviour of individuals according to their balance or imbalance. The endocrine glands appear to be a complex interdependent system which maintains the chemical balance of the body. Growth and health are significantly dependent on them and our mental and emotional lives are both the cause and the effect of their functions. Their secretions are called *hormones;* these hormones are responsible for many changes in the personality. Each gland secretes one or more types of hormones. For a detailed discussion about hormones, refer to Chapter 3. Some studies done on abnormal glandular conditions provide evidences to the fact that hormones secreted through these glands (such as thyroid, adrenal, sex glands, pituitary, pancreas, etc.) have an impact on personality. Over secretion (hyper-secretion) or undersecretion (hypo-secretion) by any of these glands may exert a tremendous influence upon an individual's development and consequently upon his personality (Hoskins, 1933) Insufficient secretions from the thyroid gland, for example, can make a person lethargic and sluggish. Personality changes, as shown in altered attitudes and behaviour, can be induced by the administration of glandular extracts and similar substances.

2. **Height:** Height frequently has a noticeable effect on personality. We are all familiar with the tendency of many short people to be pugnacious or argumentative or confrontational and "cocky" or boastful and, we can attribute this tendency partly to an effort to compensate the feeling that one is less adequate physically than a taller person. Research indicates that leaders tend to be taller and heavier than the average, but whether the height of a leader is due entirely to inherited tendencies or to others factors—for example, better nutrition—is yet to be discovered.

3. **Heredity:** Heredity or inherited pre-dispositions is an important determinant of personality. "Heredity" means the biological transmission of genetic characteristics from parent to offspring or child. Many psychologists hold that the differences in personalities are due to the differences in zygote or cell from which life of an individual begins or

originates. Some characteristic features of personality, such as intelligence, interests, talents, emotional expressions, stress tolerance, etc. is thought as inherited pre-dispositions. Heredity does not completely determine any characteristic or trait but it provides basis or potential for the development of any personality trait. Training and experiences in the environment contribute to the development of traits. Heredity influences physique, motor-sensory equipment and level of intelligence. Recently, it has also been established that certain diseases and temperamental characteristics are also inherited from forefathers or ancestors.

4. **Nervous System:** According to Kempf, the author of "*The Autonomic Function of Personality*", the nervous system is one of the important determinants of personality. The autonomic nervous system plays an important role. Several research studies have documented the role of nervous system in extraversion, introversion, neuroticism—the important traits of personality and in emotions.

5. **Physique or Physical Structure:** Another important biological determinant affecting personality is physique. "Physique" is the structure and anatomical organization of the body. Physique constitutes size of the body, complexion of the skin, general health, physical deformities, etc. A balanced combination of all these features is an eye-catching and attractive personality. But owing to poor physique, people are subject to humiliation, bias, and prejudice, which arouses inferiority complex in them. It is also observed that people's behaviour towards other individuals is modified, to some extent, according to their physique or physical structure.

6. **Pigmentation of the Skin:** Skin pigmentation has implications for personality, particularly if it differs from the pigmentation of the dominant group of the society. What effect it has depends partly on the culture. Commonly, those with dark skin are considered unattractive.

7. **Temperament:** Temperament has important implications for personality. Individual's first personality is temperamental in nature and it is on this initial behaviour pattern that the framework of his personality is erected. The personality of an infant is constituted almost entirely by its temperament, and this is what forms the basis of the reaction of others to the child. Parents always have certain expectations (largely unconscious) from their newly born or unborn children. Parents are upset by infants who demand much attention, and do not expect them to be nuisances, and are pleased by those who do not. The temperament of an infant is not only an important ingredient in her or his budding or growing personality, but it directly affects and conditions the emotional climate of her or his family, which in turn, has effect on her or his personality. The emotional climate not only tends to persist into childhood

but also forms the basis of the child's expectations of herself or himself, her or his self-structure. In this way, the temperament of the infant sets up waves and counterwaves of feelings, which constitute the forces moulding her or his personality during its earliest stages.

8. **Body Type:** To some psychologists, body type appears to be related to certain characteristics. W.H. Sheldon has related certain personality types to certain body types. However, the methodology Sheldon used, raised serious questions as to the validity of his findings. Even if Sheldon's findings are accepted, it cannot be said that the personality traits he demonstrated are caused by the type of body structure. It may be that to have a certain kind of temperament and to grow up in a certain kind of emotional climate means that one will develop a certain kind of body. Or, what is more likely, all these factors may be interrelated without one necessarily causing another.

DDrugs, deficiency of different vitamins in the body, long illnesses also causes some changes in the personality.

Psychologists differ in the emphasis they place on the importance of biological-constitutional factors in personality development.

Socio-cultural determinants

Hereditary factors, including the biogenic determinants and environment in which one grows and develops, interact with each other in shaping and developing of one's unique personality. The environments of different individuals are very much different from one another and also their effects. Environmental influences begin since the time of the conception of the foetus in the womb of the mother. Mother's physical, mental, and emotional health or conditions influence the growth and development of the foetus. Physical, geographical, and social conditions of the external environment play an important role in shaping the personality of individuals. Environmental factors include mainly the geographical or physical and the home and the school environment.

Some of the important socio-cultural determinants affecting personality of an individual are discussed below:

1. **Home:** The home environment or atmosphere plays an important role in shaping the personality pattern of an individual. The first environment, the child moves in, is her or his home. In fact, home is a place where the foundations of personality are laid. Family is the major socializing agent during early years of life in the development of personality. The relation of the child with the parents, especially mother, is most intimate. Presence of parental love is very essential for the development of healthy personality. Family warmth is an important contributor to personality. Children coming from homes where good morale pattern dominated were better adjusted, more independent, and more satisfactorily related to their

parents than were the average adolescents of the group (Stott, 1939). The child learns various socially valued skills, etiquettes, manners, habits, beliefs, attitudes, ways of adjusting to problems, and values in the family. Child rearing practices adopted by parents, rewards and punishments used, parental expectations, parental attitudes, interpersonal relationships help in determining and developing personality traits. Within the family, parents become models for their children. Albert Bandura (1977), a social learning theorist, concluded that a child learns much by imitation.

The parents' attitudes towards the child, towards each other, and towards other people, events, and objects exercise a potent or powerful influence upon the child's developing personality (Symonds, 1939). Margaret Ribble (1944) reported that lack of adequate cuddling and other close physical contact with some friendly adult or family member can impose serious handicaps on the growing infant. Hilgard (1952) and Baldwin (1942) found that the parents usually unconsciously relieve their own childhood problems through their children. Factors such as enjoyment of group, family life, little if any work done away from by the mother, amount of punishment, welcoming of the child's friends to the home, emotional control and good health of parents, and sharing of joys and sorrow with the parents may lead to good adjustment on the part of adolescents (Crow and Crow, 1973; Landis, 1952). Many other factors, such as size of the family, ordinal position of the child, sex-distribution, sibling rivalry, sex compositional pattern of siblings in the family, etc. are also important familial correlates of personality. Disturbed family structure exposes the children to stressors, conflicts and feelings of insecurity and rejection. Those coming from homes showing family discord pattern were, generally, poorly adjusted in their social environment (Stott, 1931; 1941). So, a congenial home atmosphere with good relations with parents and other family members is essential for a healthy personality.

2. **Neighbourhood:** People who live in the neighbourhood, influence the development of personality. Neighborhood is like second home where the child interacts with other children. This interaction helps the child to learn various traits, skills, and responses. A stable neighborhood permits the development of cooperation, sympathy, affection, and caring attitude.

3. **School:** School, a primary social group, is another factor that influences personality because a significant part of a child's life is spent in school. Obviously, much of the child's personality is already shaped in home before she or he comes to school. The child interacts with teachers, classmates, schoolmates, and school administrators. The suitability of curricular offerings, type of curriculum and examination, attitudes of the teachers, teacher-taught relationships, relationships of the child with her or his fellow classmates and schoolmates, playground activities,

institutional rules and regulations, competitiveness, emotional tone, social climate, instructional process are all important correlates for the makeup of the child's personality. The school has an important role to shape, mould, and regulate the personality of children by creating better emotional atmosphere, better teaching methods, use of catharsis, and by providing guidance and counselling.

The companions, classmates, friends, schoolmates influence the child's ideas, attitudes, intellect, morals, conduct, and personality. The teacher or the teachers substitute the parents. Her or his behaviour plays a significant role in the development of child's personality. The teacher is an important constituent in the instructional process. The attitude of the teacher towards teaching is an important variable. The teacher must have a positive attitude toward teaching and life, in general. The primary attribute of a good and effective teacher is the ability to create a warm, friendly atmosphere. The democratic atmosphere is flexible and child-centered; it permits maximum personality development for the child, prepares her or him for group living and for making her or his own decisions and gives superior training in emotional self-control. Teaching should be tailored or geared to the needs of the children. The teacher must have sympathetic attitude towards the slow learners, delinquents, and other deviant children.

4. **Economic Factors:** Economic factors greatly determine some of the important personality traits. Poverty of parents and lack of money to fulfil the legitimate needs of their children lead directly to frustration. Socio-economic inferiority is a well-known cause of the development of undesirable personality traits among young people. A low economic status and a maladjusted personality often go together, though not in all cases. A number of studies have documented a strong relationship between the poverty status of parents and lower IQs in children at least up to 5 years of age, with persistent poverty having the most adverse effects (Duncan et al., 1994; McLoyd, 1998). These adverse effects of poverty on cognitive functioning seem to occur as a function of a variety of factors associated with poverty, including poor physical health or low birth weight at birth, higher risk of prenatal exposure to drugs, higher risk of lead poisoning, and less cognitive stimulation in the home environment (McLoyd, 1998). Antisocial personality disorder is strongly related to social class, occurring at three times the rate in the lowest income category as in the highest income category, whereas depressive disorders occur only about 50 percent more often in the lowest income category as in the highest income category (Kessler et al., 1994).

Unemployment, coupled with slow down or recession and inflation, is a source of chronic anxiety for many people. Unemployment can be damaging financially as well as psychologically. Periods of extensive unemployment are typically accompanied by financial hardships, self-devaluation, demoralization, emotional distress, somatic complaints, depression, hostility, marital problems, and physical violence among couples. The wives of unemployed men suffer from anxiety, depression, and hostility (Dew, Bromet, and Schoolberg, 1987). Many studies report that the unemployed fathers engage in child abuse (Cicchetti and Lynch, 1995; Dew et al., 1991).

5. **Ordinal Position in The Family:** Ordinal position in the family—whether oldest, middle, youngest or only child—influences the personality pattern to a great extent. Alfred Adler emphasized the importance of birth order in the development of personality. Adler believed that the pattern of child's personality depends upon her or his position in the family. The birth order of the child fixes her or his status in the family which decides her or his roles that affect the personality. Whether the child strives for superiority or feels inferior or isolated, as also her or his emotional relationship with her or his parents, brothers and sisters, and several other personality traits depend upon this position. Her or his position in the family has much to do with the role—hence, the personality—of the individual. Oldest sons in patriarchal families frequently develop "crown-prince" characteristics of behaviour; they look upon themselves as "assistant fathers", are dominant, have a strong sense of responsibility, are self-sufficient, and tend to take themselves very seriously. The birth of another child in the family has an important influence on the first child, since it takes away her or his monopoly in affection and sometimes she or he is neglected altogether. Hence, she or he feels jealous with the younger child and tries to regain her or his rights. Frequently, the oldest child is the object of more anxiety on the part of the parents than are younger children; she or he is also likely to be more jealous. So, an eldest child may be of authoritarian type of personality. The middle child finds herself or himself faced by the choice of competing with her or his older siblings, criticizing and depreciating them, or falling back to the level of the younger siblings. The youngest child in the family is treated with love and affection by everyone, hence she or he becomes overdependent. The youngest child tends to have her or his "babyhood" prolonged by her or his parents and siblings. Discipline tends to be less strict with him, and his siblings are likely to fight his battles for him. A single child may be of careless temparament. But, the parental attitude is more important in determining the personality of the child.

6. **Early Childhood Experiences:** Childhood experiences are decisive determinants of personality in later life. Most theories of personality development emphasise the importance of early childhood experiences in importance shaping her or his personality and the main directions that a person's coping style will be. In fact, every experience from the moment of conception till death affects the personality. Traumatic experiences or

psychic traumas in the childhood temporarily shatter our feelings of security, adequacy, and worth, and influence our perceptions of ourselves and our environment. Parental deprivation in childhood, according to Sigmund Freud (1856–1939), might result in fixation at the oral stage of psycho-sexual development; according to Erik Erikson (1902–1994), it might interfere with the development of basic trust; according to Harry Stack Sullivan (1892–1949), it might stunt the development of the child's capacity for relatively anxiety-free exchanges of tenderness and intimacy with others; according to B.F. Skinner (1904–1990), it might retard the attainment of needed skills because of a lack of available reinforcements; according to Aaron Temkin Beck (Born in 1921), it might result in the child acquiring dysfunctional schemas and self-schemas in which relationship are represented as unstable, untrustworthy, and without affection. Feeding, weaning, toilet training, child-rearing practices, parents' attitudes, inconsistent discipline play an important role in the development of personality.

7. **Inter-Personal Relations:** An individual interacts with different members of the society as she or he grows and these interpersonal interaction and relations are important means which help in the development of certain social personality characteristics and traits, which in turn result in dynamic changes in response tendencies to make better adjustment. Subgroups within a general socio-cultural environment—such as family, sex, age, class, occupational, ethnic, and religious groups foster beliefs and norms of their own, largely by means of social roles that their members learn to adopt. When social roles are conflicting, unclear, or uncomfortable, or when an individual is unable to achieve a satisfactory role in a group, healthy personality development may be impaired.

8. **Parenting Styles:** Parenting styles can have a significant impact on a child's development. Four types of parenting styles have been identified that seem to be related to different developmental outcomes for the children. These styles vary in the degree of parental warmth (amount of support, encouragement, and affection versus shame, rejection, and hostility) and in the degree of parental control (extent of discipline and monitoring versus being largely unsupervised).

(i) *Authoritative parenting style:* In authoritative parenting style, parents are both very warm and set clear limits and restrictions to the behaviour of children and this parenting style is related with positive outcomes.

(ii) *Authoritarian parenting style:* In authoritarian parenting style, parents are high on control and low on warmth. This parenting style is related with negative outcomes; conflicted, irritable, moody children, poor, social and cognitive skills, and aggressive behaviour.

(iii) *Permissive-Indulgent parenting style:* In permissive-indulgent parenting style, parents are high on warmth, low on control and discipline. This style of parenting is associated with impulsive and aggressive behaviour and children. Much permissiveness and little discipline in the home is associated with antisocial and aggressive behaviour. Overly indulged children are spoiled, selfish, impatient, inconsiderate, and demanding. Indulged children enter readily into inter-personal relationships, but they exploit people for their own purposes in the same way that they have learned to exploit their parents (Million and Davis, 1945).

(iv) *Neglectful-uninvolved parenting style:* In neglectful-uninvolved parenting style, parents are low both on warmth and control. In neglectful parenting style, infants or children suffer from inadequate care at home. Parents typically neglect or devote little attention to their child or children and are generally rejecting. Parental rejection of a child may be demonstrated by parents in various ways—by physical neglect, denial of love or affection, lack of interest in child's activities and achievements, failure to spend time with the child, lack of respect for the child's feelings and rights, cruel and abusive treatment. This deprivation and rejection may lead to retarded growth and development, physiological disturbance, poor linguistic development, personality disorders, anger, and aggression.

Uninvolved parenting style is associated with moodiness, low self-esteem, conduct problems, problems with peer relations and with academic performance, and disruptions in attachment.

9. **Child Abuse:** Abuse (physical or sexual or both) of children has also been associated with negative effect on the development of child's or victim's personality. Child abuse has become a major public health problem, according to the World Health Organization (WHO). The findings on child abuse are so scary that each home appears unsafe for our young children, especially females. Abused children often have a tendency to be overly aggressive, socially withdrawn, self-injurious and suicidal behaviours, problems in social and emotional functioning, impaired relationships, depression, atypical or insecure attachment, relationship difficulties, anxiety, lower IQ and reading ability, lower academic achievement, inability to trust, and low self-esteem.

10. **Value Patterns:** The broader aspects of personality are shaped by the value patterns of the culture. The culture determines what the standards of right and wrong behaviour shall be—that is, what the norms are—what is important in the environment, what kinds of behaviour shall be rewarded or penalized, and what the rewards and penalties shall be. Cultural values are pervasive, permeating virtually all aspects of group

and individual life. The personalities of most individuals in our culture are also moulded by the pattern of values that is the core of our middle-class ideology.

11. **Self-Concept:** Self-concept influences our personality development in two ways. One is that if other people hold high positive attitudes towards us, this enhances our self-image and self-acceptance. The other is that if others hold negative attitudes toward us, it creates feelings of worthlessness or triviality and consequently may lead to self-defence or withdrawal from social situations.

12. **Sexual Function or Sex Roles:** The role of sex is well-defined in each culture is the sex role—the behaviour, attitudes, and personal qualities society expects of each person according to her or his sex. Whether one is male or female has pronounced effects on personality, although many of the personality traits that were once considered to be biologically determined now appear to have their origin in the culture—that is, they are related to what the culture expects of its females and males rather than to any inherent, biological predisposition. For example, common sense tells us that women are born to be passive, dependent, and submissive, whereas men are born to be active, dominant, and aggressive. Girls tend to be less active than boys, they prefer to play with dolls, and they are more verbal. Some of these differences may be related to inherited temperament, but for the most part they are the result of the expectations of the adults who dominate society. Girls are as strong as boys through childhood and early adolescence; but our insistence that girls play subordinate roles makes it necessary for them to gain their ends by less direct means than those available to boys. Thus, girls learn to express themselves verbally rather than physically. In other words, girls behave the way they do largely because we expect them to do so; we encourage and reward them when they act like “little ladies;” we express disapproval when they do not conform to this stereotype. If boys behave like the little-lady stereotype, we shame them by referring to them as “sissies;” and we arrange situations, select companions, and promote experiences that will cause them to act in accordance with the little boy stereotype. As a result, children who do not conform to the expectations of their sex roles learn to be ashamed of their deviant behaviour. It, therefore, appears that the personality characteristics that we associate with womanhood (submission, co-operation, aesthetic expression, etc.) are not so much biologically determined as they are the result of what the culture has led us to expect of women and what women have come to expect of themselves. Undoubtedly, the childbearing function of women places them in situations where they are required to be tender, kind-hearted, and motherly, and the larger size and strength of men lead them to engage in activities calling for vigour, dynamism, and aggression. Similarly, many of

the personality characteristics we have come to associate with manhood (dominance, independence, aggression, etc.) are the result of the fact that our culture expects men to play competitive occupational roles in our patriarchal society.

However, these differences are not as crucial as they were in former days, nor are they as important as we commonly believe. The middle-class way of life, with the father becoming more closely involved in the care of children, has demonstrated that he can be as tender and as considerate as the mother. The larger size of the male is no longer the advantage it was formerly, because in modern life there is less and fewer premiums placed on muscular strength in the performance of the tasks of daily life. Indeed, there are few occupations today in which women could not compete successfully with men. It is interesting to note, too, when women enter occupations that are highly competitive, they can become as aggressive as any man.

Margaret Mead
(1901–1978)

Yet, the anthropologists find cultures where the men have personality traits we call "womanly" and where women not only possess "manly" traits but play occupational and social roles that are monopolized by males in our culture. Probably the best study of cultural influences on masculine and feminine qualities is that made by Margaret Mead (16 December, 1901–15 November, 1978) of three New Guinea tribes who were racially similar and living in the same general area. She found the Arapesh to be peaceful, co-operative people, who minimize sex differences and accept human nature as intrinsically good. According to the Arapesh ideal, both men and women are non-aggressive, permissive, kindly, and maternal. The Mundungumor are a Spartan people in many ways the opposite of the Arapesh. Both men and women of this tribe are expected to be sexually aggressive, jealous, violent, competitive, and vengeful. The Tchambuli have created a culture that emphasizes artistic skills and ritual. Whereas the Arapesh and the Mundungumor have not developed differentiated sex roles for their members, the Tchambuli have clear and separate concepts of the kinds of person's women and men should be. Women should be persons who fish, manufacture, and control the power and economic life of the community. They should take the initiative in courting and be tolerant and appreciative of male activities. Men should be persons who are dependent, coquettish, who place much stress on show, and who spend much time in games and theatricals. Thus, with the Arapesh, the ideals for both sexes correspond to our ideals of feminine personality and behaviour; with the Mundungumor, the pattern is similar to our masculine stereotype; and the Tchambuli have assigned sex roles that are in sharp contrast to the expectations of men and women we have developed in Western culture.

Nevertheless, the fact that women are smaller, weaker, slighter, and are peculiarly equipped for child-bearing has a pronounced effect on their personalities, irrespective of the culture they belong to.

13. **Occupational Role:** Of prime interest to the college student and psychologist is the part played in personality development by the occupational role. That certain personality traits are traditionally related to certain occupations is widely known. The general population frequently confuses good "role-playing" with "good adjustment". The doctor who conforms exactly to his stereotype and is precisely what his patient and his fellow workers expect of him, may be markedly less successful in his other life roles. Is a man well-adjusted who has the same mannerisms, outlook, and approach to people, regardless of whether he is in his office, at his club, in the "bosom of his family", out hunting with his friends, playing golf, or playing chess? Many persons learn to play their occupational roles so skillfully that we are often misled into overestimating their general level of adjustment.

An interesting variety of the occupational role is that played by the marginal businessman. He is an excellent illustration of how cultural forces, expectations of the dominant social groups, and self-expectations combine to form a rather pronounced personality pattern, which tends to be characteristic of marginal businessmen, irrespective of race or colour.

Marginal businessmen have existed since the dawn of history. They are the individuals who do not "belong" to a community, who come in from the outside and endeavour to obtain and maintain a foothold in order, at first, to gain livelihood, and later, to flourish and become economically, socially, and politically powerful. Well-established members of the community usually view the outsiders with suspicion and hostility, and history is full of bloody persecutions of such newcomers.

Because the marginal businessman must subsist on leavings, because he is not established, and because life is grimmer and more hazardous for him than it is for more secure members of the community, he tends to develop rather well-defined personality traits. He may find it necessary to become striving, aggressive, and ruthless. He learns how to stretch the mores of the community just as far as they will go and still remain inside the law. He works long hours; he cuts corners; he tries to produce more per hour and per day than do other workers in his occupation. These traits are both the result and the basis of his exclusion from normal social intercourse with the dominant culture, many of whose members may display the same personality traits. The members of the dominant culture tend to resent, despise, and fear him, even though they are responsible for his deprived status by refusing him participation in the normal economic life of the community.

At any stage of life in our culture, we commonly play a variety of roles. Roles are learned by the individual through a process of identification with another person or persons. Some of these roles are compatible; others may conflict. A common example of conflicting roles is that of the travelling salesman who also tries to be a good husband and father. His situation is difficult because being a successful travelling salesman often involves being "on the road" twenty-five days out of the month, whereas being a good family man involves being at home most of the nights of the week. Similar situations are faced by persons in the entertainment industry: musicians, actors, and their agents. For these people, building a stable home life is exceedingly difficult, and divorce is much more frequent in their families than it is among the general population.

Conflict in role is also much in evidence when an individual changes his way of life; at these times he must go through an adjustment period that is often very painful for both him and his associates. There are others times in life when a change of role is accompanied by conflict and anxiety: the change from being the only child to being the older child; the change from the role of high school student to that of an employee; the change from a civilian to a solider and back again; the change from the role of bachelor or maiden to that of spouse; the change from the role of a childless spouse to that of a parent. The fact that some of these changes have joyful connotations in our culture, sometimes blind us to the realities. For example, parenthood has its own special joys, but there are bound to be times when children are something less than satisfying and when each parent longs—momentarily, of course—for the days when he had fewer and less pressing responsibilities. There is no change of role that does not bring with it some problem of adjustment; in fact, change is stressful; and the more unrealistic the individual's expectations are, the more difficult the shift is likely to be.

14. **Minority or Racial Group:** Being one of the unprivileged or unfavoured or dependent minority or backward or racial group has a considerable impact on the personality of that individual. Members of such groups at one time reflected and still reflect in their personality, the bias, prejudice, discrimination, and injustice constantly directed against them by the members of the majority or privileged group. Some of the members belonging to these minority groups accept their inferior status in the society and do not protest against it, while others resist, protest, revolt, and develop aggressive attitudes, which result in the social changes taking place rapidly and also in transformations of the society.

15. **Culture:** The importance of cultural forces in the development of personality is very great. Personality is determined by culture which represents the environment in its totality. Customs, traditions, rituals, standards, norms, values, needs, attitudes, beliefs, religious faiths, aspirations, childhood training, and ways of living of an individual are regulated by the culture she or he belongs to. C. Kluckhohn, emphasizing the importance of culture in the life of an individual said, "Culture regulates our lives at every turn. From the moment we are born until we die there, whether we are conscious of it or not, constant pressure upon us to follow certain types of behaviour that other men have created for us." Personality of an individual is gradually shaped by the culture; she or he is born in. E.B. Tyler, famous anthropologist, defined culture as, "It is that complex whole which includes knowledge, beliefs, morals, law, custom, and many other capabilities and habits acquired by man as a member of society." "Culture" refers to the total activities of a society. It leaves permanent impressions on the personality of an individual. All the behaviour patterns which the parents transmit to their children are cultural products. Culture is in fact, the ground from which personality emerges.

Differences in personality due to differences in socializing norms of different cultures are best demonstrated in the studies of primitive societies. Margaret Mead concluded that cultural conditions play an important role in moulding the personality patterns of individuals. According to her findings, the development of the sense of security seemed to be one of the chief factors determining the formation of personality.

The "natural" family ties that we accept as a norm in our culture are not found in all groups of people. For example, Balinese children learn not to depend on members of the family for warmth and affection. When Balinese children are about three years old, their mothers deliberately frustrate them by fondling other children in their presence and by offering them the breast and then withdrawing it. Because of this kind of treatment during childhood and because of the general atmosphere of the Balinese culture, its members learn to withdraw into themselves and not to depend on siblings or parents for emotional support.

It is important to remember that no one is consciously aware of having been influenced by the personality determinants that inhere in his biological heritage or his social and physical environment. Most of us accept the facts of our existence as natural phenomena, unaware that they are to a large extent the creation, in part, of the emotional and social climate that we ourselves, through our cultural group, have created.

There has been a constant warfare between hereditarians and environmentalists as regards the contribution of these factors in the development of personality. There are some psychologists who over-emphasize the environmental influences to the exclusion of heredity in the growth and development of personality and there is another group of psychologists who claim the superiority of heredity over environment in the development of personality. As a matter of fact, no definite line of demarcation can be drawn between the contributions of heredity-environment in the development of personality. Development of personality depends upon both heredity and environment. Some of these are more important during the early stages of development, while some at later. Heredity sets the limit of the maximum development of a characteristic which cannot be crossed by providing best environment. The best environment cannot make an idiot, a talented person. Good training and experiences definitely improve the performance of children. Bad environment can suppress good inheritance but good environment is not a substitute for bad heredity. Thus, it is clear that personality development results from many influences that operate in and upon a child. Each factor has its influence in its own way and multiplicative product of factors is what we call—“Personality”.

13.4 THEORIES OF PERSONALITY BASIC CONCEPTS OF FREUDIAN THEORY OR FREUD’S THEORY OF PERSONALITY OR PSYCHO-ANALYTIC VIEWPOINT

Sigmund Freud (1856–1939) was born on 6 May, 1856 at 117, Schossergasse (Frendova Ulice) in a small town, Freiberg, in Moravia and grew up in Jewish family in Vienna, Austria. He was trained in medicine, with specific interests in neurology and psychological problems. He died of the cancer of the mouth and jaw that he had suffered from for the last 20 years of his life. Freud is generally considered the single most important theorist in the field of personality. His theory has been called “The single most sweeping contribution to the field of personality” (Phares, 1979).

Sigmund Freud
(1856–1939)

The important concepts of childhood experiences and unconscious motivation originated with Freud. Motivation that is not in the conscious awareness of the person is called the “unconscious motivation”. The reasons for the “motives” behind behaviour are often not obvious to the individual. One of the major aspects of Freud’s theory of personality is the principle of “psychic determinism”. The gist of this principle is that there is no such thing as accidental or meaningless behaviour because all behaviour is assumed to be caused or motivated by psychological factors which operate unconsciously. Slips of the tongue (“Freudian slips") are probably the best known examples of psychic determinism. Freud's principle posits a connection between all behaviour and psychological factors. Freud (1938) argued that free will is psychologically determined. In essence, most of Freud's work is concerned with establishing the unconscious meaning of overt and covert (dreaming, thinking, etc.) behaviour.

Instincts also play an important role in Freud's personality theory. According to Freud, the direction of behaviour is influenced by the interaction of instincts, the environment, and inhibitory forces (social prohibitions). Environmental stimuli and instinctual energy arouse tension and provide the impulse to action, while inhibitory forces prevent indiscriminant tension reduction. "Instincts" are biological sources of energy that exert demands on the mind. They are classified according to their aim (the conditions necessary for satisfaction), object (the action which reduces the instinctual energy), and source (the physical basis of the instincts). Instincts are further categorized according to whether they are life instincts (Eros)—those related to survival (hunger, thirst, sex, maternal attachment, etc.)—or death instincts (Thanatos)—those related to destructive energies (violent aggression, suicidal tendencies, etc.).

13.4.1 The Structure of Personality or the Structure of Human Psyche (Mind)

Freud divided the human psyche into three separate but interacting elements: the id, the ego, and the super-ego. According to Freud, personality includes three systems: the id, the ego, the super-ego. The id, the ego, and the super-ego are not physical divisions of the brain. Instead, they are names given to strong psychological forces, the existence of which is inferred from the ways that people behave. The ability of these three systems to interact effectively determines the quality of an individual's mental health. When the systems interact harmoniously, the individual is likely to be well adjusted. When there is discontinuity—caused, for example, by an overwhelming id or super-ego—the individual is likely to be maladjusted.

The ID

In psychoanalytic theory, "id" is the instinctual drive and the first structure to appear in infancy. Humans are born with an id, which is immature and illogical. Freud described the id as a reservoir or storehouse of psychic energy, the pool of biological drives that arise from our needs for food, water, warmth, sexual gratification or satisfaction, avoidance of pain, and so forth. Freud believed that these drives (biological forces) power and direct all human behaviour. Fenichel (1945) describes the id as the "dynamic, driving chaos of forces which strive for discharge and nothing else." More colloquially, the id is known as the seat of all drives and instincts and is concerned with the alleviation of hunger, self-preservation, love, and preservation of the species (Brill, 1938). In psychoanalytic theory, "libido" is a term used to describe the instinctual drives of the id. Libido is the most prominent instinct in Freud's theory of personality. It is the basic constructive energy of life, primarily sexual in nature. It is the energy directed by the ego towards the object of its sexual or pleasurable desires (Freud, 1935). The ego "attaches" the libido to objects from which it expects to receive satisfaction. Freud referred to this attachment as "Cathexis". Presently, Cathexis is used to describe the relationship between the ego and its objects of satisfaction. For Freud, sexual energy, or libido, was the main life-affirming force in the human psyche or Eros. "Eros" is the Greek god of love. In Freudian theory, "Eros" refers to the whole complex of life-preservative instincts. Included among these, of course, are the sexual instincts. There is also a negative, life-destroying tendency in the human psyche, which is called *Thanatos*. "Thanatos" is the Greek god of death. In Freudian theory, "Thanatos" refers to the totality of death instincts; theoretical generalized instinct for death as expressed in such behaviours as denial, rejection, and the turning-away from pleasure.

The id is an unconscious force, with no link to objective reality. It seeks one thing only; the discharge of tension arising from biological drives. The id is the primeval, impulsive part of the personality, demanding instant gratification of all of its demands. It is unrealistic, selfish, and demanding, working on what Freud described as the Pleasure Principle, the idea that every impulse should be satisfied, immediately. The "Pleasure Principle" means that the id desires immediate gratification and tension reduction. The Pleasure Principle can be understood as a demand to take care of needs immediately. Pleasure Principle demands that an instinctual need be immediately gratified, regardless of reality or moral considerations. The id's exclusive devotion to gratification—without regard for logic or reason, reality or morality—is called the *Pleasure Principle*. Id consists of such ambitions, desires, tendencies, and appetites as are guided by the Pleasure Principle. One of the methods by which the id achieves this objective is "primary process thinking", that is, thinking devoid of reality, time, order, or logical constraints, such as dreams, image, or fantasies. When an adult responds to extreme stress by reverting to very childish behaviour (laughing and crying inappropriately, hallucinating, etc.), this adult is relieving tension by allowing the id to reign. In this case, the id, whose objective is to reduce tension, achieves this goal through an extreme form of primary process thinking.

Id is the raw savage and immoral basic stuff of a man's personality that is hidden in the deep layers of her or his unconsciousness. Id has no values, knows no laws, follows no rules, does not recognize right or wrong, and considers only the satisfaction of its needs and appetites to be paramount or highly important.

Freud also maintained that the id lacks moral judgment. It cannot distinguish between good and evil. The id is unconscious, without contacts to the external world. The id is like a demanding, impulsive, selfish child. It seeks only its own pleasure, has no inhibitions, and cannot abide or tolerate frustration or deprivation of any kind. The id seeks satisfaction of bodily needs, but has no way of determining which means of doing so are safe and which are dangerous. This task falls to the ego.

The Ego

In psychoanalytic theory, the "ego" is the rational part of the personality that mediates between the demands of the id and the constraints of the super-ego, and the realities of the external world. The ego, according to Freud, begins to develop soon after birth, but does not become apparent until the age of about six months or ego begins to function at about the age of six months. Although a child is born with an id, the ego does not develop until the id starts interacting with its environment. The ego relates the organism to reality by means of its consciousness, and searches for objects to satisfy the wishes that id creates to represent the organism's needs. The ego develops because of the need to deal with the outside world. The ego's primary role is to serve as a mediator between the id and reality (Freud, 1920, 1932). At the age of six months, infants can start to take past experiences into account. Unlike the id, most of the ego operates or functions according to the Reality Principle, taking into account past experiences, it seeks the best time to obtain the most pleasure with the least pain or damage to the self. In psychoanalytic theory, "Reality Principle" means the recognition of the reality environment by a child, the growing awareness of its demands and the need to accommodate to them or trying to balance the demands of the unconscious mind with what is practical. Freud believed that the Reality Principle was the guiding force behind the ego's operation. The Reality Principle says, "Take care of a need as soon as an appropriate object is found". It represents reality and, to a considerable extent, reason. The aim of Reality Principle is to postpone the discharge of energy until a socially acceptable object is available. As opposed to the Pleasure Principle, the Reality Principle uses only "secondary process thinking". This includes reasoning, planning, making evaluations, and so on.

According to Freud, the ego maintained a state of dynamic equilibrium between different pressures (from id and super-ego), and a kind of balancing act, giving in a little to one source and then compensating by giving in a little to another.

The ego, functions, as a policeman to check the unlawful activities of the id. It is the executive unit with the power of veto. It follows the principle of reality and acts with the intelligence to control, select, and also decides what appetites have to be satisfied and in which way they may be satisfied.

The ego is not solely an inhibitor and repressor. Not only must the ego hold back or repress certain impulses or motives but more importantly, it must arrange, schedule, and control the manner in which other motives are to appear. The ego, consistent with psycho analytic theory, is viewed as the central organizer or integrator of behaviour. The strength and effectiveness of the ego is an important determinant of individual's adjustment.

The Super-ego

Freud's third personality component is the "super-ego", which includes individual's conscience, ideals, moral, and values. In psycho-analytic theory, super-ego is the conscience, ethical or moral dimensions or attitudes of personality. The super-ego is the component of personality that represents the ideals and moral standards of the society as conveyed to the child by her or his parents or other elders. Just as the ego grows out of the id's interaction with its environment, the super-ego develops out of the ego's response to parental controls. Super-ego includes rules, principles, and duties. As the child attains maturity, the rules become internalized into the personality, rather than an external one, the child develops from kind of internalized unconscious "parent" which contains strict ideas of propriety, duty, conscience, and obligations. This is known as *super-ego*. The super-ego absorbs all the prohibitions, inhibitions, and standards that are expressed by parents and society, thereby acting as a conscience in its attempts to direct behaviour according to parental, societal, and "ego" ideals.

The super-ego in Murray's theory as in Freud's, is considered to be a cultural implant. It is an internalized subsystem that acts within the id to regulate behaviour in much the same manner that agents outside the individual's once acted. These agents typically the parents but also one's peers, teachers, public personalities, and fictional characters act as representatives of the culture so that internalizing their prescription represent a move in the direction of internalizing cultural prescription

The super-ego is the ethical or moral arm of the personality. It is idealistic and does not care for the realities. Perfection rather than pleasure is its goal. It is a decision-making entity which decides what is good or bad to the social norms and therefore acceptable or otherwise.

There are two aspects to the super-ego: one is the conscience, which is an internalization of punishments and warnings. The other is called the *ego ideal*. It derives rewards and positive models presented to the child. The conscience and the ego ideal communicate their requirements to the ego with feelings like pride, shame, and guilt.

Freud put forward a dynamic concept of personality by conceptualizing the continuous conflict among the id, the ego, and the super-ego, while the id operating on the pleasure principle, continuously presses for the immediate discharge of bodily tension, the super-ego concerned with morality prohibits such gratification. Thus, a war-like situation is created between the id and the super-ego with the ego attempting to mediate. The extent to which the ego is able to discharge its responsibilities decides the personality make-up of the individual.

Individuals who have a strong or powerful ego are said to have a strong or balanced personality because the ego is capable of maintaining a balance between the id and the super-ego. In case, an individual possesses a weak ego, she or he is bound to have a maladjusted personality. Here, two situations may arise. In one situation, the super-ego may be more powerful than the ego, and so does not permit desirable fulfilment of the repressed wishes and impulses. This situation results in a neurotic personality. In neurotic personality, the individual is moody, touchy, anxious, or restless. If, on the other hand, the id is more powerful than the ego, the individual may indulge in unlawful or immoral activities leading to the formation of a delinquent or antisocial or psychotic personality

ID	EGO	SUPER-EGO
(Pleasure; immoral or unlawful activities; unconscious)	(Reality; partly conscious, rest unconscious)	(Perfection; neurotic personality; partly conscious, rest unconscious)

The ego must perform a delicate balancing act (between the id and the super-ego). The ego acts as a supervisor. It must satisfy both the pleasure-seeking demands of the id and the equally powerful perfection-seeking commands of the super-ego. It must negotiate a compromise between the id's drives and the super-ego's rules about moral behaviour. Finally, the ego must continually assess reality, delaying action when appropriate.

The conflict among the id, the ego, and the super-ego is central in Freudian theory. Freud proposed that the ego tries to resolve this conflict. Often, it resolves the conflict via defense mechanisms, which are mental activities that prevent dangerous thoughts or wishes from becoming directly effective. Defense mechanisms are discussed later in this theory.

These three structures—the id, the ego, and the super-ego are critically important in Freudian theory because personality and behaviour are created by the constant conflict and interplay among the id, the ego, and the super-ego (Domjan, 1996).

The id, the ego, and the super-ego are related to a person's level of awareness. Conscious and the unconscious, of course, is one of Freud's greatest contributions. Even if he did not invent the terms, he certainly was responsible for popularizing them. Freud compared the human mind to an iceberg: only a small part of the iceberg rises above the surface of the water. This portion is the *conscious*, which includes everything you are aware of at a particular moment, your present perceptions, memories, thoughts, fantasies, feelings. Our "conscious experiences" refer to our sensory awareness of the environment and of ourselves. Only the ego and the super-ego are included in the conscious. The ego and the super-ego are partly unconscious also (Figure 13.1).

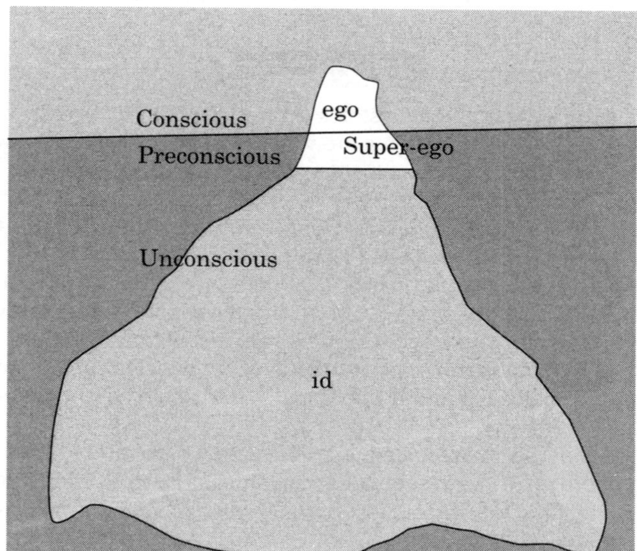

Figure 13.1 The id, the ego, and the super-ego.

Some additional material that is not in awareness at a particular time can be retrieved or recalled with a little effort, this material is called the **preconscious** or **subconscious**. Working closely with the conscious mind is what Freud called the pre-conscious or the sub-conscious, what we might today call "available memory": anything that can easily be made conscious, the memories you are not at the moment thinking about but can readily bring to the mind. The nature of the material in the preconscious is not different from the material in the conscious; thoughts move fairly easily from one state—conscious, to the other—subconscious (Cloninger, 1993).

Now no one has a problem with these two layers of mind. But Freud suggested that these are the smallest parts.

Freud was especially interested in the **unconscious**, which holds thoughts and desires that are far below the level of a person's awareness. The largest part by far is the unconscious. Most of the iceberg lies below the surface of the water. It includes all the things that are not easily available to awareness, including many things that have their origins there, such as our drives or instincts, and things that are put there because we can't bear to look at them, such as the memories and emotions associated with trauma. According to Freud, the unconscious is the source of our motivations, whether they are simple desires for food or sex, neurotic compulsions, or the motives of an artist or scientist. And yet, we are often driven to deny or resist becoming conscious of these motives, and they are often available to us only in disguised form.

AMAZING FACT

In 1912, the luxury liner, *Titanic*, struck an iceberg on her maiden voyage and sank with 1500 passengers and crew in the North Atlantic. It was on its maiden voyage from Southampton to New York.

Icebergs are giant chunks or large masses of ice floating in the sea that break off the ends of glaciers and drift out to sea and are found mainly to the south of Greenland. They are formed where glaciers meet the sea. The part of the iceberg which is visible is only its tip and the rest of it is under water. Only about a tenth of an iceberg shows above water. The rest is hidden under the sea. It is seven to ten times as large under the water. This makes them very dangerous to passing ships and boats. Icebergs are a major hazard to the ships. A collision with an iceberg can be disastrous.

Icebergs may be many kilometers long and weigh millions of tones. The biggest iceberg ever was seen near Antarctica. It was about the size of Belgium (near France). The tallest iceberg was more than half as high as the Eiffel Tower in Paris (France).

Freud argues that most psychic processes are not conscious; they are hidden from the outside world, for example traumatic childhood memory. Although a traumatic memory will not reach consciousness during normal daily activities, Freud proposed that it may influence your behaviour without your being aware of it. The id is totally unconscious, and parts of the ego and the super-ego are also unconscious.

To Freud, the unconscious was both a reservoir of instinctual drives and a storehouse of all the thoughts and wishes we conceal from conscious awareness because they cause us psychological conflict. *Inf act*, Freud maintained that the unconscious is the major motivating force behind human behaviour. According to him, much of what we say and do is either an effort to find some socially acceptable way of expressing unconscious impulses or an effort to keep those impulses from being expressed. Table 13.1 gives summary of Freud's "Model of the Mind".

Table 13.1 Summary of Freud's "Model of the Mind"

	id	*Ego*	*Super-ego*
What it does	Expresses sexual and aggressive instincts; follows the Pleasure Principle	Mediates between desires of the id and demands of the super-ego; follows the Reality Principle; uses defense mechanisms to ward off unconscious anxiety	Represents conscience and the ego ideal; follows internalized moral standards
How conscious it is	Entirely unconscious	Partly conscious, partly unconscious	Partly conscious, partly unconscious
When it develops	Present at birth	Emerges after birth, with early formative experiences	Last system to develop; becomes internalized after the oedipal stage
Example	"I'm so mad. I could kill you." (felt unconsciously)	Might make a conscious choice ("Let's talk about this") or resort to an unconscious defense mechanism, such as denial ("What me angry? Never")	"Thou shall not kill."

13.4.2 How Personality Develops

Sigmund Freud developed an extensive theory about the shaping of adult personality by early life experiences. According to Freud, the experiences that children have during the first five years of life are very important. Their personalities are developing during that period, and adult personality depends very much on the experiences of early childhood. Freud argued that during each stage in the child's life, the drive for pleasure centres around a particular area of his body, first the mouth, then the anus, and finally the genitals. Freud believed that adult personality is shaped by the way in which the conflict between these early sexual urges and the requirements imposed by society (weaning, toilet training, etc.) are resolved. According to him, failure to resolve any of these conflicts can result in fixation, in which the person becomes "stuck" in that particular psychological battle, repeating the conflict in symbolic ways. The basic energy remains attached to that stage during adulthood.

13.4.3 Stages of Psycho-sexual Development

Freud noted that at different times in our lives, different parts of our skin or body give us greatest pleasure. Later theorists would call these areas erogenous zones. It appeared to Freud that the infant found its greatest pleasure in sucking, especially at the breast. Freud contended that infants are capable of sexual expression because they experience sexual drive in the form of instinctual energy, although the genitals are not necessarily the source of satisfaction. In fact, babies have a penchant or fondness for bringing nearly everything in their environment into contact with their mouths. A bit later in life, the child focuses on the anal pleasures of holding it in and letting go. By three or four years, the child may have discovered the pleasure of touching or rubbing against his genitalia. Only later, in our sexual maturity, do we find our greatest pleasure in sexual intercourse. In these observations, Freud had the makings of a psychosexual stage theory.

According to Freud's psychodynamic approach to personality, all children, regardless of culture, go through or pass through several biologically programmed stages of development called the *five stages of psycho-sexual development*—the oral stage, the anal stage, the phallic stage, the latency stage, and the genital stage, during which different parts of the body are capable of providing the necessary satisfaction and tension reduction. Sometimes children have problems with one of the stages. This leads to fixation, in which basic energy remains attached to that stage during adulthood. In Freudian theory, "fixation" is the process whereby a person becomes excessively attached to (or affectively fixated on) an object or person appropriate to an earlier stage of development. Fixation is apt to occur if the individual experiences either excessive satisfaction or excessive frustration at a particular stage. However, when trauma becomes inordinate, the individual may also regress to the last successfully completed stage. Freud points out that fixation and regression go hand in hand. The stronger the fixation, the more likely is that frustration will produce regression to that earlier stage. The person is thus said to have become affectively fixated at an immature stage. This condition is assumed to produce a variety of neurotic behaviours, such as excessive or irrational attachments to people or objects and an inability to form normal, mature relationship. When an adult has great problems, she or he shows regression; with their behaviour becoming more like the behaviour they showed when they were children. Adults normally regress to a psychosexual stage on which they fixated as children. Fixation gives each problem at each stage a long-term effect in terms of our personality.

The oral stage (lasts from birth to about 18 months)

The ego starts developing at this stage (6 months of age). Freud believed that during the first year of life—the oral stage, a child's sexual pleasure focuses on the mouth. The focus of pleasure is, of course, the mouth. Sucking, he maintained, is a source of intense pleasure in its own light. Sucking and biting are favourite activities. In the young infant, Freud believed, the libido or the sexual energy was focused on the mouth, and infants could derive great satisfaction from oral activity; at this time, the young child would automatically put anything new to its mouth. Freud called this the *oral stage*. Young children in the oral stage enjoy various activities involving their mouths, lips, and tongues.

Children may experience problems at this stage, for example, because of rapid weaning. A child who became orally fixated at this time, through weaning which was either too early or too late, would, according to Freud, be likely to become an adult with an excessive interest in oral stimulation. These problems can produce adults with an oral personality. Those with oral receptive or passive personality are very dependent on other people, whereas those with oral aggressive characters are aggressive. If you, in the first eight months of your life, are often frustrated in your need to suckle, perhaps because mother is uncomfortable or even rough with you, or tries to wean you too early, then you may develop an oral-passive character. They often retain an interest in "oral gratifications". They might become a gourmet, enjoying the taste of food (eating), or they might smoke (smoking), drinking, or be constantly thumb-sucking, and the like. Fixation at the oral stage can lead to a passive, overly dependent, unenterprising adult. When we are between five and eight months old, we begin teething. One satisfying thing to do when you are teething is to bite on something, like mummy's nipples. If this causes a great deal of upset and precipitates an early weaning, you may develop an oral-aggressive character. These people retain a life-long desire to bite on things, such as pencils, gum, finger nails, and other people. They have a tendency to be verbally aggressive, argumentative, sarcastic, and so on.

The nature of the pleasure which the child experienced in the oral stage could leave a lasting effect on personality. Essentially, the child could derive pleasure from two types of activity: sucking and swallowing, or biting and chewing. Too much of either, Freud considered, could have lasting effects. A child which derived excessive pleasure from sucking and swallowing would become highly gullible or susceptible (easily deceived) and trusting (liable to "swallow" any story).

The anal stage (18 months—3 or 4 years)

The anal stage occurs during the second year of life, when children begin to develop voluntary control over their bowel movements. It is the time during which stimulation is focused on eliminative functions through either holding back (anal retention) or letting go (anal expulsion) of the body's waste material. The anal stage involves the anal areas as the major source of satisfaction. The focus of pleasure is the anus. It is during this stage that the toilet training occurs. Holding it in and letting it go are greatly enjoyed. Strict toilet training or fixation at this stage results in personality traits that are very much the opposite of uninhibited defecation—such as fastidious orderliness, and excessive neatness. If parents were too strict during toilet training, Freud agued, then the child could become an anal-retentive (able to retain things) personality. Anal retentive types are presumed to adopt abstinent and stingy behaviours. Children who have problems at the anal stage may develop an anal retentive character, making them mean and stubborn, and liking things to be arranged neatly. Another possibility is that they will become very generous and giving.

In the anal stage, children are fascinated with their "bodily functions". The infant seeking to hold on to its faeces (waste matter discharged from the bowels) would eventually become the adult seeking to hold on to its possessions, and it would develop into a miser, or perhaps an obsessional collector. If parents are strict in toilet training, they may use punishment or humiliation. This child will likely become constipated as she or he tries desperately to hold it in at all times, and will grow up to be an anal retentive personality. She or he will tend to be especially clean, perfectionist, dictatorial or authoritarian, very stubborn, and stingy. In other words, the anal retentive is tight in all ways. But if the parents were too lenient, or put themselves at the child's mercy in the process of toilet training, the child would become anal-expulsive, becoming sloppy or careless, disorganized, and overtly generous to a fault and giving in adult life. They may be cruel, destructive, and given to vandalism and graffiti, and adopt disruptive and disorderly behaviours.

However, individuals fixated at the anal stage are likely to exhibit ambivalent or contradictory behaviour because they have not resolved their conflict between retaining and expelling waste material. In cases where there is a partial resolution of the anal stage, Freud assumed that there would be an exaggeration of one of the two anal traits (retentive or expulsive).

Freud's theory presented infant care as a tortuous path: mothers had to ensure that the child was not weaned too early or too late, and that it (infant) was toilet-trained at exactly the right age, and so on. They were told, moreover, that failure to achieve these things could result in lasting damage to their child.

The phallic stage (3 or 4 years—5, 6 or 7 years)

The phallic stage is the third and final stage of infantile sexuality. Although there are two more stages of psychsexual development (latency stage and genital stage), the initiation of genital stimulation marks the end of the "infantile" period of sexual expression (that is, oral and anal stimulation). This stage spans the years from about three or four to 5 or 6 or 7 years. The child finds pleasure in self-stimulation of the genitals. The focus of pleasure is the genitalia. During this stage, the penis or clitoris becomes the major source of satisfaction. Freud assumed that masturbation begins during the phallic stage and has several important consequences for later development. When it has been disrupted or when the child has been made to feel guilty about it, inhibition as an adult is likely to occur (Abramson, 1973; Abramson and Mosher, 1975). Since infantile masturbation is also a means of learning to respond to sexual arousal (Fenichel, 1945), its absence is sometimes associated with certain types of sexual dysfunctions in women (for example, orgasmic dysfunction; Loppicolo and Lobitz, 1972). Presently, research is demonstrating that masturbation at all ages is an integral part of normal sexual development, and can have the effect of enhancing the capacity for sexual expression (Abramson, 1973; Abramson and Mosher, 1975, 1979; Mosher and Abramson, 1977). Those who have problems at this stage, develop what is known as a *phallic character*. Men with a phallic character are vain and self-assured. Women with a phallic character fight hard for superiority over men. Individuals who are fixated at the phallic stage are likely to constantly relieve the Oedipal situation or experience a lack of sexual interest.

The phallic stage is said to be particularly important to a person's psychosexual development because this is the period when the Oedipus or Oedipal complex presumably occurs. **Oedipus** or **Oedipal Complex** or **Crisis**, named after the ancient Greek story of king Oedipus, who inadvertently killed his father and married his mother, is a conflict in which a boy's sexual impulses are directed towards his mother and he views his father as a rival. In boys, sexual desires for the mother are accompanied by fear of retaliation by the father. The type of fear which the boy experiences is called "castration anxiety". Freud felt that this situation represents the final phase of infantile sexuality because the source of sexual satisfaction has become external to the child's body. A boy who develops normally will reduce this fear by identifying with his father, internalizing his father's values, and developing a strong super-ego.

Freud maintained that little girl experiences the **Electra Complex**. She develops hostile feelings for her mother while her love of her father grows. Freud believed that girls resolve their Electra Complex by identifying with their mothers.

Unsuccessful resolution of the phallic stage can cause a person to be either overly proud or overly timed (Fenichel, 1945).

The latency or latent stage (5, 6 or 7 years—puberty, that is, somewhere around 12 years old)

The latency stage follows the phallic stage, and lasts until puberty, and is believed to be a time when the sexual instincts remain dominant. This stage lasts from age of 5, 6 or 7 years to puberty. Children's sexual feelings remain in the repressed state. Freud believed that the sexual impulse was suppressed in the service of learning. Children are ashamed and disgusted about sexual issues, and so they tend to avoid members of the other gender. During this stage, boys and girls tend to ignore each other. Child is busy learning a range of social and cognitive skills.

The genital stage

The final stage is the genital stage. The genital stage begins at puberty, and represents the resurgence or recovery of the sex drive in adolescence, and the more specific focusing of pleasure in sexual intercourse. In this stage, the main source of pleasure is in the genitals, which is similar to the phallic stage. However, there is the key difference that the focus in the genital stage is on sexual pleasure with another person. During puberty, sexual urges reappear and the genital pleasure during the genital stage arises from sexual relationships with others. Children who have avoided problems during the earlier stages develop a genital character. Adults with a genital character are mature, and are able to love and be loved. Heterosexual relationships normally result if excessive trauma and conflict have been avoided. With the successful resolution of conflicts, a person is capable of forming deep and mature love relationships and of assuming a place in the world as a fully independent adult.

This is a true stage theory, meaning that Freudians believe that we all go through these stages, in this order, and pretty close to these stages (Freud, 1894).

13.4.4 Defence Mechanisms

Freud's use of the term "defense" was his first reference to a psychodynamic principle. He used this term to refer to the process by which the ego unconsciously defends itself against undesirable thoughts, feelings, or impulses. This defence process was further categorized (most notably by Anna Freud, 1946 and Otto Fenichel, 1945) into different mechanisms that represent different tactical maneuvers used by the ego to shield it from unacceptable instinctual (id) demands. "Defense mechanism" is a term applied to any enduring pattern of protective behaviour that functions to provide a defense against the awareness of that which is anxiety-producing. The ultimate objective of a defense mechanism is to shield the ego from unacceptable thoughts, feelings, and

Anna Freud
(1895–1982)

impulses by translating them into acceptable material. If translation into acceptable material does not occur, the undesirable impulse will merely re-emerge. These defense mechanisms (repression, regression, reaction formation, rationalization, sublimation, displacement, projection, denial, introjection and isolation) allow the energy associated with these dangerous ideas to be channelled into other thoughts and behaviours.

These irrational protective measures are referred to as ego-defense mechanisms or psychic mechanisms, and Sigmund Freud, his daughter Anna Freud (1895–1982) and other disciples have discovered quite a few. The ego deals with the demands of reality, the id, and the super-ego as best as it can. But when the anxiety becomes overwhelming, the ego must defend itself. It does so by unconsciously blocking the impulses or distorting them into a more acceptable, less threatening form. These discharge or soothe anxiety by helping a person push painful ideas out of consciousness rather than coping with an anxiety-provoking or anxiety-producing situation. These are usually unconscious and reality distorting. Note that, to be a true example of a defense, it should function unconsciously. And yet Freud saw defenses as necessary. You can hardly expect a person, especially a child to take the pain and sorrow of life full on!

A brief introduction of the above-mentioned defense mechanisms is given below:

1. **Repression:** "Repression" means a mental process or operation that functions to protect the individual from ideas, impulses, and memories which would produce anxiety, apprehension or guilt. It means preventing painful or dangerous thoughts from entering consciousness. Repression, which Anna Freud also called "motivated forgetting" is just that; not being able to recall a threatening situation, person, or event. Repression is considered to be operative at the unconscious level. It is regarded as an ego function. Repression is an unconscious process whereby unacceptable impulses or feelings are purposefully forgotten in order to avoid the possible consequences of acting upon them, as well as to avoid the pain of being aware of them. This, too, is dangerous, and is a part of most other defenses. For example, a mother's occasional impulse to kill her troublesome child is denied access to awareness or consciousness.

However, the major problem with repression is that it does not work. When repression is used, conflicts continue to occur because new experiences that are related to the repressed material re-arouse the "forgotten" impulses. Moreover, since the "forgotten" or repressed impulses continue to remain in the unconscious, they are also continuously seeking gratification. Note that repression differs from denial because with repression, impulses may be experienced, but are then forgotten, whereas with denial, the existence of the impulses is never acknowledged.

2. **Regression:** "Regression" means reverting to an earlier, more primitive or more child-like pattern of behaviour. It means retreating to an earlier developmental level or stage involving less mature behaviour and response ability. Regression is a movement back in psychological time when one is faced with stress. When we are troubled or frightened, our behaviour often become more childish or primitive. For example, a 12 years old boy may show regression by thumb-sucking even though he never sucked his thumb as an infant. A child may begin to suck his thumb again or wet the bed when they need to spend some time in the hospital. Teenagers may giggle uncontrollably when introduced into a social situation involving the opposite sex.

3. **Reaction formation:** "Reaction formation" is a process through which unacceptable feelings or impulses are controlled by establishing the behaviour patterns which are directly opposed to them. It means preventing the awareness of expression of unacceptable desires by an exaggerated adoption of seemingly opposite behaviour. Reaction formation is a defense mechanism that replaces an unacceptable impulse by rigid adherence to a set of attitudes or beliefs that are the opposite of the unacceptable impulse. Reaction formation, which Anna Freud called "believing the opposite", is changing an unacceptable impulse into its opposite. According to psychoanalytic theory, reaction formation operates by repressing the original impulse, which is assumed to continue to exist unconsciously in its original form and is, thus, likely to emerge under some circumstances. For example, a father who was obsessed with thoughts of harming his daughter, might become a "super father". So a child, angry at her or his mother, may become overly concerned with her and rather dramatically shower her with affection. For instance, an excessive concern about cleanliness may be a reaction formation against a need to be dirty.

Perhaps the most common and clearest example of reaction formation is found in children between seven and eleven or so: most girls will tell you in no uncertain terms how gross boys are, and boys will tell you with equal vigour how disgusting girls are. Adults watching their interactions, however, can tell quite easily what their true feelings are!

4. **Rationalization:** "Rationalization" is a process to conceal the true motivations for one's actions, thoughts or feelings. It means using contrived "explanations" to conceal or disguise unworthy motives for one's behaviour. Rationalization is the cognitive distortion of "the facts" to make an event or an impulse less threatening. We do it often enough on a fairly conscious level when we provide ourselves with excuses.

5. **Sublimation:** "Sublimation" is the process whereby primitive, libidinous impulses are redirected and refined into new, learned, non-instinctive behaviours. It means channelling frustrated sexual energy into

substitutive activities. Sublimation is the transforming of an unacceptable impulse, whether it is sex, anger, fear, or whatever, into a socially acceptable, even productive form. So, someone with a great deal of hostility may become a hunter, a butcher, a football player, or a mercenary. Someone suffering from a great deal of anxiety in a confusing world may become an organizer, a business person, or a scientist. For Freud, in fact, all positive, creative activities were sublimations, and predominantly of the sex drive. Freud himself suggested that there was one positive defense, which he called "sublimation".

Sublimation is successful because it involves the channelling of instinctual energy into social acceptable endeavours without blocking the discharge of this energy (Fenichel, 1945). What differentiates sublimation from all other defenses is that the remaining defenses are constantly working to prevent re-eruption of warded-off id impulses. This is the case because the instinctual energies are never allowed sufficient gratification. Thus, in those situations in which the instinctual energy is afforded no release, it merely continues to exert pressure for gratification.

Psychoanalysts often suggest that creativity is actually a sublimated form of sexual impulses. Psychoanalysts (therapists who use Freud's form of therapy) are fond of suggesting that creativity is actually a sublimated form of sexual impulses. That is, to some psychoanalysts, all of the energy that goes into a creative product is nothing other than redirected libidinal energy. Of course, there are many artists, writers, musicians, psychologists, and so on who have very different opinions about what constitutes creative energy.

6. **Displacement:** "Displacement" is the transference of affect or wishes and desires from their original object or person to another object or person. It means discharging pent-up feelings, often of hostility, on objects less dangerous than those arousing the feelings. Displacement is the redirection of an impulse onto a substitute target. For example, a man harassed and exploited by his boss at work initiates an argument with his wife or children. Someone who is frustrated by her or his superior or superiors may go home and kick the dog, beat up a family member, or engage in cross-burnings. Someone who hates her or his mother may repress that hatred, but direct it instead towards, say, women in general. Someone who has not had the chance to love someone may substitute cats or dogs or pigeons for human beings.

7. **Projection:** "Projection" is the process by which one ascribes one's own traits, emotions, dispositions, etc. to another. It means attributing one's unacceptable motives or characteristics to others. Projection is the process of getting rid of impulses that are objectionable to the ego by attributing the impulses to other people. Projection, which Anna Freud also called *displacement outward,* is almost the complete opposite of

turning against the self. It involves the tendency to see your own unacceptable desires in other people. In other words, the desires are still there, but they are not your desires anymore. There is an accompanying denial that one has these feelings or tendencies. It functions to protect oneself from anxiety. A husband, a good and faithful one, finds himself terribly attracted to the charming and flirtatious lady next door. But rather than acknowledge his own, hardly abnormal lust, he becomes increasingly jealous of his wife, constantly worried about her faithfulness, and so on.

So, for instance, when an angry, bitter young man complains about all of the hostile people around him, he is unconsciously projecting his own feeling of anger to other people. Thus, he no longer experiences his own bitterness and anger because it has now been attributed to others. Actually, Fenichel (1945) suggests that people use projection because they prefer to feel dangers and threats from sources external to themselves, given that it is easier to blame others, than to blame oneself.

8. **Denial:** "Denial" means protecting the self from an unpleasant reality by the refusal to perceive or face it. Denial is a defense mechanism that simply disavows or denies thoughts, feelings, wishes, or needs that cause anxiety. Denial is simply the tendency to refuse to believe in the existence of painful experiences and memories. The term is used purely for unconscious operations that function to "deny" that which cannot be dealt with consciously. Denial involves blocking external events from awareness. If some situation is just too much to handle, the person just refuses to experience it. It is one of the most common defense mechanisms used by children: "That mean-looking man over there who is trying to scare me isn't really there." Freud believed that refusing to acknowledge a painful experience may actually be a compromise between the conscious realization of the painful experience and the tendency to deny it. For example, the statement, "Although I cannot recognize that person in my dream, I am sure it is not my mother", may mean "I think this person represents my mother, but I am still able to deny it" (Freud, 1923).

As you might imagine, this is a primitive and dangerous defense—no one disregards reality and gets away with it for long! It can operate by itself or, more commonly, in combination with other, more subtle mechanisms that support it. For example, a chain-smoker concludes that the evidence linking cigarette use to health problems is scientifically worthless.

9. **Introjection:** "Introjection" sometimes called identification, involves taking into your own personality characteristics of someone else, because doing so solves some emotional difficulty. For example, a child who is left alone frequently, may in some way try to become "mom" in order to lessen her or his fears. Identification is very important to Freudian theory as the mechanism by which we develop our super-egos.

10. **Isolation:** "Isolation" is a defence mechanism by which the memory of a previous experience is isolated from the emotional content associated with that experience. It operates unconsciously and functions by severing the conscious psychological ties between some unacceptable act or impulse and its original memory source. In this sense, the original experience is not forgotten but it is separated from the effect, originally associated with it. Isolation actually allows the individual to think about a particular experience devoid of its emotional connections. Freud (1924) believed that isolation occurs frequently in relation to the intimate or emotional aspects of sexuality. That is, he reasoned that since the Oedipal conflict involves retribution for feeling sexually attracted to a loved parent, individuals who do not adequately resolve this conflict are not likely to be able to feel sexual towards a loved one, because such feelings are too painfully reminiscent of the Oedipal situation. Therefore, they isolate the tenderness from sexuality and are only able to become sexually involved with individuals whom they either feel ambivalent about or actually dislike.

While each of the defense mechanisms discussed thus far are usually thought of as means of defending the ego from threatening impulses, they obviously are also used in lesser degrees in all of our everyday lives. The distinction between the pathological and normal use of a defense mechanism is that when the use is pathological, it is exaggerated and rarely conscious, and when it is conscious, its use is often very disturbing or bothersome to the individual. Moreover, pathological defense mechanisms usually have an overriding effect on the functions of the ego. In this sense, the ego actually becomes a slave to its defenses.

Advantages of Freud's Approach or Psycho-Analytic Theory of Personality

(i) Freud was the earliest of the modern day personality theorists.

(ii) The impact of Freud's ideas has been greater than that of any other personality theorists. Moreover, he was probably the most prolific and honoured writer of all times in the field of psychology.

(iii) Adult personality depends in part on the experiences of early childhood.

(iv) The various personality types suggested by Freud do seem to exist. For example, Freud argued that adults with an anal retentive character are stubborn, mean, and like neatness. It has been found (for example, Pollak, 1979) that these three personal features do tend to be found together in the same person. In a similar way, Kline and Storey (1977) found that some people possess all of the features of the oral receptive character, with others showing all the features of the oral aggressive character.

Disadvantages or Criticism of Freud's Approach or Psycho-Analytic Theory of Personality

(i) Freud exaggerated the importance of early childhood; personality also depends on heredity and on the experiences of adolescence and adulthood.

(ii) Supporting data have not been collected and analyzed in rigorous scientific ways.

(iii) The sample on which psychoanalytic theory is based is small and atypical—namely, individuals undergoing psychoanalysis.

(iv) Many Freudian concepts are untestable. It is very hard to test Freud's theory of psychosexual development.

(v) The most controversial aspect of Freud's theory of personality is his notion of infantile sexuality.

(vi) It has not been shown that adult personality depends on the specific experiences of, for example, toilet training, in the way that Freud argued.

(vii) Freud theory is biased against women. Freud maintains that women have inferior moral judgment, a gender bias that is not supported by research.

(viii) Freud's psychoanalytic theory is too pessimistic about human nature. We act ethically because we fear punishment from our super-ego.

13.5 PSYCHOMETRIC THEORIES

These are concerned with identifying and quantifying distinctive personality traits, or characteristics, of personality. These theories are sometimes referred to as psychometric theories, because of their emphasis on measuring personality by using psychometric tests. The following are included in this category:

- Allport's trait theory
- Cattell's theory (16 PF or personality factors theory)
- Murray's theory of personality
- Eysenck's theory (trait cum type approach; temperament theory)

13.5.1 Allport's Trait Theory

Gordon Allport (1897–1967) was a pioneer in trait psychology. Gordon Allport was born in Montezuma, Indiana, in 1897. Allport received his Ph.D in Psychology in 1922 from Harvard. His career was spent developing his theory, examining such social issues as prejudice, and developing personality tests. He died in Cambridge Massachusetts in 1967. He wrote the first textbook on Personality, published in 1937, and continued to develop and refine his ideas for almost forty years.

Gordon Allport
(1897–1967)

Gordon Allport believed that the words (adjectives) people use to describe themselves and others provide a window to personality. One of his first steps was to comb or scrutinize an unabridged dictionary for words used to describe people (Allport and Odbert, 1936). He found almost 18,000. The psychologists who subscribe to this approach believe that the personality of an individual is but a combination or sum total of these personality or behavioural traits that can be discovered through the continuous and objective observation of her or his behaviour. Allport believes that traits are essentially unique to each individual. Two, personality theories, namely Allport's theory and Cattell's theory are said to be the best examples of trait approach.

Traits, according to Allport, are the basic units of personality. Each of us develops a unique set of such organized tendencies termed traits in the course of our continuous and gradual development. Traits are long-lasting aspects of a person which influence her or his behaviour. "Traits" have been defined as "Broad, enduring, relatively stable characteristics used to assess and explain behaviour" (Hirschberg, 1978). A trait is a consistent tendency to have certain kinds of beliefs, desires, behaviours, and so forth (Wakefield, 1989). Personality traits have most often been measured by means of questionnaires.

Traits may be defined as relatively consistent general behaviour patterns that an individual exhibits in most situations. These patterns are said to be the basic units of one's personality that can be discovered through observing one's behaviour in a variety of situations. In a trait approach, the personality is viewed in terms of various traits, for example, honest, shy, sociable, aggressive, humourness, lazy, dull, dependent, etc.). Allport (1937, 1961) decided to organize this overwhelming task by proposing three levels or types of traits:

Cardinal traits

The word "cardinal" means important, primary, central, and fundamental. A "cardinal trait" is one that dominates and shapes a person's behaviour. These are the traits that some people have which practically define their life. Some one who spends their life seeking fame, or fortune, or sex is such a person. Cardinal traits are the primary traits so dominant in one's personal disposition that they colour virtually every aspect of one's behaviour and attributes. These traits, if found in an individual are limited in number—just one or two. Perhaps, you know someone who is obsessed with becoming wealthy, or another person whose life focus is religion. If a person has humorousness as a cardinal trait, she or he will bring a sense of humour into almost all situations irrespective of its actual demands. In fact, such cardinal traits, although very few in number, overrule other traits and thus drift the whole personality of the individual along with them. Allport proposed that these cardinal traits are rare; however, most of us lack a single theme in our lives.

Often we use specific historical people to name these cardinal traits: Scrooge (greed), Joan of Arc (heroic self-sacrifice), Mother Teresa (religious service), Marquis de Sade (sadism), Machiavelli (political ruthlessness), and so on. Relatively few people develop a cardinal trait. If they do, it tends to be late in life.

Central traits

A "central trait" is a general characteristic, found to some degree in every person. These basic building blocks of personality shape much of our behaviour, though they are not as overwhelming influential traits as cardinal traits. Central traits represent those few characteristic tendencies which can be ordinarily used to describe a person, for example, honesty, kindness, submissiveness, etc. Allport found that when people are asked to characterize an individual, they tend to use the same or similar words, and these words fall into categories such as honest, gregarious, independent, extraversion, cheerfulness. He called these *central traits*. According to Allport, for knowing an individual's personality, we need to know only five to ten such central traits. When you describe someone, you are likely to use words that refer to these central traits: smart, dumb, wild, shy, sneaky, dopey, grumpy... . He noted that most people have somewhere between five and ten of these.

Secondary traits

"Secondary traits" are not as dominant as cardinal or central traits. Secondary traits are not quite so obvious, or so general, or so consistent. A secondary trait is a characteristic seen only in certain situations. Preferences, attitudes, situational traits are all secondary. These appear in only a relatively small range of situations and are not considered strong enough to be regarded as integral parts of one's personality. These must be included to provide a complete picture of human complexity. For example, some typical secondary traits might include "uncomfortable in large crowds" and "likes to drive sports cars".

Allport argued that a person's pattern of traits determined her or his behaviour. No two people are completely identical, and as a result no two people respond completely to the same environmental situation. Allport (1937) said, "The same fire that melts the butter hardens the egg."

Allport believed that traits unify and integrate a person's behaviour by causing that person to approach different situations with similar goals or plans in mind. A person who is highly competitive, for example, will view a variety of situations as opportunities to "beat" other people, to show that she or he is superior in strength, intelligence, or talent. Although acknowledging that situations do influence behaviour, he maintained that the way a person interprets situations depend on her or his inner disposition.

Allport also believed that two people who possess the same trait often express that trait in different ways. For example, one ambitious person may strive to achieve in the business world, another becomes a social climber, and another is a marathon runner. Allport saw each individual as having a unique personality profile; regardless of general traits she or he shares with others. For this reason, he is sometimes referred to as an idiographic theorist, that is, his primary focus was on unique, idiosyncratic cluster of traits that distinguishes each person from all others. He maintained that individuals can be only partially understood by administering standardized tests and comparing the results to group norms. In-depth case studies are necessary to do justice to the uniqueness of each human being. In contrast to the idiographic strategy is the nomothetic approach, which searches for general, all-encompassing laws of personality.

Allport lists seven characteristics of "psychological maturity", Allport's term for mental health:

1. Specific, enduring extensions of self that is involvement.
2. Dependable techniques for warm relating to others (for example, trust, empathy, genuineness, tolerance...).
3. Emotional security and self-acceptance.
4. Habits of realistic perception (as opposed to defensiveness).
5. Problem-centeredness and the development of problem-solving skills.
6. Self-objectification—insight into one's own behaviour, the ability to laugh at oneself, etc.
7. A unifying philosophy of life, including a particular value orientation, differentiated religious sentiment, and a personalized conscience.

Allport is one of those theorists who were so right about so many things that his ideas have simply passed on into the spirit of the times.

His theory is one of the first humanistic theories, and would influence many others, including Maslow and Rogers. One unfortunate aspect of his theory is his original use of the word "trait", which brought down the wrath of a number of situationally oriented behaviourists who would have been much more open to his theory if they had bothered to understand it. But that has always been a weakness of psychology in general and personality in particular.

3.5.2 Cattell's Theory of Personality or Cattell's Research Approach

Raymond Bernard Cattell (20 March 1905–2 February 1998), a British-born American researcher and psychologist and student of Spearman developed most advanced theory of personality based on the trait approach. Raymond Cattell is a nomothetic theorist, nomothetic approach searches for general, all-encompassing laws of personality. Raymond Cattell (1973) firmly believed that Psychology could become as exact and rigorous a science as chemistry and that it should be possible to identify the basic elements of personality, classify them, and understand the general laws by which the elements combine. He wanted to identify all of the personality traits possessed by humans. Cattell's main aim was to provide a complete account of all personality traits, even if some of these were rather similar to each other.

Raymond Bernard Cattell
(1905–1998)

Like Allport, Cattell believed that the vocabulary people use to describe themselves and others provided essential clues to the structure of personality. He claimed that the words in the English language provide useful information about personality. The reason is that any important way in which people differ from each other should be represented by some relevant words. He made use of a list of 4500 words that are used for personality description. These words were reduced to 160 trait words by removing unfamiliar words and words of the same meaning. Cattell then added eleven traits from personality literature, producing a total of 171 trait names which were claimed to cover almost everything of importance in personality. Cattell used factor-analysis to identify the basic or primary traits underlying the huge array of descriptive adjectives. "Factor-analysis" is a complex statistical or mathematical technique or procedure for identifying underlying sources of consistency. He applied factor-analysis to subjective ratings of personality (how people describe one another) in order to identify underlying or source straits. He used this information or life data to devise questionnaires which were administered to thousands of people of different ages and backgrounds. He also used several hundred objective tests to explore how traits might be expressed. Figure 13.2 shows cattell's sixteen factors of personality.

	1	2	3	4	5	6	7	8	
reserved									outgoing
less intelligent									more intelligent
affected by feelings									emotionally stable
submissive									dominant
serious									happy-go-lucky
expedient									conscientious
timid									venturesome
tough-minded									sensitive
trusting									suspicious
practical									imaginative
forthright									shrewd
self-assured									apprehensive
conservative									experimenting
group dependent									self-sufficient
uncontrolled									controlled
relaxex									tense

Figure 13.2 Cattell's sixteen factors of Personality (16 PF).

Cattell concluded that personality is composed of sixteen (16) primary or source traits, which he described in terms of opposing tendencies (Figure 13.2 and Table 13.2). Cattell's main contribution was the Sixteen Personality Factor Test (16 PF), which was designed to measure 16 aspects of personality. Table 13.2 shows Cattell's sixteen personality traits or factors (16 PF):

Table 13.2 Cattell's 16 personality traits or factors (16PF)

S.No	*Characteristics*	*Traits*	*Characteristics*
1	Reserved	A (Warmth)	Outgoing
2	Less intelligent	B (Intelligence)	More intelligent
3	Stable, ego strength	C (Ego-strength)	Emotionality, Neuroticism
4	Humble	E (Assertiveness)	Assertive
5	Sober	F	Happy-go-lucky
6	Expedient	G	Conscientious
7	Shy	H (Venturesome, character)	Venturesome
8	Tough-minded	I	Tender-minded
9	Trusting	L	Suspicious
10	Practical	M	Imaginative
11	Forthright	N	Shrewd
12	Self-assured, Placed	O	Apprehensive
13	Conservative	Q_1	Experimenting
14	Group-dependent	Q_2	Self-sufficient
15	Uncontrolled, Undisciplined	Q_3	Controlled
16	Relaxed	Q_4	Tense

Virtually all traits theorists credit Cattell with introducing and refining the quantitative approach to the study of Personality. But many feel that his table of personality elements is too complex, that it includes too many "surface" (as opposed to underlying "source") traits. One of these is Hans Eysenck. Howarth and Browne (1971) by using factor-analysis were able to identify only ten different factors in the 16 PF. They concluded that "The 16 PF does not measure the factors which it purports to measure." The great similarity among different personality factors on the 16 PF has led most experts to conclude that the 16 PF actually contains far fewer than 16 different personality factors.

Advantages of cattell's approach

(i) Cattell has put considerable effort into the task of providing a complete account of human personality.

(ii) Cattell has done more than anyone else to study personality in several different ways—by obtaining L, Q, and T data. Life data (L) is observer's ratings of other people's behaviour. Questionnaire (Q) data is obtained from self-report questionnaires. Objective test (T) data is careful assessment of some aspects of behaviour under controlled conditions. Cattell had hoped that the same personality traits would appear in L, Q, and T data.

(iii) Cattell's approach adopts an entirely scientific approach to the study of human personality, relying on the relatively objective evidence of questionnaire data or behaviour.

(iv) Cattell's theory emphasizes the importance of physiology and biology in human personality.

(v) It is accepted that behaviour depends in large measure on internal factors, for example, self, traits, and that external factors like rewards and punishments are not all important.

Disadvantages of Cattell's approach

(i) The evidence suggests that far fewer than 16 different personality traits are measured by the 16 PF.

(ii) Cattell's theory does not have an adequate account of the role played by heredity, environment, and physiology in producing individual differences in the various personality dimensions.

(iii) Cattell's theory pays little or no attention to the role of cognitive factors in personality.

(iv) Cattell argues that personality normally changes very little over time.

13.5.3 Murray's Theory of Personality or Henry A. Murray's Personology

The focus of Murray's theory is upon individuals in all their complexity and this point of view is highlighted by the term "Personology"; which was introduced by Murray (1936) as a label for his own efforts and those of others who were primarily concerned with a full understanding of the individual case. He has emphasized consistently the organic quality of behaviour; indicating that a single segment of behaviour is not to be understood in isolation from the rest of the functioning person. A further contrast to some holistic (treating the whole person rather than just the symptoms) theorists is his "field" orientation; his insistence that the environmental context of behaviour must be thoroughly understood and analyzed before an adequate account of individual's behaviour is possible.

Henry A. Murray
(13 May, 1893–23 June, 1988)

The past or history of the individual is fully as important in Murray's view as the present individual and her or his environment. His theory shares with psychoanalysis the assumption that events taking place in infancy and childhood are crucial determinants of adult behaviour. A further similarity between this position or theory and psychoanalysis lies in the considerable importance attributed to unconscious motivation and the deep interest displayed in the subjective or free, verbal report of the individual including imaginative productions. A further unusual feature of this theory is the consistent emphasis upon the coexisting and functionally linked physiological process that accompanies all psychological processes.

Urray agrees with Freud in conceiving of the Id as the repository or a storage place of primitive and unacceptable impulses. Here is the origin of energy, the source of all innate motives, the unseeing and the unsocialized self. Murray insists that the Id includes impulses that are acceptable to the society and self. Not only does the Id contain impulses towards both good and evil, but the strength of these tendencies varies between individuals.

13.5.4 Eysenck's Theory of Personality or Eysenck's Bio-Social Theory or Eysenck's Trait Type Theory or Eysenck's Dimensions of Personality

Hans Eysenck (4 March, 1916–4 September, 1997), a prominent British psychologist, was born on March 4, in Germany in 1916. He has written 75 books and some 700 articles, making him one of the most prolific writers in the field of Psychology. Eysenck taught at the University of London, as well as serving as the director of the Psychology department of the Institute of Psychiatry, associated with Bethlehem Royal Hospital. He retired in 1983 and continued to write until his death on September 4, 1997.

Eysenck believed in the biological basis of personality. Eysenck's theory is based primarily on physiology and genetics. Although he is a behaviourist who considers learned habits of great importance, he considers personality differences as growing out of our genetic inheritance. A biological substrate is responsible for individual differences on fundamental dimensions of personality. He is, therefore, interested in what is usually called *temperament*. "Temperament" is that aspect of our personalities that is genetically based, inborn, therefrom birth or even before. Eysenck's theory is also called "Temperament" theory. Thus, Eysenck focuses on "biological dimensions of personality", and his approach is "biosocial" in that the characteristic functioning of the central nervous system predisposes individuals to respond in certain ways to their environment.

Behaviour results from a person's position on these dimensions (biological, learning, and environmental), combined with the circumstances to which she or he is exposed. That is, behaviour typically reflects an interaction of person tendencies and environmental forces.

Eysenck distinguishes between the concepts of trait and type. A "trait" refers to a set of related behaviour that co-vary or repeatedly occur together. A person with a trait of sociability goes to parties, talks with friends, and likes to spend time with people, and so on. A "type" is a higher order or superordinate construct comprised of a set of correlated traits. An extravert, for example, is sociable, assertive, and venturesome.

Both concepts refer to continuous dimensions in contrast to the tendency to think of a type as and either—or set of categories. The distinction is that a type is more general and inclusive.

H.J. Eysenck argued that it was better to focus on a small number of really important personality traits (sometimes known as super factors). These *super factors* were chosen in such a way that they were not at all similar to each other. In technical terms, that was achieved by making sure that none of the factors was correlated or associated with any of the others.

Eysenck's original research found two main dimensions of temperament: Neuroticism and Extraversion-Introversion (Figure 13.3). Eysenck later proposed that three major dimensions—E, N, and P, defined as clusters or group of correlated traits (Figures 13.3 and 13.4) or three typological dimensions or three major personality traits or superfactors account for most of human behaviour, all of which are measured by Eysenck Personality Questionnaire—EPQ (Eysenck, 1947, 1953, 1975, 1992). These factors are as follows:

E (EXTRAVERSION): Introversion versus Extraversion

Introversion versus Extraversion is a dimension or type of personality fairly similar to Jung's categorization of people as either introverts or extraverts. Introversion-Extraversion is the extent to which people are socially withdrawn or socially outgoing. Introversion versus Extraversion describes the extent to which people are shy or outgoing. It includes such traits as being silent or talkative, reclusive or talkative, cautious or adventurous, inclined to stay in the shadows or eager to be in the limelight (Figure 13.3). On one hand are those who are passive, quiet, cautious, and reserved. On the other hand are those who are socially outgoing, active, optimistic, gregarious, impulsive, excitement-oriented, and jolly people. Those scoring high on Extraversion (extraverts) are more sociable and impulsive than those scoring low (introverts). Extraversion as opposed to introversion refers to the out-going, uninhibited, sociable proclivities of a person. Extraversion is associated with positive emotionality, the inclination to be enthusiastic, lively, and cheerful (Figures 13.3 and 13.4). However, Eysenck notes that few perfect introverts or extraverts exist. Instead, a person can be placed anywhere between these two extremes, that is on a continuum ranging from Introversion to Extraversion instead of naming types as Introverts and Extraverts.

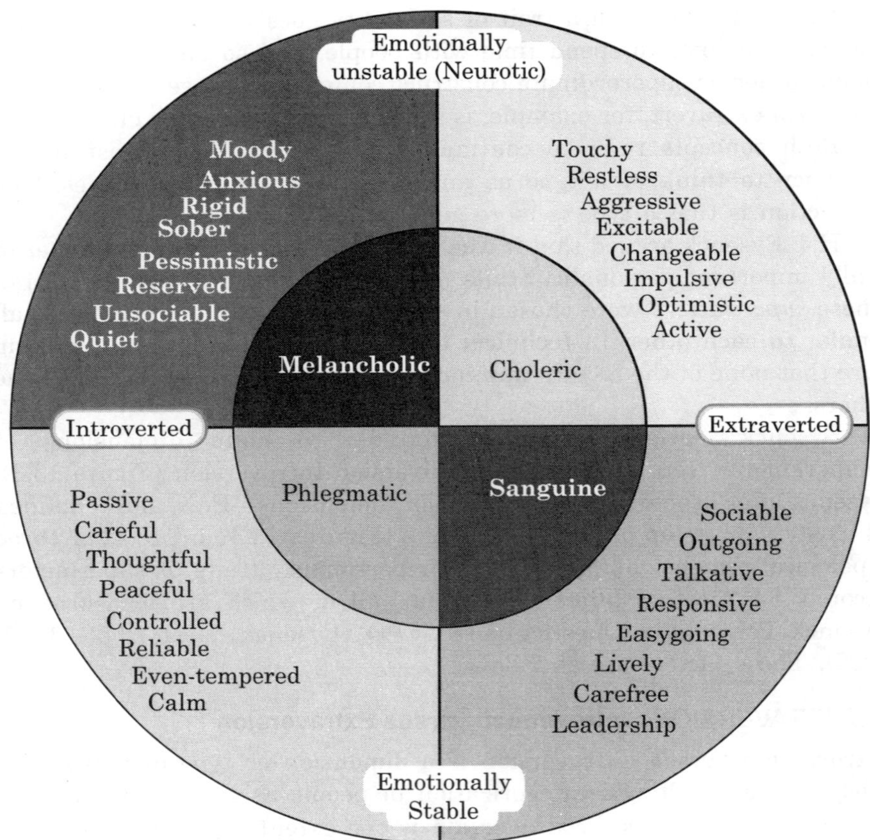

Figure 13.3 Characteristics of various personality types.

Eysenck concluded that differences in personality have a biological basis. He reported that introverts and extraverts differ in their level of arousal in a specific structure of the brain, the reticular formation (Eysenck, 1970). So far as extraversion is concerned, introverts were assumed to have a higher level of cortical arousal (activity in the brain) than extraverts. This occurs because of individual differences in activity in a part of the brain known as the ascending reticular activating system. In general, introverts have higher levels of arousal internally, so they tend to avoid external stimulation. So, the introvert seeks out situations that minimize stimulation, thus preventing cortical arousal from becoming too great. In contrast, extraverts tend to have lower levels of arousal internally in the cortex of the brain. As a result, they seek high levels of external stimulation to raise cortical arousal to an optimum level. Nervous system is insensitive. The nervous system is not very sensitive and they seek the arousal.

Extraversion-Introversion dimension is found in everyone, but the physiological explanation is a bit more complex. Eysenck hypothesized that Extraversion-Introversion is a matter of the balance of "inhibition" and "excitation" in the brain itself. Excitation is the brain-waking itself up, getting into an alert, learning state. Inhibition is the brain-calming itself down, either in the usual sense of relaxing and going to sleep, or in the sense of protecting itself in the case of overwhelming stimulation.

Someone who is extraverted, hypothesizes and has good, strong inhibition: when confronted by traumatic stimulation—such as car crash—the extravert's brain inhibits itself, which means that it becomes "numb", you might say, to the trauma, and therefore will remember very little of what happened. After the car crash, the extravert might feel as if he had "blanked out" during the event, and may ask others to fill them in on what happened. Because they do not feel the full mental impact of the crash, they may be ready to go back to driving the very next day. One of the things that Eysenck discovered was that violent criminals tend to be non-neurotic extraverts.

The introvert, on the other hand, has poor or weak inhibition: when trauma, such as the car crash, hits them, their brains do not protect them fast enough, do not in any way shut down. Instead, they are highly alert and learn well, and so remember everything that happened. They might even report that they saw the whole crash "in slow motion!" They are very unlikely to want to drive anytime soon after the crash, and may even stop driving altogether.

This makes sense in terms of the observed behaviour of extraverts and introverts. Extraverts spend much more of their time than introverts with other people, whereas introverts adopt a more cautious and reserved approach to life.

Evidence relating to cortical arousal in introverts and extraverts was reviewed by Gale (1983). He considered studies of electroencephalography (EEG that is brain-wave activity). Out of 38 experiments, introverts were more critically aroused than extraverts in 22 experiments, the opposite was the case in 5 experiments, and the two groups did not differ in the other 11 experiments. Thus, introverts are generally more cortically aroused than extraverts, but this is by no means always the case.

More recent experiments have confirmed and refined Eysenck's biological hypothesis. These studies show that introverts and extraverts differ not in their resting or baseline levels of arousal, but in their response to stimulation or arousability (Stelmack, 1990).

Characteristics of Extraverts: The following are the characteristics of the extraverted person:

- Outgoing and loud
- Lively, full of high spirits
- Carefree
- Impulsive
- Optimistic
- Quiet social, sociable
- Takes interest in other people
- Insensitive to social criticism
- Practical kind or type of person
- Risk-taking
- Very talkative
- Helpful
- Has many friends
- Adventurous
- Has spontaneous interests
- Has rapid movement
- Mobile
- Inclined towards direct action
- Takes interest in other people, in outward activities, more than in their own ideas and emotions
- Thick-skinned
- Not easily offended or embarrassed
- Man of action
- Sportive
- Acts before she or he thinks
- Do not confine herself or himself to a particular routine work.
- Magnify or exaggerate her or his success and ignore failures.
- Show much love to the external world, physical and social objects.
- Do not set up defensive attitude. So, it is easier to make friendship with such persons
- Less emotional. Life for these persons is less emotional
- Has poor occupational histories
- Has sexual difficulties
- Has poor performance on intelligence tests
- Adjusts very easily to different situations and circumstances

Actors, doctors, engineers, sales representatives, advertising agents, social workers belong to this type.

According to Eysenck and Eysenck (1975), "The typical extravert is sociable, likes parties, has many friends, needs to have people to talk to, and does not like reading or studying by himself. He craves excitement, takes chances, often sticks his neck out, acts on the spur of the moment, and is generally an impulsive individual. He is fond of practical jokes, always has a ready answer, and generally likes change; he is carefree, easy-going, optimistic, and likes to laugh and be merry. He prefers to keep moving and doing things, tends to be aggressive and loses his temper easily; altogether his feelings are not kept under tight control, and he is not always a reliable person."

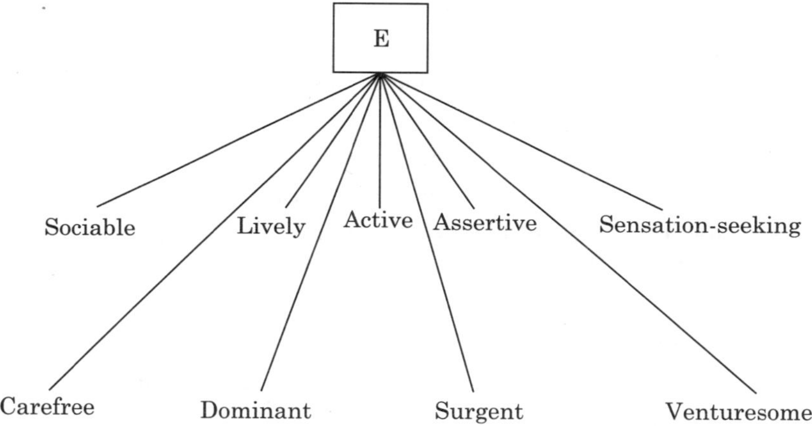

Figure 13.4 Characteristics of extraversion.

Extraversion declines with age. It is more marked for men than for women. The usual superiority of men appears to be found only in the below-forty groups; above that age, women appear more extraverted (Figure 13.4).

Characteristics of Introverts: "Introversion" is a combination of two words, "intro" and "version", which means life energy turning inside. The introvert person is more interested in her or his thoughts and ideas than in the immediate social environment (Figure 13.3). Jung says that minds of introverts can be compared with very deep lakes. The following are some of the features of an introverted person:

- Quiet, careful, passive, and reserved
- Introspective and reflective
- Disciplined and well-ordered people
- Likes to stay alone, remain alone

- Imaginary, indecisive, socially reserved
- Magnifies her or his failures too much
- Extremely self-analytical and self-criticized
- More theoretical
- Persistent and rigid
- Subjective
- Fond of day-dreaming, have day-dreaming
- Afraid of external realities
- Tactless
- Cold and shy
- Socially sensitive, feels offended easily
- Indecisive, unable to make decisions
- Has her or his own world of thinking
- Always dissatisfied with her or his work
- Sad kind of person
- Possesses refined tastes and interests
- Choosy and remain moody most of the times
- Unable to express her or his feelings
- Has her or his own likes and dislikes
- Has slowness in moving
- Has poor attention
- Obtains satisfaction from her or his mental imagery
- Repressive type of person
- Likes to brood all the while
- Irritable
- Prone to thought than to action, prefers thinking than action
- Worries too much even for small matters and incidents
- Not very friendly; rather has a few friends
- Centre her or his interests around herself or himself
- Prefers thinking than action
- Not very practical
- Sometimes suffer from inferiority complex
- Takes long time to make a decision and decisions are personalized
- Usually lean and thin
- Suffers from stomach troubles
- Likes jobs which require thoughtful planning and systematic organizations

Scientists, philosophers, teachers, poets, artists belong to this group.

According to Eysenck and Eysenck (1975), "The typical introvert is a quiet, retiring sort of person, introspective, fond of books rather than people; he is reserved and distant except to intimate friends. He tends to plan ahead, "looks before he leaps" and distrusts the impulse of the moment. He does not like excitement, takes matters of everyday life with proper seriousness, and likes a well-ordered mode of life. He keeps his feelings under close control, seldom behaves in an aggressive manner, and does not lose his temper easily. He is reliable, somewhat pessimistic, and places great value on ethical standards."

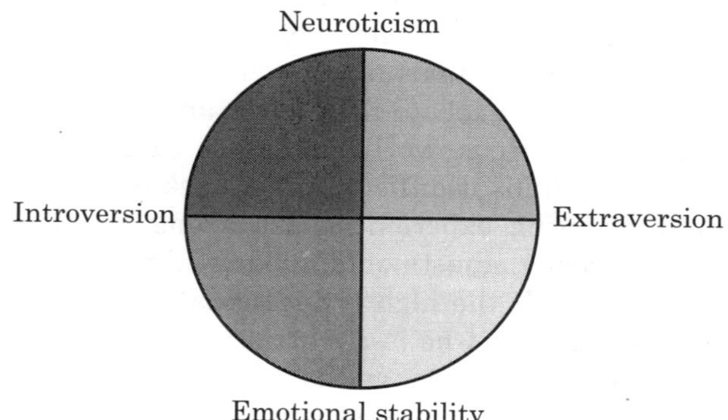

Figure 13.5 Extraversion and Neuroticism.

N (Neuroticism): Emotional stability versus neuroticism or stability versus neuroticism or stability versus instability

Neuroticism is the name Eysenck gave to a dimension that ranges from normal, fairly calm, and collected people to one's that tend to be quite "nervous". His research showed that these nervous people tended to suffer more frequently from a variety of "nervous disorders" we call *neuroses*, hence the name of the dimension (Figure 13.5). "Stability versus instability" refers to a person's general moodiness. In different terms, it can be emotional stability versus neuroticism, the degree to which people have control over their feelings. Those scoring high on neuroticism are more tense and anxious than those scoring low. Again, however, a person can be placed at any point along the stability-instability continuum. At one extreme is the very emotionally stable person. A stable person or emotionally stable or who is not neurotic or who is low on neuroticism is calm, carefree, even-tempered, dependable, reliable, controlled, unworried, almost never falling to pieces (Figure 13.3). A person who is unstable or neurotic or emotionally unstable is moody, touchy, anxious, restless, aggressive, and quick to fly out of control (Figure 13.3). At the other extreme is the highly neurotic person. Neuroticism or emotional instability includes such traits as anxiety and inability to control impulses, a tendency to have unrealistic ideas, and general emotional instability and negativity. "Neuroticism" refers to the general emotional liability of a person, his emotional over-responsiveness and his liability to neurotic breakdown under stress. Neuroticism is sometimes called negative emotionality because of the neurotic person's tendency to feel anger, scorn, revulsion, guilt, anxiety, and other negative moods (Watson and Clark, 1992). Neurotic individuals are worriers, complainers, and defeatists, even in the absence of any major problems (Figures 13.3 and 13.6). They complain about different things at different ages, but they are always ready to see the sour side of life and none of its sweetness.

According to Eysenck and Eysenck (1975), neurotic is a "The typical high N scorer as being an anxious, worrying individual, moody, and frequently depressed. He is likely to sleep badly, and to suffer from various psychosomatic disorders. He is overly emotional, reacting too strongly to all sorts of stimuli and finds it difficult to get back on an even keel after each emotionally arousing experience. His strong emotional reactions interfere with his proper adjustment, making him react in irrational, sometimes rigid ways.... If the high N individual has to be described in one word, one might say that he is a worrier: his main characteristic is a constant preoccupation with things that might go wrong, and a strong emotional reaction of anxiety to these thoughts. The stable individual, on the other hand, tends to respond emotionally only slowly and generally weakly, and to return to baseline quickly after emotional arousal: he is usually calm, even-tempered, controlled and unworried."

So far as neuroticism is concerned, Eysenck argued that neuroticism depends on activity within the visceral brain, which consists of the hippocampus, amygdala, cingulum, septum, and hypothalamus. He argued that those high in neuroticism have a more active visceral brain than those low in neuroticism. However, physiological studies have usually found no difference in physiological responding between those high and low in neuroticism (Fahrenberg, 1992).

Neuroticism is a genetically-based, physiologically-supported dimension of personality. He, therefore, went to the physiological research to find possible explanations. The most obvious place to look was at the sympathetic nervous system. This is a part of the autonomic nervous system that functions separately from the central nervous system and controls much of our emotional responsiveness to emergency situations. For example, when signals from the brain tell it to do so, the sympathetic nervous system instructs the liver to release sugar for energy, causes the digestive system to slow down, opens up the pupils, raises the hairs on your body (Goosebumps), and tells the adrenal glands to release more adrenalin (epinephrine). The adrenalin in turn, alters many of the body's functions and prepares the muscles for action. Adrenaline (a-DREN-a-lin), also called *epinephrine*, (ep-e-NEF-rin), is a hormone, or chemical messenger, that is released. In response to fear, anger, panic, and other emotions, it readies the body to respond to threats by increasing heart rate, breathing rate, and blood flow to the arms and legs. These and other effects prepare the body to flight (run away) or fight. The traditional way of describing the function of the sympathetic nervous system is to say that it prepares us for "fight or flight".

Eysenck hypothesized that some people have a more responsive sympathetic nervous system than others. Some people remain very calm during emergencies; some people feel considerable fear or other emotions; and some are terrified by even very minor incidents. He suggested that this latter group had a problem of sympathetic hyperactivity, which made them prime candidates for the various neurotic disorders.

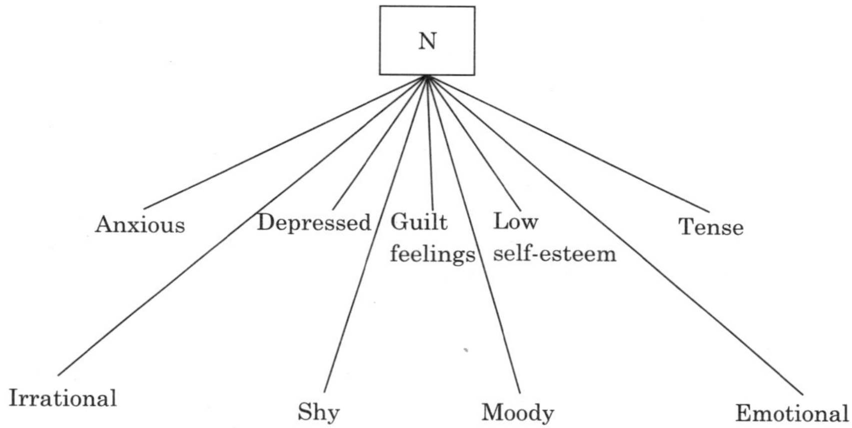

Figure 13.6 Characteristics of Neuroticism.

N, too, declines with age. Perhaps, rather less precipitately than P and E and here males and females run parallel for all interests and purposes. The decline is not large, but nevertheless quite definite.

P (Psychoticism): Psychoticism versus impulse control

In more recent years, Eysenck (1976) has expanded his original two-dimensional descriptive model by adding a third descriptive dimension of Psychoticism—P. The third dimension is what Eysenck called "Psychoticism" or what American psychologists usually call "Psychopathology", a lack of feeling for others, a tough matter of interacting with others, and a tendency to be different to defy social conventions. Psychoticism can indicate a psychological disorder in extreme cases, but Eysenck proposed that it is a personality characteristic that can be applied in varying degrees to everyone. Those scoring high tend to be aggressive, hostile, and uncaring. Psychoticism is an independent dimension which describes the personality as cold, solitary, ego-centric, impersonal, impulsive, cruel, hostile to others, inhuman, not caring, troublesome, sensation-seeking, and insensitive, not showing any loyalty or concern for others, lacks empathy and feelings, liking for odd and unusual things, and opposed to accepted social norms (Figure 13.7). The kinds of qualities found in high psychotic people include certain recklessness, a disregard for common sense or conventions, and a degree of inappropriate emotional expression. A person who is low on P is more empathic, less adventurous, and bold.

According to Eysenck and Eysenck (1975), "A high scorer, then, may be described as being solitary, not caring for people; he is often troublesome, not fitting in anywhere. He may be cruel and inhuman, lacking in feeling and empathy, and altogether insensitive. He is hostile to others, even his own kith and kin, and aggressive, even to loved ones. He has a liking for odd and unusual things, and a disregard for danger; he likes to make fools of other people, and to upset them. This is the description of adult high P scorer; as far as children are concerned, we obtain a fairly congruent picture of an odd, isolated troublesome child; glacial and lacking in human feelings for his fellow-beings and for animals; aggressive and hostile, even to near-and-dear ones. Such children try to make up for lack of feeling by indulging in sensation-seeking "arousal jags" without thinking of the dangers involved. Socialization is a concept which is relatively alien to both adults and children; empathy, feelings of guilt, sensitivity to other people are notions which are strong and unfamiliar to them."

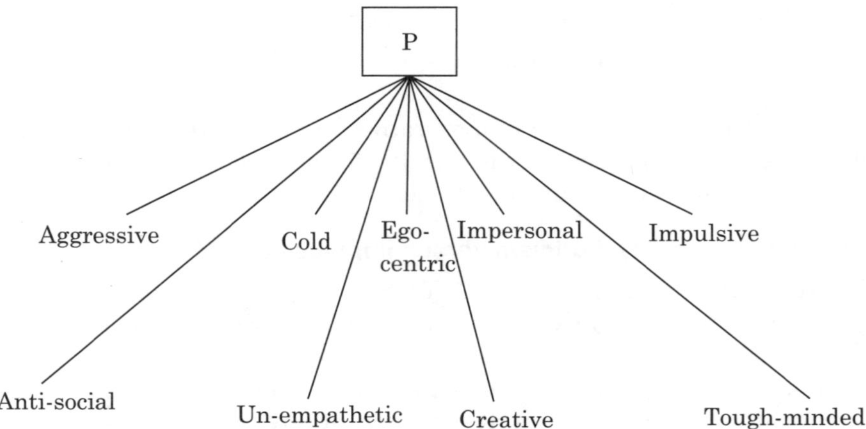

Figure 13.7 Characteristics of Psychoticism.

There is decrease in P score with age (more marked for males than for females).

According to Eysenck (1967), individual differences in these dimensions are due in large part to heredity. The degree of similarity can be expressed in terms of correlation. A correlation of 0.00 indicates no similarity at all, whereas a correlation of + 1.0 indicates perfect similarity. Shields (1962) found that the correlation between identical twins brought up together was + 0.38 for neuroticism and + 0.42 for extraversion, which indicates some degree of similarity in personality. This compared with correlations of + 0.11 for neuroticism and –0.17 for extraversion between fraternal twins, which indicates little or no similarity. Surprisingly, identical twins brought up apart were even more similar in personality than those brought up together, producing correlations of + 0.53 for neuroticism and of + 0.61 for extraversion. The fact that identical twins (and especially identical twins brought up apart) were more similar in personality than fraternal twins indicates that heredity plays a part in determining personality.

According to H.J. Eysenck, "Heredity influences the responsiveness of parts of the physiological system."

Eysenck is also primarily a research psychologist. His methods involve a statistical technique called *factor-analysis*. This technique extracts a number of "dimensions" from large masses of data. For example, if you give long lists of adjectives to a large number of people for them to rate themselves on, you have prime raw material for factor-analysis. Eysenck concludes that his three factors consistently emerge from factor-analytic studies of personality questionnaires.

Eysenck (1947, 1990) believes that a model of personality must be hierarchical. He proposes a hierarchy containing four levels. At the bottom level are specific responses such as talking before class on a single occasion. At the second level are habitual responses, which include frequent or recurring behaviours such as talking before class on a regular basis. The third level is that of traits, which are defined in terms of inter-correlated sets of habitual responses. A person who is sociable, for example, talks before class, enjoys talking with other people, likes to go to parties, and so on. At the highest level of generality are types, which in turn, are defined as inter-correlated sets of traits. For example, the Psychoticism type subsumes the traits of aggressive, impulsive, and anti-social. Eysenck identifies the three types using factor-analysis. In factor-analytic terms, a trait is a primary factor and a type is a second-order factor. Eysenck proposes that Psychoticism, Extraversion, and Neuroticism structure individual differences in temperament, or the non-cognitive domain of personality. He acknowledges intelligence as a separate characteristic that structures individual differences within the cognitive domain.

Eysenck (1990) advances three arguments that biological factors play a critical role in determining individual differences on the three types:

1. These same factors consistently have emerged in investigations of personality structure in widely divergent cultures (Barratt

and Eysenck, 1984); this cross-cultural unanimity is difficult to explain except in terms of biological factors.

2. Individuals tend to retain their position on these dimensions across time (Conley, 1984, 1985).
3. There is evidence of a substantial heritable component in individual on the three dimensions (Eaves, Eysenck, and Martin, 1989; Loehlin, 1989).

Both of these last two findings clearly suggest to Eysenck that biological factors contribute to individual differences on the typologies. It is assumed that all three factors are determined to a large extent by heredity. In addition, there is a large body of work that directly supports the biological bases of Extraversion and Neuroticism (for example, Bullock and Gilliland, 1993; Eysenck, 1967; Eysenck, H.J., 1985; Gale and Eysenck, 1989; Matthews and Amelang, 1993; Smith, 1983; Smith, Rockwell-Tisher and Davidson, 1986; Stelmack, 1981, 1990; Stelmack and Geen, 1992; Stelmack, Houlihan, and Mc Garry-Roberts, 1993; Sternberg, 1992; Strelan and Eysenck, 1987).

Advantages of Eysenck's theory of personality

(i) Later work has confirmed that extraversion and neuroticism are major personality traits; it is not clear that psychoticism is a major trait.

(ii) There is much support for the view that there are a small number of major traits; many argue that there are five such traits: extraversion, neuroticism, conscientiousness, agreeableness, and openness (McCrae and Costa, 1987).

(iii) Heredity plays a role in determining an individual's level of extraversion, neuroticism, and psychoticism, but much less than was assumed by Eysenck.

Disadvantages of Eysenck's theory of personality

(i) Little progress has been made in finding the physiological systems associated with the super factors, with the possible exception of extraversion.

(ii) Reducing personality to only three traits leaves out much of the richness and complexity of personality.

13.6 TECHNIQUES OF ASSESSMENT (PSYCHOMETRIC AND PROJECTIVE)

Psychological testing of personality is based on two general types—self-report inventories and projective tests. Self-report inventories pose questions about personal habits, attitudes, beliefs, and fantasies. Some of the psychometric measures to assess personality are discussed below:

13.6.1 The Minnesota Multiphasic Personality Inventory (MMPI)

The Minnesota Multiphasic Personality Inventory was developed by J.C. McKinley and S.R. Hathaway. MMPI consists of 550 items. Each item is printed on a separate card. The answers to the items included in this inventory indicate certain personality traits of the individual. The subject has to respond to the questions of the inventory by giving the answers in "yes", "no", or "doubtful" in the space provided for the answer. Responses are then evaluated. The MMPI has become the most widely used psychological test in the clinical setting (Helmes and Reddon, 1993; Lubin and others, 1984).

13.6.2 The Sixteen Personality Factor Inventory (16 PF)

The Sixteen Personality Questionnaire (16 PF) is an objectively scorable test devised by basic research in psychology to give the most complete coverage of personality. The test was designed for use with individuals aged sixteen years and above. Forms A, B, C, and D are most appropriate for individuals whose educational level is roughly equivalent to that of the normal high school student. Form E is designed for individuals with marked educational and/or reading deficiency. The 16 PF can be scored by hand or by a computer, and various types of answer sheets are available. The personality factors measured by the 16 PF are not just unique to the test, but, instead, rest within the context of a general theory of personality. Nearly ten years of empirical, factor-analytic research preceded the first commercial publication of the test in 1949. Since this time, five major revisions of items and many additional improvements, such as supplementary validity scales, have been incorporated into the 16 PF.

The dimensions of 16 PF are set out in Table 13.2. Each factor is listed with its alphabetical designation and brief descriptions of high and low scores. These 16 dimensions or scales are essentially independent. 10–13 items are provided for each scale in Form A and B. In Form C and Form D, there are 8 items. Three alternative answers are provided for each of the questions.

13.6.3 The Eysenck Personality Questionnaire (EPQ)

The Eysenck Personality Questionnaire is the result of many years of developmental work. The questionnaire presents three-dimensional analysis of personality E–I (Extraversion-Introversion), N (Neuroticism),

P (Psychoticism), and some L (lie scale) items. Each of these three traits is measured by means of 100 questions, carefully selected after lengthy item-analysis and factor-analysis. The final version of the EPQ is described in considerable detail in the book titled *Psychoticism: A Dimension of Personality* (Eysenck and Eysenck, 1975). The test-retest reliability of the test lies in the .80 to .90 region. The EPQ is not inferior to any other published personality test. The subject has to answer the questions of the test by putting a cross mark in the box following "Yes" or "No". The subject is instructed not to think too long about the exact meaning of the question. Scoring is done with the help of scoring key. The raw scores are then converted to sten scores. The stens are converted to centiles.

13.6.4 The California Personality Inventory

The California Psychological Inventory (CPI) is a self-report inventory created by Harrison Gough and currently published by Consulting Psychologists Press. It was created in a similar manner to the Minnesota Multiphasic Personality Inventory (MMPI), but unlike the MMPI, it is not concerned with maladjustment or clinical diagnosis, but concerned itself with more "normal" aspects of personality.

Test design: The CPI is made up of 434 true-false questions, half of which were taken from the original version of the MMPI. The test is scored on 18 scales, three of which are validity scales. Eleven of the non-validity scales were selected by comparing responses from various groups of people. The other four were content validated.

The test is typically used with people aged 13 years and older. It takes about 45–60 minutes to complete.

The revised third edition of the CPI contains 434 items. This latest version requires that the patient's false and true answers be transformed at an additional cost into raw scale and standard scores by the publisher, who will also provide interpretative report writing. The older CPI with the 462 items is still available for sale by the publisher, Consulting Psychologists Press, and comes with plastic scoring keys and profile sheets, thus allowing each research or clinical psychologist to score the test by hand, an admittedly less convenient but nonetheless a less expensive alternative, one ideally suited for use in training psychology students.

Scoring: The inventory contains 434 items which can be scored to yield 18 scales. The 18 scales are further grouped into four classes: (1) measures of poise, ascendancy, self-assurance, and interpersonal adequacy; (2) measures of socialization, responsibility, intrapersonal values, and character; (3) measures of achievement potential and intellectual efficiency; (4) measures of intellectual modes and interest modes.

This paragraph will discuss what are referred to as the structural scales of the CPI-462 version, using information being provided by the manual for that version, the CPI Administrator's Guide from 1987. Alpha, Beta, Delta, and Gamma personality types are conveniently illustrated by a score's placement on a grid defined by the two dimensions—the degree to which the person is norm-favouring or norm-questioning on one dimension (called the v.2 scale), and the degree to which she or he is more externally or internally focused (the v.1 scale). Alpha personality types are more enterprising, dependable, and outgoing. Betas are reserved, responsible, and moderate. Gammas are adventurous, restless, and pleasure-seeking. Finally, Deltas are withdrawn, private, and to some extent disaffected. In a separate measure known as *Realization*, also referred to as the v.3 scale, a tester's score may reflect the degree to which she or he is reflective, capable, and optimistic about the present and future, when the score is high, or possesses the opposite characteristics when low. Thus, research scientists or medical or psychology graduate students tend to score high on this scale, while psychiatric patients, juvenile delinquents, prison inmates and even high school students in general (who lack life experience and are still forging a solid sense of identity) tend to score low.

Another components of this test are the 20 Folk Concept Scales (18 in the CPI-434 version)—measuring Dominance, Capacity for Status, Sociability, Social Presence, Self-acceptance, Independence, Empathy, Responsibility, Socialization, Self-control, Good Impression, Communality, Well-being, Tolerance, Achievement via Conformance, Achievement via Independence, Intellectual Efficiency, Psychological-mindedness, Flexibility, and Femininity/Masculinity. These scales are called "folk" as they attempt to capture personality themes that should be broadly cross-cultural and easily understood around the world. This test is thus an attempt to tap into personality factors that arise without exception to some, varying, degree, in all humans regardless of cultural context, and which provide a picture of people's relatively stable tendencies and characteristics, which is as good as any definition for what is loosely termed their unique "Personality".

Validity: Correlations between CPI scales and related external criteria tend to fall in the .2 to .5 ranges. This degree of correlation is typical for much of personality research. Extremely high correlations are not likely to be found for personality measures because the scales typically try to assess rather broad behavioural tendencies.

Norms are available for males only, females only, and male/female data combined. The CPI has been very popular in research and in individual assessments of adolescents and adults. The fact that it was developed and normed on non-psychiatric or non-clinical populations is regarded almost universally as part of its positive reputation and usefulness among psychologists.

Advantages of the personality inventories and questionnaires

(i) Inventories and questionnaires are economical in terms of time and money. Use of these measures makes possible the study of a number of subjects in minimum of time and money because it can be administered on a number of subjects at a particular time.

(ii) We can obtain information many times from the same respondents and thus reliable data can be collected. Questionnaires are reliable and valid, that is these are standardized (objective, accurate, and precised measures).

Disadvantages of the personality inventories and questionnaires

(i) It is difficult to establish rapport with all the subjects if these are administered in groups.

(ii) It is difficult to get answers or responses to all the questions from the subjects.

(iii) Subject may not give the true answers or may be ignorant of her or his own traits or characteristics. Questionnaires are often, justifiably, considered susceptible to distortion and deliberate faking.

(iv) Objective tests are not a good way of measuring personality. They are unreliable, with people often obtaining different scores when given the same objective test twice.

13.6.5 Projective Techniques

Projective techniques are based on the phenomena of "Projection". According to Anastasi (1988), "The material used in these techniques or tests represents "a sort of screen" on which the subject "projects" his characteristics through processes, needs, anxieties, and conflicts." Projective techniques make use of ambiguous or unstructured material in order to permit individuals to express their own perception of the material. In projective testing, the subject's responses to ambiguous or unstructured situations are assumed to reflect inner reality. Projective tests assess the way people respond to and interpret ambiguous stimuli such as inkblots and pictures in which the motives and feelings of the characters are not clear. The test takers describe what they see in these materials. Presumably, in doing so, they project their own uncontrolled feelings, conflicts, needs, and personality characteristics. Someone who repeatedly sees peering eyes/and threatening figures in abstract blots of ink is projecting onto the inkblots the fears and suspicious typical of paranoia. The main projective techniques are discussed below:

The Rorschach inkblot test

Hermann Rorschach
(1884–1922)

The Rorschach inkblot test was developed by Hermann Rorschach (8 November, 1884–2 April, 1922), the Swiss psychiatrist. The Rorschach test is a projective test, developed in the year 1921, consisting of a series of inkblots, about which the subject reports her or his perceptions; the assessor subsequently interprets these responses. The Rorschach inkblot test is the best projective test. It is composed of 10 cards each containing a rather elaborate inkblot; 5 inkblots are in colour and 5 in grey and black (Figure 13.8). These inkblots are completely unstructured—the shapes of the blots do not have any specific meaning. The unstructured material gives the subject or the respondent the freedom to give as many responses as she or he wants.

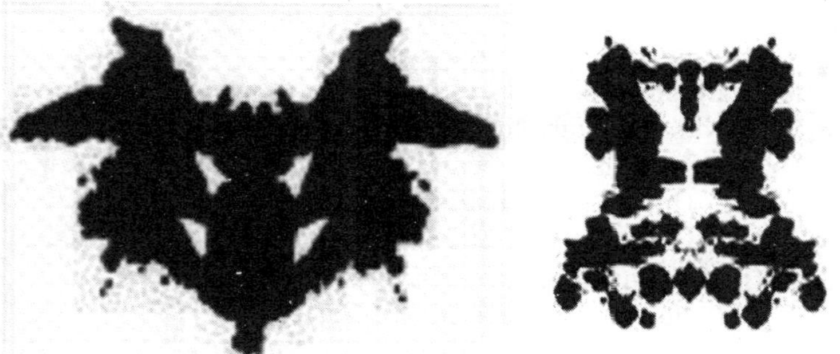

Figure 13.8 A card of Rorschach inkblot test.

The subject studies one blot at a time and tells what she or he thinks each blot resembles. The cards are presented one at a time in a specified order. The subject is allowed to give as many responses as she or he wants and is permitted as much time as she or he needs. The subject is also allowed to turn the card around as she or he pleases and looks at it from any angle. In this way, the subject reveals her or his inner self by going deeper in the unconscious mind and projecting repressed thoughts, feelings, wishes, desires, fears, hopes, ambitions, etc. The responses and time taken are recorded, and then cards are shown to the subject a second time and the subject is asked to elaborate any ambiguous interpretations and explain which parts of the inkblots led to her or his responses. Results are scored against three main criteria—do their responses involve movement, form, colour or all the three combined? Is the form clear or blurred? Do subjects see human figures (H), or animal figures (A), or natural objects (N) like rivers, green fields, etc., or inanimate objects like pot, etc.? Seeing whole figures indicates high intelligence and the ability to synthesize. Predominance of forms in motion, especially human forms, shows vivid imagination. Marked responses to colour show impulsiveness, if not emotional instability. The seeing mostly of animal forms shows lower intelligence and stereotyped thinking. The noting of small, unusual details shows introversion and possible emotion conflicts, and the noting of three-dimensional shading effects shows anxiety. A preponderance of responses determined by shape or form means good control and harmony between the intellectual and emotional aspects of personality (Klopfer and Kelley, 1942).

The Thematic Apperception Test (TAT)

The Thematic Apperception Test or TAT was introduced in 1943 by Henry A. Murray (13 May, 1893–23 June, 1988) to measure the need for achievement. Later, it was fully developed for the assessment of personality with the help of the psychologist C.D. Morgan. The TAT is considered to be the most elaborate and systematic study of personality.

Henry A. Murray
(1893–1988)

The TAT was first developed in 1935 by Henry Murray, Christiana Morgan, and their colleagues at the Harvard Psychological Clinic. The early versions of the TAT listed Morgan as the first author, but later versions dropped her name. One of the controversies surrounding the history of the TAT concerns the long and conflict-ridden extramarital relationship between Morgan and Murray, and its reinforcement of the prejudices that existed in the 1930s against women in academic psychology and psychiatry.

It is generally agreed, however, that the basic idea behind the TAT came from one of Murray's undergraduate students. The student mentioned that her son had spent his time recuperating from an illness by cutting pictures out of magazines and making up stories about them. The student wondered whether similar pictures could be used in therapy to tap into the nature of a patient's fantasies.

The Thematic Apperception Test, or TAT, is a projective measure intended to evaluate a person's patterns of thought, attitudes, observational capacity, and emotional responses to ambiguous test materials. In the case of the TAT, the ambiguous materials consist of a set of cards that portray human figures in a variety of settings and situations (Figure 13.9). The subject is asked to tell the examiner a story about each card that includes the following elements: the event shown in the picture;

what has led up to it; what the characters in the picture are feeling and thinking; and the outcome of the event.

Because the TAT is an example of a projective instrument—that is, it asks the subject to project her or his habitual patterns of thought and emotional responses onto the pictures on the cards—many psychologists prefer not to call it a "test", because it implies that there are "right" and "wrong" answers to the questions. They consider the term "technique" to be a more accurate description of the TAT and other projective assessments. The TAT is one of the oldest projective measures in continuous use. It has become the most popular projective technique among English-speaking psychiatrists and psychologists, and is better accepted among clinicians than the Rorschach's.

The TAT is often administered to individuals as part of a battery, or group, of tests intended to evaluate personality. It is considered to be effective in eliciting information about a person's view of the world and her or his attitudes towards the self and others. As people taking the TAT proceed through the various story cards and tell stories about the pictures, they reveal their expectations of relationships with peers, parents or other authority figures, subordinates, and possible romantic partners. In addition to assessing the content of the stories that the subject is telling, the examiner evaluates the subject's manner, vocal tone, posture, hesitations, and other signs of an emotional response to a particular story picture. For example, a person who is made anxious by a certain picture may make comments about the artistic style of the picture, or remark that she or he does not like the picture; this is a way of avoiding telling a story about it.

Figure 13.9 A card of the Thematic Apperception Test (TAT).

The subject has to interpret a picture by telling a story about it—what is happening, what led upto the scene and what the outcome will be. Like the Rorschach test, the material or the stimulus is unstructured. The pictures chosen are somewhat vague, and allow varied interpretations. Thus, the responses are dictated by the past experiences, conflicts, and wishes of the subject. Essentially, the subject projects himself into the scene, identifying with a character. Unlike in the Rorschach test, the major analysis is based on the content of responses rather than on the formal aspects. TAT identifies the subject's drives, conflicts, and attitudes towards himself. The test is composed of 30 pictures or cards—10 for males, 10 for females, and 10 for both sexes. The test is usually administered in two sessions. The subject has to make up a story for each of the pictures or cards presented to her or him, within a fixed period of time. The subject is led to believe that her or his imagination is being tested and that there is no right or wrong responses. In making up the stories, the subject unconsciously projects several characteristics of her or his personality. Final interpretation is made by studying all the stories of a subject. The pictures or cards are presented one at a time. All the pictures or cards are numbered. The degree of ambiguity increases with the increasing numbers. According to Murray, the test should take one hour at the most for its administration. The general quality of his thinking, originality, logic, ability to exercise control under emotional stress, bizarre language, habits of attacking problems, inhibitions, and several other aspects of personality are revealed in almost all stories—as in these stories, he raises problems or situations, delves into reasons for them and attempts to solve or finalize those problems for the characters in the pictures. He identifies himself with the situations and his own personality is thrown in, which the psychologist receives as if on a platter (Murray, 1943). TAT is used for selection and guidance purposes. It is also used for the diagnosis of various mental disorders. TAT works well with adults.

Students in medicine, psychology, or other fields who are learning to administer and interpret the TAT, receive detailed instructions about the number of factors that can influence a person's responses to the story cards. In general, they are advised to be conservative in their interpretations, and to err "on the side of health" rather than of psychopathology when evaluating a subject's responses. In addition, the 1992 Code of Ethics of the American Psychological Association requires examiners to be knowledgeable about cultural and social differences, and to be responsible in interpreting test results with regard to these differences.

Experts in the use of the TAT recommend obtaining a personal and medical history from the subject before giving the TAT, in order to have some context for evaluating what might otherwise appear to be abnormal or unusual responses. For example, frequent references to death or grief in the stories would not be particularly surprising from a subject who had recently been bereaved. In addition, the TAT should not be used as the sole examination in evaluating an individual; it should be combined with other interviews and tests.

One precaution required in general assessment of the TAT is the absence of a normative scoring system for responses. The original scoring system devised in 1943 by Henry Murray, one of the authors of the TAT, attempted to account for every variable that it measures. Murray's scoring system is time-consuming and unwieldy, and as a result has been little used by later interpreters. Other scoring systems have since been introduced that focus on one or two specific variables—for example, hostility or depression. While these systems are more practical for clinical use, they lack comprehensiveness. No single system presently used for scoring the TAT has achieved widespread acceptance. The basic drawback of any scoring system in evaluating responses to the TAT story cards is that information that is not relevant to that particular system is simply lost.

A recent subject of controversy in TAT interpretation concerns the use of computers to evaluate responses. While computers were used initially only to score tests with simple yes/no answers, they were soon applied to interpretation of projective measures. A computerized system for interpreting the Rorschach was devised as early as 1964. As of 2002, there are no computerized systems for evaluating responses to the TAT; however, users of the TAT should be aware of the controversies in this field. Computers have two basic limitations for use with the TAT: the first is that they cannot observe and record the subject's vocal tone, eye contact, and other aspects of behaviour that a human examiner can note. Second, computers are not adequate for the interpretation of unusual subject profiles.

The TAT is often used in individual assessments of candidates for employment in fields requiring a high degree of skill in dealing with other people and/or ability to cope with high levels of psychological stress—such as law enforcement, military leadership positions, religious ministry, education, diplomatic service, etc. Although the TAT should not be used in the differential diagnosis of mental disorders, it is often administered to individuals who have already received a diagnosis in order to match them with the type of psychotherapy best suited to their personalities. Lastly, the TAT is sometimes used for forensic purposes in evaluating the motivations and general attitudes of persons accused of violent crimes. For example, the TAT was recently administered to a 24-year-old man in prison for a series of sexual murders. The results indicated that his attitudes towards other people are not only outside normal limits but are similar to those of other persons found guilty of the same type of crime.

The TAT can be given repeatedly to an individual as a way of measuring progress in psychotherapy or, in some cases, to help the therapist understand why the treatment seems to be stalled or blocked.

In addition to its application in individual assessments, the TAT is frequently used for research into specific aspects of human personality; most often needs for achievement, fears of failure, hostility and aggression, and interpersonal object relations. "Object relations" is a phrase used in psychiatry and psychology to refer to the ways people internalize their relationships with others and the emotional tone of their relationships. Research into object relations using the TAT investigates a variety of different topics, including the extent to which people are emotionally involved in relationships with others; their ability to understand the complexities of human relationships; their ability to distinguish between their viewpoint on a situation and the perspectives of others involved; their ability to control aggressive impulses; self-esteem issues; and issues of personal identity. For example, one recent study compared responses to the TAT from a group of psychiatric inpatients diagnosed with dissociative disorders with responses from a group of non-dissociative inpatients, in order to investigate some of the controversies about dissociative identity disorder (formerly called *multiple personality disorder*).

The large numbers of research studies that have used the TAT have indicated that cultural, gender, and class issues must be taken into account when determining whether a specific response to a story card is "abnormal" strictly speaking, or whether it may be a normal response from a person in a particular group. For example, the card labelled 6GF shows a younger woman who is seated turning towards a somewhat older man who is standing behind her and smoking a pipe. Most male subjects do not react to this picture as implying aggressiveness, but most female subjects regard it as a very aggressive picture, with unpleasant overtones of intrusiveness and danger. Many researchers consider the gender difference in responses to this card as a reflection of the general imbalance in power between men and women in the larger society.

The TAT is usually administered to individuals in a quiet room free from interruptions or distractions. The subject sits at the edge of a table or desk next to the examiner. The examiner shows the subject a series of story cards taken from the full set of 31 TAT cards. The usual number of cards shown to the subject is between 10 and 14, although Murray recommended the use of 20 cards, administered in two separate one-hour sessions with the subject. The original 31 cards were divided into three categories, for use with men only, with women only, or for use with subjects of either sex. Recent practice has moved away from the use of separate sets of cards for men and women.

The subject is then instructed to tell a story about the picture on each card, with specific instructions to include a description of the event in the picture, the developments that led up to the event, the thoughts and feelings of the people in the picture, and the outcome of the story (Figure 13.10). The examiner keeps the cards in a pile face down in front of her or him, gives them to the subject one at a time, and asks the subject to place each card face down as its story is completed. Administration of the TAT usually takes about an hour.

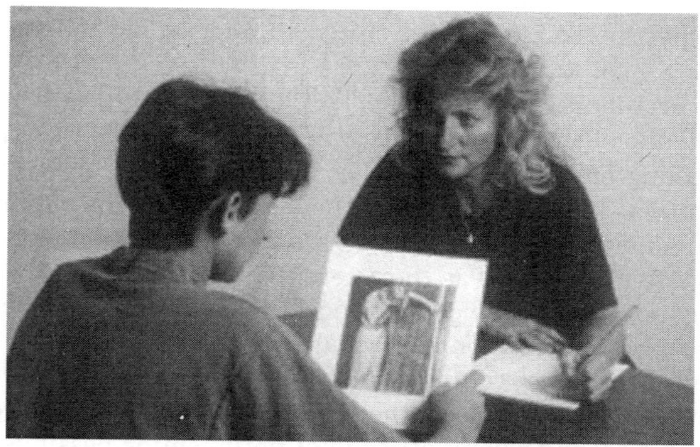

Figure 13.10 Administration of the Thematic Apperception Test (TAT).

In the TAT, the test subject (the boy shown here) examines a set of cards that portray human figures in a variety of settings and situations, and is asked to tell a story about each card. The story includes the event shown in the picture, preceding events, emotions and thoughts of those portrayed, and the outcome of the event shown. The story content and structure are thought to reveal the subject's attitudes, inner conflicts, and views.

Race is another issue related to the TAT story cards. The original story cards, which were created in 1935, all involved Caucasian figures. As early as 1949, researchers who were administering the TAT to African-Americans asked whether the race of the figures in the cards would influence the subjects' responses. Newer sets of TAT story cards have introduced figures representing a wider variety of races and ethnic groups. As of 2002, however, it is not clear whether a subject's ability to identify with the race of the figures in the story cards improves the results of a TAT assessment.

Murray's original practice was to take notes by hand on the subject's responses, including her or his non-verbal behaviours. Research has indicated, however, that a great deal of significant material is lost when notes are recorded in this way. As a result, some examiners now use a tape recorder to record subjects' answers. Another option involves asking the subject to write down her or his answers.

There are two basic approaches to interpreting responses to the TAT, called *nomothetic* and *idiographic* respectively. "Nomothetic interpretation" refers to the practice of establishing norms for answers from subjects in specific age, gender, racial, or educational level groups and then measuring a given subject's responses against those norms. "Idiographic interpretation" refers to evaluating the unique features of the subject's view of the world and relationships. Most psychologists would classify the TAT as better suited to idiographic than nomothetic interpretation.

In interpreting responses to the TAT, examiners typically focus their attention on one of three areas: the content of the stories that the subject tells; the feeling or tone of the stories; or the subject's behaviours apart from responses. These behaviours may include verbal remarks (for example, comments about feeling stressed by the situation or not being a good storyteller) as well as non-verbal actions or signs (blushing, stammering, fidgeting in the chair, difficulties making eye contact with the examiner, etc.) The story content usually reveals the subject's attitudes, fantasies, wishes, inner conflicts, and views of the outside world. The story structure typically reflects the subject's feelings, assumptions about the world, and an underlying attitude of optimism or pessimism.

The results of the TAT must be interpreted in the context of the subject's personal history, age, sex, level of education, occupation, racial or ethnic identification, first language, and other characteristics that may be important. "Normal" results are difficult to define in a complex multicultural society like the contemporary United States.

The Children's Apperception Test (CAT)

Dr. Leopold Bellak developed this test for use with children between 3–10 years of age. This test consists of 10 cards having pictures of animals as children could identify themselves more readily with animal figures. Animals in these cards are shown in real-life situations. These cards are used for both girls and boys. The child has to tell a story relating to that picture. All the cards are presented one by one.

The Word Association Test (WAT)

The Word Association Test is another projective test. It was devised by Jung, and is an important psychoanalytic technique. According to Galton (1879), "One of the oldest projective techniques for studying personality is the word association test." In this, the subject is given stimulus words and asked to respond as quickly as possible with the very first word that comes into her or his mind, the time of reaction being noted with a stop watch. The interpretation of the responses is based on the response word and the reaction time. When the reaction time is unusually long, or the response is unusual, the existence of a repressed complex is suspected.

Inability to respond or mere repetition of the stimulus word is also significant in understanding emotional blockings of the subject. This test is employed for detecting complexes or areas of emotional conflicts. The method is also useful for exploring the mental content and the various interests of the individual.

The Sentence Completion Test (SCT)

Originally, this test was devised by Ebbinghaus as a test of intellectual ability. Work of Payne and Tendler used it as a method of assessing personality. The Sentence Completion Tests consist of incomplete sentences and require the subject to complete a sentence in one or more words. The subject is asked to respond or answer the questions as quickly as possible with the very first thought that comes to her or his mind. The subject is instructed not to give more thoughts to the answer to a particular question. This test is useful in detecting inner emotional conflicts, attitudes, aversions, etc. Incomplete Sentence Blank by Rotter is an example of Sentence Completion Test (SCT).

The Sentence Completion Test (SCT) is based on the same principles on which the Word Association Test (WAT) is based. The Sentence Completion Tests (SCTs) are considered superior to Word Association Tests (WAT) because the subject can respond in more than one word. So, it becomes possible to have great flexibility and variety of responses as a result of which a wider area of personality and experiences may be revealed.

Advantages of the projective techniques

(i) These are the only techniques which study and reveal the unconscious mind of the person.
(ii) The subject is free to give any response.
(iii) The interference of the examiner is less.

Disadvantages of the projective techniques

(i) These techniques deal with the unconscious mind which is 1/10th part of the individual mind.
(ii) These techniques require an expert service and experience for their administration, scoring, and interpretation.
(iii) These techniques are time consuming.
(iv) These techniques cannot be administered in groups.
(v) These techniques are more applicable to maladjusted and abnormal person.

EXERCISES

The below mentioned are some of the questions that have been asked in the examinations conducted by the Guru Nanak Dev University or can be asked. Knowledge of these answers can help the students to get success in the examinations.

Section A

Answers to the following questions in **five** lines or 50 words.

1. Define Personality.
2. What is persona?
3. What is extraversion?
4. What is fixation?
5. Explain Eysenck's personality questionnaire.
6. Difine Trait.
7. What do you mean by temperament?
8. What is sixteen personality factor (16 PF) test?
9. What is neuroticism?
10. What is psychoticism?
11. Define id.*
12. Define ego*
13. Define super-ego.*
14. What is the literal meaning of the term "personality"?
15. What is TAT?
16. What is 16 PF.
17. Define source traits.*
18. Define surface traits.*
19. What is electra complex?
20. What is oedipus complex?*
21. Explain Catharsis.
22. Describe the components of personality given by Freud.
23. Stages of psychosexual development given by Freud.
24. What is defence mechanism?
25. Define reaction formation.
26. What are the projective techniques?
27. Explain the cardinal traits.
28. Explain the central traits.
29. What is inkblot test?

30. Explain the Word Association Test (WAT)
31. What do you mean by Sentence Completion Test (SCT)
32. Define intellectualization.

Section B

Answers the following questions up to **two** pages or 500 words.

1. Discuss the concept of personality.
2. Write briefly the Freud's theory of personality.
3. According to Freud, what are the three levels of consciousness?
4. In Freud's theory, what are the three basic components of personality?
5. According to Freud, what are the psychosexual stages of development?
6. What are the central traits and source traits?
7. What are the strengths and weaknesses of the trait approach?
8. What are the projective tests of personality?
9. Explain the main elements of personality.
10. Explain the Eysenck's personality theory.
11. Explain the Murray's theory of personality.
12. What is a trait? Explain briefly the trait theories of personality.
13. Can personality be described on the basis of traits? Discuss.
14. Describe the Cattell's theory of personality.
15. Describe the Freud's theory of personality.
16. Explain the structure of personality given by Freud.
17. Explain Allport's theory of personality.
18. Distinguish between "Type" and "Trait". Explain the Allport's theory of personality.
19. Discuss any two projective techniques of personality assessment.
20. Highlight the contribution of Murray towards the understanding of personality.
21. What is a trait? Differentiate between the type and trait theories of personality giving examples?

Section C

Answer the following questions up to **five** pages or 1000 words.

1. Describe two trait theories of personality. What do they have in Common? How do they differ?

2. Can personality be described on the basis of traits? Discuss.
3. What are the social-cultural determinants of personality?
4. What is the role of environment in shaping the personality of the child? Illustrate your answer with examples.
5. What is the contribution of heredity and environment in the development of personality?
6. What is personality? Discus Freud's theory of personality.
7. What are the different techniques of measuring personality?
8. What is projection? What are the projective methods of measuring personality?
9. Explain the Freudian theory of personality.
10. Define personality. Discuss the different techniques of personality assessment.
11. What are the various techniques of assessing personality?
12. What is personality? Write various determinants of personality in detail.
13. Discuss the various defence mechanism used to reduce anxiety and guilt.
14. Explain Freud's stages of psychosexual development.
15. Define personality and what are the characteristics of personality?
16. Describe the Cattell's theory of personality?

REFERENCES

Adler, A., *Individual Psychology of Alfred Adler: A Systematic Presentation in Selections From His Writings,* New York: Harper Collins, 1989.

Allport, G.W., *Personality—A Psychological Interpretation,* New York: Holt, 1937.

Allport, G.W., *Personality—A Psychological Interpretation*, New York: Holt, 1948.

Allport, G.W., *Becoming: Basic Considerations for A Psychology of Personality*, New Haven, CT: Yale University Press, 1955.

Allport, G.W., *Personality and Social Encounter: Selected Essays,* New York: Beacon Press, 1960.

Allport, G.W., *Pattern and Growth in Personality,* New York: Holt, Rinehart and Winston, 1961.

Allport, G.W., and Odbert, H.S., 'Trait Names: A Psycho-lexical Study,' *Psychological Monographs*, **47** (1, Whole No. 211), 1936.

Anastasi, A., *Psychological Testing* (6th ed.), New York: Macmillan, 1988.

Baldwin, A.L., 'Personal Structure Analysis: A Statistical Method for Investigating the Single Personality,' *Journal of Abnormal and Social Psychology*, **37**, 163–183, 1942.

Bandura, A., *Principles of Behavior Modification*, New York: Holt, Rinehart, and Winston, 1969.

Bandura, A., *Aggression: A Social Learning Analysis,* Englewood Cliffs, NJ: Prentice-Hall, 1973.

Barrat, P., and Eysenck, S.B.G., 'The Assessment of Personality Factors Across 25 Countries,' *Personality and Individual Differences,* **5**, 615–632, 1984.

Beck, A.T., *Depression,* New York: Hoeber, 1967.

Bellak, L., *Conceptual and Methodological Problems in Psychoanalysis,* Annals of the New York Academy of Science, **76**, 971–1134, 1959.

Bootzin, R., Bower, Crooker and Hall, *Psychology Today*, New York: McGraw-Hill, INC, 1991.

Bullock, W.A. and Gilliland, K., 'Eysenck's Arousal Theory of Introversion—Extraversion: A Converging Measures Investigation,' *Journal of Personality and Social Psychology*, **64**, 113–123, 1993.

Cattell, R.B., *Personality,* New York: McGraw-Hill, 1950.

Cattell, R.B., *Personality: A systematic, Theoretical, and Factual Study,* New York: McGraw Hill, 1950.

Cattell, R.B., *Personality and Social Psychology,* San Diego: Knapp, 1964.

Cattell, R.B. (Ed.), *Handbook of Multivariate Experimental Psychology* (2nd ed.), Chicago: Rand McNally, 1966.

Cattell, R.B., *Abilities: Their Structure, Growth, and Action,* Boston: Houghton Mifflin, 1971.

Cattell, R.B., *Personality and Mood by Questionnaire,* San Francisco: Jossey-Bass, 1973.

Cattell, R.B., *The Inheritance of Personality and Ability: Research Methods and Findings,* New York: Academic Press, 1982.

Cattell, R.B. and Child, D., *Motivation and Dynamic Structure,* New York: John Wiley, 1975.

Cattell, R., Eber, H., and Tatsuoko, M., *Handbook for the Sixteen Personality Factor Questionnaire (16 PF)*, Champaign, IL: Institute for Personality and Ability Testing, 1988.

Conley, J.J., 'The Hierarchy of Consistency: A Review and Model of Longitudinal Findings on Adult Individual Differences in Intelligence, Personality and Self-opinion,' *Personality and Individual Differences*, **5**, 11–26. 1984a.

Conley, J.J., 'Longitudinal Consistency of Adult Personality: Self-reported Psychological Characteristics Across 45 Years,' *Journal of Personality and Social Psychology*, **47**, 1325–1333, 1984b.

Conley, J.J., 'Longitudinal Stability of Personality Traits: A Multitrait-Multimethod-Multioccasion Analysis,' *Journal of Personality and Social Psychology*, **49**, 1260–1282, 1985.

Crow, L.D. and Crow, A., *Educational Psychology,* New Delhi: Eurasia Publishing House, 1973.

Domjan, M., *The Essentials of Conditioning and Learning,* Pacific Grove, Calif: Brooks/Cole, 1996.

Duncan, L.E. and Agronick, G.S., 'The Intersection of Life Stage and Social Events: Personality and Life Outcomes,' *Journal of Personality and Social Psychology,* **69**, 558–658, 1995.

Eaves, L., Eysenck, H.J., and Martin, N., *Genes, Culture and Personality: An Empirical Approach,* New York: Academic, 1989.

Erikson, E.H., *Insight and Responsibility*, New York: Norton,1964.

Eysenck, H.J., *Dimensions of Personality,* London: Routledge and Kegan Paul, 1947.

Eysenck, H.J., *Uses and Abuses of Psychology,* Baltimore: Penguin Books, 1953a.

Eysenck, H.J., *The Biological Basis of Personality*, Springfield, IL: Charles C. Thomas, 1967.

Eysenck, H.J., *The Structure of Human Personality* (3rd ed.), London: Methuen, 1970.

Eysenck, H.J. (Ed.), *Readings in Extraversion-Introversion, Vol. 3: Bearings on Basic Psychological Processes,* New York: Wiley-Interscience, 1971a.

Eysenck, H.J., *The IQ Argument: Race, Intelligence, and Education,* New York: Library Press, 1971b.

Eysenck, H.J., *The Structure of Human Personality* (3rd ed.), New York: Methuen, 1971.

Eysenck, H.J., *The Learning Theory Model of Neurosis—A New Approach,* Behavior Research and Therapy, 14, 251–267, 1976a.

Eysenck, H.J., *Case Studies in Behavior Therapy,* London: Routledge and Kegan Paul, 1976b.

Eysenck, H.J., 'Personality, Cancer and Cardiovascular Disease: A Casual Analysis,' *Personality and Individual Differences,* **6**, 535–556, 1985.

Eysenck, 'H.J., Biological Dimensions of Personality,' in L.A. Pervin (Ed.), *Handbook of Personality: Theory and Research* (pp. 244–276), New York: Guilford, 1990.

Eysenck, H.J., 'Four Ways Five Factors are Not Basic,' *Personality and Individual Differences*, **13**, 667–673, 1992.

Eysenck, M.W., *Individual Differences: Normal and Abnormal,* Hove, UK: Lawrence Erlbaum Associates Ltd. 1994.

Eysenck, H.J. and Eysenck, S.B.G., *Psychoticism: A Dimension of Personality,* London: Routledge and Kegan Paul, 1975.

Fenichel, O., *The Psychoanalytic Theory of Neurosis,* New York: Norton, 1945.

Freud, S., *The Origins of Psychoanalysis, Letters to Wilhelm Fliess, Drafts and Notes: 1887–1902 (Includes Project for a Scientific Psychology),* New York: Basic Books, 1887–1902/1954.

Freud, S., *The Ego and the Id*, London: Hogarth Press, 1923.

Freud, S., *Inhibition, Symptoms and Anxiety*, London: Hogarth Press, 1926.

Freud, S., *A General Introduction to Psychoanalysis*, New York: Liveright, 1935.

Freud, S., *The Problem of Anxiety*, New York: W.W. Norton & Co., 1936.

Freud, A., *Ego and the Mechanisms of Defence*, New York: International Universities Press, 1946.

Freud, S., *An Outline of Psychoanalysis*, New York: Norton, 1949.

Freud, S., *Beyond the Pleasure Principle*, New York: Liveright, 1950.

Freud, S., *An Outline of Psychoanalysis*, London: Hogarth Press, 1953.

Freud, S., *The Standard Edition of the Complete Psychological Works,* J. Strachey (Ed.), London: Hogarth, 1953–1974.

Freud, S., *The Interpretation of Dreams*, London: Hogarth, 1953/ 1990.

Freud, S., *The Question of Lay Analysis,* in Standard edition (Vol. 20), London: Hogarth, 1959.

Freud, S., *Inhibitions, Symptoms and Anxiety*, in Standard edition (Vol. 20), London: Hogarth, 1959.

Freud, S., *Three Essays on the Theory of Sexuality*, New York: Basic Books, 1962.

Freud, S., *Psychopathology of Everyday Life*, New York: W.W. Norton & Company, 1971.

Friedman, H.W., and Schustack, M.W., *Personality: Classic Theories and Modern Research,* Boston: Allyn and Bacon, 1999.

Gale A., and Eysenck, M.W. (Eds.), *Handbook of Individual Differences: Biological Perspectives,* New York: Wiley, 1989.

Galton, F., *Psychometric Experiments,* Brain, **2**, 149–162, 1879.

Goode, W.J., and Hatt, P.K., *Methods of Social Research*, New York: McGraw-Hill, 1952.

Gough, H.G., *California Psychological Inventory Administrator's Guide.* Palo Alto, CA: Consulting Psychologists Press, Inc., 1987.

Gough, H.G., and Bradley, P., "*CPI Manual*", Ed. 3, Palo Alto, CA: Consulting Psychologists Press, 1996.

Hall, C.S., and Lindzey, G., *Theories of Personality*, New Delhi: Wiley Eastern Ltd., 1940.

Hall, C.S., and Lindzey, G., *Theories of Personality* (3rd ed.), New York: John Wiley, 1978.

Harrison, P.L., 'Thematic Apperception Methods,' in B.B., Wolman (Ed.), *Handbook of Clinical Psychology* (pp. 562–620), New York: McGraw-Hill, 1965.

Hathaway, S.R. and McKinley, J.C., 'A Multiphasic Personality Schedule (Minnesota): I. Construction of the Schedule,' *Journal of Psychology*, **10**, 249–254, 1940.

Hathaway, S.R., and McKinley, J.C., *The Minnesota Multiphasic Personality Inventory* (rev. ed.), Minneapolis: University of Minnesota Press, 1943.

Helmes, E., and Reddon, J.R., 'A Perspective on Developments in Assessing Psychopathology: A Critical Review of the MMPI and MMPI-2,' *Psychological Bulletin*, **113**, 453–471, 1993.

Hilgard, E.R., 'Experimental Approaches to Psychoanalysis,' in E. Pumpian-Mindlin (Ed.), *Psychoanalysis as Science* (pp. 3–45), Stanford, Calif: Stanford University Press, 1952.

Jung, C.G., *Conscious, Unconscious and Individuation*, in G. Adler, M. Fordham, and H. Read (Eds.), *The Collected Works of C.G. Jung*, London: Routledge, 1959.

Kessler, R.C., McGonagle, K.A., Zhao, S., Nelson, C.B., Hughes, M., Eshleman, S., Witchen, H-U., and Kendler, K.S., 'Lifetime and 12-month Prevalence of DSM-III-R Psychiatric Disorders in the United States,' *Archives of General Psychiatry*, **5**, 8–19, 1994.

Kline, P., *Fact and Fancy in Freudian Theory*, London: Methuen, 1972.

Kluckhohn, C., and Murray, H.A., *Personality in Nature, Society, and Culture,* New York: Knopf, 1949.

Loehlin, J.C., 'Partitioning Environmental and Genetic Contributions to Behavioral Development,' *American Psychologist*, **44**, 1285–1292, 1989.

Lubin, B., Larsen, R.M., and Matarazzo, J.D., 'Patterns of Psychological Test Usage in the United States: 1935–1982,' *American Psychologist*, **39**, 451–454, 1984.

Maddi, S.R., *Personality Theories: A Comparative Assessment,* Homewood, Illinois: Dorsey, 1976.

Maddi, S.R., *Personality Theories: A Comparative Analysis* (6th ed.), Pacific Grove, Calif: Brooks/Cole, 1996.

Maslow, A.H., *Motivation and personality* (2nd ed.), New York: Harper & Row, 1970.

Maslow, A.H., *The Farther Reaches of Human Nature,* New York: Viking, 1971.

Matthews, G., and Amelang, M., 'Extraversion, Arousal Theory and Performance: A Study of Individual Differences in the EEG,' *Personality and Individual Differences*, **14**, 347–363, 1993.

McCrae, R.R., and Costa, P.T., Jr., 'Validation of the Five-Factor Model of Personality Across Instruments and Observers,' *Journal of Personality and Social Psychology*, **52**, 81–90, 1987.

McCrae, R.R., and Costa, P.T., Jr., *Personality in Adulthood,* New York: Guilford, 1990.

Mead, M., *Sex and Temperament in Three Primitive Societies,* New York: Dell, 1935.

Michel, W., 'On the Future of Personality Measurement,' *American Psychologist*, **32**, 246–254, 1977.

Millon, T. and Davis, R.D., 'The Development of Personality Disorders,' in D. Cicchetti and D.J. Cohen (Eds.), *Developmental Psychopathology: Vol. 2. Risk, Disorder, and Adaptation* (pp 633–76), New York: Wiley, 1945.

Morgan, C.D., and Murray, H.A., 'A Method for Investigating Fantasies,' *Archives of Neurology and Psychiatry*, **34**, 289–306, 1935.

Munn, N.L., *An Introduction to Psychology* (2nd ed.), New Delhi: Oxford and IBH, 1967.

Murray, H.A., 'Basic Concepts for a Psychology of Personality,' *Journal of General Psychology*, **15**, 241–268, 1936.

Murray, H.A., *Manual of Thematic Apperception Test,* Cambridge, Mass: Harvard University Press, 1943.

Nelson, L.J., and Miller, D.T., 'The Distinctiveness in Social Categorization: You Are What Makes You Unusual,' *Psychological Science*, **6**, 246–249, 1995.

Pervin, L.A., *Personality: Theory and Research* (5th ed.), Chichester: Wiley, 1989.

Phares, E.J., *Clinical Psychology: Concepts, Methods, and Profession,* Homewood, IL: Dorsey, 1979.

Prince, M., *The Unconscious* (2nd ed.), New York: Macmillan, 1929.

Rogers, C.R., *On Becoming a Person,* Boston: Houghton Mifflin, 1961.

Rorschach, H., *Psychodiagnostics: A Diagnostic Test Based on Perception* (P. Lemkau and B. Kronenberg, Trans.), Berne: Huber. (1st German ed. Published 1921; U.S. distributor, Grune & Stratton).

Rotter, J.B., 'Word Association and Sentence Completion Methods,' in H.H. Anderson and G.L. Anderson (Eds.), *An Introduction to Projective Techniques* (pp. 279–311). Englewood Cliffs, NJ: Prentice-Hall, 1951.

Rotter, J.B., 'Generalized Expectancies for Internal Versus External Control of Reinforcement,' *Psychological Monographs*, **81** (1, Whole No. 609), 1966.

Schultz, D., and Schultz, S.E., *Theories of Personality* (6th ed.), California: Brooks/Cole, 1998.

Sheldon, W.H., *The Varieties of Temperament: A Psychology of Constitutional Differences,* New York: Harper, 1942.

Skinner, B.F., *About Behaviorism,* New York: Knopf, 1974.

Smith, B.D., 'Extraversion and Electrodermal Activity: Arousability and the Inverted-U,' *Personality and Individual Differences*, **4**, 411–420, 1983.

Smith, B.D., Rockwell-Tisher, S., and Davidson, R., 'Extraversion and Arousal: Effects of Attentional Conditions on Electrodermal Activity,' *Personality and Individual Differences*, **7**, 293–303, 1986.

Stelmack, R.M., 'The Psychophysiology of Extraversion and Neuroticism,' in H.J. Eysenck (Ed.), *A Model for Personality* (pp. 38–64), Heidelberg: Springer-Verlag, 1981.

Stelmack, R.M., 'Biological Bases of Extraversion: Psychophysiological Evidence,' *Journal of Personality,* **58**, 293–311, 1990.

Stelmack, R.M., and Geen, R.G., 'The Psychophysiology of Extraversion,' in A. Gale and M.W. Eysenck (Eds.), *Handbook of Individual Differences* (pp. 227–254), New York: Wiley, 1992.

Stelmack, R.M., Houlihan, M., and McGarry-Roberts, P., 'Personality, Reaction Time, and Event-Related Potentials,' *Journal of Personality and Social Psychology*, **65**, 399–409, 1993.

Sternberg, G., *Personality and the EEG:* 'Arousal and Emotional Arousability,' *Personality and Individual Differences*, **13**, 1097–1113, 1992.

Strelau, J., and Eysenck, H.J. (Eds.), *Personality Dimensions and Arousal,* New York: Plenum, 1987.

Sullivan, H.S., *The Interpersonal Theory of Psychiatry,* New York: Norton, 1953.

Tyler, L., *Individuality: Human Possibilities and Personal Choice in the Psychological Development of Men and Women,* San Francisco: Jossey-Bass, 1978.

Wakefield, J.C., 'Levels of Explanation in Personality Theory,' in D.M. Buss and N. Cantor (Eds.), *Personality Psychology: Recent Trends and Emerging Directions* (pp. 333–346). New York: Springer-Verlag, 1989.

Warren, S., 'Toy Makers Say Bye to "Plasticizers,' *Wall Street Journal*, pp. B1, B8, 1999.

Watson, J.B., The Place of The Conditioned Reflex in Psychology, *Psychological Review*, **23**, 89–116, 1916.

Watson, J.B., *Behaviorism,* New York: Norton, 1925.

Watson, J.B., *Behaviourism*, London: Kegan Paul, 1930.

Weiss, A.P., 'Conscious and the Unconscious,' *Psychological Bulletin*, **16**, 9–12, 1919.

Woodworth, R.S., *Dynamic Psychology,* New York: Columbia University Press, 1918.

Woodworth, R.S., *Dynamics of Behavior,* New York: Holt, Rinehart and Winston, 1958.

Wade, C., and Tavris, C., *Psychology,* New York: Harper and Row, 1998.

Zuckerman, M., 'Good and Bad Humors: Biochemical Bases of Personality and Its Disorders,' *Psychological Science*, **6**, 325–332, 1995.

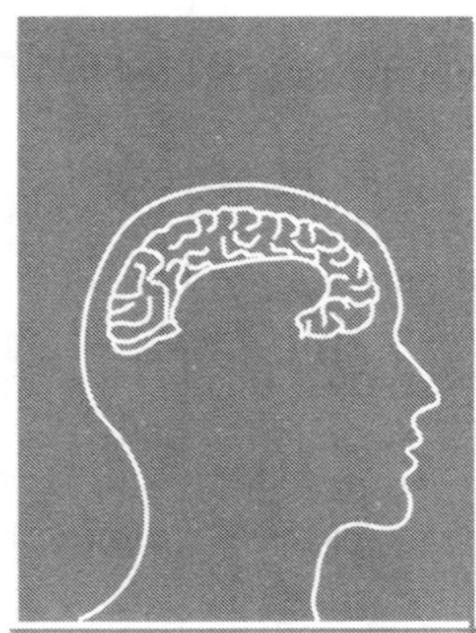

Index